Japan
Economic
Almanac

The Nikkei Weekly
1996

From Japan's leading publisher
of business information

NIHON KEIZAI SHIMBUN, INC.

Edited by

THE NIKKEI WEEKLY

Nihon Keizai Shimbun, Inc.
1-9-5 Otemachi, Chiyoda-ku,
Tokyo 100-66
Tel: (03) 3270-0251

President and Publisher
Takuhiko Tsuruta

Editor
Nobuo Ikeda

Circulation Manager
Makoto Takekuma

Advertising Sales Manager
Kazuo Onodera

Articles in this almanac were written
by the staff of *The Nikkei Weekly*,
or compiled, translated and edited
by the staff of Nikkei News Bulletin Inc.

THE JAPAN ECONOMIC ALMANAC

Editor
Sumio Kido

Editor and Production Coordinator
Yutaka Negishi

Production Editor
James McDonald, NNB
with   Marc Anthonisen
        Peter Currie
        Keiko Hachiya
        David Hurwitz
        Sharon Houghton
        Peter Langan
        Kay Larsen
        Jeanmarie McNiff
        John Rutherford

Design Editor
Kenichiro Tachibana, NNB
with   Nobuko Oinuma
        Yuko Yajima
        Keiko Ishikawa

Cover illustrated by
Susan McNab, The Nikkei Weekly

Printed by
Dai Nippon Printing Co., Tokyo

All rights reserved.
Copyright ©1995
Nihon Keizai Shimbun, Inc.

ISBN 4-532-67505-7
ISSN 0915–830

NOTICE

ABOUT *THE NIKKEI WEEKLY*

The Nikkei Weekly is Japan's only English-language business newspaper covering the entire spectrum of the nation's economy, financial sector and industry. Each week, the paper provides concise but comprehensive reports and analysis of developments in Japan's overall business trends, international trade, banking, government finance, securities markets, commodities and industries. Other features include Asia-Pacific news, new products, personal profiles, guest columns and opinions.

The Nikkei Weekly is published by Nihon Keizai Shimbun, Inc. and draws on the vast editorial resources of *The Nihon Keizai Shimbun* (The NIKKEI), Japan's sole business daily, with a circulation of 3 million and an editorial staff of well over 1,300 in Japan and abroad. In addition to The NIKKEI, Nihon Keizai Shimbun, Inc. publishes three Japanese-language newspapers – *The Nikkei Industrial Daily, The Nikkei Financial Daily,* and the *Nikkei Marketing Journal* — plus electronic information services and a wide variety of books and magazines. *The Nikkei Weekly* prints numerous summaries of important articles from these four Japanese papers, as well as articles by its own staff writers. It is printed simultaneously in Tokyo, Los Angeles and Heerlen (The Netherlands).

Since its start in 1963 as *The Japan Economic Journal, The Nikkei Weekly* has become the definitive source of English-language information on Japan's economy for the international business community. □

JAPAN'S LEADING
BUSINESS NEWSPAPER

THE NIKKEI WEEKLY

Dear Reader,

While every year is meaningful and memorable as we live through it, 1995 has been very special, a year to be treasured in memory and recounted to future generations.

In commemorating the historic 50th anniversary of the end of World War II, Japan had the opportunity to look back on its accomplishments since then and review how it has contributed to the world over this half century. That brought with it a grand opportunity to consider what we as a nation could not accomplish in the past, and what we should accomplish in the future. Japan's direction had not been discussed so widely and with such enthusiasm for many years.

Unfortunately, other factors made 1995 memorable in less pleasant ways — two events in particular that none welcomed. The Great Hanshin Earthquake, the worst disaster of its kind in this half century, wreaked havoc and claimed more than 5,000 lives. Then came the truly frightening incidents in which the sinister Aum Shinrikyo cult released deadly sarin gas in Tokyo subways and other sites.

The former exposed the unexpected fragility of modern cities; the latter shattered our long-held myth of Japan as a safe society, which along with economic prosperity seemed a defining characteristic of the nation. That these events coincided 50 years after the war is a dramatic irony.

On the economic scene, *endaka* bogged down progress toward economic recovery and spread fear of deflation through the business world. Making matters worse, many financial institutions struggled to deal with mountains of bad debt. Japan's skies remain cloudy.

After breaking through the once-inconceivable ¥100 barrier, the yen snowballed to a record 79.75 to the dollar in April. Though this extreme was short-lived, and we've since seen some correction, that peak in the value of the currency cast a long shadow over the economy.

The effects of a strong yen are pervasive: deflationary steps that go beyond so-called price breaking, apprehension about deindustrialization precipitated by the hollowing-out of industry and higher unemployment.

In addition, every solution of a trade issue between Japan and the U.S. seems to drag a new problem behind it, like ripples on a pond. Even as auto trade negotiations reached a last-minute resolution, contention over airline access came to the fore.

The list of worrisome factors seems endless. Bad debt continues to plague financial institutions, and the collapse of several credit unions this year showed just how seriously ill the Japanese economy has been since the bursting of the infamous speculative bubble.

This was also a difficult year in government. Aftershocks from the political earthquake that ended 40 years of Liberal Democratic Party rule continued to alter the political landscape through 1995. Both the business world and the public look with reproach on politicians who simply react to economic problems but are unable to take effective action.

Today's dramatically changing world demands continuous adaptation by human society. This is essential if all nations are to live and prosper in harmony. We see the sharing of accurate information as a good place to start.

Japan Economic Almanac 1996 presents a diverse and, we hope, helpful body of factual information selected to enable our readers to form an accurate, up-to-the-minute picture of Japan. If this book helps readers better understand our rapidly evolving nation, I will consider my job well done.

Nobuo Ikeda
Editor
The Nikkei Weekly
November 1995

Table of Contents

CHRONOLOGY 1995

Kobe quake, Aum cult, soaring yen dominate news as economy wilts

January

1 Law on state subsidies to political parties takes effect.

4 Dollar hits four-month high at ¥101.

6 1994 auto sales up 0.5% to 4.91 million vehicles: Japan Automobile Dealers Association.

1994 year-end foreign exchange reserves post $122.8 billion: MOF

SDP faction plans new political party.

9 Government and BOJ offer $1 billion loan for Mexican financial crisis.

Japan, U.S. reach agreement in financial services talks.

Itochu, Toshiba, Time-Warner, US West agree on joint cable TV venture in Japan.

10 1994 imported auto sales jumped 49.6% to record 301,391 vehicles: Japan Automobile Importers' Association

11 Japan-U.S. Summit: finance offered to convert North Korean nuclear reactors; APEC asked to liberalize trade and investment

Mexico requests $3 billion from banks in U.S., Europe and Japan; four Japanese banks tapped for $800 million.

15 Japanese-German ¥16 billion Express satellite lost after launch.

17 Quake devastates Kobe and surrounding areas; Japan's worst postwar disaster kills over 5,000.

Stocks, bonds and yen plunge after earthquake.

SDP faction postpones new party inauguration due to earthquake.

18 Government sets up earthquake task force.

Tokyo government OKs ¥30 billion bailout of Tokyo Kyowa Credit Association and Anzen Credit Bank.

19 Prime Minister Tomiichi Murayama visits Kobe.

20 Opening of 132nd Diet session; Murayama calls for quake recovery aid.

Government apology prompts end to Narita airport opposition.

23 Nikkei index dips below 18,000 for the first time in for a year; earthquake blamed.

Sony and Microsoft agree to develop multimedia hardware and software.

24 Government declares earthquake-stricken region a disaster area.

Japan's trade surplus up 0.8% in 1994; record high for third straight year.

Auto output down 6.0% in 1994; fourth straight yearly decline.

Matsushita Electric Industrial, Toshiba, U.S. and European partners promote industry standard for digital videodiscs.

27 Sumitomo Bank predicts ¥280 billion pretax losses for FY 1994 due to ¥800 billion bad loan write-off.

Large retail store sales down 2.1% in 1994; third straight year of declines: MITI

30 Seiyu offers ¥130 billion grant to subsidiary, Tokyo City Finance, for bad debt write-off.

February

1 U.S. Fed raises discount rate by half a point to 5.25%, highest in four years.

Showa Denko and Nippon Petrochemical to merge synthetic resin divisions.

2 Ford Motor (Japan) to run pre-delivery car inspections at Nissan Motor's Zama plant.

3 G-7 finance ministers and central bank heads start two-day confab on preventing currency crises.

6 Hokkaido Colliery & Steamship wins court protection from creditors; group liabilities total ¥160 billion.

7 Government to extend validity of passports from five years to 10.

8 1994 current account surplus dipped 1.6%, first drop in four years.

Machine tool orders notch 7.8% gain in 1994.

9 Deposit Insurance Corp. to put up ¥400 billion for bailout of Tokyo Kyowa and Anzen credit unions.

10 Economy on recovery track despite Kobe earthquake: Economic Planning Agency.

13 Tokyo Kyowa and Anzen credit unions to be taken over by Tokyo Kyodou Bank.

NEC and Hitachi develop world's first 1-gigabit DRAM chip; NEC to start test-marketing in 1998.

16 Japan and EU start two-day talks on auto trade; EU opposes Japanese request for larger export quota in 1995.

Dollar sinks below 98 yen to mark three-month low.

17 1994 U.S. trade deficit with Japan hit record high $65.6 billion, up 10.6% from 1993.

21 U.S. puts together $20 billion aid package to solve currency crisis in Mexico.

22 Supreme Court rejects appeal by two remaining defendants in Lockheed bribery case.

23 Daiei ditches Suntory beer; Suntory wine and soft drinks pulled from Daiei shelves following day.

26 U.K. merchant bank Barings Plc loses over 500 million pounds on derivatives trading.

27 Nikkei index slides below 17,000 to 14-month low; investors scared off by Barings debacle.

Fiscal 1995 budget clears lower house, quickest passage in postwar history.

Tokyo Kyowa and Anzen credit unions accuse ex-presidents of breach of trust.

28 NTT and AT&T to jointly offer corporate telecommunications services.

Daiei and Suntory mend fences, agree on new sales partnership.

29 Diet approves extra budget to rebuild Kobe; move brings FY94 government bond issues to record ¥16.49 trillion.

March

3 Japan's economy to pick up modestly on corporatre earnings recovery and stall in pace of capital investment decrease: BOJ tankan for February.

January international balance of payments tumbles 47% from year ago to $3.694 billion.

4 Finance Minister Masayoshi Takemura announces G-7 agreement on concerted intervention to halt dollar's plunge; dollar hits record low of ¥93.70 in New York on March 3.

7 Dollar dives to ¥88.75 in Tokyo.

8 U.S. Fed Chairman Alan Greenspan tells House of Representatives a weak dollar is unfavorable.

10 Nikkei index closes at 15-month low of 16,358.38.

U.N. to remove "enemy clause," referring to Germany, Japan, and others.

11 PM Tomiichi Murayama attends U.N. World Summit for Social Development.

14 Government to merge Export-Import Bank of Japan and Overseas Economic Cooperation Fund.

17 EPA says 1994 4th quarter GDP fell 0.9% in real terms from preceding quarter, annualized growth at -3.4%, first negative growth in one year.

Steelmakers and trade unions agree on 0% base wage hike.

Long-term interest rate tumbles, with yield on key No. 174 10-year bond slipping to 3.94%.

Average household savings falls 0.1% in 1994 to ¥12.34 million, marking first decline since the start of statistics compilation in 1963: Management and Coordination Agency.

20 Fatal sarin nerve gas planted in Tokyo subway system, killing 12 and injuring more than 5,000 passengers.

22 Sony announces appointment of Managing Director Nobuyuki Idei as president and chief operating officer, effective April 1.

23 Average price of land fell 3.0% in 1994: National Land Agency.

Dollar falls to postwar low of ¥87.97 in New York.

26 Police launch investigation of Aum Shinrikyo religious cult on suspicion of involvement in sarin nerve gas attack.

28 Mitsubishi Bank and Bank of Tokyo agree to merge to create Tokyo Mitsubishi Bank, with deposits and bank debentures topping ¥50 trillion.

30 Takaji Kunimatsu, head of the National Police Agency, wounded by gunman in front of his Tokyo residence.

Bundesbank cuts official discount rate by 0.5 percentage point to 4%.

Japanese and North Korean ruling parties agree to resume talks for normalization of bilateral diplomatic ties.

31 Mitsui Petrochemical Industries and Ube Industries agree to merge polypropylene divisions.

Cabinet approves government's five-year deregulation plan.

BOJ takes accommodative stance on money market to guide short-term interest rate lower.

Dollar dips to record low of ¥86.30 in New York.

April

1 Kansai railway companies, Kansai Electric Power and Osaka Gas decide to ask banks for ¥350 billion to rebuild after quake.

2 Ruling coalition officials start two-day visit to South Korea.

5 February current account surplus hits record high of $12.325 billion.

7 Dollar sets new low of ¥83.61 in Tokyo.

9 Independents take governor seats in Tokyo and Osaka.

10 Dollar skids to ¥80.15 in Tokyo.

Matsushita Electric Industrial agrees to sell 80% of MCA to Seagram of Canada for $5.7 billion.

12 GE of U.S. announces to start credit card business in Japan.

13 Medical expenses for elderly to hit ¥71 trillion or 10% of national income in 2025: Health and Welfare Ministry.

NEC ups stake in state-run French computer maker Bull from 3.74% to 17%.

Government decides on ¥58 billion loans to Vietnam for fiscal 1994.

14 Cabinet OKs measures to cope with yen's rise and flagging economy.

18 Vice-minister talks fail to solve Japan-U.S. auto trade dispute.

19 Dollar dives to new global low of ¥79.75 in Tokyo.

21 Orix and Daikyo announce they will tie up in housing market.

25 G-7 finance ministers and central bank governors call for orderly reversal of yen's climb.

26 Governor Aoshima cancels Tokyo World City Expo scheduled for March 1996.

NTT Data Communications Systems listed on TSE second section.

27 Japan-U.S. expert-level talks make no progress in auto trade spat.

30 U.S. slaps trade and investment embargo on Iran.

May

2 In China, PM Tomiichi Murayama begins four days of meetings with Premier Li Peng and Communist Party leader Jiang Zemin

5 Japan-U.S. auto-trade talks break down; MITI chief Hashimoto, USTR Kantor fail to agree on Japan buying more U.S. parts.

10 Failed auto-trade talks prompt U.S. to plan sanctions on Japanese auto imports. U.S. files with WTO; claims closed Japanese market.

Investigators conduct 60 raids over alleged illegal lending by two failed credit cooperatives.

15 Law promoting decentralization passes Diet.

16 Japan's FY94 direct investment in Asia hits record $9.7 billion, up 47% year on year. Asia overtakes Europe, becomes second largest recipient region after North America.

Export financing criteria relaxed by Ex-Im Bank.

Aum Shinrikyo cult leader Shoko Asahara arrested, charged with deadly March sarin gas attack in Tokyo subways.

17 U.S. names 13 Japanese luxury-car models subject to 100% tariffs. Tokyo appeals to WTO.

18 Securities houses report bleak FY94 results; red ink at 23 of 25 listed brokerages, including three of The Big Four.

19 First supplementary budget for FY95 enacted.

Honda, Mitsubishi, Mazda temporarily halt exports of luxury cars to U.S.

22 Japan threatens to reduce grant aid to China in protest of underground nuclear tests.

Mining production index for FY94 rises — first time in four years: MITI .

Real economic growth forecast for 1995 revised down to 1.3% from 2.5% by OECD.

23 Japan-U.S. aviation talks fail. Japan rejects U.S. demand for more cargo routes.

24 Five major nonlife insurers report 18.2% rise in combined FY94 pretax profits.

25 Eleven city banks post 92.3% dive in combined FY94 pretax profits, non-performing loans rise by ¥1 trln.

Possible economic downturn: BOJ Governor Matsushita.

26 North Korea seeks rice aid due to poor 1994 harvest.

27 SDP adopts 1995 platform without word "socialism."

28 Sakhalin, Russia, rocked by 7.5 Richter quake; death toll tops 2,000.

29 Toyota tops corporate earnings list for FY94.

30 Concern rises over economic downturn as major indicators point to weakness: diffusion index drops below 50%; monthly mining-output index falls for first time in three months.

31 Tokyo Governor Aoshima cancels World City Expo Tokyo '96.

Combined central-bank intervention to prop up dollar by Japan, U.S., Germany.

June

1 Strong yen leads Toyota Motor and Nissan Motor to slash prices on vehicles built at U.S. and European plants.

2 Japan's 10 electric power suppliers say additional rate cuts to take effect in July.

5 Government enacts law to guarantee employee leave to care for the elderly and sick family members, to become effective in April 1999.

6 MOF estimates financial institutions have an aggregate ¥40 trillion in bad loans.

8 14.7% fare hike on major private railways and subways to take effect in September.

9 BOJ's May tankan: diffusion index for major industries marks minus 16, up 5 points from February; margin of rise decreases from previous survey.

Lower house adopts "no-war resolution" to mark the 50th anniversary of the end of the Second World War.

12 Japan-U.S. auto trade talks open at WTO.

Seven of eight major life insurers see fiscal 1994 pretax profits fall.

June monthly economic report shows some industry sectors suffering from yen's strength.

U.S. and North Korea reach agreement in light-water nuclear reactor talks.

No-confidence vote turned down in lower house.

Chirac announces France's resumption of nuclear testing.

15 Postal savings deposits exceed ¥200 trillion.

Japan, U.S. agree to try harder to reach accord in auto trade talks.

From three-day G-7 meeting, joint communique pledges to stabilize currency rates.

19 U.S. warns of sanctions against Japanese cargo flights as conflict over the opening of new air routes results in a breakdown of talks.

21 FTC warns Shiseido about price control on products sold via major retailers, pointing to a violation of the Anti-Monopoly Law.

Japan Securities Dealers Association announces plan to create a second OTC market by easing regulations for registration.

22 EU complains to WTO that Japan's liquor tax laws are unfair, with levies for whiskey set higher than that for shochu.

ANA jumbo jet headed for Hakodate, Hokkaido, hijacked. The perpetrator, a former bank employee, is apprehended 16 hours later and all 365 passengers are released unharmed.

Three-day Japan-U.S. vice-ministerial talks on auto trade held in Geneva.

23 Securities Exchange Surveillance Commission files complaint with Tokyo prosecutors, charging TSD Corp.'s former president of stock price manipulation.

Supreme Court dismisses appeal by victims suffering from side effects of the drug Chloroquine, upholding a lower court ruling that the state bears no responsibility.

26 Asahi Breweries and Miller Brewing of the U.S. to cooperate globally.

27 Government's supplementary economic stimulus package includes possible early use of public funds to cover bad loans at financial institutions.

Chrysler acquires Seibu Motor Sales, becoming the first of the Big Three to control its own Japanese sales unit.

Harunori Takahashi, former president of Tokyo Kyowa Credit Association, and Shinsuke Suzuki, former president of Anzen Credit Bank, are arrested on charges of breach of trust on dubious loans.

29 Japan and the U.S. reach accord in the auto trade talks.

30 Ruling coalition parties draw up policy to reduce Japan's current account surplus to below 2% of GDP by 1998.

Tokyo Metropolitan Government and prosecutors seek court order to disband Aum Shinrikyo religious cult.

July

1 Product Liability Law takes effect.

3 Nikkei 225 Stock Average hits nine-year low, dropping to 14,295.90 yen.

USTR announces investigation of Japan's photo film market under Section 301 in response to allegations by Eastman Kodak Co. that anti-competitive practices such as price maintenance, price fixing, and rebate schemes create unfair market barriers against foreign products.

Shiseido Co. notifies Fair Trade Commission (FTC) it will ignore warnings of violations of Anti-Monopoly Law, objecting to FTC claim it forces retailers to sell products at suggested retail prices.

5 Former Prime Minister Takeo Fukuda dies.

Nishiyodogawa Ward, Osaka residents win court battle against factory, auto exhaust pollution.

6 Japan, U.S. simultaneously ease monetary policy. U.S. Federal Reserve Board lowers short-term federal fund rate to 5.75%.

Tsutomu Matsuzaki arrested for spreading false rumors relating to firm's development of anti-AIDS vaccine to prop up stock price.

7 Bank of Japan announces short-term market rates to fall below 1.0% official discount rate; guides overnight call rates down to all-time low of 0.8%.

Japanese, U.S. monetary authorities intervene in New York forex market selling yen for dollars.

10 Long-term prime rate cut to all-time low of 2.7%. Japan's three long-term credit banks, including Industrial Bank of Japan, cut prime lending rates starting July 12 following BOJ's lowering of short-term interest rates.

U.S., Canada join European Union in requesting bilateral talks with Japan at World Trade Organization (WTO) to resolve dispute over liquor taxes; claim it is unfair to place higher levies on imported whiskey than on shochu.

11 U.S. announces normalization of diplomatic relations with Vietnam.

Economy's moderate recovery in standstill, and down from previous month: EPA July report

Federation of Electric Power Companies requests government to reconsider construction of new advanced thermal nuclear reactor, claiming that electricity generated would cost three times that of light-water reactors.

13 Japan, U.S. resume three-day vice-ministerial aviation talks.

16 Murayama acknowledges some government responsibility in Minamata mercury poison case.

19 Second over-the-counter market launched; easier for firm's with growth potential to register.

20 Japan, European Union begin two-day negotiations on liquor taxes. Deliberations on whiskey and shochu tax differences end in stalemate.

Japan, U.S. aviation talks resolved; Federal Express granted seven routes allowing stopovers in Japan, Japan obtains approval for Chicago-bound flights from Kansai International Airport.

23 Social Democratic Party of Japan suffers major setback in Upper House elections winning only 16 seats in worst performance ever; tripartite ruling coalition retains majority; voter turnout lowest ever at 44.52%.

24 Intel Corp. of U.S. agrees to make desktop personal computers for Toshiba Corp.

25 1995 Economic White Paper cites need for deregulation to stimulate economy.

May economic indicators slip below 50% boom-or-bust line for first time in 17 months, diffusion index at 30%, leading indicator at 20%.

26 Japan accepts European Union proposal for temporary global financial services accord under WTO; U.S. not a party to agreement.

First auctions of foreign rice held.

28 June industrial output falls 0.8% month-on-month to 94.8; third consecutive month of decline.

Yoshio Nakajima, head of Finance Ministry research institute, resigns after discovery he had signed private contract to form health drink company with man linked to recent credit union scandal.

Fair Trade Commission investigates more than 10 major department stores for violating Anti-Monopoly Law.

31 Tokyo Metropolitan Government orders failed Cosmo Credit Cooperative to suspend operations; BOJ extends special emergency loans, first such relief measure in 30 years.

August

1 MOF plans measures to deal with bank failures, including expanding Deposit Insurance Corp.

2 Finance Minister Masayoshi Takemura announces emergency measures to cap strong yen.

Dollar rises to 91 yen on concerted intervention by Japan and the U.S.

American Airlines Inc. invests in JAL unit, ties up with JAL for ticketing.

3 Nikkei Stock Average tops 17,000 points on halt to yen's rise.

4 Diet adopts resolution opposing nuclear testing by China and France

Ceilings set for FY96 budget; general expenditure at ¥43.93 trillion, up 4.2% from the initial FY95 budget. Defense spending grows 2.9%.

7 Net purchase in overseas bonds of $42.67 billion for January-June, the third highest six-monthly total.

Five Aum Shinrikyo cult members, including leader Shoko Asahara, are indicted for murder and attempted murder in the June 1994 sarin gas attack in Matsumoto, Nagano Prefecture.

8 PM Tomiichi Murayama reshuffles cabinet; retains Foreign Minister Yohei Kono, Finance Minister Masayoshi Takemura and MITI chief Ryutaro Hashimoto. Economist Isamu Miyazaki appointed to head EPA.

Taito Corp., Kyocera Corp. and 52 others set up multimedia service firm.

10 Land prices drop in a further 54 residential and 21 commercial districts, says National Land Agency survey.

Toyota Motor Corp. Vice President Hiroshi Okuda replaces ailing Tatsuro Toyoda as president.

Sony Corp. says it will pay part of executive salaries with warrants.

15 July trade surplus shrinks 23% year on year to $9.43 billion.

50 firms from Japan, the U.S. and Europe agree to unify standards for future UNIX operating system.

16 Dollar surges above 99 yen in Tokyo for the first time since early February, gaining 4.20 yen.

Finance Ministry investigates debt-ridden Nippon Housing Loan Co.

Foreign entrants total a record 1.35 million, up 2.5% year on year, reports Justice Ministry.

17 General Motors Corp. of U.S. says it will sell subcompact Saturn, dubbed a Japanese car killer, in Japan.

18 Failed Cosmo Credit Cooperative to transfer operations to Tokyo Kyodou Bank, conclude Tokyo government, Finance Ministry and BOJ.

Land values tumble an average of 40%, nearly 50% in Tokyo and Osaka, over the three years to Jan. 1, 1995, National Tax Administration reports.

21 MITI chief Ryutaro Hashimoto declares candidacy for LDP presidency.

Japanese banks receive downgraded credit ratings from Moody's Investors Service Inc. and other U.S. agencies.

International Monetary Fund criticizes Japan's banking policy in its annual report on global capital markets.

23 Commercial banks' contributions to bailout Cosmo Credit Cooperative are finalized by the Finance Ministry.

24 Negotiations on standardizing digital videodisc formats start between rival Toshiba- and Sony-led groups.

The 1995 rice harvest is expected to be average, says the Agriculture Ministry.

25 U.S. Treasury Department urges Japan to cut key interest rate.

28 Yohei Kono decides not to stand for re-election as LDP president.

Settlement details for failed Cosmo Credit Cooperative finalized by Tokyo Metropolitan Government, Finance Ministry and BOJ.

29 Japan Satellite Systems Inc. launches broadcasting satellite JCSAT-3 to start digital transmissions from spring 1996.

30 Ailing Kizu Credit Cooperative ordered to suspend operations by Osaka Prefectural Government.

Salvage plan for bankrupt Hyogo Bank, a large regional institution, announced by Finance Minister Masayoshi Takemura.

31 FY96 budget requests total ¥79.19 trillion, up 11.6% from the initial FY95 budget.

Industrial production index for July fell 2.4% from June to 92.6, the fourth consecutive month of decline, says MITI.

September

1 Takashimaya absorbs five department store operator units.

Fourteen major private railway firms in the Tokyo, Osaka and Nagoya areas and a Tokyo subway operator raise fares.

4 U.N. Fourth World Conference on Women starts in Beijing.

Tokyo Electric Power ranks top FY94 income earner: National Tax Administration.

5 Top five steelmakers, including Nippon Steel, say they will post profits for first-half of FY95, the first time in three years. The firms' pretax profits total ¥60 billion.

6 July current account surplus falls 20.5% year on year to $9,218 million, the second straight month of decline.

8 Political party income in 1994 totals ¥148.4 billion, down 13.4% year on year, and falls for third year in a row for the first time.

Bank of Japan cuts official discount rate by a half percentage point to another record low 0.5%. Dollar surges to over ¥100 at one point, and Nikkei Stock Average tops 18,000-point level.

Budgetary requests for FY96 general account total 11.6% more than FY95 original budget.

9 ASEAN, Japan and Australia hold economic talks.

11 Toyoda Machine Works, Toshiba Machine and four other firms agree on joint development of personal computer numerical-control equipment.

Economic Planning Agency deletes "recovery" in its monthly economic report for the first time in a year.

12 Prime Minister Tomiichi Murayama leaves for Middle East.

Mitsubishi Estate says it will retreat from Rockefeller Center.

Dollar closes in Tokyo above ¥100 for the first time in eight months, at ¥100.63-100.66.

14 Nonperforming loans at eight housing loan companies total ¥8.4 trillion, of which ¥6.3 trillion is seen as irrecoverable: Finance Ministry.

15 Michio Watanabe, former deputy prime minister, passes away.

Two opposing blocs in digital videodisc standard row agree to unify standard. A seven-firm consortium, including Toshiba and Matsushita Electric Industrial on one side, and the Sony-Philips camp on the other to outline details by month-end.

18 1995 April-June quarter sees annualized 3.1% inflation-adjusted growth in gross domestic product.

19 Land prices nationwide as of July 1 fall for fourth year in a row. The average dips 2.1% year on year. Drop in commercial districts widens to 6.9%.

20 Toyota Motor raises stake in Daihatsu Motor to 33% to acquire management rights.

Government approves pump-priming package of over ¥14 trillion.

22 Liberal Democratic Party elects Ryutaro Hashimoto as president. Hashimoto wins 304 votes, far above the 87 posted for Junichiro Koizumi, the former minister of posts and telecommunications.

25 New Liberal Democratic Party executives assume office, with Ryutaro Hashimoto as the 17th president, Koichi Kato as secretary general, Masajuro Shiokawa as general council chairman and Taku Yamasaki as policy research council chief.

26 Daiwa Bank reveals ¥110 billion loss in U.S. Treasury bond dealings, concealed by a New York office trader for 11 years.

27 Finance Minister Masayoshi Takemura announces early bad-debt disposal policy, with plans to establish a body to collect problem loans at housing loan firms, and that use of public funds and other measures will be worked out by year-end.

Tokyo Governor Yukio Aoshima confirms he retracted a campaign pledge not to use taxpayers' money to dispose of bad loans incurred by bankrupt Tokyo Kyowa and Anzen credit unions.

28 NTT says its local telephone line networks will be fully opened to other common carriers.

Sega Enterprises to build mini-theme parks in U.S. with Spielberg's DreamWorks SKG and MCA.

29 Extraordinary Diet session convenes.

Victims of sarin nerve gas on a Tokyo subway platform. The terror attack by a religious cult killed a dozen people and injured more than 5,000.

Police in protective gear conduct tests at a subway station to determine the cause of the poisoning.

The U.S. dollar touched a historic low at ¥79.75 on April 19, before settling into range trading around ¥82-85 until Japanese, American and German monetary authorities jointly intervened in the market to push the yen down late in the summer.

Hundreds of meters of the Hanshin Expressway swayed, tilted and finally collapsed, providing one of the most illustrative examples of the damage wrought by the January 17 quake.

Kyodo Photo

A bus tilts precariously over the edge of a fallen section of expressway in downtown Kobe. The Great Hanshin Earthquake and resultant fires killed an estimated 5,500 residents of Kobe, Ashiya and Nishinomiya, and left almost a quarter of a million people homeless during a bitterly cold winter.

YEAR IN REVIEW

Japan in the year the goalposts moved

BY MICHIO
KATSUMATA
Senior Staff Writer

It is difficult to write a commentary on Japan in 1995 without falling into understatement in an attempt to avoid overstatement of the extraordinary events that took place in the year.

1995 was barely ushered in when the most destructive earthquake to hit the Japanese archipelago in over 70 years struck; the struggling economy was then rocked by banking failures; citizens looked for leadership and reassurance and found only a morally bankrupt political system; and in the year celebrating 50 years of peace in Japan since the end of World War II, a fanatical religious group embarked on a campaign of mayhem and terror.

Every year brings a transition of some kind, but 1995 for many Japanese was a watershed marking the end of an era and jarring the foundations of confidence in the country's post-war political, economic and social systems.

HEADLINE GRABBERS

The Kobe earthquake and the Aum Shinrikyo religious cult shook up Japan physically and psychologically in 1995.

The Great Hanshin Earthquake on Jan. 17 killed more than 5,000 people and injured thousands more. It was the worst natural disaster in Japan since the 1923 Great Kanto Earthquake in the Tokyo region that caused 142,000 deaths.

Businesses in Kobe and Osaka were heavily damaged by the earthquake, which further delayed national economic recovery after four years of stagnation.

Then in March, members of Aum Shinrikyo released the deadly sarin nerve gas on Tokyo subways in the morning rush hour, killing 12 people and causing injury to thousands more. The cult was also accused of kidnapping and murdering a lawyer and his family and several others who opposed the group.

Evidence also surfaced that Aum experimented in production of chemical weapons and imported assault rifles from Russia to prepare to overthrow the government later in the year. Cult leader Shoko Asahara and many of his closest disciples were arrested, but the very existence of such a bizarre, extremist cult was difficult for most to come to terms with.

BUM BANKS

Meanwhile, Japan's venerable and seemingly all-powerful banking industry discovered a serious chink in its armor.

Financial institutions in the post-war era enjoyed ever expanding business as financiers to industry. Banks

When land prices dropped in succeeding years, banks came down to earth with a bump

were regarded as the safest bet around, on par with government-backed public institutions.

College students always ranked banks high on their list of desired employers, not least because of generous welfare policies. Parents were proud to say their sons or daughters worked in the "rock solid" banking industry. Banks also outdid government posts in terms of salary and bonuses.

However, these rock solid institutions found themselves on shifting sands in 1995 as bad debt held by the banks moved from the billions of yen into the trillions.

"Trustworthy," "reliable" and "accountable" no longer leap to mind when discussing Japan's bankers, because it became clear most of them, too, were taken in by the greed that characterized the bubble economy of the mid to late 1980s.

Banks loaned out money hand over fist during the asset-inflated bubble years, most if it secured against sky-high property prices. When land prices dropped in succeeding years, banks came down to earth with a bump and found themselves sitting on a heap of nonperforming loans.

Sumitomo Bank bit the bad debt bullet earlier than most, posting pretax losses of ¥335 billion in the fiscal year ended March 1995 by writing off bad loans of ¥800 billion. It was the first red-ink at a city bank since the chaos that followed the end of the war in the 1940s.

Many smaller institutions, such as credit unions, faced more serious debt problems. In the past, city banks offered a helping hand to credit unions in financial difficulty, but this time the banks themselves lacked the reserves, and the will, to help out.

This forced the Ministry of Finance and the Bank of Japan to come up with rescue plans. The BOJ went so far as to set up a public-funded bank to retire debt at two bankrupt credit unions in Tokyo. Later, chief executives of the two companies were charged with breach of trust. In summer, a bank and two credit unions in the Kansai region went under, causing further anxiety and distrust among depositors.

Other developments served to undermine confidence in the global banking system. Barings Plc, Britain's oldest merchant bank, went bankrupt in February after a derivatives dealer in Singapore caused losses exceeding 500 million pounds (¥130 billion). In a similar vein, Daiwa Bank in September disclosed that a dealer at its New York office caused ¥110 billion in losses through fraudulent bond deals.

Another event in the banking industry made the headlines. In March, Mitsubishi Bank and Bank of Tokyo agreed to merge within a year to form the biggest bank in the world with deposits of around ¥50 trillion. Officials at the banks said international competition and financial deregulation prompted the move.

Industry analysts believe further mergers and acquisitions in the banking industry are likely.

In the meantime, the Japanese economy continued to be hammered by the strong yen. The ¥100 mark against the dollar was long regarded as the resistance line, but the Japanese currency surged past that marker in June 1994, and hit ¥96 in October. The yen remained in the record-breaking mood in 1995, clearing another psychological line of ¥90 to the dollar in March, and crashing through ¥80 in April.

Few expected this dramatic jump in the value of the yen, considering the weakened economy and tougher competition from U.S. industry and emerging Asian economies. The yen's behavior in 1995 pushed policy makers to re-examine the structure of the Plaza Accord, an arrangement for cooperative intervention in foreign exchange markets set up by industrialized nations in September 1985.

POLITICAL THEATER

A circus of scandal and corruption has never been far from center stage in Japanese politics over the last two decades. Japanese politicians repeatedly threatened to clean up their act, but always managed to somehow put on a similar show; only the players were different.

Prospects for change did improve in 1995, but this focused on electoral reform, with a token swipe at cutting private funding for political parties. Little was done to try and curb the excesses that many politicians seem to see as a perquisite of public office.

A mixture of a single seat and proportional representation system was introduced in November 1994 and state funding for political parties made a controversial passage through the Diet. The new system will be tested in the next general election expected to be held sometime in the early part of 1996.

The birth of the Shinshinto conservative party in December 1994 was the result of battles for dominance among factions in the Liberal Democratic Party, but another factor was the new election system favors large parties.

Local elections held in April 1995, however, put the jitters into major political parties after independent candidates took the governorships of Tokyo and Osaka.

New Tokyo Governor Yukio Aoshima was a former TV scriptwriter and actor, while new Osaka Governor Isamu Yamada enjoyed a former life on the stage as a comedian. Although both were former upper house members, commentators were quick to latch onto the background of the new governors, suggesting a couple of comedians had joined the other jokers in public office.

Unkind comments aside, Aoshima and Yamada beat candidates from the big parties — Aoshima did not even bother to campaign — which clearly showed voter antagonism toward conventional politics.

Another shock for the ruling coalition was the upper house election in July. Though the three coalition parties, the LDP, SDP (Social Democratic Party of Japan) and Sakigake, expected some losses, the results were worse than anticipated. Prime Minister Tomiichi Murayama reportedly wanted to resign, but was eventually convinced to stay on to help hold the coalition together.

Still, the Murayama cabinet's public approval rating continued to slip, reflecting disappointment about the lack of leadership as the economy remained in a five-year slump.

Yohei Kono, a Murayama supporter, was forced out as LDP head in September and replaced by the hawkish Ryutaro Hashimoto. The socialists, meanwhile, were reorganizing with the aim of establishing a new party in preparation for the next general election.

Japan has a reputation for bureaucratic stability and propriety despite upsets caused by political struggles and shenanigans. However, civil servants were also tarred with the scandal brush in the year.

A high ranking Finance Ministry official was found to have made heavy investments in the stock market using "donations" from some shady associates. The official, who neglected to inform the tax authorities about the income invested in shares, also ran what the press called "side-businesses." Hardly the behavior of a public servant.

Other reports surfaced of large amounts of taxpayers' money being used by local government officials to entertain central government bureaucrats at swank restaurants and other watering holes.

WAR APOLOGIES

Prime Minister Murayama tried to have a formal Diet resolution passed offering apologies for Japanese aggression in World War II. However, strong opposition among ruling coalition members and the conservative opposition vetoed the move and the final Diet resolution in June was a watered down political compromise with no apology.

This upset many neighboring nations that felt the brunt of Japan's colonialism and militarism before and during the war. Murayama did make a public apology for the war in his role as prime minister on the memorial day of Japan's surrender, August 15.

In the 50 years since the end of the war, Japan has established itself as an economic power, but there still remains the question of whether it is welcomed in the world community as a political power.

Japan is now seeking to identify more with Asia, seeing the next century as the beginning of the Asia-Pacific era. The country is the biggest donor of economic aid to the region, an effort highly appreciated by Asian nations. But Asia remains very wary of Japan's political aspirations, fearing the possible resurgence of the country as a military power.

It is, therefore, Japan's basic position to clearly oppose militarism, and particularly nuclear arms as the only nation to be subjected to atomic bombings. For this reason, the government opposed the nuclear weapons tests by China and France in 1995, although the authorities were criticized in some quarters for not being vigorous enough in protesting the tests.

Japan is still seeking permanent membership of the United Nations Security Council, but discussions are still ongoing as to whether the U.N. should maintain its Cold War structure or reform itself to work more effectively on global issues.

On this issue, Japan needs to show clearer vision about what it sees as its international role in and outside the U.N.; a task, once again, held over to another year.

POLITICAL SCENE

'Odd-couple' coalition nears end as general election approaches

BY HIDENAKA KATO
Staff Writer

To general astonishment, the tripartite coalition under Prime Minister Tomiichi Murayama survived to enter its second year in June 1995. But with all parties gearing up in autumn for a yet-unscheduled general election to the lower house of the Diet, most observers were predicting a swift demise for the odd-couple coalition.

On September 21, Murayama's Social Democratic Party of Japan decided to terminate itself — having recognized that commitment to socialist dogma was hardly likely to bring success at the polls given the political winds of the post-Cold War era. Members planned to form a new party, hoping to build a larger tent with a more broad-based agenda.

One day later, the coalition linchpin Liberal Democratic Party chose high-profile Minister of International Trade and Industry Ryutaro Hashimoto as its new president. A bitter setback in July voting for upper house seats convinced the Liberal Democrats they needed a strong leader to fight a general election, and many felt no one filled that role better than Hashimoto — who had projected the image of a tough and outspoken negotiator during auto-trade talks with U.S. Trade Representative Mickey Kantor through June 1995.

The very next day, political tectonics had to give way to geological forces

As of early autumn, few analysts were willing to predict the results of a general election, especially given that it would be the first held after adoption of a new electoral system combining single-seat districts and proportional representation. But there was general agreement that the runup to voting would be Murayama's swan song, and that either the LDP or the largest opposition force, Shinshinto, would lead the next administration.

The coalition of the longtime archrival SDP and LDP, with the splinter Sakigake as a junior partner, was viewed as unstable even as it formed a government in June 1994. But the Murayama cabinet managed to avoid collapse by compromising over some major items on the political agenda — a Diet resolution marking the 50th anniversary of the end of World War II, for example — and simply postponing others, such as tax reform.

By mid-1995, however, circumstances were limiting the ability of the Murayama administration to continue its high-wire act, even though close supporters wanted Murayama to continue as premier for as long as possible. Opinion polls revealed support rates for the cabinet declining; business leaders were disgusted at the lack of strong initiatives to stimulate the economy; and, perhaps most telling, the coalition members had all performed under expectations in two significant polls: the unified regional elections in April and the July upper house vote. In July, Murayama's SDP won only 16 seats against its target of 22, reducing its strength in the upper chamber from 63 to 38. The LDP failed to win as much as expected, picking up only 46 seats to reach 110. Sakigake, which had aimed at five seats, won just two.

The primary factor keeping Murayama in office was less admiration for him than the hard reality that there was really no viable replacement. As a result, most coalition members wanted to keep Murayama as the cabinet's front man until a budget for fiscal 1996 was compiled — a process obviously favorable to those in charge — sometime early in the year.

Coalition leaders thus put their best efforts into avoiding any mishaps that might force an election, and events conspired with them to help hold the coalition together through a long, hot summer.

WHITHER JAPANESE SOCIALISM?

On January 16, a long-simmering fissure within Murayama's SDP suddenly exploded into a seemingly unbridgeable gap. Led by former party chairman Sadao Yamahana, the less ideologically oriented members voted to abandon the Socialists and form their own party, a move certain to pull the rug out from under the coalition.

But the very next day, political tectonics had to give way to geological forces. The Great Hanshin Earthquake forced all parties to pull together; Yamahana stood down his revolt; and even the main opposition Shinshinto, which had hoped to take advantage of an SDP breakup to regain power, could do nothing but collaborate with the government to pass a fiscal 1995 budget and other measures to cope with the devastation in Kobe and the surrounding regions.

Shinshinto had coalesced in December 1994 as a mega-merger of nine opposition political groups. Behind the move lay the simple political idea that the winner-takes-all nature of single-seat constituencies would favor a larger party. But with little in common on sensitive political issues, Shinshinto leaders ran into frequent difficulties in forming party consensus, and this weakness too helped keep the coalition in power.

Shinshinto kept a low profile during the political cease-fire that followed the earthquake. Among other things, the fact that the largest faction within the party was an LDP spinoff prevented Shinshinto from appealing to voters on the basis of distinct policy differences with the ruling coalition.

This political stalemate disgusted voters, who displayed their dissatisfaction in the form of apathy. The July upper house election saw a record-low voter turnout of just 44.52%.

RISE AND FALL

Changes of major parties' number of seats in both houses

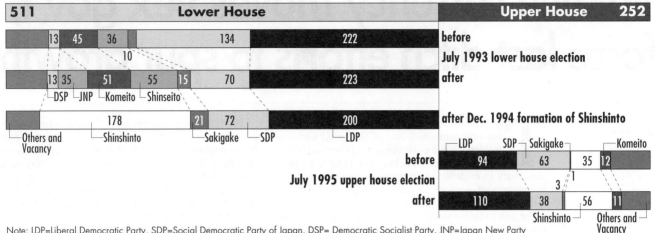

Note: LDP=Liberal Democratic Party, SDP=Social Democratic Party of Japan, DSP= Democratic Socialist Party, JNP=Japan New Party
Source: The Nikkei Weekly

ALL THE (POLITICAL) WORLD'S A STAGE?

Japan's political establishment was upset in April, when voters chose two former comedians as governors of Tokyo and Osaka. In Tokyo, almost all parties supported a candidate who had served as deputy chief cabinet secretary, the nation's senior career bureaucrat, for no less than seven years. In Osaka, the choice of all parties but the Japan Communist Party was a former Environment Agency administrative vice minister, top bureaucratic post in that organization.

Both were defeated.

Professional politicians had argued that the experience and connections those candidates enjoyed with the nation's powerful central government would contribute to smooth management of the mammoth governments of Japan's two largest urban centers. But the voters were sick and tired of the faceless ex-bureaucrats and senior officials of business organizations who so often dominate candidate lists in local elections.

Later, analysts interpreted the results as a show of public disgust at the back-room collusion of ostensibly rival parties, leading even their traditional supporters to turn away and become so-called "non-affiliated" voters. So, when it came to the House of Councilors election in July, the parties raced to sign up celebrity candidates, ranging from a one-time professional wrestler, to a TV commentator, an Olympic medalist, an actress and a novelist, hoping to attract those floating votes.

Surprise! Relatively few of these celebrities passed muster with the voters to win upper house seats.

Even so, the parties have not ruled out fielding celebrity candidates in the next general election, though judging from the results they had better not rely too much on former movie stars and athletes, analysts said.

Both Yukio Aoshima and Knock Yokoyama, the comedians-turned-governors, have indeed experienced difficulties in handling their offices. "They are, after all, amateurs," comments one veteran Diet legislator. Then, too, the municipal assemblies they're trying to deal with are dominated by party warhorses.

LIBERALS SEEK A HOME

As the Shinshinto took form late in 1994, a senior Socialist leader proposed a new 'liberal' party to offer voters a clear alternative to the two conservative camps. The idea aimed at attracting Sakigake, but that moderate conservative group demurred. In any event, strong opposition from the left wing of the party — including some legislators, union officials and local supporters favoring the traditional pacifist party line — prevented the Socialists from acting on the proposal for almost a year.

UNIFIED REGIONAL ELECTIONS

Voting for local officials take place every four years in April, and offers a de-facto national election. The two-stage balloting of 1995, for examples, included 13 of 47 prefectural governorships as well as thousands of mayoralties and tens of thousands of municipal assembly seats. The results are crucial to political parties, as a reflection of the strength of each party's grass-root organizations.

YEN APPRECIATION

Volatile currency moves vex gov't, force last-ditch efforts to spur growth

BY KATSURO
KITAMATSU
Deputy Editor

It remains

uncertain

when the

Japanese

economy

will get back

to solid

growth

The yen's volatile behavior on foreign exchange markets remained one of the most serious problems for the Japanese economy in 1995. Late night head-scratching and table thumping was much in evidence as government and industry ran brainstorming sessions to work out measures to deal with the yen's surge against the dollar.

The yen's climb started in March and although it ran out of steam later in the year, the currency's appreciation clobbered business activities, deflated domestic prices and put economic recovery on hold.

The stronger yen also forced industries, in particular export-oriented manufacturers, to further streamline domestic operations and shift overseas.

Apparently, the speed of the yen's uphill sprint surprised the government and did far more damage to the economy than the authorities expected.

The Bank of Japan on March 3 orchestrated a massive market intervention with U.S. and European financial authorities to support the greenback. The central bank also cut the official discount rate by a half point to 1% on April 14 as another measure to discourage yen buying.

On the same day, the government announced an emergency spending package of ¥7 trillion. The package, financed by a supplementary budget, included additional implementation of public-works projects, deregulation, and encouraging imports, along with a reduction in public utility rates to pass on the benefits of the higher yen to consumers.

The currency markets took a quick look at these efforts, gave a big yawn, and went on with enthusiastic buying of the yen. The buying spree culminated on April 19 when the dollar hit a record low of ¥79.75 in Tokyo. The U.S. currency remained below ¥100 for the next few months.

Hoping to alleviate the yen shock and get the economic recovery on track, the government on June 27 made public the specifics of the April 14 stimulus package, along with some additional measures to spur domestic demand. Once again, however, currency markets were far from impressed.

The seemingly unstoppable advance of the yen turned Japan's economic climate even bleaker in the second half of the year.

According to the BOJ's quarterly *tankan* survey of business sentiment released on Sept. 8, the business conditions index for major manufacturers stood at minus 18 in August, down from minus 16 in May. The index is calculated by subtracting the percentage of companies which report their business conditions as unfavorable from the percentage of firms with a favorable outlook.

Likewise, the government's official diagnosis of the economy was cheerless. In its monthly economic report in September, the Economic Planning Agency deleted "recovery" from its descriptions of the economy, pointing out that business at many corporations was stalled and inventories were piling up. Since September 1994, the agency had been asserting that the economy was on a gradual recovery path.

However, the EPA report denied that the economy had plunged into another downward spiral, asserting that the dollar's rebound against the yen in July and a recovery in stock prices in the summer would help revitalize business activities toward 1996. The sentiment of both currency and stock markets changed, the report said, since the dollar turned stronger through yen-selling intervention by Japanese, U.S. and European monetary authorities on July 6 and 7.

RECORD-LOW DISCOUNT RATE

In further attempts to put some life into the economy, both the Bank of Japan and the government undertook additional stimulus measures in September.

On Sept. 8, the BOJ reduced the official discount rate by another half point to a record low 0.5%. At the same time, it allowed the overnight call rate — the short-term interest rate banks charge each other for overnight loans — to drop further.

The government on Sept. 20 took the wraps off another spending package worth ¥14.22 trillion, with over ¥12 trillion allocated for public-works projects. A high priority was placed on revitalizing the real estate market. It also included funds to promote science and technology projects and expand telecommunications networks.

Still, it remains uncertain when the Japanese economy will get back to solid growth. Although the dollar recovered to ¥100 and above at one stage later in the year, it remained relatively weaker against the yen compared with recent years.

According to a Nihon Keizai Shimbun survey of 1,604 listed companies (excluding financial institutions and companies with irregular business terms) pretax profits for the year through March 1996 are expected to grow 14.1% on average from a year earlier. This is thanks mainly to cost-cutting and the dollar's rebound in July.

But recovery at small and midsize companies will be slower due to lingering difficulties caused by the higher yen.

The survey says non-manufacturers also expect sluggish profit growth because domestic demand looks likely to remain dormant for the foreseeable future.

MAJOR ECONOMIC EVENTS AND CURRENCY MOVES

Yen-dollar spot rate in Tokyo

April 19: Dollar hits record ¥79.75 at one time

July 6-7: Dollar-buying intervention by G-7

Sept. 8: BOJ cuts official discount rate to 0.5%

April 25: Conference of G-7 finance ministers and central bankers

April 14: BOJ cuts official discount rate to 1%. Govn't unveils economic stimulus package

Sept. 14: Dollar rises to ¥102.8 in Tokyo
Sept. 20: Govn't announces new stimulus measures

'95 Jan | Feb. | March | April | May | June | July | Aug. | Sept.

Source: The Nihon Keizai Shimbun

THAT HOLLOW FEELING

In preparation for the yen's long-term strength against the dollar and intensified competition around the world, Japanese companies plan to shift more operations from Japan to China, Southeast Asia and other locations overseas. Although this threatens to shut down plants at home and put more Japanese out of work, many companies believe they have little choice.

"Our priority is to expand production capacity overseas and minimize the cost of domestic operations," said an official at Showa Corp., a parts supplier affiliated with Honda Motor Co.

In the year through March 1996, the company plans to invest ¥6 billion in its plants in China, Thailand, the U.S. and other countries, almost 2.5 times the figure spent a year earlier. It will also be the first time for the company to spend more overseas than in Japan.

Showa is not an isolated case. According to a Nihon Keizai Shimbun survey of 335 Japanese manufacturers, 57% said they have plans to increase investment in plant and equipment overseas. Perhaps more serious, 82.4% said they expect the so-called hollowing out of domestic industry to continue.

The ratio of offshore production at these companies to domestic output reached 14.18% in fiscal 1995 on average, up from 13.31% a year ago. They plan to increase the number of overseas employees by 4.4% from the previous year and 5.0% in fiscal 1996. Employment of domestic workers in the same years, however, is expected to fall by 0.5% and 0.2%, the survey shows.

The average boom-or-bust dollar/yen exchange rate at these firms was ¥94.98, but the level varies widely by industry. Pharmaceutical companies, for example, said they can remain profitable at around ¥90. But textile firms, steelmakers and food producers said they need the rate above ¥100.

"Neither the extreme strengthening or weakening of the dollar is welcome for our business," said Heiichi Hamaoka, a managing director at Nissan Motor Co. He expects the yen to remain stronger against the dollar in the long run, but hopes the U.S. currency will stabilize at around ¥100.

KEY WORD

YEN'S GLOBALIZATION

The dollar's plunge against the yen in 1995 touched off debate on whether the Japanese currency could replace the dollar as the key currency in Asia. Asian central banks reduced dollar holdings in favor of the yen, but the size of yen-denominated trade remains far smaller than dollar-denominated deals. Economists said the Japanese government needs to deregulate financial markets if it wants to raise the yen's status in Asia.

KEY WORD

OFFSHORE R&D

To improve competitiveness in foreign markets, more Japanese companies set up research and development facilities overseas. Although the majority of firms still keep essential R&D at home, electric appliance manufacturers, such as Sony Corp., are taking advantage of overseas expertise and manpower by establishing R&D facilities outside of the country. Red tape and high cost are two other reasons why Japanese R&D is moving offshore.

ASIAN ECONOMIES

East Asian economic growth, trade continue on fast track

BY TOSHIYA
KAWAHARA
Deputy Editor

Despite the continued recession in Japan since 1991, there have been no signs of decline in the economies of East Asia

The economies of Asia continued to expand in 1995, fueling economic growth worldwide. By one estimate, the total population of Asia will hit 4.9 billion in 2025, or 58% of the world's population. The importance of the emerging economies of East Asia, in particular, is increasing in the global marketplace as ever-larger flows of capital are moving eastward.

East Asia will see an 8.1% increase in actual economic growth in both 1995 and 1996, according to a forecast by the World Bank in its annual report released in April 1995. The report said that developing nations overall would post 4% economic growth for the same period.

The report also predicted that both exports and imports in East Asia would continue to grow by around 9% annually, with average growth estimated at 7.7% over the next 10 years through 2004. It noted that China, India and Indonesia would likely join the ranks of the world's six largest economies as measured by purchasing power parity in coming years.

Toshio Watanabe, a professor at Tokyo Institute of Technology, said that in East Asia, comprising the newly industrialized economies (NIEs) of South Korea, Taiwan, Hong Kong and Singapore, members of the Association of Southeast Asian Nations (ASEAN, comprising Brunei, Indonesia, Malaysia, the Philippines, Singapore, Thailand and Vietnam) and China, a "self-supportive recycling structure" has been established, based on supplies of capital funds and goods within the region since the end of the 1980s when expansion first began.

Watanabe observed that despite the continued recession in Japan since 1991, there have been no signs of decline in the economies of East Asia. On the contrary, the East Asian economies have continued to support growth in neighboring countries, maintaining the vitality of the region as a whole.

"The role of the NIEs, in this respect, is crucial because they are emerging as importers as well as investors in the ASEAN region and China," he said.

But the Asia Pacific region will need a combined $1.2 trillion to $1.5 trillion in infrastructure investment in the next 10 years to maintain the current growth rate, according to another report released by the World Bank in September.

The developing economies of Asia grew 7.7% in 1994 and are likely to mark 7.5% growth in 1995, according to the 1995 annual report by the Economic and Social Commission for Asia and the Pacific (ESCAP).

Bangkok-based ESCAP traced high economic growth to rapid expansion of exports, a massive influx of private capital, government-initiated deregulation and liberalization measures and strong domestic demand spurred by rising incomes and living standards in the region.

Trade in the Asia Pacific region grew by an average 15% annually from 1990 to 1993. This performance was three times stronger than the showing in industrialized countries. Intra-regional trade increased nearly 50% in 1994, further stoking growth in the area.

The average gross domestic product (GDP) of developing Asia Pacific countries showed growth of 8.2% in 1994, according to a report released by the Asian Development Bank in April. The report projected 7.6% growth in 1995 and 7.4% in 1996.

The NIEs — often referred to as the Four Dragons — achieved an increase of 7.4% in average GDP growth in 1994, against 6.2% the previous year. Hong Kong marked a slight fall to 5.5% while South Korea saw growth of 8.3%.

China's economy grew 11.8% in 1994, down from 13.4% the previous year. Growth is expected to slip further to 9.8% in 1995. Inflation there should cool to around 15% in 1995 from 21.7% in 1994, the report said.

Southeast Asian economies showed average GDP growth of 7.5% in 1994, up 0.7 percentage point from 1993, with improved performances in virtually all sectors.

Trade between Japan and Asia has also been expanding. Two-way trade surged to $252.2 billion in 1994, up 17% from the previous year. This figure is close to the $273 billion in combined trade between Japan and the U.S. and European Union, according to a report released in March by the Ministry of Finance. Trade expansion between Japan and Asia stemmed from economic growth in the region and increased investment by Japan, the report said.

On the political stage, ASEAN is raising its profile in the Asia Pacific region as it moves closer to uniting all 10 Southeast Asian nations under the ASEAN umbrella.

In July, Vietnam became the seventh member of the association. Cambodia has now joined Laos as an ASEAN observer while Myanmar has edged closer to observer status by acceding to the Treaty of Amity and Cooperation in Southeast Asia.

ASEAN is becoming increasingly assertive in political and security issues. The ASEAN foreign ministers' meeting in July called for a settlement of the Spratly islands issue through negotiation in response to the growing threat to the region from China.

The member states of ASEAN were expected to play key roles at the Asia-Pacific Economic Cooperation forum held in Osaka in November.

EMERGING TRADE ZONES

1 ASEAN Free Trade Area
Thailand, Indonesia, The Philippines, Malaysia, Singapore, Brunei

2 South China Economic Zone
Hong Kong, Taiwan, Fujian, Guangdong

3 Indian Ocean Free Trade Group (Proposed)
Australia, South Africa, India, Indonesia, Malaysia, Singapore

4 Japan, NIEs, ASEAN, China

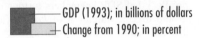
— GDP (1993); in billions of dollars
— Change from 1990; in percent

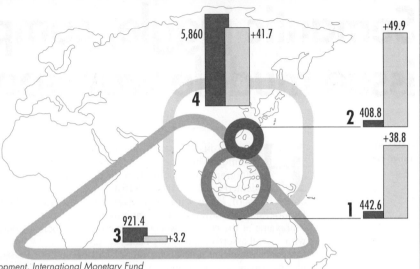

5,860   +41.7   +49.9
4
2 408.8
+38.8
1 442.6
921.4
3 +3.2

Source: Organization for Economic Cooperation and Development, International Monetary Fund

EMERGING ECONOMIES IN ASIA

Asian economies have seen explosive growth as the markets of Vietnam, Myanmar and India attract investors worldwide. Having joined ASEAN in July, Vietnam has surfaced as an economy offering massive business potential. The normalization of U.S.-Vietnam diplomatic relations in 1995 cleared the path for many foreign investors seeking business opportunities in the country.

Myanmar has also started to relax its policy of isolationism, in a bid to grab some of the capital flowing into Asia. The ruling State Law and Order Restoration Council (SLORC) made a significant policy shift in July when it released dissident Aung Sang Suu Kyi after six years of house arrest. The military junta took the step to improve its human rights image with the aim of obtaining development assistance from the West.

India stepped into the spotlight in 1995 as economic liberalizations instituted by Prime Minister Narasimha Rao began to take root, drawing foreign funds. The economies of South Asia will average annual growth of 5.4% in the next 10 years, with India becoming one of the six largest economies in the world by 2010, according to estimates by the World Bank.

TOP 10 FOREIGN INVESTORS IN VIETNAM

Cumulative amount from January 1988 through June 1995; in millions of dollars, number of projects in parentheses

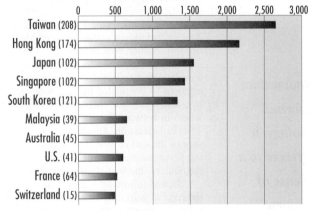

Taiwan (208)
Hong Kong (174)
Japan (102)
Singapore (102)
South Korea (121)
Malaysia (39)
Australia (45)
U.S. (41)
France (64)
Switzerland (15)

0   500   1,000   1,500   2,000   2,500   3,000

Source: State Committee for Cooperation and Investment of Vietnam

SPRATLY ISLANDS

A group of uninhabited islands and reefs in the South China Sea believed to be rich in oil and other resources. China, Vietnam and Taiwan have each claimed the entire group, while Malaysia, the Philippines and Brunei claim rights to parts of the chain. Construction by China on Mischief Reef drew protests from the Philippines. China says it will accept only bilateral negotiations, but the other claimants want multilateral talks. The various claims represent an Asian crisis waiting to happen.

APEC (ASIA-PACIFIC ECONOMIC COOPERATION)

APEC was established in 1989, with a membership of 18 countries from Asia, Oceania and the Americas. It was initially conceived as a forum for the exchange of views among finance ministers. But recently its scope has widened. The APEC Bogor Declaration adopted in Indonesia in November 1994 called for liberalization of trade and investment in industrialized nations by 2010 and in industrializing countries by 2020. APEC leaders met in Osaka in November 1995, to hammer out details.

50 YEARS AFTER WORLD WAR II

Semantic juggle, compensation issue muddle war apology

BY MIHOKO IIDA
Staff Writer

How will history remember Prime Minister Tomiichi Murayama? Undoubtedly, several paragraphs will be written on the unprecedented coalition of his leftist Social Democratic Party of Japan with the conservative Liberal Democrats; the alliance of convenience that put Murayama at the steering wheel of government, albeit with several assertive and unruly back-seat drivers.

Another important note on his record will be apologies for Japanese aggression in World War II. To mark the 50th anniversary of the end of the war in 1995, Murayama went further than any previous post-war prime minister in attempting to atone for the country's wartime onslaught.

But for victims of Japanese aggression in WWII, the expression of remorse was far too little, much too late.

Critics were also quick to state that Murayama should have done more, considering the SDP spent much of the post-war era supporting a clear apology for Japan's wartime offensive, as well as compensation for individual war victims. Past LDP administrations shut the door on individual claims. Under Murayama, the door to compensation remained firmly closed.

This situation served to muddle Murayama's apology; a muddle that reflected the nature of the Japanese government — dominated by the conservative LDP, topped by a leftist premier, and mixed with a dash of the somewhere-in-between Sakigake party.

Nevertheless, on August 15, 1995, the 50th anniversary of the end of WWII, a Japanese prime minister for the first time admitted that a flawed national policy led the country into war. Part of his statement went:

"...Japan, following a mistaken national policy, took the road to war, only to ensnare the Japanese people in a fateful crisis, and, through its colonial rule and aggression, caused tremendous damage and suffering to the people of many countries, particularly in Asia."

Referring to the "irrefutable facts of history," Murayama expressed his "feelings of deep remorse" and "heartfelt apology." The statement was generally well received worldwide. But Asian governments and media commentators did not hide their lingering distrust of a country where top government officials regularly deny that Japan was an aggressor in WWII.

Doubters overseas found grounds for such distrust in the first half of 1995 when the coalition could not decide on how to word a Diet resolution addressing Japan's record in WWII. Compiling the resolution was one of the platforms upon which the Murayama coalition was established in June 1994.

SDP lawmakers initially pressed for inclusion of an apology, but the LDP refused to entertain the idea. Not only were LDP members afraid of alienating party support groups — such as the Japan War-Bereaved Families Association, which believes an apology would dishonor Japanese soldiers and civilians who died in the war — but a hard core of LDP lawmakers believe an apology is not required.

The deadlock led SDP lawmakers to tone down their demand and urge a statement of *hansei* (a Japanese word that falls short of an outright apology) on three issues: the colonization of the Korean Peninsula, acts of aggression against China, and Japanese behavior in Asia during the Pacific War.

After the opposition Shinshinto boycotted the Diet vote on the issue, a watered-down version of the resolution was passed by the lower house on June 9. Rather than a formal apology, it referred to a "sense of remorse toward acts our country carried out in the past."

Fudged atonement is better than none was also the message conveyed when the government launched a fund to compensate women used as sex slaves by the Japanese Imperial Army during WWII. The fund was launched in July 1995 after much squabbling within the coalition as to how the government should commit itself to the project.

Finally, it was stipulated that direct compensation for the victims must come from private-sector donations. The government was left responsible for setting up the fund as well as promising to provide medical and welfare services through the fund for the former so-called comfort women.

The Japanese government maintains that wartime compensation matters were settled following the signing of the San Francisco Peace Treaty. Tokyo's stance is that its former colonies in Asia waived the right to individual claims when they accepted reparations in the 1950s and 1960s in the form of economic aid.

Foreign war victims weren't the only ones denied adequate redress. The Murayama administration also attempted to resolve the issue of compensation for victims of the U.S. atomic bombings of Hiroshima and Nagasaki and raise the matter to one of national redress. The SDP, traditionally been supported by pacifists and nuclear opponents, was in favor of such legislation.

But, again under LDP pressure, the final draft omitted the words "national redress," the statement backers of the bill had fought for to testify Japan owes a special debt to individuals who suffered from the bombings.

All in all, it is difficult to discern whether history will look kindly upon the Murayama government's record during the 50th anniversary year. But for all his limitations and failings due to the nature of the coalition, critics generally agree that Murayama accomplished more in terms of atonement for the war than would have been possible under any LDP administration.

Rather than a formal apology, it referred to a "sense of remorse"

THE FUND OF LITTLE COMFORT

In 1995, the government finally addressed the issue of compensating women forced to provide sex to Japanese troops during World War II.

However, in deciding to set up a fund to collect private donations, the authorities left it unclear as to how much money will be collected and who will receive it.

What was clear is that direct compensation from the Japanese government will not be forthcoming.

Despite these drawbacks, even critics admit that something is better than nothing. For one thing, the women forced into wartime prostitution are getting old. For another, 1995 was the 50th anniversary of the war's end, which fund advocates used as a focus point to build support for the plan within the government.

The crux of the controversy over how to atone for the humiliation and suffering endured by these women was the question of government compensation. Conservative forces in government have repeatedly argued that war-compensation payments have been settled at the government-to-government level.

In order to balance the desire to help the victims and not appear to be providing direct compensation, the government has structured the Asian Women's Fund as a joint government and private venture. The authorities agreed to set up and operate the fund — so far ¥500 million has been collected — but will not disburse compensation payments. Also, such payments will come from private donations only.

The fund launched its cash drive on Aug. 15 with full-page advertisements in six of the nation's largest newspapers. The campaign is expected to run through February 1996.

Prime Minister Tomiichi Murayama donated ¥150,000 to the fund followed by a ¥100,000 voluntary contribution from each cabinet member.

Fund advocates estimate ¥1-2 billion will be needed to provided payments to the former comfort women.

But reality has been harsher than expectations.

While activists say the success of the fund depends on major contributions from corporate Japan, the country's largest business group Keidanren has turned down a government request that it assist in collecting contributions from its members.

CHRONICLE OF JAPANESE ECONOMY

1949 Occupation Army's G.H.Q. sets the rate of yen at 360 per U.S. dollar

1950 Korean War boosts demand for Japanese goods, spurring economic growth

1951 San Francisco Peace Treaty is signed

1952 Japan becomes a member of the IMF and the World Bank

1955 Japan joins GATT

1956 Government economic white paper says the postwar period is over; Japan joins the United Nations

1957 Japan is selected as a nonpermanent member of the U.N. Security Council

1964 Japan becomes a member of the OECD

1966 Japan's GNP exceeds $100 billion

1967 Capital inflow is liberalized

1968 Japan's GNP is second only to the U.S.

1971 Yen appreciates to 308 to the dollar under the Smithsonian agreement

1973 Floating exchange rates are adopted; first oil crisis

1975 Industrialized nations hold their first summit meeting including Japan

1978 Japan-China Peace and Friendship Treaty is signed

1979 G-7 summit is held in Tokyo; second oil crisis

1985 Plaza Accord is signed to lower the value of the dollar

1989 Nikkei Stock Average records a historic high of 38,915; consumption tax is introduced

1990 Stock prices fall sharply

1991 Securities and financial scandals erupt

1993 Rice imports are partly liberalized under GATT Uruguay Round agreement

1994 Yen rises above 100 per dollar

1995 Great Hansin Earthquake hits Kobe area; yen tops 80 per dollar temporarily

Source: The Nihon Keizai Shimbun

KEY WORD

HANSEI

An expression that falls between reflection and repentance, often translated as remorse. A child can feel *hansei* for forgetting to do homework and a political statement can express *hansei* for Japan's aggression in World War II. The Diet resolution on the country's war record refers to a "sense of hansei," because conservative lawmakers opposed an outright apology.

KEY WORD

COMFORT WOMEN

A translation of the Japanese word *ianfu,* a euphemism for women enslaved by the Japanese Imperial Army to provide sex to soldiers during World War II. Historians estimate the number of comfort women to be in the thousands, but no official figure is available. Most of the women were from Korea, but women from China, Indonesia, the Philippines, the Netherlands and Japan were also used as sex slaves in military brothels.

TRADE FRICTION

Japan, U.S. continue brinksmanship in item-by-item negotiation waltz

BY MASATO
ISHIZAWA
Staff Writer

During the Cold War, the perceived threat of Soviet communism meant politics and security tended to take precedence over economics in Japan-U.S. relations. At that time, the majority of Americans and Japanese considered that national interests on both sides of the ocean best served by a strong trans-Pacific alliance. But five years on from the collapse of the Berlin Wall there is no longer a common enemy to unite Japan and the U.S. Fears that economic conflict will undermine Tokyo-Washington ties are currently mounting in both countries.

Crisis was narrowly averted on June 28 when Japan and the U.S. struck a last-minute agreement on automobile and auto parts trade. But many observers reckon the accord is unlikely to offer a long-term solution to trade-related conflict as the two countries continue to bicker over other issues such as access to Japan's photographic-film market.

Japan and the U.S. were at loggerheads for more than 20 months over auto-sector trade differences. The major sticking point in negotiations was the "voluntary" purchase of U.S. auto parts by Japan.

Autos and auto parts account for some 60% of Japan's trade surplus with the U.S., which in the year through March 1995 totaled $65.7 billion. In 1992, Japanese automakers buckled under pressure from both Tokyo and Washington to buy foreign-made auto parts to the tune of $19 billion by the end of March 1995. The U.S. insisted that this should be expanded from 1995 in subsequent rounds of negotiations.

But Tokyo was adamant that enforcing overseas procurement by automakers was completely beyond the scope of government. The U.S. responded in May with a threat to impose 100% tariffs on Japanese luxury automobiles. An 11th-hour agreement was eventually reached on June 28 at a ministerial meeting in Geneva between MITI minister Ryutaro Hashimoto and U.S. Trade Representative Mickey Kantor.

Tokyo pledged to eliminate unfair business practices between automakers and dealerships, if any were found to exist, as a means of boosting sales of U.S. cars and auto parts in Japan.

Hashimoto also promised to take steps to deregulate repair shops in Japan. In addition, Japanese automakers announced voluntary steps to boost overseas production and parts procurement.

As an illustration of Tokyo's refusal to yield to unreasonable U.S. demands, Japanese government officials and auto-industry executives hailed the agreement as a major turning point in the bilateral relationship.

But U.S. pressure did not ease. Instead, Washington applied similar threats of punitive sanctions to the simmering dispute over Japan's photographic-film market.

Washington's success in the dispute with China over intellectual property rights encouraged strong-arm tactics against Japan

Furthermore, doubts remain as to the viability of the auto agreement. The Clinton administration reminded Tokyo late in September that it means to ensure full implementation of the June 28 auto agreement. If not, was the implication, sanctions are still an option.

"We have many options," Kantor said. Some commentators read this as an indication that the U.S. could either invoke Section 301 of the U.S. Trade Law or file a complaint with the new World Trade Organization.

In the past, Japan and the U.S. have haggled over a variety of trade issues. So why has the punitive-sanctions card been played by Washington only recently?

Many observers reckon the Clinton administration's first priority is to shore up its position ahead of next year's presidential election. Clinton needs to woo back the constituency of workers he alienated with his strong backing for the North American Free Trade Agreement. In Japan his tough stance on Japan-U.S. trade is widely viewed as a crowd-pleasing act performed for the benefit of the autoworkers and other labor unions.

But MITI officials believe there is another explanation. The hardline U.S. approach, they claim, crystallized in Beijing. They believe Washington's recent success in the dispute with China over intellectual property rights encouraged the Clinton administration to adopt strong-arm tactics against Japan too.

The theory undoubtedly contains some elements of truth. But the track record of U.S. sanctions against Japan is uneven, to say the least. Punitive tariffs imposed in 1987 by the U.S. to force open Japan's allegedly closed semiconductor market initially targeted 14 Japanese imports worth $4 billion. But pressure from American consumers and companies forced the Reagan administration to scale down the targets to just three items — personal computers, color TVs and machine tools — worth just $300 million. This amount represented a tiny fraction of the $80 billion worth of goods Japan was selling to the U.S. at the time.

Once a compromise of sorts had been reached on auto parts, the next potential flash point in Japan-U.S. trade relations was the issue of photographic film and paper sales. The Office of the USTR announced in July its decision to pursue a complaint by Eastman Kodak Co. of unfair tactics to restrict the U.S. firm's market share in Japan. That set the stage for the imposition of sanctions under Section 301 of U.S. Trade Law.

Kodak claimed that Fuji Photo Film Co. and other industry leaders were, with the acquiescence the Japanese government, contriving to keep Kodak products from reaching Japanese stores. The "illegal" methods alleged by Kodak included "highly progressive rebates" which made distributors financially reliant on Fuji to the exclusion of other firms.

AUTOMOBILE ACRIMONY

May 5	Auto talks between Japan and the U.S. break down in Canada
May 10	U.S. announces intention to file complaint against Japan at WTO within 45 days
May 16	U.S. says 100% punitive tariffs to be imposed on some Japanese luxury-car imports
	MITI requests emergency meeting with U.S. under WTO auspices within 10 days
May 26	U.S. rejects MITI request and proposes meetings in Washington on June 20-21
May 30	MITI head Ryutaro Hashimoto sends letter to USTR Mickey Kantor requesting talks before June 15 in Geneva
June12, 20-21	Talks held in Geneva and Washington
June 28	U.S., Japan strike a deal in Geneva

Source: Nikkei Weekly

NEXT ACT IN THE LONG-RUN SHOW

In 1995, Tokyo and Washington locked horns over cars, air routes and film. Could personal handy phones trigger the next in a continuing series of trade disputes? That possibility emerged in September when U.S. officials insisted a new group of companies affiliated with Japan's telecommunications behemoth Nippon Telegraph and Telephone Corp. should be covered under a long-standing bilateral agreement on NTT procurement. The agreement was initially concluded in 1980 and most recently extended in October 1994. It was designed to make NTT procurement procedures more transparent and boost foreign equipment sales. NTT's overseas procurement is monitored under the agreement and reviewed annually by the U.S. government. Under the agreement, NTT is required to publish its components shopping list in government publications a few months ahead of actual purchasing. The telecommunications ministry maintained that it could not compel the NTT subsidiaries to adopt the procurement procedures. But three subsidiaries wholly owned by NTT — NTT Data Communications Systems Corp., NTT Mobile Communications Network Inc. and NTT Power and Building Facilities Inc. — were following the guidelines voluntarily.

CAR IMPORTS AT ISSUE

Share of imported vehicles in the world's leading markets in 1994; in percent

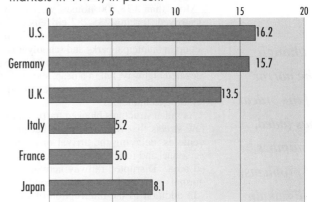

U.S.	16.2
Germany	15.7
U.K.	13.5
Italy	5.2
France	5.0
Japan	8.1

Note: Figures for U.S., Germany, U.K., Italy and France exclude intra-NAFTA or EU trade.
Source: Ministry of International Trade and Industry

KEY WORD

WORLD TRADE ORGANIZATION

The trade watchdog established in January 1995 played a major role in the Japan-U.S. auto trade dispute. Its scheme for dispute settlement provided an opportunity for Japanese negotiators to bring the issue before a third party and deflect undue pressure or sanctions by the U.S.

KEY WORD

NEW STRATEGIC ALLIANCE

This was proposed by U.S. Commerce Undersecretary Jeffrey E. Garten on his visit to Japan in August 1995. He called for renewed cooperation between Japan and the U.S. and suggested a new framework in addition to existing bilateral trade framework talks started in 1993.

KOBE EARTHQUAKE

Slow response to damage reveals inadequate disaster-preparedness

BY TOSHIO
SHINMURA
Staff Writer

Although the horror of the ordeal has faded, a number of problems still remain

In the wee hours of January 17, 1995, the citizens of the southwestern port city of Kobe awoke to horror. At 5:46 a.m., a massive earthquake measuring 7.2 on the Richter scale devastated the city and neighboring areas. The temblor was Japan's deadliest since the Great Kanto Earthquake of 1923, which claimed some 143,000 lives in greater Tokyo.

Known as the Great Hanshin Earthquake, the Kobe quake toppled office buildings, houses and train stations and damaged highways, railways and port facilities. Fires broke out immediately and spread quickly, charring more than 100 hectares of Japan's sixth largest city before firefighters could get the blaze under control.

Unable to free themselves from collapsed houses or escape from the flames, more than 5,500 citizens of Kobe and neighboring cities such as Nishinomiya and Ashiya were killed, while over 26,000 were injured.

More than 178,000 houses were fully or partially destroyed, forcing 235,282 citizens of Kobe alone to evacuate to school gymnasiums, public halls and tents set up in municipal parks and schoolyards.

A 200-meter portion of the Hanshin Expressway, an elevated highway, fell in a heap, shocking the Construction Ministry and questioning Japan's quake-resistant building technologies.

As fallen structures blocked traffic on many roads, the few streets that remained open became jammed with vehicles, delaying the arrival of emergency medical personnel and food and water from outside the devastated area. Disrupted railway networks did not resume normal operation for two to six months.

In addition to the interruption of transportation systems, the indispensable so-called lifelines, or the supply of water, gas, electricity and telephone services, were also cut off. Restoration of such public utility services took days and in some cases weeks.

Mitsubishi Research Institute estimated material damages, including that suffered by public utilities, housing, private and corporate assets and inventories, amounted to ¥6.27 trillion. To restore and rebuild what was lost, the think tank projected ¥9.48 trillion would need to be invested.

The earthquake not only shattered the local economy, but left deep scars on the national economy. Consumer spending in the January-March quarter rose only 0.1% because the quake chilled consumer sentiment, even outside the damaged region.

Overall, first quarter real GDP growth over the preceding quarter was a mere 0.1%.

The Great Hanshin Earthquake revealed the lack of disaster preparedness on the part of the local and central governments. For the first several hours after the quake, the Prime Minister's Office obtained information necessary to deal with the situation through televised reports because the office did not have its own independent network to gather information.

SLOW RESPONSE

The Hyogo prefectural governor was criticized for failing to promptly seek assistance from the central government by requesting mobilization of Self-Defense Forces personnel to help in rescue efforts. If local authorities do not make a request, the SDF cannot begin rescue activities.

Critics said the errors committed in such a critical situation were due to the lack of a clear chain of command, or crisis management system.

In July, half a year after the quake, the Hyogo prefectural government finished compiling a 10-year relief plan, named Hyogo Phoenix Plan. The plan calls for total investment of ¥12.1 trillion for the first five years through 2000.

Of the funds, ¥8 trillion is to be appropriated for urban-infrastructure projects, such as repairing port facilities and rebuilding roads; ¥2.1 trillion will be earmarked for the restoration of housing and social-welfare needs; and ¥1.5 trillion is expected to be allocated to assist private-sector industries, including low-interest loans and subsidies.

For the full 10 years of the plan, the authors estimate expenditures will total ¥17 trillion.

The central government has provided a wide range of support measures, most recently ¥1.4 trillion was set aside for reconstruction projects in its economic stimulus package announced in September.

Although the horror of the ordeal has faded into memory as the first anniversary of the quake approaches, a number of problems still remain.

Thousands of people are still living in evacuation shelters since losing their homes in the quake. Local authorities had built a total of 48,300 temporary housing units as of early August. But many of the units remain vacant because they are situated in somewhat remote locations relative to the shelters, which are more convenient for commuting to work or going to the hospitals. And some evacuees said they do not want to leave the friends they have made in the shelters.

Kobe closed its evacuation shelters by suspending food services at the facilities on Aug. 20 and ordered some 6,600 quake victims to move to temporary apartments. Even so, about 2,700 citizens have remained in the shelters.

The rebuilding of devastated neighborhoods is proceeding very slowly, as coordination between local governments and former residents is time consuming.

DAMAGE REPORT

TIME: Jan. 17, 1995, 5:46 a.m.

CASUALTIES: (as of July 1995)

Killed: 5,502

Missing: 2

Injured: 36,929

Destroyed houses (full and partial): 208,150 units

People left homeless: 314,169 (at peak)

Source: Local government and the police

RECONSTRUCTION DEMAND SLUGGISH

When the Great Hanshin Earthquake shook Kobe, economists predicted damage to the local economy would slow Japan's growth in the short term. But demand related to reconstruction would more than make up for the losses over the medium term, they said. It now appears this medium term will be a bit longer than they thought.

The construction industry is disappointed over sluggish orders for reconstruction once emergency repair work peaked. For one thing, tearing down damaged structures took more time than expected. Right after the quake, contractors increased personnel in the region, but were forced to scale back again before summer because due to the lack of orders. Reconstruction of office buildings and private condos were especially slow, one construction industry source reported.

The slow pickup of construction contracts had an adverse impact on the building materials market. After padding inventories on expectations of a rush of orders, steel companies had to trim production of H-beams because prices dipped due to excess supply. Crude steel output had to be curtailed as well.

Funding was a key obstacle to getting reconstruction projects up and running in both the private and public sectors. Small and midsize enterprises, such as shoe factories in Kobe's Nagata Ward, are being squeezed out of rebuilding funds.

"As reconstruction-related demand from the private sector is unlikely to increase during fiscal 1995, there is little hope that such demand will have a positive impact on the overall economy," said Tsutomu Nishimura, deputy chairman of the Japan Research Institute.

ESTIMATED DAMAGES CAUSED BY QUAKE

In billions of yen; based on 1990 prices

		Asset	Damage	Expected Investment
Social Infrastructure	Road	4,552.0	364.0	700.0
	Port	1,301.4	650.5	1,040.0
	Railway	2,064.0	310.0	420.0
	Communication	3,115.0	93.0	100.0
	Electricity	4,646.0	278.0	300.0
	Water/Gas	1,105.8	98.0	98.0
	Sewage /Industrial Water /Waste Treatment	2,347.0	176.0	176.0
	Education	3,556.0	362.7	400.0
	Park	247.1	18.5	18.5
	Disaster Control	1,267.3	63.4	63.4
	Sub Total	24,191.5	2,414.1	3,315.9
Housing	Housing	23,528.0	1,259.7	2,052.6
	Household Effects	10,164.0	575.6	667.2
	Sub Total	33,692.0	1,835.3	2,719.8
Corporate Asset	Building	7,759.0	968.5	1,915.4
	Equipment	7,082.0	663.5	1,141.0
	Sub Total	14,841.0	1,632.0	3,056.4
Inventory	Retail Goods Inventory	979.0	141.0	141.0
	Manufacturers' Inventory	1,990.0	249.0	249.0
	Sub Total	2,969.0	390.0	390.0
	Total	75,693.5	6,271.4	9,482.1

Source: Mitsubishi Research Institute

KEY WORD

RECONSTRUCTION PLANS

Quake-related rebuilding plans are being formed at many levels. The central government's seven-member Hanshin-Awaji Reconstruction Committee, chaired by a former vice minister of the National Land Agency, discusses basic policies and concrete measures. The committee then makes recommendations to Hyogo Prefecture and the city of Kobe, which have outlined their own 10-year restoration blueprints as well.

KEY WORD

RISK MANAGEMENT

The Great Hanshin Earthquake clearly revealed that Japan's central and local governments are severely unprepared for effectively handling large-scale disasters. After exposure to harsh criticisms, risk management became a priority issue. The Prime Minister's Office strengthened its capability to gather information in an emergency and the central government revamped in July its master plan for handling national disasters.

AUM SHINRIKYO

Tokyo nerve-gas attack reveals murderous truth behind wacky cult

BY HIDENAKA KATO
Staff Writer

Commuters at many Tokyo train stations in February 1990 were taken aback at the sight of weirdly costumed young people imploring passers-by to elect the leader of their little-known religion to a seat in the National Diet.

The campaigners drew many a laugh, especially for their rather unusual headgear — more commuters thought it was some kind of outlandish elephant mask than recognized it as a portrayal of the group's guru.

The vaguely comical cult was already suspected by some of having a more sinister side. But it was only five years later those commuters learned only too well the deadly truth behind Aum Shinrikyo.

Aware they were about to be investigated in connection with several alleged abductions, members of the cult released nerve gas on Tokyo subways March 20, 1995 — presumably targeting passengers heading into the government district of Kasumigaseki. The death toll from the deadly sarin gas reached 12, with more than 5,500 hospitalized.

That attack, and the ensuing revelations as police investigated, rocked Japan's sense of security and prompted reassessments of its education system, police, media and religious groups.

Two days after the gassings, 2,500 police in riot gear and gas masks raided Aum facilities in Tokyo and in Yamanashi and Shizuoka prefectures. What they eventually found was not just the raw materials to produce sarin, but military hardware, sophisticated lab equipment and hundreds of metal drums filled with toxic chemicals.

Aum members claimed the chemicals were for agricultural use. The group wanted to become completely self-sufficient and cut itself off from the rest of the world, which it viewed as filled with enemies. Cult leader Shoko Asahara had established a rigid hierarchy that mirrored the structure of the Japanese government and sought to militarize the group in preparation for doomsday, which he said would come by the end of the century.

A DEADLY TEST

Aum is now believed to have also perpetrated an earlier sarin attack, in July 1994 in Matsumoto, Nagano Prefecture. There, seven were killed and 200 injured. Police report Aum also abducted Kiyoshi Kariya, a Tokyo notary public, and tried to force him to reveal the whereabouts of his sister. She had fled Aum's complex in Yamanashi and was in hiding because of a dispute over a donation of her assets. The group is belived to have killed Kariya and cremated his corpse in a microwave incinerator designed by cult members.

And the group is suspected as well of sending a letter bomb addressed to Tokyo Governor Yukio Aoshima, who had told the press he would consider seeking a court order to disband the religion. Subsequently, Aum attempted to release hydrogen-cyanide gas at Shinjuku Station, Tokyo's busiest train terminal, near the metropolitan government offices.

Asahara and other Aum leaders have been indicted on charges of murder. The police believe the cult took as many as 24 lives by poison gas, strangling and lethal injection. The cult is also suspected of kidnapping, manufacturing guns and even a plan to purchase Russian military tanks.

Asahara founded the group that was to become Aum in 1984. Combining yoga with "scientific" analysis of the state of enlightenment, he attracted primarily young followers — especially students in science and engineering at graduate schools. Experts point to weakening family ties, a growing sense of insecurity about the future and young people's difficulty in finding an identity as making Aum and other fad religions attractive.

THE MISSING LAWYER

Japanese society was poorly equipped to help anyone who quit, or tried to quit, the cult. Experts point out that, unlike in the U.S. and other nations, there are few in Japan capable of counseling former cult followers and assisting them to rejoin society. Following the raids on cult sites, authorities took into protective custody more than 100 children of Aum followers, many in need of medical and psychological care, some with signs of split personalities.

Criticism of the police mounted as a result of the sarin attacks. One puzzle was why it took the police six years to link the cult to the 1989 kidnapping of Tsutsumi Sakamoto — a lawyer who had tried to help Aum members leave the sect. Because an Aum badge was found at Sakamoto's house after he and his family suddenly disappeared, Sakamoto's colleagues and several journalists had long argued Aum was responsible. But the police failed to establish any connection until Aum members in custody after the Sarin incident finally confessed. Remains of Sakamoto, his wife and their year-old son were then found buried in the mountains of central Japan.

Police insist there was a lack of direct evidence in the case, but analysts say the police were afraid of a public relations disaster — Aum had already been accusing the cops of trying to suppress its legal religious activities. Any investigation of a religious group might have triggered outcrys of protest from those who remember the intolerance of prewar days.

Remains of Sakamoto, his wife and their year-old son were then found buried in the mountains

LOSING FAITH

The events surrounding Aum Shinrikyo brought the role of religions in Japanese society into question. "Before Aum, the typical Japanese believed religious groups were harmless," says Hiroo Takagi, a former professor of Toyo University. "Now, people are bound to think twice about choosing to join or even contribute to religious groups." After the sarin gassings, debate grew over the need to revise the Religious Corporation Law. Under this law, almost all applications to establish a religion are approved by the central or regional governments. Once approved, the religion has legal protection and tax exemption, and is not required to report publicly on its activities.

Those favoring revision of the law argue it allows bizarre cults such as Aum to thrive. The three parties of the ruling coalition intended to revise the legislation during a Diet session in late 1995.

Religious groups voiced opposition to revision, however, warning that any attempt to tinker with the law would turn into a battle over Japan's constitutional guarantees of freedom of religion. "It wasn't tax exemption that made Aum what it became," stressed an official of Soka Gakkai, Japan's largest lay Buddhist organization. Others pointed to the fact that Aum apparently broke numerous laws, including regulations on construction and the use of pharmaceuticals, but no attempt is being made to question the legitimacy of those laws.

The issue is extremely delicate for politicians, since religious organizations also comprise powerful voting blocs. Thus the largest opposition party, Shinshinto, which draws support from Soka Gakkai, argued against revision of the law. On October 9, Justice Minister Tomoharu Tazawa resigned following media reports that he made a secret deal with Shinshinto to oppose the revision.

INCIDENTS INVOLVING AUM

Feb.	1984	Shoko Asahara forms Aum Shinsen no Kai.
July	1987	Aum Shinsen no Kai is renamed Aum Shinrikyo.
Aug.	1989	Aum is registered as a religious corporation by Tokyo Metropolitan Government.
Nov.	1989	Tsutsumi Sakamoto, a lawyer helping Aum members wishing to leave the sect, is abducted from his home along with his wife and 1-year-old child.
Feb.	1990	Asahara and 24 other Aum members run in general elections for the lower house, but none win seats.
June	1994	Sarin is released in a residential area in Matsumoto, Nagano Prefecture. killing seven and leaving over 200 injured.
July	1994	Foul smells are reported near Aum complex in Yamanashi Pref. Sarin residue is found in the soil near the complex.
■1995		
Feb.	28	Kiyoshi Kariya, a notary public whose sister has been trying to quit the cult, is kidnapped in Tokyo.
Mar.	20	Sarin is released in the Tokyo subway system, killing 12 and injuring more than 5,000.
Mar.	22	Police begin raids on 25 Aum facilities throughout the nation, citing Aum's alleged involvement in the abduction of Kariya.
Mar.	30	Takaji Kunimatsu, commissioner general of the National Police Agency, is shot and seriously injured by an unidentified gunman. Aum denies any involvement .
Apr.	14	Police raid 120 Aum facilities throughout the nation. Fifty-three children of Aum followers in Kamikuishiki are taken into protective custody.
Apr.	23	Hideo Murai, Aum's "Science & Technology Minister," is stabbed to death in front of the cult's Tokyo headquarters by a self-proclaimed member of a right-wing organization.
Apr.	28	The Defense Agency punishes two Ground Self-Defense Force officials on charges of leaking inside information to Aum.
May	5	Lethal chemicals are discovered inside a restroom at an underground passage in Tokyo's Shinjuku Station. Police claims the chemicals could have produced enough lethal cyanide gas to kill more than 10,000 people.
May	16	Asahara is arrested on charges of murder in connection with the March 20 sarin attack in Tokyo.
May	16	A parcel bomb destined to Tokyo Governor Yukio Aoshima explodes and injures Aoshima's secretary. Police claims Aum sends the parcel.
June	6	Asahara and six other leaders are indicted on charges of murders.
June	30	Tokyo Government and Tokyo Prosecutors' Office ask a court order to disband Aum.
Sept.	6	Police find bodies of lawyer Sakamoto and his wife in mountains central Japan.

KEY WORD

SARIN

This nerve gas was developed in Nazi Germany before World War II. Sarin is fairly simple to synthesize given basic knowledge of chemistry and appropriate lab equipment. All necessary ingredients can be easily and legally purchased. Production or possession of sarin was not illegal until May 1, 1995, when the government passed legislation banning the substance.

KEY WORD

AUM

The word Aum derives from an acronym for the Sanskrit words for the creation, maintenance and destruction of the universe. Massive media coverage of the cult brought other Sanskrit terms to the fore, including *satian* (truth) which Aum used to designate cult-owned buildings. Another term was *poa*, the moving of a soul to a higher plane. Asahara allegedly ordered cult members to "poa" the family of Tsutsumi Sakamoto, which they interpreted as an order to kill.

NONPERFORMING LOANS

Financial investment lesson in 1995? Don't bank on banks!

BY YUZO SAEKI
Staff Writer

For several years, 1995 included, Japanese banks have taken most of the top ten spots in world asset rankings for financial institutions. Lucky for Japanese bankers there is no feel-good league in their sector, because confidence in the Japanese banking system in 1995 hit the lowest point since the Showa financial panic of the 1930s.

As with many other problems in the Japanese economy, there was a clear trail from the plight in the banking sector back to the asset-inflated bubble economy of the late 1980s, or rather its bursting. The collapse of the bubble free-for-all finally left the banking industry with trillions of yen in bad debt, most of it secured on property — with most of the property built on the myth that land prices only go up.

Critics say financial institutions spent most of the 1990s elbowing the bad loan issue to one side, hoping it would somehow go away, with the result the debt snowballed; the day of reckoning only delayed.

The seriousness of the problem became clear in 1995, when the Ministry of Finance estimated total bad loans at financial institutions at around ¥40 trillion.

Around the same time, the failures began.

Credit cooperatives in Tokyo and Osaka went under, followed by Hyogo Bank, the country's largest regional bank. Hyogo was the first Japanese commercial bank to go belly up in the post-war era.

The government scrambled to contain the threatening crisis, providing funds in the form of special loans from the Bank of Japan and grants from the Deposit Insurance Corp. The MOF also raised the question of using public funds to bail out financial institutions, including seven heavily indebted mortgage loan companies. Nevertheless, the financial authorities were lambasted by domestic and overseas critics for failing to deal with bad loans before they reached such proportions.

The International Monetary Fund added its own criticism to the chorus, stating in its annual report in August 1995 that the authorities' hands off approach compounded the problem.

Meanwhile, Moody's Investors Service announced credit ratings for banks in August under its new so-called financial strength ratings system. The rating aims to assess the strength of individual banks on a stand-alone basis; that is, without assistance from other group companies or a government, Moody's explained.

Japanese banks didn't do well in Moody's new league. On average, they rated D, which translated as possessing adequate financial strength, but threatened by such factors as vulnerable business structure, wobbly financial fundamentals and unstable operating environment.

Major U.S. banks received an average rating of C-plus, two ranks higher than Japanese institutions.

In the same month, Standard & Poor's placed Mitsubishi Bank, Sanwa Bank, Dai-Ichi Kangyo Bank, Fuji Bank and Sumitomo Bank on its credit watch list for possible downgrading. Furthermore, Japanese banks were required to pay additional interest margins of about 0.05 of a percentage point on Eurodollar loans in comparison with Western banks, financial sources said.

Despite these woes, the Japanese government faced a tough time convincing the public of the need to use tax money to restore stability in the financial system.

Public anger erupted in December 1994 when the government announced the establishment of Tokyo Kyodou Bank to take over two scandal and debt-ridden Tokyo credit unions — Tokyo Kyowa Credit Association and Anzen Credit Bank. Citizens were enraged by the prospect of their tax yen being used to pay off the thrifts' debts, particularly when it became clear the credit unions had been used as something akin to personal piggy banks by their executivess.

Tokyo's local assembly in March refused to endorse a ¥30 billion low-interest loan from the Tokyo government as part of the bail out. The newly elected governor of Tokyo, Yukio Aoshima, had campaigned on a vow that not a yen from public coffers would be spent on the rogue thrifts.

Financial authorities also faced resistance from private banks asked to help foot the bill.

Under the bail-out package for Cosmo Credit Cooperative, Tokyo's largest credit union which went bust at the end of July, banks with outstanding loans to the thrift will write off ¥63 billion, or 60% of the total.

Banks with close links to Osaka-based Kizu Credit Cooperative, which went bankrupt in August, were also asked to cough up. In Kizu's case, Osaka authorities sought Sanwa Bank's cooperation on the grounds problems at the credit union stemmed in large part from Sanwa's introduction of large-lot depositors to Kizu, which was offering unusually high interest rates.

Sanwa, however, disclaimed any responsibility for how Kizu handled its funds.

Worries about the vulnerability of private-sector banks prompted depositors to shift money to postal savings, which refueled an on-going argument between the public and private financial sectors.

The crux of the conflict is that banks complain the post office takes away a considerable portion of their business because of the unfair advantage of government backing. Total postal savings deposits reached ¥200 trillion in 1995, with the system seeing a net increase of ¥3.3 trillion in the half-year ended September. This perhaps illustrates the public cares little for the banks versus post office debate and more about a safe place to deposit hard earned cash.

Tokyo's local assembly in March refused to endorse a ¥30 billion low-interest loan as part of the bail out

THIEVES IN THE BOARDROOM?

Recent bankruptcies in Japan's financial sector is certain to stoke debate over the structure of smaller financial institutions, including credit cooperatives and regional banks.

Financial deregulation has brought down protective barriers around small and locally based banks, which intensified competition with large institutions. This is one factor behind the recent spate of failures, as it prompted smaller financial institutions to offer unusually high interest rates on deposits and to indulge in risky lending.

Allowing directors of credit cooperatives to own other businesses only created a conflict of interest that led to illegal loans.

Harunori Takahashi, former chairman of Tokyo Kyowa Credit Association, was arrested in June 1995 for alleged breach of trust related to shady lending.

The Tokyo District Public Prosecutors office also arrested Shinsuke Suzuki, a former chairman of Anzen Credit Bank. Prosecutors said Anzen extended billions of yen in loans to golf course and real estate developers without any tangible collateral. A portion of the loans was also used to pay off debts at a car dealership owned by Suzuki.

On the issue of using tax money to pay off debts at the corrupt and defunct thrifts, the Diet heard testimony from financial experts and individuals directly involved.

Tetsuya Horie, former president of Long-Term Credit Bank of Japan — the main lender to the E.I.E International group led by Kyowa's Takahashi — was among those summoned.

From the testimonies, including those from Takahashi and Suzuki, and findings by prosecutors, it became clear that the former chairmen were using the credit cooperatives like personal bank accounts.

Loans extended to companies operated by the former chairmen also violated the rule that total loans to a single borrower must be less than 20% of the cooperative's own capital or less than ¥800 million.

MOF'S BAD-LOAN MEASURES

The Finance Ministry's Policy Toward Resolving the Bad-Loan Problem Announced Sept. 27 '95

More Disclosure

Requesting regional banks to disclose amount of loans whose interest payments have gone arrears for more than six months

Requesting shinkin banks to disclose part of the loans in which the borrowers have gone bankrupt

Disclose the aggregate amount of non-performing loans at all financial institutions as of the end of Sept. 1995

Reforming Deposit-Insurance System

Present a revised Deposit Insurance Act to the next regular Diet session to allow the system to collect emergency funds from members in case a large-scale failure appears possible

Raising premiums paid by private banks for deposit-insurance system

Improving Management of Credit Cooperatives

Establish an institution for taking over operations of failed credit cooperatives

Restricting credit cooperative executives from holding positions in other companies

On the Jusen Problem

Draw up the scheme for resolving the bad-loan problem at the seven housing-loan companies before the end of 1995

Further

Consider use of public funds to help financial institutions write off loan lossed

Source: The Nihon Keizai Shimbun

KEY WORD

INTRODUCTORY DEPOSITS

Credit unions and other local financial institutions received "introductory deposits" from large commercial banks and used the funds as real estate loans. The big banks persuaded corporate clients to issue commercial paper and deposit the fund at the thrifts to gain higher interest rates. The large bank would in turn profit from handling charges on issuing the commercial paper.

KEY WORD

DEPOSIT INSURANCE CORP.

Set up in 1971 with funds from a premium of 0.012% on deposits at private banks. The institution covers up to ¥10 million per depositor. Bank failures depleted funds at the DIC, so the government is considering reform of the institution, which may include giving the DIC authority to shut down troubled financial institutions. The DIC's reserve totaled ¥820.5 billion in March 1994.

DEFLATION

Price decline becomes 'too much of a good thing' explain economists

BY TOSHIO
SHINMURA
Staff Writer

The drop in corporate earnings will, in turn, take a bite out of salaries, push up unemployment and dampen consumer sentiment

Deflation was the dreaded scare word in the Japanese economy in 1995. Much debate and controversy surrounded the issue: was the economy on the verge of entering a deflationary spiral, or had it already done so?

While advocates of both views argued the point, scattered signs of deflationary trends were clearly surfacing.

In the fiscal year ended March 1995, nominal gross domestic product grew only 0.3%, the lowest since the authorities started compiling statistics in 1955. Worse, nominal GDP fell short of real GDP growth of 0.6%.

Such a reversal of nominal and real GDP growth, partly the result of a decline in consumer prices, was quite extraordinary; but it happened again early into fiscal 1995. In the April-June 1995 quarter, nominal GDP was up 0.2% over the previous quarter while real GDP rose 0.8%. The GDP deflator, an inflation indicator, fell 1.2%, the fourth straight quarter of negative readings.

The national consumer price index, excluding prices of perishables, remained below year-earlier levels for five consecutive months through August, the first such straight decline ever for the index.

"Lower prices are good for consumers, because it boosts real purchasing power, but the CPI decline has actually gone beyond a level to benefit consumers," said Kenji Yumoto, senior economist at the Japan Research Institute.

Yumoto explained that the falling CPI caused serious damage to industry, because of the decline in sales and profits. The drop in corporate earnings will, in turn, take a bite out of salaries, push up unemployment and dampen consumer sentiment. This then leads to a fall in production and eventually slows economic growth.

PROPERTY PROBLEMS

Condominium prices are another example of the deflationary trend. Housing starts, led by condominiums, increased three straight years through fiscal 1994, when total starts stood at 1.56 million. Historically low interest rates and falling land prices ignited heated competition among developers to build condominiums priced much lower than apartments available during the bubble economy years, and relatively young first-time buyers bought them. But that boom peaked, and housing starts were expected to dip to around 1.47 million in fiscal 1995, in spite of even lower interest rates and prices.

The fall in prices for new condos had a negative ripple effect. Prices of used condominiums declined in line with those of new ones, which convinced many potential used-condo buyers to wait and see if prices would fall further. Unable to find buyers, owners of used condos were unable to return to the market to purchase a new home.

BLAME YEN, BUBBLE

Economists point to two deflationary factors that pushed prices lower.

One is the extraordinary appreciation of the Japanese yen, which started around March 1995. In April, the Japanese currency touched a record ¥79.75 to the U.S. dollar.

The stronger yen caused two problems. First, it spurred imports of low-priced manufactured goods, ranging from clothing, textiles, and food to home appliances and furniture. The flood of imports hurt domestic manufacturers, as they had to cut prices to compete. But, even with the price cuts by Japanese firms, imports took a bigger share of domestic markets.

Second, the yen's appreciation damaged the cost-competitiveness of Japanese products in overseas markets. To recover or maintain competitiveness, many domestic manufacturers shifted production overseas.

All told, the high yen hurt corporate earnings, helped shrink domestic markets, pushed production offshore and added more Japanese to the unemployment line.

LAND SLIDES

The other deflationary factor was the remnants of the asset-inflated bubble economy in the late 1980s and early 1990s. During the period, prices, especially real estate and stocks, soared and the adjustment after the burst of the bubble is still going on.

The most striking example of this adjustment is the fall in land prices. According to the National Land Agency, overall commercial land prices as of July 1, 1995 fell 6.9% from the previous year, while the prices of residential land fell 0.9%. Average prices in both land categories thus fell for a fourth straight year. In Tokyo, prices of commercial real estate skidded 16.9%, while residential land dipped 3.3%.

Declining land prices produced a mountain of nonperforming loans at financial institutions, which had extended the loans during the bubble years using real estate as collateral. Estimates put the total of this bad debt in the region of ¥40 trillion.

Weighed down by this bad loan burden and its dampening effects on profitability, commercial banks have been extremely cautious about extending new loans to the private sector, which, in turn, hampered economic recovery.

USING THE 'D' WORD

The government and the Bank of Japan showed a marked reluctance to use the dreaded term "deflation" when issuing reports on the economy in fiscal 1995.

The Economic Planning Agency compromised by saying the economy is going through a "disinflation" period. The EPA's usage was based on the view the economy continued to grow, though very modestly, as consumer prices fell.

The Bank of Japan maintained until June that deflation was not an issue of concern.

In arguing against the deflation theorists, both the government and the central bank maintained the economy was gradually recovering, and some indicators, such as private-sector capital investment and corporate earnings, were expected to rebound.

The conviction behind this argument, however, weakened in July, when then EPA director general Masahiko Komura said that if the government did not take proper action, the economy would move into a deflation phase.

Other senior EPA officials said the central bank should boost money supply to avoid deflation.

In response, the BOJ guided money market rates lower, aiming to encourage borrowing and economic growth. But the beneficial effects were limited.

When a cluster of financial institutions failed in August and industrial output fell, the BOJ finally decided to cut the official discount rate from 1% to 0.5% on September 8.

In explaining the reason for the rate cut, BOJ Governor Yasuo Matsushita told a press conference there was growing concern about the continued standstill of the economy.

The cutting of the official discount rate to an historic low was aimed at preventing the spread of "deflationary phenomena," the governor explained.

Following this, the government put together another spending package on Sept. 20 to encourage economic growth and, hopefully, finally shake off the deflation demon.

The stimulus plan amounted to a massive ¥14.22 trillion, with around ¥12.8 trillion earmarked for public works projects.

ECONOMY APPROACHING DEFLATION?

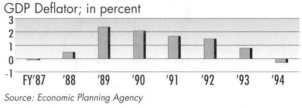

Real GDP Growth; in percent

Nominal GDP Growth; in percent

GDP Deflator; in percent

FY'87 '88 '89 '90 '91 '92 '93 '94

Source: Economic Planning Agency

LAND PRICES AND GDP

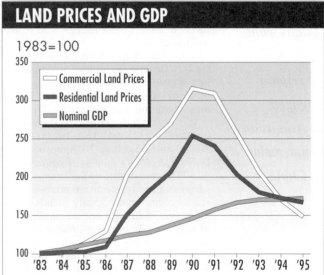

1983=100

- Commercial Land Prices
- Residential Land Prices
- Nominal GDP

'83 '84 '85 '86 '87 '88 '89 '90 '91 '92 '93 '94 '95

Note: Land prices are in Tokyo, Osaka and Nagoya areas. 1983 prices are based as 100. GDP figures are those of the previous fiscal year.
Source: National Land Agency, Economic Planning Agency

KEY WORD

DEFLATION

Deflation is defined as a sustained fall in prices, often accompanied by declines in production and employment. Private economists said the economy was close to or in deflation in 1995, pointing to a drop in prices and the sluggish economy. The government and the BOJ agreed the economy was in serious trouble, but refused to call it deflation, because corporate earnings were picking up and wages were gradually increasing.

KEY WORD

DISINFLATION

Before the cut in the official discount rate on Sept. 8 and drafting of the huge economic stimulus package on Sept. 20, the government had insisted the economy was in a disinflation phase, or inflation was falling, not a deflation phase. To support its view, the government said falling prices were helping economic growth. Inflation-adjusted gross domestic product in fiscal 1993 was down 0.2%, but rebounded to 0.6% in fiscal 1994.

DEFENSE POLICY

Alliance with U.S. remains key to maintaining East Asia security

BY SATOSHI ISAKA
Staff Writer

Sensible Asians want the U.S. to remain engaged in Asia as a counterbalance to China.

In recent years, a key question for Japanese foreign-policy makers has been how to convince skeptics at home and in the U.S. that the bilateral security arrangement instituted in the 1950s remains as important as ever, even though no visible military threat looms.

Since President Bill Clinton took office three years ago, Japanese officials have been very worried that overall relations with the U.S.— especially the security pact— could weaken because of a White House preoccupation with rectifying the bilateral trade imbalance.

That concern was especially strong in 1995, when it increasingly appeared U.S. leaders would find it difficult to win voter support for continuing strong commitments to protect other nations with American soldiers and money.

In this regard, a comprehensive policy statement by the U.S. Defense Department in March, clearly committing Washington to a continued role as premier provider of security for Japan and the rest of East Asia, was the most reassuring statement to date.

"It is most significant that the Pentagon report explicitly states the U.S. will keep 100,000 personnel in East Asia," notes Tetsuya Nishimoto, chairman of the Defense Agency's joint staff council. Of that force, 44,800 troops are stationed in Japan.

China's recently assertive posture— evidenced by territorial claims on the Spratly Islands, an uncompromising pursuit of stronger nuclear capabilities and attempts to intimidate Taiwan with missile tests— has aroused concern in many Asian nations about its potential threat. Hence, for all the anti-American rhetoric of Malaysian Prime Minister Mahathir Mohamad and some others, sensible Asians want the U.S. to remain engaged in Asia as a counterbalance to China.

For this reason, Japan and other Asian nations were worried about the possibility of a continuing gradual decline of the regional U.S. military presence following the collapse of the Soviet Union. Indeed, that was the recommendation of Defense Department reports issued in 1990 and 1992. From 1990 to 1994, U.S. forces presence in Asia fell from 135,000 to 100,000.

Such fears tightened a notch early in 1995, when the conservative think tank Cato Institute published a study favoring an end to the Japan-U.S. military alliance. The same idea was advanced by leading "revisionist" Chalmers Johnson in a controversial article in Foreign Affairs magazine.

Japanese diplomats and analysts thus welcomed the Pentagon report as a reflection of the importance Washington attaches to its security arrangement with Tokyo. Titled "U.S. Security Strategy for the East Asia-Pacific Region," the document calls the alliance with Japan "the linchpin of U.S. security policy in Asia." It was initiated by Joseph Nye, assistant secretary of defense for international security affairs, apparently intended in part to persuade Americans with isolationist views that it is in the military and economic interests of the U.S. to "maintain our strong military presence" in Japan and in other Asian countries. "Japan supplies by far the most generous host-nation support of any of our allies," it notes.

Particularly significant concerning ties with Japan is the report's admonition, "We must not allow trade friction to undermine our security alliance."

Yukio Okamoto, former director of the Foreign Ministry's North American division, commented, "After two years of an excessive emphasis on trade, U.S. policy toward Japan is finally returning to a sound one," aimed at creating a balance among security considerations, economic ties and political cooperation on bilateral and global affairs.

MUTUAL PROGRESS REQUIRED

This U.S. confirmation of the worth it attaches to bilateral security should not, however, be used by Japan as an excuse to scuttle ongoing efforts at correcting its own economic faults, such as excessive regulations, Okamoto continued.

That concern is echoed in the U.S. report: "If public support for the relationship is to be maintained over the long term, progress must continue to be made by both sides in addressing fundamental economic issues."

At a Sept. 27 meeting in New York, Foreign Minister Yohei Kono and Defense Agency Director General Seishiro Eto signed an agreement with U.S. counterparts Warren Christopher and William Perry, increasing Japanese coverage of the costs of maintaining American forces in Japan. In addition to the salaries of Japanese employees at U.S. bases, and utility fees, Japan will now also cover transportation costs within the country. This new agreement, taking effect April 1996, was seen paving the way for a November summit in Japan between Prime Minister Tomiichi Murayama and President Bill Clinton.

Officials at the Defense Agency and Foreign Ministry say they are also impressed by the Pentagon report's reference to multilateral forums for discussing confidence-building measures to improve regional security.

Although both Japan and the U.S. believe such forums should only complement and not replace existing bilateral security arrangements, the report gives high marks to the ASEAN Regional Forum, an ambitious attempt to build an Asian equivalent to the Conference on Security and Cooperation in Europe.

CHINA OPPOSES THEATER MISSILE DEFENSE

One crucial question in the post-Cold War period is how to maintain balance in East Asia among the three key regional powers: the U.S., Japan and China. A measure of the intractability of this question is the depth of concern China has shown over steps by Japan and the U.S. toward development of a so-called Theater Missile Defense system. Although this idea originally emerged as a counter to suspected North Korean development of nuclear weapons, Chinese officials repeatedly voiced dissatisfaction in 1995 that such a system "would disturb the Asia-Pacific regional situation."

At bilateral talks in Tokyo early in 1995, the Japanese side told China such a defense system would be deployed for purely defensive purposes, and pointed out that Tokyo is holding off a final decision on the project while it weighs huge development costs against effectiveness.

Those security talks were the first ever to include both military and diplomatic officials from the two countries. Japan proposed them as an means of building confidence between Asia's two major powers.

On other matters, Japanese officials urged Beijing to make its military policy more transparent. Japan and other neighboring nations have expressed concern over the rapid growth in Chinese military spending. The Chinese representatives replied that spending is going only to "modernize" China's outdated materiel, noting much of the increase is the result of inflation.

Japan also criticized China's repeated nuclear testing as undermining global efforts to forestall nuclear weapons programs under the Nuclear Non-Proliferation Treaty, because such moves erode the confidence of non-nuclear states in that treaty. But Tokyo's requests to limit testing fell on deaf ears.

Even so, Japan viewed the talks as a useful starting point in terms of confidence-building,. been absent until now.

For their part, the Chinese showed considerable interest in the latest status of the Japan-U.S. security arrangement. During the Cold War, China viewed the pact as a menacing alliance of hostile powers. In recent years, though, China is said to appreciate the positive role the pact has had in preventing any re-emergence of a militarily powerful Japan.

Japan is also exploring the possibility of detailed bilateral security dialogues with other regional powers. The aim is to help reduce post-Cold War uncertainty in the region, by promoting greater communication between the military planners and officers of countries like South Korea and Russia.

U.S. TROOPS IN ASIA-PACIFIC REGION

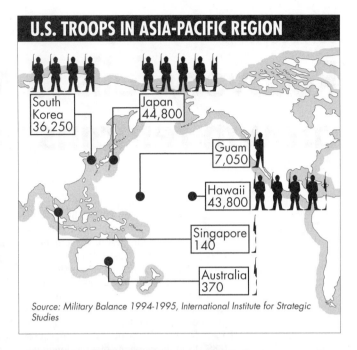

Source: *Military Balance 1994-1995, International Institute for Strategic Studies*

THE WORLD'S LARGEST MILITARY FORCES

Army		Navy			Air Power	
Country /area	Size of troops (1,000)	Country /area	Thousand tons	Number of ships	Country /area	Number of active fighters
N.Korea	1,000	China	1,024	1,080	U.S.	4,380
Russia	780	U.K.	830	320	Ukraine	1,220
S.Korea	550	France	451	330	India	890
U.S.	533	India	263	170	France	870
Pakistan	520	Peru	235	40	N.Korea	770
Vietnam	500	Taiwan	220	390	Turkey	620
Turkey	393	Turkey	210	240	U.K.	610
Iraq	350	Brazil	199	180	Syria	590
Iran	345	Italy	195	180	Egypt	560
Egypt	310	Germany	189	200	Germany	540
Ukraine	308	Spain	187	160	Israel	510
Syria	300	Indonesia	181	210	S.Korea	490
Taiwan	289	Canada	164	70	Taiwan	470
Japan	151		344	160		510

Source: Defense Agency

BALLISTIC MISSILE

The concept of defending against ballistic missiles with anti-missile systems and satellites designed to detect, track and shoot down enemy missiles. The U.S. has proposed such systems to allies, including Israel and Japan, given the potential emergence of regional aggressors armed with nuclear-capable missiles and other weapons of mass destruction (such as Iran, North Korea and others). In fiscal 1996 Japan is to spend ¥2 billion on evaluation research of the concept.

ASEAN REGIONAL FORUM (ARF)

This multilateral framework on security opened in 1994 in Bangkok with 18 members, including the U.S., Russia, China, Japan, Australia and the European Union, as well as the six ASEAN states. At the 1995 annual meeting in Brunei, where Cambodia joined, members agreed to make military policies more transparent by annually publishing defense papers. To many Asian nations, the ARF is valuable because it provides a rare formal and multilateral channel for addressing problems related to China.

GDP/ECONOMY

Recovery fails to take effect; growth remains near zero in FY95

BY TOSHIO
SHINMURA
Staff Writer

Though some sectors of the Japanese economy improved in 1995, the recovery remained extremely fragile. To the disappointment not only of Japanese taxpayers, but of other countries hoping for a boost to the world economy, Japan was expected to record a fourth year of near-zero growth in the fiscal year through March 1996.

Even before January-March results were announced in the summer, economists revised their forecasts for real gross domestic product growth in fiscal 1995 to below 1%. Real GDP in the April-June quarter increased 0.8% from the previous quarter, logging an annual rate of 3.1% However, on a six-month, January-June basis, GDP growth was minus 0.1%, compared with 0.4% growth in the previous six months. Therefore, some economists concluded, the relatively high rise of GDP in the April-June quarter was more a reflection of the weak previous quarter, and economic recovery is not as strong as it appeared.

Others, like Tsutomu Tanaka, advisor at Mitsubishi Research Institute, pointed out the April-June quarter does not include such minus factors as the yen's appreciation during the spring and consecutive declines in industrial output.

Compared with previous recoveries, the one in 1995 displayed several differences that could perhaps explain its sluggishness. First, private capital spending, one of the key elements of economic growth, rebounded only very slowly from a three-year decline. A Nikkei survey forecast that capital investment would rise a modest 3.9% in fiscal 1995. Japan Credit Bank put the figure even lower at 1.7%. The restriction in capital outlays was seen as natural in the aftermath of the bubble economy, in which industries such as automobiles and steel invested heavily in production capacity.

While some manufacturers, including electric machinery and pulp and paper makers, planned to boost capital spending, non-manufacturers, especially in the construction and real estate sectors, were looking to cut back further. In the case of electric machinery, a rebound in capital spending was supported by brisk demand for semiconductors and recovering demand for some appliances.

Consumer spending also displayed slower-than-usual improvement. Though sales in some merchandise categories marked record year-on-year increases, overall sentiment remained weak. Household spending, according to a Management and Coordination Agency survey, was down 1.1% from a year earlier in July for the eighth month of decline in 10 months..

Sales at department stores and supermarkets continued to decline. August department store sales were down 0.8 % from a year earlier, recording a 42nd month of decline. Sales at supermarkets also fell 1.4% year on year, posting a sixth month of decline.

Economists pointed to a number of factors dampening consumer sentiment. Unemployment ran at a record high 3.2% in August for a third month and appeared unlikely to improve in the near term as companies continued to cut costs. The appreciation of the yen to a record high of just under ¥80 to the dollar undermined exports such as automobiles and electric machinery and put added pressure on export-oriented industries to restructure, prompting consumer fears that the delayed improvement in corporate earnings would result in slower wage growth.

Although the yen fell to a level of around ¥100 to the dollar during the summer, and earnings forecasts for export-oriented companies were accordingly adjusted upward, that did not put an end to corporate restructuring efforts.

CONSUMERS STILL TIGHTFISTED

Furthermore, psychological shockwaves from the Great Hanshin Earthquake in January, which devastated the city of Kobe and neighboring areas, claiming over 5,500 lives; and then from the sarin nerve gas attacks on the Tokyo subway system in March, further knocked the wind out of consumer sentiment.

The government's game plan for the recovery had been for public spending, along with private housing investment, to sustain the economy until capital investment and consumer spending could kick in. However, both public spending and housing investment started to slow prematurely. While housing starts had been far above average in fiscal 1994 amid brisk construction of condominiums, a dip in such construction in fiscal 1995 dragged starts back down.

Net external demand — the difference between exports and imports — also limited GDP growth. While the strong yen eroded the price competitiveness of Japanese exports, it invited a flood of imported manufactured goods.

Thus, to avoid a double-dip in the economy, the Ministry of Finance unveiled a deregulatory package in August to weaken the yen. The thrust of the package was aimed at encouraging Japanese institutional investors to buy foreign securities and extend loans overseas. Coupled with concerted market intervention, the package pushed the yen back to near ¥100 to the dollar within a few weeks.

On Sept. 8, the Bank of Japan cut the official discount rate to an all-time low of 0.5%, further suppressing the yen and boosting the Nikkei Stock Average to above 18,000 points.

Appreciation of the yen to a record high of just under ¥80 to the dollar undermined exports

CAPITAL INVESTMENT AND CONSUMER SPENDING

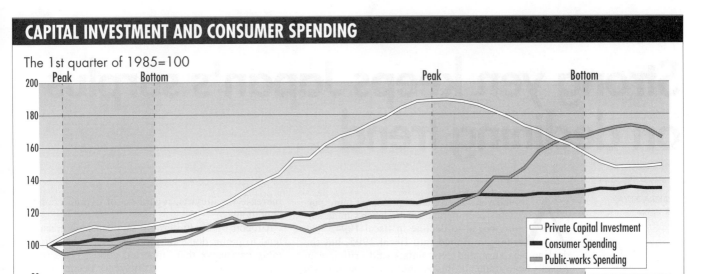

The 1st quarter of 1985=100

Peak Bottom Peak Bottom

Legend:
- Private Capital Investment
- Consumer Spending
- Public-works Spending

'85 '86 '87 '88 '89 '90 '91 '92 '93 '94 '95

Note: Seasonally adjusted in real terms, with the 1st quarter of 1985 set as the base of 100.
Source: Economic Planning Agency

PUBLIC-WORKS SPENDING LOSES PUNCH

During the latest recovery, officially declared to have begun in the October-December quarter of 1993, the economy responded little to injections of tens of trillions of yen. In fiscal 1995, the Murayama administration offered two stimulus packages, the first in April and the second in September, and drafted two supplementary budgets. Some ¥2.7 trillion was allocated in the first supplementary budget, ¥2 trillion of which went to public-works (excluding land purchases) and relief for the earthquake-devastated Kobe area. In the second supplementary budget, an additional ¥8 trillion was allocated for public spending, with ¥910 billion to promote advances in science, technology and telecommunications, and to improve the educational and social infrastructure. Economists said that traditional public-works spending to build roads, bridges and ports could no longer stimulate adequate final demand. According to an estimate, ¥1 trillion in public spending, mainly on building roads and bridges, could generate only ¥1.85 trillion in GDP output, while the same amount of spending on research and development could stimulate about ¥2.17 trillion.

REAL GDP RECOVERY AFTER RECESSIONS

Legend:
- After "Mini" Recession ('77)
- After First Oil Crisis ('73-'74)
- After Second Oil Crisis ('80-'82)
- After "Endaka" Recession ('85-86)
- After Latest Recession ('93-present)

0 1 2 3 4 5 6 7 8 9 10 (quarters)

Note: GDP indexed 100 at the beginning of each expansion phase through the peaks.
Source: Economic Planning Agency

ENDAKA

The yen's rise to the dollar, called *endaka* in Japanese, boosted consumer purchasing power in 1995 by lowering the price of imports. However, it also undercut products manufactured in Japan, dampening corporate earnings and, eventually, the job market. The rising yen accelerated the shift of production overseas, particularly to Southeast Asia. While leading export-oriented companies could breath easier after the yen returned to ¥100 to the dollar, most smaller businesses still had break-even points above ¥105.

ECONOMIC STIMULUS PACKAGE

The Japanese government drafted pump-priming measures every year starting in 1992, including two in 1993. Three out of the four packages earmarked spending in excess of ¥10 trillion. Major features were public-works spending, deregulation, subsidies for housing purchases, low-interest loans to smaller businesses and tax cuts. Economists and government officials said that without the extra spending, the recession could have been worse. But even with more than ¥45 trillion spent in about three years, the economy failed to recover.

TRADE

Strong yen keeps Japan's surplus on declining trend

BY AKIRA IKEYA
Staff Writer

As the yen's appreciation prompted more purchases of imported goods, Japan's trade surplus began to decline in fiscal 1994. The trend continued into fiscal 1995, but the decline was slow and economists said criticism of Japan's huge trade surplus is unlikely to quiet down soon.

In fiscal 1994, ended March 1995, Japan saw a customs-cleared trade surplus of $117.98 billion, down 3.2% from fiscal 1993 and the first drop since fiscal 1990, according to the Ministry of Finance.

RECORD IMPORTS

That decline is attributed to a sharp increase in imports, which totaled almost $290.49 billion for the year, a rise of 18.9%. In addition to strong imports of semiconductors and personal computers, extensive importing of clothing from China and of automobiles from Europe and the U.S. resulted in a record value for imports in the term.

The strong yen should have held down Japanese exports by forcing exporters to raise prices on overseas markets, thus curbing their competitiveness. But that apparently didn't happen, at least in fiscal 1994. The value of exports totaled just under $408.47 billion for the year, up 11.5%.

Economists explain the increase in the value of exports as caused by the "J-curve" effect. When the yen appreciates against the dollar, the value of yen-denominated exports balloons when calculated in dollars. The dollar averaged ¥99.77 in fiscal 1994, against ¥108.17 in fiscal 1993 — effectively an appreciation of 8.4% for the yen.

The Finance Ministry claims the downward trend in Japan's surplus is clearer in yen terms. The surplus was ¥11.76 trillion in fiscal 1994, down 10.6% from a year earlier. The value of exports was ¥40.75 trillion, up 2.9%, while imports totaled ¥28.98 trillion in value, up 9.6%.

J-CURVE KICKS IN

According to the J-curve theory, yen appreciation initially expands the value of Japanese exports, but will eventually hold them down. This second stage of the J-curve effect apparently emerged in fiscal 1995. For example, the trade surplus dropped 23% in dollar terms year on year in July 1995.

The ministry says steady imports should continue to reduce the surplus. But some economists doubt there will be further increases in imports. Asahi Mutual Life Insurance Co. forecasts a slowing of the pace of increase for imports, regardless of overall economic conditions.

A report by the life insurer says Japanese consumers tend to prefer domestic products even when they are more expensive than imported goods. This pattern changed somewhat in recent years because of low growth in incomes, but should the economy recover even moderately, consumers will again begin to buy domestic goods. And, if economic conditions instead worsen, overall consumption, including imports, will shrink.

Imports rose 15.3% in volume in fiscal 1994. Asahi Life estimates import volume will grow an average 7.4% in fiscal 1995 and in fiscal 1996, if domestic demand expands an average of 2% per year and consumers continue to prefer cheap imported goods.

On the other hand, a sharp decline by the yen which began in August 1995 could have a very strong impact on the expansion of import value, given that a larger percentage of imports than exports is settled in dollars.

Ministry of International Trade and Industry statistics show that in March 1995, 37.6% of Japan's exports were settled in yen compared with 24.3% of imports.

SURPLUS SWELLS

Japan's politically sensitive trade surplus with the U.S. continued to expand. In fiscal 1994, it totaled $55.66 billion, up 8.9% for a fourth straight year of increase. The increase stemmed from steady growth in the U.S. economy during in the year while Japan's domestic demand was weak, economists said. As the pace of U.S. growth slowed in fiscal 1995, the rise in Japan's surplus flattened out.

Some economists say the U.S. trade deficit with China will eventually grow and its deficit with Japan will shrink, shifting the focus of American criticism from Japan to China.

Japan's trade surplus with the European Union approached $21.38 billion in fiscal 1994, down 12.3% for the second year of decline.

The surplus with the rest of Asia totaled $63.68 billion, up 13.9% for a fifth year of increase. The Asian surplus was higher than that with the U.S. for a second straight year.

Meanwhile, Japan's current-account surplus, which incorporates the trade balance on payment basis, the services balance and the unrequited transfers balance, was $125.01 billion for fiscal 1994, down 4.2% for the first decline in four years.

In yen terms, the current-account surplus totaled ¥12.39 trillion, down 11.8% for a second consecutive year of decline.

OFFICIALS TARGET STRONG MARKET IMPACT

In September 1995, the Ministry of Finance changed its time schedule for releasing data on the trade balance and international balance of payments to 8:50 a.m., from the previous 3:30 p.m.

Such statistics are typically released before market openings in other industrialized countries, the ministry said, claiming it only wanted to follow international custom. Tokyo markets begin trading at 9 a.m.

But traders say the ministry shifting to releasing the data in the morning obviously in order to have a greater impact on the markets. Because both surpluses have been on the decline recently, the impact of these figures on currency rates should be significant, they added.

The first morning announcement made no significant difference, however, traders say. On Sept. 6, the ministry released data on the balance of payments in the morning. The dollar advanced by a full ¥1, but that was mainly attributable to market intervention by the Bank of Japan, the traders explain.

Some expect the ministry to change its release schedule again before long if the pattern of the surpluses changes, and if the announcement of figures does not have the desired impact on the market.

One other change already scheduled for 1996 will start from the data for January. The ministry will release the balance of payments figure only in yen terms, instead of in both yen and dollar terms as it previously did.

Data on the services balance will also be broken down into 11 subcategories instead of four. This change in format reflects the expansion in global services trade. Recognizing the rapid expansion of derivatives trading on financial markets, the new formula will include an independent subcategory for derivatives.

Under the new formula, some components of the unrequited transfers balance will be excluded from the current-account balance. If the data for fiscal 1994 is calculated according to the new formula, the current-account surplus amounts to ¥12.43 trillion, an increase of ¥108.9 billion over the figure yielded by the current formula, according to the ministry.

Ministry officials say the formula change follows standards set by the International Monetary Fund.

CURRENT ACCOUNT SURPLUS

In billions of dollars

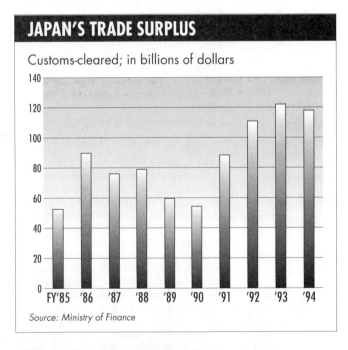

Source: Ministry of Finance

JAPAN'S TRADE SURPLUS

Customs-cleared; in billions of dollars

Source: Ministry of Finance

RATIO OF FINISHED GOODS IMPORTS

This compares imports of finished goods to total imports. In fiscal 1994, the ratio hit a record 55.8%, up from 53.0% a year earlier. Japan previously imported materials to process into export goods. The higher ratio means that industrial pattern has changed, and also reflects the shift to overseas production by Japanese manufacturers, who now assemble electric appliances and other products abroad and import the finished goods into Japan.

SERVICES BALANCE

The current-account surplus includes the services or non-trade balance. The services balance includes transportation, travel and investment income. Recently, Japanese foreign travel has affected this balance. In fiscal 1994, almost 13.74 million Japanese traveled overseas, an 11% increase. Their spending boosted the fiscal 1994 transportation deficit to $13.75 billion and the travel deficit to $28.55 billion — both record figures.

OVERSEAS INVESTMENT

Industry shifts more high-tech R&D overseas to tap foreign talent pool

BY MASATO
ISHIZAWA
Staff Writer

As the yen strengthened to record highs in 1994 and 1995, increasing numbers of Japanese firms expanded direct investment in Asia. During the year through March 1995, Japanese direct investment in other Asian countries outstripped Japan's investment in Europe for the first time in 11 years, according to the Ministry of Finance.

Japanese manufacturing investment in Asia in fiscal 1994 was, at $5.18 billion, greater than similar investment by Japan in North America, which totaled $4.76 billion. Overall direct investment by Japan in other Asian countries ranked second after North America at $17.82 billion. But it outstripped the $6.23 billion in Japanese direct investment channeled toward Europe, which fell 21.5% from fiscal 1993.

Worldwide, Japanese overseas investment was up 14% to $41.05 billion in fiscal 1994, with funds directed toward 2,478 projects. Japanese investment in Asia was up 46.1% in the same period. It approached $9.7 billion and helped finance 1,305 projects.

Indonesia received nearly $1.76 billion, up two-fold from the previous year. Investment to the Philippines tripled to $668 million. China-bound investment from Japan increased a hefty 51.7% to $2.56 billion in fiscal 1994. But this figure actually marked a decline in investment growth, which the previous year had hit 58%. Ministry officials said Japanese companies appeared to be favoring the Association of Southeast Asian Nations (ASEAN), where comprehensive deregulation is currently under way.

Japan's investment in Latin America surged to $5.23 billion, up 55.2% from the previous year. Much of the increase was due to funds channeled into a shipbuilding project in Brazil and an auto project in Mexico.

In the five years from fiscal 1986-90, Japan invested $227.2 billion overseas. During that period, North America got the biggest piece of the pie, totaling $109 billion, or 48.1% of total investment. Other countries in Asia received a $28 billion slice representing just 12.4% of the total. From fiscal 1992 through 1994, too, around 40% of Japan's overseas investment flowed into the U.S., while Asia pocketed less than half at around 18% in fiscal 1992 and fiscal 1993. But in fiscal 1994 the proportion rose to 23%.

Many industries in the developing economies of Asia have benefited substantially from an influx of Japanese funds in recent years. Malaysia now has an exporting auto industry in the form of the Proton group, a venture between local firms and Mitsubishi Motors Corp. The Philippines also stands to gain from the partnership as Proton makes moves to set up a manufacturing plant there. Singapore has attracted virtually all Japan's large electronics firms, who have set up operations there including semiconductor manufacture and assembly of television sets. Sony Corp., for example, manufactures wide-screen television tubes at its Singapore factory.

The shift to offshore production has been a major talking point in recent years. But moves by many firms to establish offshore research and development sections are having an equally strong impact.

Japanese manufacturers such as Casio Computer Co. and Sharp Corp. are establishing and expanding R&D facilities in Europe and the U.S. in a bid to tap the experience and expertise of local experts and researchers.

The move is not unprecedented. It has always made good business sense to develop new products within the target market. Japanese companies have done R&D in the U.S. and elsewhere for many years. This time around, though, they are heavily dependent on the U.S. and European research units to generate winning ideas.

There are numerous benefits to be gained from setting up R&D bases overseas: fewer regulations to hamper entry into new areas of business; more advanced telecommunications infrastructures; and many other industrialized countries are outstripping Japan when it comes to basic digital research.

One reason for the recent scramble to set up R&D units abroad is the progress evident in the U.S. toward creating an advanced telecommunications infrastructure. Japan is lagging here. Most of the recently established or planned Japanese R&D units overseas center on digital and telecommunications-related technology, key areas in the multimedia market.

Sharp opened a third U.S. R&D facility in 1995 in Camas, Washington, to focus on digital-processing technology. Pioneers in offshore R&D like Sony, Matsushita Electric Industrial Co. and NEC Corp., have recently been reorganizing overseas research units.

And the overseas R&D wave is not limited to consumer-electronics companies. Toppan Printing Co.'s new unit in California, its first overseas, studies image processing and network technology. The firm is counting on the facility to expand its consulting operations on use of the Internet and other aspects of multimedia.

Japanese companies also see R&D units in the U.S. as an excellent base from which to expand their marketing scope. Casio, a manufacturer of digital watches, calculators and electronic organizers, set up its first overseas R&D unit in October 1994 in California. The firm is looking to develop telecommunications technology.

The same month, Olympus Optical Co. opened a unit in New York to gain expertise in systems integration. "Demand is rising in the medical field for (advances in) image processing and computer-related technology," said spokesman Nobuo Shinozaki. "The U.S. has a concentrated pool of talented people in these areas."

There are numerous benefits to be gained from setting up R&D bases overseas

LEASING FIRMS FOLLOW MAKERS OVERSEAS

As components manufacturers follow manufacturers overseas, fears are mounting that the very backbone of Japanese industry has been broken. And manufacturers and parts makers are not alone in moving offshore. Japan's leasing firms are also joining the rush abroad, hot on the heels of small and midsize manufacturers, their main clients.

Vietnam is a particularly attractive destination. There, many of Japan's leading electrical-machinery firms are preparing to embark on joint-venture production of home electronics.

Foremost among Japanese leasing firms moving into Asia is Orix Corp., the industry leader. The Tokyo-based firm's latest plan is to establish a leasing company in Hanoi together with the Vietnam Investment and Development Bank.

Japan Leasing Corp. also intends to set up a leasing firm in Hanoi jointly with the Bank for Foreign Trade of Vietnam by the end of the year under similar conditions to the Orix arrangement. Japan Leasing will provide some 30% of the capital in the firm, which will lease equipment and facilities to Japanese and other foreign companies setting up operations in the country.

In Indonesia, Diamond Lease Co., a major leasing firm affiliated with Mitsubishi Bank, set up at the end of April a wholly owned subsidiary in Jakarta. The unit is headed by an executive from the Japanese parent, but the bulk its work force have been hired locally. The firm will initially target small and midsize Japanese firms operating in Indonesia, but plans to cater to local businesses in the future. It is Diamond Lease's second subsidiary in Asia, following its unit in Hong Kong.

The value of leasing contracts concluded on the domestic market in fiscal 1994 rose 2.3% to ¥7.3 trillion, the first gain in three years. But this is still far below the industry's fiscal 1991 peak of ¥8.8 trillion.

The leasing sector at home cannot be expected to return to strong growth until conditions indicating genuine economic recovery emerge. But observers do not expect to see the green shoots of recovery for some time yet.

JAPAN'S EXTERNAL INVESTMENT

In billions of dollars

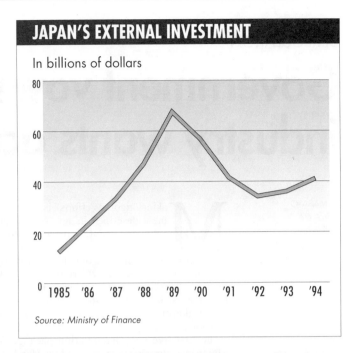

Source: Ministry of Finance

EXTERNAL INVESTMENT BY AREA

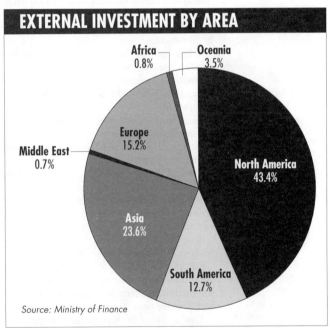

Source: Ministry of Finance

KEY WORD

HOLLOWING OUT

The Japanese economy is undergoing a period of hollowing out similar to the one experienced by the U.S. in the first half of the 1980s. The shift to overseas production has been triggered by the yen's appreciation, high wage levels and the economic recession. The U.S. managed to regain international competitiveness by restructuring and fostering new businesses. But creating new businesses may prove more difficult for export-oriented Japan.

KEY WORD

OVERSEAS INVESTMENT INSURANCE

The Ministry of International Trade and Industry's trade insurance program provides coverage for losses on loans and investments made by Japanese corporations. The screening procedure for each investment or loan application was recently replaced with ceilings for each country ranging from ¥1 billion to ¥10 billion. In 1995, MITI expanded coverage to the six members of ASEAN in response to the 10% annual growth there in investment by Japanese companies.

DEREGULATION

Government vows to cut red tape; industry wants action, not words

BY MASATO
ISHIZAWA
Staff Writer

Making "rigorous efforts" is how the government described its attempts to dismantle rules and regulations widely derided at home and overseas as obstacles to economic growth and inhibitors of industrial activity.

Such deregulation efforts received a lukewarm response from economists, with many lauding the intention, but quick to criticize the government's ponderous and tinkering — as opposed to dismantling — approach.

The first five-year deregulation package from the Murayama administration, released on March 31, 1995, touched on virtually all areas of the economy, from finance, transportation and real estate to energy and employment.

A highlight of the plan is a commitment by the Fair Trade Commission to take up the issue of whether to allow the formation of holding companies in Japan, a subject the FTC had refused to address during the post-war period.

Elimination of the Anti-Monopoly Law's ban on holding companies has long been sought by the Ministry of International Trade and Industry and a large number of business organizations.

The FTC has resisted calls to abolish rules prohibiting establishment of holding companies on grounds such a move would further strengthen *keiretsu,* or cross-share-holding, business groupings in Japan. This, the FTC maintains, would provoke sharp criticism from U.S. authorities, who have in the past labelled the keiretsu practice a barrier to free trade.

But in August 1995, the watchdog panel finally agreed to "exchange opinions with the private sector (on the holding company issue) and investigate the subject over the next three months."

Also included in the deregulation package are studies on setting up a bidding system for allocating radio-frequency bandwiths for the booming cellular telephone and personal handy-phone system markets and review of the Large-Scale Retail Store Law. Both reviews are to be complete by the end of March 2000.

Easing, if not eliminating, existing government criteria for public offerings of company stock is another part of the deregulation plan. This, of course, aims to resuscitate the nation's stock markets.

Employment agencies, tobacco sales and railway fares are also on the red-tape-removal list.

The Ministry of Agriculture, Forestry and Fisheries added 44 deregulation provisions to the 86 it had previously drawn up, but its efforts are unlikely to win enthusiastic applause from overseas trading partners. The ministry plans to reduce or abolish export inspections on only a handful of products, such as soy sauce,

green tea, dried *shiitake* mushrooms, mandarin oranges and apples, hardly the stuff of controversial trade disputes.

Meanwhile, the five-year timeframe of the March 31 deregulation package was shortened on April 14 to three years when the Murayama administration launched a series of measures to cope with the strong yen.

"Each deregulation provision by itself will have only a small impact on economic recovery, but the deregulation plan as a whole will have positive benefits on expansion of imports, promotion of new entries into the market and narrowing of the wide price gap between Japan and other nations," said Murayama.

He noted that the package includes review of major issues, such as regulations on holding companies and the Large-Scale Retail Store Law.

STEP 1

Kosaku Inaba, chairman of the Japan Chamber of Commerce and Industry, welcomed the deregulation plan on the premise that it is just the first step in the government's comprehensive deregulation policy.

"There is much room for improvement in the plan," was the more guarded comment from Shoichiro Toyoda, chairman of Keidanren, Japan's most powerful business organization.

The second climax of the government's deregulation efforts came on Aug. 2 when the Ministry of Finance unveiled deregulatory measures on investments in foreign equities. As the move by the monetary authorities was unexpected, it won the approval of market players — at least in the initial stages.

Encouraging Japanese institutional investors to buy foreign securities and extend loans overseas was part of the ministry's goal. A not unintended spin-off from this was buying of the dollar to bring down the yen.

The ministry's deregulatory plan, which took effect immediately, also lifted the ban on life insurers extending loans in foreign currencies and eliminated the so-called 50% rule, which barred insurers from providing more than half the funds in overseas syndicated yen lending.

To encourage Japanese institutional purchases of U.S. Treasuries and other foreign-currency denominated bonds, the ministry gave holders the go-ahead to valuate the instruments either at cost or market value.

"We welcome the ministry's deregulation measures because they should help in bringing down the yen," said Josei Ito, president of Nippon Life Insurance Co. and chairman of the Life Insurance Association of Japan.

NEW ZEALAND SHOWS THE WAY

New Zealand's success at deregulating itself out of an economic slump has drawn increasing attention from Japan's Economic Planning Agency, not least because New Zealand now posts faster economic growth than any other member of the Organization for Economic Cooperation and Development.

Isamu Miyazaki, who took office as director general of the EPA in September, chose Wellington for the first overseas stop-over in his new job.

During the Aug. 23-24 visit, Miyazaki met with New Zealand's finance minister, central bank governor and other high-ranking government officials to discuss the nation's accomplishment. The deregulation measures in the country follow the basic policy of stressing market mechanisms, privatizing state-run enterprises and liberalizing entry into the banking sector.

Until early in the 1980s, New Zealand had the most restrictive government regulations among industrialized economies. As a result of limiting imports and repeated cycles of easing credit and expanding spending from a short-term perspective, the country had seen its real economic growth rate falter.

That, coupled with the simultaneous rise in unemployment and inflation, compelled the government to take emergency steps, such as freezing commodity prices, wages and interest rates.

But the situation changed in 1984, when the Labor Party government, with Roger Douglas as finance minister, began to revamp the economic structure. Of special note was the policy accord between the government and the central bank under which the bank gained more independence, but was required to keep the annualized increase in commodity prices below 2%.

Included in the accord was a requirement that the central bank governor would resign if commodity prices rose more than 2% year on year. That policy was carried over by the National Party upon its return to power in 1990.

The new government continued to push ahead with drastic measures to reform the country's economic structure, including selling postal savings and communications businesses to overseas concerns, halving the number of public employees and simplifying the tax system.

The EPA is now looking at the program adopted by New Zealand as a possible blueprint for deregulation and streamlining of Japan's economic structure.

NEW DEREGULATION PLANS

Package launched on March 31

From Fair Trade Commision:
Review by end of March 1998 a law banning holding companies

Offer by end of March 1996 more freedom to offer discounts and prizes

From Ministry of International Trade and Industry
Review by end of March 2000 Large-Scale Retail Store Law

From Ministry of Posts and Telecommunications
Consider by end of March 2000 introduction of a bidding system for radio-frequency allocation

From Ministry of Home Affairs
Review by end of March 1998 regulation banning self-service gasoline station

From Ministry of Finance
Review by end of March 1996 criteria for public offering of stock

Review by end of fiscal 1999 criteria for approving tobacco retail sales

Review by end of fiscal 1996 requirements on corporate bond issuances

From Ministry of Labor
Expand from fiscal 1996 job categories that private employment agencies can cover

From Ministry of Transport
Ease regulations after fiscal 1995 on fares charged by railway companies

Allow by end of March 1996 used cars to be exported without governments permission

From Ministry of Agriculture, Forestry and Fisheries
Abolish by end of fiscal 1996 export inspection of items including soy sauce, green tea, dried *shiitake* mushrooms, mandarin oranges and apples

Source: Ministries

KEY WORD

LARGE-SCALE RETAIL STORE LAW

The law restricting opening and operation of large retail stores has long been blamed as a major factor in keeping Japan's retail prices higher than in other industrialized nations. In May 1994, the government liberalized rules on opening retail stores with a sales floor under 1,000 sq. meters and promised to further review the law later. However, the authorities did not specify a date for further deregulation of the retail industry.

KEY WORD

STOCK OPTIONS

The government's September stimulus package eases restrictions on the offering of stock options to company employees. The idea was to fuel growth for venture businesses, but the deregulation step failed to impress industry executives since it restricts options to a small number of venture firms. Only 25 firms meeting the criteria of a 1989 law on venture businesses, and another 40 firms now under examination, can qualify to offer stock options to their employees.

BUDGET/TAXATION

More spending, less tax revenue may mean additional deficit bonds

BY AKIRA IKEYA
Staff Writer

Although the scale of public works projects had recently expanded, the stimulative effect on the economy was weaker

Although the burden of stimulating the economy falls on the Japanese government, its room to maneuver became increasingly narrow in fiscal 1995 amid a deterioration in the state of the nation's finances. Because of the economic slump that followed the bubble economy of the late 1980s, the nation's tax revenues dropped for four straight years through fiscal 1994, at which point revenues came to ¥51.03 trillion, down 5.7% from fiscal 1993. Though the general account logged a surplus of ¥607.6 billion, an official at the Ministry of Finance commented that the additional issue of deficit-covering bonds worth ¥810.6 billion was the only reason.

In addition to the decline in tax revenues, government officials also became concerned about the country's mounting debt. Outstanding government bonds were expected to total ¥216 trillion, up 5.9% from a year earlier. The portion of fiscal 1995 revenue that would come from bond issues was estimated at 20.9%.

Japan used to be famous for its fiscal health. By calendar 1994, however, Japan's fiscal deficit amounted to 3% of its gross domestic product, according to the International Monetary Fund. The comparable figure in the U.S. was 2%.

Economists predicted that the impact of the fiscal 1996 budget on the economy would be limited since the increase in public works was to change little from previous years. Requests for the fiscal 1996 general account totaled ¥79.19 trillion, up 11.6% from the initial budget for fiscal 1995. The double-digit increase seemed appropriate given the need for economic stimulus. However, a significant part of the expansion came from a 32.2% jump in debt servicing costs to ¥17.47 trillion. Requests for grants to local governments also rose 20.5% to ¥15.92 trillion.

On the other hand, requests for general expenditures (including public works and ministry operating costs) rose only 4.2%, matching a ceiling set previously by the government. In the initial budget for fiscal 1995, the increase in general expenditures was 3.1%.

With limited financial resources, the government tried to appear serious about addressing changes in Japan's economy. As the appreciation of the yen exposed the weakness of export-oriented manufacturing, the government tried to prod domestic producers toward higher value-added industries.

For the first time, the government set aside ¥140 billion for non-capital investment, including research and development, information technology and relief for the earthquake-stricken Kobe area. Ministries vied for shares of these funds as well. While the government pushed the spending as the focal point of the fiscal 1996 budget, economists felt it would be too small to be

effective. Furthermore, R&D investment would not have an immediate impact on the economy, they said.

Typically, public works spending patterns need to be adjusted to suit structural changes in the economy. However, the allocation among major public works categories seemed unlikely to change in the fiscal 1996 budget. In the requests from the Ministry of Construction, which typically receives 68% of the public works budget, the shares of four large categories — roads, forestation and flood control, city planning and public housing — changed little from the previous year. The most significant divergence was an increase of 0.09 of a point for forestation and flood control. Although the scale of public works projects had recently expanded, the stimulative effect on the economy was weaker, economists claimed.

A more serious problem was the expected shortfall in fiscal revenue, which would force the government to issue additional deficit-covering bonds. The Finance Ministry estimated the government's revenue for fiscal 1996 at ¥70.14 trillion, down 0.1% from the projected revenue for fiscal 1995. The amount would fall ¥9.05 trillion short of requested spending.

SEMI-OFFICIAL LENDING

Meanwhile, requests for the Fiscal Loan and Investment Program (FLIP) came to ¥49.64 trillion, up 3% from the initial plan for fiscal 1995. Funded by sources such as postal savings and the national pension scheme, FLIP allocates money to quasi-governmental corporations, including the Government Housing Loan Corp., Japan Development Bank and Export-Import Bank of Japan. FLIP funds also go to non-financial institutions, including the Japan Public Highway Corp.

The low 3% increase in demand for FLIP funds for fiscal 1996 partly reflected criticism that the program was crowding out private-sector lending. Requests from Japan Development Bank dropped 15% from the previous year. Still, the Finance Ministry was to scrutinize requests from the quasi-public corporations to ensure that their projects were appropriate.

As for the annual revision of the tax system, the Tax Commission, an advisory panel to the prime minister, seemed likely to recommend keeping the landholding tax in fiscal 1996. Some in the private sector had called for abolishing the tax which, they said, put an unreasonable burden on large landowners.

The commission was also expected to call for a higher liquor tax on *shochu,* a distilled spirit, after the European Union, the U.S. and Canada complained the tax was too low compared with that on imported whisky, but the change may come later than fiscal 1997.

OUTLINE OF FISCAL 1995 BUDGET

On an initial-budget basis; in billions of yen

REVENUES	AMOUNT	CHANGE*
Tax and stamps	53,731	0.1%
NTT stock proceeds	172	0.0%
Other revenues	4,485	-19.9%
Bond issues	12,598	-7.7%
Total	70,987	-2.9%
EXPENDITURES	**AMOUNT**	**CHANGE***
General expenditures	42,141	3.1%
Social security	13,924	3.3%
Defense	4,723	0.86%
Public works	9,239	-17.1%
ODA	1,035	3.6%
Debt servicing	13,221	-7.9%
Tax grants to local governments	13,215	3.6%
Other expenditures	2,408	-32.4%
Total	70,987	-2.9%
FISCAL LOAN & INVESTMENT	**40,240**	**2.1%**

*Change form initial FY94 budget

THE LIMITS OF HIDDEN DEFICITS

If tax revenues fall short of planned expenditures amid concerns over government bond issues, the Ministry of Finance can sometimes create "hidden deficits" to make ends meet. For the fiscal 1996 budget, however, MOF officials said the room for such deficits, from borrowing from special accounts and postponing payments, was limited.

In fiscal 1995, total hidden deficits amounted to ¥2.9 trillion. That included borrowing from special accounts such as the foreign exchange fund as well as delays in payments to the pension program and employment insurance. The deficit also included the postponement of the more than ¥800 billion paid annually toward debts from the now-privatized Japanese National Railways.

In addition, the government postponed, for the third year, payment to a special account targeting the national debt. The government was supposed to set aside 1.6% of the value of outstanding bonds as of the beginning of the previous year. Not paying this in fiscal 1995 saved ¥3.25 trillion for the general account. The government was to resume the payments in fiscal 1996, increasing debt-servicing costs for the year.

OUTSTANDING GOVERNMENT BOND ISSUES

In trillions of yen

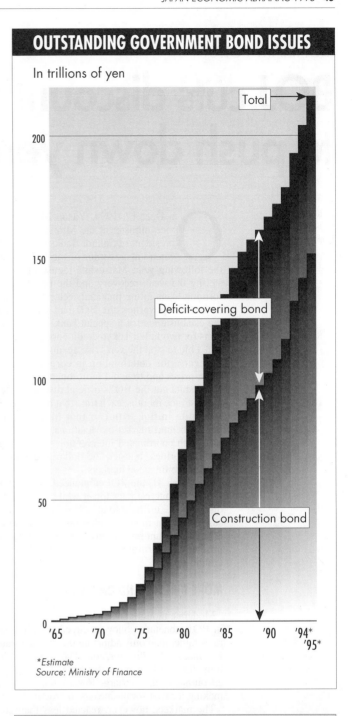

*Estimate
Source: Ministry of Finance

DEFICIT-COVERING BONDS

Funds raised through construction bond issues must be used, by law, for public works and capital contributions. To make up for revenue shortfalls, the government issues deficit-covering bonds, which first appeared from fiscal 1976 through fiscal 1989 after the passing of a special law. The government resumed issuing the bonds in fiscal 1994 to finance income tax cuts. The outstanding balance of deficit-covering bonds at the end of fiscal 1996 was expected to come to ¥65 trillion.

GRANTS TO LOCAL GOVERNMENTS

A certain portion of revenue from five sources —income, corporate, liquor, consumption and tobacco taxes — is pooled for grants to local governments to meet their revenue shortfalls. Among 3,281 prefectures, cities and towns, only 154 entities do not receive the grants. Among the 47 prefectures, only Tokyo is able to make ends meet without support from the national government.

MONETARY POLICY

BOJ cuts discount rate to record low to push down yen, boost markets

BY KAORU
MORISHITA
Staff Writer

On Dec. 17, 1994, Yasuo Matsushita, former vice minister at the Ministry of Finance and president of Sakura Bank, succeeded Yasushi Mieno as governor of the Bank of Japan. In the following year, Matsushita focused heavily on bolstering the weak recovery and the problem of nonperforming loans in the financial sector. The week before he became governor, the BOJ had already announced the establishment of a special bank to take over operations for two failed Tokyo credit cooperatives.

In a bid to stop the yen's rise against the dollar, as well to reverse the deterioration in corporate earnings and share prices and to avoid more financial-sector failures, Matsushita cut the BOJ's official discount rate twice in his first nine months, each time to a new record low.

Despite initial criticism that Matsushita's moves lagged behind market expectations, his rate cuts, coupled with coordinated intervention with foreign monetary authorities, boosted the dollar and sent a positive message to financial markets.

On March 31, the BOJ announced that it would guide short-term interest rates lower while keeping the official discount rate unchanged at 1.75%. A BOJ official even suggested that money market rates could go below the official discount rate. Following the announcement, the unsecured overnight call rate declined from 2.2% to around 1.75%.

MORE DIRECT HAND ON RATES

Moderate though the action was, it heralded a new era in BOJ monetary policy of directly guiding short-term rates rather than only adjusting the discount rate. Kunio Kojima, a BOJ director, told The Nihon Keizai Shimbun that guiding money market rates lower would encourage banks to charge lower interest rates on loans, making it easier for businesses to procure funds.

The markets, however, reacted less than enthusiastically, with the Nikkei Stock Average sinking to 15,381.29 points on April 3, its lowest since August 1992, while the yen remained firm against the dollar.

On April 14, the BOJ cut the official discount rate by 0.75 of a percentage point to a record low 1%. Matsushita announced that, "Although the economy is still in a modest recovery phase, the further appreciation of the yen and continued asset deflation is posing a threat to a sustained recovery." In the following three months, the overnight call rate hovered around 1.3%.

On April 26, the G-7 finance ministers and central-bank heads issued a communique after a closed-door meeting in Washington, D.C. calling for "an orderly reversal" in the dollar's decline. The communique also said that exchange rates had gone beyond levels justified by the economic fundamentals of the major industrialized nations. Finance Minister Masayoshi Takemura hailed the statement as "unprecedented in its straightforwardness" and "epoch-making".

Although the markets discounted the communique soon after it was released, timely coordinated monetary policy in the following months eventually led to an upturn in the dollar against the yen.

FEAR OF DEFLATION

On July 6, Matsushita announced to the press that the economic recovery had stalled. Following his announcement, the central bank started guiding short-term money market rates even lower. The next day, Kojima explained that the BOJ "took the step to dispel possible deflation concerns." As a result, the unsecured overnight call rate declined to around 0.75%, a quarter of a percentage point below the official discount rate.

The reversal in position of the official discount rate and short-term money market rates limited the usefulness of the discount rate and BOJ lending in monetary policy. Jesper Koll, vice president and head of economic and market research at J.P. Morgan Securities Asia Ltd., commented that the official discount rate became "a penalty for banks that failed to square their positions after a day's business."

On Aug. 30, the failure of two financial institutions, Hyogo Bank, the largest of second-tier regional banks, and Kizu Credit Cooperative, the country's second largest credit union, was announced.

On Sept. 8, the BOJ cut its official discount rate by half a percentage point to 0.5% — a record low not only for Japan, but for any industrialized nation in the post war era. The BOJ also announced that it would guide short-term money market rates to slightly below the new official discount rate.

Analysts said the September rate cut was aimed at dispelling concerns over financial instability rather than bolstering the stagnant economy.

TO THE RESCUE

Loans and assistance to financial institutions from Deposit Insurance Corp.; in billions of yen

Period		Amount	Recipient	Purpose
1992	April	8.0	Iyo Bank	Loan to help finance bailout merger of troubled Toho Sogo Bank
	October	20.0	Sanwa Bank	Grant to assist takeover of ailing Toyo Shinkin Bank
1993	October	26.0	Bank of Iwate	Grant to assume business of bankrupt Kamaishi Shinkin Bank
	November	19.9	Osaka Koyo Credit Coop.	Grant to assist takeover of Osaka Fumin Credit Coop.
1995	March	2.5	Kansai Kogin Credit Coop.	Grant to acquire Gifu Shogin Credit Coop.
	July	40.0	Tokyo Kyodou Bank	Grant to assume business of bankrupt Tokyo Kyowa and Anzen credit cooperatives
	July	2.8	Kanagawa Labor Credit Association	Grant to assist takeover of Yuai Credit Coop.
1996		110.0*	Tokyo Kyodou Bank	Grant to assist takeover of Cosmo Credit Coop.
		400.0*	A new bank	Grant to assume business of Kizu Credit Coop.
		400.0*	A new bank	Financial aid to take over business of Hyogo Bank

*Estimate
Source: The Nihon Keizai Shimbun

BOJ VOWS TO PROTECT DEPOSITORS

On Aug. 1, the Bank of Japan offered more than ¥10 billion in unsecured loans to Cosmo Credit Cooperative, Tokyo's largest credit cooperative, which had been ordered to suspend operations the previous day amid a run by depositors. This was the first instance of special lending by the BOJ since Yamaichi Securities Co. was rescued from the brink of bankruptcy in 1965.

Article 20 of the Bank of Japan Law states that the BOJ has to demand collateral when it makes loans. At the same time, however, Article 25 says that the BOJ may, with permission from the finance minister, undertake such steps as are necessary to foster and maintain the credit system. Based on Article 25, the BOJ extended to Cosmo the special unsecured loans in order to prevent a chain reaction of bank runs.

BOJ Governor Matsushita cited three conditions for special BOJ lending to prevent the failure of a financial institution. First, the BOJ's absence would have to otherwise risk depositor unrest, threatening the nation's financial stability. Second, the funds would have to be indispensable for solvency and there would be no other possible lenders. Third, steps would be taken so that management and shareholders shared the burden of bailing out the institution.

On Aug. 30, the nation's second largest credit cooperative, Osaka Prefecture-based Kizu Credit Cooperative, became the next to fail and faced a run by depositors. On the same day, Finance Minister Takemura announced that Hyogo Bank, the nation's largest second-tier regional bank, would be liquidated as a result of bad loans and would transfer operations to a newly established bank. BOJ Governor Matsushita stated that, "If a shortage in funds for deposit withdrawals should arise, all necessary steps will be taken to secure necessary funds, including the extension of loans under Article 25 of the Bank of Japan Law."

By mid September, cumulative special lending to the three financial institutions amounted to more than ¥500 billion. Toshihiko Fukui, deputy governor at the BOJ, told The Nikkei Weekly that there were limits to the amount of special loans the BOJ could make. If such loans were to become unrecoverable, he said, the credibility of the yen would be undermined.

WIDENING GAP

Official discount rates of Germany, Japan and the U.S.; in percent

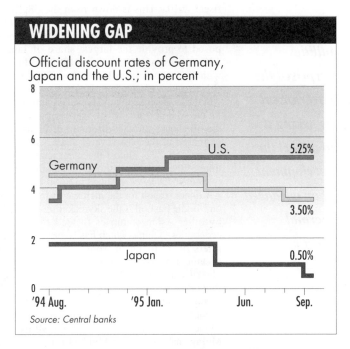

Source: Central banks

CREDIT COOPERATIVES

These are membership-based financial institutions that serve small businesses and individuals. Both deposits from and loans to nonmembers are limited to less than 20% by law. There were some 370 credit co-ops as of September 1995. Starting late in 1994, five have collapsed, requiring emergency assistance from financial authorities. Several of the failed cooperatives had accumulated a substantial amount of nonmember deposits in a bid to move closer to commercial banking.

RESOURCES/ENERGY

Continued reliance on foreign oil spurs domestic nuclear industry

BY SATOSHI ISAKA
Staff Writer

Japanese utilities surprised the government by asking it to cancel the development of an advanced thermal reactor

Japan has traditionally placed great importance on energy security due to the lack of its own supply. With awareness of vulnerability heightened by the two oil shocks of the 1970s, the government has set a long-term goal of reducing Japan's dependence on Middle East oil by developing alternative forms of energy and securing oil from other sources.

According to the latest revision of the government's long-term supply targets drawn up in September 1994, oil will make up 48% of Japan's total energy requirement, equivalent to 635 million kiloliters of crude oil, in fiscal 2010. This is down from the 58.2% of Japan's actual energy needs that oil filled in fiscal 1992.

Among non-oil energy sources, nuclear power is supposed to provide the largest share of Japan's needs, 17%, up from 10% in fiscal 1992, followed by coal with 15%, down from 16.1%, and liquefied natural gas (LNG) with 13%, up from 10.6%.

In terms of oil suppliers, however, Japan's dependence on the Middle East, which had temporarily fallen after the oil shocks through efforts to diversify, has steadily increased in the past several years. In fiscal 1994, it returned to 77%, almost the same level as in 1978, the time of the second oil shock, and a substantial increase from the 67% level achieved in fiscal 1987.

A major reason for the increase in Japan's dependence on Middle East oil is the skyrocketing demand for crude by other Asian countries to feed their fast-growing economies. China, which has been one of the few suppliers of oil to Japan from outside the Middle East, became a net oil importer in 1994, though it still supplied Japan with 5.3% of its oil imports in fiscal 1994. Indonesia, which has long been the largest oil exporter to Japan outside the Middle East, is also expected to become a net importer in several years.

One major reason behind Prime Minister Tomiichi Murayama's visit to the Middle East in September 1995 was thus to strengthen ties with Saudi Arabia in anticipation of Japan's greater dependence on the region for oil, which many experts believe will exceed 90% of Japan's need in the next century. During talks held in Jidda, Murayama called on King Fahd to renew the offshore drilling rights of Arabian Oil Co., the largest Japanese oil field operator in the Middle East. Japan presently imports 1 million barrels a day from Saudi Arabia, about 20% of its total oil imports in fiscal 1994.

A similar motive is clearly behind the unusually blunt line Japan took against China's territorial claims in the South China Sea. Chinese moves in the area threaten Japan's oil lifeline to the Middle East and Indonesia and its supply of LNG from Indonesia, Malaysia and Brunei, Japan's three largest suppliers of LNG, who together account for nearly 80% of total LNG imports.

When Foreign Minister Yohei Kono met his counterparts from the seven ASEAN nations in Brunei in August 1995, he made it clear that Japan will side with ASEAN on the method by which the dispute over the Spratly islands is negotiated. China has insisted on discussing the issue on a bilateral basis with the other countries claiming ownership, including the Philippines, Vietnam, Brunei and Indonesia. ASEAN has called for multilateral discussions such as those held at the 19-member ASEAN Regional Forum.

In February, Tokyo was embarrassed by the international outcry over the first shipment to Japan of highly radioactive waste reprocessed in France. The protests from anti-nuclear groups and countries along prospective shipping routes, however, were a relatively temporary concern for Japan, whose own reprocessing plants are expected to come on line in the year 2000.

The real problem for Japan — and other nations that rely on nuclear power — is that it has yet to find a feasible way to safely dispose of high-level radioactive waste, a term used by experts to denote waste with a radioactive half-life of tens of thousands of years.

In July, Japanese utilities surprised the government by asking it to cancel the development of an advanced thermal reactor (ATR), a 30-year project that has already cost Japanese taxpayers nearly ¥300 billion, on the grounds that it will not be cost-efficient. This was an unprecedented act in the post-war history of close collaboration between the government and utilities in promoting nuclear energy.

Construction costs of the demonstration ATR had ballooned to nearly double the original estimates, and it was shown that the electricity it produced would cost three times as much as that generated by conventional light-water reactors. The cost analysis forced the government in late August to accept the utilities' request to cancel the ATR project.

Still, both the government and the utilities firmly maintain that it is vital to reprocess the nation's spent nuclear fuel, separating plutonium and uranium from the waste for reuse.

From this standpoint, the government's cancellation of the ATR project did relatively little damage because the much more important project of developing fast-breeder reactors to recycle nuclear fuel was not substantially affected. The ATR project was to be a transitional step, consuming the growing amount of plutonium produced from reprocessed spent nuclear fuel until fast-breeder reactors begin full operations early next century.

In late August, after 10 years and nearly ¥600 billion, the Monj, prototype fast-breeder reactor went on line, the first time the project has produced electricity.

KEEPING TRACK OF THE PLUTONIUM

The substantial amount of plutonium that will result from the proliferation of nuclear power plants in Asian countries in the next few decades is bound to raise concerns among the nations in the region. To prevent this from happening, Japanese experts are urging the creation of a pan-Asian nuclear pact. Such a pact is intended to make nuclear programs within the region more open to outside scrutiny and to facilitate the peaceful use of plutonium or its storage until an effective method of disposal is developed. It is also aimed at dispelling concerns among nations in the region over the stockpiling of plutonium, which can be extracted from spent nuclear fuel and used to make atomic weapons.

More specifically, Atsuyuki Suzuki, a professor of nuclear engineering at the University of Tokyo, has called for an "Asian equivalent of Euratom," the European Atomic Energy Community. Under this program, countries that recycle nuclear fuel follow strict safeguards to prevent its diversion for military use. Other experts have said that because gaps in nuclear technology between nations are wider and mutual suspicions deeper in Asia than in Europe, the basic idea should be expanded beyond the Euratom concept and deal with a wide range of cooperation to help the region's less-developed members learn to use nuclear energy safely. No formal blueprint has been forthcoming from Japan, but nuclear experts from South Korea, Taiwan, Southeast Asian nations and Australia were strongly supportive of an initiative floated along these lines by Japanese officials at various forums in 1995.

The essence of this ambitious idea is to expand the system of voluntary disclosure of information that Japan applies to its own fuel-recycling program to other countries in the region. Ideally, experts from each country would be permitted to freely inspect any and all facilities within the region, a step which would help both to build confidence among Asian counties as well as reduce the global inspection burdens of the hard-pressed International Atomic Energy Agency (IAEA).

A major reason for the keen interest in Japan's idea within Asia, especially among the smaller countries, is the lack of space to store spent fuel. Storage facilities in Taiwan and South Korea are already approaching their limits. According to South Korean sources, the country's storage capacity will be used up by 2006, even if the on-site storage facilities at its 23 reactors are expanded to their maximum. South Korea is thus faced with a clear choice: follow Japan's lead and separate plutonium from its spent fuel to minimize waste or stop operating nuclear reactors altogether.

COMPOSITION OF POWER PRODUCTION

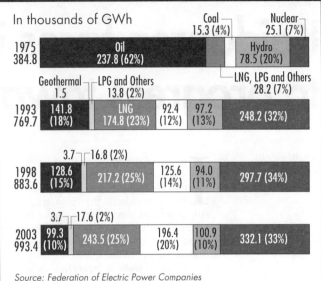

Source: Federation of Electric Power Companies

JAPAN'S CRUDE OIL IMPORTS (FY1994)

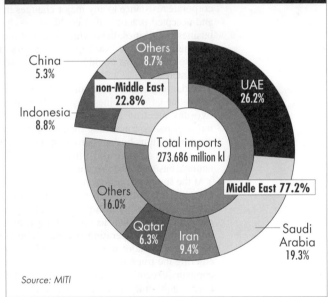

Source: MITI

ATR (ADVANCED THERMAL REACTOR)

Convertors and breeders are the two major kinds of nuclear reactors that use plutonium as fuel. The difference is that the former is always a net consumer of plutonium while the latter can either increase or decrease the amount of plutonium it uses by adjusting its fuel-assembly design. An ATR is a Japanese-style convertor that can burn not only plutonium and enriched uranium, but also natural uranium.

ASIATOM (ASIAN ATOMIC ENERGY COMMUNITY)

ASIATOM is a proposed regional cooperation arrangement aimed at promoting the safe use of nuclear energy in Asia and preventing the possible diversion of nuclear materials to military use. Japanese experts say that any such setup is unlikely to work without U.S. participation or support because the U.S. virtually controls the nuclear policy of many countries in the region through its supply of nuclear fuel and technology.

BUSINESS ORGANIZATIONS

Keidanren faces internal opposition to progress toward deregulation

BY HIJIRI INOSE
Staff Writer

In light of the drastic changes sweeping over Japan's political and economic systems in recent years, the nation's major business organizations — traditionally one side of the "iron triangle" along with politicians and bureaucrats — have been asking themselves what their new raison d'etre should be.

And this year, some business leaders finally seemed to find the answer to that question. They came to the conclusion that business organizations should turn themselves into crusaders leading Japan Inc. into the 21st century rather than continue their traditional role of fund suppliers to conservative political parties.

Those business leaders found it extremely difficult, however, to execute their new role in the face of strong corporate resistance to any major changes in regulations and accepted practices that could adversely affect their businesses. Critics, meanwhile, sneer at those self-proclaimed crusaders, saying the leaders themselves oppose changes that could work against their own business interests.

Keidanren, (the Federation of Economic Organizations), the largest business organization in Japan, held a two-day meeting in the summer to discuss a broad range of issues concerning member companies. As the most prestigious business group in the country, Keidanren wanted to take the initiative in reforming the nation's business customs and practices.

At the summer meeting, Keidanren leaders challenged the chief executive of a truck transport company to debate the necessity of a government regulation on the minimum size of the fleet a trucking firm must own in order to win an operating license. The law has been considered a major obstacle preventing outsiders from entering the truck transport business. But the transport company executive insisted that the regulation was not blocking the entry of newcomers.

One Keidanren member who took part was pleased with the debate, saying that it was significant just to discuss such issues long considered taboo. But critics say that discussion itself will not bring about any change to everyday business.

NEED 'BORDERLESS' ENVIRONMENT

Nearly all Keidanren members — senior executives of long established businesses such as automakers and steel manufacturers — agree that the Japanese business system needs to be reformed in order to adapt to a new environment often characterized as "borderless." They claim that Keidanren, as a crusader, needs to work with politicians and bureaucrats to change or abolish numerous government regulations that work against the vital interests of Japanese consumers.

But when it comes to individual issues, those same members tend to make any excuse possible to keep their own industries from being a target of reform. The inclination of executives to protect their own turf has also been seen in other business organizations.

For example, Keizai Doyukai, (the Japan Association of Corporate Executives), has questioned the system of fixed commissions for securities transactions that, it claims, is causing Japan's stock markets to hollow out. But some Keizai Doyukai members from the securities industry oppose liberalization of commissions. They insist that regulatory changes should come first to permit securities houses to enter other financial markets, such as banking and insurance, as is becoming more common in the West.

A CHANGING GAME

Through the postwar period, leading business organizations have engaged in aggressive lobbying to protect their interests and to resist regulatory changes that could work against those interests. Under the old regime, when foreign companies were not as interested in the Japanese market as they are now, Japanese firms could enjoy, and profit from, operating in virtually closed markets.

But as national borders come to mean less and less and as competition with foreign companies gets tougher and tougher, Japanese business leaders have realized that their industries cannot survive without radical change.

For example, fixed commissions for securities transactions do guarantee brokerages a certain profitability for the moment. But high commissions have already begun to turn many foreign investors away from the Japanese stock market to other Asian exchanges where commissions are much lower. If the trend continues, many business leaders worry that it would make it more costly for Japanese companies to raise funds at home, which would eventually make them less competitive abroad.

Many critics doubt that even the leading business organizations will be able to change Japan Inc. drastically enough to keep up with the pace of change outside traditional business circles. The reason for that, the critics say, is that Japanese prefer arriving at a consensus to holding a vote in making a decision. Such a decision-making system inevitably slows down change, they point out. In particular, major business organizations such as Keidanren and Keizai Doyukai have a large number of member companies, which makes it even more difficult and time-consuming to win a consensus.

POLITICAL DONATIONS CONTINUE TO DECLINE

Political donations, which have long been a symbol of Japanese money politics, dropped sharply in 1994. But that does not necessarily mean that the intimate relationship between politicians and business circles is deteriorating, critics say.

According to the Ministry of Home Affairs, the amount of political donations from both companies and individuals declined to ¥148.4 billion in 1994, down 13.4% from the previous year. Donations have now fallen for three consecutive years.

The decline was attributed to the fact that companies contributed less money to political groups than before. Few companies were able to keep the amount of their contributions at previous levels due to the prolonged business downturn. At the same time, the emergence of new political parties and realignments among the parties in power made it difficult for many corporate donors to decide which party to support. Also there was no major election last year, which was another reason for shrinking contributions since political donations primarily are used to fill campaign war chests.

On top of all that, political analysts agree that Keidanren's landmark decision in 1993 to cease making political contributions strongly influenced companies' decisions on political donations. Keidanren had long allocated donations to conservative parties, based on each member company's capital assets or profit levels. But faced with harsh criticism from the public that grateful politicians were, in turn, making policies that favored business over public interest, Keidanren declared an end to the practice in September 1993.

Political donations from companies have never died out, however, as both politicians and businessmen see the donations as a kind of necessary evil.

In 1994, despite being mired in a swamp of bad debt, the banking industry made the largest single contribution among all industries. It is unclear how the donations influenced policy-making of the political parties that received the money. But to say the least, it is true that the parties that were the recipients of the banking industry's largesse are now strongly urging the government to use taxpayers' money to save the industry from its own excesses.

It remains to be seen if corporate political largesse will continue to shrink. Some analysts predict the introduction of single-seat constituencies will mean lower demand for political funding; others remain skeptical, saying corporations will continue to dominate political funding unless individuals give more.

EARNINGS OF FORMER LDP FACTIONS

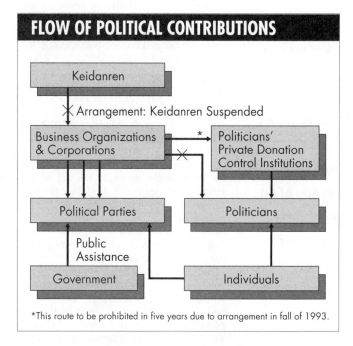

In billions of yen

Legend: Komoto, Miyazawa, Mitsuzuka, Watanabe, Obuchi

1991   '92   '93   '94

Source: Political parties

FLOW OF POLITICAL CONTRIBUTIONS

Keidanren

✗ Arrangement: Keidanren Suspended

Business Organizations & Corporations → * → Politicians' Private Donation Control Institutions

Political Parties   Politicians

Public Assistance

Government   Individuals

*This route to be prohibited in five years due to arrangement in fall of 1993.

KEY WORD

MINRYO

"Minryo" was coined on the pattern of "kanryo," or government bureaucrats, to designate career staff at Keidanren. While kanryo have great influence on policy making, minryo help Keidanren leaders formulate suggestions for the government. Kanryo have often been criticized for working for their own ministry's, rather than the national, interest. Similarly, it is said that minryo often represent the narrow interests of a particular industry rather than industry as a whole.

KEY WORD

PACS

The Keidanren has begun considering the introduction of an American-style political donation system, called Political Action Committees. Under the PAC system, individuals wanting to make political donations do so through PACs set up in companies, labor unions and other groups. Corporations and other organizations, often criticized for being too cozy with politicians, would then be prohibited from making political donations.

EMPLOYMENT

Recession, industrial hollowing-out threaten lifetime employment deals

BY AKIRA IKEYA
Staff Writer

One of the most serious overmanning problems can be found in the white-collar section of the work force, comprising mostly middle-aged men

Japan's unemployment rate rose to record high levels in 1995. Industry in Japan is facing fundamental structural changes as domestic production loses the competitive edge it once enjoyed amid the country's longest recession since 1945. Clearly, as Japanese manufacturers increasingly shift production to offshore subsidiaries, new industries will have to be nurtured to absorb the surplus labor force at home.

According to the Management and Coordination Agency, the unemployment rate in Japan averaged 2.9% in fiscal 1994 through March 1995, up from 2.6% in the previous year and the highest since fiscal 1953 when the agency began to track the data in the present form. In fiscal 1995 from April, the already-shaky situation deteriorated further, with the rate hitting a record monthly high of 3.2% in April.

The job-offers-to-applicants ratio, another indicator of employment trends, stood at 0.61, or 61 jobs for every one hundred job seekers, in June 1995. In fiscal 1994 the ratio was 0.64, declining from 0.71 the previous year, according to the Ministry of Labor.

The government has been claiming that the economy bottomed out in October 1993 and has since been on the road to recovery. But some economists suspect that the fragile economic recovery ran out of steam in spring 1995 and has been worsening since then.

Improvements in the economy tend to take some time to translate as demand for labor. But recovery in the labor market has been a long time coming, suggesting that the recession is just one of several factors at work here, according to economists.

Since Japan's speculative bubble of the late 1980s burst, many firms have attempted to combat weak sales with cost cutting, including labor expenses. Meanwhile, the steady appreciation of the yen since 1993 prompted many firms to shift to overseas production. The two factors have combined to significantly reduced employment opportunities in Japan, economists said.

Moreover, this is likely to be a long-term trend. In the future more companies are expected to introduce computerization to facilitate reductions in human labor. Meanwhile, there is a vast pool of inexpensive labor in the developing countries of Asia which is gradually taking over low-tech manufacturing processes from Japan. As the 20th century draws to a close, the Japanese work force will be forced to seek out employment opportunities in new industries.

From 1994 to 2000, employment in the construction and manufacturing sectors will rise by only 1.1% to 21.81 million, while in the service sector it will jump 6.5% to 41.79 million, according to a study panel set up by the Ministry of Labor. The service sector includes public utilities, wholesalers, retailers, restaurants, banks, brokerage firms, transportation and telecommunications companies.

Between 2000 and 2010, the total number of jobs will fall by 1.5% to 65.59 million, the panel says. During that period, employment in construction and manufacturing will shrink 4.4% to 20.84 million while service-sector employment will rise 0.8% to 42.12 million.

The surplus work force no longer required by manufacturers is likely to be absorbed by nonmanufacturers, keeping the unemployment rate at around 2.7% in 2000, according to the panel's predictions.

But some economists believe this outlook is too optimistic, being based on the assumption that surplus labor can make a smooth transition from the manufacturing and construction sectors to nonmanufacturing activity. The panel, they argue, has failed to recognize incongruities between the types of jobs available and the age of the surplus work force.

For example, one of the most serious overmanning problems can be found in the white-collar, middle-management section of the work force, comprising mostly middle-aged men.

In 1995, the Ministry of Labor introduced a scheme to encourage worker mobility from industries unable to maintain payrolls to sectors looking to take on more staff.

The ministry had already been paying so-called labor adjustment subsidies to companies which kept workers on the payroll though their services were not actually required. These subsidies were taken from the national employment system, which is funded by mandatory payments from both employers and workers.

In July 1995, the ministry added a new subsidy system to promote mobility in the work force. Under the new program, the ministry identifies those industries undergoing structural recession. When workers move from these hardest-hit industries to other sectors of the economy, the government will subsidize their wages for up to a year. The government also extends subsidies for personnel training where required.

If companies in sectors recognized to be facing structural difficulty decide to move into other areas of business, the government will also subsidize training schemes to allow the firm to make the switch successfully.

Nevertheless, the future still looks grim. There are strong indications that many firms are moving away from hiring full-time personnel and are increasing the part-time staff on their books instead.

According to the Management and Coordination Agency, the number of part-time workers showed a sharp increase in June 1995 while the full-time employment rate scarcely rose.

UNEMPLOYMENT LEVEL & JOB OFFERS TO APPLICANTS RATIO

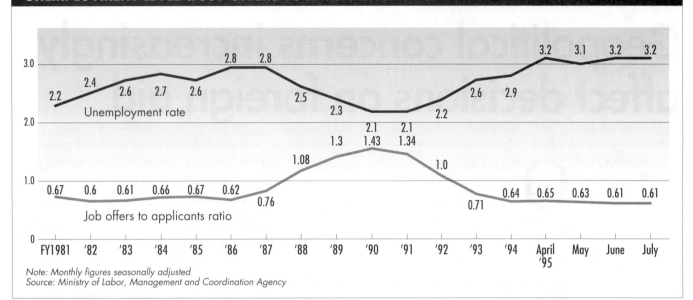

Note: Monthly figures seasonally adjusted
Source: Ministry of Labor, Management and Coordination Agency

'95 COLLEGE GRADS FIND JOB MARKET COLD

The job market may have been chilly in 1994, but in 1995 the climate was decidedly harsh for undergraduates seeking their first full-time position. The flagging economy has prompted many companies to pare labor costs in a bid to boost profits. Japan's tradition of lifetime employment has prevented massive redundancies, forcing management to curtail or halt hiring instead, to keep payrolls lean.

Japanese students graduate in March and generally start full-time work in April. Students generally start hunting for a job at the beginning of their final year. To date, most have expected to have secured a position with a company by the end of the summer. But at the end of April 1995, there were still around 160,000 new graduates without jobs, up 10,000 from a year earlier, according to the Management and Coordination Agency. This was the largest figure recorded since the agency started tracking the data in 1984.

According to Recruit Research Co., a private research agency, as of July 1995, private companies were planning to hire 391,000 newly college graduates to start work in the spring of 1996, a 2.4% drop from the previous year's survey. The job-offers-to-applicants ratio for new college graduates consequently stood at 1.08, down 0.12 point from the previous year, marking a decline for the fifth consecutive year. The figure may not appear particularly low, but it is the female graduates who have borne the brunt of the cutbacks. The job-offers-to-applicants ratio for female graduates stood at 0.45 for the same period. In other words, more than 50% of newly graduated female students were unable to secure a position.

Female students have complained that there is active discrimination against them. In some cases they are not even allowed the opportunity to apply for positions that are available to their male contemporaries. But the 1986 Equal Opportunity Law is little more than a guideline. Companies contravening the law cannot be penalized. The Ministry of Labor can do no more than advise companies practicing discrimination on gender grounds to refrain from doing so.

UNCERTAIN FUTURE

Number of college graduates who failed to get jobs*; in thousands

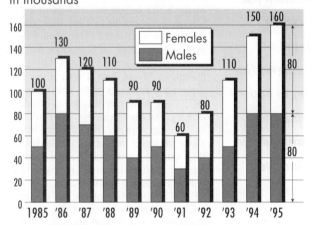

*At end of April each year
Source: Management and Coordination Agency

UNEMPLOYMENT RATE

Japan's unemployment rate stood at 2.9% in 1994, below the 6.1% in the U.S., 8.2% in Germany and 9.3% in the U.K., says the Management and Coordination Agency. Japan's low jobless rate compared with other industrialized nations is attributed to the traditional lifetime employment system. Companies tend to hold on to surplus workers and some analysts reckon that the unemployment rate in Japan would rise by 2 percentage points if companies were to let their unproductive workers go.

OFFICIAL DEVELOPMENT ASSISTANCE

Geopolitical concerns increasingly affect decisions on foreign aid

BY SATOSHI ISAKA
Staff Writer

Even the three parties of the coalition put pressure on the Foreign Ministry to both terminate grant aid and reduce yen loans

Official development assistance is undoubtedly the most significant foreign-policy instrument available to Japan. But events in 1995 underscored for Japan the message that there are some things money just can't buy. Japanese officials were repeatedly frustrated in their efforts to influence controversial policies in some of the developing countries that are large beneficiaries of aid from Japan.

China is a case in point. Beijing went ahead with its nuclear testing program in 1995 despite repeated, high-level official requests from Tokyo that it should refrain from doing so. Given China's determination to upgrade its nuclear arsenal, it is likely that Beijing will continue to ignore Tokyo's threat of reductions in economic aid and conduct further tests in the future.

Japan has been by far the largest supplier of foreign aid to China for some years, disbursing more than 60% of the $2.25 billion in ODA that China received from foreign governments in 1993 (the latest year for which figures are available). Underlying this largess is the tacit understanding on both sides that Japanese aid is a substitute for war reparations. Beijing dropped official claims for World War II reparations from Japan when diplomatic relations with Tokyo were normalized in 1972. And until recently, Japan avoided open criticism of its gargantuan neighbor. Tokyo's lack of assertiveness stemmed partly from the fact that China has been Japan's cultural mentor for two millennia. In addition, the Japanese government recognizes that China suffered heavy casualties due to the aggression of Imperial Japan before and during World War II.

But China's policy of nuclear testing in recent years has provoked Tokyo to make repeated threats that Japanese taxpayers will soon tire of handing over billions of yen to a regime that persists in upgrading its nuclear capacity. And Japanese antipathy to nuclear weaponry was particularly pronounced in 1995, the 50th anniversary of the bombing of Hiroshima and Nagasaki.

After China's nuclear tests in May 1995, Japan finally lost patience and took the unprecedented step of announcing a cutback in grant aid to China in fiscal 1995, from the previous year's budget of ¥7.8 billion ($79.59 million), although the actual amount was not immediately announced. In light of Tokyo's principles on the disbursement of aid, the decision was overdue. Under the 1992 ODA Charter, the government is supposed to consider factors including the military spending, the development of weapons for mass destruction and the arms trade in recipient countries before a decision to grant aid is reached.

Nevertheless, just three months after the first test in 1995, China exploded another nuclear device for testing purposes. Beijing's audacity incensed Japanese politicians and government officials. Discussions began immediately in Japan on reducing yen loans, concessional lending that accounts for the bulk of Japanese ODA to China.

Foreign Ministry officials expressed reluctance to trim yen loans because Tokyo had already made a formal agreement with Beijing to extend a new three-year, ¥580 billion tranche, from fiscal 1996.

Government officials have acknowledged their unwillingness to tamper with the yen loans stems from fears of further disruption in Japan-China relations, already ruffled by issues such as the controversial opinions voiced by Japanese politicians on Japan's wartime aggression and Japan's policies toward Taiwan.

But the caution of the professional diplomats does not necessarily reflect public opinion in Japan.

Increased military spending by China, saber-rattling over the Spratly Islands, military exercises off Taiwan and other displays of assertiveness have prompted widespread caution in Japan. The opposition Shinshinto party called for immediate suspension of all aid to China. Even the three parties of the ruling coalition jointly put pressure on the Foreign Ministry to both terminate grant aid and reduce yen loans.

Iran is another nation that has continuously perplexed policy makers in Tokyo. Japan was providing yen loans to support Tehran's project to build what will become the country's largest hydroelectric power plant.

But the Islamic republic's suspected backing of international terrorism, sabotaging of the Middle East peace process and development of nuclear weapons has placed Japan in an awkward position.

A general principle comes into play when dealing with questionable regimes, according to Hiroshi Hirabayashi, former head of the Foreign Ministry's economic cooperation bureau. "Japan's approach is not confrontational. We value friendly persuasion and quiet diplomacy over isolation or open confrontation."

Japanese officials believe the most effective way to rectify Tehran's behavior is by supporting the pragmatic foreign and economic policies pursued by President Hashemi Rafsanjani, while pointing out the reasons for international suspicion of Iran. But this approach runs contrary to the stand taken by the U.S. In fact, Washington has repeatedly urged Japan and other countries to follow its lead in putting pressure on Tehran through economic and diplomatic isolation.

Japan is keenly aware of U.S. concerns. But "the government has already decided to extend the second tranche of official yen loans to Iran," said Sadayuki Hayashi, vice foreign minister. Japan extended the first tranche of ¥38.6 billion in 1993.

PROBLEMS WITH ODA ADMINISTRATION

In its frankest admission yet of shortcomings in Japan's ODA strategy, the Foreign Ministry in 1995 published a list of aid projects judged to have been inefficient. Problems were identified in 30 of the 128 projects, or 23%, reviewed by independent experts or the ministry's own auditors in fiscal 1993. Insufficient knowledge of local conditions and misuse and poor maintenance of equipment were just some errors cited.

The assessment revealed that Japanese aid largely yielded the intended results in 98 of the projects. But three grant projects were considered particularly ineffective:

• In Thailand, ¥4 billion was spent to irrigate 5,110 hectares of seaside land. But less than half the land, just 1,478 hectares, was actually irrigated, due mainly to vacillation on the part of the Thai government and delays in land appropriation.

• In Nepal, 16,951 portable power poles (worth ¥900 million) were supplied to help spread electricity to mountain areas. About half the poles were found to have been used in areas where cheaper, concrete poles would have sufficed.

• In Mali, most of ¥120 million spent on parts for farm vehicles was wasted because so many of the vehicles were already beyond repair. Given the road conditions in the central African state, the parts should have been delivered much earlier, acknowledged the report's authors.

The ministry has published audit reports every year since 1982, but this was the first to actually rate project efficiency. Officials explained they were trying to make ODA policy more accountable to Japanese taxpayers, as financiers of the world's largest foreign-aid program. Previously, audit reports were crammed with detailed descriptions and comments on a project-by-project basis, making for a 600-page tome that was read by few. But since aid projects are not subject to Diet approval, being simply selected at the discretion of Foreign Ministry bureaucrats, the report is the only way for taxpayers to keep tabs on how their money is being spent overseas.

The Foreign Ministry's new steps toward greater accountability are also evident in the section of the report calling for feedback on policy problems. For example, the report said that when making aid decisions, Japan should consider the changing policies in countries that are rapidly liberalizing their economies, like Argentina, India and China.

Hiroya Ichikawa, of Keidanren notes that if a project proves commercially successful, then Japan should be flexible enough to shift the money already earmarked for that project to other less-successful but meaningful projects.

ODA SHARES OF 21 DAC COUNTRIES

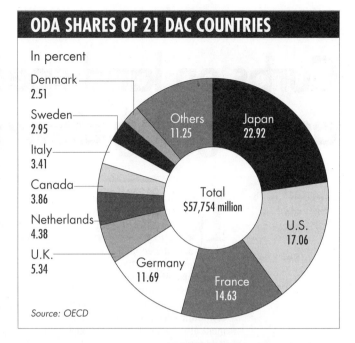

In percent

Source: OECD

ODA BY COUNTRY

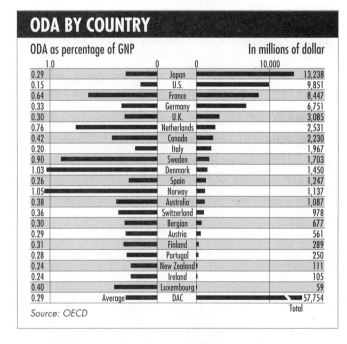

ODA as percentage of GNP			In millions of dollar
0.29		Japan	13,238
0.15		U.S.	9,851
0.64		France	8,447
0.33		Germany	6,751
0.30		U.K.	3,085
0.76		Netherlands	2,531
0.42		Canada	2,230
0.20		Italy	1,967
0.90		Sweden	1,703
1.03		Denmark	1,450
0.26		Spain	1,247
1.05		Norway	1,137
0.38		Australia	1,087
0.36		Switzerland	978
0.30		Bergian	677
0.29		Austria	561
0.31		Finland	289
0.28		Portugal	250
0.24		New Zealand	111
0.24		Ireland	105
0.40		Luxembourg	59
0.29	Average	DAC	57,754 Total

Source: OECD

SOUTH-SOUTH COOPERATION

A new priority in ODA policy is support for so-called South-South cooperation. Under this principle, a developing country that has received assistance from richer nations will then pass on its new-found expertise to neighbors with similar cultural and geographical landscapes. Already Japan is offering funds and equipment to Egypt, Indonesia, Peru and Singapore, where local experts trained under Japanese aid schemes are now themselves training personnel from less-developed neighbors.

THE DAC LIST

The OECD's Development Assistance Committee periodically meets to review which nations qualify as "developing countries," making them eligible for ODA. In May 1995, the DAC agreed that countries with per capita GNP above $8,356 would no longer qualify. Consequently, economies like Taiwan, Brunei and Cyprus will "graduate" in three years. Thereafter, while donor countries will still be free to extend aid to these economies, the contributions will not be counted as ODA.

LAND/HOUSING POLICY

Curbs on land speculation now seen as dragging down overall economy

BY KATSURO
KITAMATSU
Deputy Editor

The MOF
obviously
does not want
to give up
revenue
from the
landholding
and fixed
property taxes

Real estate prices continued falling into 1995 and showed no signs of a pickup. The weak real estate market has become a major obstacle to the recovery, not only of related industries, but of the economy as a whole.

The government has adopted a package of measures to stimulate the real estate market, such as advance land purchases for future public works, on the grounds that the vitalization of land transactions holds the key to economic recovery. In the same context, the government also began looking seriously at the idea of easing land taxes.

However, the proposal to reduce landholding taxes, a focal point in tax reform, faces tough opposition from within the ruling coalition, notably the Social Democratic Party of Japan (SDP).

The downturn of real estate prices was triggered directly by the burst in the early 1990s of the asset-inflation bubble economy. Since then, price falls have exceeded the range of "correction of bubble prices" and started showing signs of what could be called a structural deflation spiral.

In other words, a vicious circle has arisen in which falls in land prices caused by weaker demand depress corporate earnings in the form of declining asset values and act as a drag on economic recovery. At the same time, the growth of wages and employment slows, further dampening demand for real estate.

According to a National Land Agency report released July 1, land prices throughout the country in the first half of 1995 declined 2.1% on average from a year earlier, compared with a 2.3% fall in 1994. Prices dropped 0.9% in residential areas, compared with 1.2% in 1994, and 6.9% in commercial areas, the same rate as the previous year. Indeed, prices declined for five years in a row for the first time since the agency began compiling data in 1975.

Although the margin of price drops in residential areas narrowed from a year earlier, commercial areas saw an increase in the rate of price falls.

Compared with land prices in the pre-bubble days of 1983, prices in residential and commercial areas in the three major urban regions — Tokyo, Osaka and Nagoya — are now 1.68 and 1.47 times higher, respectively. But when the growth of wages since is taken into account, land prices have effectively fallen back to pre-bubble levels.

Even as low land prices have been a drag on the investment of assets by individuals and companies, they are also slowing the settlement of problem loans by financial institutions. In September, therefore, the governmentt included measures to revitalize the real estate market in its economic stimulus package.

The package sees stimulating the property market as a key policy and envisages achieving the target through the government's advance purchases of land for future public works — for which ¥3.23 trillion was set aside.

To stimulate housing investment by individuals, the government also added ¥500 billion to the budget of the Housing Loan Corp. Meanwhile, homeowners are taking advantage of record-low interest rates at private-sector financial institutions to make advance repayment on loans from the Housing Loan Corp.

The latest set of measures to stimulate the real estate market is significantly larger than any in the five previous stimulus packages adopted since 1992. But relevant tax reforms, which drew strong attention as another key land policy issue, faced opposition both within the government and the ruling coalition.

The debate keyed on whether to freeze on the landholding tax, introduced in 1992 to curb speculative trading, and whether to lower the fixed property tax which is widely seen to have become more onerous with the decline in real estate prices.

The prevailing view in the Liberal Democratic Party has been for an easing of land taxes as an economic stimulus since at least June 1994, when the LDP joined the three-party coalition led by SDP chief Tomiichi Murayama, who thus became prime minister. Ryutaro Hashimoto, overwhelmingly elected LDP president in September, called for freezing the landholding tax and lowering the fixed property tax during his campaign.

But the SDP and the Sakigake, the LDP's smaller partners in the ruling coalition, have persistently opposed an easing of land taxes for fear that speculative land trading could re-emerge and drive up land prices again.

The Ministry of Finance has taken a neutral stance on a wholesale review of land taxes. "The taxation system should not be amended without reviewing land policy as a whole," said a senior official at the tax bureau.

The MOF obviously does not want to give up revenue from the landholding and fixed property taxes. In addition, a cut in land-related taxes runs counter to its policy of "lowering the ratio of direct taxes and raising that of indirect taxes," and makes it difficult to increase the consumption tax as planned for April 1997.

Nevertheless, measures to ease land-related taxes are slated for implementation in fiscal 1996 in line with recommendations by the Tax Commission.

While the government and the ruling coalition agree that the revitalization of the real estate market is essential to economic recovery, opinion diverges sharply on the likelihood of a recurrence of speculative land trading as well as on the very definition of "speculative." The economic effects of tax reform have thus come into question in a private sector wary of the whole idea.

MOVING THE CAPITAL

When calls for revitalizing the real estate market as a key economic stimulus began to increase in 1995, the long-running debate on the idea of transferring some of the functions of the nation's capital out of Tokyo got a fresh burst of steam.

Studies to select a candidate for a new capital and decide the date of transfer got under way, especially within the ruling coalition, thus increasing the possibility that a transfer could be realized.

The basic idea is to move the capital's legislative and administrative functions, which center on the Diet and government ministries and agencies, to a regional city.

The project is expected to help expand economic activity by arousing construction demand. It is also expected to contribute to disaster prevention, decentralization of power and deregulation by correcting the over-concentration of political and government functions in the economic capital, Tokyo.

An interim report released in June by a government research commission calls for separating politics and economics and moving the parliament out of Tokyo to begin with.

The report envisages a new capital with a population of 100,000 in the first stage and a span of 10 years from the start of construction to the opening of parliament.

The government planning sector would follow the Diet into the new capital, and the population grow to around 300,000 by that time, the commission says.

The National Land Agency estimates that the transfer of the capital would cost some ¥14 trillion.

The final decision on a candidate for the new capital — the focal point of interest, for obvious reasons — is expected by the end of 1997, at the earliest. So far, a total of 16 prefectures have declared their candidacy and the competition is likely to intensify.

In addition to transferring the capital functions away from Tokyo, government officials, politicians and pundits are discussing two different ideas for creating a new Japanese capital. One of these is the remodeling of Tokyo into a more convenient and less congested city; the other is geographically expanding the capital area by relocating some of Tokyo's existing functions to neighboring municipalities.

These two idea seem less realistic than simply establishing a new capital, however. Taichi Sakaiya, a well-known author and strong advocate of a new capital, says it would take ¥140 trillion and half a century to remodel Tokyo given today's land prices, and expanding the city would also be too expensive.

PLUNGING INTO NEGATIVE ZONE

Year-on-year changes in land price indexes for urban districts, surveyed every March

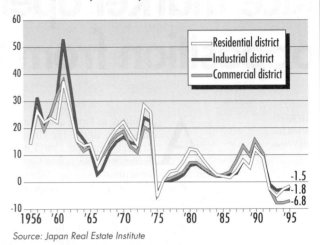

Source: Japan Real Estate Institute

LAND LESS PRICEY

Six prefectures showing largest year-on-year drops in so-called roadside land prices, based on National Tax Administration survey of sites near main streets

	Roadside land price (Per sq. meter)	Year-on-year change
Tokyo	¥804,000	−19.4%
Osaka	¥468,000	−19.3%
Hokkaido	¥94,000	−13.8%
Aichi	¥177,000	−13.7%
Chiba	¥222,000	−10.8%
Miyagi	¥144,000	−10.0%

Source: National Tax Administration

KEY WORD

LANDHOLDING TAX

The landholding tax was introduced in January 1992 to discourage short-term, speculative real estate dealing by imposing additional taxes at a set rate applied to appraised inheritance taxes on land held by individuals and companies. Reform of the landholding tax was a focal point of the debate on fiscal 1997 tax reform, with the MOF arguing that freezing or abolishing the tax, which applies mainly to large companies, would do little to contribute to economic recovery.

KEY WORD

LAND TRUST

Trust banks receive land in trust from owners, raise funds, construct buildings and manage them for the owners. The system greatly attracted land owners during the bubble economy as a way to profit from idle assets. But trust banks have lost interest in the system as using land as security to raise funds became less viable against a background of falling land prices. Land trust projects therefore are being canceled in quick succession across the country.

AGRICULTURE

Rice market opens slightly despite opposition from farm lobby

BY TOSHIO
SHINMURA
Staff Writer

Agriculture in Japan underwent some sweeping changes in 1995. The Uruguay Round of the General Agreement on Tariffs and Trade in December 1993 called for drastic upheavals in Japan's agricultural sector. Many of the measures went into effect in fiscal 1995, from April 1995 through March 1996.

The liberalization of regulations on rice imports had the biggest global impact. Before the GATT agreement, the Japanese government banned imports of rice by the private sector. Only the government was allowed to import rice and then only in the event of a shortage. This did, in fact, occur in 1993, when a total of 2.5 million tons of foreign rice was imported from the U.S., China, Australia and Thailand.

Under the GATT agreement, Japan accepted the principle of 'minimum access' which commits signatories to imports equivalent to at least 4% of domestic demand. Japan undertook to import rice from 1995 through 2000, starting out with 4% of domestic demand, or 400,000 tons, and rising to 8% by the year 2000.

Acceptance of minimum access enabled Japan to avoid rice tariffication, or the liberalization of imports through tariff imposition. Market access from 2001 is to be renegotiated at the World Trade Organization.

Of the 400,000 tons of foreign rice imported in fiscal 1995, 5,000 tons were brought in by trading firms through an auction method known as simultaneous buy and sell (SBS). The remainder was imported by the government Food Agency to be sold to the private sector using SBS auction prices as a yardstick.

The first SBS auction was initially scheduled for May, but was postponed until July after opposition from politicians representing Japan's rice farmers.

In September, the first bags of imported rice appeared on retailers' shelves. A 5-kilogram bag of Australian rice, called 'Mirin,' was priced at ¥2,140, scarcely cheaper than the ¥2,200 price tag on domestic rice. Mirin's price had been pushed up at auction by retailers anxious to get it into their stores to lure customers.

The opening of the Japanese rice market to imports actually came at an inopportune time for Japanese farmers. In 1995 there was a surplus of domestically produced rice. The 1994 rice crop was a record 11.9 million tons, thanks to the long, hot summer in 1994. About 1.9 million tons also remained from the 1994 crop while about 0.9 million tons of foreign rice imported to combat the domestic shortage in 1993 also remained unsold. On top of that, the 1995 harvest produced a bumper yield.

With an additional 400,000 tons of imported rice swelling inventories still further, analysts are predicting a sharp decline in rice prices in 1996.

In the past, rice farmers could only sell their produce to middle men

April 1995 also saw the liberalization of imports of other agricultural products including wheat, starch and powdered skimmed milk. From April, any importer was able to import the products on payment of tariffs.

Tariffs on wheat and starch were set high enough to prevent imports from making a large dent in the domestic market in 1995. But imports of beef grew sharply after tariffs were reduced from 50% in 1993 to 48.1% in 1995. Imports in the April-June period increased 22% year on year, topping the 17% level established to safeguard domestic produce. Consequently, tariffs on beef were temporarily returned to 50%. They are scheduled to fall to 29.8% by 2000, however.

Another change in 1995 which had far-reaching repercussions throughout Japanese agriculture was the replacement of the 1942 Staple Food Control Act by the new Food Control Law. The new law went into effect in November 1995.

The 1942 law was formulated when rice production was still insufficient to meet domestic demand. Under the law, every aspect of the rice business, from production through retailing, was effectively controlled by the government. But five decades later this is no longer appropriate.

A major feature of the revised food control law is the liberalization of Japan's rice distribution system. In the past, rice farmers could only sell their produce to middle men who would then sell it to wholesalers. They then sold it to licensed retailers, mostly small-capital outlets. Leading national supermarket chains were excluded from this system, so they borrowed licenses from smaller outlets.

This convoluted distribution channel has been simplified under the new law. The law also allows farmers to sell as much as they wish directly to retailers provided the retailers are registered with the agriculture ministry.

Prices are now determined by different methods, too. Previously, the government's Rice Price Council set rice prices, and rice producers' demands took precedence over a fair deal for consumers. But since the enactment of the new law, prices are determined at retailers' auctions and should more accurately reflect supply-demand conditions.

The new law also has a profound effect on the operations of producers. In the past, the government provided incentives for rice farmers to reduce production. But production adjustments are now left entirely to the discretion of each individual farmer.

The measures have sparked fierce competition among retailers and farmers. According to simulations carried out by agricultural organizations, the retail price of rice is expected to fall 20% by 2000. Agricultural cooperatives will likely be the hardest hit by these upheavals.

MORE VEGETABLES COMING IN

In thousands of tons

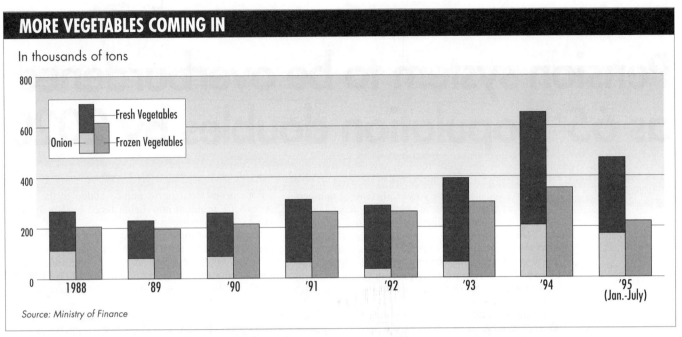

Source: Ministry of Finance

VEGETABLE IMPORTS GROW

As the yen strengthened against the dollar, a wide variety of reasonably priced imported vegetables, including onions, garlic, potatoes, asparagus, tomatoes and cauliflower, appeared in Japan's supermarkets. Imports were further spurred by the poor growing weather in the summers of 1993 and 1994 which produced bad domestic yields.

Imports of fresh vegetable in 1994 surged 70% from the previous year to 600,000 tons. The trend continued in 1995, rising 38% during the January-July period, according to the Ministry of Agriculture, Forestry and Fisheries.

Trading companies and supermarkets emerged as major importers of vegetables grown overseas.

An affiliate of Seiyu Ltd., the supermarket operator, supplied onion and garlic seeds to China and then imported the produce to Japan. Other leading supermarkets including Daiei Inc. and Jusco Co. have also been extending overseas vegetable production operations.

Vegetable imports from the U.S., Australia, New Zealand, Mexico and the Philippines also rose.

Meanwhile, foreign vegetable producers have been targeting Japan's vegetable market independently. Dole Food Co. has made approaches to the Japanese market, offering lettuce, broccoli, asparagus and cauliflower, as well as banana and pineapple. The company is hoping to export vegetables worth ¥20 billion to Japan by 1996.

Del Monte Fresh Produce Inc. started trial exports of vegetables to Japan in 1994 and aims at exports worth ¥40 billion in 1998.

But imports of vegetables fell on a monthly basis in July from a year earlier for the first time in 18 months, partly due to lower overseas production. And as the Japanese yen started to weaken against the U.S. dollar and domestic production returned to normal, the pace of vegetable imports looked likely to slow down toward the end of 1995.

RICE INVENTORY

As of October; in thousands of tons

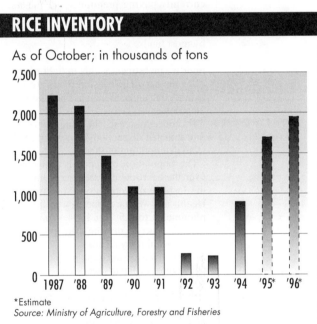

*Estimate
Source: Ministry of Agriculture, Forestry and Fisheries

KEY WORD

1995 NEW FOOD CONTROL LAW

Under this law, which replaced the 1942 Staple Food Control Act in November 1995, the government has only partial control over the production, marketing and pricing of rice. It will continue to purchase some rice for resale to retailers, but "black market" channels outside government routes are now officially recognized. Diversification and simplification of rice marketing channels is expected to bring lower retail prices. In the future, the government will focus on inventory policy and rice imports.

AGING POPULATION

Pension system to be overburdened as 65+ population doubles by 2020

BY YUMIKO SUZUKI
Staff Writer

As Japanese society ages, increasing numbers of elderly people are becoming dependent on corporate annuities as their chief source of income.

But the financial health of pension funds is deteriorating, jeopardizing future annuity payments. In November 1994, a corporate pension fund actually went bankrupt, sending shock waves throughout Japan's working population.

The financial difficulties of corporate pension funds arises from an imbalance between the number of people currently paying premiums and the number of those drawing annuities, analysts say. This problem is exacerbated by the low returns on investments experienced by most funds.

Few corporate pension funds have managed to improve investment yields in light of the sluggish securities market. The pension funds are instead requesting parent companies to increase premiums to cover investment losses.

As concern spread, the Ministry of Health and Welfare initiated discussion of measures to prevent matters from deteriorating further.

The population of Japan is expected to age rapidly over the next few decades, according to estimations by the Institute of Population Problems at the Ministry of Health and Welfare, due to a falling birth rate, which plummeted to 1.5% in 1994. Japan's population will actually start to decline after peaking 130 million in 2011, the ministry reckons.

The number of Japanese people aged between 15 and 64, or most of Japan's work force, will start falling from 1995.

But the number of people over 65 will have doubled to 32 million by 2020. In that year, the over-65s will make up around 25% of the entire population of Japan, the highest proportion in the world.

But with an ailing pension system, some economists say the younger generation are unlikely to see the annuities they expect after retirement.

SHOCKWAVE

The 1994 collapse of an Osaka-based pension fund, the first in nine years, highlighted the gravity of the current scenario. The fund covered 36 small and midsize companies and groups in the spinning industry.

The number of policyholders in the fund had decreased to about 2,200 at the end of fiscal 1994 as the industry went into decline. But those drawing pensions from the fund totaled about 4,400. Eventually it became clear that continued annuity payments would not be possible and the fund collapsed.

Poor investment performance added to the fund's woes — a problem now being faced by a number of other corporate pension funds.

Average investment yields at Japan's corporate pension funds fell for three consecutive years to around 3% in fiscal 1994, the worst on record. The funds' latent losses were estimated at around ¥3 trillion in March 1995, due for the most part to tumbling Japanese share prices since 1990.

Funds are now looking to strengthen investment strategies. In recent years, some corporate pension funds have turned to investment management companies, as well as the life insurers and trust banks which previously handled their assets.

But only 20% of pension funds are following this course, mostly those attached to larger corporations. The majority of funds set up jointly by small and midsize companies have fewer assets and lack investment expertise, analysts said.

HIGHER PREMIUMS

Pension plans were originally set up on the assumption that investments would yield annual returns of 5.5%. Many of the funds are looking to parent companies for additional contributions to compensate for these losses. But analysts believe that a further hike in premiums will be inevitable if investment performance by corporate pension funds remains less than 5.5% annually in years to come.

Some companies have started to take action. The pension fund of Marubeni Corp. organized a committee in June to discuss investment policy. Committee members included both employees of the trading house and fund staff.

Some economists warn that the actual structure of pension schemes will not be viable in coming years in light of the speed at which Japan's population is aging.

The Ministry of Health and Welfare set up a study group of private-sector experts and individuals from the pension-fund industry in late September 1995, to consider ways of restructuring the pension funds.

The panel is reviewing the assumed investment performance and the possibility of adopting a pension system under which contributions remain fixed but pension payouts differ based on the performance of the fund's investments. This system is widespread in the U.S.

The ministry has also urged the Ministry of Finance, which oversees money management, to deregulate the management of pension fund assets to improve investment performance.

YIELDS OF EMPLOYEES' PENSION FUNDS BASED ON THE BOOK VALUE

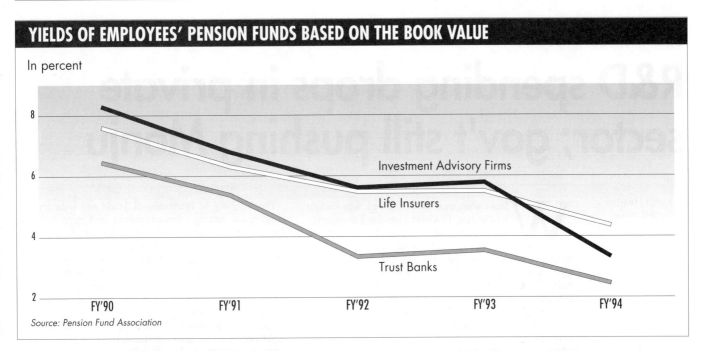

In percent

Investment Advisory Firms
Life Insurers
Trust Banks

Source: Pension Fund Association

PREMIUMS TO DOUBLE BY 2025

The public pension plan for salaried workers also increased its premiums. A revised national pension law came into effect in November 1994. The legislation increased the premium paid by salaried workers from 14.5% to 16.5% of their monthly salary. The premium is scheduled to rise every five years until it hits 29.6% in fiscal 2025.

But premiums could top 30% if Japanese society grays even more rapidly than anticipated and investment performance does not improve, predict industry observers.

The public pension fund's yield on investments has been falling since fiscal 1989. It hit 2.67% in fiscal 1994, down 4 percentage points in six years, due to the falling securities market. Accumulated losses amounted to nearly ¥700 billion at the end of last fiscal year.

The public pension plan had assets of about ¥111 trillion at the end of fiscal 1994. About 20% of these assets was entrusted to trust banks and life insurance companies by the Pension Welfare Service Public Corp. (Nempuku), an organization affiliated with the Ministry of Health and Welfare.

PENSION ASSETS IN JAPAN

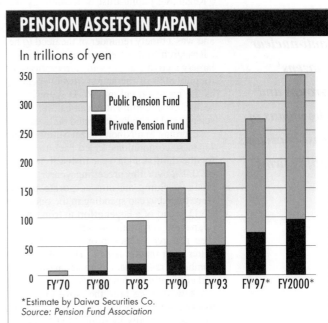

In trillions of yen

Public Pension Fund
Private Pension Fund

*Estimate by Daiwa Securities Co.
Source: Pension Fund Association*

CORPORATE PENSION FUNDS

Companies establish corporate bodies to handle annuity payments to employees after retirement. Larger companies tend to set up individual funds while small and mid-size firms in the same line of business often collaborate. There were nearly 1,900 pension funds in Japan in September 1995 and one third of the salaried population was covered by these schemes. The total balance of assets held by the funds amounted to ¥38 trillion at the end of fiscal 1994.

REGULATION OF INVESTMENT

Money managers have been grumbling that investment regulations regarding allocation of assets are too rigid. Under the so-called 5-3-3-2 rule recommended by the Ministry of Finance, individual fund managers must place 50% or more of assets in relatively safe investments such as bonds or cash, 30% or less in stocks and foreign currency-denominated assets and 20% or less in real estate.

SCIENCE/TECHNOLOGY

R&D spending drops in private sector; gov't still pushing Monju

BY JUNICHI UMEDA
Senior Staff Writer

Angry jeers of anti-nuclear citizens' groups and the moans of cost-conscious utility firms

When public trust in technology was shaken by the Jan. 17 Great Hanshin Earthquake, the government was quick to respond. In its 1995 white paper on science and technology released in mid-July, the Science and Technology Agency called for the utilization of technology to build a safe, human-oriented society. In reference to medical care, environmental protection and energy conservation, the white paper stressed that technology must be adjusted to the needs of people, and not the other way around.

Regaining public trust in technology has become an urgent task for those engaged in research and development. The earthquake shook the arrogance of engineers and was a timely reminder of the need to be humble.

Research and development activities in Japan are largely a private affair, with corporations accounting for roughly 80% of the nation's R&D spending. But even as the recession cut into R&D spending by the private sector, the government began calling for an increase in science and technology-related budgets.

According to a Nihon Keizai Shimbun survey, leading Japanese corporations scaled back their R&D spending for the third straight year in fiscal 1994, cutting funds by 0.9% over the preceding year. As the prolonged business slump ate into corporate profits, managers were forced to cap spending in the once-sacred house of R&D as part of a larger effort to trim operating costs.

Japanese corporations started narrowing the focus of their research themes in order to develop products that better meet market needs. They also began cutting the number of researchers by reorganizing research systems and eliminating redundancies.

Noteworthy has been the move to set up R&D facilities overseas. Electronics makers and pharmaceutical firms are hurriedly locating R&D bases in the U.S. and major European countries. Some consumer electronics firms even plan to set up R&D units in China to be ready to meet the potentially huge local demand.

Corporate R&D spending is expected to rise in fiscal 1995. The Nikkei survey projects a 2.4% increase on a planning basis.

In stark contrast to the scale-back in the private sector, the government began aggressively promoting science and technology. During compilation of the fiscal 1996 budget, concerned ministries and agencies increased their R&D-related budgets in an effort to "create new industries" toward the 21st century.

For example, the Science and Technology Agency will inaugurate a ¥15 billion "strategic basic study promotion project," under which it will provide funds to researchers engaged in the development of technologies like environment-friendly waste disposal systems.

The Ministry of International Trade and Industry has singled out cutting-edge electronics and biotechnology for special treatment. In the electronics field, the ministry wants to emphasize development of a 4-gigabit-class memory device and also support commercialization of truly portable computers. In the biotechnology field, the ministry will help scientists increase their ability to analyze bacterial DNA and create a special system for the analysis of protein structures.

These are two broad areas of research with tremendous promise but also substantial risk, where private industry hesitates to invest resources. Calls for a governmental commitment in such basic areas of study have been strong. The share of public sector R&D spending still stands low at 21.6% in Japan, compared with 42.3% in the U.S. and 37.1% in Germany.

NUCLEAR & SPACE DEVELOPMENT

Japan's nuclear power program entered a new stage in August 1995 when the prototype fast-breeder reactor Monju began producing electricity for the first time. The milestone was passed amid the angry jeers of anti-nuclear citizens' groups and the moans of cost-conscious utility firms.

It took the governmental Power Reactor and Nuclear Fuel Development Corp. 30 years and ¥600 billion to bring the 280,000-kilowatt fast breeder reactor on-line.

Monju burns a mixture of uranium and plutonium, which can be used for nuclear weapons. Japan faces international criticism for its plutonium-based nuclear power program, since it could undermine international efforts to promote nuclear non-proliferation.

Costs are another issue. The electricity generated by Monju is more than twice as expensive as power generated by Japan's existing 49 light-water reactors.

In the field of space development, the National Space Development Agency (NASDA) posted steady achievements in 1995. In March, its H-II rocket successfully launched two satellites into geostationary orbits.

The H-II has thrust equal to the European Space Agency's Ariane-4 rocket and is capable of launching a 2-ton satellite. However, launching costs can reach around ¥18 billion, which is almost double that of the Ariane, which dominates 60% of the world's satellite launching business.

In August, NASDA and the Science and Technology Agency decided to postpone until August 1996 the launch of an earth observation satellite that was originally planned to go up in February 1996. The postponement was made due to delays in development of the satellite, but it means there will be no launch on an H-II rocket for a year and half.

JAPAN'S TRADE IN TECHNOLOGY LICENSES IN FY93

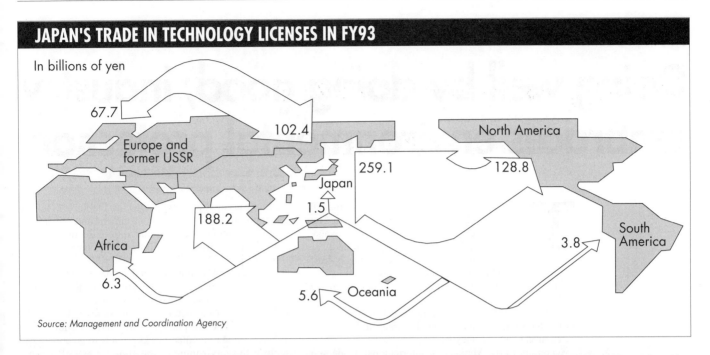

In billions of yen

67.7 — Europe and former USSR
102.4
259.1 — Japan
1.5
188.2
Africa
6.3
5.6 — Oceania
North America
128.8
South America
3.8

Source: Management and Coordination Agency

PUBLIC/PRIVATE R&D SPENDING

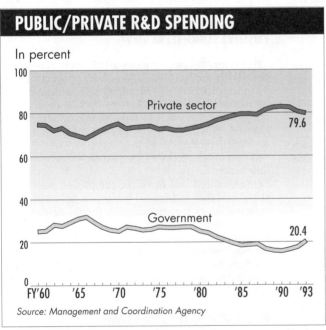

In percent

Private sector — 79.6
Government — 20.4

Source: Management and Coordination Agency

10 BIG R&D SPENDERS

FY'95 R&D spending ranking; in billions of yen, year-on-year percent changes in parentheses

Rank	Company Name	R&D Spending	
1	Toyota Motor Corp.	400	(N.A.)
2	Hitachi Ltd.	380	(-0.7)
3	Nippon Telegraph and Telephone Corp.	300	(+3.2)
4	NEC Corp.	300	(+3.5)
5	Toshiba Corp.	290	(+4.6)
6	Fujitsu Ltd.	280	(+1.6)
7	Honda Motor Co.	205	(+5.0)
8	Mitsubishi Electric Corp.	170	(+3.0)
8	Nissan Motor Co.	170	(+10.4)
10	Canon Inc.	135	(-0.6)

Ranking of R&D cost-to-sales ratio (%); R&D spending in million of yen in parentheses

Rank	Company Name	% Ratio to Sales	
1	Chugai Pharmaceutical Co.	16.1	(26,900)
2	Olympus Optical Co.	15.4	(27,500)
3	Fujisawa Pharmaceutical Co.	14.4	(32,000)
4	Eisai Co.	14.0	(35,385)
5	Green Cross Corp.	13.1	(11,408)

Source: The Nihon Keizai Shimbun

KEY WORD

R&D SPENDING PER RESEARCHER

Japan lags other major industrialized nations in R&D expenditures per researcher. Japanese R&D spending per researcher stood at ¥22.03 million in 1993, according to a Science and Technology Agency survey. Calculated on OECD purchasing power parity terms, the comparable 1989 figure for the U.S. was ¥29.51 million, for Germany in 1989 ¥35.16 million, and for France in 1992 ¥35.46 million. The Japanese figure for university researchers is especially low at ¥11.55 million in 1993.

KEY WORD

TECHNOLOGY TRADE BALANCE

The balance of trade in technologies is a gauge of whether or not a country is technologically "independent." Japan's technology exports in fiscal 1993 rose 20.8% from the preceding year to ¥400 billion, while imports fell 0.2% to ¥363 billion, reported the Management and Coordination Agency. It was the first time exports exceeded imports since the agency began recording statistics in 1972. But Japan still incurred technology trade deficits with industrialized countries.

ENVIRONMENT

Doing well by doing good; industry embraces environmental protection

BY MIHOKO IIDA
Staff Writer

The government anticipates the environmental business will be a leading industry in the 21st century; but corporate Japan has yet to display much enthusiasm for this cutting-edge field.

In particular, the rapidly expanding economies of East Asia are expected to provide lucrative markets for companies already manufacturing environment-friendly equipment, analysts say.

Since late 1994, several Japanese ministries have sponsored studies on the potential markets to be created by environmental businesses.

According to the Ministry of International Trade and Industry, the current domestic market — from garbage disposal equipment to recycled products — stands at ¥15 trillion.

If the field continues to expand at an annual rate of 6%, the market would reach ¥23 trillion in 2000; given sustained annual growth of 4% thereafter, the figure comes in at ¥35 trillion in 2010.

The Environment Agency's estimate is on the light side; a market of ¥13 trillion in 2000 and ¥26 trillion in 2010.

The discrepancies center on MITI's inclusion of such eco-businesses as the recycling of autos, clothes and books.

SHARING RECYCLING COSTS

Potential markets were also included in MITI figures. In June 1995 the government adopted recycling legislation requiring manufacturers to pay part of the costs incurred in recycling plastics and metals, materials making up half of household garbage. This has prompted official estimates that new markets will total ¥100 billion within 10 years. The law is to take effect in fiscal 1997.

The legislation — compiled by MITI and four other ministries (Health and Welfare; Agriculture, Forestry and Fisheries; Finance; and Environment) — aims to slash the amount of consumer waste. Food manufacturers who utilize containers, as well as container manufacturers themselves, will be responsible for a percentage of recycling expenses. At the same time, large retailers who package products will bear some of the costs as well.

Health officials calculate that companies will foot roughly ¥100 billion for recycling efforts; recycling costs are projected at ¥1.3 per PET bottle and ¥0.1 per glass bottle. Manufacturers will incorporate these expenses into retail prices; in the end it will be the consumers who pick up the tab.

Although the market for environmentally conscious businesses is expected to expand, an Environment Agency survey found few companies that have concrete programs to preserve the environment and still fewer willing to spend the time and money to incorporate environmental friendliness into future business activities.

The survey on environmental management targeted 2,177 listed companies. Of the 906 companies responding, 414 (45.7%) said they have policies to preserve the environment. But merely 304 companies (33.6%) said they have concrete plans to carry those policies out. When it came to regular checks on how to go about protecting the environment, the figure was still lower, standing at only 253 companies (27.9%).

POSITIVE LONG-TERM VIEW

By sector, the picture looks a little more promising, but only if viewed from a long-term perspective. Of 593 manufacturers and electricity and gas suppliers, a little more than half said they are working on developing products that will have minimal impact on the environment. Similarly, 36.1% said they are planning and developing products that can be recycled.

Results of the agency's survey on eco-businesses fared little better.

One hundred and forty-six companies out of 906 (16%) said they had created businesses dedicated to the preservation of the environment, for example, selling waste-disposal equipment. Only 91 (16%) said they are planning to enter the field, or conduct research into and develop environmental businesses.

Indeed, Japanese companies appear slow to catch onto what has become a worldwide phenomena: developing an environment-friendly business climate.

WASTE-DISPOSAL BRINGS CASH

But new enterprises have sprung up. For instance, the 146 firms which have created eco-businesses have started 416 such enterprises. Sixty-seven businesses deal with treatment facilities for water pollution, 55 for air pollution and 44 for waste disposal.

The market for waste-disposal plants, a mainstay of environmental businesses, is estimated at roughly ¥500 billion a year in Japan.

In May 1995, Mitsubishi Heavy Industries Ltd. bid to build a municipal waste-disposal plant in Thailand, leading industry analysts to conclude Japanese companies are eying the rapidly growing economies of East Asia as potential markets for future environmental businesses.

IMPACT ON THE BOTTOM LINE

The Environment Agency's 1995 white paper targets the industrial sector, introducing for the first time the concept of cost efficiency in the fight to preserve the environment. This is a long-overdue reversal of the conventionally held belief that environment-friendly measures are costly, labor-intensive and time consuming. The report emphasizes that, in the long run, businesses can save money by implementing measures that will prevent environmental disasters.

A case in point is Minamata disease, a disorder of the nervous system caused by mercury poisoning. People living in the area of Minamata, Kumamoto Prefecture, were poisoned by eating fish contaminated with mercury discharged by a nearby factory. Had the company taken effective prevention measures, the resulting deaths and disabilities and suffering would never have occurred.

In addition to prevention, the agency lists six other measures needed to tackle environmental concerns:

1. Get to the root of the problem; many socio-economic structures may need to be changed.
2. Approach the question as an entity, understanding the symbiosis between water, air, etc.
3. Link environmental measures with other measures, such as uniting car emission standards with traffic measures.
4. Utilize market mechanisms; for example, implement an environmental tax on products that damage the environment.
5. Arm consumers with information concerning the environment.
6. Establish a network among industry officials and consumers.

Though cost-efficiency is key, the agency admits there is currently no method to calculate the economic impact of pollution. The Minamata case is unusual in that the consequences could be assessed in monetary terms, leading analysts to conclude the agency has yet to devise a plan to calculate the economic bottom line.

The annual report also focused on the Asia-Pacific region as an area in need of immediate environmental measures. By 2025, 60% of the world's population will live in the region and consume 30% of the global energy supply. As levels of carbon dioxide emissions increase, bringing about a subsequent rise in global temperature, the report warned China and India — currently large producers of corn and wheat — are likely to face sharp drops in production.

ENVIRONMENT COST – WHO PAYS?

Will company foot the bill?

Regardless of business profits 8.3%
Don't know 6.1%
Others 4.6%
At the least 13.1%
906 companies surveyed
As much as possible 67.9%

Source: Environment Agency FY1995 White Paper

ECO-PRODUCTS ON RISE

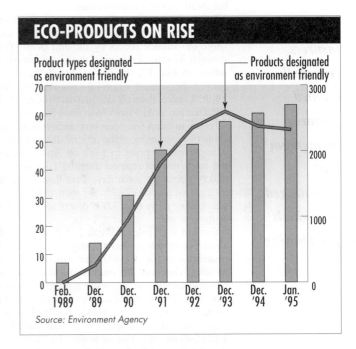

Source: Environment Agency

ECO-BUSINESS

An all-encompassing term involving many sectors. Usually refers to businesses which offer products or services that act to alleviate negative impact on the environment. It can also refer to a business supplying technology and systems. The Environment Agency has designated four categories: equipment which alleviates environmental impact; products that have minimal impact on the environment; services which contribute to environmental preservation; and social infrastructure facilities.

RECYCLING PROMOTION LAW

This legislation, enacted in June 1995 and to take effect from April 1997, is overseen by five ministries. It holds companies responsible for the recycling of containers and packaging. Manufacturers of soft drinks and packaged foods will be required to help finance recycling efforts; manufacturers of containers, such as the plastic materials industry, as well as large retailers that package products, are also targeted.

STOCKS

Market stubbornly refuses to rise as domestic investors stay cautious

BY MASAKO FUKUDA
Staff Writer

Selling by life insurers repeatedly stymied upward momentum and discouraged individuals from buying

The Nikkei Stock Average hit a post-bubble low in July 1995, but rebounded after persistent government effort helped reverse the yen's surge and boost expectations for an improvement in corporate earnings. Foreign investors were the most active buyers, while domestic investors remained cautious.

Average daily turnover on the Tokyo Stock Exchange fell to 237 million shares in April, but rebounded to above 400 million in July after brokerage-account dealing was deregulated. Average daily volume in September swelled to 464 million shares.

Tokyo share prices declined from the beginning of the year on selling by institutional investors looking to shore up balance sheets by the end of the fiscal year through March. Following the Great Hanshin Earthquake on Jan. 17, the Nikkei Stock Average, which started the year at 19,684.04 points, dropped below 19,000, even though reconstruction-related issues attracted buy orders from individual investors.

To try to keep the economic recovery on track, the Bank of Japan reduced the official discount rate by 0.75 of a percentage point to 1.0% on April 14. However, the stock market reacted unenthusiastically, plunging 390.90 points the same day. Five days later, the dollar hit a record low of ¥79.75. By then, the Nikkei average was trading more than 3,000 points lower than where it started the year.

Toward the Golden Week holidays of early May, share prices rebounded slightly on arbitrage buying, returning to the 17,000s for the first time in two months. However, the market's topside was capped by rebound selling from domestic institutional investors.

In spite of the bilateral auto trade accord with the U.S. on June 29, the Nikkei average declined to 14,445.40. The index then slipped to a post-bubble low of 14,295.90 on July 3 amid selling by domestic institutional investors locking in paper profits. Blue chip stocks hit their lowest prices in several years.

The broader-based TOPIX index, which covers all shares on the first section of the TSE, dropped back to 1,194.28, just above its low of 1,193.16 from June 13 and down significantly from 1,553.40 at the beginning of the year.

On July 7, U.S. and Japanese monetary authorities intervened in tandem in the forex market, pushing up the dollar. Encouraged by the move, investors chased the Nikkei index up more than 1,000 points to the 16,000 level. TOPIX rose 62.20 points to 1,298.99.

The Ministry of Finance introduced measures on Aug. 2 to correct the appreciation of the yen, combined with coordinated intervention in New York. The Nikkei index recovered to the 17,000 level the next day. The driving force was buying by foreign investors on expectations that a rebound in the dollar would boost corporate earnings and reduce firms' paper losses on equities.

On Aug. 15, the monetary authorities of Japan, the U.S. and, unexpectedly, Germany, engaged in joint dollar-buying in London and New York, pushing the dollar to ¥96. The Nikkei average surged above 18,000 by the next day for the first time since Feb. 22, rising nearly 1,300 points in two days.

As the index began to settle back, the BOJ lowered the official discount rate to another record low of 0.5% on Sept. 8. The move boosted the stock average 658.37 points by the end of the day. Foreign investors bought continuously, targeting export-oriented high-tech issues, including electronic blue chips NEC, Toshiba and Hitachi, as well as precision machinery issues.

TWICE SHY

Much of the downward pressure on the market in 1995 came from domestic life insurers, Japan's largest institutional investors. In January-March, life insurers sold to lock in profits before the end of the fiscal year. From April, they kept on selling to limit losses on their portfolios. Net equity sales by life insurers in 1995 exceeded ¥1 trillion as of Aug. 4.

Life insurers were reluctant to take on new equity investments, opting instead to reduce their ratio of stocks to total assets. Selling by life insurers repeatedly stymied upward momentum in the stock market and discouraged individuals from buying on the first section.

Another worrying factor for the market is the swelling volume of cash long positions bought against futures contracts for arbitrage — piled up to a record 2.19 billion shares as of October 5.

This is one of the factors blocking upward momentum, since it has a deteriorating effect on the market's supply-demand condition. A flood of arbitrage-related selling can easily send the key index plunging even in thin volume. This prevents active trading, due to persistent fears of downside risk.

NIKKEI STOCK PRICE AVERAGE

Weekly changes

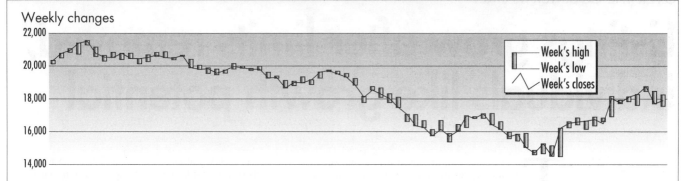

TSE first section turnover; in millions of shares

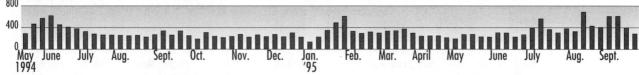

THE COLLAPSE OF BARINGS

In 1995, the Nikkei 255 futures market was the setting for the collapse of one of the U.K.'s most prestigious banks, Barings Plc. Nick Leeson, a trader for the bank in Singapore, managed to run up over $1 billion in losses on futures in the early part of the year — enough to scuttle the bank.

Based on the Nikkei Stock Average, Nikkei 225 futures are frequently used as a hedge against movements on the Japanese stock market. From early 1995, however, Leeson made a bet that the stock market wouldn't fall much below 19,000 in the coming months. But on January 17, the Great Hanshin Earthquake unsettled an already nervous market. On January 23, the Nikkei index fell over 1,000 points. In hopes of boosting the market by himself, Leeson bought more futures, further increasing his exposure. But the Nikkei failed to recover. No longer able to keep his wager afloat, Leeson fled Singapore on February 23. Barings collapsed and was cautiously taken over by ING Bank of the Netherlands within a month.

Leeson had bought Nikkei futures in both Singapore and Osaka. Fortunately, the Osaka Securities Exchange managed to weather the debacle without much panic. The OSE transferred the positions of Baring Securities Ltd., the bank's Japanese subsidiary, to Daiwa Securities Co. The contracts were unwound by early March at levels that enabled Baring's losses to be covered by margin payments it had already made.

A major factor in the collapse of Barings was a lack of internal controls. Barings made the mistake of allowing Leeson, initially sent to Singapore to manage back-office oprations, to keep that position when he was promoted to trader on the Singapore exchange. By booking his own trades, Leeson was able to take long bets on the way markets would move without attracting attention.

The same mistake — allowing a trader to book his own trades — would result in a scandal of striking similarity in New York seven months later. There, it was revealed that Toshihide Iguchi, a bond trader for Daiwa Bank, had managed to canceal $1.1 billion in bond trading losses that began in 1984.

OVER-THE-COUNTER MARKET

Listings grow after limits removed; individuals like growth potential

BY ASAKO ISHIBASHI
Staff Writer

The Japanese over-the-counter market saw strong expansion amid sweeping reforms in 1995. In April, the ceiling on the number of new OTC listings per week was abolished. As a result, the number of OTC-registered issues reached 617 in July — up from 568 at the end of 1994. By year-end, the number of issues was expected to surpass 700. However, the market was still modest in size compared with the more than 5,000 issues on the NASDAQ market in the U.S.

OTC shares went through a downward correction in the first half of 1995 amid selling by institutional investors at home and abroad. The benchmark Nikkei OTC index dropped nearly 40% from its July 1994 high of 2,002 points to 1,194 in June 1995.

OTC shares bounced back from July as domestic investment-trust funds and foreign investors returned as strong buyers. Ten investment-trust funds targeting OTC issues were launched in June through August, compared with just two in January through May. OTC trust funds gained more popularity among individual investors, who were attracted by the growth potential of younger companies.

Many fund managers maintained that the OTC market was the place to be as Japan exited an era of growth built on government protection of selected export-oriented industries and entered an economy driven by new services and consumer demand.

Earnings at OTC companies generally grew faster than those at larger companies listed on the Tokyo Stock Exchange. According to a Nihon Keizai Shimbun survey, aggregate pretax profits at 392 OTC companies were expected to grow 30.0% in the fiscal year through March 1996, compared with 14.1% for 1,604 listed companies.

Many OTC businesses boosted sales and profits by tapping domestic niche markets. Analysts said sectors related to personal computers and video game software were likely to remain strong earners. Softbank Corp., a PC software wholesaler, became an OTC market leader. Since debuting in July 1994, the issue was consistently the highest-priced on the market.

Meanwhile, companies listed on the big boards tended to rely heavily on cost-cutting and exports to eke out profits amid slow domestic sales.

DEREGULATION

Japanese entrepreneurs have to wait an average of 25 to 30 years for their businesses to be profitable enough to meet the tough criteria for OTC registration. In contrast, entry to the NASDAQ market in the U.S. usually occurs about five years after companies are established.

Japan's OTC entrants are required to have minimum assets of ¥200 million, plus at least 2 million shares outstanding and pretax profits of ¥10 per share during the year preceding their initial public offering (IPO). In practice, however, even stricter standards are applied.

Venture capitalists in Japan tend to invest only in mature companies that will be strong enough to go public within five to 10 years. As a result, new companies are left to struggle through their start-up years on their own. In most cases, they rely heavily on bank loans.

The justification for tough OTC criteria has been that they minimize investment risk. The trade-off has been a delay in IPOs by many emerging businesses.

NEW MARKET FOR HIGH-TECHS

In July, however, the Japan Securities Dealers Association opened a second OTC market for high-tech ventures. Actual trading in the new market was not expected to begin until November, after pricing methods for new issues were worked out.

Rules were being designed to greatly speed entry and encourage early investment in new businesses. The new market will be open to research-oriented ventures with ratios of R&D spending to sales of at least 3%. Entrants can even be unprofitable at the time of their IPO provided their lead managers are confident in their innovative ability and growth potential.

Lead managers will be able to price IPO shares at their discretion without the usual pre-offering auction. Issuers in the new market will have to convince Japanese investors, many of them risk-averse in the wake of the bubble economy, to buy on growth prospects. To encourage investors, the new rules call for more detailed and frequent financial disclosure.

An increasing number of investment-trust funds targeting OTC issues have been launched since early in the summer of 1995.

Brokers say these new OTC funds are attracting retail investors, who recognize the high growth potential of the OTC market but find investment in individual ventures overly risky.

From June through September, the number of new OTC investment-trust funds totaled 14, against just two launched in the first five months of the year.

NUMBER OF REGISTERED OTC ISSUES

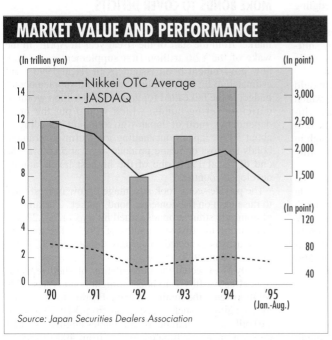

'90	342
'91	430
'92	436
'93	477
'94	568
'95 July	617

Source: Japan Securities Dealers Association

500 OTC COMPANIES BY SECTORS

In percent; as of April 1994

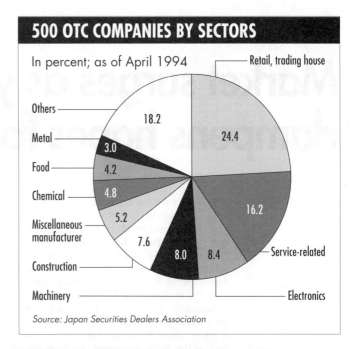

- Retail, trading house — 24.4
- Service-related — 16.2
- Electronics — 8.4
- Machinery — 8.0
- Construction — 7.6
- Miscellaneous manufacturer — 5.2
- Chemical — 4.8
- Food — 4.2
- Metal — 3.0
- Others — 18.2

Source: Japan Securities Dealers Association

MARKET VALUE AND PERFORMANCE

(In trillion yen)   (In point)

— Nikkei OTC Average
---- JASDAQ

'90 '91 '92 '93 '94 '95 (Jan.-Aug.)

Source: Japan Securities Dealers Association

OTC ENTRY CRITERIA

Second OTC Market	**Existing OTC Market**
Profitability No set requirements (Losses not prohibitive)	Pretax profits of ¥10 per share during year preceding public offering
Number of Shares No set requirements for outstanding shares prior to OTC entry	At least 2 million outstanding shares
For Public Offering More than 500,000 shares	250,000 shares, plus 12.5% of the outstanding shares
Number of Shareholders More than 50	More than 200
Net Assets More than ¥200 million on the day of public offering	More than ¥200 million at end of fiscal year preceding public offering
Disclosure Financial statements for two most recent years Risk data, such as new technologies and outlook on new businesses After IPO, quarterly financial reports	Financial statements for two most recent years

Source: Japan Securities Dealers Association

KEY WORD

VENTURE CAPITAL FIRMS

Venture capital firms specialize in funding new enterprises. Such investors reap capital gains by selling their stakes in the ventures at the time of public offerings. Most Japanese venture capital firms are affiliated with big banks, security houses or insurance companies. For example, Japan Associated Finance Co., the nation's largest venture capital company, is affiliated with Nomura Securities Co.

KEY WORD

LEAD MANAGER

This is the leading investment bank in an underwriting syndicate for a new equity issue or other security. For the second OTC market, the lead manager will be responsible for determining if businesses are ready to go public based on analysis of growth potential. The lead manager will set the public offering price after sounding out institutional investors.

BONDS

Market surges as yen's appreciation dampens hopes for recovery

BY ASAKO ISHIBASHI
Staff Writer

Japan's weaker-than-expected recovery boosted the bond market in 1995 as the Bank of Japan drastically eased credit, cutting the official discount rate (ODR) twice to a historic low of 0.50% by September. The BOJ's looser rein on money was intended not only to prod the economy, but to give Japan's ailing financial institutions a chance to recover.

At the beginning of the year, few market watchers expected the BOJ to maintain its easy monetary policy, let alone implement additional rate cuts. Still, the bond market rallied from mid February as the yen's surge against the dollar dampened prospects for the fledgling economic recovery.

Domestic financial institutions bought Japanese government bonds in a process of elimination as they shifted money from the teetering Tokyo stock market while avoiding foreign bonds amid fears of currency risk.

On April 7, the BOJ publicly announced it would lower the overnight call rate as far as the ODR, which then stood at 1.75%. While the BOJ action was criticized as half-hearted and insufficient to prop up the dollar against the yen, the move was still a breakthrough in that the central bank took the initiative in pushing money market rates lower.

Market and political pressures eventually convinced the BOJ to also cut the ODR to 1% on April 14. On July 7, the central bank again announced it was guiding money market rates lower, this time to below the 1.0% ODR. The overnight call rate dropped to below 0.80% and the yield on the benchmark No. 174 10-year Japanese government bond fell to a low of 2.495%. September bond futures contracts rose to ¥122.65.

LOCKING-IN PROFITS

The bond market entered a correction after hitting a ceiling in July. Japan's city banks and long-term credit banks were net sellers between April to July, dumping ¥5.2 trillion worth of yen bonds. Most of the selling was done in July as banks locked in profits ahead of the half-year book-closing in September.

Agricultural credit institutions bought a net ¥2.2 trillion worth of yen bonds during the same period. In July alone, they made their biggest net monthly purchase ever of ¥900 billion while also actively trading in bond futures and options.

Life insurers were even bigger buyers — purchasing over a net ¥4.2 trillion — as yen bonds remained their core investment. While the Ministry of Finance tried to encourage Japanese institutional investors to buy more foreign bonds with a deregulatory package in August, participation by Japanese life insurers in the quarterly U.S. Treasury refunding later in the month was relatively low-key. Japanese life insurers were estimated to have bought only about 7% of the three-year Treasuries offered and 5% of the 10-year notes.

Japanese money managers began running out of investment options as returns on Japanese government bonds started to lose appeal. Coupon rates on newly issued 10-year government bonds were cut every month from March to July. The July issue carried a coupon rate of 3%, a level many fund managers considered unattractive for long-term investment.

MORE BONDS TO COVER DEFICITS

On the other hand, supply concerns loomed over the market from the start of the fiscal year in April. In the wake of the ¥2.6 trillion first supplementary budget, new government bond issuances in fiscal 1995 were estimated to hit ¥40.8 trillion. A second supplementary budget in the fall called for another ¥10 trillion worth of deficit-covering bonds, which would put the bond dependency ratio of Japan's government spending at about 30%. Japan's outstanding long-term government bonds to gross domestic product stood at 53.6% at the end of fiscal 1994, one of the highest levels among developed countries.

The private sector took advantage of low interest rates to raise cash on the domestic bond market. The amount of domestic straight bonds issued hit a record ¥2.22 trillion during the first six months of 1995. The total for the year was expected to surpass the record ¥3.71 trillion issued in 1993.

Analysts expected the deregulation of shelf registration, effective July 1, to boost straight bond issues. The MOF lowered the minimum capitalization for a company engaging in shelf registration from ¥100 billion to ¥10 billion. The number of companies eligible for shelf registration was estimated to rise from 400 to around 900.

Meanwhile, retail investors hunting for higher yields at a time of record-low interest rates in Japan have flocked to foreign bonds.

The dollar's recovery against the yen since August was also encouraging, by reducing currency-exchange risk.

Sales of foreign bonds at Nomura Securities Co. totaled some ¥50 billion in the April-June quarter. Volume then surged to ¥120 billion in July, and to ¥200 billion in August.

Foreign bonds denominated in U.S. dollars, Australian dollars and German marks are among the most popular vehicles with retail investors.

5-YEAR MONEY LOOKS FOR HIGHER RETURN

In fiscal 1995, long-term credit banks and trust banks were to see massive redemptions of five-year bank debentures and loan trusts by small investors who had taken advantage of record-high interest rates in 1990. Approximately ¥6.8 trillion worth of "Wide" (fixed-rate) bank debentures and ¥4.87 trillion of "Big" (variable-rate) loan-trust funds were scheduled to mature within the year.

Both are five-year instruments with interest compounded semi-annually, payable in a lump sum upon maturity. The highest rates were offered in October 1990, when Wide bonds had an 8% coupon and a yield of 9.61% and Big loan trusts offered a yield of 9.60%.

Some ¥3.46 trillion in Wide debentures were to mature in October 1995. But, because interest rates had fallen so much by 1995, investors were looking for shorter-term investments. Some were likely to take their funds to the postal savings system. Securities companies and city banks competed to capture a portion of the redemption, but their ability to do so was limited by a lack of attractive instruments, analysts said. Brokers touted bond investment trust funds or straight bonds, while city banks started offering five-year time deposits in November 1994.

Long-term credit banks and trust banks pitched five-year renewals as well as shorter investment instruments, such as one-year discount bank debentures or one-year money trusts. In the first rush of redemptions in April and May, nearly 75% of the investors kept their money in the same bank.

NEW ISSUES

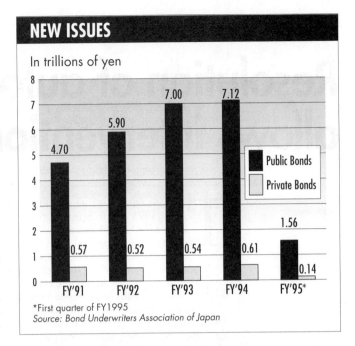

In trillions of yen

*First quarter of FY1995
Source: Bond Underwriters Association of Japan

KEY RATE MOVES

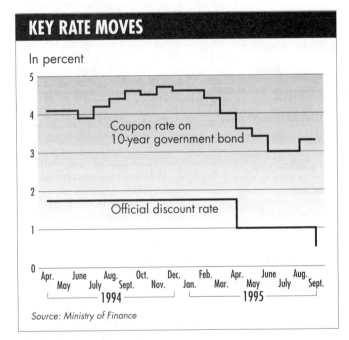

In percent

Source: Ministry of Finance

5-YEAR GOVERNMENT BOND FUTURES

The Tokyo Stock Exchange was expected to list five-year Japanese government bond futures by the end of 1995 or early 1996. Five-year JGB futures would be the third kind of bond futures to be listed on the TSE. Deliverable bond grades included interest-bearing JGB's with a maturity of five years, including four-year and six-year JGB's that are not listed on the TSE. The new hedging instrument was expected to help smooth the yield curve by adding more liquidity toward the middle.

MONEY MARKET OPERATIONS

Trading hours for money market operations were expanded to 9 a.m. to 5 p.m. in March 1993. However, most activity was still concentrated in the early morning.

The BOJ announces its projections for the next day's supply and demand of money market funds at 5:20, 5:50 or 6:20 p.m. every day. Additional revisions are announced at 10 a.m. the following day. Regular BOJ operations are conducted at 9:20 and 10:10 a.m.

FOREIGN EXCHANGE

Resolution of auto-trade talks allows intervention to boost dollar

BY JOSHUA OGAWA
Staff Writer

The U.S. dollar hit a record low of ¥79.75 in April 1995 due to pressure from Japan-U.S. trade talks, the Mexican peso crisis, developments in Europe and speculative selling. While close cooperation and intervention by Japan and the U.S. in the summer helped the dollar rebound more than 20%, many players in the forex market remained skeptical about the currency's long-term prospects.

The trade imbalance between Japan and the U.S., despite slight contractions, continued to limit the dollar's rise. Also, the pace of deregulation in Japan, which was expected to weaken the yen, remained slow.

The dollar started 1995 at ¥100.88, carrying over the positive sentiment seen around Christmas 1994. But a financial crisis in Mexico sent the dollar falling against major currencies within a few days. The greenback soon dipped below ¥100 as those who had hoped for a quick settlement of the Mexican crisis started unloading dollar positions.

Despite two economic packages arranged by the international financial community to help Mexico's borrowers, the dollar continued to slide against the yen. By the end of February, the dollar was fully submerged below ¥100 and would not resurface until early September.

While the U.S. was busy with the peso crisis, Europe saw increased political turmoil in Bosnia and Chechnya, which pushed the German mark higher against other European currencies as investors looked for a safe haven. The mark consequently strengthened further against the dollar, pulling the yen with it.

The dollar fell below ¥90 by late March, causing anxious Japanese exporters to rush to cash earnings into yen. Japanese companies also sold dollars ahead of the fiscal year-end in March, further weighing down the currency. To limit the dollar's decline and the related drop in Tokyo share prices, the Bank of Japan guided money market rates lower. However, forex players, most of whom had expected the BOJ to cut the official discount rate instead, chased the greenback even lower.

The U.S. government responded little to the yen's rise to the dollar. Since the dollar remained very strong against the currencies of Canada and Mexico — the U.S.'s largest trading partners — concern about a rising yen was not as strong as in Japan.

By the time the Bank of Japan cut the official discount rate by 0.75 percentage point to 1% on April 14, the market had already fully discounted the move. Speculators, looking to cash in on discord between Tokyo and Washington pushed the dollar to a record low of ¥79.75 on April 19.

On April 25, the finance ministers from the Group of Seven industrialized nations, meeting in Washington, called for the "orderly reversal" in the dollar's decline.

Some market watchers said the (auto trade) settlement was a turning point for dollar/yen trading, as it allowed monetary policy to take the spotlight

But since no concrete measures were announced, positive effects on the dollar were muted.

On May 31, the Bank of Japan and the monetary authorities of the U.S. and major European countries stepped into the New York market, pushing the dollar back to ¥84. The dollar then fluctuated narrowly, bounded by exporter selling at higher levels while supported from below by expectations of intervention.

In late June, agreement between Japan and the U.S. on auto and auto-parts trade eliminated significant political pressure on the dollar. It moved to around ¥86 as market players expected the accord to help reduce Japan's huge trade surplus. Some market watchers said the settlement was a turning point for dollar/yen trading, as it allowed monetary policy to take the spotlight.

That assessment rang true in early July as Japan and the U.S. coordinated monetary policy and forex intervention. The U.S. Federal Reserve Board cut its key federal funds rate by 0.25 percentage point to 5.75%, confirming expectations of a strengthening U.S. economy and warding off fears of more rate cuts. Meanwhile, the Bank of Japan guided money market rates lower again. As a result, the dollar jumped to around ¥89. Although the rise was later slowed by profit taking by hedge fund operators and Japanese exporters, the unit's upward momentum remained intact.

On August 2, Finance Minister Masayoshi Takemura announced a deregulation package aimed at promoting overseas investment by Japanese institutional investors, particularly life insurers. Coupled with concerted intervention by the Bank of Japan and the Federal Reserve the same day, the announcement boosted the dollar above ¥90. Another round of coordinated intervention on August 15, this time joined by the German Bundesbank, pushed the greenback above ¥96.

On September 8, the Bank of Japan cut the official discount rate to an unprecedented 0.5% while repeatedly intervening in the forex market. The dollar reached a 15-month high of ¥104.50 on September 18. Although the dollar later went through several corrections, the sharpest of which came after the market responded unenthusiastically to an economic stimulus package revealed on September 20, bullish sentiment on the dollar for the near term remained intact.

Difficulties in the creation of a European Monetary Union — which would again boost the mark against the dollar — or another cut in U.S. interest rates could drag the dollar lower against the yen some analysts warned. Still, a steep decline below ¥90 seemed unlikely, at least before the end of the year, they said.

On October 7, the G-7 finance ministers confirmed their commitment to a stronger dollar. The unit moved little from its range near ¥100 immediately afterward.

DOLLAR/YEN SPOT • TOKYO

Weekly Chart

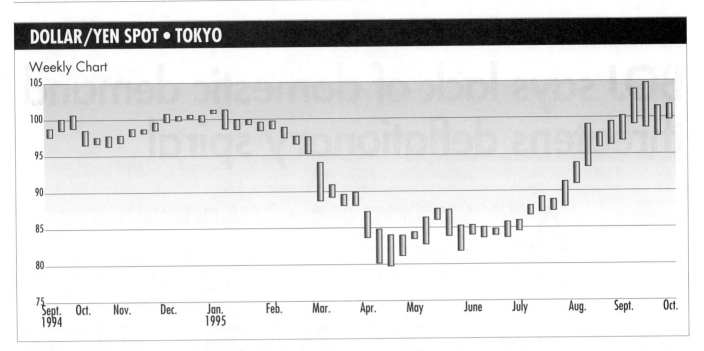

Sept. 1994 — Oct. (1995)

FOREIGN EXCHANGE

Trading volume of dollar-yen exchange via brokers on the Tokyo foreign exchange market (spot plus forward swap); in trillions of dollars

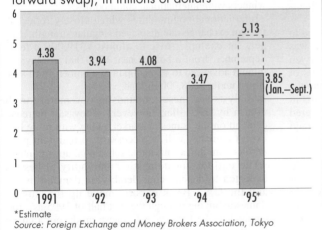

1991	4.38
'92	3.94
'93	4.08
'94	3.47
'95*	3.85 (Jan.–Sept.) / 5.13

*Estimate
Source: Foreign Exchange and Money Brokers Association, Tokyo

SHARE OF ELECTRONIC BROKING

In Tokyo Foreign-Exchange Market, dollar-yen spot trading; in percent

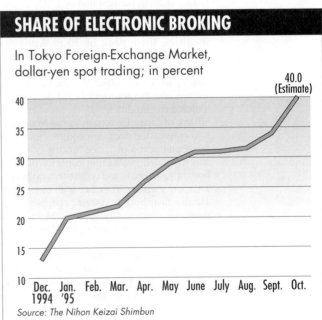

40.0 (Estimate)

Dec. 1994 — Jan. '95 — Feb. Mar. Apr. May June July Aug. Sept. Oct.

Source: The Nihon Keizai Shimbun

KEY WORD

CONCERTED INTERVENTION

Central banks sometimes enter the currency market to try to move exchange rates. Such intervention is most effective when several central banks act together. The Bank of Japan repeatedly bought dollars in 1995 to curb yen's appreciation, which was hurting domestic economic recovery by undermining export profitability. On August 15, dollar buying by the Bundesbank in addition to intervention by the Bank of Japan and the Federal Reserve came as a surprise and prompted a strong surge in the dollar.

KEY WORD

ELECTRONIC BROKING

Increasingly, foreign exchange orders in 1995 were being matched automatically by computers rather than by traders. Because of the significant cost advantage, electronic broking gained wide acceptance in Tokyo. The share of electronic broking in dollar/yen spot trading in Tokyo increased to 31% by August 1995, compared with 6% in March 1994. Even the Bank of Japan was said to have started using electronic broking to intervene in the market in September.

COMMODITIES

BOJ says lack of domestic demand threatens deflationary spiral

BY KAORU
MORISHITA
Staff Writer

After leveling off in 1994, Japanese commodity prices resumed falling in 1995. An increase in lower-priced imported materials due to the appreciation of the yen against the dollar, coupled with stagnant overall demand, pushed the Nikkei Commodity Index of 42 items to a 22-year low in July.

The index, based on an average of 100 in 1970, dropped from a peak of 157 in September 1990 to around 117 at the end of 1993. Though the index seemed to bottom out around 118 in 1994, it started falling again in the first half of 1995.

Meanwhile, the Nikkei World Commodity Index, which tracks the dollar prices of 14 international commodities, hit a peak of 70 in April due to strong economies in Asia and the U.S. However, in Japan, the steep rise of the yen against the dollar during the first quarter more than offset the rise in dollar prices. Nonferrous and precious metals led decliners among international commodities.

Bank of Japan Governor Yasuo Matsushita pointed to two reasons for declining commodity prices. One was the phenomenon of "price busting". With a higher yen and expanded production capacity in Asia, imports of both raw materials and consumer goods flooded into the Japanese market. Together with streamlining efforts in Japan's distribution system, cheaper imports lowered domestic commodity prices. Matsushita welcomed price declines of this nature as a step toward closing the price gap between domestic and overseas markets.

But commodity prices also fell on shrinking domestic demand. Toshihiko Fukui, senior deputy governor of the BOJ, told The Nikkei Weekly that this would remain a matter of concern since, once shrinking demand started to erode business sentiment, there would be a risk of a deflationary spiral.

Prices of domestic industrial materials were already sinking. Steel product prices weakened across the board. Average H-beam prices dropped to ¥34,700 a ton in August 1995, down 9.9% from a year before. Steel bar prices weakened to ¥29,800, down 17.9%, while angle was also down 10.8%.

Steel producers expected construction demand to pick up as a result of the devastating Great Hanshin Earthquake. Still, declining housing starts kept overall demand in check while increased imports of finished steel products hurt domestic downstream producers, leading to lower steel prices.

Analysts pointed out that the psychological blows of the earthquake in January, followed by the sarin nerve gas attacks on the Tokyo subway system in March, dampened consumer sentiment, causing the supply-and-demand situation for commodities to slacken. For example, the average price of wool yarn used in suits stood at ¥964 per kilogram in August, down 24.5% from a year before.

Sluggish sales of consumer durables such as automobiles and home appliances prompted final producers to put pressure on material suppliers to cut prices, particularly after the yen surged as far as ¥80 in April. As a result, prices of materials like steel sheet and plastics were weak.

As the dollar recovers against the yen, from a bottom at below ¥80 in April to around ¥100 in September, commodity prices recovered their earlier losses. In September, the monthly average of the Nikkei Commodity Index of 42 items recovered to 115.260 points, up from a low of 112.116 in July. The index of 17 commodities rose to 90.080 in September, from a low at 84.338 in July. The greater advance by the more internationally oriented 17-item index signifies the main winners were international commodities.

International commodities which closely reflect the foreign exchange rate displayed singular strength. Copper, for example, rose to almost ¥319,000 a ton in September, from a bottom near ¥260,000 in May; aluminum advanced to ¥206,000 in September, from a low at just under ¥178,000 in June.

Analysts see these rebounds as due merely to the upturn by the dollar, however. They say increased demand on the domestic market, along with more brisk export demand, will be necessary to maintain prices until commodities shift into a substantial upward phase.

The outlook for domestic commodity prices was expected to depend considerably on demand in Asia and the U.S. Brisk exports made up for sluggish domestic buying through the first half of 1995 as strong demand in the U.S. gave Japanese producers a chance to sell in Asia. If the economies of Asia or the U.S. were to turn sluggish, exports from Japanese producers were expected to fall, further dampening domestic prices.

COMMODITY FUTURES BROKERAGES GO PUBLIC

In 1990, the Ministry of International Trade and Industry and the Ministry of Agriculture, Forestry and Fisheries changed their policy on commodity futures markets from one of regulation to promotion, adopting an amended commodity markets act. Thus, after keeping a low profile for half a century, Japanese commodity futures brokerages started going public in 1995.

On Sept. 12, Ace Koeki Co., a leading such brokerage, registered on the over-the-counter market. In October, second-ranked Okato Shoji Co. followed suit. Several others were preparing to go public within the next year.

Because of the high-risk/high-return nature of commodity futures (investors can trade large amounts of commodities on margins only one-tenth the actual trading prices), the market traditionally has had an image of a gambling den. As a result, institutional investors have tended to stay away. Rather, 90% of the trading is by individual investors looking for speculative gains. The remainder of trading is by firms that actually deal in commodities — producers, wholesalers, trading houses — who use futures to hedge against price fluctuations.

Japan has 80 commodity futures brokerages. It was hoped that OTC registration would help expand the commodity futures market by boosting its credibility. "Because of the shady image from the past, many individual investors still refuse to trade, even if brokers encourage them," said Yuko Taniwaki, financial analyst at Nomura Research Institute. "But, if commodity futures brokerages enjoy higher credibility, it will be easier for them to attract new investors," he said.

Enhanced credibility was also expected to help promote the listing of new items. Previously, firms that actually dealt in commodities blocked the introduction of futures, in part because of the speculative image. This was especially the case with nonferrous metals.

Unlike U.S. futures markets, which trade both commodities and financial products, Japanese commodity futures list only commodities. Moreover, the market lacks large-scale items such as oil and nonferrous metals. Commodity futures brokerages expected the future listing of major products to help attract institutional investors.

NIKKEI COMMODITY INDEX (42 ITEM)

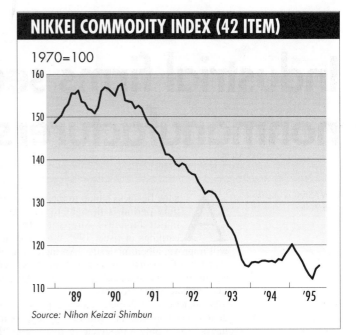

1970=100

Source: Nihon Keizai Shimbun

COMMODITY MARKET MOVES

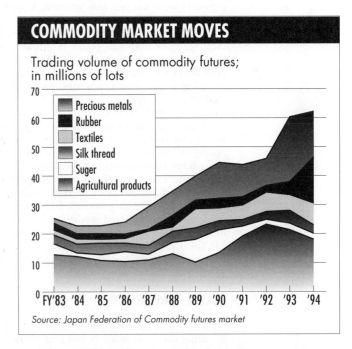

Trading volume of commodity futures; in millions of lots

- Precious metals
- Rubber
- Textiles
- Silk thread
- Suger
- Agricultural products

Source: Japan Federation of Commodity futures market

KEY WORD

NIKKEI COMMODITY INDEX

Printed weekly by The Nihon Keizai Shimbun, this index covers 42 items including steel, nonferrous metals, textiles, timber, petrochemicals, paper and foodstuffs. The index is based on an average of 100 in 1970. Since the prices of the commodities covered reflect domestic demand and supply, the index is used as an indicator of the economy. In addition to the weekly index, Nikkei prints an index of 17 items daily.

KEY WORD

COMMODITY FUNDS

After the Commodity Fund Act went into effect in April 1992, Japanese commodity futures brokerages, non-banks and securities brokerages began offering commodity funds through commodity trading advisers. CTAs establish funds and invest money collected from investors in items such as precious metal futures.

CORPORATE EARNINGS

Industrial firms see profits recover; nonmanufacturers remain in funk

BY MASAKO FUKUDA
Staff Writer

As the business slump in the post-bubble economy period is thought to have hit bottom, major Japanese companies forecast their earnings in fiscal 1995 through March 1996 will improve, albeit modestly. An increase in the profitability of exports, thanks to the yen's weakening against the dollar since the summer of 1995, is expected to contribute to the recovery.

Manufacturers anticipate sales and profits will continue to expand, as seen in fiscal 1994, while nonmanufacturers predict only a moderate recovery from the earnings decline of the previous year due to still stagnant domestic demand.

According to a Nikkei survey of 1,604 listed companies, aggregate corporate pretax profits are forecast to rise 14.1% year on year in fiscal 1995. The survey covered companies that close their books on March 31, excluding banks, securities houses, nonlife insurers and credit/leasing companies.

In fiscal 1994, pretax profits at major companies increased 9.3%, pulled up by the 24.8% growth in profits at manufacturers, who made big strides in their cost-cutting efforts and were quick to turn to overseas markets where the business climate was good.

In contrast, nonmanufacturers saw pretax profits decrease by 4.3% due to slumbering domestic demand. Among poor performing sectors, construction and real estate companies suffered notable declines in profit due to slow demand after the bubble economy period.

In fiscal 1995, manufacturers expect pretax profits to increase 25.1%, while nonmanufacturers project a gain of 1.6%, the Nikkei survey found.

ROLLER-COASTER YEN

The double-digit profit growth forecast by the manufacturing sector depends heavily on exports and the yen's value to the dollar. The yen surged to a post-war record high of 79.75 against the dollar on April 19, 1995.

As most companies calculated initial fiscal 1995 earnings projections based on an in-house yen-dollar rate of 85-95, analysts warned of a possible scenario of much lower corporate earnings.

But the yen started losing ground against the dollar from July 7, 1995, when Japan and the U.S. both lowered short-term interest rates. The concerted dollar-supporting stance of major industrialized nations, including the U.S., Japan and Germany, also helped the dollar recover the ¥100 level by the fall.

Among manufacturers, the materials industry will probably manage to mark a recovery in pretax profits in fiscal 1995, most research institutions predict. The steel

sector will return to the black for the first time in three years on the strength of corporate restructuring, including payroll cuts and rationalization of manufacturing processes.

The paper/pulp sector will see higher profits because the tight supply-demand situation pushed up product prices, the think tanks say.

Companies in the assembly industry will benefit from the dollar hitting a bottom. Electronics and precision instrument manufacturers will mark a large increase in profits due to overall strong demand for semiconductors and personal computers as well as the improved profitability of exports.

CARMAKERS IMPROVE

Profits at automakers will grow on the strength of cost-cutting efforts and the yen's appreciation. Nissan Motor Co. will likely post ¥10 billion in pretax profits in fiscal 1995, marking a turnaround from pretax losses of ¥61 billion incurred in fiscal 1994.

On the other hand, a recovery of nonmanufacturer companies' profits will remain moderate due to poor domestic sales, most research institutes say.

Among the think tanks affiliated with the Big Four securities houses, Nomura Research Institute was the most optimistic, projecting a 7.1% profit increase for nonmanufacturing companies, while Daiwa Institute of Research forecast growth of 1.6%. Nikko Research Center and Yamaichi Research Institute of Securities & Economics both predict pretax losses for nonmanufacturing companies.

The exception among nonmanufacturers is the telecommunications sector. Companies in this field will likely post a rise in pretax profits, led by the good performance of Nippon Telegraph and Telephone Corp.

The Bank of Japan cut the official discount rate to a historic low of 0.5% on September 8, 1995. The low rate will support the recovery of companies with large debts, such as electronics or electric power companies, analysts say.

FOREX RATES WILL RULE

Corporate earnings will brighten if the dollar appreciates further to the yen. But the picture will grow bleak if the dollar weakens and the stagnant domestic economy turns for the worse, most research institutes agree.

For fiscal 1996, the research institutes affiliated with the Big Four brokerages — Nomura Securities Co., Daiwa Securities Co., Nikko Securities Co. and Yamaichi Securities Co. — project pretax profits of listed companies will rise around 15% year on year.

CORPORATE PROFITS IN MAJOR INDUSTRIES

Year-on-year percentage change in pretax profits; in percent

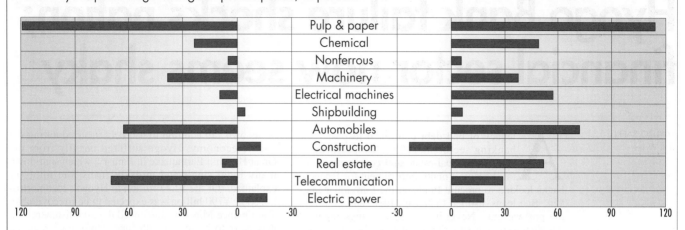

Note: Left diagram presents projections for fiscal 1995; right graph plots fiscal 1994 figures
Source: Nikkei Financial Daily

CORPORATE PROFITS

Year-on-year percentage change in pretax profits

-0.3 -14.7 -25.0 -18.0 9.3 14.1
FY1990 FY'91 FY'92 FY'93 FY'94 FY'95*

Note: Listed companies whose accounting year ends in March.
Excludes banks, securities houses and insurance firms.   *Estimate
Source: The Nihon Keizai Shimbun

CONSOLIDATED/PARENT RATIO

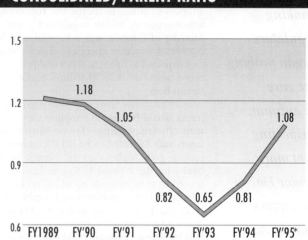

Note: Surveys focused on business results as of the end of March each
year, by listed companies excluding banks, securities and insurance
houses.   *Estimate
Source: The Nihon Keizai Shimbun

KEY WORD

CONSOLIDATED FINANCIAL STATEMENT

Nonconsolidated financial statements were the norm until Japanese firms began globalizing, which required adopting international accounting standards. In fiscal 1994, the Finance Ministry abolished the so-called 10% rule, which allowed parent firms to exclude any results from subsidiaries accounting for less than 10% of assets, sales and net profits of all units covered in the statement. Many firms increased the coverage of their group statements, making them a better gauge of performance.

KEY WORD

CROSS-SHAREHOLDING

As holding companies are prohibited in Japan, many firms hold shares in each other. This cross-shareholding relationship enables a company to secure stable stockholders. Firms started selling off cross-held shares recently, however, to put the money to better use or obtain profits before closing their books. Notable among such selling was that of bank issues by nonfinancial institutions. Latent profits of major banks have fallen considerably from the peak in fiscal 1988.

BANKS

Hyogo Bank failure shocks nation; financial sector now seems shaky

BY YUZO SAEKI
Staff Writer

American banking regulators began probing the case in autumn, suspecting that more senior Daiwa executives may have known about the trades, and submitted false reports

A legacy of bad debt continued to pester the banking sector in 1995. Nonperforming loans to the real-estate and construction sectors became a major impediment for Japanese banks looking to procure funds on the Eurodollar market. Bad loans also led to Japan's first bank failure in the postwar era. Nevertheless, some banks reported that they were able to write off most of their bad loans from the bubble economy by the end of fiscal 1994.

Outstanding nonperforming loans at 21 major banks (11 city banks plus three long-term credit banks and seven trust banks) totaled ¥12.55 trillion at the end of March, down from ¥13.33 trillion six months earlier.

In April, Mitsubishi Bank and Bank of Tokyo announced plans to merge the following year. The announcement, which was quickly endorsed by the Ministry of Finance, was a hopeful sign that the banking sector would re-energize. Tokyo Mitsubishi Bank was expected to open its doors in April 1996, with combined assets of ¥72.79 trillion making it the world's largest bank.

Some analysts, however, wondered whether the two banks would be able to structure their merger so as to reap efficiency gains. Tokyo Mitsubishi's return on assets was expected to be 0.11%, some 0.04 of a percentage point higher than the average for Japanese city banks but far behind U.S. and European standards, according to an estimate by a U.S. brokerage firm.

Japan's 11 city banks reported combined core business profits of ¥2.06 trillion in fiscal 1994 through March, down 13.6% from the previous year. Earnings were hurt by a weak domestic bond market and lower income from international operations. Combined pretax profits fell 92.3% from fiscal 1993 to ¥43.1 billion, dropping for the sixth year in a row. City banks increasingly set aside funds to write off bad debt, allocating a record ¥3.78 trillion, up from ¥2.34 trillion a year earlier.

The stock market's decline became a major concern, as banks were relying on paper gains on stocks to write off bad debt. As of the end of March 1995, unrealized profits on city-bank stock portfolios fell to ¥5.2 trillion, down 58.4% from a year earlier.

Sumitomo Bank and Hokkaido Takushoku Bank posted the first pretax losses of any major commercial bank in the postwar era. Sumitomo saw pretax losses of ¥335.7 billion and net losses of ¥335.4 billion in fiscal 1994 after setting aside ¥826.4 billion for loan losses. Hokkaido Takushoku reported pretax losses of ¥8.7 billion, mainly due to a sharp plunge in stock prices toward the end of March.

On Aug. 30, the Ministry of Finance deemed Hyogo Bank, a Kobe-based regional bank with deposits of ¥2.53 trillion, incapable of returning to financial health on its own. In addition to bad debt incurred during the bubble economy, Hyogo suffered heavily from the Great Hanshin Earthquake in January, which shut down many local small and midsize firms, the ministry explained. Of the ¥2.77 trillion in Hyogo's loan portfolio, some ¥790 billion was expected to be irrecoverable. The Finance Ministry announced the establishment of a new bank to be set up with funds from other regional banks and the local business community to take over Hyogo's operations.

As foreign banks became increasingly apprehensive about the financial health of their Japanese counterparts, funding costs to Japanese banks on the Eurodollar market rose. Major Western banks began charging Japanese banks 60 to 80 basis points over the LIBOR (London inter-bank offered rate), compared with the maximum of 30 basis points charged to other Western banks. In September, a $1.1 billion bond-trading scandal at Daiwa Bank's New York office compounded concerns about Japan's banking system, pushing the spread charged to Japanese banks to roughly 1 percent above LIBOR.

Japanese banks made an effort to improve business practices, including introducing new loan-screening methods. Bank of Tokyo introduced a policy toward the end of 1994 of rating corporate clients and outstanding loans on a scale of one to 10.

Banks also reduced staff by limiting the hiring of new graduates. City banks took on only 4,300 new college graduates in April 1995, down 35% from a year earlier. The figure represented a dramatic drop from the 13,500 new graduates hired in April 1991. Still, industry analysts said that Japanese banks need to cut back on staff even more to remain competitive with foreign counterparts.

In October, Toshihide Iguchi was indicted in New York on charges stemming from more than a decade of trading losses that left Daiwa Bank $1.1 billion short of its paper holdings of U.S. government bonds.

Iguchi was Daiwa's main trader for the government bonds from 1984 to July 1995, when he wrote a letter to the bank's Osaka headquarters disclosing the losses and the more than 30,000 unauthorized transactions he had hidden with false paperwork.

American banking regulators began probing the case in autumn, suspecting that more senior Daiwa executives may have known about the trades, and submitted false reports on the financial state of its New York branch.

Moreover, observers were appalled by the fact that Daiwa issued ¥50 billion in preferred stock just two days after management had received the written confession from Iguchi.

CITY BANKS

Financial results for fiscal 1994; in billions of yen, with change from previous year in parentheses

Banks	Core Business Profits		Pretax Profits		Net Profits	
Sanwa	304.8	(-14.8%)	49.2	(-45.1%)	36.7	(-29.7%)
Fuji	288.2	(-20.4%)	38.1	(-27.5%)	34.3	(+28.4%)
Mitsubishi	246.6	(-12.9%)	45.0	(-28.6%)	35.1	(+19.3%)
Sumitomo	243.5	(-19.4%)	-335.7	(—)	-335.4	(—)
Dai-Ichi Kangyo	225.1	(-4.4%)	54.1	(+43.7%)	30.2	(-6.8%)
Tokyo	172.4	(-6.8%)	54.1	(-26.2%)	45.9	(-9.0%)
Sakura	160.1	(-22.8%)	66.0	(+4.8%)	24.4	(-29.8%)
Asahi	146.6	(-11.3%)	33.6	(+10.2%)	19.1	(-7.4%)
Tokai	145.7	(-19.1%)	29.6	(-15.8%)	20.9	(+1.1%)
Daiwa	93.1	(+32.5%)	17.5	(-55.5%)	13.9	(+6.8%)
Hokkaido Takushoku	32.0	(0.0%)	-8.7	(—)	5.2	(+24.5%)

Source: Banks

DEPOSITS SLIDING

Year-on-year change in deposit balances; in percent

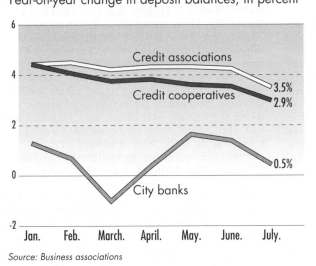

Source: Business associations

GROWTH IN BAD LOANS AT 21 MAJOR BANKS

Total value of loans non-performing for more than six months or made to bankrupt clients; in trillions of yen

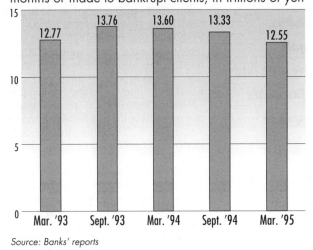

Source: Banks' reports

KEY WORD

HOLDING COMPANIES

Japan's large commercial banks pressed the government to lift its ban on holding companies. After city banks were allowed to enter the securities business in 1994, the holding company structure became more desirable as a way of isolating risk among group operations than the parent-subsidiary arrangement. In its five-year deregulation plan announced in March 1995, the government promised to reconsider the ban within the next three years.

KEY WORD

DERIVATIVES

Both city and smaller banks in Japan rapidly increased their use of derivatives. These financial instruments, based on the value of underlying securities, allow banks to offer new services such as long-term fixed-rate loans. But increased use of derivatives exposes banks to more market risk. The outstanding notional principal of derivatives at 11 city banks totaled ¥1,021 trillion at the end of March 1995. Should the counterparties of the contracts default, losses could reach as high as ¥26.45 trillion.

SECURITIES

Big 4 return to black ink; smaller brokers still suffer on low turnover

BY YUMIKO SUZUKI
Staff Writer

Thirsty for high investment returns, small investors had a favorable response

For brokerage houses, 1995 started as another difficult year. The yen's sharp appreciation to the dollar, as well as the tremendous blow of the Great Hanshin Earthquake on January 17, knocked the wind out of the domestic economic recovery, discouraging investors. Concerns about Japan's financial system further eroded investor confidence.

But sentiment changed in July as the yen began to retreat. Stock market trading volume picked up along with share prices, thanks in great part to the return of foreign bargain-hunters. This brought about a substantial increase in commission income at some brokerages.

Larger securities firms benefited more than others. By the end of September, the Big Four brokerage houses — Nomura, Daiwa, Nikko and Yamaichi — projected that pretax profits in the fiscal year through March 1996 would likely meet or slightly surpass initial estimates. Daily trading value on the first and second sections of the Tokyo Stock Exchange averaged some ¥312 billion in the first half of fiscal 1995, far above their break-even levels around ¥250 billion. Active bond trading supported by lower short-term interest rates and strong sales of foreign-currency-denominated bonds to small investors also boosted profits.

Nomura Securities Co. posted about ¥32 billion in pretax profits in the first fiscal half, up ¥9.6 billion from a year earlier. The other three major brokerages projected pretax profits between ¥5.2 billion and ¥27 billion.

Analysts attribute their recovery of profitability to a strategy of focusing on a specific arena. Nomura, for example, emphasized sale of foreign-currency-denominated bonds to retail investors as a core business at its branch offices. The brokerage targeted individual investors, mainly in urban area, assuming they would be conscious of interest rates. Thirsty for high investment returns, small investors had a favorable response to the broker's active sales, especially after summer when the dollar regained ground against the yen.

Daiwa Securities Co. strengthened its marketing of investment trust funds. The company's commissions on fund sales added up to ¥12 billion in the April-August period, surpassing the results of the other three leading houses, which earned from ¥6.5-8.5 billion.

Nikko Securities Co. fought hard to sell stocks and convertible bonds to small investors. The brokerage enjoyed activate equities sales from July, when the key stock index dipped to its lowest level since August 1992. Nikko earned more than ¥10 billion in commissions in September alone, almost equal to the earnings of Nomura, the largest brokerage house.

Yamaichi Securities Co. also put extra energy into equities sales, earning fully as much in commissions during both July and August as it had seen for the entire April-June period.

Unlike the Big Four, most second-tier and smaller brokerages still depended heavily on commissions, particularly from individual investors. Their break-even level for average daily trading value on the TSE was around ¥350 billion.

Although daily trading value on the TSE increased during the summer, due to trading by domestic and foreign institutional investors, most individuals stuck to the sidelines. As a result, all second-tier brokerages except Kokusai Securities Co., which posted ¥3 billion in pretax profits, saw losses for the first half.

Second-tier brokerages faced increasing competition from bank securities subsidiaries, some of which started operating from the summer of 1993. Some bank units grabbed a substantial share of straight-bond underwriting, taking advantage of close ties to corporations. According to a research institute, IBJ Securities Co., a subsidiary of Industrial Bank of Japan, took 6% of such underwriting from April to mid-September. The share was topped only by the Big Four. Other bank subsidiaries Fuji Securities Co. and Sakura Securities Co. were also among the top 10 underwriters, each taking a 2% share. Altogether, bank securities units took over 20% of the straight-bond underwriting market, double the figure from all of fiscal 1994.

Second-tier brokerages also suffered from a legacy of overinvesting during the bubble era. Some of them are troubled by the burden of reconstructing affiliated nonbanks. Sanyo Securities Co. posted about ¥13 billion in pretax losses in the first fiscal half, almost the same amount as in the first six months of the previous fiscal term. The broker had to shoulder the cost of stabilizing a failed credit/leasing affiliate, in addition to computer-related expenses of ¥10 billion.

The expanding profitability gap between the second-tier brokers and larger firms led to further restructuring. Kankaku Securities Co., which recorded pretax losses of around ¥10 billion during the April-September half, slashed the number of departments at its headquarters from 47 to 34 through integration and closure. Okasan Securities Co., which posted pretax losses of ¥2 billion for the period, planned to transfer 200 headquarters employees — one-third of its headquarters staff — to sales branches.

Even the securities affiliate of Dai-Ichi Kangyo Bank cut 202 employees by July through a voluntary early retirement program. Some expected an industry-wide reshuffling, since mounting losses from the early 1990s onward were seriously eroding capital strength.

DAILY TURNOVER

Average daily trading volume on TSE 1st section (in millions of shares)

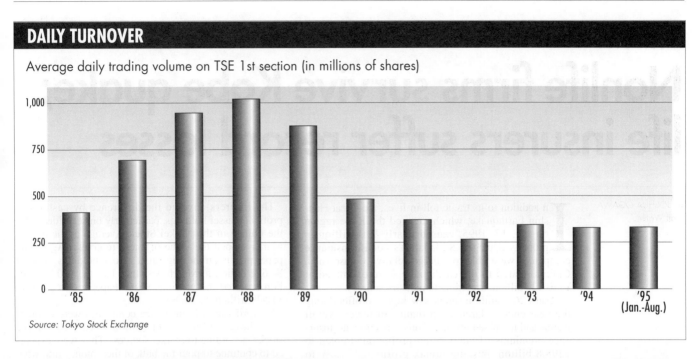

Source: Tokyo Stock Exchange

BOND FUTURES

Transactions by securities houses (in trillions of yen)

Source: Tokyo Stock Exchange

SECURITIES INDUSTRY EMPLOYMENT

In thousands

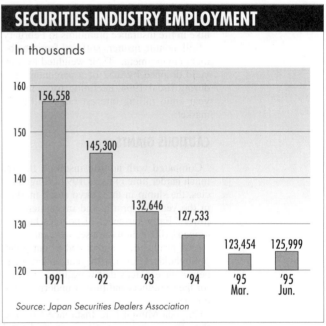

Source: Japan Securities Dealers Association

KEY WORD

CAPITAL STRENGTH

The MOF puts a brokerage under strict surveillance when its capital-adequacy ratio falls under 150%. The ministry may suspend operations if the ratio slips below 100%. Some smaller brokerages tried to boost their ratios by issuing new shares or by taking on partners. Kankaku raised ¥60 billion in July by issuing shares bought by Dai-Ichi Kangyo Bank and group firms. Meanwhile, the oil-rich Sultanate of Brunei became the largest shareholder of Century Securities Co., another midsize brokerage.

KEY WORD

SMALL SUCCESSES

While many brokerages posted huge pretax losses, several small brokers managed profits. Their success reflected sharp cost cutting as well as distinctive ways of doing business. Matsui Securities Co. of Tokyo, which posted ¥112 million in pretax profits for fiscal 1994, attracted margin trading from small investors with low-key newspaper ads instead of pushy salesmen. Kosei Securities Co., based in Osaka, saw ¥322 million in pretax profits for fiscal 1994, mostly from derivatives transactions.

INSURANCE

Nonlife firms survive Kobe quake; life insurers suffer record losses

BY JOSHUA OGAWA
Staff Writer

In addition to its tragic toll in lives, the Great Hanshin Earthquake, which ravaged the Kobe region on Jan. 17, 1995, caused nearly ¥10 trillion in property damage. Still, Japan's nonlife insurance companies were able to emerge relatively unscathed. Claims related to the earthquake were estimated at ¥120-130 billion, according to industry sources.

Japan's 26 nonlife insurers saw higher profits during the year ended March 1995 thanks to fewer overall claims and increased revenue from a hike in auto-insurance premiums. Underwriting profits quadrupled to ¥298.8 billion, pushing pretax profits up 31.0% to ¥360.4 billion. In the year through March 1996, underwriting profit was expected to grow further following a hike in fire insurance premiums in February 1995.

Still, nonlife insurers suffered from the bearish investment environment. Their weighted average investment yield dropped by 0.52 of a percentage point to 4.22% during fiscal 1994, declining for a fourth consecutive year amid falling interest rates and a sluggish stock market.

CAUTIOUS GIANTS

Compared with nonlife insurers, life insurers had a much harder time in fiscal 1994. Stagnant sales of policies, the slump in the Tokyo stock market and the rise in the yen sent profits and investment returns sharply lower. Early surrender of policies held by individuals topped ¥100 trillion for a second year.

As a result, life insurers had to cut dividends paid to policyholders for a fifth year and raise premiums on new policies: steps that were likely to weaken demand for their products and further undermine their long-term business.

Chiyoda Mutual Life Insurance Co., the smallest of the "Big Eight", as well as six midsize life insurers reported losses for the year ended March 1995, marking the first time in the postwar era that several life insurers incurred losses simultaneously.

Life insurers are Japan's largest institutional investors. Combined assets of the Big Eight at the end of March 1995 totaled ¥137.45 trillion, putting them in the ranks of the largest institutional investors in the world. However, their assets had grown only 5.4% in the prior year, compared with 8.4% in fiscal 1993.

Combined premium revenues rose just 0.9% to ¥22,467 billion, compared with 2.3% the year before and double-digit increases in the late 1980s.

The eight insurers reported average investment yields of 1.31-3.29% during fiscal 1994, down from 3.36-4.25% the year before and far below the slightly more than 5% they had to pay in terms of policy dividends.

The insurers covered the difference by cashing in profits on asset holdings, particularly on securities. But the plunge in the Nikkei Stock Average at the end of March sapped the value of latent reserves. Aggregate paper profits on the Big Eight's stock holdings stood at ¥4,622 billion in March, less than half the ¥10,813 billion reported the previous year. Paper losses came to ¥1,539 trillion, up 160%.

In April-July, life insurance companies were estimated to have sold nearly ¥1 trillion worth of Japanese stocks, according to market sources. They were expected to continue to pour the bulk of their money into what they called "safe" assets, namely yen-denominated bonds and loans.

In the summer, the yen receded and Tokyo share prices recovered. On Aug. 2, the Ministry of Finance announced deregulation on overseas investment and lending. While the changes helped reverse a portion of the paper losses and rekindle some appetite for foreign securities, the majority of life insurers continued to move away from riskier assets and foreign markets.

At the same time, life insurers decided to cut labor costs to deal with their negative yields and improve their financial positions. Nippon Life Insurance Co. — Japan's largest life insurer — announced it would cut 3,000 of its 14,000 workers in the three years starting spring 1996. Sumitomo Life Insurance Co., the third largest life insurer, also planned to eliminate 2,000 jobs within three years.

CROSSING INTO NONLIFE

Deregulation will likely be the focus of the industry in 1996. The revised Insurance Business Law, which was enacted in May 1995, will take effect in spring 1996. The new law will lower the barrier between life and nonlife insuring, allowing firms from either side to cross over by opening subsidiaries.

Most insurers expressed willingness to set up such subsidiaries as early as fall 1996. But except for Nippon Life, none had made definite plans since their financial positions continued to weaken as policy sales slumped and investment returns dropped.

Nippon Life said it expected to launch a nonlife insurance subsidiary that would start business from fall 1996 with capital of at least ¥30 billion and some 300 employees. The majority of the workers were to be transferred from the parent company.

INSURERS SLIDE

Financial highlights of Big 8 life-insurance companies for year ended March 31, 1995; in billions of yen, except for investment yield

	Premium Revenue		Unrealized Stock Profit		Pretax Profits		Net Profits		Investment Yield		Total Assets	
Nippon	5,662.2	-2.2	2,343.2	-41.4	233.5	-13.7	268.5	-12.0	2.94%	-0.54	36,681.1	5.7
Dai-ichi	4,083.5	1.2	879.5	-57.1	105.5	-50.0	182.0	-16.7	2.94%	-0.42	26,009.0	6.2
Sumitomo	3,694.8	2.2	38.4	-95.1	184.3	-7.4	205.8	-6.5	3.18%	-0.73	22,526.4	5.3
Meiji	2,621.1	1.3	1,002.2	-50.7	60.0	-32.2	145.6	-8.1	3.29%	-0.87	15,661.9	5.6
Asahi	1,959.9	2.0	210.2	-73.8	49.2	-6.5	71.2	-25.9	3.25%	-0.75	11,751.3	5.2
Mitsui	1,684.9	1.3	36.3	-90.6	5.1	-86.2	51.0	-41.2	2.00%	-1.61	9,690.4	4.7
Yasuda	1,652.3	0.9	102.8	-80.7	48.1	-11.1	116.2	-3.7	3.32%	-0.60	8,733.9	6.8
Chiyoda	1,108.2	8.7	10.1	-95.0	-41.1	—	25.1	-46.0	1.31%	-2.94	6,396.2	1.3
Total	22,466.9	0.9	4,622.7	-57.2	644.6	-31.5	1,065.4	-14.9	2.77%*	-1.06*	137,450.2	5.4

Note: Right-hand columns in each category are year-on-year percent changes except for investment yield, where figures are percentage-point changes   *Average
Source: Companies

EXPECTED INSURANCE DEREGULATION

To remove inter-market barriers

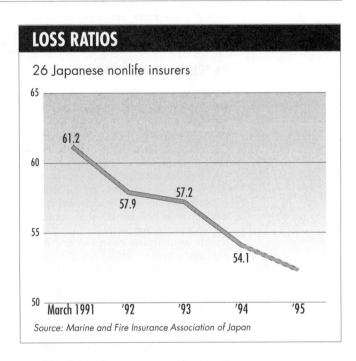

Source: The Nihon Keizai Shimbun

LOSS RATIOS

26 Japanese nonlife insurers

March 1991	61.2
'92	57.9
'93	57.2
'94	54.1

Source: Marine and Fire Insurance Association of Japan

EARTHQUAKE INSURANCE

Earthquake insurance is sold by nonlife firms as a rider on fire policies, and reinsured by the government through Japan Earthquake Reinsurance Co. The Finance Ministry will revise the current scheme effective January 1996, extending the limit on claims to ¥50 million per dwelling, and to ¥10 million for contents. After the January quake, the number of policyholders dramatically increased. Premium revenue from earthquake insurance at the "Big Six" nonlife insurers grew to ¥2.4 billion at the end of March 1995, a 37% increase from a year earlier.

NEW INSURANCE BUSINESS LAW

The new Insurance Business Law was enacted May 31, 1995 and will take effect April 1, 1996. The revised law permits both life and nonlife insurers to enter the other business through subsidiaries. It also introduces a notification system for certain products and premium rates, as well as an insurance brokerage system – allowing brokers to handle policies for more than one insurer.

NONBANKS

Red ink swamps mortgage lenders; city banks disclaim responsibility

BY YUZO SAEKI
Staff Writer

Japan's nonbank financial institutions, particularly housing-loan companies, were at the heart of the nation's financial difficulties in 1995. Struggling under mounting bad debt as real-estate prices continued to collapse, housing-loan companies, known as *jusen*, were hard pressed to repay creditors that included such major financial players as commercial banks and agricultural credit cooperatives.

In the 1970s, commercial banks played a key role in setting up Japan's eight jusen so that they themselves could concentrate on corporate lending. However, within a few years, banks started to move back into retail lending. This prompted the jusen to shift much of their business to the real-estate and construction sectors.

¥6 TRILLION IRRECOVERABLE?

After the real-estate market crashed in the early 1990s, many of the jusen's borrowers defaulted. By the end of September 1994, four jusen — Jyuso Inc., Chigin-Seiho Housing Loan Co., Housing Loan Service Co. and Sogo Jukin Co. — held liabilities in excess of assets.

As they entered their second year of a 10-year rehabilitation plan devised jointly by the Ministry of Finance, parent banks and other lenders, the companies seemed unlikely to be able to stay above water. This posed a serious problem for parent banks and other lenders, primarily agricultural cooperatives, which alone had extended a combined ¥13.6 trillion. In March 1995, Jyuso asked agricultural cooperatives to extend the deadline on ¥40 billion of the ¥60 billion it was scheduled to repay in fiscal 1995.

On Sept. 14, the ministry reported that the eight jusen had bad debt totaling roughly ¥8.4 trillion as of the end of June, much higher than the ¥6 trillion earlier reported. After liquidation of collateral, about ¥6.3 trillion of the debt was expected to prove irrecoverable.

Vowing to resolve the problem before the end of 1995, the government prepared to use public funds to help the jusen's creditors absorb the losses. However, agricultural cooperatives and commercial banks were at odds over who should accept responsibility. Doing so would be an admission of guilt for excessive lending and would result in resignations or demotions.

Agricultural cooperatives argued that parent banks should absorb the losses since they exercised virtual control over the jusen by putting their officials in top positions. Meanwhile, banks contended that it was a generally accepted principle that all creditors should share the risks of lending.

In addition to housing-loan firms, Japan's nonbank financial institutions include leasing firms, credit-card issuers and other credit institutions. According to a ministry survey of 300 major nonbanks, to which 278 responded, outstanding loans totaled ¥55.8 trillion in March 1995, down 4.8% from a year before, marking the largest decline since the ministry began conducting the survey in September 1990.

SHUTTING DOWN

Lending to the real-estate sector fell 5.1% to ¥20.4 trillion, though the sector remained the strongest borrower from nonbanks with a 37% share. Loans to the construction sector declined 8.9% to ¥2.1 trillion and corporate lending fell 6.8% to ¥46.3 trillion.

In 1995, some banks moved to dissolve their affiliated nonbanks after failed attempts at rehabilitation. In March 1995, three regional banks — Bank of Osaka, Fukutoku Bank and Hanwa Bank — applied in court to liquidate 11 affiliated nonbanks.

In contrast to the adversity that most of nonbanks faced, consumer credit companies boomed. Consumer lending showed 5.8% growth to ¥9.5 trillion. Takefuji Corp., the largest such company, saw its net profits grow 73% to ¥41.6 billion in fiscal 1994.

POINTS OF LIGHT

While large commercial banks continued to prefer lending only to employees of elite companies, consumer credit companies lent individuals small amounts — ¥500,000 maximum — with little time or paperwork involved.

The credit-card business also improved. Despite a weak performance at department stores, which saw sales decline for a 41st straight month in July 1995, consumers opened their wallets at suburban retail outlets, according to the Japan Consumer Credit Industry Association.

A survey by the association found that 30 major credit-card issuers had extended a combined ¥952.4 billion as of June, up 8.0% from a year earlier. The monthly survey reported year-on-year increases for eight consecutive months. The 30 companies accounted for about 70% of all credit-card lending.

Profitability of these firms improved also thanks to lower interest rates, reducing their funding costs. Rapid business expansion is also prompting them to recruit the 1995 crop of college grads aggressively, in contrast to the cutbacks in recruiting by city banks. For example, Aiful Co. of Kyoto plans to increase its 1996 recruitment by 11.1% to 210.

TROUBLED LOANS

How deposits at agricultural cooperatives flow

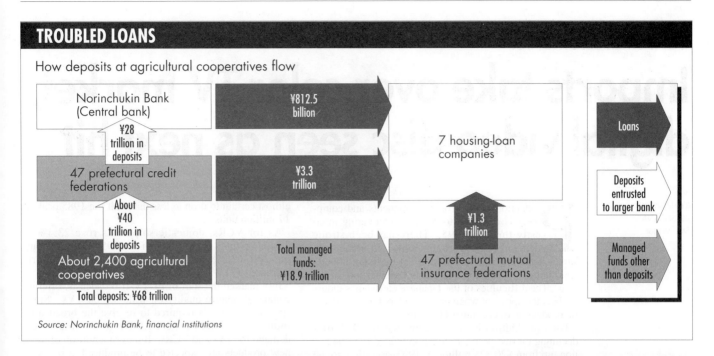

Norinchukin Bank (Central bank)

¥28 trillion in deposits

47 prefectural credit federations

About ¥40 trillion in deposits

About 2,400 agricultural cooperatives

Total deposits: ¥68 trillion

¥812.5 billion

¥3.3 trillion

Total managed funds: ¥18.9 trillion

7 housing-loan companies

¥1.3 trillion

47 prefectural mutual insurance federations

Loans

Deposits entrusted to larger bank

Managed funds other than deposits

Source: Norinchukin Bank, financial institutions

TARGETING SMALL BORROWERS

Market share of Japan's consumer-loan companies; as of March 1994

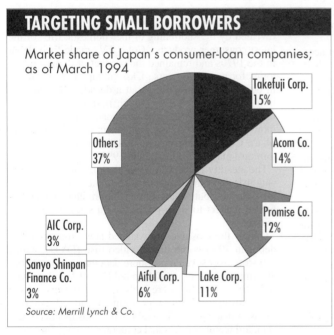

Takefuji Corp. 15%

Acom Co. 14%

Promise Co. 12%

Lake Corp. 11%

Aiful Corp. 6%

Sanyo Shinpan Finance Co. 3%

AIC Corp. 3%

Others 37%

Source: Merrill Lynch & Co.

NON-BANK LENDINGS

Outstanding loans at 300 major non-banks; in trillions of yen

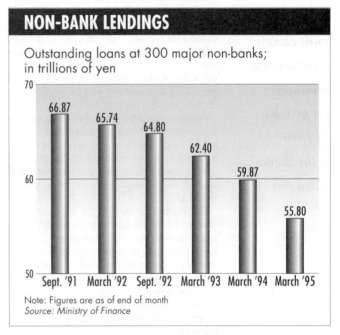

Sept. '91	66.87	
March '92	65.74	
Sept. '92	64.80	
March '93	62.40	
March '94	59.87	
March '95	55.80	

Note: Figures are as of end of month
Source: Ministry of Finance

MODIFIED PARENT BANK RESPONSIBILITY

Whereas the "parent bank responsibility" principle holds that financial institutions are fully responsible for the failure of their affiliated nonbanks, the "modified parent bank responsibility" theory says other lenders should be asked to absorb losses in proportion to their lending. If the "parent bank responsibility" concept is adopted regarding the jusen, some major banks may not be able to bear the resulting losses, observers say.

AGRICULTURAL CREDIT COOPERATIVES

Agricultural cooperatives operate financial services for farmers and other local customers. The nation's 2,400 cooperatives have total deposits of ¥68 trillion. More than two-thirds were entrusted to the cooperatives' 47 prefectural credit federations. Such prefectural federations collectively extended ¥3.3 trillion to *jusen* housing-loan companies. The farm credit unions stand to lose about ¥2.5 trillion if creditors are forced to write off losses in proportion to their lending.

CONSUMER ELECTRONICS

Imports take over color TV market; digital video disc seen as next hit

BY HISAYUKI
MITSUSADA
Staff Writer

One of the most closely watched new products set to debut in 1996 is the digital video disc

Production of electronic components and equipment is expected to continue recovering modestly through 1995. There has been strong demand for key components and some consumer items, but this has been offset by rising imports spurred by the yen's appreciation in the early part of the year. The difficulties of the Japanese electronics industry become apparent when one considers falling domestic production of consumer electronics.

Total production in Japan recovered in 1994 after declining for two years. Production totaled ¥21,404 billion, up from ¥20,828 million in 1993, according to the Electronics Industries Association of Japan. The EIAJ predicts growth will likely continue in 1995, albeit at a modest pace, rising 2.2% to ¥21,719.7 billion.

Output of components and devices including semiconductors, liquid crystal displays, switches and cathode ray tubes will increase 4.5% to ¥8,834.4 billion, supported by demand for parts for personal computers, copiers and telecommunications equipment.

Prospects are also good for office equipment, testers, telecommunications products, and other commercial equipment. This sector will likely grow 2.4% to ¥10,269.5 billion, supported by corporate investments in information networks and the start of new services such as the personal handy-phone system, according to the EIAJ.

The picture is less bright for consumer electronics goods. Domestic output is projected to decline for the fourth consecutive year, dropping 5.3% to ¥2,615.8 trillion. Even though minidiscs and wide-screen television sets have stimulated consumer demand, the overall market is becoming increasingly dependent on imports, the association noted.

The continuing shift of production overseas is best represented by color television sets and videocassette recorders.

In June, for the first time, color televisions imports surpassed domestic production. Output fell 27.1% to 602,000 units as domestic factories focused mostly on lucrative wide-screen televisions, according to the EIAJ. Imports, meanwhile, reached a record monthly high of 615,000 units, according to the Ministry of Finance. Among major suppliers were Malaysia and Thailand, favorite Asian production bases of Japanese companies.

In the first six months of 1995, domestic shipments of color TVs rose a robust 15% year on year to 4,189,000 units. But domestic production fell 14.1% to 4,016,000 units, while imports surged 22.5% to 3,312,000 units. The trend is likely to continue despite the weakening of the yen in the summer. Domestic color TV production in 1995, based on major suppliers' production plans, is

almost certain to drop to less than half the 1985 peak of 17 million units.

As for VCRs, domestic shipments rose 23.4% to 2,515,000 units in the first half of 1995. Domestic output fell 12.2% to 6,557,000 units, while imports increased 181.2% to 1,356,000 units.

July marked the start of EDTV-II broadcasts, offering enhanced picture quality on wide screen TVs. Since special circuitry is required to receive the broadcasts, industry watchers expect EDTV to stimulate new demand for TVs and VCRs. But even a portion of these new products are expected to be produced at overseas factories.

The momentum of the shift to overseas production is revealed by the shortening of the "domestic life" of the latest consumer products. Color TVs made their debut in the 1970s and remained the product of domestic factories for nearly 20 years. Cassette tape players stayed in domestic factories for about a decade. But production of wide-screen TVs, which first appeared on the market in 1991, started to shift abroad in 1994. And the mini disc may only have a domestic life of two years. Sharp Corp. is shifting assembly of about 45% of its minidisc players to Malaysia in 1995.

The steadily rising yen is not the only reason for the sluggish domestic consumer electronics market. Analysts also attribute a lack of new hit products, which has forced makers to slash prices to win sales in saturated markets.

One of the most closely watched new products set to debut in 1996 is the digital video disc (DVD), which can store over seven times more data than a conventional compact disc, or enough to hold a full-length movie. Industry expectations are high because the discs have applications in both entertainment and information fields, replacing the CD-ROM, which has fast become a standard feature of personal computers.

The Sakura Institute of Research, an arm of Sakura Bank, estimates the market for DVD players alone will reach ¥150 billion in the year 2000.

Some industry estimates put the size of the overall market at several trillion yen.

The other product which Japanese electronics manufacturers hope will keep their factories humming is the flat-screen television. Sony Corp., Fujitsu Ltd., NEC Corp. and Matsushita Electric Industrial Co. separately announced plans to start volume production in 1997 of flat color screens measuring up to about 42 inches.

Each company plans to use a different format, but the deciding factor here as far as sales are concerned will be picture quality, including color and response time, and quick acceptance, which will boost demand and help bring prices down, analysts say.

COLOR TELEVISION STATISTICS

In millions of units

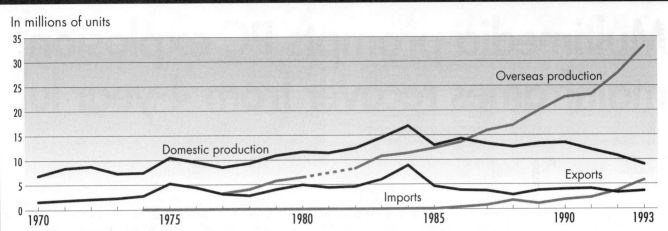

Note: 1. Overseas production data is for the fiscal period from April 1 through March 31 of the following year.
2. Domestic production figure for 1987 includes chassis and kits.
3. Export figures for 1970-1977 include chassis and kits.
Source: MITI, MOF and Electronic Industries Association of Japan.

CAPITAL SPENDING: ELECTRIC/ELECTRONICS

In billions of yen

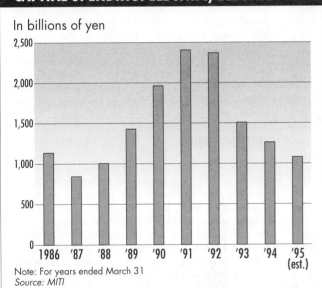

Note: For years ended March 31
Source: MITI

ELECTRONICS PRODUCTION BY CATEGORY

In trillions of yen

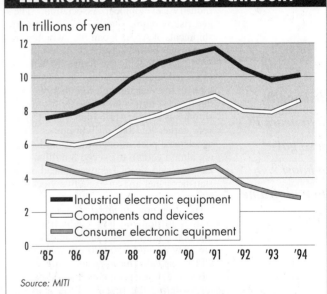

Legend:
- Industrial electronic equipment
- Components and devices
- Consumer electronic equipment

Source: MITI

KEY WORD

LARGE FLAT-PANEL DISPLAYS

Conventional picture tubes are impractical for TV monitors greater than 30 inches. Three competing technologies for new displays emerged in 1995 as viable candidates for commercial introduction in late 1996. The plasma display, pushed by NEC and Fujitsu, has the comparative advantage of high production yields; Sharp is promoting LCD monitors; Sony has adopted a format called the Plasmatron, invented by Tektronix of the U.S., which combines LCD and plasma technologies.

KEY WORD

DIGITAL VIDEO DISC

An advanced data storage medium the size of a conventional CD, but capable of storing a full-length movie or massive amounts of computer data. Initial discs, due in late 1996, will be read-only, but rewritable media are expected on the market by the end of the century. In mid-September, the rival camps of Toshiba and six other firms versus Sony/Philips agreed on standard specifications for discs capable of holding 4.7 gigabytes of data per side.

COMPUTERS

Multimedia prompts PC explosion; mainframes recover from 4-year lull

BY HISAYUKI
MITSUSADA
Staff Writer

*Ironically,
it appears PCs
also gave
a boost
to mainframe
sales*

The Japanese computer market will remember 1995 as an amazing year, with active shipments of all kinds of computers from the smallest to the biggest pieces of iron.

The most spectacular growth occurred in the personal computer market, where strong demand from individual consumers and corporations helped boost shipments by more than 30% from 1994 through 1995. It was a busy time for domestic and foreign PC makers alike, revising production plans and forging new alliances amid an increasingly fierce price war.

Volume was tremendous. In the year through March 1995, domestic shipments of PCs shot up 40.5% to 3.348 million units, according to the Japan Electronic Industry Development Association. The real percentage rise remains a hefty 35% when corrected for the shipments of Apple Japan Inc., which were not included in statistics before July 1994.

When announcing the figures in May, the association predicted shipments would increase to 4.2-4.3 million units in the year through March 1996. But by summer, the forecast turned out to be far too modest. Domestic shipments in the April-June quarter rose 53% from a year earlier to 1.08 million units. "Judging from the accelerated pace through the second quarter, shipments are almost certain to exceed 5 million units" for the fiscal year, said Yoshi Takayama, head of the association's statistics panel and an executive vice-president of NEC Corp.

The steep downtrend in PC prices has helped fan the flames of demand. PCs which sold for ¥200,000-300,000 in mid-1994 with an Intel 486 microprocessor are now around ¥50,000 cheaper, yet feature faster CPUs, expanded memory and more accessories.

Because of the price cuts, the 53% increase in volume terms during the first fiscal quarter translated into a more modest but still strong rise of 27% rise in value terms.

Exports, comprised almost entirely of notebooks and other portables, increased 20% year on year to 266,000 units. Meanwhile, the value of exports inched up 4% to ¥80.5 billion.

Computer manufacturers also reported strong sales of workstations and network software and equipment. Much of the demand came from companies seeking to raise the efficiency of their white-collar workforce in the face of the prolonged economic slump.

Strong demand in this sector is normally taken as evidence of the corporate trend to downsize, shifting from powerful but expensive mainframes to smaller, cheaper and more flexible machines. But the lucrative mainframe business has life in it yet, as seen by a recovery in shipments.

STILL KICKING

Domestic shipments of mainframes in the year through March 1996 are set to rise for the first time in four years. Hitachi Ltd., IBM Japan Ltd., Fujitsu Ltd. and NEC all estimated double-digit year-on-year growth in orders for the April-September period. IBM Japan foresees a record high for the fiscal year.

Mainframe makers acknowledge the downsizing trend, but have successfully boosted the cost-performance of their big iron. In April, Hitachi introduced mainframes with two to three times the cost-performance of previous models, and especially attractive prices at the high end. In May, Fujitsu released a model with about three times higher cost-performance. Mainframe lease fees used to be in the millions of yen, but NEC lowered its monthly lease fee for the AX7300 to ¥580,000.

Ironically, it appears PCs also gave a boost to mainframe sales. "The spread of PCs has deepened understanding among users that such machines cannot replace all the functions of a large computer," explained Kakutaro Kitashiro, president of IBM Japan.

SHIFTING SANDS

The PC price wars have led to some interesting new alliances. NEC, Japan's leading PC maker with a commanding share of over 45% of the market, entered into a tie-up with Packard Bell Electronics Inc., a top U.S. vendor, acquiring close to 20% of the company. One of the announced aims was to combine their purchasing prowess for components such as CD-ROM drives.

Toshiba Corp., the top seller of notebook PCs in the U.S., showed renewed interest in the domestic market by introducing a series of new models, from notebooks to high-end desktop PCs. But it decided to focus development efforts on notebooks, and consigned all desktop production to Intel.

Packard Bell raised its stake in Japan by setting up a sales subsidiary, and U.S. clone maker Gateway 2000 Inc. also set up a Tokyo subsidiary.

Microsoft Corp. dominates the market for PC operating systems. Hoping to check that company's spread in the workstation field, a group of 58 workstation and software makers including NEC and Sun Microsystems Inc. united in 1995 to develop a next-generation 64-bit Unix operating system. The current 32-bit Unix operating system was hindered by delays in developing unified standards and gradually gave way to Windows NT, released in 1993.

DOMESTIC PERSONAL COMPUTER SHIPMENTS

In thousands of units

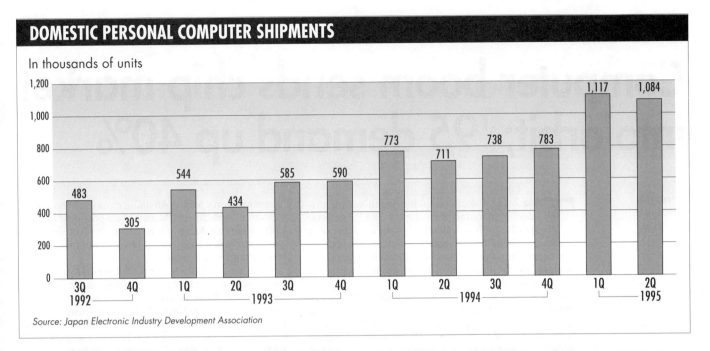

Source: Japan Electronic Industry Development Association

MAINFRAME COMPUTER SHIPMENTS

In trillions of yen

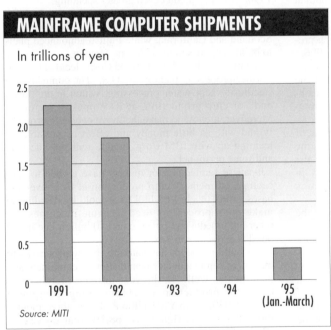

Source: MITI

WORLD PC MAKER CONNECTIONS

Arrows show capital participations
Lines show other tie-ups

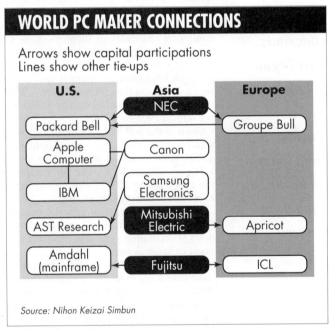

Source: Nihon Keizai Simbun

UNIX

A multitasking, multi-user operating system, used mainly by workstations and servers, but portable to any platform, from PCs to mainframes. First developed in 1969 by AT&T Bell Laboratories and licensed for a low fee, Unix has since evolved into several variations. The lack of a unified standard has made it costly to develop application software. And while two organizations vied to set the standards between 1988 and 1994, Windows NT gained popularity as an easier-to-use 32-bit OS.

MAINFRAME COMPUTERS

Powerful computers that can be applied to many different tasks, from scientific calculations to graphics processing to database management. They form the core of on-line banking systems and industrial order processing systems. The mainframe market expanded fast until around 1990, when corporations began reining in their investments and users began turning to increasingly powerful lower-priced workstations and PCs. The need for dedicated computer rooms for mainframes has been another negative factor.

SEMICONDUCTORS

Computer boom sends chip market into orbit; '95 demand up 40%

BY HISAYUKI
MITSUSADA
Staff Writer

Chip-related companies have begun taking over excess capacity from slumping audio-visual equipment makers

The biggest decision facing Japan's semiconductor manufacturers during 1995 was how much and how quickly to boost capacity, as a worldwide explosion in sales of information equipment stimulated demand for all kinds of semiconductors, from commodity DRAM memory chips to microprocessors.

While major chip makers cheerfully surfed the steady expansion in demand in 1994, the mood changed to a sense of crisis as severe shortages emerged. Companies belatedly began to accelerate their capital spending through the summer of 1995, building new lines both at home and abroad to fill the chip gap.

The boom spread to semiconductor manufacturing equipment and materials suppliers, some of which predict record profits for fiscal 1995 through March 1996.

Industry executives were predicting strong demand early in 1995, and by summer few doubted that the boom would continue through 1996. World Semiconductor Trade Statistics estimates global demand growing 40% in 1995 over 1994.

Much of the pull has come from the increasing use of semiconductors in electronic equipment. During the 1970s, semiconductors accounted for around 4% of the value of such products. The percentage rose to 7% in the 1980s and to 10% in 1990-1994. But the figure is expected to jump to 15% in 1995.

The widening spread of personal computers plus the introduction of Microsoft Corp.'s memory-hungry Windows 95 operating system is expected to give a major boost to future demand.

PC unit sales in Japan alone are expected to grow more than 40%, exceeding 5 million units. The internal RAM memory required for the Japanese version of Windows 95 is said to be 8 megabytes, which is double the amount sufficient for Windows 3.1. Add to that the increasingly common addition of CD-ROM drives and advanced sound and graphics functions, and you have a mix that spells huge demand for chips of all kinds.

As of August, major PC manufacturers planned to purchase roughly 80% more semiconductors (on a bit-count basis) in 1996 than in 1995, which surpasses the 60-70% rise predicted by chip makers.

The semiconductor book-to-bill ratio in July remained high at 1.22 despite a 36% year-on-year increase in output, and there was a severe shortage in dynamic random access memory (DRAM) chips. "Only about 80% of demand is probably being met, and it will likely stay in the 90-95% range," said Akira Minamikawa, an analyst at Dataquest Japan KK.

In the face of the shortage, the Japanese chip makers even had good things to say about rival South Korean makers, whose emphasis on memory chips has been an increasing worry here. "Anything easing the shortage is welcome," said Shigeki Matsue, vice president of NEC Corp.'s semiconductor group, about the Korean firms' moves to expand capacity. "Meeting customer demand is our top priority at present."

Not to miss out on the market opportunity, Japanese companies are making large plant and equipment investments. As of the end of August, the top five chip makers' semiconductor-related capital spending plans for the year through March 1996 totaled ¥635 billion, far exceeding the record ¥566 billion spent in fiscal 1990. Analysts predict even greater spending.

The buildup both at home and abroad continues. NEC moved forward its plan to build new DRAM lines in Scotland and California, while Fujitsu announced plans to build new lines in the U.K. and Oregon.

In a major policy shift, Toshiba Corp. decided to build a wafer-processing plant in the U.S. The company had steadfastly kept wafer processing, which is the "front end" of chip production, at its domestic factories. Moreover, it chose to make the move overseas as quickly and with as little money and effort as possible by teaming up with IBM Corp., which will provide land and some personnel.

Japanese semiconductor makers have tended to concentrate on memory chip production at their overseas bases. But Hitachi Ltd. broke the mold by deciding to make microprocessors used in game machines and other multimedia equipment on a ¥40 billion line it will build at its factory in Texas.

The building boom has naturally brought benefits to makers of semiconductor manufacturing equipment and materials as well. In the year through March 1995, domestic production of chip making equipment increased 39.1% to ¥703 billion. In the three months through June, the figure rose 68.1% year on year to ¥220 billion. Equipment maker Tokyo Electron Ltd., air compressor maker SMC Corp., and chip package maker Kyocera Corp. are expecting record profits in the current fiscal year.

In a telling sign of the shifting fortunes of different industries, chip-related companies have begun taking over excess capacity from slumping audio-visual equipment makers.

For example, chip testing equipment maker Advantest Corp. took on some of the 300 workers from Akai Electric Co.'s Saitama factory, which gave up production of videocassette recorders. Shinkawa Ltd. will take over a Teac Corp. factory to produce IC manufacturing machines, and IC tester maker Lasertec Corp. is nearing a decision to acquire part of the Yokohama factory from VCR maker Shintom Co.

PLANNED INVESTMENT PLAN FOR 16M-DRAMS AND 64M-DRAMS

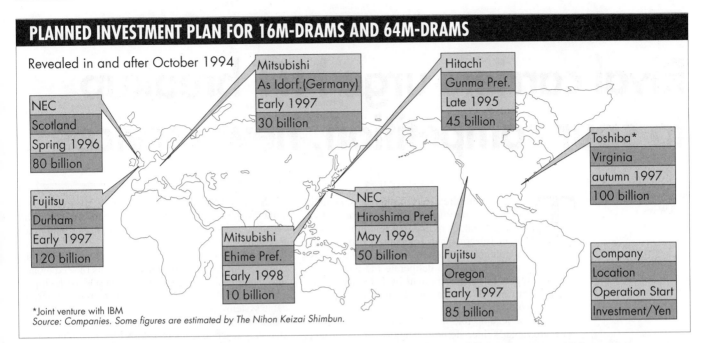

Revealed in and after October 1994

Mitsubishi / As Idorf.(Germany) / Early 1997 / 30 billion

Hitachi / Gunma Pref. / Late 1995 / 45 billion

NEC / Scotland / Spring 1996 / 80 billion

Toshiba* / Virginia / autumn 1997 / 100 billion

Fujitsu / Durham / Early 1997 / 120 billion

Mitsubishi / Ehime Pref. / Early 1998 / 10 billion

NEC / Hiroshima Pref. / May 1996 / 50 billion

Fujitsu / Oregon / Early 1997 / 85 billion

Company / Location / Operation Start / Investment/Yen

*Joint venture with IBM
Source: Companies. Some figures are estimated by The Nihon Keizai Shimbun.

FOREIGN MARKET SHARE IN JAPAN

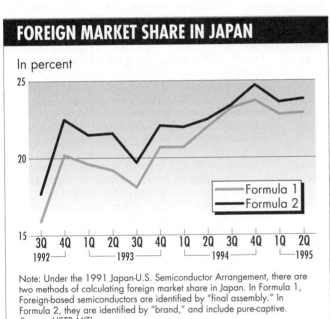

In percent

- Formula 1
- Formula 2

| | 3Q | 4Q | 1Q | 2Q | 3Q | 4Q | 1Q | 2Q | 3Q | 4Q | 1Q | 2Q |
| 1992 | | 1993 | | | | 1994 | | | | 1995 | | |

Note: Under the 1991 Japan-U.S. Semiconductor Arrangement, there are two methods of calculating foreign market share in Japan. In Formula 1, Foreign-based semiconductors are identified by "final assembly." In Formula 2, they are identified by "brand," and include pure-captive.
Source: USTR,MITI.

EARNINGS ESTIMATES BY CHIP-RELATED FIRMS

Results for the year through March 1996 on an unconsolidated basis estimated as of September 1995; the initial projections at term's start in parentheses

Chip makers	Pretax profits (billion yen)	Yr-on-Yr Change (%)
Hitachi	110 (100)	24
Toshiba	90 (72)	26
NEC	80 (67)	32
Fujitsu	75 (65)	25
Mitsubishi	70 (65)	10
Oki	38 (20)	-8
Equipment makers	**Pretax profits (billion yen)**	**Yr-on-Yr Change (%)**
Tokyo Electron	*38 (28.5)	104
Advantest	*20 (14)	134
SMC	*18.5 (16)	25
Nikon	13 (10)	121
THK	8.5 (8.0)	245

*Record profits

FAST SRAM

Fast static RAM devices with access speeds of less than 10 nanoseconds have come into large demand now that Intel's Pentium processor has made the scene. Pentium-based machines now account for 70% of PC sales, and the less expensive DRAMs are not fast enough to take full advantage of this powerful chip. PC makers are using fast SRAM for cache memory. Following the lead of NEC and Hitachi, Mitsubishi Electric, Sony and Sharp have started SRAM production. The market is expected to hit $400 million in 1995 and triple by the year 2000.

FLASH MEMORY

A memory technology that could replace hard disks, flash memory retains data even without power, and allows fast erasure and rewriting. Toshiba developed flash memory in 1980, but Intel now holds about 50% of the roughly $1.3 billion market. Several formats are competing for leadership, and major chip makers are forming alliances. Heralding the rising status of South Korean chip makers, Toshiba joined Samsung Electronic in April to develop an advanced 64-megabit flash memory. Dataquest Inc. predicts a $6 billion market in the year 2000.

TELECOMMUNICATIONS

Rival carriers urge NTT breakup to spur competition, new services

BY NORRI KAGEKI
Staff Writer

One potential group of rivals that has surfaced in the local market are the cable television companies

The telecommunications industry is keenly tracking the national debate concerning the possible breakup of Japan's telephone giant Nippon Telegraph and Telephone Corp.

The special committee set up by the Ministry of Posts and Telecommunications to deliberate the issue is to submit a report to the government by February 1996. The government will then decide on the future of NTT by the end of March.

Playing the leading role in promoting the breakup of NTT are Japan's three domestic long-distance carriers DDI Corp., Japan Telecom Co. and Teleway Japan Corp. These firms insist that NTT's long-distance unit should be separated from the local telephone division.

The three complain that they are not provided equal access to NTT's local telephone lines and are being unfairly charged higher access fees than NTT's long-distance unit.

Some stock analysts argue that the breakup would be advantageous to NTT's shareholders because it would improve the firm's profitability and support long-term growth.

But NTT itself strongly opposes the move. The telecom behemoth says that a breakup would diminish its global competitiveness and weaken its research and development capabilities. Taking the debate to the national level, it also claims the breakup would not be good for Japan.

One likely breakup scenario has NTT split into separate long-distance and local providers, with the local division separated into 2 or 5 regional operators. Once that happens, the Japanese telecommunications industry is expected to go through a major reorganization, which may involve mergers among telephone companies.

Despite the hopes of the telecommunications ministry, few industry watchers believe the telecommunications sector can be stimulated by the simple breakup of NTT because the local telephone market would still be dominated by the NTT spin-offs. What is needed are policies that generate competition in local markets, they say.

One potential group of rivals that has surfaced in the local market are the cable television companies. Held back for so long by excessive regulation, the cable industry began to show new signs of life in 1993-1994 as deregulation measures were introduced.

As part of the deregulation, cable operators are now allowed to provide telecommunications services, and some major cable firms have already announced plans to forge into the telephone market. Their main objective is to lure more subscribers by using their cable network to supply cheap telephone services along with television programs.

U.S. cable titans like Tele-Communications Inc. and Time-Warner Entertainment have taken interest in the Japanese market and are expected to play an important role in the evolution of cable here.

These U.S. firms have tied up with major trading houses, which are pouring large amounts of seed money into cable businesses, and formed MSOs, or multiple-system operators, to manage and operate numerous cable systems in local markets.

But much depends on whether cable operators can smoothly reach agreement with NTT concerning access to its vast telephone network. That arrangement must materialize before cable firms can offer subscribers the chance to make phone calls outside of their cable TV regions.

Luckily NTT is being cooperative about the matter, at least on the surface. Outright rejection would play into the hands of those who are calling for the breakup of NTT on grounds that it is too predominant.

Meanwhile, an entirely new mobile communications service came into being in the summer of 1995 with the long-awaited arrival of the personal handy-phone system, or PHS.

Subsidiaries of NTT and DDI launched the new phone service in July with limited operations in and around Tokyo and Sapporo. A third player, backed by a group including Japan Telecom, Tokyo Telecommunication Network Co., and major trading firms, followed suit with a PHS service in October. All four operators plan to gradually expand their services to other parts of the country.

The initial response was overwhelming as people rushed to subscribe to the PHS services. One projection has 40 million subscribers signed up by the year 2010. But it remains to be seen whether PHS can live up to its billing.

The telecommunications ministry and NTT are cheering for a success because both want to export the technology overseas, especially in Asia. Seminars and trial-operations have already been carried out in 10 localities, including China, Hong Kong, Malaysia and Indonesia, and foreign concerns are closely watching to see how PHS flies in Japan.

PHS handset manufacturers are also eager to sell their products abroad. NEC Corp., for example, is performing trials independently outside of Asia.

Traditional cellular telephone operators, worried that the PHS companies might steal their customers, are working to lower their rates. In one swipe, initial subscriber fees for cellular phones were slashed by around 75% to ¥10,000, which at least approaches the PHS startup fee of ¥7,200.

NUMBER OF MOBILE PHONE SUBSCRIBERS

In millions of subscribers

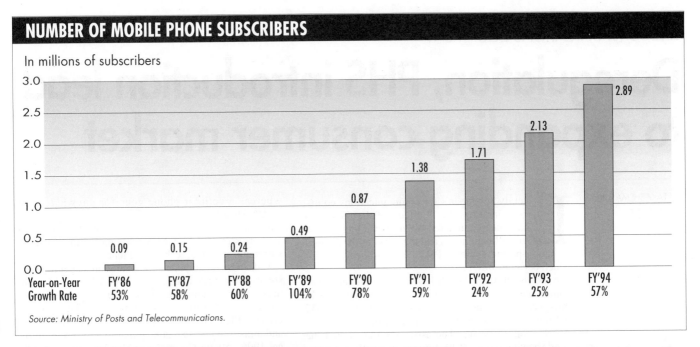

Year-on-Year Growth Rate	FY'86 53%	FY'87 58%	FY'88 60%	FY'89 104%	FY'90 78%	FY'91 59%	FY'92 24%	FY'93 25%	FY'94 57%
	0.09	0.15	0.24	0.49	0.87	1.38	1.71	2.13	2.89

Source: Ministry of Posts and Telecommunications.

DOMESTIC MARKET SHARE

Number of calls; as of March 1995

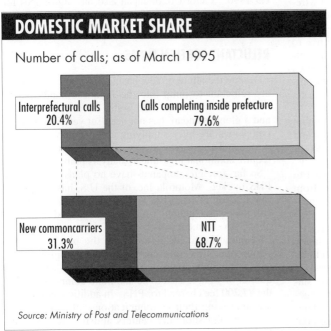

Interprefectural calls 20.4%

Calls completing inside prefecture 79.6%

New commoncarriers 31.3%

NTT 68.7%

Source: Ministry of Post and Telecommunications

GROWTH OF INTERPREFECTURAL CALLS

Market share of New common carriers; in percent

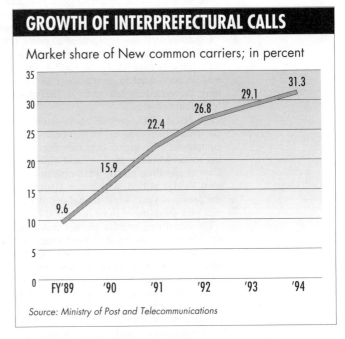

9.6 — FY'89
15.9 — '90
22.4 — '91
26.8 — '92
29.1 — '93
31.3 — '94

Source: Ministry of Post and Telecommunications

KEY WORD

MULTIPLE-SYSTEM OPERATOR (MSO)

A company that operates many cable TV systems to take advantage of economy of scale. An MSO is in better position to negotiate lower prices with equipment manufacturers and companies that lay cable.
Tele-Communications teamed with Sumitomo Corp. to establish Japan's first MSO — Jupiter Telecommunications Co. Later, Time-Warner Entertainment and common carrier US West Inc. have set up Titus Communications Corp. with Itochu Corp. and Toshiba Corp.

KEY WORD

PERSONAL HANDY-PHONE SYSTEM (PHS)

A new portable technology that lies between cordless and cellular phones. PHS is cheaper than cellular services, but offers fewer functions. A three-minute local PHS call costs ¥40, less than one-third the cost of a cellular call. But PHS cannot be used from fast-moving vehicles, and users must be near a base station because PHS antennas are weaker than those of cellular phones.
For the service to prosper, PHS operators will have to saturate their service areas with base stations.

TELECOMMUNICATIONS EQUIPMENT

Deregulation, PHS introduction lead to expanding consumer market

BY TAKASHI MASUKO
Deputy Editor

Luckily for Japan's telecommunications equipment industry, the ill effects of the rising yen have been countered by an expanding market for cellular phones and the debut of the personal handy-phone system (PHS), limited services for which began in July 1995.

In the year through March 1995, overall production of communications equipment rose for the first time in three years, climbing a year-on-year 1.1% to ¥2.5032 trillion, according to the Communications Industry Association of Japan. The association attributed the good showing to the 20.2% surge in production of wireless communications equipment following liberalizations which allowed retail sales of cellular phones.

Communications equipment exports fell 6.6% to ¥782.5 billion amid the yen's steep rise against the dollar. Imports rose 45.9% to ¥207.4 billion as foreign makers scrambled to grab a share of Japan's telecommunications equipment market, including the market for cellular phones.

For fiscal 1995, mobile communications equipment companies plan to invest ¥878.6 billion yen in plant and equipment, 50% higher than the previous year, according to the Ministry of Posts and Telecommunications. Capital spending among PHS operators is expected to total ¥191.4 billion, which is a 10-fold increase from the previous year, while digital cellular phone companies plan spending of more than ¥300 billion.

The benefit of cellular phones was made clear after the Jan. 17 Great Hanshin Earthquake, when ordinary telephone services were suspended for days but cellular phone subscribers retained a dial tone in many areas.

Cellular phones would be useless if all the base stations were destroyed, but the overall cellular infrastructure is much less vulnerable than the vast wired telephone web. If one cellular base station is knocked out of service, users need simply move to a nearby functioning area to make and receive calls.

Interestingly, cellular phone operators had their busiest sign-up month in July 1995, when the first PHS services were inaugurated. In that month, a record-high 474,700 cellular phones were registered. The number represents a 200% jump from July of the previous year. By August, the cumulative total surpassed 6 million units.

In July, the long-awaited personal handy-phone system hit the streets. PHS services are cheaper than cellular phone services, but offer fewer functions. It costs just ¥2,700 a month to subscribe to PHS, compared with around ¥7,000 for cellular phone services, and a 3-minute call using a handy-phone costs between ¥40 and ¥200, compared with ¥150 to ¥230 for a cellular call. Moreover, PHS handsets are priced around ¥40,000, whereas a cellular phone goes for anywhere from ¥40,000 to ¥90,000.

In the first month of service, a total of 87,000 subscribers signed up for PHS, although some operators suffered from initial technical glitches.

Audio-visual equipment companies are eager to grab a share of the PHS market. Kenwood Corp., a leading maker of car audio equipment, hopes to make handy-phones one of its major lines of business. The company projects PHS handset sales of ¥7 billion in fiscal 1995 and aims to more than double that to ¥15 billion in fiscal 1996. Victor Co. of Japan also has high hopes for PHS, aiming for sales of around ¥4 billion in fiscal 1995, rising to ¥10 billion in fiscal 1996.

RELUCTANT FOREIGN FIRMS

Despite the allure of new business, foreign companies are reluctant to jump into the Japanese handy-phone market, partly because PHS is still a local phenomenon and a global standard has not been set yet. The foreign companies are busy supplying cellular phones worldwide, and the introduction of a new standard will require additional investment, analysts point out.

So far, foreign companies have no plans to enter the PHS market. Motorola Inc. of the U.S. has postponed introduction of handsets, and Finland's Nokia Corp. is still undecided, although it has been engaged in handy-phone development work.

Responding to the new kid on the block, cellular phone operators have cut their rates, bringing initial subscriber fees down to around ¥10,000, which is a quarter of what it used to be and more competitive with the ¥7,200 fee charged for PHS. In addition, companies are improving their communications infrastructure in underground shopping centers and in tunnels along highways and national routes.

Another promising new telecommunications market is asynchronous transfer mode (ATM) switching systems, which are capable of transmitting audio and video as well as data signals quickly over existing networks. Fujitsu Ltd. plans to supply ATM switches to regional telephone companies in the U.S., including Atlanta-based BellSouth Corp. and New York-based Nynex Corp.

ATM switches, tailored for complex multimedia networking, can transfer data at rates of up to 156 megabits per second, which is more than 100 times the speed of conventional digital switching systems. ATM switches lie at the heart of advanced information networks such as B-ISDN (broadband integrated services digital network). Recently, ATM switches have also begun showing up in advanced corporate office networks.

WIRELESS TELECOM DEVICE OUTPUT

In billions of yen

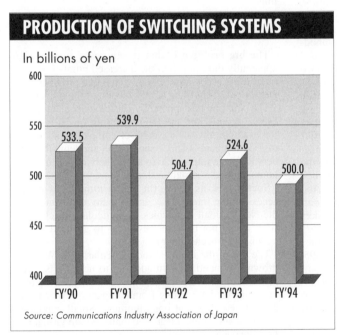

	FY'90	FY'91	FY'92	FY'93	FY'94
	642.0	720.7	658.3	631.7	759.1

Source: Communications Industry Association of Japan

PRODUCTION OF TELEPHONES

In billions of yen

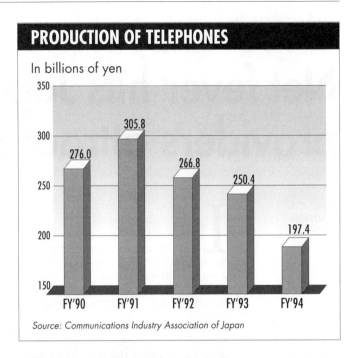

	FY'90	FY'91	FY'92	FY'93	FY'94
	276.0	305.8	266.8	250.4	197.4

Source: Communications Industry Association of Japan

PRODUCTION OF SWITCHING SYSTEMS

In billions of yen

	FY'90	FY'91	FY'92	FY'93	FY'94
	533.5	539.9	504.7	524.6	500.0

Source: Communications Industry Association of Japan

PRODUCTION OF TELECOM EQUIPMENT

In billions of yen

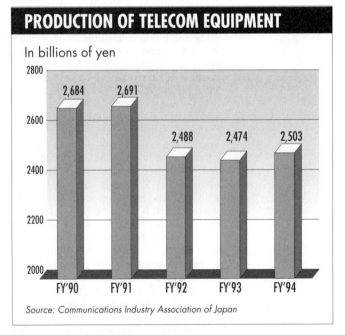

	FY'90	FY'91	FY'92	FY'93	FY'94
	2,684	2,691	2,488	2,474	2,503

Source: Communications Industry Association of Japan

KEY WORD

CELL RELAY

In the fall of 1995, NTT plans to launch a cell-relay service offering data transmissions at 6 megabits per second. That compares with 64 kilobits per second for packet exchange and 1.5 megabits for frame relay. Designed to accommodate corporations that use LANs for large-volume data transmissions, this will be the first commercial communications service using asynchronous transfer mode switches. NTT rival Japan Telecom Co. intends to soon follow with a similar service.

KEY WORD

ATM-LANS

Asynchronous transfer mode (ATM) technology is sophisticated and complex. It may eventually become widespread, but the first applications are in ATM-local area networks. ATM switches can be installed in LAN backbones without a need to replace existing hardware. Both universities and corporations have begun using ATM-LANs. Fujitsu Ltd. will supply an ATM switching system to Toray Industries Inc., which plans to construct an in-house multimedia network.

INTERNET

Net fever hits Japan; new service providers attract 1 million users

BY HISAYUKI
MITSUSADA
Staff Writer

Internet World magazine claims Internet use is growing so fast that at current rates everyone on earth will be connected by the year 2004. The growth of the Internet has created a broad range of business opportunities, from network providers to page designers and set-up firms. It has put small businesses on an equal footing with the largest companies, because in cyberspace the customers determine what they want to see.

According to the Internet Society, there were 96,000 host computers in Japan serving clients on the Internet at the end of 1994. This is up 30% from a year earlier. By the middle of 1995 there were approximately 1 million Internet users in Japan.

The rising tide dubbed the "multimedia age" embodied in the computer and the "information highway" symbolized by the Internet reached Japan in 1993. Two commercial providers — AT&T Jens Corp. and its InterSpin and Internet Initiative Japan (IIJ) Inc. began offering connections to the Internet that year. These companies mainly provided dedicated lines to corporate customers at hefty prices. The first network to offer Internet access to individuals was TWICS.

In response to the increased hoopla surrounding the Net, more that 40 access providers had established operations by September, up from four last year. And with more and more companies, large and small, joining the fray, it is hard to know just how many providers there really are, computer industry people say.

BNN, a Tokyo publisher of computer magazines which started its dial-up service at the end of June 1995, is one such newcomer. As with many other small companies providing Internet access, its competitive advantage is a low flat rate of ¥1,000 per month. This compares with companies who charge based on usage, starting at ¥10 a minute.

The low price is possible because many of these new providers are trying to create a potential customer base for future or related businesses rather than create a stand-alone connection service.

Another example of the trend is Bekkoame Internet Inc. of Tokyo, which started as an electronic bulletin board. Its membership has now grown to around 18,000 users. Even it does not intend to be profitable only with the connection service. "Using the member network, we hope to provide on-line games," said President Toru Fujita.

On-line services are beginning to tap the rising popularity of the Internet, particularly the graphical World Wide Web. PC-Van operated by NEC Corp. and Nifty-Serve, a Fujitsu Ltd. affiliate, were planning to offer connection to the WWW by the end of 1995, while software house Justsystem Corp. offers access to the Web by using a function built into its popular Ichitaro word-processing program.

Small access businesses are relatively easy to start because IIJ, for example, offers a package with workstations and other necessary hardware, technical assistance and maintenance for ¥15 million. The monthly operating cost is relatively low at around ¥40,000. The companies then lease lines to the dedicated server. They can simply lease more lines as their user base expands. Subleasing is less expensive, but the trade off is speed and a limit on the number of users for each line.

TRAFFIC JAMS ON THE INFOBAHN

The big problem is that the increase in providers apparently did not match the increased number of computer users accessing the Net, which one provider compared to the "Big Bang at the creation of the universe."

The situation has apparently caused discontent among users. A look into the Internet forum on Nifty-Serve, for example, reveals a wealth of complaints about cut-offs during access and a shortage of modems that renders it almost impossible to access services during peak hours, around midnight in Japan.

Such concerns aside, the rising number of people accessing the Internet has drawn many companies onto the Net — small companies, in particular, which otherwise would not have the resources to go head-to-head against well-heeled conglomerates.

The use of the Internet, and particularly the Web, has grown exponentially. In addition to news, arts, and a plethora of amusement sites, a Net surfer can find business information ranging from company profiles to catalogs to employment opportunities. Small companies benefit from joining electronic malls, where virtual traffic is heavier.

Setting up shop on the Internet is far cheaper than conventional marketing. All that's needed is a computer to act as the server and an Internet address, called a URL, available from a link-up provider. The next logical step is a site Internet users can access from the World Wide Web.

In this way, a small company can provide information on its goods at much lower costs than, say, running a 15-second ad on TV. And if done right, the effort can reach an audience estimated at 60 million.

Nomura Research Institute says there were 94 online businesses based in Japan using the Internet as of September 1, 1995. Of these, 14 were so-called electronic shopping malls combining services from a number of companies registered on an Internet site.

A WIDENING WEB

Small Internet service providers face big competition in Japan

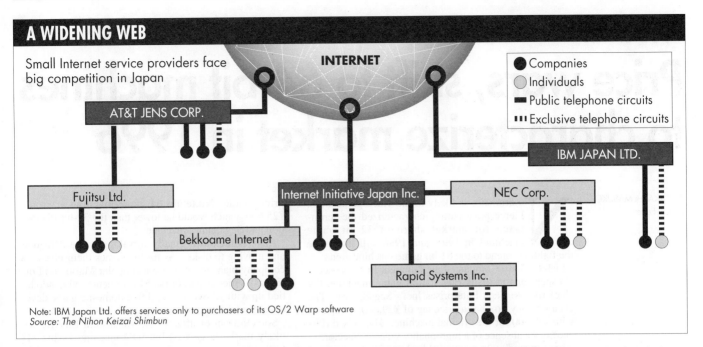

INTERNET

- ● Companies
- ○ Individuals
- ▬ Public telephone circuits
- ⫶⫶⫶ Exclusive telephone circuits

AT&T JENS CORP.

IBM JAPAN LTD.

Fujitsu Ltd.

Internet Initiative Japan Inc.

NEC Corp.

Bekkoame Internet

Rapid Systems Inc.

Note: IBM Japan Ltd. offers services only to purchasers of its OS/2 Warp software
Source: The Nihon Keizai Shimbun

WORLD'S INTERNET SERVERS BY COUNTRY

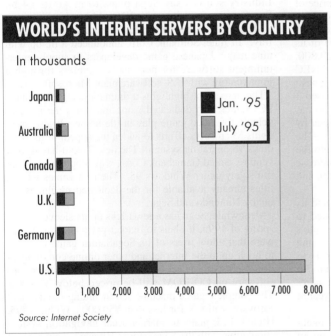

In thousands

- Japan
- Australia
- Canada
- U.K.
- Germany
- U.S.

Legend:
- ■ Jan. '95
- ▨ July '95

0   1,000   2,000   3,000   4,000   5,000   6,000   7,000   8,000

Source: Internet Society

JAPAN'S MAJOR NETWORK PROVIDERS

Fees for Public line connection (¥)

	Registration fee	Monthly basic fee	Additional per-min. charge
IIJ	30,000	2,000	—
NEC	10,000	5,000	20
Tokyo Internet	30,000	19,000	—
IBM Japan	2,000	2,000	6**
Fujitsu	5,000	2,000	20
Bekkoame	10,000	20,000*	—

*Per year   **Per 36 seconds
Source: Companies

WORLD WIDE WEB

Created in 1990, the World Wide Web — commonly called either WWW or simply 'The Web' — refers to the hypertext linkage of information resources, whereas the Internet refers to the physical links making up the global network. Data resources are accessible through the use of software known as net browsers. The Web has become very popular thanks to browsers such as Netscape and Mosaic, which offer online access/display for graphics, sound and digital movies.

DIAL-UP IP

Any circuit which connects computers through telephone lines, commonly through a modem, is called dial-up. Dial-up connections are maintained only as long as the online session lasts. The letters IP stand for Internet Protocol and are specific instructions the computer issues to connect with the server allowing it to be connected directly to the Internet.

VIDEO GAMES

Price wars, shift to 64-bit machines to characterize market in 1996

BY TAKASHI MASUKO
Deputy Editor

Sega has a few tricks up its sleeve...it plans to market peripherals and software that allow users of its machine to hook up to the Internet

No armistice is likely in the video game wars. Fierce price cutting characterized the scrimmage for market share in 32-bit game machines in 1995, and 1996 will likely see the fighting spread to the 64-bit game machine arena.

In July, Sony Computer Entertainment Inc. released a cheaper version of its PlayStation game machine, the chief rival to Sega Enterprises Inc.'s SegaSaturn. The cheaper Sony box has a price tag of ¥29,800, compared with ¥39,800 for the original machine. The only difference is the absence of a high-quality video connector.

Sega immediately responded by lowering the price of its SegaSaturn from ¥44,800 to ¥34,800 and bundling its popular Virtual Fighter game with the machine.

Matsushita Electric Industrial Co. cut the price of its 3DO Real game machine from ¥44,800 to ¥29,800. And Victor Co. of Japan, Sanyo Electric Co., and NEC Corp. also plan to slash prices on their 32-bit machines.

Total sales of 32-bit machines have already passed 3 million, thanks partly to aggressive price cuts. So far, Sony has managed to hold a slight lead over Sega by continually introducing attractive game software. The competition will only intensify further coming into the 1995 Christmas sales season. Sony plans to increase the number of its software titles to more than 200, and Sega plans to offer more than 150.

Nintendo Co. does not have a 32-bit machine and its presence in the video game market has continued to decline. According to Nikkei statistics, Nintendo's share of fiscal 1994 domestic shipments of game machines dropped a sharp 20 percentage points to 55.4%. Sega held second place with 19.1%, up 7.6 points, and Sony stood third with 15.1%. Nintendo's share will likely drop further in the current fiscal year at the expense of sales of rivals' 32-bit machines.

Nintendo's operating profits in fiscal 1995 will likely shrink 22% from a year earlier to ¥91 billion on an expected 6% decline in sales to ¥330 billion. However, pretax profits are projected to increase 27% to ¥124 billion on the back of exchange gains from the dollar's recent rise against the yen.

The company's mainstay 16-bit Super Famicon (the Super Nintendo overseas) is encountering intense competition at home and abroad. Moreover, first-year sales of a 32-bit handheld 3-D game machine called Virtual Boy are expected to total just 500,000 units. The company had an initial sales target of 1.5 million units, but the product has failed to spark demand because of the poor quality of the three-dimensional software.

Nintendo originally planned to release a next-generation 64-bit game machine in the fall of 1995, but later decided to postpone the introduction until the end of the year at the earliest. The company is working to set the price of the Nintendo 64 game machine at around ¥25,000, which would be lower than the 32-bit PlayStation and SegaSaturn machines.

Also, Nintendo is finally forsaking game cartridges and moving to disks. As for the games themselves, the company plans to introduce its popular Mario and Final Fantasy series as part of the 64-bit lineup. Nintendo has tied up with 12 overseas and five domestic game developers for 64-bit game software.

Sometime in or after 1995, Matsushita Electric will likely market a new 64-bit 3DO machine — the M2. Industry sources say Sega plans to make its 64-bit SegaSaturn compatible with 3DO's M2 architecture.

Meanwhile, a newcomer has entered the video game fray. In June, Softbank Corp. announced a tie-up with nine major Japanese game developers to supply entertainment software for personal computers through a joint venture with U.S. software giant Microsoft Corp.

The agreement highlights a dramatic attempt to make PCs rather than dedicated game machines the primary vehicle for video game play in the home. It also spotlights Microsoft's efforts to widen the appeal of its Windows 95 operating system. The new Tokyo-based joint venture, called Gamebank Corp., will supply games that run solely under Windows 95. The first games will be titles already available for the dedicated machines put out by Nintendo and Sega.

Meanwhile, Sega has a few tricks up its sleeve. In the spring of 1996, it plans to market peripherals and software that allow users of its SegaSaturn game machine to hook up to the Internet and other online communications services. A set of modem and communications software on CD-ROM will be priced below ¥15,000. The complete game machine set, including modem and software, will sell for less than ¥50,000. Within 1995, Hitachi Ltd. plans to market a car navigation system compatible with the SegaSaturn. Hitachi's machine will play Sega games as well as video compact disks.

Matsushita Electric has the same idea. It has already built a prototype car navigation system based on the 32-bit 3DO Real game machine, and has started developing a unit based on the 64-bit M2.

As for arcade games, Sega in September tied up with a Hollywood dream team to develop more than 100 amusement theme parks across the U.S. Its partners will be U.S. entertainment giant MCA Inc. and DreamWorks SKG, the company co-founded by Steven Spielberg, former Disney movie chief Jeffrey Katzenberg and music mogul David Geffen. Sega will provide game machines and management know-how, while Spielberg will be responsible for creating main park themes The three parties are also discussing the use of MCA's video technology and its library of movies.

SALES OF MAJOR GAME SOFTWARE HOUSES

In billions of yen

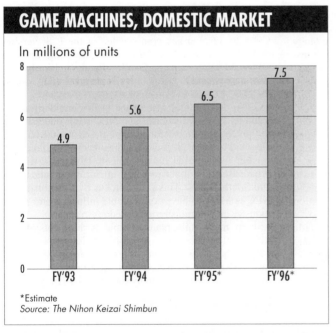

Capcom
Konami
Square
Enix

*Estimate
Source: Companies

SALES OF NINTENDO AND SEGA

In billions of yen

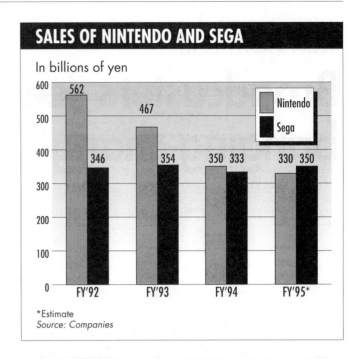

	Nintendo	Sega
FY'92	562	346
FY'93	467	354
FY'94	350	333
FY'95*	330	350

*Estimate
Source: Companies

GAME MACHINES, DOMESTIC MARKET

In millions of units

FY'93	FY'94	FY'95*	FY'96*
4.9	5.6	6.5	7.5

*Estimate
Source: The Nihon Keizai Shimbun

DOMESTIC VIDEO GAME MARKET

Sales scale in fiscal 1993

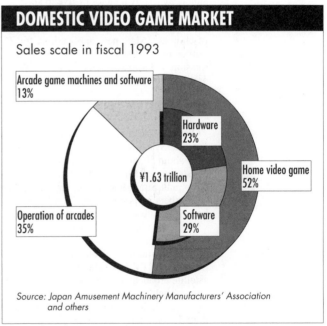

Arcade game machines and software 13%

Hardware 23%

¥1.63 trillion

Home video game 52%

Operation of arcades 35%

Software 29%

Source: Japan Amusement Machinery Manufacturers' Association and others

---

KEY WORD

64-BIT GAME MACHINE

The next-generation of 64-bit video game machines will enable advanced display of three-dimensional graphics, providing high-quality images that come close to the real thing. Thanks to their high-performance 64-bit microprocessors, these machines might also find use in the home as a set-top multimedia platform controlling various on-line services.

KEY WORD

AMUSEMENT THEME PARKS

Amusement theme parks, or location-based entertainment centers, take up just 1,000 to 4,000 sq. meters of space, compared with the tens of hectares required of large theme parks like Disneyland. They operate under specific themes, and feature advanced video arcade games, high-tech interactive attractions, and simulators. In Japan, Sega has succeeded in transforming several conventional arcades into such theme parks.

MEDIA & ADVERTISING

Broadcasters see digital technology bringing change, more competition

Compiled from Nikkei
Publications: NNB

The year 1996 will see the start of digital television broadcasting in Japan. Initiating digital TV will be satellite-based and cable providers, according to proposals from Ministry of Posts and Telecommunications panel in March 1995. That group suggested a shift of all conventional TV broadcasting to digital format early in the next century.

Digital broadcasting allows the transmission of far more data at a given frequency than the analog technology currently in use. Switching from analog to digital broadcasts will expand the possible number of television channels by a factor of five to six.

Once digital TV takes hold, new broadcasting firms will appear and audiences will enjoy a far wider range of choices. Also, new applications for TV technology will come into play, including synchronized data transmission and software-on-demand services for computers and game machines.

50 CHANNELS

One possible pioneer in such business fields is Japan Satellite Systems Inc., which plans to start broadcasting over about 50 channels in April 1996. This company, a consortium of Mitsui & Co., Itochu Corp., Nissho Iwai Corp. and Sumitomo Corp., targets 120,000 household subscribers in its initial year, and hopes to top 1 million household subscribers by the fourth year.

Nippon Television Network Corp., a nationwide broadcaster, is also taking a look at digital broadcasting over the communications satellite of Japan Satellite Systems. NTV has scheduled a trial series of digital satellite broadcasts of its conventional programming.

In the field of cable TV, where competition is increasing as a number of foreign providers move into Japan, digital technology will soon gain momentum. One of the great concerns about digital cable service, which means a major expansion of channel availability, is programming. Having sufficient programs enough to fill the expanded transmission capability will be a serious problem in Japan, which already imports a large amount of programming from the U.S.

The ministry's advisory group, while it set a tentative schedule for shifting to digital broadcast, satellite and cable systems, failed to decide whether or not high-definition TV broadcasting via satellite should be digital or analog. The ministry, jointly with NHK (Japan Broadcasting Corp.), Sony Corp., Matsushita Electric Industrial Co. and others, has developed an analog technology for high-definition satellite broadcasting.

For its part, the publicly funded NHK announced in January 1995 it will continue to promote its analog HDTV technology for the immediate future, while it

studies the long-term potential of digital HDTV.

Regarding the proposed shift to digital technologies for conventional TV broadcasting, Sony is eying joint development of technology with the BBC (British Broadcasting Corp.) and British Telecommunications Plc. The U.K. is scheduled to introduce digital broadcasting in 1997. Japan will start preparation in 1996 to set standards for digital broadcasts, and Sony hopes cooperation with the BBC will help it take the lead role.

TIE-UPS

When it comes to hardware for digital broadcasting, Mitsubishi Electric Corp. has joined forces with AT&T Corp. to develop key components for the U.S. version of high-definition TV. NEC Corp. has come up with advanced microchips to handle digital satellite broadcast signals, and the technology is already taking root in the U.S., Europe and much of Asia.

Given the near-collapse of the analog standard advocated by NHK, Mitsubishi and NEC seem interested in the potential demand for satellite-based digital HDTV. Demand in the U.S. is expected to reach 2 million subscriber households by the end of 1995, and digital broadcasting is about to begin in Europe, Hong Kong and South Korea. This shift in focus by Mitsubishi and NEC is likely to have considerable influence on related industry and administration decisions in Japan.

Sharp, meanwhile, plans to triple its shipments of digital satellite receivers to 3 million devices in fiscal 1995. That decision came in response to growing sales in the U.S. and expected demand growth in Europe. Sharp has a virtual monopoly on the U.S. market.

MULTIMEDIA

In the multimedia area, Nippon Telegraph and Telephone Corp., AT&T and Sony organized a joint venture in September 1995 to deliver multimedia communications services in Japan. The venture was to launch in early 1996 an English-language service providing advanced electronic mail capabilities for personal digital assistants (PDAs), based on software developed by General Magic Inc. of the U.S. Japanese-language service is to begin by the end of 1997.

General Magic is owned by 16 firms, including Mitsubishi Electric, Matsushita Electric Industrial Co. and Fujitsu Ltd., as well as NTT, AT&T and Sony.

Japan's multimedia market swelled 35.1% to ¥1,622.5 billion in 1994. This includes ¥909 billion from sales of hardware, up 69.6% from the preceding year, ¥651.8 billion from software sales, up 4.8%, and ¥61.7 billion from services, up 43.5%.

TOTAL ADVERTISEMENT COST AND GDP

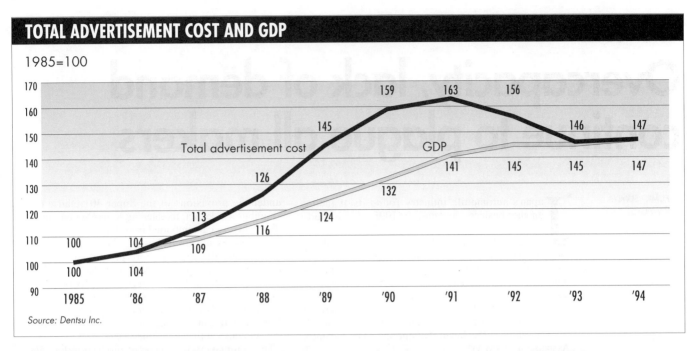

1985=100

Total advertisement cost: 100, 104, 113, 126, 145, 159, 163, 156, 146, 147
GDP: 100, 104, 109, 116, 124, 132, 141, 145, 145, 147

Source: Dentsu Inc.

TOTAL AD COST BETWEEN 1990 AND 1994

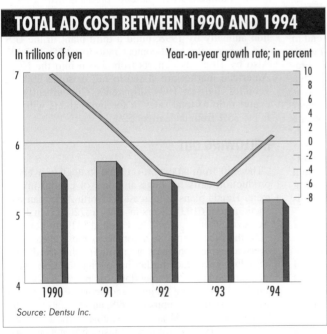

In trillions of yen / Year-on-year growth rate; in percent

Source: Dentsu Inc.

1994 AD-COST GROWTH RATE BY SECTOR

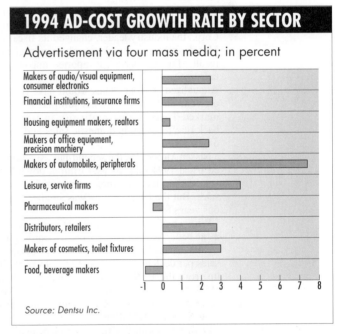

Advertisement via four mass media; in percent

Makers of audio/visual equipment, consumer electronics
Financial institutions, insurance firms
Housing equipment makers, realtors
Makers of office equipment, precision machiery
Makers of automobiles, peripherals
Leisure, service firms
Pharmaceutical makers
Distributors, retailers
Makers of cosmetics, toilet fixtures
Food, beverage makers

Source: Dentsu Inc.

ADVERTISING

Total Japanese advertising billings grew 0.8% in 1994 to ¥5,168.2 billion, according to leading advertising agency Dentsu Inc. The growth was a boon to domestic agencies, which had seen overall billings fall in both 1992 and 1993. For more than four decades, ad billings had expanded consistently except for 1965, which saw a falloff of 1.5%, until 1992 and 1993.

Dentsu attributed the 1994 growth in advertising expenditures to a general economic recovery in Japan, improved corporate earnings, brisk sales of housing and durable goods, falling prices thanks to the strong yen, tighter competition due to deregulation, an income-tax cut and an unusually hot summer.

Advertising through the four mass media — newspapers, magazines, radio and television — increased 2.0%. Growth was sharpest in TV advertising at 3.4%. Newspaper ads, which had decreased for three straight years, saw a 1.1% increase. Among magazines, women's magazines saw ad placements rise 1.6%. But radio advertising fell a sharp 4.0%, a third consecutive losing year.

By industrial sector, auto and auto accessory makers boosted advertising most strongly at 7.4%. They were followed by housing and leisure equipment at 5.6%, service and leisure firms at 4.0%, publishing at 4.0%, cosmetics and toilet fixture makers at 3.0% and distributors and retailers at 2.8%.

By agency, Dentsu increased its market lead, expanding billings 1.5%, followed by Hakuhodo, which achieved growth of 4.4%, and Daiko Advertising Inc., 3.5%. Billings by the top 10 agencies increased 1.3% to ¥2,594.2 billion. That was sharper growth than the overall 0.8% market rise, showing increased dominance by the leading agencies. Ad billings are seen rising some 3% in 1995.

AUTOMOBILES

Overcapacity, lack of demand continue to plague all makers

BY FUMIO SUMIYA
Staff Writer

Japan's automobile industry found itself facing another business downturn in 1995, after a short-lived dream of sales recovery. That follows a three-year slump in sales of new cars amid the longest postwar period of economic sluggishness.

In fiscal 1994, domestic sales of new vehicles, including minicars — with engine displacement of 660cc or less — rose to 6,698,407 units, up 4.8% from the previous year. This marked the first year-on-year increase since 1990, the longest sales slump ever for the industry, according to the Japan Automobile Manufacturers Association (JAMA).

As a result of the upturn in the market, automakers posted a business recovery in fiscal 1994. Toyota Motor Corp., the industry leader, changed its fiscal year end to March from June, and so only reported nine-month results. For that period, it reported unconsolidated pre-tax profits of ¥236.2 billion on sales of ¥6.16 trillion. Annualized, Toyota's sales would have risen 0.8% year on year and pretax profits jumped 47%. This year marked Toyota's first profit rise in five years on the back of a recovery in domestic sales and deep cost cutting.

Nissan Motor Co., the second-largest automaker, posted fiscal 1994 sales of ¥3.4 trillion, down 4.9% from a year earlier, marking three consecutive years of falling sales. But the latest decline was smaller than the previous year's 8%.

With a recovery in new car sales, auto dealers enjoyed a far better year in fiscal 1994. According to a survey by the Japan Automobile Dealers Association, average sales per dealership climbed 12.5% to ¥8.9 billion, well up from the ¥7.9 billion recorded in a dismal fiscal 1993. Sales of new vehicles rose 15.2% to ¥6.3 billion. Revenues from service, including safety inspections, grew 8.6% to ¥1.2 billion.

With cost-cutting efforts in place, dealers' average pretax profits increased to ¥69.4 million, a welcome change from the average ¥1.25 million of pretax losses in fiscal 1993.

BAD PORTENTS

But industry watchers warn that the recovery of sales will not continue for long. Sales of new cars, excluding minicars, in August stood at 296,411 units, up only 0.4% from a year earlier. Ominously sales of subcompact cars, with engine displacements of 2,000cc or less, which account for half of all new car sales, dropped by 12.4%.

In September 1994, Japan and the U.S. failed to reach agreement on cars and car parts in the framework trade talks. As a result, Washington started an investigation

under the provisions of the Super 301 clause of the Omnibus Trade Act, threatening to impose punitive tariffs on luxury cars imported from Japan.

Facing pressure from Washington and the Big Three automakers demanding more procurement of U.S.-made auto parts and the opening of the Japanese auto market, the five leading carmakers — Toyota, Nissan, Mitsubishi, Honda and Mazda — announced voluntary programs to boost production at their transplants in North America at the final moment of Tokyo-Washington auto talks at the end of June 1995.

The automakers will increase production by 25% to 2.65 million units in 1998. Toyota plans to raise its North American output by 365,000 vehicles to 1.1 million annually by 1998, build a third plant in the U.S. and increase the local-content ratio to 62.5% in 2002. Also by 1998, its exports from Japan into the North American market are slated to fall to some 300,000 vehicles, half its 1994 shipments. Concurrently, its export ratio to total sales in foreign markets will also fall to 35% from the current 52%.

HOLLOWING OUT

The shift from an export-oriented strategy to overseas production calls for huge amounts of capital investment. Honda plans to increase its North American production from 610,000 cars in 1994 to 720,000 in 1997. Achieving that target will cost around $310 million.

On the other hand, as automakers press ahead with overseas expansion, fears are mounting that the domestic industry will face further hollowing out. One industry estimate has it that total domestic passenger car production by the five major manufacturers will sink to around 7.48 million units in 1998, an 11% fall from the 8.37 million of 1994 and comparable to the level seen in the early 1970s, before the industry began its massive exports to the U.S. and Europe.

Assuming that exports decrease by 500,000 cars between now and 1998, at least two domestic assembly plants with a total of roughly 4,000 employees will have to be shut down, industry watchers warn.

According to JAMA, Japan's 1995 auto exports are likely to fall more than 10% below the 1994 level of 4.46 million vehicles. That would represent the lowest level of exports in 19 years for the industry. Vehicle exports in July fell a sharp 29.3% year on year to 286,866 units, marking the second largest drop ever and the seventh straight month of decline. Automakers' shift to production in North America will accelerate the tendency of exports to decrease, observers point out.

BREAKDOWN OF JAPANESE CAR MARKET FOR IMPORTS

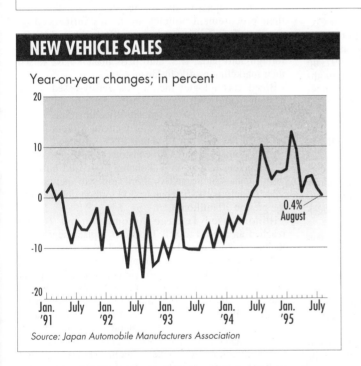

U.S.					U.K.		Germany					France	Italy	Sweden	
GM	Ford	Chrysler	Honda U.S.A	Toyota U.S.A.	Rover	Jaguar	VW Audi	BMW	Mercedes Benz	Porche	Opel	PSA	Fiat	Saab	Volvo

Note: Figures are as of fiscal 1994.
Source: Japan Automobil Importers Association

NEW VEHICLE SALES

Year-on-year changes; in percent

0.4%
August

Source: Japan Automobile Manufacturers Association

AUTO INDUSTRY PRODUCTION

In millions of cars

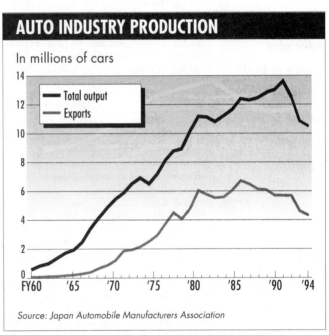

- Total output
- Exports

Source: Japan Automobile Manufacturers Association

KEY WORD

MINI RV

Japan's auto industry refers to a wide range of sport-utility cars as recreational vehicles or RVs; including off-road 4WDs, station wagons, minivans and camping cars. Suzuki sold 17,300 units of its Wagon-R in July alone, up 40% from a year earlier. Mitsubishi's Pajero Mini, radically downsized from its successful big brother, came out in December 1994 and within six months had a waiting list of 40,000. Average monthly sales of mini RVs were expected to hit 29,000 vehicles in 1995.

KEY WORD

ADVANCED SAFETY VEHICLES

Japanese carmakers are working on the development of so-called Advanced Safety Vehicles. Honda's approach is to stress accident prevention through collision-avoidance technology, including radar to help compensate for driver errors in perception and judgment. Nissan started testing ASVs focusing on systems to detect driver dozing and sound an alarm. Carmakers aim to commercialize ASVs early in the 21st century.

AUTO PARTS

Shift to production abroad weakens keiretsu ties among parts makers

BY FUMIO SUMIYA
Staff Writer

Japanese auto parts makers, struggling to cope with declining orders from automakers themselves hit by weak sales, have begun seriously looking abroad for ways to survive the bad times. In 1995 they were active in expanding their overseas manufacturing operations, increasing procurement of foreign-made parts and materials, and sometimes setting up joint ventures with their rivals.

In the move overseas, of course, they are also following the lead of their clients, as Japanese automakers continue to shift production offshore.

Honda Foundry Co., affiliated with Honda Motor Co., decided to set up a new factory in the U.S. to turn out engine parts. Honda intends to increase its output of vehicles in North America to 720,000 units in 1997, up 20% from 1994. Musashi Seimitsu Industry Co., another Honda affiliate, plans to build a continuous production facility for automotive suspension systems in the U.S. in 1996.

Kansei Corp., a Nissan Motor Co. affiliate that makes automotive meters and gauges, decided to establish a joint venture in China to produce indicators and measuring equipment starting in 1996.

Amid expansion of overseas operation, two major parts makers tied up to cooperate in business in China, transcending their keiretsu — interlocking business group — ties.

In May, Aisin Seiki Co., a Toyota affiliate, and Unisia Jecs Corp., a member of the Nissan group, reached an accord to set up a company to make clutches in Nanjing, in order to reduce investment costs and business risk.

Parts makers have also begun to look overseas for parts and materials supplies

Additionally, parts makers have also begun to look overseas for parts and materials supplies. Nissan affiliate Fuji Univance Corp., a transmission maker, procures casting parts worth 1 billion yen a year from South Korea, Indonesia and other Asian countries, aiming to reduce procurement costs by 20%.

Mazda Motor Corp. affiliate U-Shin Ltd., a manufacturer of electrical equipment parts, will purchase foreign materials worth 1.6 billion yen in fiscal 1995, well up from 1 billion yen in the previous year.

Eleven Japanese automakers purchased 19.86 billion dollars of U.S.-made parts in fiscal 1994, according to the Japan Automobile Manufacturers Association (JAMA). Back in January 1992, on the occasion of a visit to Japan by U.S. President George Bush, Japan's automakers said that they would buy 19 billion dollars worth of U.S. parts in fiscal 1994.

While their local parts procurement in North America totalled 16.6 billion dollars, surpassing the 15 billion dollar target, imports to Japan stood at 3.2 billion dollars, falling short of the 4 billion dollar goal.

Toyota Motor purchased 5.69 billion dollars worth of U.S. parts in fiscal 1994, 8% over its initial target. Nissan Motor bought 4.1 billion dollars worth, surpassing its goal of 3.5 billion dollars. Mitsubishi Motors laid out 1.78 billion dollars on U.S. parts, 11% more than its target. Neither Honda nor Mazda reached their targets, however, with Honda purchasing 4.83 billion dollars and Mazda 2 billion dollars.

Japanese automakers explain that they have to increase their purchases of foreign auto parts in order to offset the impact of the strong yen. They deny that their procurement policies are in any influenced by pressures from foreign government and parts makers.

As Japanese automakers began seeking lower-cost foreign auto parts, U.S. auto parts makers have raised their marketing profile in Japan.

Breed Technologies Inc., a New Jersey-based airbag system manufacturer with a 60% share of the world market, opened a Tokyo branch office in spring. Delco Electronics Co., an affiliate of General Motors Corp., set up its Tokyo office in March 1995.

Ford Motor Co. started to construct a parts design and development facility in Yokohama to expand business with Japanese automakers. Ford hopes to increase its sales of auto parts in Japan to 300 million dollars from the present 10 million.

Illinois-based Tenneco Automotive and Toyota reached an accord to sell Tenneco's replacement parts, including shock absorbers, through Toyota's network of 5,000 outlets nationwide, starting October 1995.

Automakers also began to use common parts to cut costs. For instance, Nissan Diesel Motor Co., which uses more than 400,000 parts in truck production, revealed its intention to reduce the number of parts, such as transmissions and accelerators, by 40-70% by 1997, using common parts over a range of models.

Such measures by Japanese automakers are expected to have adverse effects on the domestic auto parts industry.

According to a June survey on the business results of 72 major Japanese auto parts makers by the Japan Auto Parts Industries Association (JAPIA), total sales of the companies surveyed fell to 7.13 trillion yen in fiscal 1994, down 0.1% from the previous year and down 8.1% from fiscal 1991. This was attributed to a decline in domestic automobile production as automakers moved instead to expand their overseas operations.

Net profits at the 72 companies surveyed, however, rose a full 66.1% to 115.8 billion yen in fiscal 1994, supported by tough streamlining and strictly limited capital spending. The association says that the business environment for the auto parts industry will remain poor as long as vehicle production stays sluggish.

IMPORTED CAR MARKET

Backed by the strong yen, at least through early 1995, foreign automakers saw their sales shoot up in Japan. In fiscal 1994, sales of imported vehicles rose to a record 332,952 units, up 53% from the previous year. While the parade of imports was led by Volkswagen AG — VW alone held more than 10% of the import market — and other German car makers, Detroit's Big Three intensified their marketing efforts in Japan.

Chrysler Corp. took over Seibu Motor Sales Co., a Tokyo-based auto dealership, in August. Chrysler plans to spend an estimated 100 million dollars in an attempt to create its own distribution channel in Japan. The company also reached an accord with Osawa & Co., a trading house, under which the U.S. automaker increased its equity stake in Chrysler Japan Sales Ltd., which handles importing.

Chrysler sold 13,625 units in fiscal 1994, up 60% from the previous year, with the Cherokee accounting for the lion's share of that. The automaker hopes to expand annual sales to around 50,000 vehicles in the next few years, and then double that by 1999, with the establishment of its own marketing and pricing policy.

Chrysler's decision indicates the American automaker has decided it cannot wait for Japanese manufacturers to open up their sales channels.

Also, Chrysler is investing approximately $180 million to develop three additional right-hand drive vehicles for Japan and other appropriate markets — the Chrysler Neon, Jeep Cherokee and a new minivan now under development. The U.S. firm will pitch the Neon subcompact on the Japanese market in 1996, and the minivan in 1997.

General Motors plans to establish a new subsidiary in Tokyo in January 1996 to import and wholesale the Saturn to domestic dealers. By the end of 1997, the world's largest automaker hopes to be selling 5,000 Saturns annually through several hundred dealer outlets, and, eventually, 30,000 units a year.

GM has already begun negotiating with Toyota-affiliated dealers, and is also discussing a new dealership network with Mitsui & Co., currently the exclusive importer of GM commercial vehicles. The American automaker does not plan to invest directly in such a network, but will instead contract separately with individual dealers.

The tentatively named Saturn Japan will be the first wholesaler of GM cars in this country. At present, Yanase & Co. holds exclusive import rights to GM models, and its dealerships will play a large role in selling Saturns to Japanese consumers.

While GM saw its sales slip 1.1% to 8,624 units in fiscal 1994, Ford sales jumped 114% to 13,357 units.

Ford Motor Co. (Japan) and Chiba Toyopet Corp., a Toyota group dealer, agreed in September that Chiba Toyopet would market Ford cars at all 50 of its Chiba Prefecture outlets.

The firm plans to remodel dealerships as two-story showrooms, displaying Toyota cars on the ground floor and Ford's Taurus, Mustang and other models upstairs.

Chiba Toyopet started selling Fords in 1994, and will invest some ¥600 milion in the remodeling program. During the January-August period of 1995, it sold a total of 200 Fords.

Setting up a dealership in the Tokyo metropolitan area typically costs about ¥1 billion, including the price of land. The deal between Ford and Chiba Toyopet is seen as the first example of a new idea for expanding sales of foreign cars.

PROCUREMENT OF U.S. AUTO PARTS

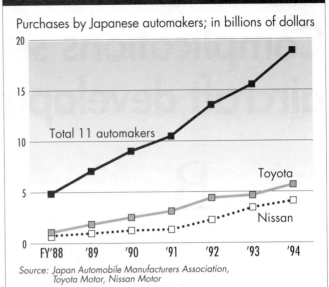

Purchases by Japanese automakers; in billions of dollars

Source: Japan Automobile Manufacturers Association, Toyota Motor, Nissan Motor

AUTOMAKER PURCHASE PLANS FOR U.S. PARTS

Japan automakers' voluntary plans to procure U.S. auto parts; in billions of dollars

	Fiscal Year	Local Procurement	Parts Imports	Total
Toyota Motor Corp.	93	3.51	1.14	4.65
	94	4.35	1.34	5.69
	96*	5.15	1.30	6.45
NIssan Motor Co.	93	3.03	0.42	3.45
	94	3.48	0.62	4.1
	97*	3.40	0.88	4.28
Mitsubishi Motors Corp.	93	0.65	0.27	0.92
	94	1.40	0.38	1.78
	96*	1.40-1.63	0.40	1.80-2.03
Honda Motor Co.	93	—	—	—**
	94	4.45	0.38	4.85
	95*	4.65	—	—
Mazda Motor Corp.	93	1.65	0.16	1.81
	94	1.77	0.25	2.02
	97*	1.90	0.35	2.25

*Voluntary targets   **Not unveiled   Source: Automakers

KEY WORD

ONE ON ONE MEETING

JAMA, in association with the Motor and Equipment Manufacturers Association (MEMA) of the U.S., in 1990 began to hold meetings bringing together Japanese automakers and U.S. parts suppliers. The aim was to promote private deals between the two sides, so as to ease trade conflict between Tokyo and Washington. Five such meetings have been held in the U.S. so far. The most recent, in June 1995, drew some 60 U.S. parts makers.

AEROSPACE & DEFENSE

Complications set back 2 domestic aircraft development projects

BY FUMIO SUMIYA
Staff Writer

Business fell off in the aerospace industry in fiscal 1994, affected by both sluggish economic conditions and a slowing of defense procurements. Production in the industry fell to ¥826.3 billion, down 4.3% from the previous year, said the Society of Japanese Aerospace Companies.

Aerospace has been hurt by the long recession in the airline industry. Export products, including components for foreign aircraft manufacturers, decreased 3% to ¥96.7 billion. Employment at aerospace firms dropped to 27,525 as of the end of fiscal 1994, from 28,674 a year earlier.

Demand from the Defense Agency, which accounts for 70% of total aerospace demand, is not expected to see any major increase, say industry watchers. With budget growth on the decline, Japan's defense industry is pinning its hopes on the FSX, an advanced support fighter. A prototype FSX underwent its first taxiing tests at an Air Self-Defense Force base in September 1995.

In August, the Defense Agency decided to request an initial procurement of 12 FSXs, at a cost of about ¥148 billion. In all, the agency hopes to buy 141 FSXs over the dozen years through 2007, including some for use as training aircraft.

Japan initially budgeted ¥165 billion for development of the FSX, a figure that later swelled to ¥327 billion.

Mitsubishi Heavy Industries Ltd. led the industrial consortium that developed the fighter, in cooperation with Lockheed Corp. whose F-16 jet served as the basic airframe.

U.S. officials unofficially requested that Japan target a fleet of 130 support fighters — American defense contractors shared some 40% of the development work on the plane — but the feeling now in Tokyo is that would be excessive given the steady decline in defense spending here since the end of the Cold War.

The government's initial planning was to deploy 25 FSX fighters in each of three ASDF squadrons. This would result in a total fleet of 120-130 aircraft, including those for reserve and training. Because the international defense situation has so drastically changed during the past six years, however, the defense budget for fiscal 1995 was reduced by 6.5%.

The ASDF currently deploys 170 of its F-15 mainstay fighters, and 74 F-1 support jets. A panel on defense policy advised in the fall of 1994 a reduction of overall aircraft deployments.

The FSX employs state-of-the-art technology, including an active phased-array radar and a co-cured composite wing structure. The radar equipment, developed by Mitsubishi Electric Corp., has already gone into service with the U.S. Air Force and its capabilities are said to have significantly influenced development of the F-22 Stealth fighter.

Joint development on an international basis is a trend in the civil aviation industry as well as in defense, though cooperation there is even more problematical.

The Ministry of International Trade and Industry decided in September 1995 to postpone development of the YSX, an advanced jetliner with seating for 90-100 passengers, though feasibility studies are to continue through March 1997. The original schedule called for joint development of the YSX to begin as early as spring of 1996, with the U.S. and China participating. The aircraft was to go into service shortly after the turn of the century.

Yen appreciation put an end to those plans, however. Though the Japanese currency began to ease back early in the autumn of 1995, it remained about 20% stronger than when the YSX was conceived in 1989. The strong yen pushed development costs to a level far beyond all expectations.

Also, China has a similar project underway in cooperation with South Korea, and was undecided about joining the Japanese project. Domestic industry sources cite difficulty in attracting Chinese interest because China wants to develop larger aircraft. Without a Chinese market, the YSX is viewed as too costly for airlines.

The objective of the YSX program was development of a small airliner under Japanese initiative, targeting a market sector expected to expand in the late 1990s as short-distance flights become more common.

Japan and Boeing Co. signed a letter of understanding in July 1995. But in September, a senior Boeing official said it would be difficult to proceed with the YSX because of questions about the scale of the potential market for a small jetliner and its profitability.

A number of similar projects are underway in Asia, including the China-South Korea program and a development effort in Indonesia. Boeing wants the countries to integrate these into a single plan, fearing so many different projects will leach all profitability from a small-range passenger jet. But the would-be developers are not enthusiastic about joining forces.

Except as a supplier of components to foreign manufacturers, Japan has stayed out of the commercial aircraft business since abandoning the YS-11 in 1972. That small turboprop airliner turned out to be a commercial flop.

Japan's aerospace industry depends on defense orders for 75% of its sales. With the Defense Agency cutting back procurement of fighter planes, success for the YSX is viewed as crucial.

JAPAN'S AIRCRAFT INDUSTRY

Value of output; in billions of yen

	Airplane orders from Defense Agency	Private Aircraft Demand	Reparation for the U.S. Air Force in Japan	Exports	Total
'85	538.5	54.2	3.1	46.7	642.5
'86	516.7	59.9	3.3	42.6	622.5
'87	535.2	77.5	4.4	52.0	669.1
'88	520.9	77.0	2.2	61.3	661.4
'89	556.1	84.6	1.8	88.4	730.9
'90	599.5	90.4	1.7	110.0	801.6
'91	637.5	92.6	1.4	119.3	850.8
'92	638.5	97.3	1.9	120.5	858.2
'93	620.9	116.6	1.7	103.4	842.6
'94	662.4	101.5	1.5	99.6	865.0

Source: Society of Japanese Aerospace Companies

LIFTOFF: HOW ROCKETS COMPARE

Major satellite launch vehicles; weight, payload capacity in metric tons

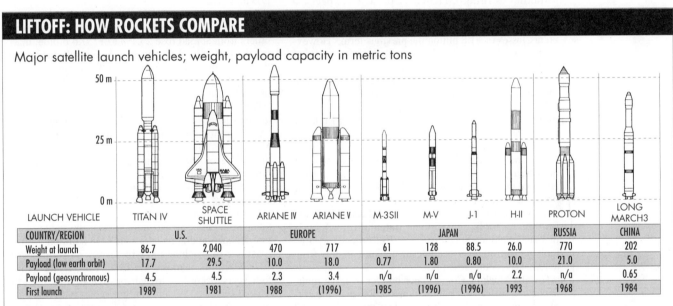

LAUNCH VEHICLE	TITAN IV	SPACE SHUTTLE	ARIANE IV	ARIANE V	M-3SII	M-V	J-1	H-II	PROTON	LONG MARCH3
COUNTRY/REGION	U.S.		EUROPE		JAPAN				RUSSIA	CHINA
Weight at launch	86.7	2,040	470	717	61	128	88.5	26.0	770	202
Payload (low earth orbit)	17.7	29.5	10.0	18.0	0.77	1.80	0.80	10.0	21.0	5.0
Payload (geosynchronous)	4.5	4.5	2.3	3.4	n/a	n/a	n/a	2.2	n/a	0.65
First launch	1989	1981	1988	(1996)	1985	(1996)	(1996)	1993	1968	1984

Note: Dates in parentheses are forecasts

Source: NASDA, Arianespace, Society of Japanese Aerospace Companies

THEATER MISSILE DEFENSE

The U.S. started research into Theater Missile Defense after the Gulf War in 1991. This comprises a regional system for satellite detection of enemy ballistic missiles and interception by medium-range anti-missile missiles. The Defense Agency began research into such systems in March 1995, after Japanese companies including Mitsubishi Heavy Industries Ltd., the leading manufacturer of missiles, started their own research.

H-II ROCKET

Japan's space program experienced a serious setback in 1995. The National Space Development Agency scrubbed the August launch of an H-II rocket due to delays in completing the satellite slated to ride the H-II into orbit. The launch was to be the first step toward commercial use of the H-II, and observers say the postponement to summer 1996 may hurt Japan in the severe competition for a commercial space program.

MACHINE TOOLS

Specialist makers see improvement but others still suffer order draught

BY MASAHIKO
CHONAN
Staff Writer

Barring a further appreciation of the yen, Mori Seiki Co. will likely post ¥3 billion in pretax profits in the business year ending March 1996, according to company president Yukio Mori. If the projection comes true, it would be the first pretax profits in four years for Japan's top maker of numerically controlled lathes and machining centers. Production is now running at 450 units a month, or 30% above the previous year's levels, and Mori Seiki says it can secure a profit even if the Japanese currency strengthens to around ¥80 to the dollar.

Makino Milling Machine Co. also expects a turnaround in fiscal 1995. The leading machine tool maker projects ¥600 million in pretax profits, versus pretax losses of ¥1.8 billion the previous term. However, this would be attained largely through cutbacks of over ¥1 billion in personnel expenses.

Apart from these two firms, no optimism is warranted for Japan's machine tool industry in fiscal 1995. The value of machine tools orders soared 45% year on year in April according to the Japan Machine Tool Builders' Association. But on a month-on-month basis it was the second consecutive monthly decline.

With the economic recovery beginning to show signs of petering out, hurt by the strong yen, worries have emerged that the value of machine tool orders will taper off more toward the end of the year.

On a year-on-year basis, orders have been recovering for smaller tools, replacement demand for which is increasing among smaller users. But orders for large tools remain sluggish as domestic demand, mainly from automakers, continues to lull.

Toshiba Machine Co., a major builder of large tools, expects to suffer ¥3.5 billion in pretax losses in the current business year, though this is less than half the red ink spilled the previous term. Specialist large tool maker OKK Corp. will likely post pretax losses of ¥2.5 billion.

Smaller machine tool builders are also reeling under severe conditions, largely because of their weaker price competitiveness. With some now operating with more debts than assets, industry analysts have begun predicting a shakeout in Japan's machine tool industry.

After three depressing years, the machine tool industry finally had something to smile about in the latter part of 1994. Domestic demand for machine tools remained sluggish as automakers and machinery makers continued to curb their capital spending, but demand from abroad, mainly from the U.S. and Asia, picked up steadily.

Machine tool orders received in 1994 increased 7.8% to ¥573.1 billion, marking the first rise in four years, according to the Japan Machine Tool Builders' Associa-

tion. However, that figure is still only 41% of the all-time high of ¥1,412.1 billion yen posted in 1990.

On a year-on-year basis, monthly orders began gaining momentum after rising in June for the first time in 43 months. The value of orders booked recovered to the ¥50 billion level in September and reached the year's monthly high of ¥58.4 billion in December.

Numerically controlled machine tools accounted for 88.0% of the total value of orders received in 1994, up 3.6 points from 1993. Orders for ¥504.2 billion worth of NC machine tools were booked, up 12.4% from the previous year.

Total machine tool orders received from domestic users fell 2.2% year on year to ¥315.5 billion while orders from abroad rose 23.1% to ¥257.6 billion, marking the first gain in four years. As a result, the proportion of export orders reached 44.9%, continuing to rise steadily from 25.7% in 1991, 33.2% in 1992 and 39.3% in 1993.

The value of production of machine tools declined for the fourth consecutive year in 1994, dropping 6.5% to ¥554.1 billion, according to statistics released by the Ministry of International Trade and Industry. That is only 43% of the all-time high of ¥1,303.4 billion marked in 1990. After June, monthly production moved around ¥40-50 billion. August marked the first year-on-year increase in production in 35 months.

NC machine tools accounted for a record 79.2% of total production, up 1.9 points. But the value of NC tool production dropped 4.3% to ¥438.8 billion.

Exports of machine tools increased 7.4% in 1994 to ¥328.8 billion, marking the first year-on-year gain in four years, according to statistics released by the Ministry of Finance. As a result, the export ratio (the value of exports divided by the total value of production) reached 59%, up 7 points from the previous year. NC machine tools accounted for ¥258.3 billion or 79% of the total value of exports.

By market, exports to the U.S., the largest market, rose 22% to ¥117.9 billion, accounting for 36% of total exports. Exports to the European Union fell 13% to ¥36.2 billion, accounting for 11% of the total.

Exports to Asia fared well, with shipments to South Korea rising 27% to ¥51.01 billion and shipments to Thailand climbing 28% to ¥18.66 billion.

Japan imported ¥25.2 billion worth of machine tools in 1994, almost unchanged from the preceding year, according to the MOF.

Imports from the U.S. rose 11% to ¥12.1 billion, representing 48% of total imports. Imports from Germany fell 9% to ¥3.9 billion, and those from Switzerland decreased 20% to ¥2.7 billion. These three countries accounted for 74% of total imports.

MACHINE TOOL ORDERS

Annual total; in billions of yen

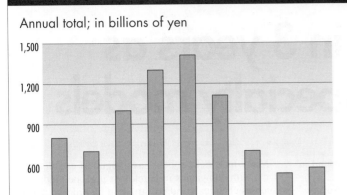

Source: Japan Machine Tool Builders' Association

Orders received by sector in 1994; in millions of yen

Steel & Non-Ferrous Metal
Metal Products
Machinery
Electric machinery
Autos
Shipbuilding
Precision machinery
Other manufacturers
Public sector demand
Others
Trading houses
Exports

Source: Japan Machine Tool Builders' Association

MACHINE TOOL EXPORTS AND EXPORT RATIO

In billions of yen   In percent

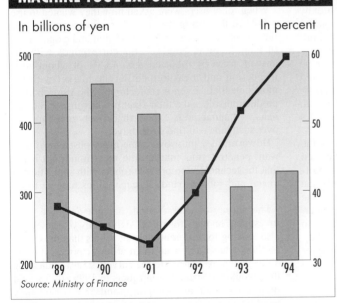

Source: Ministry of Finance

EMPLOYMENT IN MACHINE TOOL INDUSTRY

In thousands of person

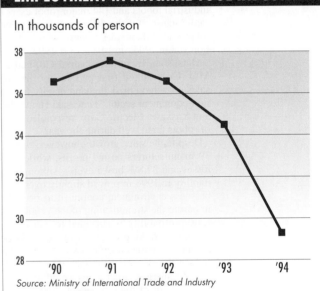

Source: Ministry of International Trade and Industry

KEY WORD

POLLUTION PREVENTION AND SAFETY

Pollution prevention and safety have become major selling points. In the past, Japanese machine tool makers devoted much of their research activity developing ways to enhance efficiency and productivity. But now, in order to fend off increasing competition from rivals in the U.S. and Europe, they have begun to pay more attention to technologies and systems that can help machine tools operate cleaner and safer.

KEY WORD

MAN-MACHINE INTERFACE

Optimizing the man-machine interface is another area where technical breakthroughs are urgently sought by Japanese machine tool makers and their users. The goal of the interface is to enable operators to run machine tools as efficiently as possible.

Other technical themes on the drawing board include super-high speed operations; greater mechanical reliability and dimensional accuracy; cost reductions; new processing know-how; and higher mechanical standards.

INDUSTRIAL ROBOTS

First sales growth in 3 years as demand shifts to specialty models

Compiled from Nikkei
Publications: NNB

The industrial robot market saw a turnaround in sales in 1994 after two years of decline. The Nikkei's "14th Robot Manufacturer Survey" found that manufacturers expect the recovery to continue on demand from the automobile and electronics industries. But another Nikkei survey of major robot users indicated that user needs have clearly changed, shifting from conventional robots used in volume production to lower-priced, more diverse specialty robots for smaller-volume production. It also showed that most users plan to restrict their investment in robots in 1995 to the amount spent in 1994, indicating that the robot industry will continue to face lean times ahead.

Questionnaires were sent to 111 manufacturers of industrial robots and 144 major robot users for return by mid-August. Of the 50 manufacturers that responded, 39 provided their sales figures, which totaled 454.2 billion yen in 1994, up 14.3% over 1993.

Matsushita Electric Industrial Co. and Fuji Machine Mfg. Co., ranked first and second in sales, reported sales growth on brisk demand mainly from the information-equipment sector. Kawasaki Heavy Industries Ltd. and Yaskawa Electric Corp. responded that export sales of robots fared well during the year.

Despite the sales growth, however, only 17.8% of the 39 manufacturers posted profits, while 44.4% suffered losses and 37.8% broke even. Although industry profitability in 1994 improved slightly over 1993 levels, the business environment continued to be unfavorable due in part to the strengthening of the yen against the dollar. Low profitability is expected to cause the industry to continue shrinking — 36.7% of the respondents predicted that many manufacturers would leave the industry or reduce the size of their operations, while 40.6% said industry mergers and tie-ups would increase.

Two-thirds of the respondents forecast either a gradual or strong recovery in demand, while 26% projected flat demand and 8% expected demand to be lower this year. Though 16 robot manufacturers said the automotive sector would lead a demand recovery, 32 thought that the electric machinery and electronic parts sectors would be the driving forces behind a recovery.

Though poor profitability worried 64% of the manufacturers, 46% said the industry is overly dependent on specific sectors, such as cars and electric machinery.

Robot manufacturing is a typical order-based business, susceptible to changes in the financial health of its customers. Manufacturers are apparently worried that an excessive dependence on a few industries could undermine the robot industry as a whole.

Some even say the market has almost matured, pointing to the need to cultivate new demand through technological innovation and promotional efforts.

Many makers of robots have begun to establish contacts with companies in heretofore untapped industries, such as chemicals and construction, in order to develop industry-specific robotic systems. Kawasaki Heavy Industries, for example, says it will close its first deal for such system development in the near future.

Yaskawa Electric has been enjoying brisk sales of robots to the housing industry, a relative laggard in the use of robots. Home building, which is a labor intensive business involving dangerous, strenuous and dirty jobs, is a rich potential market for robot makers.

POTENTIAL DEMAND

When robot users were asked how they wanted to use robots in the future, the most common response was they would use them in the inspection and examination of manufactured goods. This corresponds with the answer given by robot makers, 43.5% of whom cited inspection and measurement as the market with the most potential. Even manufacturers who use robots in production still make their final product inspections by hand. Manufacturers expect that robots made to take over such jobs will find eager buyers.

However, they must overcome many obstacles if they want penetrate this market, the most important being that the technology to provide robots with sophisticated visual and object-handling capabilities has yet to be developed.

The survey of users found that not only are their investment budgets for robots tighter this year, they are also looking for different types of robots than those currently available and want them at lower prices. Of the 43 users that responded to the survey, 25.6% indicating they would cut spending on robots in 1995, 16.3% said they would increase spending, and 58.1% said they would maintain the same level of spending as in 1994.

In answer to a question asking them to cite the factors they thought were important in selecting robots (multiple answers were allowed), 88.6% cited price, 56.8% said they wanted a wider range of robots suitable for use in plants that make various kinds of products in small volumes, and 47.7% said they would choose robots requiring less floor space.

The survey highlighted the shifting demand among users, with 90.9% hoping to buy robots for small-volume, variable production. Less than 10% of the respondents wanted to buy conventional types of robots designed for mass production.

Robot manufacturers are well aware of the current unfavorable market environment, with 53.1% of the manufacturers citing intensifying price competition as a leading negative factor in the industry.

Demand for industrial robots is growing particularly fast at construction sites.

This robot is preparing sushi for sale at a supermarket.

ROBOT INVESTMENT

Fewer
25.6%

More
16.3%

Same Level
58.1%

Source: Nikkei Survey of 43 Industrial Robot Users

ROBOT MANUFACTURERS' SALES

RANK FY94 (FY93)	COMPANY	FY94 SALES (¥ MILLIONS)	GROWTH (%)
1 (1)	Matsushita Electric Industrial Co.	96,100	20.1
2 (2)	Fuji Machine Mfg. Co.	56,588	13.1
3 (3)	Fanuc Ltd.	50,000	5.7
4 (4)	Yaskawa Electric Corp.	37,100	38.9
5 (5)	Kawasaki Heavy Industries Ltd.	18,000	20.0
6 (11)	Mitsubishi Electric Corp.	13,000	8.3
7 (6)	Nachi-Fujikoshi Corp.	11,300	−17.5
8 (10)	Yamaha Motor Co.	9,820	36.3
9 (7)	Daihen Corp.	9,600	−8.5
10 (9)	Star Seiki Co.	9,400	−1.2
11 (7)	Hitachi Ltd.	7,000	−33.3
12 (13)	Fuji Yusoki Kogyo Co.	6,100	10.9
13 (13)	NEC Corp.	6,000	9.9
13 (12)	Kobe Steel Ltd.	6,000	0.0
15 (–)	Yushin Precision Equipment Co.	5,845	11.1

Source: The Nihon Keizai Shimbun

KEY WORD

OFFSHORE PRODUCTION

Robot manufacturers are increasing their use of foreign-made parts and components. Yamaha Motor Co. has been buying CRTs from Taiwan, saving about 35% by doing so, and this includes shipping expenses. Kawasakai Heavy Industries has begun to shift production of welding robots for the U.S. market to the U.S. It also plans to import U.S.-made robots to Japan in the near future.

KEY WORD

OVERSEAS PROCUREMENT

The Nikkei survey found that 9.1% of robot manufacturers are buying parts from overseas and plan to maintain their current overseas procurement level, another 9.1% are buying from overseas and plan to increase such procurement in the future, and 63.6% are not buying overseas but intend to do so in the future.

CHEMICALS

Mergers to reduce excess capacity continue as profits keep leaking away

BY SUMIO KIDO
Deputy Editor

Reorganization of Japan's chemical industry was in full swing in 1995, in particular the integration of specific operations among rival companies. This trend should continue as the industry enters an era of global competition, with giant U.S. and European firms butting heads with Japan and new entries from the emerging economies of Asia.

Nippon Zeon Co., Sumitomo Chemical Co. and Tokuyama Corp. merged their vinyl chloride resin operations in July 1995 with the establishment of Shin Dai-Ichi Vinyl Corp. The new firm has surpassed Shin-Etsu Chemical Co. to become the largest maker of vinyl chloride in Japan, targeting annual sales of ¥40 billion the first year and annual production of 430,000 tons.

Showa Denko KK and Nippon Petrochemicals Co. formed a new synthetic resin firm, Japan Polyolefin Co., in June 1995. The new firm, which started operations in October, has a production capacity of 1 million tons a year and an annual sales target of ¥100 billion.

In July 1994, Showa Denko swapped its polystyrene business for the polypropylene business of Asahi Chemical Industry Co., letting both companies concentrate on making and selling their strongest products.

Mitsui Petrochemical Industries Ltd. and Ube Industries Ltd. integrated their polypropylene businesses as Grand Polymer Co., in July 1995. The firm started operations in October with an annual production capacity of 400,000 tons and yearly sales target of ¥60 billion.

Tosoh Corp., Mitsui Toatsu Chemicals Inc. and Denki Kagaku Kogyo KK agreed in September 1995 to combine their polyvinyl chloride resin businesses. They will set up Japan's largest such business in January 1996 and start operations that April at an annual production capacity of 580,000 tons.

All these moves were undoubtedly stimulated by the megamerger of Mitsubishi Kasei Corp. and Mitsubishi Petrochemical Co. into Mitsubishi Chemical Co. in October 1994. The new company is now the largest firm in the Japanese petrochemical industry with a combined annual production capacity for polyethylene and polypropylene of more than 1 million tons. The firm's president has said, however, that even this level of integration of production and sales is not sufficient, suggesting possible affiliations with other chemical firms.

Why are Japan's chemical firms rushing into such alliances? The petrochemical industry has an aggregate annual production capacity of some 7.4 million tons for ethylene, the fundamental chemical material, and some 10 million tons for general-purpose resins such as polyethylene and vinyl chloride resin. But this production capacity, second only to the U.S., is divided among 11 firms in the ethylene sector and 15 in the vinyl chloride sector as of April 1995.

"Too many firms in Japan are specializing in the same small-scale business sectors, so none of them can compete independently with foreign rivals," an industry analyst says.

In fact, it was oversupply, in addition to the collapse of the bubble economy in the early 1990s, that caused industry earnings to deteriorate. Although losses have recently been declining thanks to higher demand and a price recovery, the domestic synthetic resin business lost ¥100 billion in fiscal 1993.

The chemicals industry overseas has also been turning to mergers and acquisitions over the past few years.

For example, The Royal Dutch Shell Group, an international oil major jointly operated by the U.K. and the Netherlands, combined its resin business with that of Montedison S.p.A of Italy and established a new firm in March 1995. The firm's production capacity for resin totals about 3 million tons a year, an amount equivalent to about 20% of the world's capacity.

Du Pont E.I. de Nemours & Co. of the U.S., the world's largest chemical firm, purchased the nylon business of Imperial Chemical Industries Plc of the U.K. in 1993. Its total sales expanded to $39 billion in 1994, far larger than Mitsubishi Chemical's $10 billion.

As a result of restructuring and achieving economies of scale, production costs at U.S. and European chemical firms have fallen. According to industry analysts, it now costs ¥20 more on average for Japanese chemical firms to produce polyethylene resin worth ¥100 a kiloliter than for their Western counterparts.

Japanese chemical firms are also concerned about the expansion of petrochemical plants in other parts of Asia. In Taiwan, the current annual production capacity for ethylene will be doubled by the end of 1998 to 2.70 million tons. Indonesian and Malaysian chemical firms are also constructing new plants to produce ethylene and other petrochemical products.

Total ethylene production capacity of five of the seven ASEAN countries — Thailand, Malaysia, Singapore, Indonesia and the Philippines — will probably reach 5 million tons a year by the beginning of the 21st century.

The rapid expansion of the chemical industry elsewhere in Asia is attributable to economic growth and the growing transfer of production of cars and electric appliances by western and Japanese manufacturers.

In 1994, Japan exported a record 1.175 million tons of petrochemicals using ethylene as a base. The increase in production capacity in the rest of Asia along with lower production costs there, about 20-40% lower than in Japan, will eventually cause a steep reduction in Japanese exports of petrochemical products. Moreover, Japan will eventually see mounting pressure to open its domestic market to imported petrochemicals.

REORGANIZATION OF PETROCHEMICAL INDUSTRY

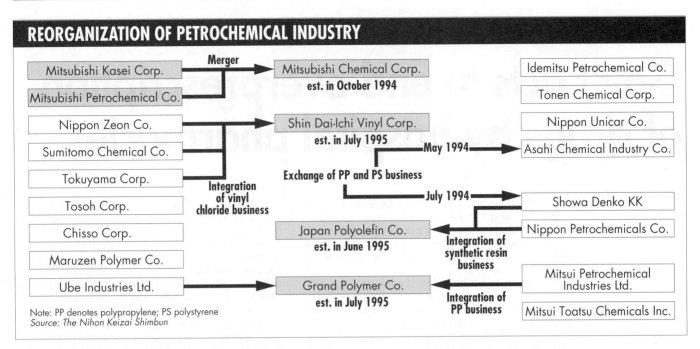

Note: PP denotes polypropylene; PS polystyrene
Source: The Nihon Keizai Shimbun

ETHYLENE PRODUCTION

In millions of tons

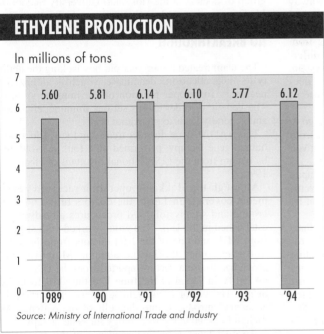

Year	Production
1989	5.60
'90	5.81
'91	6.14
'92	6.10
'93	5.77
'94	6.12

Source: Ministry of International Trade and Industry

PETROCHEMICAL PRODUCTION CAPACITY

In thousands of metric tons; per year

Product	Capacity	Year-on-year change
Ethylene	6,478	0.2%
Low-density polyethylene	2,258	0.0%
High-density polyethylene	1,286	0.7%
Polypropylene	2,581	0.5%
Ethylene oxide	924	4.5%
Styrene monomer	2,976	20.1%
Polystyrene	1,351	-0.4%
Acetaldehyde	424	-0.2%
Acrylonitrile	607	0.0%
Synthetic rubbers	1,040	2.2%

Note: Figures are as of August 1994
Source: Ministry of International Trade and Industry

KEY WORD

GENERAL-PURPOSE RESINS

Synthetic resins widely used for packaging materials, sundries and household goods. The term generally includes five resins: low-density and high-density polyethylene, polypropylene, polystyrene and vinyl chloride resin. These five resins account for about 70% of the total synthetic resin production in Japan.

KEY WORD

JOINT-SALES COMPANIES

Sales companies for petrochemical products established by separating the sales divisions of synthetic resin manufacturers and integrating them under MITI guidance in a bid to prevent excessive competition. These companies are now being dissolved as petrochemical firms prefer complete integration with other firms, including R&D and production as well as sales.

PHARMACEUTICALS & BIOTECHNOLOGY

Gov't acts to end overprescription of drugs by hospital pharmacies

BY NORRI KAGEKI
Staff Writer

Visit any home in Japan and you are likely to find a box full of medicine — some old, some new, and none marked. This is a medication-happy country, and part of the reason is that hospitals and clinics do not only prescribe drugs, they sell them as well.

The Ministry of Health and Welfare is now promoting a policy to encourage hospitals to cut off their drug dispensing divisions and just write prescriptions, which would be filled by outside pharmacies.

The government's aim is to prevent hospitals from over-prescribing medications and wean them away from their reliance on rebates from pharmaceutical companies.

Incidents of sickness and even death resulting from cross-reactions between drugs prescribed by two different hospitals highlight the risks of the current system. When patients bring prescriptions from different doctors to the same pharmacy, there is a better chance of preventing these types of accidents.

At present, only around 17% of patients in Japan go to an outside pharmacy after getting prescriptions from hospital doctors, according to the latest statistics given by the ministry.

There are now 33,000 dispensing pharmacies in Japan doing around ¥1 trillion worth of business. The government predicts the market will expand to ¥3 trillion by the year 2000.

Several large corporations entered the pharmacy market in 1995, giving credence to the government's projection. For example, Mitsui & Co., a major trading company, teamed up with Daiichi Clinical Laboratories Inc., which operates a chain of drug stores. The first store of their joint venture, Ain Medical Systems Inc., opened in central Tokyo in the spring of 1995. The store is one of Japan's largest pharmacies, handling 800 to 1,000 prescriptions daily.

Ain Medical Systems is just one of several companies which have not only begun to dispense drugs in lieu of hospitals, but have also taken on some of the trappings of the family doctor. Pharmacists will visit patients at home and perform such tasks as giving nutrient drip infusions.

PRODUCT LIABILITY

The government took other steps in 1995 to protect the general public from medical hazards. But one indirect step was the July 1 enactment of legislation establishing the concept of product liability. The law entitles consumers to compensation for injury caused by a defective product without having to prove that the manufacturer was negligent.

One of the first effects of the law was to scare away two major manufacturers of silicone used to coat hypodermic needles and reduce pain during injections. Japanese hypodermic needle makers told the silicone manufacturers not to worry about lawsuits because the same material has been in use for 20 years. But ultimately the needle makers were forced to buy the silicone from foreign makers. Experts on product liability law say such cases of Japanese manufacturers retreating from specific markets may increase in the medical field.

A medical milestone was passed in 1995 when a group of doctors at the Hokkaido University School of Medicine performed Japan's first case of gene therapy.

NO BREAKTHROUGH

The team treated a four-year old boy lacking the ability to make adenosine deaminase, which is an enzyme necessary for proper function of the immune system. The genetic disorder causes serious immunodeficiency and generally leads to premature death.

This was the same disorder treated in the world's first human gene therapy, performed on a four year-old girl by a team from the U.S. National Institutes of Health in 1990.

Although the Hokkaido operation received heavy media coverage in Japan, the doctors broke no new ground and simply followed procedures already well-established in the U.S. The group worked with support from NIH, and one of the NIH doctors from the 1990 trial even joined the Japanese team. Moreover, the group had to use a vector imported from the U.S., since no entity in Japan at the time had the skill to make them. The vector is the vehicle by which therapeutic genes are introduced into the cells of the patient. As such, it is the enabling technology for gene therapy.

To give Japan some independence in this important new medical field, the government and seven pharmaceutical companies including Hisamitsu Pharmaceutical Co. and Kyowa Hakko Kogyo Co. jointly established a research and development firm that will independently develop new vectors.

For the time being, however, several other Japanese universities plan to try their hand at gene therapy using vectors imported from the U.S.

MAJOR PHARMACEUTICAL FIRMS' EARNINGS FOR FY94

Growth from previous year in parentheses; in billions of yen

Company	Sales		Pretax Profits		Projection for FY1995 Sales	Pretax Profits
Takeda Chemical Industries, Ltd.	574.367	(2.3%)	78.809	(2.1%)	590.0	80.0
Sankyo Co.	401.466	(1.5%)	83.526	(3.9%)	405.0	85.0
Yamanouchi Pharmaceutical Co.	273.048	(5.1%)	57.990	(6.6%)	280.0	58.5
Fujisawa Pharmaceutical Co.	241.483	(2.8%)	24.009	(20.4%)	222.0	22.0
Shionogi & Co.	238.176	(3.5%)	26.192	(13.7%)	240.0	26.2
Eisai Co.	240.030	(7.0%)	36.982	(12.4%)	247.0	38.0
Daiichi Pharmaceutical Co.	211.819	(2.1%)	41.666	(8.7%)	215.0	40.0
Taisho Pharmaceutical Co.	210.936	(5.3%)	55.602	(7.7%)	218.0	56.0
Tanabe Seiyaku Co.	183.162	(0.2%)	10.515	(27.7%)	175.6	10.5

Source: Each company

R&D SPENDING BY PHARMACEUTICALS MAKERS

In billions of yen

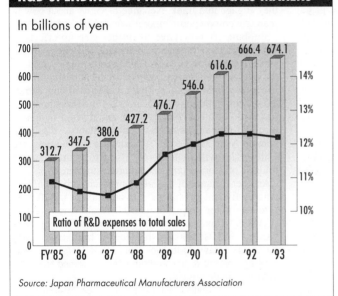

Source: Japan Pharmaceutical Manufacturers Association

GROWTH IN MEDICAL SPENDING

Growth; in percent

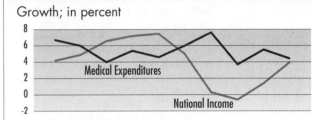

National Medical Expenditures; in trillion yen

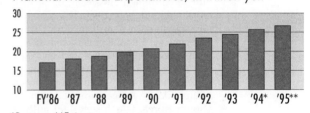

*Prospect **Estimate
Source: The Ministry of Health and Welfare

KEY WORD

PRODUCT LIABILITY LAW

Until 1995, Japan was the only one among the Group of Seven industrialized nations without a product-liability law. The Japanese law models after the European Community version, which is not as strict as the U.S. counterpart. Japanese consumers must prove that damages were suffered, that the product was defective, and that there was a cause-and-effect relationship between the defect and the injury. Since this imposes hurdles on the plaintiff, it will generally work to minimize lawsuits.

KEY WORD

GENE THERAPY

Treatment involving the introduction of genes to compensate for a missing gene or one not functioning properly. Although most gene therapy trials now being designed are to treat specific genetic disorders, the technology may also prove useful against AIDS and cancer. The vectors used to introduce genes are mostly modified viruses that retain the ability to infect human cells, but are incapable of propagating. In the U.S., several bioventures have teamed with universities to produce such vectors.

SHIPBUILDING

Japan yards regain primacy, but fear high yen will erode profits

BY MASAHIKO
CHONAN
Staff Writer

Japan bumped South Korea out of top spot in terms of tonnage of ship orders received in 1994, and in the first five months of 1995 maintained that lead, said an official of the Shipbuilders' Association of Japan. South Korean yards suffered a dramatic fall in their share of the world market as full order books made it difficult for them to hunt new business.

The world's total tonnage of ship orders received during 1994 stood at 26.14 million gross tons (or 1,576 vessels), up 15.4% over the preceding year and marking the second consecutive annual increase, according to figures compiled by the Japan Ship Exporters Association. The uptrend stemmed from growing worldwide demand for new ships, the industry body noted.

Japanese shipyards won orders amounting to 11.94 million gross tons (613 vessels), up a whopping 58.5% year on year, to regain the world's largest share at 45.7%. South Korean yards accounted for 5.73 million gross tons (144 vessels), down 31.1% from a year earlier, as their share of the world market shrank to 21.9% from 36.7%. The U.S. and European countries together accounted for 3.53 million gross tons (373 vessels), down 14.2%, with their combined share declining to 13.5% from the previous year's 18.1%.

Broken down by type of ship, bulk carriers accounted for 11.62 million gross tons, or 44.15% of the world's total ship orders in 1994. This was followed by crude oil carriers, at 7 million gross tons (26.8%), and freighters at 5.8 million gross tons (22.2%).

In terms of tonnage of ships launched, Japan remained on top with 8.6 million gross tons, or 45.4% of the world's total of 18.97 million gross tons, reported the Shipbuilders' Association of Japan. Runner-up was South Korea, which sent 4.09 million gross tons of ships down slipways, followed by the U.S. and European countries which together launched 3.21 gross tons.

The association also reported that the world's order backlog as of the end of 1994 totaled 45.79 million gross tons, up 16.7% over a year earlier. Japan held 14.66 million gross tons, up 27.9% and accounting for 32.0% of the world's total. South Korea followed with 12.24 million gross tons, up 12.2%, while the U.S. and Europe had a combined 8.2 million gross tons, up 3.0%.

Key to the strong postwar growth of Japan's shipbuilding industry is thought to be unstinting efforts to develop new types of ships to meet changing marine transport requirements and determination to improve shipbuilding technology to cut costs. Also contributing was the average 7-8% annual growth in world oil consumption, boosting demand for larger crude carriers.

As an island nation, Japan needed an increasing number of ships to bring in vast quantities of crude oil and raw materials, such as iron ore and coal, as its swift economic expansion boosted demand exponentially.

But the situation has changed in recent years. In the midst of slowing economic growth worldwide, Japan's shipbuilding industry is now being forced to keep its capacity at appropriate levels in order to stabilize the world's ship market. At the same time, the industry is trying hard to maintain as high a profitability as possible by stepping up efforts to improve productivity.

Given these circumstances, shipbuilders are under increasing pressure to promote international cooperation, such as by viewing overall supply-demand from a global viewpoint. Deserving special notice in this regard are the twice-a-year meetings of industry leaders from Japan, South Korea, the U.S. and Europe, where they engage in a frank exchange of views about how to maintain co-prosperity among world shipbuilders.

Shipbuilders now have to further step up efforts to streamline their business operations to cope with the yen's appreciation in early 1995. An example of this is the internal realignment planned by Ishikawajima-Harima Heavy Industries Co. (IHI), which will concentrating all shipbuilding at its Kure yard in Hiroshima Prefecture and its Tokyo No.1 yard, and transfer hydraulic machine production at the Nagoya plant to the Chita plant in Aichi Prefecture. Abandoning shipbuilding, the Chita plant will then devote itself to manufacturing bridges, oil storage tanks and marine structures.

Another instance of this new approach is the joint bidding by five major shipbuilders on an order for 10 midsize container ships for United Arab Shipping Co. (UASC). This was the first time the five major shipyards — IHI, Mitsubishi Heavy Industries Ltd., Kawasaki Heavy Industries Ltd., NKK Corp. and Mitsui Engineering & Shipbuilding Co. — joined forces to bid for a single project.

Japanese shipbuilders have been closely watching the dramatic advance of their South Korean rivals in recent years. About two years ago, Japanese shipbuilders were said to be behind the Koreans on a price competitive basis by 20% or more, but that gap narrowed considerably as Japanese stepped up streamlining efforts. Recently it seemed to have shrunk to around 10%, according to figures from a major Japanese research institute. But it began to widen again in early 1995 due to the postwar highs marked by the yen on foreign exchange markets from March through the summer.

The stronger yen is shaving shipbuilding profits. Particularly hard hit are midsize yards with bottom lines severely damaged by the depressed shipping business and softening ship prices in the wake of the sharpening rivalry with their Korean rivals. Most midsize shipyards appear likely to post either thin pretax profits or even losses in the current fiscal year.

SHIPBUILDING ORDERS

In millions of gross tons

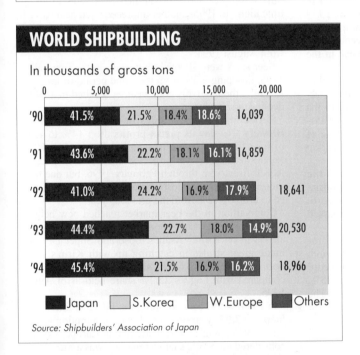

Source: Japan Ship Exporters' Association

WORLD SHIPBUILDING

In thousands of gross tons

Year	Japan	S.Korea	W.Europe	Others	Total
'90	41.5%	21.5%	18.4%	18.6%	16,039
'91	43.6%	22.2%	18.1%	16.1%	16,859
'92	41.0%	24.2%	16.9%	17.9%	18,641
'93	44.4%	22.7%	18.0%	14.9%	20,530
'94	45.4%	21.5%	16.9%	16.2%	18,966

■ Japan □ S.Korea ▨ W.Europe ■ Others

Source: Shipbuilders' Association of Japan

SHIP ORDERS RECEIVED BY TYPE IN 1994

In thousands of gross tons

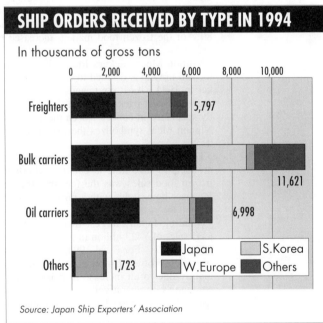

Freighters 5,797
Bulk carriers 11,621
Oil carriers 6,998
Others 1,723

■ Japan □ S.Korea ▨ W.Europe ■ Others

Source: Japan Ship Exporters' Association

KEY WORD

MEGAFLOAT

To utilize marine space, the last usable space remaining on the globe, a super-large floating steel structure called Megafloat is under development by 13 leading ship-builders and four steelmakers, with government support. In April 1995, they organized the Megafloat research consortium to undertake a ¥7.5 billion, three-year project to produce prototypes of floating structures to be used as platforms for waste disposal plants, oil and gas storage tanks, warehouses, airports and power plants.

KEY WORD

ALUMINUM-ALLOY CAR FERRY

The Kawasaki Jet Piercer, a high-speed catamaran car ferry, christened "Hayabusa" in Japanese, is the world's largest car ferry made primarily of aluminum alloy. Built at the Kobe plant of Kawasaki Heavy Industries Ltd., the ferry is now in service between Kyushu and the island of Shikoku in the Inland Sea. It is designed to carry 460 persons and 94 passenger cars and can also handle large trucks and buses. The ferry has attained a maximum cruising speed of 35.5 knots.

FOODSTUFFS

Domestic brewers look to China; Virgin enters local cola wars

BY MAKOTO SATO
Staff Writer

The food processing industry remained in the midst of a structural change, brought on by intense competition. With the abolition of the long tradition of rebates, major frozen food producers, such as Ajinomoto Co. and Nichirei Corp., introduced open-pricing systems in the frozen food market. Although the frozen food market neared maturation, the market for cooked frozen food continued to grow. This segment thus drew some newcomers, which intensified competition among producers.

According to the Japan Frozen Food Association in Tokyo, annual production of frozen food in 1994 reached 1.32 million tons, up 4.4%. In comparison, production of cooked frozen meat, which accounts for 80% of the frozen food market, increased 6.4% in the year.

Nippon Meat Packers Inc., a leading meat packer located in Osaka, decided to enter the frozen food market in 1994. As it commands the largest share in the domestic meat-packing market, Nippon Meat could easily specialize in cooked frozen meat. The challenge of Nippon Meat symbolizes the expansion of the market itself.

The association said more consumers took to the products to save time in cooking. Further supporting frozen food sales was the fact that the percentage of Japanese households with a microwave oven surpassed 86% in the year.

Nichirei, Japan's largest frozen food producer, projects sales of ¥423 billion in fiscal 1995 through March 1996, up 2%. For fiscal 1994, Nichirei marked record operating profits of more than ¥12.3 billion, up 25%, mainly due to an increase in frozen food sales. The company's comparatively low earnings projection for fiscal 1995 is due to a fall in sales of marine products.

COLA, BEER, ETC.

In the beverage market, the cola wars took on a new twist when Coca-Cola (Japan) Co.'s dominance was challenged by Richard Branson's Virgin Cola introduced in July 1995. Branson, founder and chairman of the British Virgin group, hoped to expand his success from the commercial aviation and entertainment fields to the cola market.

Coca-Cola commands a greater-than-90% share of Japan's cola market. Although there are no trade barriers for newcomers, Coca-Cola's deep-rooted hold is very hard to penetrate, most beverage industry experts agree.

Branson managed to obtain shelf space for Virgin Cola in the supermarket outlets of Daiei Inc. and Daiei Convenience Systems Inc.'s Lawson convenience stores. But Virgin Cola has yet to appear in any vending machines as more than half of the machines in Japan are owned by Coca-Cola.

Many market analysts are skeptical about Virgin Cola's potential. "Japanese consumers rarely buy several cans of cola at one time, as the British do. So, having a beverage sold through the vending machine network is very important in Japan," explained Masaaki Yamaguchi, an analyst of Nomura Research Institute.

The scorching summer of 1994 made the Japanese thirsty for beer and sent summer beer sales to an all-time high. In 1995, another unprecedented heat wave in August pushed up beer sales at five Japanese breweries to a record 7.128 million liters in the month, up 5% from August 1994.

Beer sales were sluggish, however, in the first half of 1995, dropping 5.3% from the same period of last year. For July, the relatively cool weather resulted in a 19.8% decline in sales.

Reflecting poor beer sales in most of 1995, Kirin Brewery Co. saw its pretax profits drop 14% to ¥31.1 billion for the six months ended September 1995. Japan's leading brewer projected a 2% gain in sales for its full fiscal year through February 1996, but due to an increase in operating costs, operating profits are expected to drop by 12% from the previous year.

Competition in the beer market reached new heights. Asahi Breweries Ltd., Japan's second largest brewer, closed in on Kirin. Asahi's top brand Super Dry beer made great strides in catching up with Kirin's Lager beer by increasing its domestic market share to 23.1%, compared with Lager's 25.2% share held as of August 1995.

In 1994, world beer consumption hit 123 million kiloliters, up 2.9% year on year. Beer consumption in Asia grew a whopping 11.4%, while that in Europe, which is considered the world's largest market, was a mere 0.2%.

Given these conditions, Kirin decided in April 1995 to establish breweries in China, where the thirst for beer appears unquenchable. Also, Kirin agreed to provide licenses to Chinese breweries for local production and sales of Kirin brand beer. The Chinese were the second biggest beer drinkers in the world in 1994, gulping down more than 14.1 million kiloliters, up 15.1%.

Japanese breweries weren't the only ones setting up production and sales bases in China, however. Breweries of other industrialized countries have already established production bases and sales networks in the country. The battle in China and other Asian beer markets is expected to heat up in 1996.

FOOD SELF-SUFFICIENCY RATE BY ITEM

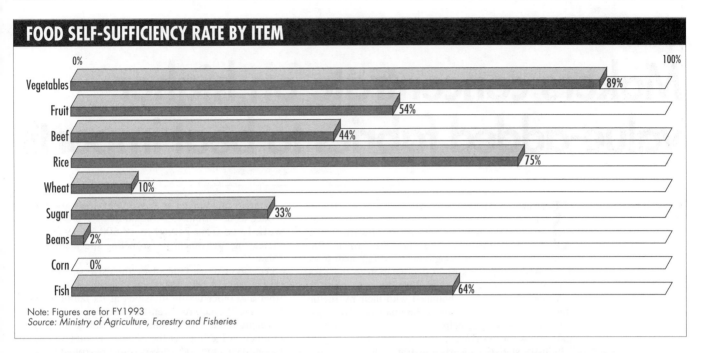

Vegetables 89%
Fruit 54%
Beef 44%
Rice 75%
Wheat 10%
Sugar 33%
Beans 2%
Corn 0%
Fish 64%

Note: Figures are for FY1993
Source: Ministry of Agriculture, Forestry and Fisheries

ANNUAL FROZEN FOOD PRODUCTION

In thousands of tons

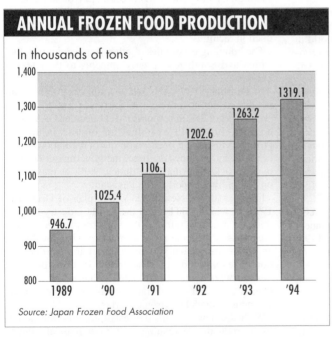

946.7 (1989), 1025.4 ('90), 1106.1 ('91), 1202.6 ('92), 1263.2 ('93), 1319.1 ('94)

Source: Japan Frozen Food Association

BEER PRODUCTION

In thousands of kiloliters

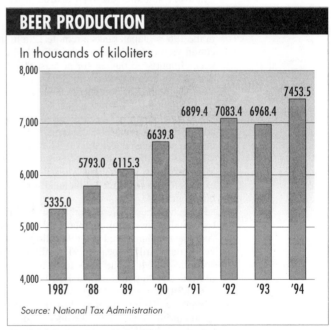

5335.0 (1987), 5793.0 ('88), 6115.3 ('89), 6639.8 ('90), 6899.4 ('91), 7083.4 ('92), 6968.4 ('93), 7453.5 ('94)

Source: National Tax Administration

KEY WORD

PRIVATE-BRAND BEER

Large-scale retailers, such as Daiei and Ito-Yokado Co., rushed to market their own private-brand beverages in the summer of 1995. These products are usually produced overseas, then imported and sold by retailers under their chosen brand names. Retailers can price private-brand beers lower than those supplied by a Japanese brewery. According to JETRO, beer imports totaled 324,000kl in 1994, nearly triple from a year earlier.

KEY WORD

REBATE

Once eliminated, the rebate is now reappearing in talks between frozen food producers and wholesalers in the form of sales promotion money. Previously, food producers set suggested prices and compensated merchants with rebates for any losses incurred from selling products at too-low prices. Many major food producers abolished such rebates. But now, they are providing incentives to wholesalers to promote their specific products by covering promotional costs.

TEXTILES

Makers concentrate on higher value-added fabrics to beat imports

BY SUMIO KIDO
Deputy Editor

Japanese textile producers are drowning in a torrent of cheaper imports. The industry has been battered by the flood of low-cost textiles from other Asian nations since the Plaza Accord of 1985 guided the dollar on its long downward fall against the yen. And the dollar's rapid depreciation to the ¥100 level in 1995 caused Japan's textile industry to weep.

Although companies continued with their restructuring efforts and the Ministry of International Trade and Industry stepped in to help them get back on their feet, the outlook for this domestic sector isn't good.

Industry statistics clearly illustrate a less-than-ideal picture. In 1994, cotton yarn production stood at 240,000 metric tons, less than 50% of the volume seen in the 1960s. Japan ranks a remote 12th in the world in cotton yarn output, and eighth in finished cotton products. Imports accounted for at least 80% of domestic demand for cotton products in 1994.

On synthetic fiber output, Japan was second only to the U.S. until 1989, when it was surpassed by Taiwan. Since then, Japan has been eclipsed by China in 1992 and South Korea in 1994. Japanese synthetic fiber production ranked a poor fifth in 1994 at 1.6 million tons.

The trade deficit in the textile sector has been widening since 1986, when Japan's textile imports outpaced exports for the first time. It hit an all-time high of $13.8 billion in 1994.

Reflecting these severe conditions, the number of cotton spindles owned by members of the Japan Spinners Association plummeted to 4.09 million as of May 1995, nearly one-third the peak of 11.7 million in 1963. And according to MITI, the work force in the Japanese textile industry has dropped to 1.149 million, compared with 1.391 million in 1980.

Every textile producer is thus trying to survive by restructuring operations. Teijin Ltd. decided to farm out all production of a certain type of nylon fiber to U.S. giant E.I du Pont de Nemours & Co. "We saw no chance of future growth in the business," explained Teijin President Hiroshi Itagaki.

Teijin was the first company to drastically streamline production of the three major synthetic fibers — nylon, polyester and acrylic.

A conspicuous case of restructuring in 1995 was that of Kanebo Ltd., the Osaka-based conglomerate that has diversified into cosmetics and food. In response to the yen's surge from early 1995, Kanebo announced in July that it will slash nylon and polyester fiber output by 30%.

The plan outlined a reduction of nylon fiber production at its Hofu plant in Yamaguchi Prefecture, eliminating 200 jobs there, and a cut in polyester fiber output at another plant.

Kanebo announced in November 1994 its plan to reduce its debt from ¥555 billion to ¥475 billion and its work force from 21,960 to 18,600 by 1998, while increasing investment in cosmetics and pharmaceuticals.

Daiwabo Co., an Osaka-based midsize spinning firm, said in August 1995 that it will scale down its synthetic fiber and other textile divisions at its Izumo plant in Shimane Prefecture, eventually stopping cotton and synthetic fabric production. It will shift some 30% of production facilities at the plant to a joint venture in Indonesia, taking 200 workers off its payroll at home.

Among others, Asahi Chemical Industry Co. reduced polyester output and Unitika Ltd. streamlined its production facilities.

The booming economies of other Asian countries, like China and South Korea, gave impetus to their textile exports.

In February 1995, the Japan Spinners Association petitioned the government to introduce import quotas on cotton goods. In response, MITI decided in April to begin a full-scale examination on the issue and promised to reach a decision on quota regulations within the year. At the same time, the government decided in August to levy dumping duties, 9.9% at maximum, on cotton fiber imports from Pakistan.

In line with the New Fiber Vision plan of December 1993, in which MITI urged the textile industry to continue its structural reforms, the ministry pledged to help the industry become more competitive by developing an online transaction system to streamline the distribution of textile products. The project involves developing software to facilitate data exchange on product planning, inventory and transactions. It also envisions setting up a model electronic market.

With the new system, the textile distribution period from production to retailing will be dramatically cut to some 20 weeks from more than 60 weeks at present, and allow a substantial reduction in inventories, the ministry said.

Meanwhile, Japanese textile firms are urged to come up with higher value-added products to compete with foreign products.

"Shape memory" textiles are just one such example. Toyobo Co. first introduced the product as a material for uniforms in 1992, then expanded its application to shirts, blankets and slacks. The company posted sales of ¥2.4 billion from the material in fiscal 1993 and ¥11.2 billion in fiscal 1994.

"Domestic textile firms will survive because the textile market is constantly seeking new fabrics and new applications," asserted Junji Iwamoto, vice president of trading house Itochu Corp.

EXPORTS/IMPORTS OF TEXTILE PRODUCTS

In millions of dollars

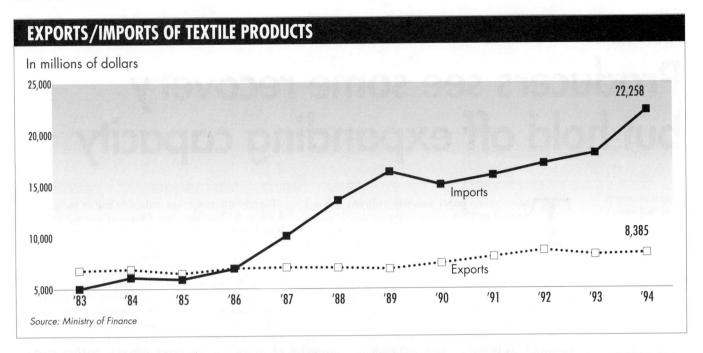

Imports: 22,258
Exports: 8,385

Source: Ministry of Finance

POLYESTER FILAMENT PRODUCTION

In thousands of tons

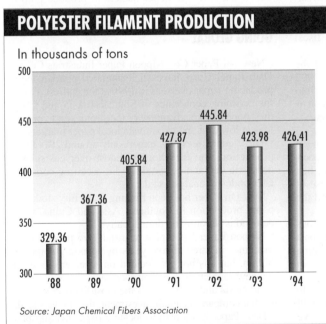

Year	Production
'88	329.36
'89	367.36
'90	405.84
'91	427.87
'92	445.84
'93	423.98
'94	426.41

Source: Japan Chemical Fibers Association

EMPLOYMENT IN TEXTILE INDUSTRY

In millions of persons; as of end of year

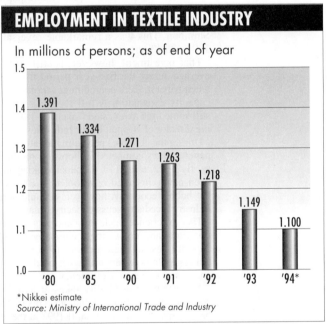

Year	Persons
'80	1.391
'85	1.334
'90	1.271
'91	1.263
'92	1.218
'93	1.149
'94*	1.100

*Nikkei estimate
Source: Ministry of International Trade and Industry

QUICK RESPONSE PROMOTION ASSOCIATION

A body set up in September 1994 by textile firms to better reflect consumer demand on product development by shortening distribution time. It aims to improve the industry's competitiveness with imports by controlling the process from production through retailing via an online network. A similar system adopted in the U.S. in the 1980s has aided the recovery of the industry there. MITI and the group hope to introduce an intra-industry electronic data exchange system for quick response by 2000.

TRANSITIONAL SAFEGUARD

An internationally accepted rule of the World Trade Organization that allows a country to impose an emergency control on textile imports when a surge in shipments threatens the domestic industry. Under the regulation, the growth of textile imports can be reduced by up to 6% from the previous year. Upon the request of Japanese textile producers, MITI is studying whether to implement the ban amid the flood of textile imports from other Asian countries.

PULP & PAPER

Producers see some recovery but hold off expanding capacity

BY JUNICHI UMEDA
Senior Staff Writer

The pulp and paper industry enjoyed revived demand in 1995. Monthly production of paper and paperboard marked a year-on-year gain for 18 consecutive months through July. Output for the year seems certain to hit a record, topping the 1991 figure.

In order to meet such strong demand, Japanese paper makers mapped out aggressive plant and equipment investment programs, after keeping a lid on capital spending since 1992.

The nation's 31 pulp and paper companies planned to earmark ¥234 billion for plant and equipment investment in fiscal 1995, up 50.5% from the preceding year, according to an August survey by The Nihon Keizai Shimbun. This was a remarkable reversal from fiscal 1994's 28.4% drop.

That investment, however, is still only 70% of the average during the five-year period from 1988 to 1992 when paper makers poured huge amounts of money into capacity expansion. A full recovery in investment is still some time away, said Takehiko Takayama, managing director of Nippon Paper Industries Co.

During the "bubble" period in the late 1980s, pulp and paper makers competed in boosting production capacity. By 1992, a total of 42 paper-making machines had been newly installed or retooled. With the collapse of the bubble economy, however, demand shrank and the industry faced an excess-capacity situation.

That experience made pulp and paper makers cautious this time, and not a single company planned to boost capacity. Instead their focus in 1995 was on renovating boilers, pulp digesters and other production facilities in an attempt to improve efficiency.

A paper making facility takes at least two years to come on stream after installation. This means there will be no capacity expansion until 1997 at the earliest. "We have never before seen a situation in which there is no capacity expansion for all of five years," said Takeshiro Miyashita, chairman of the Japan Paper Association.

FIRST-HALF OUTPUT UP 5.9%

Paper and paperboard production in the first half of 1995 totaled 14.8 million metric tons, up 5.9% from a year earlier, according to the industry association. Output in the entire year was estimated to hit a record, far exceeding 1994's 28.4 million tons.

Paper production in the January-June period rose 6.0% to 8.69 million tons. A recovery in newspaper advertisements helped push up newspaper production by 6.4% to 1.56 million tons. Output of printing paper also gained 7.9% to 5.20 million tons. Paper exports rose 18.6% to 287,000 tons.

Paperboard production in the first half of the year rose 5.9% to 6.12 million tons. Output of corrugated paperboard increased 7.1% to 4.51 million tons thanks to brisk demand from food processors. Cardboard output edged up 1.5% to 1.08 million tons.

Production of pulp for paper in the first half increased 7.2% to 5.46 million tons. The rate of increase exceeded the 5.9% for paper and paperboard, only the second time, following 1991, that has happened in the past 20 years. The industry body ascribed the rare occurrence mainly to a surge in pulp prices on world markets, which led domestic paper makers to produce pulp by themselves.

GOING GLOBAL

New Oji Paper Co., Nippon Paper Industries Co. and Daio Paper Corp. have all formulated plans to begin producing paper overseas in 1996 at the earliest. Eyeing the booming economies of Southeast Asia and China, they hope to take advantage of the strong yen to procure logs at low cost and to cultivate local paper markets.

These companies now export only around 2% of their production. But they hope to boost overseas sales as domestic demand is certain to hit a ceiling sooner or later, industry analysts said.

New Oji Paper has been running feasibility studies on paper production in Southeast Asia and China, where demand is shooting up dramatically.

Nippon Paper has a plan to install two paper-making machines in three to five years by spending some ¥80 billion, but has not yet decided on whethere to set up the new capacity in Japan or overseas.

Indonesia and the region is the most likely destination for the company's capital investment, the analysts said.

Daio Paper has a plan to locate a paper-making plant in China. However, details have not been worked out yet.

Paperboard manufacturers took the lead in advancing overseas. Rengo Co., a top paperboard maker, has 13 plants in five countries — China and four ASEAN members. According to a survey by the Ministry of International Trade and Industry, at least 23 Japanese-owned plants in Asia are making corrugated cardboard and other packaging materials. China has seven plants, Taiwan one, Malaysia seven, Thailand four, Indonesia and Singapore three each.

A survey by the U.N. Food and Agriculture Organization shows that the Asian paper and paperboard market has already exceeded the European market for similar products and is expected to top the North American market in 2010.

PAPER AND PAPERBOARD PRODUCTION (DOMESTIC)

In millions of tons

Year	Production
1981	16.98
'82	17.45
'83	18.44
'84	19.34
'85	20.47
'86	21.06
'87	22.53
'88	24.62
'89	26.80
'90	28.09
'91	29.06
'92	28.31
'93	27.76
'94	28.53
'95*	14.81

*Jan.-June
Source: Japan Paper Association

PAPER AND PAPERBOARD PRODUCTION

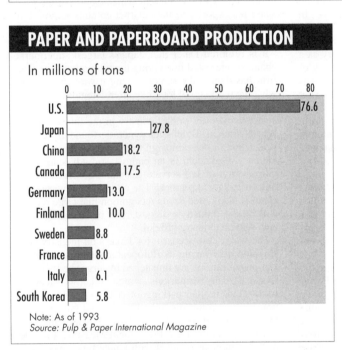

In millions of tons

U.S.	76.6
Japan	27.8
China	18.2
Canada	17.5
Germany	13.0
Finland	10.0
Sweden	8.8
France	8.0
Italy	6.1
South Korea	5.8

Note: As of 1993
Source: Pulp & Paper International Magazine

RECYCLING RATIO OF USED PAPER

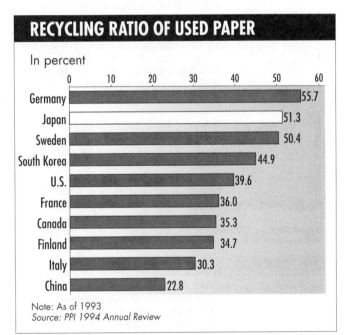

In percent

Germany	55.7
Japan	51.3
Sweden	50.4
South Korea	44.9
U.S.	39.6
France	36.0
Canada	35.3
Finland	34.7
Italy	30.3
China	22.8

Note: As of 1993
Source: PPI 1994 Annual Review

KEY WORD

RECYCLE 55 PROJECT

In an attempt to further utilize used paper, the Japan Paper Association worked out a five-year program in April 1990 to raise the recycle ratio to 55% of total paper consumption by March 1995. However, the industry failed to attain the target, with the ratio standing at an average of 53.3% in 1994. In January 1995, the industry body extended the program and set the target at 56% in the year 2000.

KEY WORD

AFFORESTATION

Japanese paper makers, which are heavily dependent on imported wood chips, are paying a good deal of attention to forest preservation these days, getting involved in afforestation projects overseas. For example, New Oji Paper's afforestation area overseas totals 150,000 hectares, almost equivalent to that in Japan. Such projects regenerate forests that not only absorb large amounts of carbon dioxide, a prime concern given global warming, but also help stabilize chip supplies.

PETROLEUM

Deregulation means oil providers will face harsh market competition

Compiled from Nikkei Publications: NNB

Japanese refiners and distributors of petroleum products face increased competition with the March 1996 expiration of the Provisional Measures Law, which prohibits companies outside the industry from importing gasoline, gas oil or kerosene. Expecting a huge market to emerge with deregulation, many companies in different fields are looking at ways to enter the oil business. The industry itself is being forced to rethink management systems which thrived under the watchful eye of government regulators.

Japanese oil companies believe that South Korean firms will be the biggest exporters of oil products. In fact, all five South Korean oil firms, including Yukong Co. and Hyundai Oil Refinery Co., are rapidly increasing their refining capacities. The Korean industry as a whole is expected to possess annual export capacity of 2 million kiloliters next year. If all that amount was shipped to Japan, South Korea's share of the market would rise to nearly 4%.

Transportation costs are critical to the petroleum industry. Fukuoka, the largest commercial center of western Japan, will form the hub of the trading area of South Korean oil companies when the import barrier disappears in March 1996.

The Hyundai group got a late start in the oil business with the acquisition in June 1993 of a refinery, which was renamed Hyundai Oil Refining. The company was expected to boost its refining capacity to 310,000 barrels a year by the end of 1995, nearly three-fold current capacity of 110,000 barrels.

The petroleum industry is also carefully watching the reaction of trading houses to the demise of the Provisional Measures Law. Leading trading firms have established nationwide networks of service stations through their affiliated sales companies. Itochu Corp., for example, has 2,300 affiliated service stations across the country. Mitsui & Co. has 1,200 stations, while Mitsubishi Corp. has 770 and Marubeni Corp. 670. Service stations affiliated with nine leading trading companies accounted for 10.9% of the total number of service stations across the country, and made up 13.6% of total sales of gasoline in fiscal 1993.

Until March 1996, trading firms are not permitted to market gasoline, gas oil and kerosene under their own brand, even though they have such extensive sales networks nationwide. They were required to procure petroleum products from designated oil companies under the Petroleum Industry Law.

But trading companies must face various challenges before they start importing petroleum products by themselves. The biggest bottleneck lies in distribution.

Petroleum companies have established systems of transporting large quantities of product to dozens of their oil tanks across the country by coastal tanker and freight car to reduce the distance of small-amount delivery by high-cost tank truck to less than 10 kilometers. In contrast, trading houses have only a few distribution bases, so they are unable to supply service stations by tank truck since that would cost just too much.

Whether a stable supply of imports can be secured remains questionable. Itochu Fuel Corp., the largest of all oil sales firms affiliated with trading firms, markets about 1.8 million kiloliters of gasoline a year. That is almost equal to the amount which South Korea could spare for exports. If new market entrants scramble for imports, the prices of imported oil will rise to the level of domestic product, and the price edge of imports lost.

It is rumored Daiei Inc., Japan's largest supermarket chain, is interested in entering the oil market. The Kobe firm has denied the rumor, saying it was just studying what the market will look like after deregulation.

However, oil companies still believe that Daiei will be a serious menace to the industry in the future, because Isao Nakauchi, Daiei's idiosyncratic founder/president, was active in the campaign to deregulate the petroleum industry. Nakauchi is an enthusiastic advocate of the introduction of self-service gas stations, which are forbidden by law at present. The oil industry's wariness of Daiei is also based on its recognition that large retailers will be the industry's biggest rival in the deregulation age, said an industry official.

The worst-case scenario for Japan's oil industry is the situation now facing its European counterpart. Service stations in Europe are threatened by large shopping centers, called hypermarkets, which sell low-priced gas from stands in their parking lots. Hypermarket gas stations now account for fully 40% of total gasoline sales in France and 10% each in the U.K. and Germany.

The expiration of the Provisional Measures Law permits the entry of retailers with ample funds into the oil business and allows large shopping centers to start selling gasoline. "We are aiming to be the first retailer in Japan to import and market gasoline," said Akira Nakano, president of Cowboy Co., which operates a chain of so-called power centers in Hokkaido.

Cowboy's power centers are collections of various types of discount stores, such as grocery and liquor shops, and have parking lots for more than 1,000 cars.

The price of regular gasoline sold by Cowboy will be 100 yen per liter or less, the company said, which is 20 yen lower than the average pump price in Hokkaido. Since South Korean gas can be imported for around 85 yen per liter, setting pump prices at about 100 yen is not impossible, even though the construction costs of oil tanks have to be added, explained an oil industry analyst at Daiwa Institute of Research Ltd.

The typical Japanese service station has six employees, twice as many as its U.S. or European counterpart, while sales volume per station is only half to one-third that of stations abroad.

VALUE OF OIL & OIL PRODUCTS IMPORTS

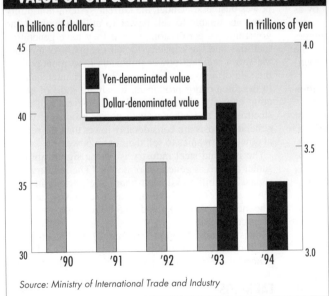

In billions of dollars | In trillions of yen

- Yen-denominated value
- Dollar-denominated value

'90 '91 '92 '93 '94

Source: Ministry of International Trade and Industry

CRUDE OIL IMPORTS

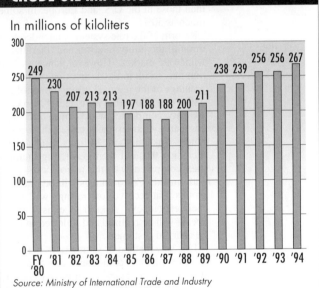

In millions of kiloliters

FY'80 249, '81 230, '82 207, '83 213, '84 213, '85 197, '86 188, '87 188, '88 200, '89 211, '90 238, '91 239, '92 256, '93 256, '94 267

Source: Ministry of International Trade and Industry

KEY WORD

SERVICE STATIONS

In sharp contrast to the situation in Europe and the U.S., the number of service stations in Japan has increased to 60,000 since the 1970s, under the protection of government regulation. But expiration of the Provisional Measures Law is expected to reduce the number of service stations.

KEY WORD

GASOLINE PRICE

The average price of regular gasoline across the country was ¥115 per liter during the April-June period in 1995, down ¥6 from the previous year. The price collapse was most conspicuous in the Tokyo area. Since domestic sales of gasoline are about 50 million kiloliters a year, the income of the entire industry will decrease by ¥300 billion if gas prices hold at around ¥115 through the year.

UTILITIES

New rates system, deregulation of power sales to transform market

Compiled from Nikkei
Publications: NNB

The revised Electricity Enterprises Act, scheduled to come into effect in January 1996, is expected to transform the provision of gas and electricity in Japan, making utilities more efficient and energy less expensive. First, the act will greatly change the way gas and electricity rates are set, by assessing the efficiency of each utility and assigning lower rates to those found to be inefficient. Such a system of punitive assessment will require utility companies to strive for efficiency if they hope to earn profits.

Second, the revised law will allow for the first time non-utility firms to sell power generated at their own facilities to electric utilities, resulting in lower rates for consumers. Japanese electricity rates are much higher than those in the U.S. and Europe, in some cases by as much as 50%.

Reform of the rate system is intended to bring competition to the utility industry and liberalize entry into the wholesale market. However, since excessive competition may result in the destruction of the financial underpinnings of the regional utility monopolies, competition will not be allowed to the extent it is in other industries.

Utility companies will be measured by a system of comparative assessment called the yardstick method. Under this method, utilities total their major costs, including those of their generating facilities, which are then compared with the major costs of other utilities and ranked. Cost rankings will be published, and companies that receive low ratings will have to improve their efficiency. A kind of quasi-competition, so to speak, will be realized and reflected in the rates that can be charged customers.

This new method of setting rates is in stark contrast to the existing rate-setting method (a total cost method), in which costs are assessed on the basis of actual expenses. Under the yardstick method, rates are determined by using uniform costs based on fixed standards, irrespective of actual expenses. As a result, "some companies will be able to achieve cost reductions and will be able to produce profits even while reducing rates, while others will not achieve cost reductions and will have their profits pressured," said an electric utility industry analyst at Daiwa Institute of Research Ltd.

Before the new rate system has even been introduced, Tokyo Electric Power Co., with its planning and technical divisions taking the lead, is planning measures to sharply reduce costs, mainly capital investment-related expenses that account for about 60% of its current expenses. The company plans to trim the managerial staff at its head office by slightly more than 30%, or about 1,000 people, over a three-year period beginning in April 1995 through personnel transfers and other means.

Kansai Electric Power Co. intends to cut capital spending and other expenses by 10% over 10 years.

Of the 10 electric power companies, three major firms — Tokyo, Kansai and Chubu — operate below the industry's average cost per unit of electricity sold, while the other seven operate above the average. When the new rate system is introduced, the difference in rates that can be charged between the three major and the seven regional firms is expected to increase, and the regional utilities will face increasing pressure to reduce costs.

The rising sense of crisis felt by the regional electric utilities is not only due to the new rate system, but also due to the liberalized rules for entering the wholesale power business. Under the current system, non-utility firms are unable to sell power to utilities without the government's permission, even if they have generating facilities and the capacity to sell energy. As a result, the seven regional power producers have monopolized the sale of power (called "specific power interchange") to the three major producers, which are short of generating capacity. The revised law, however, will allow steelmakers and other private power producers whose generating costs are considerably lower than the regional power companies to sell their extra power.

The iron and steel industry is both a significant consumer as well as generator of power. The industry consumed 73.7 billion kilowatt-hours of electricity in fiscal 1993, about 9.2% of the nation's total power demand. The industry also generated 19.5 billion kwh, or 26.5%, of its consumption.

Industry leader Nippon Steel has 10 steel plants located from Hokkaido to Kyushu, and owns a total of 35 generators (975,000kw in total output) at eight of them.

EARNINGS

The business results for electric and gas utilities for the year ended March 1995 were influenced by the unusually hot summer in 1994 and the Kobe earthquake in January 1995.

While Tokyo Electric Power marked a 31% year-on-year rise, Kansai Electric Power, which suffered damage in the earthquake, saw its after-tax profits fall by 40% year on year, posting quake-related extraordinary losses of ¥76.7 billion.

Gas utilities saw weak sales of home-use gas due to the hot summer, and three major suppliers — Tokyo Gas Co., Osaka Gas Co. and Toho Gas Co. — all saw their pretax profits decline. Osaka Gas, whose facilities were also damaged by the quake, posted a 23% drop in pretax profits and suffered net losses of ¥10.5 billion owing to quake-related extraordinary losses.

ENERGY GENERATION

Total power production; in billions of kilowatt-hour

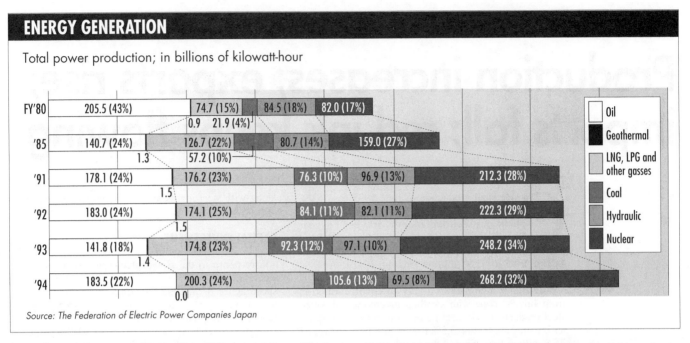

	Oil	Geothermal	LNG, LPG and other gasses	Coal	Hydraulic	Nuclear
FY'80	205.5 (43%)	0.9	21.9 (4%)	74.7 (15%)	84.5 (18%)	82.0 (17%)
'85	140.7 (24%)	1.3	57.2 (10%)	126.7 (22%)	80.7 (14%)	159.0 (27%)
'91	178.1 (24%)	1.5		176.2 (23%)	76.3 (10%)	96.9 (13%)	212.3 (28%)
'92	183.0 (24%)	1.5		174.1 (25%)	84.1 (11%)	82.1 (11%)	222.3 (29%)
'93	141.8 (18%)	1.4		174.8 (23%)	92.3 (12%)	97.1 (10%)	248.2 (34%)
'94	183.5 (22%)	0.0		200.3 (24%)	105.6 (13%)	69.5 (8%)	268.2 (32%)

Source: The Federation of Electric Power Companies Japan

ENERGY SALES OF 9 MAJOR UTILITIES

In billions of kilowatt-hour

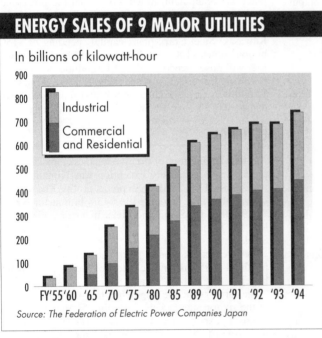

Source: The Federation of Electric Power Companies Japan

CITY GAS SALES

In billions of cubic meters

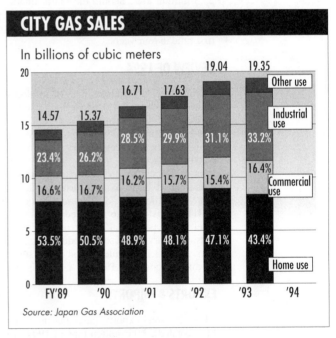

Source: Japan Gas Association

SPECIFIC POWER INTERCHANGE

Specific power interchange, whereby power is supplied at prices based on generating costs and reasonable profit, has until now been a major source of income for the regional utilities. For example, such power accounts for approximately 10% of total sales at the Tohoku, Hokuriku and Shikoku electric power companies.

PRIVATE POWER GENERATORS

Some major heavy machinery manufacturers have installed their own generating facilities since revision of the Electricity Enterprises Act will allow them to sell surplus power to utilities. Hitachi Zosen Corp., for example, has completed a power generation research facility with a 26,000kw generator, made by General Electric Co. of the U.S., and has already begun supplying power to Tokyo Electric Power.

STEEL

Production increases; exports rise; imports fall; red ink keeps flowing

BY MASAHIKO
CHONAN
Staff Writer

Crude steel production in June 1995 rose 6.9% over June 1994 to 8.69 million metric tons, the 11th consecutive month of year-on-year increases, reported the Japan Iron and Steel Federation. June brought total production for the first half of 1995 to 51.98 million tons, up 10.5% over the 1994 first half.

With major steelmakers likely to curb production from July, to cope with swelling inventories of rolled steel products, crude steel production in the third quarter is estimated to drop 3.5% from April-June, to around 25.5 million tons. Should the fourth quarter see output running at the same pace, total crude steel production for 1995 will easily surpass 100 million tons, for the first time in four years.

REVIEW OF 1994

Crude steel production in 1994 totaled 98.3 million metric tons, down 1.4%, according to statistics from the Ministry of International Trade and Industry. That broke down into 67.2 million tons (68%) produced by basic oxygen furnaces and 31 million tons (32%) by electric furnaces.

As of December 1994, Japanese steelmakers were operating 71 basic oxygen furnaces, the same number as a year earlier, and 480 electric furnaces, six more.

MITI statistics also revealed 1994 output of rolled steel products fell 2.4% year on year, to 91.6 million tons. Ordinary rolled steel products totaled 76.6 million tons, down 3.1%, while special rolled steel products hit 15 million tons, up 3.1%.

EXPORTS & IMPORTS

Iron and steel exports, including pig iron and ferroalloys, totaled 23.95 million tons in 1994, up 1.9% for a fourth straight year of advance, the Ministry of Finance reported. While dollar-based export value increased, yen-based value decreased 4.4% due to the yen's appreciation.

Exports of section steels and flat-rolled steels (sheets and plates) dropped overall, while shipments of surface-treated sheets, including galvanized sheets, scored a double-digit gain and exports of pig iron and semifinished steels slightly more than quadrupled.

Exports to the U.S., South Korea and the ASEAN states rose sharply, but shipments to China were down for the first time in four years. Exports to Taiwan marked a double-digit fall.

Iron and steel imports in 1994 totaled 8.99 million tons, down 2.1%. Imports of ordinary rolled steel products, which made up about 60% of the total, declined, along with steel ingots and semis; imports of pig iron, ferroalloys and special rolled steel products increased.

CAPITAL INVESTMENT

In response to the slower-than-expected recovery in steel demand, major steelmakers plan to trim capital spending for fiscal 1995 through March 1996, earmarking a large portion of that spending for restructuring and other measures to increase efficiency.

Nippon Steel Corp. plans to spend ¥120 billion on plant and equipment, down 7.6% from the preceding year. NKK Corp. plans to cut spending 20.4% to around ¥39 billion, its smallest figure since fiscal 1988. Kawasaki Steel Corp. plans capital spending of ¥150 billion , down 11.8%, while Sumitomo Metal Industries Ltd. will raise spending 5% to ¥110 billion. Kobe Steel Ltd. will also raise capital spending, to ¥80 billion, with ¥31 billion earmarked to rebuilt and repair facilities damaged by the Jan. 17 Great Hanshin Earthquake.

EARNINGS

In fiscal 1994, four of the five major steelmakers saw pretax losses. The only exception was Nippon Steel, which posted ¥11.2 billion in pretax profits. The red ink of the other four amounted to ¥43.8 billion for NKK, ¥26.9 billion for Sumitomo Metal Industries, ¥18.8 billion for Kobe Steel and ¥18.2 billion for Kawasaki Steel.

All five majors predict pretax accounts in the black for fiscal 1995, but say the extent of profits will depend largely on the yen-dollar rate.

The earnings picture brightened following the success of the six top steelmakers, including Nisshin Steel Co., in raising export prices to China by 18-20% beginning with August shipments. They accomplished this not through collective but by individual negotiations. Steelmakers are also finally seeing revenue from maturing diversification, mainly into semiconductor-related areas.

The higher prices for shipments to China aimed to correct the price gap between shipments to Southeast Asia and to China. Despite the increases, however, the price gap between China and Southeast Asia will likely remain to some extent, since prices to Southeast Asia were also raised for July-September shipments.

OUTPUT OF ORDINARY ROLLED STEELS & EXPORTS TO CHINA

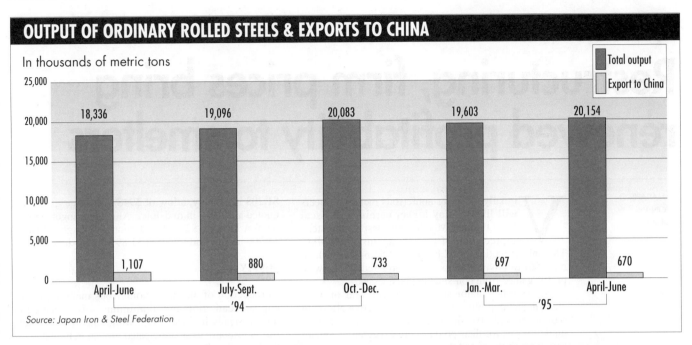

In thousands of metric tons

- Total output
- Export to China

	April-June '94	July-Sept. '94	Oct.-Dec. '94	Jan.-Mar. '95	April-June '95
Total output	18,336	19,096	20,083	19,603	20,154
Export to China	1,107	880	733	697	670

Source: Japan Iron & Steel Federation

ANNUAL CRUDE STEEL PRODUCTION

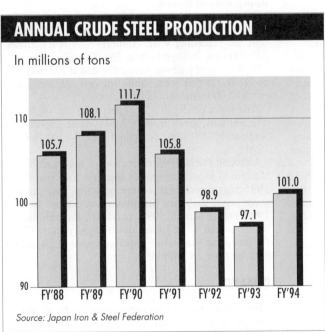

In millions of tons

FY'88	FY'89	FY'90	FY'91	FY'92	FY'93	FY'94
105.7	108.1	111.7	105.8	98.9	97.1	101.0

Source: Japan Iron & Steel Federation

IMPORTS OF STEEL PRODUCTS

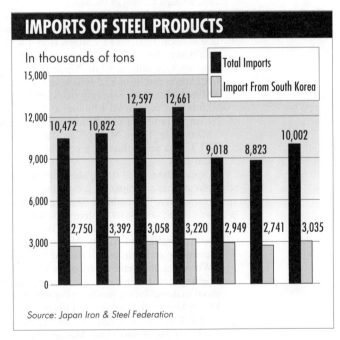

In thousands of tons

- Total Imports
- Import From South Korea

Total Imports	10,472	10,822	12,597	12,661	9,018	8,823	10,002
Import From South Korea	2,750	3,392	3,058	3,220	2,949	2,741	3,035

Source: Japan Iron & Steel Federation

KEY WORD

ELECTRIC-FURNACE PROCESS

Electric-furnace steelmaking has begun to catch on, partly because it dispenses with the upstream, costly blast furnaces and partly because operating costs are lower. But the process consumes large amounts of electric power and steel scrap, whose prices fluctuate. In April 1994, China's Ministry of Metallurgical Industry sent a mission to Japan to inspect highly efficient electric-furnace works, including operations at Nippon Steel's Kimitsu plant.

KEY WORD

SN STEEL

Steel New Structure was adopted as a Japan Industrial Standard designation in June 1994. After the Great Hanshin Earthquake in January 1995, SN steel materials for construction grabbed the spotlight for their greater quake resistance. Though more expensive, SN steels will likely take over the construction market faster than first expected. Currently, the standard covers sections, plates and strips, but will soon extend to pipe and bars, as well.

NONFERROUS METALS

Restructuring, firm prices bring renewed profitability to smelters

BY MASAHIKO
CHONAN
Staff Writer

Virtually all major nonferrous metal producers will likely enjoy higher earnings in fiscal 1995 through March 1996 despite the steep appreciation of the yen against the dollar. The only exception could be Dowa Mining Co., which may fail to cover anticipated yen-related losses with profits gained from non-smelting businesses.

The six other major smelters expect year-on-year gains in pretax profits, thanks in part to active efforts to rationalize and diversify operations, but also because market prices for their products are expected to remain firm through the rest of the year.

Mitsubishi Materials Corp., a major copper smelter, will likely see its pretax profits jump to around ¥6 billion in fiscal 1995, up ¥1.7 billion from fiscal 1994.

Sumitomo Metal Mining Co. is eying profits of ¥5 billion, up ¥3.4 billion, while Nippon Mining & Metals Co. expects profits of ¥3.5 billion yen, up ¥2.7 billion.

Mitsui Mining & Smelting Co. could post profits of ¥2.5 billion yen, up ¥0.4 billion, and Toho Zinc Co. is looking at profits of ¥1.2 billion yen, up ¥0.8 billion.

Meanwhile, Dowa Mining's profits are likely to total ¥2.1 billion yen, which is a drop of ¥0.3 billion from fiscal 1994.

Despite the overall strong showing, the smelting divisions of these companies are taking the brunt of the stronger yen. Mitsubishi Materials, for example, is likely to see sales in its nonferrous smelting division dip 5% year on year. The same divisions at Sumitomo Metal Mining and Mitsui Mining & Smelting are expected to suffer drops of 13% and 17%, respectively.

Worse yet, the yen's appreciation is cutting down on smelting fees, a major source of earnings for nonferrous metal makers. Pretax profits in the smelting division of Mitsui Mining & Smelting will likely plunge to around ¥1.5 billion, which is just 45% of the preceding year's level. At Sumitomo Metal Mining, the smelting division's pretax profits are expected to plummet by some ¥5 billion from the preceding term.

Luckily, the poor performance of these smelting divisions is expected to be more than offset by streamlining measures including payroll cutbacks, and by the diversification into new areas of business, mainly in the electronic components and advanced tool fields.

Another contributing factor this year has been the firm tone of market quotations for nonferrous metals. After hitting bottom in the fall of 1993, metal prices led by copper and aluminum continued rising and hit a high in January 1995. As of July 1995, prices remained strong in a consolidation phase.

The price for copper ingots hit a high of $3,055 per ton in January, dipped to a low of $2,715 in May, and stood at $2,923 in mid-July. Zinc ingots hit a high of $1,208 in January, a low of $948 in February, and was quoted at $1,010 in mid-July. Aluminum ingots moved from a high of $2,149 in January through a low of $1,706 in May and traded at $1,899 in mid-July.

SUPPLY

Production of all major nonferrous metal ingots — copper, lead, zinc and aluminum — is expected to remain steady in fiscal 1995, while imports will likely rise in response to an anticipated growth in both domestic demand and exports.

Output of copper ingots in fiscal 1995 is estimated to reach 1.16 million metric tons, up from 1.10 million tons the preceding year. Imports may reach around 370,000 tons, up slightly from 368,000 tons.

Production of lead ingots is estimated at 232,000 tons, up from 228,581 tons, while imports are forecast to reach 67,000 tons, up a hefty 56,100.

Zinc ingot production is expected to dip slightly to 653,500 tons, down from 673,000, while imports will surge to 95,000 tons, compared with 74,100 in fiscal 1994.

Although fiscal 1995 estimates are not available for aluminum ingots, output in the first four months of 1995 registered double-digit year-on-year growth, according to the Japan Aluminum Association. In fiscal 1994 ended March 1995, production of aluminum ingots totaled 17,627 tons, down slightly from 17,668 the preceding year, while imports jumped to 2.4 million tons, up from 2.1 million.

DEMAND

Estimated demand for copper ingots in fiscal 1995 is 1.64 million metric tons, up from 1.47 million tons the previous year. The total includes domestic demand for 1.545 million tons and exports of 100,000 tons.

Demand for lead ingots will likely total 269,000 tons, down 6,600 tons year on year. The entire amount is for domestic shipments, as no exports are expected.

Demand for zinc ingots is estimated at 750,000 tons, a slight fall of 2,000 tons from the preceding year. The total includes 721,000 tons for domestic shipment and 29,000 tons for export.

Fiscal 1995 demand estimates for aluminum ingots are not available, but in fiscal 1994 demand totaled 2.4 million tons, up 258,000 tons over the preceding year. The total included domestic shipments of 2.4 million tons and exports of 2,467 tons.

IMPORTS OF NONFERROUS ORES IN 1994

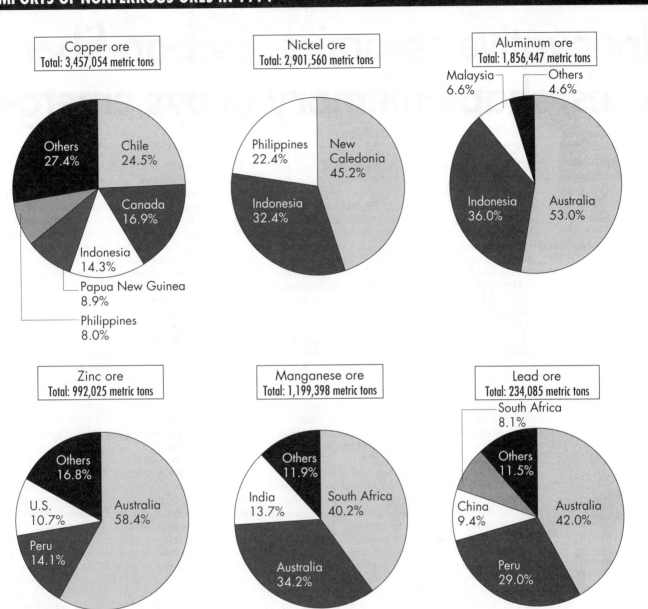

Copper ore
Total: 3,457,054 metric tons

- Others 27.4%
- Chile 24.5%
- Canada 16.9%
- Indonesia 14.3%
- Papua New Guinea 8.9%
- Philippines 8.0%

Nickel ore
Total: 2,901,560 metric tons

- Philippines 22.4%
- New Caledonia 45.2%
- Indonesia 32.4%

Aluminum ore
Total: 1,856,447 metric tons

- Malaysia 6.6%
- Others 4.6%
- Indonesia 36.0%
- Australia 53.0%

Zinc ore
Total: 992,025 metric tons

- Others 16.8%
- U.S. 10.7%
- Peru 14.1%
- Australia 58.4%

Manganese ore
Total: 1,199,398 metric tons

- Others 11.9%
- India 13.7%
- South Africa 40.2%
- Australia 34.2%

Lead ore
Total: 234,085 metric tons

- South Africa 8.1%
- Others 11.5%
- China 9.4%
- Peru 29.0%
- Australia 42.0%

Source: MInistry of International Trade and Industry

NONFERROUS METAL RECYCLING

MITI and major nonferrous metal smelters are preparing for the start of a national recycling program for nonferrous metals in home appliances and cars. Test collection is scheduled to start from the fiscal year beginning April 1996, and full operation will begin by 2000. Participating companies include Mitsubishi Materials and Sumitomo Metal Mining. Currently, only ferrous metals are recycled from scrapped home appliances and motor vehicles.

JAPAN METAL EXCHANGE

The Japan Mining Industry Association, representing about 60 nonferrous smelters and processors, opposed a proposed Japan Metal Exchange, similar to the London Metal Exchange (LME). The association argued the LME works just fine as an international barometer for prices, and that Japan's supply and demand for nonferrous metals is properly reflected on the LME. It also pointed out that different price quotations on a local exchange would cause confusion among smelters.

NEW MATERIALS

Innovative ceramics, carbon-fiber uses, shape-memory alloys emerge

Compiled from Nikkei
Publications: NNB

In fiscal 1995, the Agency of Industrial Science and Technology (AIST) launched a program to develop high-performance ceramics for power plants, aircraft and other applications. High-strength ceramics have promising uses not only as structural materials, but also in technologies that boost reliability, helping to prevent accidents and other troubles.

For example, a ceramic compound capable of withstanding temperatures up to 2,000 C could be used for the exterior surface of supersonic planes. Piezoelectric ceramics and ceramics that change shape when heated or cooled already see use in small electronic components.

In December, 1994, the AIST's Government Industrial Research Institute, Nagoya, announced the development of a silicon nitride ceramic as tough as cast iron. Because silicon nitride has tremendous heat resistance, it is considered a promising material for numerous applications. But the ceramic is normally brittle and tends to break when faced with high loads. Once the Nagoya researchers develop a way to make large pieces of the tough new ceramic, the plan is to use the material for gas turbine blades.

Japanese firms like Toshiba Corp. lead in the development of silicon nitride ceramics and hold many of the key patents. NGK Insulators Ltd. leads in the development of ceramic parts for car engines, while Kyocera Corp. and NHK Spring Co. hold important technologies for various applications, such as heaters and springs.

Another hot area of R&D concerns the so-called "wood ceramics." These new materials, made by impregnating wood with plastic resin and then firing to a hard finish, came out of the effort to develop better charcoal-making technologies, and are basically porous "reinforced charcoal." The Aomori Industrial Research Institute and Yamagata University are investigating possible uses of the material for electromagnetic radiation shields and automotive parts. And the Forestry Agency will soon launch a project aimed at bringing the technology into practical use. Wood ceramics can be made using scrap wood, and once they outlive their usefulness they can be recycled as agricultural soil improvers.

Carbon fibers are as strong as metal, lightweight, and do not rust. Mitsubishi Chemical Corp. took these features and mixed in flame-resistance to create a better carbon fiber-reinforced plastic (CFRP). This new material can be used in place of iron or aluminum for parts in the engine compartment. Carbon fibers are already being used in such familiar objects as golf clubs and fishing rods, but by imparting fire-resistance on the material, the company has opened up many more marketing avenues.

The new CFRP's heat conductivity is higher than iron and equal to aluminum. But unlike aluminum, it will not soften or deform when heated. Also, it is half the weight of aluminum, and four times lighter than iron.

The Japan Railway Rolling Stock Machinery Association has already given CFRP a nonflammable rating, so it will probably not be long before the material starts showing up in rolling stock parts.

Of course, like any material, carbon fibers have their drawbacks, the biggest being price.

Mitsubishi's new carbon fibers cost anywhere from ¥10,000 to ¥350,000 per kilogram, depending on the grade.

This is not much different from conventional CFRPs, but it is around a dozen times more expensive than metals. Because automakers and machinery makers are trying so hard to cut costs, they are unlikely to jump to the new material any time soon.

But one place where carbon fibers are taking root is in lithium-ion batteries, where their good heat, shock and chemical resistance make them an ideal material for the negative electrode.

Carbon-fiber maker Petoca Co. will begin volume production of anode materials at the end of fiscal 1995. The Kashima Oil Co. subsidiary plans to spend ¥1 billion to install production equipment at the parent firm's refinery in Kashima, Ibaraki Prefecture, which would boost its overall capacity to 40 tons per month.

Lightweight and long-lasting, lithium-ion batteries are coming into increasing demand from makers of notebook computers and other portable information terminals. In three years, annual sales could hit ¥2 billion.

Petoca's method, developed with technical help from Toshiba, uses side-products from the oil refinery process as the starting materials. The carbon fiber-based electrodes are cheaper to make than electrodes made from natural graphite or coke, and they release ions better and are more durable.

Shape memory alloys are coming into increasing demand in the medical field. Leading maker Furukawa Electric Co. sold 20% more orthodontic-use wire in fiscal 1994 than in the previous year, thanks mainly to the introduction of a new alloy wire that resists deformation from a strong force. For medical treatment purposes, the new alloys are progressively replacing stainless steel.

During the last several years, growth of the overall market for shape memory alloys has flattened out. But demand for use in cellular phone antennas is another story.

The market, worth some ¥3 billion yen in fiscal 1993, expanded nearly 30% in fiscal 1994 and is expected to grow another 20% or so in fiscal 1995.

PRODUCTION OF MAJOR ENGINEERING PLASTICS

In thousands of tons

Polyamide
Polycarbonate resin
Polyacetal resin

Polyetylene terephthalate resin (PET)
For fibers
For non fibers

Polybutyren terephthalate resin (PBT)

Source: MITI

SALES OF FINE CERAMICS

		1992		1993		1994	
		Volume*	Value**	Volume*	Value**	Volume*	Value**
Functional Materials	IC Package	964	90,961	974	96,812	1,183	125,868
	Condenser Element	73,113	127,241	83,758	132,543	101,152	141,390
	Piezo-electric Element	2,603	64,889	2,896	70,567	3,331	84,873
	Others	7,018	44,236	6,999	45,768	7,913	47,778
Structural Materials	Catalyst Carrier			16,680	15,978	13,066	16,729
	Others			448	6,493	473	6,542

*In millions of units   **In millions of yen
Source: Ministry of International Trade and Industry

KEY WORD

ENGINEERING PLASTICS

Engineering plastics refers to high-performance synthetic resins used to replace metals in machine parts and as building materials. Compared with ordinary plastics, they are highly proof against heat, corrosion and shock, and are therefore more expensive. They are known by such names as polycarbonate, used for compact discs, and polyacetal and polyamide, variations of nylon, used in components for videocassette recorders.

KEY WORD

SWIMSUITS

If you thought new materials were all a staid lot, guess again. The biggest splash in the swimsuit market in 1994 were white swimsuits that remained opaque when wet. That year, Kuraray Co. released a polyester material named Sun Snow, and Toray Industries Inc. offered a nylon material dubbed Body Shell. Both materials feature a layer of fibers mixed with ceramic particles, which prevents the white fabric from turning transparent when wet.

HOUSING/REAL ESTATE

Housing starts slow; cheaper new condos choke market for old units

BY HIDESHI SHIRAE
Deputy Editor

After bottoming out in 1991 at 1.34 million, housing starts continued to increase until 1994 when they totaled 1.56 million. But housing starts in 1995 are estimated at less than 1.5 million, including some 65,000 units built in areas damaged by the Great Hanshin Earthquake.

Even though sales of low-priced condominiums were brisk, the construction of expensive housing such as single-family homes was sluggish in the year.

Housing starts began to taper off from the October-December period of 1994 and started posting year-on-year decreases in March 1995. Housing starts in August 1995 were lower than the year-earlier level for the seventh straight month, totaling 118,726 units, down 15.0% from a year ago.

The decline in housing starts was a reaction to the rapid expansion in demand until 1994. The government-affiliated Housing Loan Corp. was flooded with loan applications in 1994 because a plunge in real estate prices and fall in housing loan interest rates made homes affordable. Moreover, interest rates were projected to start rising soon, along with the expected recovery in business.

As many people who had been waiting for the chance to buy a house did so in 1994, housing demand began to ease in 1995.

Also, the Housing Loan Corp. adopted more rigorous loan conditions from September 1994. While applicants had previously been able to borrow 100% of the money they needed for housing purchases, the corporation set a ceiling of 80% from September. The stricter conditions were introduced because the corporation's funds for 1994 had been exhausted and the number of debtors in arrears started increasing due to the business downturn.

A third reason for the fall in housing demand was a dampening of business sentiment. Concerns about the economic slump heightened. Though business activity was expected to pick up from 1994, there was little change in 1995. As the pace of growth in income was expected to remain slow and deflation became a possibility, people began to think it better to put off housing purchases. When land prices continue falling and commodity prices remain low, it is better to keep cash than to buy real estate, they concluded.

Amid slow housing starts, condo sales remained relatively strong. Of overall housing starts in July, that of condos grew 6.6% from a year earlier, marking the second straight year-on-year surge. In particular, housing developers built many low-cost condos priced around ¥40 million. The average price of a 65-sq.-meter condo in the Tokyo metropolitan area and the three surrounding prefectures plummeted 33% to ¥41.21 million in 1995 from ¥61.23 million in 1990, according to the Real Estate Economic Research Institute.

Sales of previously owned condos slowed down as the gap in their prices with newly built condos contracted. In fact, rental rates for some used condos were higher than those for new condos.

In the past, owners of condos would sell their units and purchase a single-family home. People could sell one home and buy a larger home because real estate prices spiraled up through the late 1980s. Now, however, condo owners cannot command such high prices for their units. As a result, demand for single-family housing has not grown. Latent losses on condos bought since 1988 are estimated to total ¥4 trillion, according to real estate industry statistics. Under these circumstances, demand for home remodeling expanded.

Although housing starts were weak in 1995, public anxiety about the future has eased a little. Housing purchases could get a boost from the Bank of Japan's cut in the official discount rate to an all-time low of 0.5% per annum in September and the government's plan to increase housing investment in its additional pump-priming measures.

On September 8, the Bank of Japan cut its official discount rate by 0.5 of a percentage point to a record low 0.5%. On September 20, the government announced one of its largest economic stimulus plans ever, budgeting ¥14.22 trillion to spur growth. To expand domestic demand, ¥7 trillion was added to the public works budget and policies were adopted to encourage land sales, ease regulatory burdens and help smaller companies.

To spur housing demand, the government expanded the number of units eligible for Housing Loan Corp. mortgages to 660,000, an increase of 30,000 for 1995.

With the late-summer depreciation of the yen the government's latest plan may be encouraging to consumers, but most observers still doubt it will lead to any significant recovery of housing demand. When the government mortgage agency offered its second round of 1995 loans in August and September, there were 3,000 fewer applicants (177,000) than in the second round for 1994 — this despite a record low interest rate of only 3.25%.

One reason lower HLC rates are having little effect is that demand for housing loans is shifting to private lenders. Mortgage rates from city banks have fallen to record lows near 2.3% on the first three years, well below HLC's base rate. The banks are attracting customers who are refinancing higher-interest HLC loans, as well as growing numbers of new applicants. HLC provided 35.6% of the mortgages for housing starts in the April-August period, down substantially from 42.7% for all of 1994. The private banking sector's share of mortgage lending rose to 57.5% from 50.5%.

CONDOS SUPPLY

In thousands of units

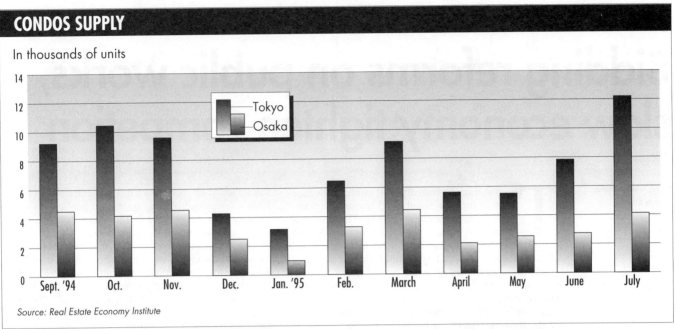

Source: Real Estate Economy Institute

HOUSING STARTS

Year-on-year change; in percent

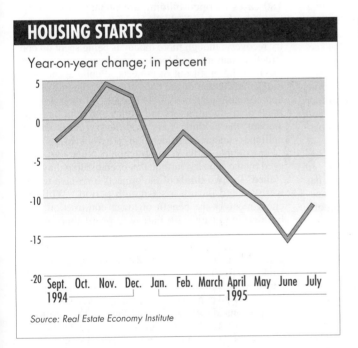

Source: Real Estate Economy Institute

NEW CONDOS

Monthly contract ratio; in percent

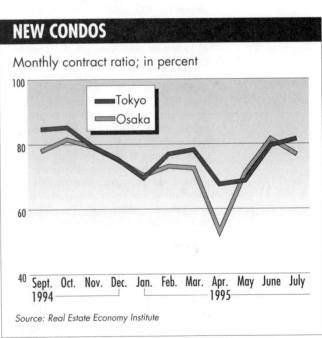

Source: Real Estate Economy Institute

KEY WORD

HOUSING LOAN CORP.

A government-affiliated financial institution established in 1950 to extend housing loans at lower interest rates and for longer terms than those offered by banks and other financial institutions. For funds, the corporation depends on government investments and borrowing from the Trust Fund Bureau. It lowered its interest rate on loans for standard housing with floor space of 125 sq. meters or less to a record low 3.15% in October 1995. This was the sixth rate cut in 1995.

KEY WORD

HOMEOWNER TAX BREAKS

Borrowers of 10-year or longer housing loans at a rate of 3% per annum or higher are eligible for income tax deductions for six years. The ceiling on the deduction is ¥300,000 a year for the first two years and ¥250,000 in and after the third. The deduction does not apply for year(s) when the annual income of buyers exceeds ¥30 million. Also, when people use income from the sale of a home toward the purchase of a more expensive home, the transferred income is exempted from taxation.

CONSTRUCTION

Bidding reforms on public works, slow economy tighten competion

BY HIDESHI SHIRAE
Deputy Editor

The construction industry will continue to face difficult times in fiscal 1995 due to the slowdown in the Japanese economy. The Research Institute of Construction and Economy (RICE) expects new construction in fiscal 1995 to remain virtually unchanged in monetary terms from the previous year, with government spending on public works projects unable to fully offset flagging construction by the private sector.

In addition, industry reforms, including modification of the bidding system for public works projects, will change the management environment.

The good news is that there have been signs that new construction in the private non-housing sector has started to bottom out. Although the investment in that sector showed sharp year-on-year declines of 21.1% in fiscal 1993 and 17.3% in fiscal 1994, it is expected to rise slightly in fiscal 1995 to ¥15.58 trillion, up 0.1% from fiscal 1994. Expectations for the rise, the first in four years, are due to the lack of existing inventory and because recent improvements in corporate business performance will result in the need for new facilities.

The amount of floor space in new construction has been increasing year on year since August 1994. In contrast, the per-square-meter cost of construction has been falling, leading to an overall decrease in the monetary value of construction. This, however, is being offset by the growth in floor space.

The floor space of factory construction is expected to rise 4.7% year on year, reflecting recovery in manufacturing, most notably in the information industry.

The floor space of new store construction is also expected to increase by 0.7%, although the total investment in monetary terms is expected to decline by 1.9% due to the falling costs of construction.

Offices construction is still in an adjustment phase.

Private housing construction, which remained strong through fiscal 1994, has ceased to grow. RICE forecasts that the value of private housing construction will total about ¥19.53 trillion in fiscal 1995, down 2.2% from the previous year. While condominium sales are still growing, the number of new construction starts for houses is expected to decrease this year.

Since private investment is stagnant, public works remain the engine of recovery. RICE estimates government investment in construction in fiscal 1995 to be about ¥31.11 trillion, up 1.4% over fiscal 1994. This alone is not enough to offset the decline in private spending, but additional public investment will be added by the second supplementary budget, giving the industry another boost.

The construction industry cannot afford to celebrate the end of the slowdown in public spending because it has to adjust to two major industry reforms: a change from a designated bidding system for public works projects to open competitive bidding, and a change in the system of guaranteeing the performance.

Open competitive bidding was tentatively introduced by some prefectures two years ago, though it was not introduced at the national level until June 1994 by public corporations directly controlled by, or affiliated with, the Ministry of Construction. In fiscal 1994, open bidding was carried out for 112 construction projects, each budgeted at ¥730 million or more. In fiscal 1995, 180 cases of open bidding are planned for projects under the direct control of the ministry.

The new system is proving to be an obstacle to industry recovery; though more money is being spent on construction, national and local governments are squeezing much of the profit out of projects. Public agencies try to take advantage of the competition in the industry by appropriating extremely tight budgets for their projects. If all of the contractors bid higher than the budgeted amount, the bidding "fails" and the project is shelved until the monetary considerations are resolved.

For example, in the reconstruction of Kobe Port, damaged by the January earthquake, open bidding may have "failed" for two-thirds of the projects for which tenders were invited during a six-month period. While the client receives the benefit of lower construction costs, builders wind up with narrower profit margins and weaker business results at the end of the year.

Until now, an industry-based system has been used to guarantee completion of public works once awarded. Under this system, a guarantor promised to complete a construction project itself if the winner of the contract was unable to complete it, for example due to bankruptcy or technical difficulties. But this has been criticized as a fertile breeding ground for *dango*, collusive bidding, as well as constituting a barrier to newcomers. Accordingly, a "performance bond system," whereby companies, such as nonlife insurers, stand as third-party guarantors for the completion of construction, was adopted as of October 1995, though only for projects under the direct control of the Ministry of Construction.

For the year through March 1996, Nishimatsu Construction Co., a midsize general contractor, is expected to be the industry's pretax-profits leader at ¥32.5 billion, topping the five largest contractors: Kajima Corp., Taisei Corp., Shimizu Corp., Obayashi Corp. and Takenaka Corp. Nishimatsu did not invest in real estate during the "bubble" economy, instead focusing on its primary business. While the decline of the major firms may be temporary, the reforms to be implemented at both central and local levels from January 1996 have the potential to change the balance of power in the industry.

COMBINED PRETAX PROFITS OF CONSTRUCTION COMPANIES

In billions of yen

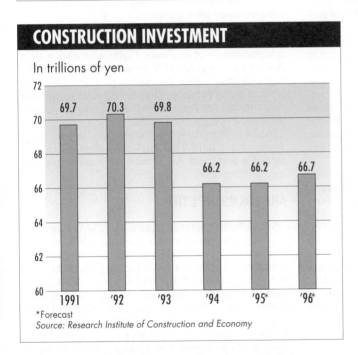

- 34 Smaller Firms
- Five Largest

FY1985 FY'86 FY'87 FY'88 FY'89 FY'90 FY'91 FY'92 FY'93 FY'94

Source: Company Reports

CONSTRUCTION INVESTMENT

In trillions of yen

1991	69.7
'92	70.3
'93	69.8
'94	66.2
'95*	66.2
'96*	66.7

*Forecast
Source: Research Institute of Construction and Economy

PERFORMANCE OF KEY CONSTRUCTORS

In billions of yen

		Sales	Pretax Profits
Kajima	FY'94	1,795	64.3
	FY'95*	1,350	20.0
Taisei	FY'94	1,557	34.9
	FY'95*	1,500	25.0
Obayashi	FY'94	1,445	39.1
	FY'95*	1,200	29.0
Shimizu	FY'94	1,860	36.5
	FY'95*	1,550	25.0
Nishimatsu	FY'94	623	31.5
	FY'95*	670	32.5

*Forecast
Source: Companies

KEY WORD

PERFORMANCE BOND SYSTEM

A system under which a guarantor, such as a nonlife insurance company, insures that a public works contract will be completed as awarded within a fixed period of time. A guarantor charges a fee for issuing such a bond, but if a firm defaults on a contract, the guarantor is responsible for fulfilling it by completing the work. Construction firms that are unable to buy a performance bond cannot be awarded a public works contract.

KEY WORD

DANGO (COLLUSIVE BIDDING)

An act by which construction firms conspire to subvert the bidding process on public works contracts. Firms bidding on contracts agree beforehand on which company will win which tender by arranging their bids on each project accordingly. Because bids exceeding the contract budget are invariably rejected, the awarder suffers no financial damage. Therefore, though such acts violate the anti-monopoly law, they have rarely been deemed criminal offenses.

AIRLINES

Recovery in domestic travel offsets lost int'l earnings from high yen

BY MAKOTO SATO
Staff Writer

Most Japanese airline operators got a bit of a break in fiscal 1994. Japan Airlines Co. (JAL) managed to end in the black for the first time in four years, posting ¥2.8 billion in pretax profits for the year ended March 31, 1995. But All Nippon Airways Co. (ANA) saw its pretax profits fall, while Japan Air System Co. (JAS) kept its pretax losses to ¥3 billion, compared with losses of ¥12.6 billion the previous year. All three airline companies are expected to do better in fiscal 1995.

A recovery in the number of airline passengers was a boon for JAL. The company's overall number of passengers reached 26.5 million in the year, up 9.9%.

Long stagnant demand for domestic flights recovered with the opening of the Kansai International Airport in September 1994. During the summer of 1995, the number of passengers on domestic flights of six Japanese airline operators increased by 7.3%.

But Japanese carriers continued to rely heavily on international flights, with such flights accounting for 70% of JAL's earnings. JAL's number of passengers for international flights gained 10.7% as the stronger yen prompted more people to head overseas.

At the same time, however, the strong yen increased the cost of international flights for Japanese airliners, particularly in comparison with American air carriers, because flight costs are calculated in dollar terms. The yen's appreciation from 100 per dollar to 80 pushed up the competitiveness of American airline operators by 20%.

In general, if several airline companies fly to the same destination, travelers will opt for the lower-priced ticket. And JAL and ANA both lost some customers to lower-priced foreign airline operators. To survive this competition, Japanese carriers must restructure their operations further to be able to provide cost-competitive flight services.

Cost cutting was one of the keys to the earnings recovery at JAL. The centerpiece of JAL's cost-cutting plan is to reduce its work force to 17,000 by fiscal 1997. The company trimmed its payroll by about 1,500 employees to 20,679 during the two years through March 1995.

JAL's personnel cost for transporting one ton of passenger/cargo a distance of one kilometer now stands at ¥17. It is trying to reduce the figure to less than ¥16.

While the number of passengers started recovering, unit fare revenues began declining because more travelers decided to fly economy class rather than first or business class. This trend was particularly notable for international flights.

Heightened competition accelerated Japanese air carriers' moves to reinforce cooperative ties with foreign companies in the field of reservation networks and mileage programs for frequent flyers. These alliances are expected to widen in 1996.

JAL and American Airlines Inc. agreed in August 1995 to link their computerized reservation systems (CRS). Under the accord, JAL obtained exclusive access to AA's CRS network called "Sabre," which is the most extensive reservation network in the world with over 114,000 terminals. Sabre will be connected to JAL's CRS network called "Axess," which with its 12,000 terminals controls more than half Japan's air transport reservation market.

Through the connection, which was the first between a Japanese and U.S. carrier, JAL hopes to increase the competitiveness of its Pacific flights on the strength of AA's wide-coverage U.S. domestic flight network. Japan's leading carrier also aims to provide value-added services for its passengers by offering AA's information on car rentals and hotels as well as ticketing services for theater and opera performances.

JAL also strengthened its code-sharing, or joint flight, arrangement with Thai Airways International and signed a pact with Air France for a partnership on mileage programs.

ANA FORMS INT'L TIES

Not to be left behind, Japan's No. 2 airline operator also expanded its cooperative arrangements with foreign airlines. ANA linked its frequent flyer program with those of Delta Air Lines Inc. and USAir, bringing the total number of flights for which ANA offers mileage points to 9,300 flights per day, up from 1,800 flights. ANA already had similar arrangements with several other major airlines, including British Airways Plc. and Cathay Pacific Airways Ltd. On code sharing, ANA inked a contract with Delta Air Lines in August 1995 to jointly operate trans-Pacific flights.

These developments in the airline industry suggest competition among international carriers has reached new dimensions. Individual airliner operators are no longer competing with each other; the battle for market share is now taking place between alliances of carriers of different countries. In other words, an airline operator must forge cooperative pacts with other major carriers to survive.

"In the current context of air transport, where competition gets tougher every day, no airline, however strong, can succeed on its own," Christian Blanc, chairman of the Air France Group, said at a Tokyo press conference held after the group's signing of an accord with JAL.

CRS COOPERATIONS OF WORLD MAJOR CARRIERS

Asia	U.S.	Europe
Axess (JAL)	Sabre (American Airlines)	Galileo (British Airways etc)
Infini (ANA)	Apollo (United Airlines)	Amadeus (Deutsche Lufthansa Air France etc)
Abacus (Cathay Pacific Airways etc)		

*Capital relationship
Source: Companies

PRE-TAX PROFITS (LOSSES) OF 3 AIRLINES

In billions of yen

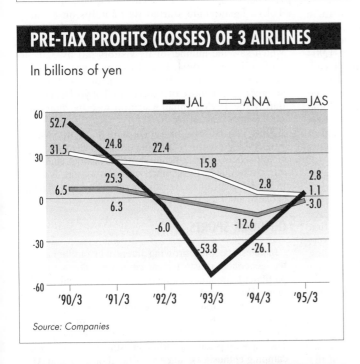

— JAL   — ANA   — JAS

JAL: 52.7, 24.8, 22.4, 15.8, -53.8, -26.1, 2.8
ANA: 31.5, 25.3, -6.0, -12.6, 2.8, 1.1
JAS: 6.5, 6.3, 2.8, -3.0

'90/3 '91/3 '92/3 '93/3 '94/3 '95/3

Source: Companies

COSTLY LANDINGS

Landing fees charged at major airports;
per Boeing 747; in thousands of yen

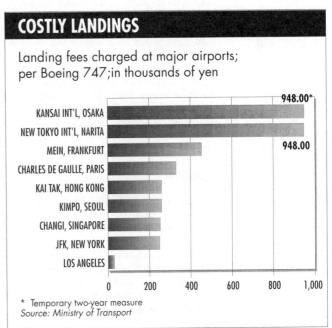

948.00*

948.00

KANSAI INT'L, OSAKA
NEW TOKYO INT'L, NARITA
MEIN, FRANKFURT
CHARLES DE GAULLE, PARIS
KAI TAK, HONG KONG
KIMPO, SEOUL
CHANGI, SINGAPORE
JFK, NEW YORK
LOS ANGELES

0   200   400   600   800   1,000

* Temporary two-year measure
Source: Ministry of Transport

KEY WORD

CRS

The computerized reservation system was originally designed for reserving and issuing airline tickets. But it has evolved into a system for providing a wide range of ticketing services and offering various information. As it provides value-added services for airline passengers, the CRS is regarded as a key tool for surviving the tough competition in the airline industry.

KEY WORD

FREQUENT FLYER PROGRAMS

Mileage accumulation programs for frequent air travelers. Members are awarded points according to distances traveled with a particular airline. The points can then be converted into free tickets. Airline operators recently started linking their mileage programs through partnerships to give passengers an incentive to use specific carriers every time they fly.

LEISURE & TOURISM

Strong yen boosts overseas touring; domestic leisure industry declines

BY JUNICHI UMEDA
Senior Staff Writer

Anemic economic activity in 1995 discouraged the Japanese from spending much time and money on leisure and entertainment. But the yen's marked appreciation against the U.S. dollar in the early part of the year prompted a record number of people to take overseas trips.

At the end of 1994, Japan's overall leisure and entertainment market was valued at ¥77.21 trillion, up 0.4% from 1993, according to the Leisure Development Center. The nearly flat growth went hand in hand with the 0.6% increase in gross domestic product for the year.

Of total spending in the leisure market in 1994, ¥5.56 trillion went for sports, ¥11.09 went for hobbies, ¥48.76 trillion for entertainment and ¥11.80 trillion for tourism.

In 1994, a Japanese worker put in an average 1,904 hours at work, down only nine hours from the preceding year, the research institute said. This indicated a stall in corporate efforts to shorten working hours and increase leisure time. The prolonged economic slump put pressure on workers to stay at the office, rather than take time off for fun. The leveling off in the amount of time set aside for recreation hurt Japan's leisure industry.

TOURISM

The mighty yen and low-priced package tours gave further impetus to the "travel abroad boom." In the first half of 1995, a record 6,821,000 Japanese headed overseas, up 8.2% from the same period of 1994, according to the Japan National Tourist Organization (JNTO). An estimated 15 million Japanese went abroad in 1995.

Despite these glowing statistics, travel companies were not altogether happy. Intensified price-cutting competition weakened the profit picture for tour operators.

The average price of the Look series of overseas package tours offered by Japan Travel Bureau Inc. in the first half of fiscal 1995 fell to a level 26.5% lower than in the corresponding period of fiscal 1991.

The number of foreign visitors to Japan in the first half of 1995 fell 2.4% from a year before to 1,625,000, according to JNTO. The Jan. 17 Great Hanshin Earthquake led many potential foreign tourists to cancel their trips to Japan.

The yen's surge in April to the 79 level against the dollar also discouraged foreign travelers.

Visitors from other parts of Asia, which normally accounts for 60% of the total, dropped markedly. In 1994, 3,468,055 foreigners visited Japan, up 1.7%. Of them, those who came for sightseeing accounted for 1,915,468, off 0.5%.

AMUSEMENT FACILITIES

The value of Japan's amusement park business shrank 3.1% to ¥567 billion in 1994, according to the Leisure Development Center. The number of visitors to amusement parks dropped in the first half of 1995 because the Kobe earthquake in January and the sarin nerve gas attack on the Tokyo subway system in March discouraged people from going out.

Amusement park operators pinned high hopes on the summer vacation season by introducing new attractions. Tokyo Disneyland started its Fantalusion evening parade of Disney characters on July 21, timed with the start of summer vacations at Japan's schools. The park, which saw the number of its visitors fall by 3.3% to 15.5 million in 1994, hoped the new parade would attract repeat visitors. Helped by the unexpectedly hot summer, the number of visitors to Tokyo Disneyland during the 1995 summer vacation rose by more than 10% from a year earlier.

Huis Ten Bosch, an amusement park in Sasebo, Nagasaki Prefecture, introduced sailboat cruising, a canoe school, a laser-beam show, fireworks and other attractions during the summer vacation season. Visitors in the first half of the season increased by two digits, a spokesman of the park said.

OUTDOOR SPORTS

Japanese people's growing interest in outdoor sports has generated a taste for car camping. The activity is particularly popular among owners of sport-utility vehicles. However, the delay in development of parking facilities at camping sites clouds the future growth potential of this leisure activity. Japan has only 900 camping sites with a total capacity for 300,000 people. The capacity is a far cry from an estimate 15 million car camping enthusiasts, noted an official of the Japan Auto Camp Association.

GOLF COURSES

The golf business remained slack in 1995. Although golf was still one of the most popular sports among Japanese businessmen, few could afford the high playing fees amid the lingering recession.

The number of golfers at golf courses in 1994 dropped for the second straight year, declining by 2.8% to 97.71 million, according to a Nikkei survey. Visitors per 18-hole golf course in 1994 declined by 5.2% to 39,713, falling short of the 40,000 mark. The rate of decrease was the largest ever.

JAPANESE OVERSEAS TRAVELERS

In 1,000 persons

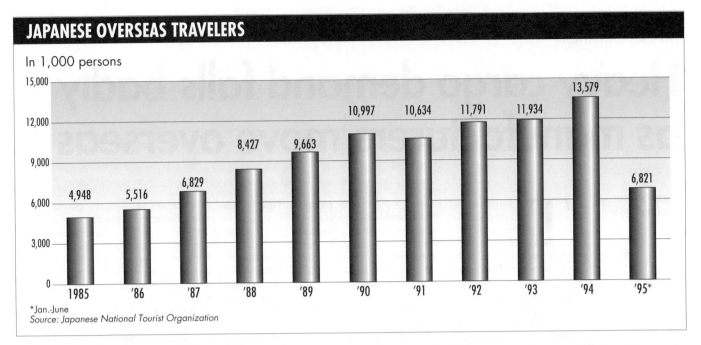

*Jan.-June
Source: Japanese National Tourist Organization

YEARLY WORKING HOURS (ALL INDUSTRIES)

In hours

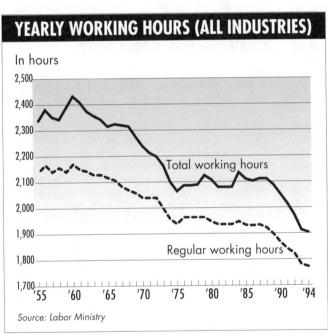

Source: Labor Ministry

NUMBER OF GOLF COURSES

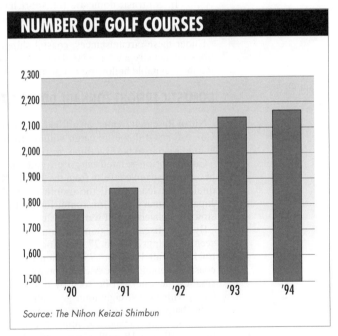

Source: The Nihon Keizai Shimbun

KEY WORD

ECO-TOURISM

Growing awareness of the necessity of environmental protection measures gave birth to the concept of "eco-tourism." Tours under this heading are designed to sustain, protect and improve the natural and cultural environment as well as deepen travelers' understanding of their surroundings. Among such package tours introduced in Japan are visits to rain forests in Indonesia and Malaysia.

KEY WORD

SECOND-BRAND TOURS

To compete with the increasing availability of discount air tickets, leading travel companies started marketing low-priced package tours several years ago. These tours fell under a series with a name different from conventional package tours and thus came to be called "second-brand tours." But some companies gave up the double-brand strategy in 1994 and 1995 as the price gap between the two brands narrowed.

TRANSPORTATION

Heavy cargo demand falls badly as manufacturers move overseas

BY JUNICHI UMEDA
Senior Staff Writer

The lingering recession is not the only factor behind poor domestic demand for physical distribution in 1995. A hollowing-out of Japanese manufacturing is even more responsible for the poor performance, as high distribution costs in Japan prompt more and more producers to shift plant and offices abroad, leaving even less domestic transportation demand.

The globalization of business has contributed to an expanded flow of cargo between Japan and overseas markets — especially between Japan and the rest of Asia. In contrast, domestic transport has dried up, reflecting low industrial production and sluggish personal consumption.

Under these circumstances, coastal shippers and the trucking industry are forced to devise means of countering the inevitable hollowing-out of manufacturing.

DOMESTIC FREIGHT TONNAGE DOWN 1.7%

Nittsu Research Center, an affiliate of Nippon Express Co., estimated domestic cargo volume for fiscal 1995, ending March, at 6,373 million metric tons, down 1.7%.

Consumption-related cargo proved specially poor because of adverse effects from the Jan. 17 Kobe Earthquake, not least of all the month-long blockage of Japan's primary trucking route. Production and construction-related freight were also sluggish.

By type: fiscal 1995 transport tonnage by railway is seen declining 2.1% to 77.4 million tons; transport by truck will fall 1.6% to 5,752 million tons; transport by coastal shipping will be 543 million tons, off 2.7%. The smallest decline will be seen by domestic airlines at 0.2%, with an air-freight tonnage totaling 744,000 tons.

In sharp contrast, international transport will be very favorable. Air transport of imports will jump 20% in fiscal 1995 to 1.18 million tons, says Nittsu Research. Freight tonnage of import containers will also rise 15.2% to 83.2 million tons. For exports, air freight will increase 13.5% to 698,000 tons and container freight 3.5% to 71.2 million tons.

SLUGGISH TRUCKING BUSINESS

Truck cargo seems the mostly severely affected by manufacturers' shifts abroad. The traffic of heavy trucks on the Tokyo metropolitan expressway, a yardstick for freight trucking, dropped 1.5% in June, the first year-on-year decline in 14 months. Traffic had increased at a double-digit rate from October 1994 to March 1995, but then slowed to a single-digit increase in April.

Trucking firms hauling freight for particular shippers on a contract basis are the most adversely affected.

Hitachi Transport System Ltd., long the primary delivery agent for parts, components and products made by Hitachi Ltd., offers a clear picture. The firm long transported TV picture tubes produced at Hitachi's Mobara plant in Chiba Prefecture to an assembly plant in Yokohama; then delivered finished color TVs to Hitachi distribution centers throughout Japan.

But Hitachi now consigns most picture tube production and TV assembly to affiliates overseas. As a result, Hitachi Transport's domestic business evaporated and it has been forced to move overseas. To keep its Japanese staff employed, the firm has been handling deliveries to convenience stores since November 1994.

COASTAL SHIPPING IN POOR SHAPE

Demand for coastal shipping dropped month by month in 1995. Slow delivery demand for steel products was a major factor behind the poor performance, said a spokesman of Nippon Shipping Co. of Tokyo. The spot charter rate for a 1,600-ton cargo vessel fell to around ¥500,000 a day in the middle of July, ¥50,000 lower than in early May.

Freight tonnage hauled by coastal tankers in May and June stood 10% to 20% below the year-earlier level, as demand for fuel oil C and gasoline was sluggish, said a spokesman of Tsurumi Yuso Co. of Tokyo.

Freight haulage by Japan Freight Railway Co., which handles most nationwide freight transport by rail, dropped 8.4% in June 1995 from a year earlier, to 4.12 million tons. That was the sixth consecutive year-on-year decline.

To counter the loss of domestic freight tonnage, transport firms are moving to cultivate their own routes to distribution bases abroad.

Nippon Express is opening shipping routes from regional Japanese ports. In June 1994, the firm began regular container service between the port of Chiba and South Korea's Pusan, an expanding hub for Asian container shipping. By the end of August 1995, the company had prompted 12 other regional ports to start service to Pusan, including Naoetsu in Niigata Prefecture, on the Sea of Japan and far closer to the South Korean port than Tokyo, Yokohama or other Pacific ports.

By taking advantage of these arrangements, Nippon Express hopes to win orders for customs clearance and cargo handling. But commissions from such activity are not enough to cover its lost trucking fees, one company official said. Finding new clients is essential.

Japanese transport firms also face challenges from foreign rivals. Federal Express Corp. is trying to expand its Asian business, using the Subic airport in the Philippines as a hub. Still-more intense competition looms.

COMPOSITION OF CONTAINER FREIGHT

Fiscal 1993; in percent

Others
14.0

Chemicals, Drugs
4.4

Rubber Products
5.2

Daily Necessities
7.0

Light Industrial Goods
8.2

Dyes, Paints, Synthetic Resins
8.9

Exports
66.5 million tons

Other Machinery
28.7

Transport Machinery
23.6

Forest Products
5.0

Chemicals
10.1

Special Products
10.7

Metal Machinery
Industrial Goods
15.1

Light Industrial Goods
16.2

Imports
63.2 million tons

Mining Products
3.3

Miscellaneous
Industrial Products
23.3

Farm And
Fishery Products
16.4

Note: Total of container freight at eight major ports – Tokyo, Yokohama, Shimizu, Nagoya, Osaka, Kobe and Kita-Kyushu.
Source: Nittsu Research Center

TOTAL DOMESTIC FREIGHT TRANSPORT

In billions of tons

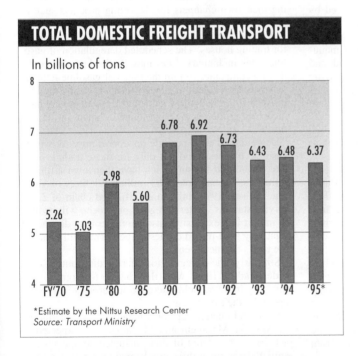

FY'70	'75	'80	'85	'90	'91	'92	'93	'94	'95*
5.26	5.03	5.98	5.60	6.78	6.92	6.73	6.43	6.48	6.37

*Estimate by the Nittsu Research Center
Source: Transport Ministry

FREIGHT TRANSPORT BY TRUCKS

In billions of tons

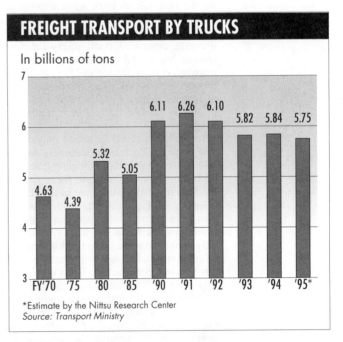

FY'70	'75	'80	'85	'90	'91	'92	'93	'94	'95*
4.63	4.39	5.32	5.05	6.11	6.26	6.10	5.82	5.84	5.75

*Estimate by the Nittsu Research Center
Source: Transport Ministry

KEY WORD

YEAR-ROUND, 24-HOUR OPERATION

Competition among the world's container terminals is intensifying as container cargo increases at a remarkably fast pace. But seven out of eight major Japanese container terminals slow down operations on Sundays, whereas other major Asian ports — Pusan, Kaoshing, Hong Kong and Singapore — observe year-round, 24-hour operation. Japanese ports will have to follow their foreign rivals to improve their competitiveness.

KEY WORD

FLAGGING-OUT

The higher yen and expanding wage differentials between Japanese and foreign sailors have aggravated the competitiveness of Japan-registered ships. To counter this situation, Japanese shipping firms have been transferring registrations to Panama and other foreign countries. With the progress of this "flagging-out," the number of Japan-registered ships dropped more than 60% during the past decade.

TRADING HOUSES

Diversification into non-Japan deals becoming key to profits, survival

BY MAKOTO SATO
Staff Writer

Appreciation of the yen continued to exert a serious influence on Japan's major "sogo shosha," or general trading houses, in 1995. Its value rose to an average ¥90.35 to the dollar in the first half of 1995, reducing the dollar value of exports by 16.8% even if the yen value of the product remained unchanged.

A report by the Japan External Trading Organization (JETRO) highlighted the effects of the yen's dramatic appreciation, showing that imports at 19 major Japanese trading houses increased 2.7% year on year for the first half of 1995, while exports decreased by 4.7%, the ninth year in a row exports declined.

The strong yen, however, is not the only cause of declining exports. Virtually every Japanese car manufacturer has moved some of its production abroad, and many electric appliance makers are also transferring production overseas. The continuing "hollowing out" of Japanese industry is also responsible for the decline in exports and thus, for declining trading house performance.

But the fall in exports is not the only cause for unease. The domestic business of Japanese trading houses is also in decline. The top six trading houses all suffered a decline in domestic trading in fiscal 1994 ended March 1995. In fiscal 1993, three out of the six largest trading houses, — Itochu Corp., Sumitomo Corp. and Marubeni Corp. — obtained more than 50% of their revenues inside Japan. In fiscal 1994, on the other hand, only Sumitomo managed to maintain the 50% level.

Lost domestic business is gradually being replaced by business conducted outside Japan unrelated to domestic importing and exporting, and sometimes not even related to trading. All of the major trading houses, except for Mitsubishi Corp., increased their business interests outside of Japan in fiscal 1994. More than 30% of the annual sales of Mitsui & Co. and Itochu came from such businesses.

A typical example of the kinds of businesses that trading houses have diversified into is the development of industrial parks in Asia. In Indonesia, the Philippines and China, major trading houses are actively competing to attract Japanese companies seeking to transfer production there.

Mitsui, for example, started to develop an industrial park in Myanmar in October. In partnership with Marubeni, it is hoping to sign an industrial park development contract with the Myanmarese government. The recent opening up of the economy in Myanmar was the impetus for such activities. However, prospects for doing business there are still unknown because of political instability and the lack of purchasing power among the local populace.

There is also a trend among trading houses toward entering the retailing business. Sumitomo has been trying to expand its business with Summit stores — a Sumitomo affiliate which operates chain supermarkets in Japan. Frozen U.S. pork imported by Sumitomo is sold at Summit shops throughout the country. Selling clothing through its subsidiaries is another key part of Sumitomo's retail strategy.

Turnabout, however, is proving to be fair play. Retailers, especially large-scale chain store operators such as Daiei Inc., Ito-Yokado Co. and Jusco Co., are expanding their own channels for importing products such as clothing and foodstuffs, by-passing the trading houses.

Deregulation may also open the door to new markets for trading houses. The scheduled deregulation of gasoline sales in January 1996 may be the last chance for trading companies to join the ranks of gasoline retailers in Japan. Deregulation, which was approved by the Diet in April 1995, will allow gas importers who do not have their own refineries to sell gasoline in Japan for the first time.

Deregulation may provide an opportunity to expand gasoline business, and not only for those trading firms like Itochu and Mitsui which have their own affiliated refineries. Itochu sold 1.83 million kiloliters of gasoline in fiscal 1994 through an affiliated chain of 2,228 service stations. After deregulation, Itochu will be able to import less expensive gasoline rather than depend on relatively high-priced domestic fuel. This will enhance the firm's competitiveness.

Similarly, the deregulation of rice distribution provides trading firms with the chance to aggressively diversify into this field, merging numerous small retailers under their own flags.

Structural changes are also underway. Major trading houses like Marubeni and Mitsubishi are expected to accelerate the listing of their affiliated companies and subsidiaries on public stock exchanges in order to reduce their administrative operations.

Major trading houses are also increasing their investment in strategic businesses such as telecommunications and multimedia,

This seems to be consistent with their long-term strategy of transforming their headquarters into a holding company which determines overall corporate group strategy and investment.

EXPORTS AND IMPORTS BY 19 TRADING HOUSES

In billions of yen

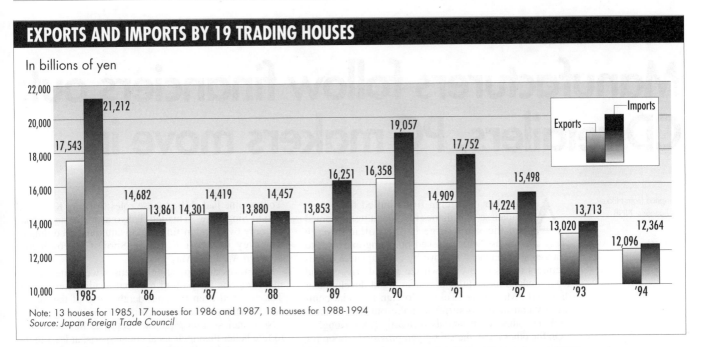

Note: 13 houses for 1985, 17 houses for 1986 and 1987, 18 houses for 1988-1994
Source: Japan Foreign Trade Council

BUSINESS RESULTS AT 9 TRADING HOUSES

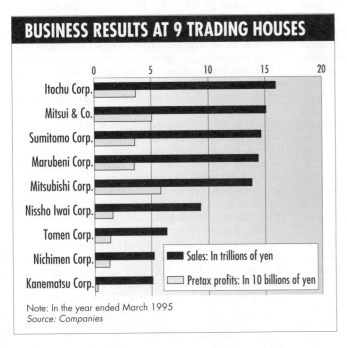

Itochu Corp.
Mitsui & Co.
Sumitomo Corp.
Marubeni Corp.
Mitsubishi Corp.
Nissho Iwai Corp.
Tomen Corp.
Nichimen Corp.
Kanematsu Corp.

■ Sales: In trillions of yen
□ Pretax profits: In 10 billions of yen

Note: In the year ended March 1995
Source: Companies

SALES BY BUSINESS AREAS

In trillions of yen; (percentage to total sales)

	Domestic Sales	Exports	Imports	In abroad
Itochu Corp.	7.754 (48.6%)	1.566 (9.8%)	1.578 (9.9%)	5.044 (31.7%)
Mitsui & Co.	6.556 (43.5%)	1.806 (12.0%)	2.027 (13.4%)	4.695 (31.1%)
Sumitomo Corp.	7.448 (50.9%)	2.025 (13.9%)	2.155 (14.7%)	3.002 (20.5%)
Marubeni Corp.	7.141 (49.7%)	2.033 (14.1%)	1.561 (10.9%)	3.637 (25.3%)
Mitsubishi Corp.	6.794 (49.2%)	2.261 (16.4%)	2.503 (18.1%)	2.254 (16.3%)
Nissho Iwai Corp.	4.068 (43.8%)	0.963 (10.4%)	1.884 (20.3%)	2.366 (25.5%)

Source: Companies

KEY WORD

LISTING AFFILIATES

Marubeni announced in August 1995 that it would list two affiliated companies — a personal computer trading company and a building utilities installer — on domestic stock exchanges, its first such listings in 18 years. Mitsubishi listed an affiliated food trading company in July, and now plans to list a company that makes prepaid-card systems for pachinko parlors. Mitsui, Itochu and Nissho Iwai also plan to list affiliates.

KEY WORD

RETAILING RICE

Deregulation of the domestic rice market in November 1995 may strongly influence the future of general trading houses. Similar to the retail gasoline market, the rice market was previously controlled by strict government regulations and a trade association, in this case the National Federation of Agricultural Cooperative Associations (Zennoh). Deregulation is expected to open this rich market to outsiders, especially trading houses.

FOREIGN AFFILIATES

Manufacturers follow financiers out; CD retailers, PC makers move in

Compiled from Nikkei
Publications: NNB

A number of foreign firms pulled the pin on Japanese subsidiaries in 1995; a trend blamed on the yen's surge to the dollar through August, which pushed operating expenses to unacceptable heights. A move by non-Japanese manufacturers to dissolve or downsize subsidiaries spread from production facilities to research and development divisions. Meanwhile, Tokyo's foreign financial community continued to suffer a shake-out as members shifted to other Asian capitals, primarily Hong Kong.

On the other hand, the strong yen provided a boon for retailers of imports. Non-Japanese music retailers, such as Tower Records Inc., made significant inroads into the market, attracting consumers with low prices for CDs. Likewise, foreign manufacturers of personal computers expanded marketing networks to promote their price-competitive imported models and capitalize on the dynamic growth in the market.

Firms maintaining research bases in Japan were particularly hard hit by the yen's surge to the dollar in April 1995. Skyrocketing personnel costs prompted Monsanto Japan Ltd. to pull the shutters down on its R&D center in Ibaraki Prefecture, a scientific research hub. The unit of the major U.S. chemical maker Monsanto Ltd. had established an agrochemical testing division at the center in 1984 and had added a chemical research division in 1993. Set-up costs for the facility, which employed some 40 scientists at one stage, were reportedly around ¥4 billion-¥5 billion. In line with global restructuring plans, however, the Ibaraki facility was put up for sale. U.S. pharmaceutical maker Upjohn Co. followed a similar game plan and abolished one of its research divisions at Upjohn Tsukuba Research Laboratories, also in Ibaraki Prefecture.

While manufacturers have been increasingly forced to shift production offshore to sidestep the adverse effects of the strong yen, this alone proved inadequate for some foreign firms. This was indeed the case for the Japanese joint venture of Olivetti & C. SpA, an Italian office equipment maker. In 1994, the firm transferred production of Olivetti-brand personal computers to Singapore from its Saitama Prefecture facility to cut costs. But, with the yen's further appreciation in 1995, Olivetti found that even development activities in Japan had become unprofitable and decided to dissolve the unit, Pegasus Inc., by November 1995. Sales had plunged below ¥1 billion in fiscal 1994, after peaking at ¥6 billion in fiscal 1992.

Meanwhile, the hollowing out of Tokyo's financial community accelerated in 1995, with a number of foreign firms relocating Asian headquarters to other cities in the region. Of the 13 non-Japanese financial institutions that previously had regional headquarters in Tokyo, nine had shifted these roles to Hong Kong and two to Singapore. This left Tokyo as the regional base for only two foreign financial institutions, according to a survey by Mori Building Shoji Co. conducted between April and May 1995.

High taxes and operating expenses were cited as the main reasons for pulling regional headquarters out of Tokyo. And even the considerable size of the market was not enough to convince foreign firms to stay.

Nevertheless, non-Japanese securities houses tended to fare better than their local counterparts, at least in the year through March 1995. Drastic belt-tightening measures, introduced earlier, began to produce results. Furthermore, foreign brokerages did not have their profits eaten away by huge personnel expenses associated with retail brokering, as their Japanese counterparts did, since non-Japanese institutions do not engage in this sector of the market.

One industry that did attract expansion from foreign concerns in 1995 was the music retailing sector. Deregulation in the laws governing the setting up of large retail outlets, together with plunging commercial rents, led non-Japanese distributors of audiovisual software to accelerate store openings. By autumn, the number of outlets had topped 50 and was expected to surpass 100 in two to three years. Tower Records opened a 5,000-sq.-meter store, reportedly the world's largest, in Tokyo's trendy Shibuya shopping district in March 1995.

Other foreign firms in the music retailing business have also made ground in Japan's notoriously obstacle-ridden distribution system. Virgin Megastores Japan Ltd. and HMV Japan KK, both subsidiaries of British music distributors, have carved out a share of the market. The largest U.S. chain of CD outlets, Musicland Group Inc., tied up with Tokyo audiovisual software wholesaler, Japan Record Sales Network Inc., to operate the SamGoody franchise.

The personal computer market also witnessed a growing presence by foreign makers in 1995. Their penetration was assisted by rapidly growing demand for PCs in general, together with the price-competitiveness of imported products in the wake of the yen's surge. Furthermore, IBM-compatible machines expanded market share strongly.

The Japanese PC market hit the 3 million units in fiscal 1994 and is expected to surpass 4 million in fiscal 1995. On size alone, Japan has become an important strategic market, second only to the U.S.

Singapore's IPC Corp. established a Japanese office in 1995 and started marketing three original models in June. Waiting in the wings were Packard Bell Electronics Inc., which became the third largest U.S. PC maker in 1994, and Gateway 2000 Inc., also of the U.S.

Tower Records runs what is claimed to be the world's largest single outlet for recorded music at this store in Tokyo's up-scale Shibuya shopping district. The shop opened in April 1995.

BUSINESS CLIMATE IN TOKYO

Survey of 32 foreign financial institutions; multiple responses; in percent

	0 20 40 60 80 100
GOOD	
Market Size	
Political Stability	
Information Availability	
Public Security	
BAD	
Income and Corporate Taxes	
Regulations	
Office Rent	
Personnel Costs	

Source: Mori Building Shoji

FOREIGN INVESTMENT IN JAPAN

	Number of Investment Projects	Amount (In millions of dollars)	Growth Rate (In Percent)
FY1989	5,688	2,860	-11.8
'90	5,939	2,778	-2.9
'91	4,212	4,339	56.2
'92	1,271	4,084	-5.9
'93	1,072	3,078	-24.6
'94	1,135	4,155	34.9

Source: Ministry of Finance

KEY WORD

FOREIGN BROKERAGES

Goldman Sachs (Japan) Corp. clocked up pretax profits of around ¥12 billion in fiscal 1994 and Salomon Brothers Asia Ltd. was just under ¥10 billion. Both topped the results posted by Nomura Securities Co.. But it should be noted that fewer than half the 47 foreign brokers who closed their books in March 1995 finished in the black, a fall from the previous year.

KEY WORD

KODAK-FUJI ROW

Accusations of a closed market in Japan sprang from Eastman Kodak Co. of the U.S. in July 1995. In a report to the office of the U.S. Trade Representative, the world's largest photographic film maker claimed Fuji Photo Film Co. was excluding foreign products from the market by using a kickback system and contracted agencies for retailing. Fuji refuted the claim, arguing Kodak's small 10% share of the Japanese market was due to inadequate product strategies.

NEW PRODUCTS & SERVICES

High-performance, status products find buyers; other markets still slow

BY ICHIRO SASAKI
Deputy Editor

As the overall economy remained stagnant, consumers tried to squirrel away money to ready for a possibly worse winter. The yen's steep rise, the Great Hanshin Earthquake in January and the deadly poison gas attack on the Tokyo subway system in March troubled consumers and caused them to tighten their purse strings. As a result, consumer prices fell sharply.

After plunging against the yen from early 1995, the dollar finally started recovering some ground at the beginning of September 1995. But this did little to alleviate public anxiety about the future.

The number of new products introduced to the market from the fall of 1994 through the summer of 1995 by producers of automobiles, household appliances and processed food items was almost the same as that of the previous comparable term. There were no particular best sellers.

Minidisc (MD) players, personal handy-phone system (PHS) terminals and the Pajero Mini sport-utility vehicle saw favorable sales. All three products did well on the strength of their high value-for-money aspect — that is, sophisticated performance at low cost.

Cosmetics and toiletries claiming to have slimming effects were bought by young women, despite their high prices. Christian Dior sold out its stock of slimming gel Svelte, for instance, at ¥6,000 a 200ml bottle. A Chinese-made soap said to help keep the pounds off also sold well at ¥2,000 a cake in major department stores.

Beer brewers introduced low-malt beer to avoid high liquor taxes. These drinks, which cannot be labeled beer by definition, had captured an estimated 4% share of the Japanese beer market by August 1995. Among popular low-malt products were Suntory Ltd.'s HOP'S (malt content: 65%), released in the fall of 1994, and Sapporo Breweries Co.'s Drafty (malt content: less than 25%), introduced in spring 1995. A 350ml can of HOP'S sold for ¥180 and Drafty went for ¥160, compared with the suggested retail price of ¥225 for a standard beer.

AUTOMOBILES

Among sport-utility vehicles, Mitsubishi Motors Corp.'s Pajero has been the favorite for more than 10 years. The release of the Pajero Mini in the fall of 1994 was an instant success.

With a price tag of ¥1.11-1.39 million, the small four-wheel drive car was a hit with women in their 20s to 40s, who have always been potential buyers of sport-utility vehicles. Total sales of the Pajero Mini reached 56,511 units in the first half of 1995 and helped propel Mitsubishi's share of the domestic new car market up to 14.2% in August 1995, closing in on Nissan Motor Co.'s 14.8%.

ELECTRONICS

High-tech products found their way into more Japanese households. Personal computers were at the top of the list. Along with declining prices, the increased popularity of online services and the Internet led many corporations and individuals to buy or replace their PCs.

NEC Corp., Fujitsu Ltd., International Business Machines Corp., Compaq Computer Corp., Dell Computer Corp., Apple Computer Inc. and other PC makers offered "all-in-one" PC models with pre-installed application software. Many of the new models that appeared in early 1995 were "multimedia" PCs with built-in CD-ROM drives and stereo speakers.

According to statistics released by the Japan Electronics Industry Development Association, 1.08 million PCs were shipped in the domestic market in the April-June quarter of 1995 alone. In the three months before that, shipments also topped 1 million units. Industry observers firmly believe the number of PC shipments will reach 5 million units in fiscal 1995.

Audio equipment manufacturers see the MD player as the steam engine that will pull the industry out of its slump. Sharp Corp. increased its production capacity 20-fold to 100,000 MD players a month in 1995. The Osaka-based electronics manufacturer thinks MD player production will prevent a hollowing out of its domestic plants.

MD players can store and play music for up to 74 minutes using rewritable 64mm-diameter floppy discs. The first MD was released to the market in 1992 by Sony Corp. After severe sales competition with digital audio tapes (DATs) introduced in the same year by Philips Electronics NV and Matsushita Electric Industrial Co., the MD player won over audiophiles with its high sound quality and user friendliness.

About 280,000 MD players were sold in 1994 and the figure is said to have topped 1 million in 1995. Some industry analysts predict 3 million MD players will sell in 1996.

SERVICES

Multimedia-related services expanded steadily. The Internet captured the hearts of Japanese cyberheads. The number of Internet users in Japan reached an estimated 1 million by mid-1995 and hundreds of companies set up sites on the World Wide Web.

The digital minidisc format quickly attracted large numbers of audio fans.

Mitsubishi Motors introduced the Pajero Mini, a compact version of its popular sports-utility vehicle, and scored a hit with young women drivers.

Beers with low malt content proved successful in the crowded market for light liquors.

KEY WORD

LOW-MALT BEER

Low-malt beer, or Happo-shu, started appearing in discount liquor shops and supermarkets. The product was the result of beer brewers' efforts to avoid exorbitant liquor taxes. The law defines beer as an alcoholic beverage with a malt content of more than 67%. The tax on beer is ¥77.7 per 350ml can. Beverages containing less than 67% malt cannot be called beer or taxed at the high rate. The tax is ¥53.4 per can for a malt content of 25%-67% and ¥29.2 for a malt content of less than 25%.

KEY WORD

HAWAII TOURS

The most popular foreign travel destination among the Japanese is Hawaii, with one out of four Japanese overseas travelers heading to the islands, according to a July consumer survey by The Nikkei Marketing Journal. The reason: cleanliness, language and safety. Travel agents offered package tours to Hawaii at discounted prices of around ¥60,000 in the off season.

SUPERMARKETS/DEPARTMENT STORES

Profits pick up after 2 years in doldrums

Compiled from Nikkei
Publications: NNB

Sales at the nation's top 500 retailers increased 2.2% in fiscal 1994, recovering from two years of virtually flat sales growth, according to the 28th annual survey of the domestic retail industry conducted by the Nikkei Marketing Journal. Aggressive expansion prompted by the easing of government restrictions on opening large-scale retail stores more than compensated for the negative effects of widespread price-cutting in the retail market.

Pretax profits increased for the first time in three years, growing 0.7% on a combination of increased sales and successful restructuring. However, the deterioration of ratios indicating operational efficiency left analysts less optimistic about the industry's recovery.

Aggregate sales of the top 500 retailers totaled ¥39.083 trillion in fiscal 1994. Convenience stores recorded double-digit growth, and specialty stores and supermarkets also did fairly well. However, sales at department stores and co-operatives declined.

Aggressive expansion and shrewd pricing policies were the keys to improved performance. Convenience stores, specialty stores and supermarkets rapidly opened new outlets. Department stores, however, which were reluctant to expand, fell victim to price competition. Co-operatives enlarged their sales space, but still lost customers to other retailer groups because they were slow in cutting prices.

Overall sales increased, but retailers saw a lower gross profit-to-sales ratio due to consumer preference for lower-priced goods. The sales value-to-sales space ratio dropped 4.6% for the same reason. The pretax profit-to-total assets ratio, an indicator of a company's operational efficiency, fell 0.1% from the previous year.

Nearly 90% of the retailers responding to the survey said they cut costs and restructured their organizations to improve performance. Despite some encouraging figures, however, retailers did not expect to see a robust recovery soon. More than 80% of them predicted that prices will continue falling, and said that themselves intend to sell lower-priced goods.

Many expected increased sales and profits in fiscal 1995. However, analysts thought that performance would depend on how quickly retailers adapted to consumer trends. Disparities in performance could even lead to a reorganization of the industry through mergers and business tie-ups.

SALES

Department stores saw sales drop by 2.7%, the third consecutive year of decline. Their share of total retail sales fell below 25% for the first time. Sales at co-operatives declined 2.3%, but sales at supermarkets, which aggressively opened new stores, increased 4.2%. Specialty store sales grew 5.2%, though they were less aggressive in opening outlets than in previous years.

The rankings of the top ten retailers in terms of sales were unchanged from fiscal 1993.

OPERATING PROFITS

Operating profits varied widely between retail groups categories. Department stores saw a large 15.5% growth in operating profits due to decisive reductions in selling costs and administrative expenses, which had swelled during their long history. The venerable department stores Mitsukoshi and Takashimaya slashed such expenses by 12.7 billion yen and 6.2 billion yen, respectively. Operating profits at metropolitan department stores, such as Mitsukoshi and Takashimaya, grew 23.0%, while stores in small, provincial cities showed a decline of 4.7%.

The operating profits at supermarkets, meanwhile, dropped 2.0%, as a result of cut-throat competition which squeezed profit margins. Operating profits at nationwide supermarket chains fell 8.9%.

The operating profits of co-operatives declined by a steep 48.4%.

PRETAX PROFITS

Similar to the trend in operating profits, department stores, specialty stores and convenience stores enjoyed growth in pretax profits, while supermarkets and co-operatives saw their pretax profits shrink.

The pretax profits of supermarkets fell 1.5% overall. The decline in profits at national supermarket chains was a particularly large 8.7%. Five major supermarket operators, Daiei Inc., Ito-Yokado Co., Jusco Co., Seiyu Ltd. and Nichii Co., suffered declines in pretax profits.

In contrast, regional supermarkets, including York-Benimaru Co., Heiwado Co., Izumi Co. and Chain Store Okuwa Co., showed a 9.6% increase.

The pretax profits-to-sales ratio at major supermarket operators of 1.5% was higher than the 1.1% ratio at department stores, but significantly lower than the 2.2% of regional supermarkets.

Pretax profits at co-operatives plunged 45.8%. This was partly due to the losses that leading co-operative Consumers Co-op Kobe suffered as a result of the Great Hanshin Earthquake after posting large profits the preceding year. Even if the performance of Co-op Kobe is excluded, however, pretax profits at co-operatives still declined more than 40%. Of the 32 co-operatives that responded to the survey, three posted pretax losses and 25 suffered declines in pretax profits.

RETAILERS RANKING FOR FY94

FY94	FY 93	COMPANY NAME	SALES (¥ MILLION)	GROWTH RATE (%)	PRETAX PROFIT (¥ MILLION)	NUMBER OF STORES	TYPE OF BUSINESS	HEAD OFFICE	BOOK CLOSING
1	(1)	Daiei	2,541,518	–	7,210	348	supermarket	Hyogo	February
2	(2)	Ito–Yokado	1,538,742	0.2%	75,054	149	supermarket	Tokyo	February
3	(3)	Jusco	1,147,413	8.2%	22,010	188	supermarket	Tokyo	February
4	(4)	Seiyu	1,032,815	–1.6%	4,123	209	supermarket	Tokyo	February
5	(5)	Nichii	1,015,017	23.5%	9,329	140	supermarket	Osaka	February
6	(6)	Mitsukoshi	767,655	–4.1%	3,695	14	department store	Tokyo	February
7	(7)	Takashimaya	706,122	–2.4%	2,126	10	department store	Osaka	February
8	(8)	Seibu Department Stores	660,337	–3.1%	–	–20	department store	Tokyo	February
9	(9)	Uny	611,233	5.9%	7,883	119	supermarket	Aichi	February
10	(10)	Daimaru	521,034	–4.1%	3,821	7	department store	Osaka	February
11	(11)	Marui	492,638	–2.8%	23,469	33	department store	Tokyo	January
12	(12)	Matsuzakaya	434,042	–5.5%	2,296	10	department store	Aichi	February
13	(13)	Isetan	410,393	–2.5%	6,373	6	department store	Tokyo	March
14	(14)	Izumiya	401,516	0.0%	10,826	76	supermarket	Osaka	February
15	(15)	Nagasakiya	378,760	–4.0%	–1,223	94	supermarket	Tokyo	February
16	(16)	Consumers Co–op Kobe	342,609	–3.8%	–269	156	co–operative	Hyogo	March
17	(17)	Tokyu Department Store	325,824	–3.9%	3,021	5	department store	Tokyo	January
18	(19)	Maruetsu	322,134	–0.7%	6,035	175	supermarket	Tokyo	March
19	(18)	Hankyu Department Store	317,184	–2.7%	3,548	7	department store	Osaka	March
20	(20)	Kintetsu Department Store	284,680	1.3%	317	6	department store	Osaka	February
21	(22)	Tokyu Store Chain	270,999	–1.4%	4,047	85	supermarket	Tokyo	February
22	(21)	Kotobukiya	269,772	–2.3%	1,257	121	supermarket	Kumamamoto	February
23	(25)	York–Benimaru	250,991	9.5%	10,494	63	supermarket	Fukushima	February
24	(23)	Yokohama Takashimaya	249,108	–2.4%	5,102	3	department store	Kanagawa	February
25	(28)	Heiwado	239,558	7.7%	8,159	72	supermarket	Shiga	February
26	(26)	Tobu Department Store	236,217	6.0%	–	2	department store	Tokyo	March
27	(24)	Sogo	232,627	–8.5%	1,715	3	department store	Osaka	February
28	(29)	Odakyu Department Store	216,935	–2.0%	–	2	department store	Tokyo	February
29	(30)	Best Denki	216,923	8.3%	9,655	468	specialty store	Fukuoka	February
30	(27)	Higashi–Nihon Kiosk	216,315	–2.8%	1,910	1,800	–	Tokyo	March
31	(31)	Seven–Eleven Japan	214,560	9.7%	93,381	5,905	convenience store	Tokyo	February
32	(34)	Life	210,722	11.8%	2,140	89	supermarket	Osaka	February
33	(32)	Joshin Denki	205,205	4.9%	2,224	195	specialty store	Osaka	March
34	(36)	Izumi	198,807	12.7%	7,588	55	supermarket	Hiroshima	February
35	(33)	Chiyoda	190,065	0.2%	8,528	1,647	specialty store	Tokyo	February
36	(–)	Miki	185,333	–	–	1,319	specialty store	Tokyo	February
37	(41)	Autobacs Seven	178,537	9.3%	15,758	381	specialty store	Osaka	March
38	(38)	Inageya	176,333	2.7%	3,263	116	supermarket	Tokyo	March
39	(37)	Daikuma	172,223	–0.9%	4,662	23	specialty store	Kanagawa	February
40	(40)	Sapporo Consumers Co–op	169,541	2.0%	1,608	115	co–operative	Hokkaido	March
41	(43)	Fuji	168,474	8.7%	2,108	42	supermarket	Ehime	February
42	(39)	Marutomi Group	168,036	–1.4%	1,435	1,787	specialty store	Aichi	February
43	(35)	Aoyama Trading	167,730	–8.0%	18,173	603	specialty store	Hiroshima	March
44	(46)	Daiichi	166,514	13.9%	4,811	291	specialty store	Hiroshima	March
45	(54)	Kojima	163,421	32.3%	6,099	158	specialty store	Tochigi	March
46	(45)	Chain Store Okuwa	160,889	6.9%	7,134	90	supermarket	Wakayama	February
47	(42)	Yaohan Japan	158,013	0.6%	4,163	83	supermarket	Shizuoka	March
48	(44)	Yokohama Sogo	147,500	–3.7%	–	1	department store	Kanagawa	February
49	(52)	Yodobashi Camera	143,210	14.1%	5,209	17	specialty store	Tokyo	January
50	(47)	Kanagawa Consumers Co–op	135,228	–6.6%	1,655	154	co–operative	Kanagawa	March

WHOLESALING

Slump in consumer spending, strong yen hit earnings

Compiled from Nikkei
Publications: NNB

The wholesale industry barely managed to eke out sales growth in fiscal 1994 after posting negative growth the previous year for the first time in 21 years. Wholesalers saw their pretax profits drop 9.9%, their fifth straight year of decline, on sales which increased a bare 0.5%, according to the Nikkei Marketing Journal's 24th Japan Wholesaler's Survey. The poor performance is attributed to the continued slump in consumer spending and the strong yen, which caused an influx of cheap imports that drove down the prices of domestically made goods.

Capital spending by wholesalers plunged 21.1% following a 29.6% drop in fiscal 1993. The average number of hours worked fell below 2,000 for the first time as firms trimmed overtime to cut personnel costs.

Amid this tough business environment, 88.7% of the wholesale companies polled said they are restructuring their operations through cost reduction, organizational streamlining or personnel reshuffling. But many respondents also noted there is a limit to what individual corporate restructuring can achieve.

A total of 63.7% said the wholesale industry will undergo rapid realignment within one year or that the pace of realignment will quicken within two or three years. In fact, 31.4% of the respondents said it will be necessary for them to tie-up or merge with one or more other firms.

FOODSTUFFS

Wholesale foodstuff sales rose a scant 0.9% in fiscal 1994, the same as in fiscal 1993, as restructuring and cost-reduction efforts failed to keep pace with falling prices. Pretax profits were down 6.6%, with the ratio of operating profits to sales dipping from 1.0% in fiscal 1993 to 0.8% in fiscal 1994.

Rice wholesalers saw their pretax profits plummet 37.7% on a 17.7% drop in sales due to a poor harvest that caused acute rice shortages. Liquor wholesalers boosted sales by 3.0% thanks to a scorching summer, but their pretax profits fell 0.7% because consumption was concentrated on lower-priced beers rather than premium brands with higher profit margins.

PHARMACEUTICALS & HEALTH-CARE PRODUCTS

Wholesalers of pharmaceuticals and health-care products saw their sales rise 5.5% in fiscal 1994 due to severe outbreaks of flu and hay fever. But their operating profits tumbled 15.1%, pretax profits dropped 12.1% and aftertax profits were down 11.7%.

The dismal profit performance is attributed to increased demands for discounts by medical institutions and a government-mandated price cut averaging 6.6% that came into effect in April 1994. Profit margins were squeezed when such cuts in wholesale prices were not matched by corresponding reductions in producer prices

Drug wholesalers are therefore stepping-up their efforts to cut costs and diversify their businesses. Suzuken Co. and Fukujin Co. plan to construct large distribution centers this fiscal year to streamline delivery. Showa Pharmaceutical Co. is separating the shipment of drugs from the transport of other products to enhance efficiency.

Kuraya Corp. is entering the information service industry with other wholesalers through the use of their computerized order-taking and placement systems. Some firms are entering health-related fields such as nursing care equipment and hospital food service.

WATCHES & JEWELRY

Watch and jewelry sales fell 4.6% in fiscal 1994 following a 6.7% decline the previous year. The sector is particularly vulnerable to economic cycles. Pricey items that sold well during the "bubble" years saw a steep fall in sales. But many wholesalers reported sales gains on a volume basis, which indicates a budding recovery in consumer spending.

While both operating profits and pretax profits were down, aftertax profits jumped 26.4%. However, that sharp increase is attributable to the soaring profits of a limited number of companies, such as Shinei Hoshoku, which posted a 214.3% gain.

In order to better survive the current, harsh business climate, Tasaki Shinju Co. and many other wholesalers located in the Okachimachi area of Tokyo are vertically integrating their businesses by moving further into the retail field.

TOP 10 FOOD WHOLESALERS

COMPANY NAME	SALES	GROWTH RATE	PRETAX PROFITS	GROWTH RATE
1. Kokubu & Co.	809,430	5.4%	3,157	21.2%
2. Yukijirushi Access Inc.	631,665	–	512	–
3. Ryoshoku Ltd.	538,612	5.7	4,055	3.9
4. Meidi-Ya Co.	510,967	3.6	351	–44.8
5. Nihon Shurui Hanbai Co.	378,932	3.0	2,071	–3.8
6. Matsushita Suzuki Co.	320,975	5.8	3,084	16.4
7. Kato Sangyo Co.	291,429	7.4	4,404	3.5
8. Koami Co.	268,032	1.6	–	–
9. Asahi Food Co.	190,713	5.7	380	–31.7
10. Yamae Hisano Co.	168,479	–	1,703	–

Note: Sales and pretax profits in millions of yen   Source: Company reports

Most apparel wholesalers are suffering declining sales.

TOP 10 MEDICINE WHOLESALERS

	COMPANY NAME	SALES	GROWTH RATE	PRETAX PROFITS	GROWTH RATE
1.	Suzuken Co.	588,476	9.3 %	15,980	–9.6%
2.	Kuraya Corp.	314,623	6.2	5,753	–10.5
3.	Sanseido Co.	259,025	6.4	6,762	–13.5
4.	Fukujin Co.	250,948	–	2,115	–
5.	Toho Pharmaceutical Co.	222,548	10.5	1,368	–44.4
6.	Nippon Shoji Kaisha Ltd.	202,446	–	4,646	–
7.	Sun-S Inc.	135,093	–	2,211	–
8.	Showa Pharmaceutical Co.	134,200	5.7	–	–
9.	Nakakita Yakuhin Co.	119,172	5.6	1,944	–23.0
10.	Akiyama Inc.	116,623	5.6	2,140	–8.1

TOP 10 WHOLESALERS OF WATCHES & JEWELRY

	COMPANY NAME	SALES	GROWTH RATE	PRETAX PROFITS	GROWTH RATE
1.	Tasaki Shinju Co.	41,214	5.4 %	2,204	–18.7%
2.	Eiko Watch Co.	30,513	–2.1	369	–5.1
3.	Tokyo Pearl Co.	24,468	–8.6	344	–58.9
4.	K. Otsuki Pearl Co.	21,613	–6.6	2,473	–35.6
5.	Nagahori Corp.	21,186	–4.4	372	–46.9
6.	Kashikey Co.	18,116	5.0	609	47.1
7.	Shinei Shokai Co.	18,063	–8.4	–	–
8.	Uchihara Co.	16,378	–2.8	234	122.9
9.	Shinei Hoshoku	15,411	–2.4	69	–26.6
10.	Bear Co.	13,537	–11.7	–	–

TOP 10 APPAREL WHOLESALERS

	COMPANY NAME	SALES	GROWTH RATE	PRETAX PROFITS	GROWTH RATE
1.	Renown Inc.	198,617	–2.6 %	–15,593	–%
2.	Takisada & Co.	181,423	–2.4	6,293	11.0
3.	Onward Kashiyama Co.	177,539	3.5	15,172	44.9
4.	Toyoshima Co.	167,736	–9.3	–	–
5.	Yagi & Co.	150,931	0.5	1,074	–20.8
6.	Gunze Sangyo Inc.	139,039	–3.9	605	–17.3
7.	Sanyo Shokai Ltd.	130,336	–2.0	417	–57.2
8.	Wacoal Corp.	127,053	1.4	10,842	6.1
9.	World Co.	124,607	–6.2	2,657	–72.5
10.	Moririn Co.	123,532	1.0	529	–48.4

TOP 10 TOY WHOLESALERS

	COMPANY NAME	SALES	GROWTH RATE	PRETAX PROFITS	GROWTH RATE
1.	Bandai Co.	114,228	–7.2 %	10,162	–0.7%
2.	Sanrio Co.	78,629	–10.0	–12,038	–
3.	HAPPINET CO.	64,903	16.7	650	–51.9
4.	Matsubaya Co.	54,373	17.5	2,223	–
5.	Yamaguchi	44,543	38.9	656	56.9
6.	Kawada Co.	44,463	–20.1	1,170	–62.1
7.	Hattori Gangu (HGK)	43,172	16.5	709	–22.8
8.	Takara Co.	42,556	–1.2	211	–
9.	Tomy Co.	24,174	–4.1	177	–
10.	Mori Toys Co.	22,167	10.9	–	–

Note: Sales and pretax profits in millions of yen   Source: Company reports

TEXTILES & APPAREL

Textile sales were off 3.5% in fiscal 1994. Though the rate of decline shrank from the 7.6% plunge in fiscal 1993, consumer belt-tightening and the growth of imports due to the strong yen continued to dampen sales. Pretax profits in fiscal 1994 were down 8.9%.

Sales of men's wear and non-kimono apparel dropped 6.7%. Though the volume of men's clothing sales did not decline greatly, discounting, especially of suits, pushed down revenues. Kimono sales tumbled 9.8% because high-priced items like kimono tend to be the ones most vulnerable to cuts in consumer spending.

Active restructuring efforts by Renown Inc. and many other firms have yet to pay off. Pretax profit per employee dropped nearly 20% to 709,000 yen, substantially below that of other wholesale sectors.

Renown in particular posted substantial operating and pretax losses due to poor sales and an increase in severance pay for workers taking early retirement.

TOYS

Sales of toys, hobby goods and leisure-time items edged up 0.7% in fiscal 1994, though operating profits were down 6.0% and pretax profits plunged 58.0%, the sharpest fall throughout the wholesale industry.

Wholesalers were hit hard by deep discounting tactics adopted by department store operators and other retailers aimed at stimulating sales.

One bright spot, however, was computer games. A great number of stores ran out of new-generation game systems released in late 1994. In particular, wholesalers dealing in Sega Enterprises Ltd.'s Sega Saturn system and Sony Computer Entertainment Inc.'s PlayStation system moved up in the sales growth rankings. Those selling Nintendo Co.'s Super Famicon games recorded lower sales.

SPECIALTY RETAILING

Profits pick up after 3-year hiatus on 4.3% rise in sales

Compiled from Nikkei
Publications: NNB

Signs of recovery are becoming apparent in the specialty retail sector. Combined fiscal 1994 sales for firms with sales of at least ¥1 billion grew a healthy 4.3% year on year, according to the Nikkei Marketing Journal's 23rd Survey of Japanese Speciality Shops. This represents the first year-on-year rise in sales growth since fiscal 1988 and is an increase of 1.8 percentage points over fiscal 1993 growth.

Consumer electronics retailers enjoyed buoyant sales, backed by brisk demand for replacement goods and strong sales of air conditioners during the hot summer. However, tougher competition served to dampen sales at men's apparel stores and toy and hobby shops.

Combined sales at 485 companies for which year-on-year comparisons were available reached ¥10.517 trillion. Pretax profits for the sector picked up for the first time in four years, expanding 3.1% on average.

Sales growth exceeded 4.2% at supermarkets and 2.7% at departments stores, thanks largely to an expansion of floor space. The number of directly-operated stores and franchises climbed 3.4% year on year, contributing to the 9.3% enlargement in retail floor space.

Restructuring efforts appear to be finally bearing fruit, as evidenced in the 0.2 point decline in the ratio of labor cost to sales to 10.2%. Pretax- and operating profits turned upward, despite the gross margin-to-sales ratio slipping 0.4 point to 28.4% in line with pressure to discount prices.

SALES AND PROFIT GROWTH

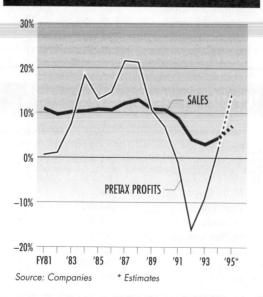

Source: Companies * Estimates

CAMERA SHOPS

Sales at retail camera shops increased 7.7%, compared with 4.7% in fiscal 1993. Top-ranking Yodobashi Camera Co. posted a hefty 14.1% rise, led by information-linked products such as personal computers.

Sales at second-ranked Bic Camera rose 7.1% and third-ranked Kitamura Co. turned around last year's decline into a 9.5% increase. But fourth-largest Doi Co. suffered a 4.9% decrease in sales.

The sector's gross margin-to-sales ratio stood at 19.4%, up 0.9 point from the year before. Meanwhile, labor costs edged down to 5.1% of sales from 5.2%. As a result, the operating profit-to-sales ratio rose 1.7 points to 3.3% and pretax profits increased 1.1 points to 3.2% of sales. Sales per capita remained unchanged from those marked in fiscal 1993.

For fiscal 1995, retail camera shops expect sales to rise 6.7% and pretax profits to expand 5.7%.

WOMEN'S & CHILDREN'S CLOTHING STORES

This sector saw sales decline 4.7% year on year. While this represents an improvement on the 7.6% drop marked the previous year, the results are none too bright. The four largest firms all suffered declining sales. On the other hand, companies with trendy new fashion labels, such as Blue Grass-affiliated Jusco Co. and casual-wear supplier Agnes B. Sunrise Inc. enjoyed brisk demand.

Pretax profits for the sector slipped 0.3 point to 0.8% of sales. And pretax losses were incurred by two of the top five companies, San-Ai Co. and Cabin Co. Sales per sq. meter of retail floor space dropped 6.8%.

For fiscal 1995, sales are projected to rise 2.7%. Nevertheless, the outlook remains bleak as apparel retailers face increasingly tough competition in the market.

MEN'S APPAREL STORES

The men's clothing sector suffered the first year-on-year drop in sales since the survey began, posting a 6.3% decline. Some 27 of the 40 firms for which year-on-year comparisons are available marked a drop in sales and almost all suit retailers saw poor results. A combination of too many new store openings, unfavorable weather, a faltering of the discount-led boom, price competition from department stores and the Kobe earthquake contributed to the lackluster results.

Although combined floor space expanded by 7.3%, this was unable to offset poor sales. Labor costs were only trimmed 0.6%, which contributed to bleak operating profits, down 37.6% year on year, and even bleaker

TOP 5 CAMERA RETAILERS

	COMPANY NAME	HEAD OFFICE	SALES (¥ million)	GROWTH RATE (%)
1	Yodobashi Camera	Tokyo	143,210	14.1
2	Bic Camera	Tokyo	100,745	7.1
3	Kitamura Co.	Tokyo	41,325	9.5
4	Doi Co.	Fukuoka	29,494	−4.9
5	Daiei Photo Enterprise	Hyogo	15,945	0.6

TOP 5 RETAILERS OF WOMEN'S & CHILDEN'S WEAR

	COMPANY NAME	HEAD OFFICE	SALES (¥ million)	GROWTH RATE (%)
1	Leilian Co.	Tokyo	84,974	−8.1
2	Suzutan Co.	Aichi	82,384	−7.1
3	San-Ai Co.	Tokyo	55,249	−11.8
4	Suzuya Co.	Tokyo	54,601	−7.2
5	Cabin Co.	Tokyo	45,902	0.6

TOP 5 RETAILERS OF MEN'S WEAR

	COMPANY NAME	HEAD OFFICE	SALES (¥ million)	GROWTH RATE (%)
1	Aoyama Trading	Hiroshima	167,730	−8.0
2	Aoki International	Kanagawa	81,538	−1.5
3	Konaka	Kanagawa	51,609	−13.5
4	Taka-Q	Tokyo	46,043	−19.8
5	Haruyama Trading Co.	Okayama	40,533	−10.1

TOP 5 CONSUMER ELECTRONICS CHAINS

	COMPANY NAME	HEAD OFFICE	SALES (¥ million)	GROWTH RATE (%)
1	Best Denki Co.	Fukuoka	216,923	8.3
2	Joshin Denki Co.	Osaka	205,205	4.9
3	Daiichi Corp.	Hiroshima	166,514	13.9
4	Kojima	Tochigi	163,421	32.3
5	Matsuyadenki Co.	Osaka	108,856	15.0

Yodobashi Camera enjoys strong sales growth that has consolidated its industry leadership.

pretax profits, which plunged 38.9%. Net profits plummeted by 70.7%, primarily since some companies reported extraordinary losses from store closings.

Depressed market conditions are likely to remain in line with an oversupply of outlets. To try and overcome the problem, a number of owners converted their stores to other businesses, such as discount liquor outlets and video rental shops.

Casual wear sales, meanwhile, rode a wave of brisk demand. Sales at Fast Retailing Co. and Right On Co. soared more than 30%. However, growth is expected to be reined in fiscal 1995.

CONSUMER ELECTRONIC STORES

Consumer electronics sales jumped 12.7%, up from 3.7% growth marked in fiscal 1993. Sparking the rise was demand for air conditioners during the exceptionally hot summer. Some stores saw air conditioner sales double from the previous year. Wide-screen TVs, consumer durables and personal computers also enjoyed brisk demand. Sales per capita expanded 10.4%.

Spectacular sales growth was recorded by Nihon Incom Co. (42.4%), Kato Denki Hanbai KK (35.8%), Yamada Denki Co. (33.1%) and Kojima (32.3%).

Operating profits for the sector expanded a huge 108.9% and pretax profits grew 54.8%. The ratio of gross margin to sales declined 0.5 percentage point but this was offset by a decline in the labor cost-to-sales ratio, which fell to 7.0% from 7.4% the previous year. Daiichi Katei Denki Co. returned to the black, posting pretax profits for the first time in four years.

The outlook for fiscal 1995 is for less spectacular growth in sales and operating and pretax profits.

SERVICE INDUSTRIES

Sales see year-on-year growth, but fall short of full-scale recovery

Compiled from Nikkei
Publications: NNB

Japan's service industry remained sluggish in fiscal 1994. According to the 13th General Survey of the Service Industry conducted by Nihon Keizai Shimbun Inc., total revenues (including outstanding loans, brokerage commissions, etc.) were up 1.5% for the 2,228 companies in 53 service sectors for which comparable results from the previous year were available.

Seventeen of the 53 sectors saw their sales decrease from a year earlier compared with 21 which fell the year before. Of those 17, five suffered year-on-year declines for the first time while the remaining 12 fell for the second straight year.

HOTELS

The hotel industry continued to experience hard times in fiscal 1994. Combined revenues were down 2.5% year on year among the 55 companies responding to this part of the survey, the third straight year they have declined. The poor showing in this sector is attributed to a plunge in revenues from corporate banquets and a decline in the average unit price per room due to severe price competition.

Only 11 hotel operators saw a rise in revenues, and of those, seven were based in regional cities. Most hotels in Tokyo suffered declining revenues.

Competition intensified nationwide. Hotel operators devised an unending series of economical banquet and lodging plans to attract customers and prevent their revenues from falling further. However, their revenues decreased because of a drop in average unit price.

Since corporate demand is not expected to pick up in the near future due to the prolonged economic downturn, the hotel industry is desperately trying to cultivate private demand, particularly for wedding receptions. Many hotels are setting up Christian-style chapels to attract young people.

All in all, most hotels expect this year to be better than fiscal 1994, with 34 of 41 hoteliers saying they expect increased revenues. However, this figure may be just wishful thinking as most of the 25 companies which forecast increased revenues for fiscal 1994 in the last survey actually posted year-on-year declines.

TRAVEL AGENCIES

Business volume increased by an average 1.7% among the 116 travel agencies for which comparable figures were available compared to a decrease of 3.4% in fiscal 1993. However, the gain was far below the 8.4% surge projected for fiscal 1994 in the previous survey due to the trend toward price cutting.

Though 81 travel agencies expect their revenues to increase by an average 5.4% in fiscal 1995, the figure is a guess rather than an estimate based on hard fact.

The Great Hanshin Earthquake of Jan. 17, 1995 was a major negative factor in fiscal 1994. Travel agencies which ended their fiscal year in or after January 1995 seem to have suffered declines in revenue of between several hundred million yen and tens of billions of yen. However, the gap in growth between travel agencies cannot be ascribed to the influence of the quake alone.

The strong yen brought about an unprecedented boom in foreign travel. Low-priced overseas package tours in particular were strongly supported by consumers. Domestic and corporate/group division business, however, remained sluggish.

Companies that aggressively sold overseas tours, including budget tours, to individual travelers, therefore, enjoyed strong growth, with some posting double-digit increases.

The four major travel agencies posted results that were basically flat from a year earlier, ranging from a decline of 1.9% to a rise of 2.4%.

Despite weak demand in domestic and corporate/group divisions, companies that anticipated the needs of consumers and then responded to those needs managed to grow.

CREDIT CARDS

Credit card shopping grew 2.1% year on year in fiscal 1994 compared to a decline of 0.5% in fiscal 1993. Though sales at department stores, which account for about 30% of credit card sales, remained slack, the use of cards for overseas purchases showed strong growth. An increase in the type and number of places other than department stores where cards can be used and a surge in the use of cash-dispensing machines by credit cards also helped to boost credit card sales.

Particularly noticeable was the growth in the number of companies affiliated with specific retailers that issued cards and cards for use at gas stations.

Retailer-affiliated Aeon Credit Service Co., Ltd. tried to achieve a high utilization rate for its card by cultivating member-establishments in commercial districts surrounding supermarkets operated by Jusco Co. Its card sales soared 28.1% in fiscal 1994 from the previous year. Daiei OMC Inc. also posted a year-on-year surge of 17.2% by encouraging its cardholders to use their cards when shopping at outlets operated by Daiei Inc., the nation's largest supermarket operator.

In a bid to boost card utilization, JCB Co. and Sumitomo Credit Service Co. introduced a system making it more convenient for cardholders to shop at supermar-

SERVICE INDUSTRY AND ECONOMY

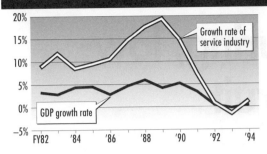

kets and department stores by not requiring them to sign for their purchases.

JOB PLACEMENT AGENCIES

The personnel placement industry bottomed out in fiscal 1994. Revenues were down 2.9% for the 99 companies for which comparable data from the previous year was available compared to an 11.7% plunge in fiscal 1993. Major corporations that had completed their restructuring programs began to fill vacancies resulting from natural attrition with temporary workers.

All of the top 10 placement agencies, except for seventh-ranking Alphastar Corp., saw smaller year-on-year increases or decreases in their sales in fiscal 1994. The placement business started to pick up in the latter half of 1993 and a full-scale recovery began in the autumn of 1994, industry sources say.

Firms in general are optimistic about fiscal 1995, with the 88 companies for which there is comparable data from the year before anticipating an average growth of 13.8%. Industry-leading Pasona Inc. projects a 19% increase.

Placement agencies are endeavoring this fiscal year to develop new businesses, enhance services and accelerate staff training to satisfy more demanding clients.

DOOR-TO-DOOR PARCEL DELIVERY

The door-to-door parcel delivery business is growing steadily overall. Total sales surged 6.9% among the 19 companies for which comparable results were available from the previous year. Fifteen companies expect their sales to increase by an average 6.7% in fiscal 1995. It should be noted that the sales gap between major companies with nationwide networks and smaller ones is widening.

The number of parcels delivered door-to-door in fiscal 1994 grew 6.7% to almost 1.33 billion, according to the Ministry of Transport. The number delivered by truck increased 6.6% while air cargo deliveries soared 28.9%.

Corporate demand for door-to-door parcel delivery grew in fiscal 1994. Demand for refrigerated door-to-door parcel delivery expanded as well due to increased mail-order sales and mid-summer and year-end gift giving. Hikes in government parcel post rates in November 1992 accelerated the shift from sending packages through the post office to private-sector door-to-door delivery services.

Yamato Transport Co. controlled 44.6% of the market in terms of volume, followed by Nippon Express Co. at 25.2%, Footwork International Corp. at 9.1% and Seino Transportation Co. at 9.0%.

TOP 5 HOTELS

	COMPANY NAME	HEAD OFFICE	SALES (¥ million)	GROWTH RATE (%)
1	Prince Hotels	Tokyo	138,752	-0.3
2	Hotel New Otani	Tokyo	56,134	-4.2
3	Tokyu Hotel Chain	Tokyo	53,732	-5.2
4	Tokyu Inn Chain	Tokyo	50,183	-2.8
5	Fujita Kanko	Tokyo	49,096	-3.6

TOP 5 TRAVEL AGENCIES

	COMPANY NAME	HEAD OFFICE	SALES (¥ million)	GROWTH RATE (%)
1	JTB	Tokyo	1,450,400	1.0
2	Kinki Nippon Tourist	Tokyo	775,966	2.4
3	Nippon Travel Agency	Tokyo	488,403	-1.9
4	Tokyu Tourist Corp.	Tokyo	289,572	-1.5
5	Hankyu Express International Co.	Osaka	217,348	5.4

TOP 5 CREDIT CARD COMPANIES

	COMPANY NAME	HEAD OFFICE	SALES (¥ million)	GROWTH RATE (%)
1	JCB	Tokyo	3,514,897	0.4
2	VISA Japan	Tokyo	2,623,522	3.1
3	Union Credit	Tokyo	1,833,376	-5.2
4	Nippon Shinpan	Tokyo	1,453,220	4.7
5	DC Card	Tokyo	1,173,030	3.0

TOP 5 TEMPORARY STAFF AGENCIES

	COMPANY NAME	HEAD OFFICE	SALES (¥ million)	GROWTH RATE (%)
1	Pasona	Tokyo	84,000	-9.2
2	Career Staff Co.	Tokyo	15,266	0.9
3	Staff Service Co.	Kyoto	13,687	1.4
4	Recruit She's Staff Co.	Tokyo	11,500	16.9
5	Adia Central Co.	Tokyo	8,396	-5.2

TOP 5 PERCEL DELIVERERS

	COMPANY NAME	HEAD OFFICE	SALES (¥ million)	GROWTH RATE (%)
1	Yamato Transport	Tokyo	455,273	8.1
2	Seino Transportation	Gifu	52,717	4.0
3	Fukuyama Transporting	Hiroshima	49,173	1.9
4	Footwork International	Osaka	44,910	9.5
5	Meitetsu Transport	Aichi	14,171	0.2

RESTAURANTS/FOOD SERVICES

Profits rise as restructuring, low-price strategies bear fruit

Compiled from Nikkei Publications: NNB

Belt-tightening measures adopted by restauranteurs over the past few years finally seem to be translating into healthier bottom lines. Aggregate sales for the top 100 restauranteurs hit ¥3.778 trillion in fiscal 1994, according to the Nikkei Marketing Journal's 21st annual survey of the industry.

This represents the first significant year-on-year sales growth in four years, expanding 3.1% (for the 97 firms for which comparisons were available). Smaller companies showed the most dramatic sales growth, with those ranked 51-100 in terms of turnover averaging 5.6%. Overall sales rose 2.9% year on year for the 315 firms for which comparisons were available.

Managers continued to devise more cost-competitive meals and reduce overhead costs, which appeared to be the industry's recipe for success. Fiscal 1994 pretax profits for the top 128 firms rose a healthy 6.4% year on year, reversing the 7.7% decline marked in fiscal 1993.

"Customers are coming back," said Hokkahokkatei Sohonbu KK, a take-out lunch chain operator, which moved up to second from fourth in the rankings, on the back of 7.3% sales growth.

BUDGET MEALS APPEAL

By sector, fast-food restaurant operators fared well, with McDonald's Co. (Japan) maintaining the top ranking in terms of sales. Thanks to strong demand for budget-combo meals, or combinations of hamburgers and drinks for a set price, the leading hamburger chain store saw sales rise 1.5% over the previous year.

Other fast-food and family restaurant chains, such as Skylark Co., Seiyo Food Systems Inc. and Lotteria Co., marked a rebound in sales growth attributed to lower-priced menus and restructuring efforts. Japanese-style taverns cut prices and clocked up a 4.3% rise in sales from fiscal 1993.

Sales at Western-style restaurants expanded 5.2%, in line with a 7.1% increase in the number of establishments. Meanwhile, pubs and night clubs saw sales rise 5.9%, compared to only 1.8% the previous year, largely attributed to a 4.5% increase in the number of new establishments.

But the stars of the restaurant sector continued to be home-delivery companies, including pizza delivery franchises. Sales expanded a whopping 26.3% in fiscal 1994, eclipsing the 20% growth of the previous year. And the number of new outlets increased by 26.7% year on year.

On the other side of the fence, hotel operators continued to suffer from declining corporate expense accounts, marking a 2.5% drop in sales (for the 55 firms for which year-on-year comparisons were available). While this represented a slight improvement over the 4.2% decline marked in fiscal 1993, the yen's appreciation and the Jan. 17 Kobe earthquake were blamed for the lack of growth.

IMPORTS CUT FOOD COSTS

Turning the yen's appreciation to their advantage, many restauranteurs stepped up imports of foodstuffs, mostly from other Asian countries. Western-style fast-food outlets imported some 80% of their supplies and the ratio rose to 65% for Chinese and Korean restaurant operators and 56.7% for western-style taverns.

Kentucky Fried Chicken Japan Ltd. is aiming to slash food costs by ¥1 billion by importing chicken from the U.S. and China. Meantime, Skylark will import spinach from China that has been grown from Japanese seeds in order to satisfy domestic taste buds.

Among Japanese-style fast-food restaurants, 28.6% recorded a substantial increase in the volume of imported foodstuffs and some 22.2% of pubs and clubs did likewise. Tsubohachi Co., a pub restaurant chain cut wholesale prices to franchisees by 10% by importing ready-to-grill yakitori from Thailand, sidestepping higher processing costs in Japan.

Prepaid cards were introduced at a growing number of establishments to boost sales. A total of 43 companies out of 224 said they had already implemented the system and a further 23 were considering doing so. McDonald's saw fiscal 1994 sales of prepaid cards jump eight-fold from 1991, when they were introduced.

Credit cards were also more widely accepted by restaurant companies, including Willy KK, a home-delivery pizza firm hoping to entice cash-strapped customers prior to pay day.

McDonald's outlets offer half-price sales.

RESTAURANTS RANKING FOR FY94

FY94	FY93	COMPANY NAME	SALES (¥ MILLION)	GROWTH RATE (%)	NUMBER OF OUTLETS	TYPE OF BUSINESS	HEAD OFFICE	BOOK CLOSING
1	1	McDonald's Japan	215,237	1.5	1,092	hamburgers	Tokyo	December
2	4	Hokkahokkatei Sohonbu	139,954	7.3	2,656	take-out lunch	Tokyo	February
3	3	Skylark	139,548	4.7	816	Western-style	Tokyo	December
4	2	Kentucky Fried Chicken Japan	132,268	–1.9	1,148	fried chicken	Tokyo	November
5	5	Mos Food Services	121,000	9.3	1,330	hamburgers	Tokyo	March
6	7	Honke Kamadoya	108,055	2.5	2,307	take-out lunch	Hyogo	March
7	8	Duskin	103,759	4.0	837	doughnuts	Osaka	March
8	9	Royal	101,229	3.5	428	Western-style	Fukuoka	December
9	6	Kozozushi Honbu	100,744	–4.7	2,000	take-out sushi	Osaka	December
10	10	Denny's Japan	95,000	2.5	471	Western-style	Tokyo	February
11	11	Seiyo Food Systems	94,320	2.2	725	multi-caterer	Tokyo	March
12	12	Yoronotaki	84,113	2.0	1,753	pub	Tokyo	March
13	13	Prince Hotels	72,410	–1.6	–	hotel	Tokyo	March
14	16	Lotteria	66,000	2.4	579	hamburgers	Tokyo	January
15	15	Yoshinoya D&C	65,900	–4.2	550	beef bowl	Tokyo	February
16	14	Kyotaru	62,931	–13.1	792	take-out sushi	Tokyo	December
17	17	Murasaki	57,746	0.3	656	pub	Tokyo	March
18	18	Tsubohachi	55,692	2.0	511	pub	Tokyo	September
19	19	Fujita Kanko (Kowakien)	49,520	–4.2	–	hotel	Tokyo	December
20	20	Ohsho Food Service	46,142	5.3	408	Chinese-style	Kyoto	March
21	21	Shidax	45,736	4.6	1,904	corporate caterer	Tokyo	December
22	23	Coco's Japan	43,003	12.8	264	Western-style	Ibaraki	February
23	22	Hotel New Otani	40,167	–		hotel	Tokyo	March
24	24	Nikkoku Trust	37,396	1.9	891	corporate caterer	Tokyo	January
25	35	Sakae Shoji	34,800	14.8	445	Chinese noodles	Tokyo	March
26	33	Doutor Coffee	34,050	10.0	602	coffee shop	Tokyo	March
27	31	Aim Service	34,000	7.8	356	corporate caterer	Tokyo	March
28	29	Dinac	33,954	5.9	211	multi-caterer	Tokyo	December
29	26	New Tokyo Restaurant	33,659	0.4	171	multi-caterer	Tokyo	December
30	36	Taisho	33,277	10.0	303	pub	Tokyo	August
31	30	Nippon Shokudo	32,653	2.3	95	dining car	Tokyo	December
32	25	TFK	32,430	–3.8	18	in-flight caterer	Chiba	March
33	32	Sapporo Lion	31,800	1.2	195	beer restaurant	Tokyo	December
34	28	Daiwa Jitsugyo	31,500	–2.0	193	multi-caterer	Osaka	March
34	34	Sato	31,500	2.4	211	Japanese-style	Osaka	March
36	27	Tokyu Hotel Chain	31,342	–5.5	–	hotel	Tokyo	December
37	44	Jonas	29,423	9.8	158	multi-caterer	Tokyo	December
38	38	Kisoji	28,850	2.2	113	Japanese-style	Aichi	March
39	169	Uokuni Sohonsha	28,563	–	577	corporate caterer	Osaka	August
40	45	Sunday's Sun	28,085	6.1	186	Western-style	Yamaguchi	March
41	48	Green House	28,000	16.2	410	corporate caterer	Tokyo	March
42	42	Folks	27,800	3.4	163	steak house	Tokyo	February
43	40	Royal Hotel	27,730	0.6	–	hotel	Osaka	March
44	37	J Diner Tokai	27,189	–5.9	321	multi-caterer	Tokyo	March
45	39	Hokkoku	27,087	–2.7	1,042	Chinese noodles	Tokyo	March
46	55	Ten Allied	26,804	19.0	140	pub	Tokyo	March
47	41	Imperial Hotel	26,670	–1.2	–	hotel	Tokyo	March
48	43	Shun Yodo	26,460	–1.4	561	take-out sushi	Kyoto	March
49	47	Gourmet Kineya	26,420	5.7	397	multi-caterer	Osaka	March
50	53	Pizza California	25,560	11.8	326	home-delivery pizza	Tokyo	October

CONVENIENCE STORES

Double-digit sales growth thanks to hot summer, aggressive openings

Compiled from Nikkei
Publications: NNB

The convenience sector enjoyed a return to double-digit growth in fiscal 1994, according to a survey of 122 companies by the Nikkei Marketing Journal. After four years of declining growth, bottoming out at 8.9% in fiscal 1993, sales expanded just over 10% in the 1994 business term. Contributing to the rebound was an unusually hot summer, which prompted a sharp increase in sales of beverages, ice creams and other seasonal items. Meanwhile, aggressive store openings provided a significant boost to overall sales. The number of outlets rose by around 9% over the previous year, for the fourth consecutive year. As a result, concerns of the market nearing saturation appear unfounded.

Midsizefirms, or those with annual sales between ¥10 billion and ¥100 billion, were the stars among convenience store operators in fiscal 1994. Aggregate sales in the segment rose 13.1% year on year, almost triple the growth rate marked by their larger competitors. In terms of new outlets, midsize chains, with a 12% year-on-year increase, also came out ahead of large firms. Operators with annual sales in excess of ¥100 billion expanded store numbers by 8.2%.

While midsize chains work toward establishing a concentration of outlets in one area, they have yet to reach the level of larger chains. "As chain store operators, midsize firms need to secure a number of profitable stores within a short period," says the chief of am/pm Japan, explaining the segment's rapid rate of expansion. Hence, regional operators in the mid-size classification and large companies ranked in the top slots in terms of store openings and sales growth. Mini Stop Kansai headed the list, followed by am/pm Japan, Hokuriku Family Mart and Poplar Co.

New outlets aside, neither midsize nor large chains were able to break out of the stagnant pattern of sales growth among existing stores (2.2% over fiscal 1993). Pressure to cut prices, in line with stiffening competition from supermarkets and discount stores, was blamed for the poor growth.

Since May 1994, major retailers have been permitted to extend opening hours under amendments to the Large-Scale Retail Store Law. With their price-competitive merchandise, the muscles of the retail business were able to lure increasingly price-conscious consumers away from convenience stores.

Changes to the retailing laws scored a direct hit on convenience stores' biggest marketing weapon: their "convenience." No less than 89.8% of convenience shop operators surveyed said their sales declined as a result of the longer opening hours for their competitors.

Rising to the challenge, convenience chains implemented aggressive price-cutting strategies. Larger companies introduced low-priced private brand merchandise and others discounted national brand goods. More than half (53.5%) of the survey respondents reduced prices of national brand goods in fiscal 1994, up 5.6 percentage points over the previous year.

Hardest hit by the price-discounting war, which spread across the retail spectrum, were the small convenience store operators. Lacking the sales volume of larger chains, they were squeezed by smaller profit margins as unit prices and per-customer sales sank. Combined sales at existing stores in fiscal 1994 grew only 1.4%, down 0.4 of a percentage point from the previous year, among small operators, or those with annual sales of less than ¥10 billion.

On a brighter note, expansion in the industry was spearheaded by operators with liquor licenses. And the trend is set to continue, with a full 82.4% of all survey respondents indicating they would increase the number of stores handling alcohol. With the difference in daily sales between licensed and unlicensed stores reportedly around ¥100,000, alcohol is a major money spinner for convenience shops.

Rice is another product operators are targeting. Permission to sell rice will shift from a licensing to a registration system in June 1996 and most convenience store firms are examining ways to capitalize on the liberalization. More than half the companies surveyed said they planned increase the number of stores selling rice.

Customers crowd convenience store counters, bringing sales growth of better than 10%.

CONVENIENCE STORES RANKING FOR FY94

FY94	FY93	COMPANY NAME	SALES (¥ MILLION)	GROWTH RATE (%)	GROUP COMPANY	HEAD OFFICE	NUMBER OF OUTLETS (GROWTH RATE)
1	(1)	Seven-Eleven Japan	1,392,312	8.6	Ito-Yokado	Tokyo	5,905 (7.9)
2	(2)	Daiei Convenience Systems	821,400	12.1	Daiei	Osaka	5,139 (6.3)
3	(3)	Family Mart Co.	486,250	8.9	Seiyu	Tokyo	2,749 (9.4)
4	(4)	Sun-Shop Yamazaki	353,203	5.3	Yamazaki Baking	Chiba	2,616 (5.4)
5	(5)	Circle K Japan	257,116	16.3	Uny	Aichi	1,622 (12.2)
6	(6)	Sunkus & Associates Inc.	185,908	18.8	Ono Group	Tokyo	1,093 (17.5)
7	(9)	Mini Stop Co.	94,009	14.6	Jusco	Tokyo	603 (18.0)
8	(8)	Kasumi Convenience Networks	89,701	6.0	Kasumi	Ibaraki	721 (8.6)
9	(7)	Kokubu & Co.	88,000	2.3	–	Tokyo	612 (0.3)
10	(10)	Seicomart Co.	83,321	12.9	Maruyo Nishio	Hokkaido	529 (11.1)
11	(11)	CoCo Store	77,300	5.5	Izumic	Aichi	553 (4.7)
12	(12)	Monmart Store Systems	69,345	-2.3	–	Tokyo	460 (1.8)
13	(13)	3F	60,993	23.8	Fuji Citio	Kanagawa	371 (23.7)
14	(14)	Save On Co.	58,292	22.9	Iseya	Gunma	497 (15.6)
15	(19)	am/pm Japan	52,000	126.9	Japan Energy	Tokyo	401 (54.2)
16	(15)	Hiroya Co.	41,000	0.2	–	Tokyo	276 (4.5)
17	(16)	Chubu Family Mart	39,430	20.5	Family Mart	Aichi	275 (15.1)
18	(17)	Poplar Co.	38,034	28.1	–	Hiroshima	301 (40.7)
19	(18)	Spar Kyushu	31,464	11.8	Kotobukiya Group	Kumamoto	229 (17.4)
20	(21)	I Family Mart	21,525	27.3	Iwataya	Fukuoka	165 (17.0)
21	(20)	Shop & Life	19,400	3.5	–	Tokyo	120 (5.3)
22	(27)	Spar Tohoku	17,300	14.3	Bell Center	Iwate	117 (11.4)
23	(26)	Tsukinotomo	17,145	12.4	–	Ibaraki	127 (12.4)
24	(22)	Spar Higashi-Kinki	16,940	5.0	Heiwado	Shiga	121 (2.5)
25	(28)	Jairo	16,647	18.2	Koami	Tokyo	123 (16.0)
26	(25)	Ryutsu	16,598	8.5	–	Tokyo	140 (7.7)
27	(29)	Circle K North Japan	15,400	20.3	Kameya Minami Chain	Aomori	111 (20.7)
28	(23)	FG My Charmy	15,144	-4.8	Hiroya	Tokyo	118 (0.9)
29	(24)	Madoka	15,000	-2.3	–	Ehime	165 (-5.7)
30	(30)	Ibaraki Seicomart	13,183	3.4	Seicomart	Ibaraki	98 (8.9)
31	(31)	M M Chain	13,100	4.5	Mizutani Shoji	Kanagawa	101 (-1.0)
32	(32)	Heart & Action Retail	12,068	15.7	West Japan Railway	Osaka	69 (6.2)
33	(42)	Matsuhaya Family Mart	9,774	36.1	Matsuhaya Convenience Store	Nagasaki	81 (20.9)
34	(34)	Familiar Kyoto	9,605	0.6	Yukijirushi Access	Kyoto	84 (7.7)
35	(38)	Pasco Retail	9,500	20.7	Pasco	Kanagawa	67 (9.8)
36	(45)	Timely	9,190	35.1		Gifu	67 (45.7)
37	(35)	Times Mart	8,906	-0.4	Sato Tokuzo Shoten	Tokyo	61 (7.0)
38	(44)	Okinawa Family Mart	8,684	26.0	Ryubo	Okinawa	71 (18.3)
39	(33)	Captain House Japan	8,640	-11.1	–	Tochigi	72 (0.0)
40	(36)	Pumpkin	7,740	-12.0	OK Corp.	Tokyo	46 (-23.3)
41	(47)	Sunny Mart	7,495	15.3	–	Kochi	52 (6.1)
42	(59)	Hokuriku Family Mart	7,419	52.4	Youth	Fukui	63 (43.2)
43	(40)	Tick Tuck Systems	7,350	-0.7	Nihonkai Shuhan	Toyama	46 (0.0)
44	(41)	Sangen	7,324	0.0	–	Tokyo	53 (3.9)
45	(46)	Shinsengumi Honbu	7,296	8.1	–	Tokyo	37 (-7.5)
46	(50)	Hokuriku Hot Spar	7,220	16.1	Albis	Toyama	63 (6.8)
47	(48)	Camel Mart Japan	7,100	10.1	Morioka Shurui Shogyo Kyodo Kumiai	Iwate	51 (10.9)
48	(39)	Sunluck Chain	7,000	-6.7	Sanraku Shoten	Aichi	61 (5.2)
49	(43)	I & Retail	6,921	0.1	Inoueki Co.	Fukuoka	59 (0.0)
50	(55)	Keiji Seicomart	6,917	25.4	Shiga Shuhan	Shiga	53 (32.5)

Directories & Statistics

LIST OF CONTENTS

Imperial Family Genealogy

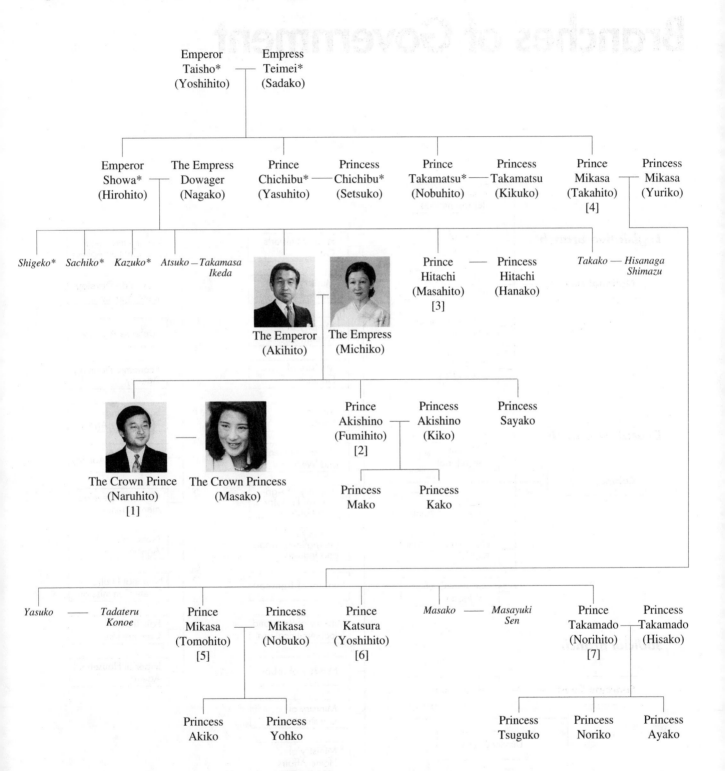

Emperor Taisho* (Yoshihito) — Empress Teimei* (Sadako)

Emperor Showa* (Hirohito) — The Empress Dowager (Nagako)

Prince Chichibu* (Yasuhito) — Princess Chichibu* (Setsuko)

Prince Takamatsu* (Nobuhito) — Princess Takamatsu (Kikuko)

Prince Mikasa (Takahito) [4] — Princess Mikasa (Yuriko)

Shigeko* Sachiko* Kazuko* Atsuko — Takamasa Ikeda

Prince Hitachi (Masahito) [3] — Princess Hitachi (Hanako)

Takako — Hisanaga Shimazu

The Emperor (Akihito) — The Empress (Michiko)

The Crown Prince (Naruhito) [1] — The Crown Princess (Masako)

Prince Akishino (Fumihito) [2] — Princess Akishino (Kiko)

Princess Sayako

Princess Mako   Princess Kako

Yasuko — Tadateru Konoe

Prince Mikasa (Tomohito) [5] — Princess Mikasa (Nobuko)

Prince Katsura (Yoshihito) [6]

Masako — Masayuki Sen

Prince Takamado (Norihito) [7] — Princess Takamado (Hisako)

Princess Akiko   Princess Yohko

Princess Tsuguko   Princess Noriko   Princess Ayako

Bracketed numbers indicate line of succession.

Italics indicate former princesses whose membership in the Imperial Family ended upon marriage, and their husbands.

* Deceased.

Branches of Government

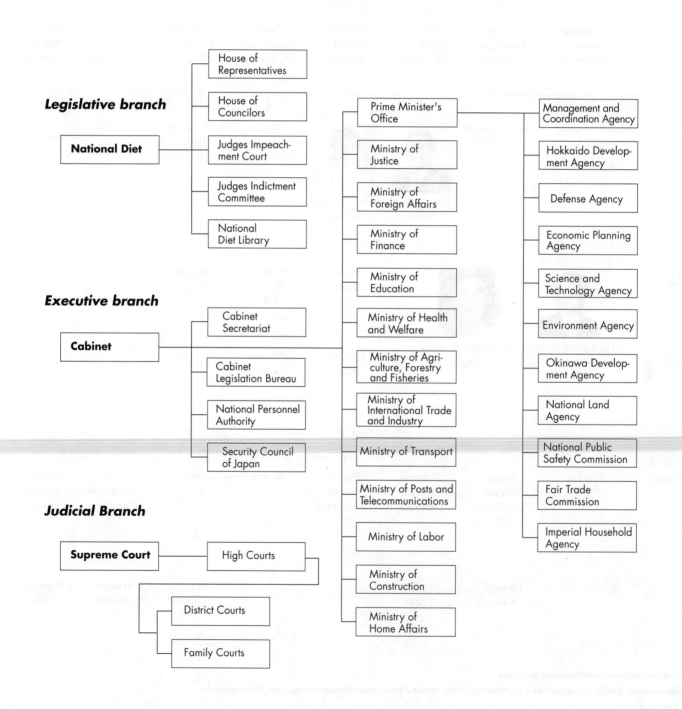

National Diet

HOUSE OF REPRESENTATIVES

7-1, Nagatacho 1-chome, Chiyoda-ku, Tokyo 100
TEL:(03)3581-5111

Speaker: Takako Doi

Vice Speaker: Hyosuke Kujiraoka

■ Secretariat
Secretary-General: Fukumaru Tani

■ Legislative Bureau
Director-General: Kazuhiro Sakamoto

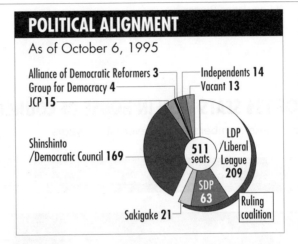

POLITICAL ALIGNMENT

As of October 6, 1995

- Alliance of Democratic Reformers **3**
- Group for Democracy **4**
- JCP **15**
- Shinshinto /Democratic Council **169**
- Sakigake **21**
- SDP **63**
- LDP /Liberal League **209**
- Independents **14**
- Vacant **13**
- **511 seats**
- Ruling coalition

Takako Doi
Speaker

BREAKDOWN OF 511 SEATS WON IN HOUSE OF REPRESENTATIVE ELECTIONS

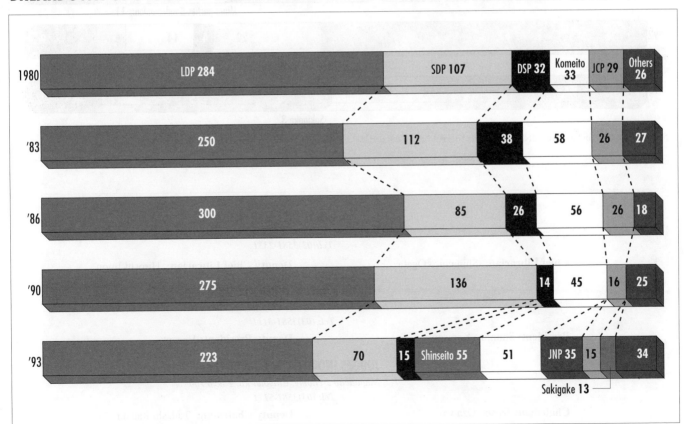

1980	LDP 284	SDP 107	DSP 32	Komeito 33	JCP 29	Others 26	
'83	250	112	38	58	26	27	
'86	300	85	26	56	26	18	
'90	275	136	14	45	16	25	
'93	223	70	15	Shinseito 55	51	JNP 35	15	34

Sakigake 13

HOUSE OF COUNCILORS

11-16, Nagatacho 1-chome, Chiyoda-ku, Tokyo 100
TEL:(03)3581-3111

President: Juro Saito

Vice President: Kanpei Matsuo

■ Secretariat
Secretary-General: Masao Tobari

■ Legislative Bureau
Director-General: Nobutoshi Tajima

Juro Saito
President

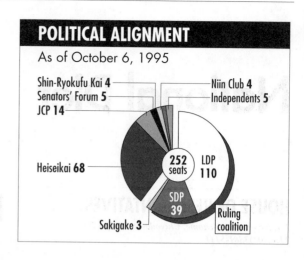

POLITICAL ALIGNMENT

As of October 6, 1995

- Shin-Ryokufu Kai **4**
- Senators' Forum **5**
- JCP **14**
- Niin Club **4**
- Independents **5**
- Heiseikai **68**
- 252 seats
- LDP **110**
- SDP **39**
- Sakigake **3**
- Ruling coalition

BREAKDOWN OF 126 SEATS WON IN HOUSE OF COUNCILORS ELECTIONS

Half of 252 upper house members elected every three years

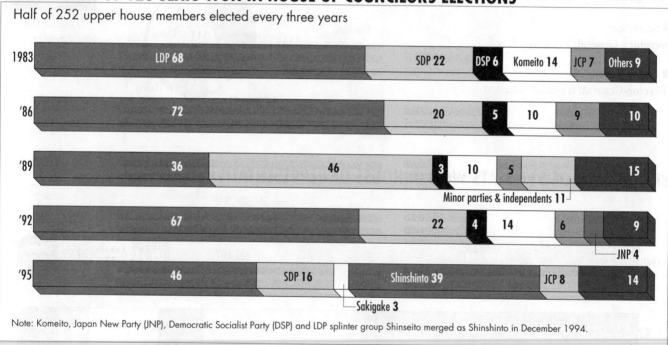

1983: LDP 68, SDP 22, DSP 6, Komeito 14, JCP 7, Others 9
'86: 72, 20, 5, 10, 9, 10
'89: 36, 46, 3, 10, 5, 15 — Minor parties & independents 11
'92: 67, 22, 4, 14, 6, 9 — JNP 4
'95: 46, SDP 16, Sakigake 3, Shinshinto 39, JCP 8, 14

Note: Komeito, Japan New Party (JNP), Democratic Socialist Party (DSP) and LDP splinter group Shinseito merged as Shinshinto in December 1994.

NATIONAL DIET LIBRARY
10-1, Nagatacho 1-chome, Chiyoda-ku, Tokyo 100
Tel:(03)3581-2331

Chief Librarian: Shinichiro Ogata   **Deputy Chief Librarian:** Hiroshi Imon

JUDGES IMPEACHMENT COURT
11-16, Nagatacho 1-chome, Chiyoda-ku, Tokyo 100
Tel: (03)3581-3111

President: Shunjiro Karasawa   **Deputy President:** Vacant

JUDGES INDICTMENT COMMITTEE
1-2, Nagatacho 2-chome, Chiyoda-ku, Tokyo 100
Tel: (03)3581-5111

Chairman: Tatsuo Ozawa   **Deputy Chairman:** Tadashi Itagaki

Major Political Parties

THREE RULING COALITION PARTIES

LIBERAL DEMOCRATIC PARTY

1-11-23, Nagatacho, Chiyoda-ku, Tokyo 100
Tel:(03)3581-6211

President: Ryutaro Hashimoto
Vice President: Vacant
Secretary-General: Koichi Kato
Acting Secretary-General: Hiromu Nonaka
Chairman of the General Council: Masajuro Shiokawa
Chairman of the Policy Research Council:
Taku Yamasaki

Chairman of the Diet Affairs Committee:
Kenzo Muraoka
Chairman of the Party Organization and Public Relations Headquarters: Shizuka Kamei

Diet Representation
House of Representatives: 202
House of Councilors: 110

Ryutaro Hashimoto
President

SOCIAL DEMOCRATIC PARTY OF JAPAN

1-8-1 Nagatacho, Chiyoda-ku, Tokyo 100
Tel: (03)3580-1171

Chairman: Tomiichi Murayama
Vice-Chairpersons: Kosuke Uehara
              Kanjyu Sato
              Keiko Chiba
General Secretary: Wataru Kubo
Deputy General Secretary: Hideyuki Maejima
              Masanori Goto

Diet Representation
House of Representatives: 64
House of Councilors: 39

Tomiichi Murayama
Chairman

SAKIGAKE

2-17-42 Akasaka, Minato-ku, Tokyo 107
Tel:(03)5570-1341

Chairman: Masayoshi Takemura
Secretary-General: Yukio Hatoyama

Diet Representation
House of Representatives: 20
House of Councilors: 3

Masayoshi Takemura
Chairman

OPPOSITION PARTIES

SHINSHINTO

No.18 Mori Bldg., 2-3-13 Toranomon, Minato-ku, Tokyo 105
Tel:(03)3502-7111

Toshiki Kaifu
President

President: Toshiki Kaifu

Vice Presidents: Tsutomu Hata, Koushiro Ishida, Takashi Yonezawa

Secretary General: Ichiro Ozawa

First Deputy Secretary Generals: Kozo Watanabe
Keiwa Okuda
Takeshi Noda

Diet Representation

House of Representatives: 169

House of Councilors: 56

JAPAN COMMUNIST PARTY

4-26-7, Sendagaya, Shibuya-ku, Tokyo 151
Tel:(03)3403-6111

Kenji Miyamoto
Chairman

Chairman of the Central Committee:
Kenji Miyamoto

Chairman of the Presidium: Tetsuzo Fuwa

Head of the Secretariat: Kazuo Shii

Vice-Chairman of the Central Committee:
Hiroshi Tachiki

Vice-Chairmen of the Presidium: Koichiro Ueda,
Mitsuhiro Kaneko

Diet Representation

House of Representatives: 15

House of Councilors: 14

Murayama Cabinet

(Reshuffled Aug.8, 1995)

Prime Minister
Tomiichi Murayama (71)
SDP

Deputy Prime Minister and Foreign Minister
Yohei Kono (58), retained
LDP

Justice Minister
Hiroshi Miyazawa (74)
LDP

Finance Minister
Masayoshi Takemura (60), retained
Sakigake

Education Minister
Yoshinobu Shimamura (61)
LDP

Health and Welfare Minister
Churyo Morii (66)
SDP

Agriculture, Forestry and Fisheries Minister
Hosei Norota (65)
LDP

International Trade and Industry Minister
Ryutaro Hashimoto (58), retained
LDP

Transport Minister
Takeo Hiranuma (56)
LDP

Posts and Telecommunications Minister
Issei Inoue (63)
SDP

Labor Minister
Shinji Aoki (69)
SDP

Construction Minister
Yoshiro Mori (58)
LDP

Home Affairs Minister and National Public Safety Commission Chairman
Takashi Fukaya (59)
LDP

Chief Cabinet Secretary
Koken Nosaka (70)
SDP

Management and Coordination Agency Director General
Takami Eto (70)
LDP

Hokkaido and Okinawa Development Agency Director General
Masaaki Takagi (66)
LDP

Defense Agency Director General
Seishiro Eto (54)
LDP

Economic Planning Agency Director General
Isamu Miyazaki (71)
unaffiliated

Science and Technology Agency Director General
Yasuoki Urano (53)
LDP

Environment Agency Director General
Tadamori Oshima (48)
LDP

National Land Agency Director General
Seiichi Ikehata (65)
SDP

Cabinet Legislation Bureau Director General
Takao Ode (62)
unaffiliated

Government

Tomiichi Murayama
Prime Minister

PRIME MINISTER'S OFFICE

6-1, Nagatacho 1-chome, Chiyoda-ku, Tokyo 100
Tel: (03)3581-2361

Prime Minister: Tomiichi Murayama
Chief Cabinet Secretary: Koken Nosaka
Deputy Chief Cabinet Secretaries: Hiroyuki Sonoda
Teijiro Furukawa

Deputy Vice-Minister of Prime Minister's Office:
Kanji Takaoka
Decoration Bureau
Director-General: Soshu Ishide

Committees and Councils

Fair Trade Commission
National Public Safety Commission
Environmental Disputes Coordination Commission
Science Council of Japan
Central Disaster Prevention Council
Conference on Environmental Pollution Control
Consumer Protection Council
Central Traffic Security Council
Public Prosecutors Qualifications Examination Committee
Executive Office of the Advisory Council on Social Security
Local Government System Research Council
Election System Council
Electric Power Development Coordination Council

Fund Operation Council
Atomic Energy Commission
Nuclear Safety Commission
Prostitution Countermeasures Council
National Development Arterial Expressway Construction Council
Council for Science and Technology
Tax Commission
Council of Foreign Economic Co-operation
Space Activities Commission
Council for Ocean Development
Trade Conference
Port and Harbour Co-ordination Council
Council for Historical Features in Ancient Capitals
Animal Protection Council

Koken Nosaka
Chief Cabinet
Secretary and State
Minister

CABINET SECRETARIAT

3-1, Nagatacho 2-chome, Chiyoda-ku, Tokyo 100
Tel: (03)3581-0101

Chief Cabinet Secretary and
State Minister: Koken Nosaka

Cabinet Councillors' Office
Councillor in Chief: Yoshitake Ota
Cabinet Councillors' Office on Internal Affairs
Councillor in Chief: Takeshi Fujii

Cabinet Councillors' Office on External Affairs
Councillor in Chief: Hiroshi Hirabayashi
Cabinet Public Relations Office
Director: Yoshihiro Handa
Cabinet Research Office
Director: Yoshio Omori

CABINET LEGISLATIVE BUREAU

Director-General: Takao Ode

BOARD OF AUDIT

2-1, Kasumigaseki 3-chome, Chiyoda-ku, Tokyo 100
Tel: (03)3581-3251

Audit Commission
President Commissioner: Yukou Sekiguchi

General Executive Bureau
Secretary General: Takeshi Abe
Assistant Secretary: Takao Nakajima

NATIONAL PERSONNEL AUTHORITY

1-2, Kasumigaseki 2-chome, Chiyoda-ku, Tokyo 100
Tel: (03)3581-5311

President: Keinosuke Yatomi
Commissioners: Minoru Hariya
               Atsunobu Ichikawa

Secretariat
Executive Director: Seinosuke Niwa

NATIONAL POLICE AGENCY

1-2, Kasumigaseki 2-chome, Chiyoda-ku, Tokyo 100
Tel: (03)3581-0141

Commissioner General: Takaji Kunimatsu
Deputy Commissioner General: Yukou Sekiguchi

Secretariat
Director-General: Kiyotaka Suganuma

IMPERIAL HOUSEHOLD AGENCY

1-1, Chiyoda, Chiyoda-ku, Tokyo 100
Tel: (03)3213-1111

Grand Steward: Shoichi Fujimori

MANAGEMENT AND COORDINATION AGENCY

1-1, Kasumigaseki 3-chome, Chiyoda-ku, Tokyo 100
Tel: (03)3581-6361

Director-General and State Minister:
Takami Eto
Parliamentary Vice Minister: Ryu Shionoya
Administrative Vice Minister: Tsutomu Sugiura
Secretariat
Director-General: Akira Kono
Personnel Bureau
Director-General: Yuji Ikenouchi

Administrative Management Bureau
Director-General: Akira Suyama
Administrative Inspection Bureau
Director-General: Toyohiko Ohashi
Pension Bureau
Director-General: Kanji Ishikura
Statistics Bureau
Director-General: Akihiko Ito

Takami Eto
Director-General
and State Minister

Committees and Councils

Council on the Policy of Regional Improvement
Pension Examination Committee

Statistics Council
Council of Youth Affairs

Isamu Miyazaki
Director-General
and State Minister

ECONOMIC PLANNING AGENCY

1-1, Kasumigaseki 3-chome, Chiyoda-ku, Tokyo 100
Tel: (03)3581-0261

Director-General and State Minister:
Isamu Miyazaki
Parliamentary Vice Minister: Yoshitaka Murata
Administrative Vice Minister: Makoto Kobayashi
Vice Minister for Economic Affairs: Shoichi Kojima
Minister's Secretariat
Deputy Vice Minister: Kazuhiko Takeshima
Coordination Bureau
Director-General: Shinpei Nukaya

Social Policy Bureau
Director-General: Michisato Sakamoto
Price Bureau
Director-General: Yoichi Ohkita
Planning Bureau
Director-General: Seiichi Toshida
Research Bureau
Director-General: Isoroku Sawada

Committees and Councils

Economic Council
Social Policy Council

Council for Stabilization of National Life

Seishiro Eto
Director-General
and State Minister

DEFENSE AGENCY

7-45, Akasaka 9-chome, Minato-ku, Tokyo 107
Tel: (03)3408-5211

Director-General and State Minister:
Seishiro Eto
Parliamentary Vice Minister: Tetsuro Yano
Administrative Vice Minister: Naoaki Murata

Joint Staff Council
Chairman: Tetsuya Nishimoto

DEFENSE FACILITIES ADMINISTRATION AGENCY

7-45, Akasaka 9-chome, Minato-ku, Tokyo 107
Tel: (03)3408-5211

Director-General: Masuo Morodomi

Committees and Councils

Fair Board
Placement Screening Committee for Self-Defense
Force Retired Personnel

Central Council on Defense Facilities

SCIENCE AND TECHNOLOGY AGENCY

2-1, Kasumigaseki 2-chome, Chiyoda-ku, Tokyo 100
Tel: (03)3581-5271

Director-General and State Minister: Yasuoki Urano
Parliamentary Vice Minister: Shizuo Sato
Administrative Vice Minister: Hiroto Ishida

Minister's Secretariat
Director-General: Toshihiro Ishii
Science and Technology Policy Bureau
Director-General: Toshio Ochiai

Science and Technology Promotion Bureau
Director-General: Shobu kudo
Research and Development Bureau
Director-General: Yasuhiro Kato
Atomic Energy Bureau
Director-General: Toshio Okazaki
Nuclear Safety Bureau
Director-General: Masayasu Miyabayashi

Yasuoki Urano
Director-General
and State Minister

Committees and Councils

Consulting Engineer Council
Council for Aeronautics, Electronics and Other
Advanced Technologies

Resources Council
Radiation Council

ENVIRONMENT AGENCY

2-2, Kasumigaseki 1-chome, Chiyoda-ku, Tokyo 100
Tel: (03)3581-3351

Director-General and State Minister:
Tadamori Oshima
Parliamentary Vice Minister: Yasu Kano
Administrative Vice Minister: Masami Ishizaka
Minister's Secretariat
Deputy Vice Minister: Kenji Tanaka
Planning and Coordination Bureau
Director: Takao Onishi

Nature Conservation Bureau
Director: Hiroshi Sawamura
Air Quality Bureau
Director: Susumu Osawa
Water Quality Bureau
Director: Michio Shimada

Tadamori Oshima
Director-General
and State Minister

Committees and Councils

Central Council for Environmental Pollution Control
Nature Conservation Council
Seto Island Sea Environmental Conservation Council

Pollution-related Health Damage Compensation
Grievance Board
Special Certification Council for Minamata Disease

NATIONAL LAND AGENCY

2-2, Kasumigaseki 1-chome, Chiyoda-ku, Tokyo 100
Tel: (03)3593-3311

Director-General and State Minister:
Seiichi Ikehata
Parliamentary Vice Minister: Gen Nakatani
Administrative Vice Minister: Yasuhisa Mitsui
Secretariat
Director-General: Yoshinobu Takeuchi
Planning and Coordination Bureau
Director-General: Takafusa Shioya

Land Bureau
Director-General: Hideo Fukasawa
Metropolitan Area's Development Bureau
Director-General: Kenji Igarashi
Regional Development Bureau
Director-General: Tadao Iwasaki
Disaster Prevention Bureau
Director-General: Koichi Murase

Seiichi Ikehata
Director-General
and State Minister

Masaaki Takagi
Director-General
and State Minister

OKINAWA DEVELOPMENT AGENCY

6-1, Nagatacho 1-chome, Chiyoda-ku, Tokyo 100
Tel: (03)3581-2361

Director-General and State Minister:
Masaaki Takagi

Parliamentary Vice Minister: Torao Tokuda
Administrative Vice Minister: Akira Watanabe

HOKKAIDO DEVELOPMENT AGENCY

1-1, Kasumigaseki 3-chome, Chiyoda-ku, Tokyo 100
Tel: (03)3581-9111

Director-General and State Minister:
Masaaki Takagi
Parliamentary Vice Minister: Eikou Kaneta

Administrative Vice Minister: Akira Kato
Hokkaido Development Bureau
Director-General: Toyoaki Kobayashi

Committees and Councils

Water Resources Development Council
Land Appraisal Committee
Land Planning Council
National Land Council

Hokkaido Development Council
Ogasawara Islands Development Council
Amami Islands Promotion and Development Council
Okinawa Development Council

Masayoshi
Takemura
Minister

MINISTRY OF FINANCE

1-1, Kasumigaseki 3-chome, Chiyoda-ku, Tokyo 100
Tel: (03)3581-4111

Minister: Masayoshi Takemura
Parliamentary Vice Minister: Genichiro Sata
                               Keigi Kajiwara
Administrative Vice Minister: Kyosuke Shinozawa
Deputy Vice-Minister for Financial Affairs:
Takatoshi Kato

Minister's Secretariat
Deputy Vice Minister: Yoji Wakui
Budget Bureau
Director-General: Takeshi Komura
Tax Bureau
Director-General: Nobuaki Usui

Customs and Tariff Bureau
Director-General: Isao Kubota
Financial Bureau
Director-General: Kouji Tanami
Securities Bureau
Director-General: Sohei Hidaka
Banking Bureau
Director-General: Yoshimasa Nishimura
International Finance Bureau
Director-General: Eisuke Sakakibara
Mint Bureau
Director-General: Akio Hanano
Printing Bureau
Director-General: Takayuki Yamamoto

NATIONAL TAX ADMINISTRATION

1-1, Kasumigaseki 3-chome, Chiyoda-ku, Tokyo 100
Tel: (03)3581-4161

Commissioner: Tadashi Ogawa

Deputy Commissioner: Shozo Wakabayashi

Commissioner's Secretariat

Deputy Commissioners for International Affairs:
Izumi Mizumori
Masanobu Hidaka

Committees and Councils

Tobacco Industries Council

Fiscal System Council

National Public Service Mutual Aid Association

Customs Tariff Council

Customs Dissatisfaction Review Committee

Central National Property Council

Securities and Exchange Council

Certified Public Accountant Examination Committee

Business Accounting Deliberation Council

Interest Rates Adjustment Council

Committee on Financial System Research

Compulsory Automobile Liability Insurance Council

Insurance Council

Committee on Foreign Exchange and
  Other Transactions

Central Council on Alcoholic Beverages

National Tax Council

Council on Tax Accountant

MINISTRY OF INTERNATIONAL TRADE AND INDUSTRY

3-1, Kasumigaseki 1-chome, Chiyoda-ku, Tokyo 100
Tel: (03)3501-1511

Minister: Ryutaro Hashimoto

Parliamentary Vice Ministers: Akihiro Ohata
                Norifumi Kato

Administrative Vice Minister: Tomio Tsutsumi

Vice Minister for International Affairs:
Yoshihiro Sakamoto

Minister's Secretariat

Director-General: Katsuhiro Nakagawa

International Trade Policy Bureau

Director-General: Hisashi Hosokawa

Deputy Director-General: Takeshi Isayama

International Trade Administration Bureau

Director-General: Katsusada Hirose

Industrial Policy Bureau

Director-General: Tsutomu Makino

Industrial Location and Environmental Protection
Bureau

Director-General: Takao Suzuki

Basic Industries Bureau

Director-General: Yasuo Hayashi

Machinery and Information Industries Bureau

Director-General: Osamu Watanabe

Deputy Director-General: Yoshio Ichiryu

Consumer Goods Industries Bureau

Director-General: Masataka Nakano

Ryutaro Hashimoto
Minister

AGENCY OF INDUSTRIAL SCIENCE TECHNOLOGY

3-1, Kasumigaseki 1-chome, Chiyoda-ku, Tokyo 100
Tel: (03)3501-1511

Director-General: Jiro Hiraishi

AGENCY OF NATURAL RESOURCES AND ENERGY

3-1, Kasumigaseki 1-chome, Chiyoda-ku, Tokyo 100
Tel: (03)3501-1511

Director-General: Tadashi Ezaki

Deputy Director-General: Seiji Murata

Director General's Secretariat

Councillor: Toru Namiki

PATENT OFFICE

4-3, Kasumigaseki 3-chome, Chiyoda-ku, Tokyo 100
Tel: (03)3581-1101/0336

Director-General: Yuji Kiyokawa

SMALL AND MEDIUM ENTERPRISE AGENCY

3-1, Kasumigaseki 1-chome, Chiyoda-ku, Tokyo 100
Tel: (03)3501-1511

Director-General: Kinju Atarashi   Deputy Director-General: Katsuhiko Tokita

Committees and Councils

Japanese Industrial Standards Committee
Industrial Structure Council
Industrial Technology Council
Board of Mine Safety Examination Committee
Central Mine Safety Committee
Export and Import Transaction Council
Export Inspection and Design Promotion Council
International Trade Insurance Council
Commodity Exchange Council
Industrial Location and Industrial Water Council
Traditional Craft Industry Council
Advisory Committee for Energy
Mining Industry Council
Petroleum Council
Coal Mining Council
Coal Mining Area Development Council
Large-Scale Retail Stores Council
Installment Sales Council

Consumer Product Safety Household Goods Quality-Labelling Council
Chemical Products Council
Aircraft Industry Council
Information Processing Promotion Council
Measurement Administration Council
Vehicle Race Council
High Pressure Gas and Explosives Safety Council
Textile Industries Council
Electricity Utility Industry Council
Patent Attorney Examination and Disciplinary Committee
Industrial Property Council
Small and Medium Enterprise Policy Making Council
Small and Medium Enterprise Stabilization Council
Small and Medium Enterprise Business Security Council
Small and Medium Enterprise Modernization Council

Issei Inoue
Minister

MINISTRY OF POSTS AND TELECOMMUNICATIONS

3-2, Kasumigaseki 1-chome, Chiyoda-ku, Tokyo 100
Tel: (03)3504-4411

Minister: Issei Inoue
Parliamentary Vice Minister: Gotaro Yoshimura
Administrative Vice Minister: Haruki Matsuno

Minister's Secretariat
Deputy Vice Minister: Masahito Tani
Postal Bureau
Director-General: Toyataro Kato
Postal Savings Bureau
Director-General: Tsuyoshi Kimura

Post Office Life Insurance Bureau
Director-General: Sadanori Amano
Communications Policy Bureau
Director-General: Akemi Yamaguchi
Telecommunications Bureau
Director-General: Mitsuo Igarashi
Broadcast Administration Bureau
Director-General: Shuji Kusuda

Committees and Councils

Postal Service Council
Examination Committee for Post Office Life Insurance and Annuities Claims

Telecommunications Council
Radio Regulatory Council
Telecommunications Technology Council

MINISTRY OF AGRICULTURE, FORESTRY AND FISHERIES

2-1, Kasumigaseki 1-chome, Chiyoda-ku, Tokyo 100
Tel: (03)3502-8111

Hosei Norota
Minister

Minister: Hosei Norota

Parliamentary Vice Ministers: Toshikatsu Matsuoka
Junji Ichii

Administrative Vice Minister: Hirofumi Ueno

Minister's Secretariat
Director-General: Yuki Takagi
Economic Affairs Bureau
Director-General: Hidetaka Tsutsumi

Agricultural Structure Improvement Bureau
Director-General: Kazuo Nonaka
Agricultural Production Bureau
Director-General: Eisuke Hinode
Livestock Industry Bureau
Director-General: Hideaki Kumazawa
Food and Marketing Bureau
Director-General: Hisashi Suzuki

Food Agency

2-1, Kasumigaseki 1-chome, Chiyoda-ku, Tokyo 100
Tel: (03)3502-8111

Director-General: Masayuki Takahashi
Deputy Director-General: Osamu Abe

Director-General's Secretariat
Director of Administration Division:
Mamoru Muguruma

Fisheries Agency

2-1, Kasumigaseki 1-chome, Chiyoda-ku, Tokyo 100
Tel: (03)3502-8111

Director-General: Hisao Azuma

Deputy Director-General: Masahiro Ishikawa

Forestry Agency

2-1, Kasumigaseki 1-chome, Chiyoda-ku, Tokyo 100
Tel: (03)3502-8111

Director-General: Hajimu Irisawa

Deputy Director-General: Isao Takahashi

Committees and Councils

Agriculture Policy Council
Statistics and Outlook Council on Agriculture, Forestry and Fisheries
Agricultural, Forestry and Fisheries Insurance Council
Irrigation and Drainage Policy Council
Agricultural Materials Council
Agricultural Mechanization Council
Sericulture Promotion Council
Fruit Agriculture Promotion Council
Livestock Industry Promotion Council
Central Milk Marketing Arbitration Council

Veterinary Affairs Council
Foodstuff Distribution Council (tentative)
Research Committee for Agriculture and Forestry Standards
Sweet Resources Council
Rice Price Council
Central Fishery Adjustment Council
Pearl Culture Industry Council
Fishing Port Council
Council for Promotion of Coastal Fishery
Forestry Administration Council
Central Forest Council

MINISTRY OF TRANSPORT

1-3, Kasumigaseki 2-chome, Chiyoda-ku, Tokyo 100
Tel: (03)3580-3111

Takeo Hiranuma
Minister

Minister: Takeo Hiranuma
Parliamentary Vice Minister: Katsuyou Ogata
Administrative Vice Minister: Minoru Toyoda

Secretariat to the Minister
Deputy Vice Minister: Hiromichi Toya
Transport Policy Bureau
Director-General: Yasutoshi Tsuchisaka
Railway Bureau
Director-General: Hisashi Umezaki

Road Transport Bureau
Director-General: Kunikatsu Yamashita
Maritime Transport Bureau
Director-Genenral: Sadao Iwata
Maritime Technology and Safety Bureau
Director-General: Kenji Ogawa
Ports and Harbours Bureau
Director-General: Hideo Kayahara
Civil Aviation Bureau
Director-Genenral: Masahiko Kurono

MARITIME SAFETY AGENCY

1-3, Kasumigaseki 2-chome, Chiyoda-ku, Tokyo 100
Tel: (03)3591-6361

Director-General: Yutaka Hatano

Deputy Director-General: Hajime Kato

METEOROLOGICAL AGENCY

3-4, Otemachi 1-chome, Chiyoda-ku, Tokyo 100
Tel: (03)3212-8341

Director-General: Kozo Ninomiya

Deputy Director-General: Yoshiro Otsuji

Committees and Councils

Council for Transport Technique
Transport Council
Council for Transport Policy
Council for Rationalization of Shipping and Shipbuilding Industries
Council for Maritime Safety and Seamen's Training

Council for Ports and Harbours
Council for Civil Aviation
Council for Tourism Policy
Shinkansen Project Council (tentative)
Japan Aircraft Accident Investigation's Committee
Meteorological Council

MINISTRY OF HEALTH AND WELFARE

2-2, Kasumigaseki 1-chome, Chiyoda-ku, Tokyo 100
Tel: (03)3503-1711

Churyo Morii
Minister

Minister: Churyo Morii
Parliamentary Vice Minister: Jinen Nagase
Administrative Vice Minister: Hiroshi Tada

Minister's Secretariat
Director-General: Takehiko Yamaguchi
Statistics and Information Department
Director-General: Akio Ono
Health Policy Bureau
Director-General: Shuichi Tani
Health Service Bureau
Director-General: Akihito Matsumura

Environmental Health Bureau
Director-General: Hidesuke Kobayashi
Pharmaceutical Affairs Bureau
Director-General: Yasuta Araga
Social Welfare and War Victims' Relief Bureau
Director-General: Fumio Sasaki
Health and Welfare Bureau for the Elderly
Director-General: Shingo Haketa
Children and Families Bureau
Director-General: Toshiaki Takagi
Health Insurance Bureau
Director-General: Nobuharu Okamitsu
Pension Bureau
Director-General: Jungoro Kondo

Committees and Councils

Council on Population Problems
Health and Welfare Statistics Council
Council on Medical Service Facilities
Medical Ethics Council
Council for those Engaged in Medical Service
Central Council for Japanese Traditional Massage,
Finger Pressure, Acupuncture, Moxacautery, Judo-
Orthopaedy, etc.
Council on Public Health
Council on Medical Care for the Atomic Bomb
Exposed
Council on the Health for the Aged
Living Environment Council
Central Council for the Improved Management of
Business Dealing With Sanitation

Food Sanitation Investigation Council
Central Pharmaceutical Affairs Council
Central Social Welfare Council
Advisory Council on Welfare of Physically Disabled
Persons
Central Council for Countermeasures for Mentally and
Physically Handicapped Persons
Central Child Welfare Council
Social Insurance Appeals Committee
Council on Health Insurance
Central Social Insurance Medical Council
Council for Pension Policy
Examination Committee for Relief Assistances

MINISTRY OF CONSTRUCTION

1-3, Kasumigaseki 2-chome, Chiyoda-ku, Tokyo 100
Tel: (03)3580-4311

Yoshiro Mori
Minister

Minister: Yoshiro Mori
Parliamentary Vice Minister: Kazuto Kamiyama
Administrative Vice Minister: Haruho Fujii
Engineer General: Takashi Toyoda
Minister's Secretariat
Deputy Vice-Minister for Administration:
Noboru Ban
Economic Affairs Bureau
Director-General: Shigeru Kowashi

City Bureau
Director-General: Shigeo Kondo
River Bureau
Director-General: Yoshio Matsuda
Road Bureau
Director-General: Kotaro Hashimoto
Housing Bureau
Director-General: Shoichiro Umeno

Committees and Councils

Central Council on Construction Contracting Business
Central Committee for Adjustment of Construction
Work Disputes
Central City Planning Council
Housing and Building-Land Council

Building Council
Central Examination Committee for Architects
Road Council
River Council
Public Use Land Council

MINISTRY OF LABOR

2-2, Kasumigaseki 1-chome, Chiyoda-ku, Tokyo 100
Tel: (03)3593-1211

Shinji Aoki
Minister

Minister: Shinji Aoki
Parliamentary Vice Minister: Chieko Noono
Administrative Vice Minister: Kunihiko Saito

Minister's Secretariat
Deputy Vice Minister: Shin Watanabe
Labor Policy Bureau
Director-General: Tokio Nanase

Labor Standards Bureau
Director-General: Nobuko Matsubara
Women's Bureau
Director-General: Yoshie Ota
Employment Security Bureau
Director-General: Noriomi Soya
Human Resources Development Bureau
Director-General: Shohei Ito

Committees and Councils

Central Labor Relations Commission

Employment Council

Labor Insurance Appeal Committee

Smaller Enterprise Retirement Allowance Mutual Aid Council

Central Labor Standards Council

Central Homework Council

Central Human Resources Development Council

Workmen's Accident Compensation Insurance Council

Pneumoconiosis Council

Central Minimum Wages Council

Council for Workers' Property Accumulation

Women's and Young Workers' Problems Council

Central Employment Security Council

Physically Handicapped Persons' Employment Council

Wages Council for Work Relief Project

MINISTRY OF FOREIGN AFFAIRS

2-1, Kasumigaseki 2-chome, Chiyoda-ku, Tokyo 100
Tel: (03)3580-3311

Yohei Kono
Minister

Minister: Yohei Kono

Parliamentary Vice Minister: Yasuo Fukuda

Administrative Vice Minister: Sadayuki Hayashi

Minister's Secretariat

Deputy Vice Minister: Tadashi Ikeda

Asian Affairs Bureau

Director-General: Ryozo Kato

North American Affairs Bureau

Director-General: Masaki Orita

Latin American and Caribbean Affairs Bureau

Director-General: Shunichi Sato

European and Oceanian Affairs Bureau

Director-General: Kazuyoshi Urabe

Middle Eastern and African Affairs Bureau

Director-General: Kensaku Hogen

Economic Affairs Bureau

Director-General: Koichi Haraguchi

Economic Cooperation Bureau

Director-General: Atsushi Hatakenaka

Treaties Bureau

Director-General: Akira Hayashi

Foreign Policy Bureau

Director-General: Yutaka Kawashima

Intelligence and Analysis Bureau

Director-General: Yushu Takashima

Committees and Councils

Foreign Service Personnel Committee

Emigration Council

MINISTRY OF HOME AFFAIRS

2-1 Toranomon 2-chome, Chiyoda-ku, Tokyo 105
Tel: (03)5574-7111

Takashi Fukaya
Minister

Minister: Takashi Fukaya

Parliamentary Vice Minister: Yu Amioka

Administrative Vice Minister: Hiromasa Yoshida

Minister's Secretariat

Deputy Vice Minister: Masahiro Futahashi

Local Administration Bureau

Director-General: Hideaki Matsumoto

Local Finance Bureau

Director-General: Yasuhiko Endo

Local Tax Bureau

Director-General: Tetsuji Sano

FIRE DEFENSE AGENCY

2-1 Toranomon 2-chome, Chiyoda-ku, Tokyo 105
Tel: (03)5574-7111

Commissioner: Toshifumi Akimoto

Committees and Councils

Central Election Management Council

Local Finance Council

Central Fixed Property Valuation Council

Council of Mutual Aid Association of Local Public Service Personnel

Fire Service Council

MINISTRY OF EDUCATION, SCIENCE, SPORTS AND CULTURE

2-2, Kasumigaseki 3-chome, Chiyoda-ku, Tokyo 100
Tel: (03)3581-4211

Yoshinobu Shimamura Minister

Minister: Yoshinobu Shimamura
Parliamentary Vice Minister: Taisuke Sato
Administrative Vice Minister: Hiroshi Nozaki

Minister's Secretariat
Director-General: Teiichi Sato
Elementary and Secondary Education Bureau
Director-General: Takayoshi Inoue

Educational Assistance and Administration Bureau
Director-General: Kohei Toyama
High Education Bureau
Director-General: Shigeru Yoshida
Science and International Affairs Bureau
Director-General: Hideki Hayashida
Life Long Learning Bureau
Director-General: Katsuhide Kusahara
Physical Education Bureau
Director-General: Keiji Kobayashi

AGENCY FOR CULTURAL AFFAIRS

2-2, Kasumigaseki 3-chome, Chiyoda-ku, Tokyo 100
Tel: (03)3581-4211

Commissioner: Atsuko Toyama
Deputy Commissioner: Motoyuki Ono
Cultural Affairs Department
Director: Yoshiyuki Nishizawa

Cultural Properties Protection Department
Director: Yasufumi Sakitani

Committees and Councils

Japanese National Commission for Unesco
Japan Academy
Japan Art Academy
Curriculum Council
Textbook Authorization Research Council
Educational Personnel Training Council
Council for University Chartering and School Juridical Person
Science Council
Geodesy Council

Central Educational Council
Council for Health and Physical Education
Council for Selection of Persons of Cultural Merits
Council on Life Long Learning
Private University Council
Council on Religious Juridical Persons
Council for the Protection of Cultural Properties
Japan Language Council
Copyright Council
Council for Science Education and Vocational Education

MINISTRY OF JUSTICE

1-1, Kasumigaseki 1-chome, Chiyoda-ku, Tokyo 100
Tel: (03)3580-4111

Hiroshi Miyazawa Minister

Minister: Hiroshi Miyazawa
Parliamentary Vice Minister: Keiji Furuya
Administrative Vice Minister: Kunihisa Hama
Minister's Secretariat
Deputy Vice Minister: Akio Harada
Civil Affairs Bureau
Director-General: Yasuo Hamasaki
Criminal Affairs Bureau
Director-General: Mamoru Norisada

Correction Bureau
Director-General: Shinichiro Tojo
Rehabilitation Bureau
Director-General: Tatsuzo Honma
Litigation Bureau
Director-General: Kazuo Masui
Civil Liberties Bureau
Director-General: Satoshi Otou
Immigration Bureau
Director-General: Chihiro Tsukada

PUBLIC PROSECUTORS OFFICE

1-1, Kasumigaseki 1-chome, Chiyoda-ku, Tokyo 100
Tel: (03)3592-5611

Prosecutor General: Yusuke Yoshinaga

Deputy Prosecutor General: Keisuke Kitajima

PUBLIC SECURITY INVESTIGATION AGENCY

1-1, Kasumigaseki 1-chome, Chiyoda-ku, Tokyo 100
Tel: (03)3592-5711

Director-General: Hiroyasu Sugihara

Deputy Director-General: Yuki Kawachi

Committees and Councils

Director-General: Hiroyasu Sugihara
Deputy Director-General: Yuki Kawachi
Committees and Councils
Legislative Council
Civil Affairs Administrative Council

Correction and Rehabilitation Council
Assistant Public Prosecutor Selection Committee
Special Examination Committee for Public Prosecutors
Selection Committee for Notaries Public
National Offenders Rehabilitation Commission

Yasuo Matsushita
Governor

BANK OF JAPAN

1-1, Nihonbashi Hongokucho 2-chome, Chuo-ku, Tokyo 103
Tel: (03)3279-1111

Governor: Yasuo Matsushita
Senior Deputy Governor: Toshihiko Fukui
Executive Directors: Kunio Kojima
Tatsuya Tamura
Akira Nagashima
Tadayo Honma
Junichi Yonezawa
Takashi Anzai
Takayuki Kamoshida
Policy Planning Department
Director: Yutaka Yamaguchi
Financial Payment System Department
Director: Minoru Masubuchi
Credit and Market Management Department
Director: Eiichiro Kinoshita
Bank Supervision Department
Director: Kagehide Kaku
International Department
Director: Shigeoki Togo

Operations Department
Director: Kensuke Tanabe
Issue Department
Director: Tasuku Horiguchi
Budget and Management Department
Director: Keiji Matsuda
Personnel Department
Director: Takehisa Toyoda
Administration Department
Director: Kiyoto Hagiwara
Information and Computer System Department
Director: Ryuzo Yokouchi
Research and Statistics Department
Director: Kunihiko Takeshima
Public Relations Department
Director: Hayashi Nakajima
Institute for Monetary and Economic Studies
Director: Iwao Kuroda

Supreme Court

4-2 Hayabusacho, Chiyoda-ku, Tokyo 102
Tel:(03)3264-8111

Ryohachi Kusaba
Chief Justice

Chief Justice: Ryohachi Kusaba

Justices: Kazutomo Ijima
Itsuo Sonobe
Toshijiro Nakajima
Tsuneo Kabe
Shinichi Kawai
Katsuya Onishi
Motoo Ono
Toru Miyoshi
Masao Ono
Mitsuo Endo
Hideo Chigusa
Shigeharu Negishi
Hisako Takahashi
Yukinobu Ozaki

Secretariat
Secretary-General: Tokuji Izumi
General Affairs Bureau
Director: Norio Wakui
Personnel Affairs Bureau
Director: Yukio Horigome
Financial Bureau
Director: Mutsuo Nitta
Civil Affairs Bureau
Director: Kimio Ishigaki
Criminal Affairs Bureau
Director: Shogo Takahashi
Administrative Affairs Bureau
Director: Kimio Ishigaki
Family Bureau
Director: Kaname Kimura
Public Information Section
Director: Katsumi Chiba
Secretary Section
Director: Katsumi Chiba

Major Business Organizations

Shoichiro Toyoda
Chairman

Federation of Economic Organizations (Keidanren)

9-4, Otemachi 1-chome, Chiyoda-ku, Tokyo 100
Tel:(03)3279-1411

Keidanren (Japan Federation of Economic Organizations) is a private, nonprofit economic organization representing all major branches of economic activity in Japan. Keidanren was established in August 1946, through the merger of various economic and industrial organizations active since the prewar period. Since then, it has grown into a nationwide umbrella organization with 123 association and 967 corporate members as of September 1995.

Officers

(Chairman)
Shoichiro Toyoda
Chairman, Toyota Motor Corp.

(Vice Chairmen)
Yutaka Kume
Chairman, Nissan Motor Co.

Seiji Suzuki
Senior Advisor, Mitsubishi Chemical Corp.

Isao Yonekura
Chairman, Itochu Corp.

Katsushige Mita
Chairman, Hitachi Ltd.

Tadahiro Sekimoto
Chairman, NEC Corp.

Shoh Nasu
Chairman, Tokyo Electric Power Co.

Kenichi Suematsu
President, Sakura Bank

Joichi Aoi
Chairman, Toshiba Corp.

Josei Itoh
President, Nippon Life Insurance Co.

Hirotaro Higuchi
Chairman, Asahi Breweries Ltd.

Sueaki Takaoka
Chairman, Seiyu Ltd.

Takashi Imai
President, Nippon Steel Corp.

**(Chairman
of the Board of Councillors)**
Hiroshi Saito
Chairman, Nippon Steel Corp.

**(Vice Chairmen
of the Board of Councillors)**
Nobuya Hagura
Senior Advisor,
Dai-Ichi Kangyo Bank

Koichiro Ejiri
Chairman, Mitsui & Co.

Kazuo Haruna
Chairman, Marubeni Corp.

Kentaro Aikawa
President,
Mitsubishi Heavy Industries Ltd.

Kenji Kawakatsu
Senior Advisor, Sanwa Bank

Katsuhiro Utada
Senior Advisor, Ajinomoto Co.

Takashi Kitaoka
President, Mitsubishi Electric Corp.

Tetsuya Katada
Chairman, Komatsu Ltd.

Yoichi Morishita
President, Matsushita Electric Industrial Co.

(Committee Chairmen)

Committee on Basic Strategy
Shoichiro Toyoda
Chairman, Toyota Motor Corp.

Committee on Corporate Ethics
Shoichiro Toyoda
Chairman, Toyota Motor Corp.

Committee on Government Reform
Takashi Imai
President, Nippon Steel Corp.

Committee on Public Affairs
Tadahiro Sekimoto
Chairman, NEC Corp.

Committee on Business and Politics
Kenji Kawakatsu
Senior Advisor, Sanwa Bank

Ad-Hoc Committee on Nurturing
Creative Human Resources
Kenichi Suematsu
Chairman, Sakura Bank

Committee on Taxation
Yutaka Kume
Chairman, Nissan Motor Co.

Committee on Economic Research
Takeru Ishikawa
Chairman, Mitsui Marine & Fire
Insurance Co.

Committee on Fiscal and Monetary
Policies
Hirotaro Higuchi
Chairman, Asahi Breweries Ltd.

Committee on International Finance
Tsuneo Wakai
President, Mitsubishi Bank

Committee on Economic Structure
Takahide Sakurai
President, Dai-Ichi Mutual Life
Insurance Co.

Japan Federation of Employers' Associations (Nikkeiren)

4-6, Marunouchi 1-chome, Chiyoda-ku, Tokyo 100
Tel:(03)3213-4474

Jiro Nemoto
Chairman

Nikkeiren is Japan's most widely representative organization of employers, dealing primarily with labor and social issues from the employers' viewpoint. It currently includes 47 regional (prefectural) associations and 55 industrial associations — representing virtually all private industries except agriculture and forestry. The group's objective is to promote cooperation among employers' associations and coordinate corporate strategies for labor-management relations. Nikkeiren was organized April 12, 1948, by a group of employers seeking to establish orderly labor-management relations to facilitate Japan's postwar economic reconstruction.

Officers

(Chairman)
Jiro Nemoto
Chairman, Nippon Yusen Kabushiki Kaisha

(Vice Chairmen)
Akira Miki
Senior Advisor, Nippon Steel Corp.

Sugiichiro Watari
Advisor to the Board, Toshiba Corp.

Kuniji Miyazaki
Chairman, Dai-Ichi Kangyo Bank

Keiichi Konaga
President, Arabian Oil Co.

Toshio Miyoshi
Chairman, Matsushita Electric Works Ltd.

Ken Moroi
Chairman, Chichibu Onoda Cement Corp.

Tadao Suzuki
President, Mercian Corp.

Masami Iwasaki
Vice Chairman, Toyota Motor Corp.

Yoshihiro Fujii
Chairman, Hitachi Zosen Corp.

Shunji Kono
President, Tokio Marine & Fire Insurance Co.

Masahiko Furukawa
Chairman, Mitsubishi Chemical Corp.

(Director-General)
Michio Fukuoka

(Deputy Directors-General)
Takeo Naruse
Makoto Saito

Japan Association of Corporate Executives (Keizai Doyukai)

4-6, Marunouchi 1-chome, Chiyoda-ku, Tokyo 100
Tel:(03)3211-1271

Jiro Ushio
Chairman

Keizai Doyukai is a private, nonprofit organization formed in 1946 by 83 business executives seeking to contribute to the reconstruction of Japan's economy. Keizai Doyukai members include some 1,558 executives representing 900 corporations — all sharing a common belief that corporate managers should lend their talents to a broad range of economic and social issues. Keizai Doyukai members participate as individuals, expressing opinions and ideas distinct from their positions within company or industry.

Executive Board

(Chairman)
Jiro Ushio
Chairman, Ushio Inc.

(Vice Chairmen)
Tasuku Takagaki
President, Bank of Tokyo

Tatsuro Toyoda
Vice Chairman, Toyota Motor Corp.

Masaji Shinagawa
Advisor, Nippon Fire & Marine Insurance Co.

Yotaro Kobayashi
Chairman, Fuji Xerox Co.

Yoshihiko Miyauchi
President, ORIX Corp.

Hiroshi Araki
President, Tokyo Electric Power Co.

Takeo Shiina
Chairman, IBM Japan Ltd.

Hiroshi Watanabe
Chairman, Sanwa Bank

Susumu Tenporin
Chairman, Mitsui O.S.K. Lines Ltd.

Yuzaburo Mogi
President, Kikkoman Corp.

Japan Chamber of Commerce and Industry (Nissho)

2-2, Marunouchi 3-chome, Chiyoda-ku, Tokyo 100
Tel:(03)3283-7866

Kosaku Inaba
Chairman

The first chambers of commerce and industry in Japan were established in Tokyo, Osaka and Kobe in 1878. Today, there are chambers in every major city, 509 in all, with some 1.5 million members. Local chambers devote themselves to regional development of commercial and industrial activity and to contributing to the communities they represent. The umbrella Japan Chamber works on a nationwide, and international basis collecting and coordinating the views of local chambers and making policy recommendations to government agencies.

Officers

(Chairman)
Kosaku Inaba
President, Ishikawajima-Harima
Heavy Industries Co.

(Vice Chairmen)
Masafumi Onishi (Osaka)
Chairman, Osaka Gas Co.

Seitaro Taniguchi (Nagoya)
President, Nagoya Railroad Co.

Kojiro Tsushima (Yokohama)
Chairman, Sagami Railway Co.

Yutaka Ueno (Yokohama)
President, KK Ueno Unyu Shokai

Kazuo Inamori (Kyoto)
Chairman, Kyocera Corp.

Fuyuhiko Maki (Kobe)
Advisor, Kobe Steel Ltd.

(Special Advisors to the Chairman)
Shinroku Morohashi
Chairman, Mitsubishi Corp.

Takuya Okada
Chairman, Jusco Co.

Tetsuo Fujimori
Advisor, Dai-Ichi Kangyo Bank Ltd.

Norio Ohga
Chairman, Sony Corp.

Atsushi Kobayashi
President, Lion Corp.

Kiyoshi Kawashima
Superme Advisor, Honda Motor Co.

Masahiko Nakanishi
President, Benkan Corp.

Kazuo Sugiyama
President, Electric Power Development Co.

Michio Mizoguchi
Advisor, Japan-China Association on Economy and Trade

Eimei Yamashita
Councillor, World Order Study Association

(Senior Managing Director)
Shoichi Tanimura

(Managing Director)
Teiichi Nishikawa

Other Organizations

Japan Federation of Smaller Enterprise Organizations
2-8-4 Nihonbashi Kayabacho,
Chuo-ku, Tokyo 103
Tel:(03)3669-6862
Fax:(03)3668-2957

Japan Junior Chamber, Inc.
2-14-3 Hirakawacho,
Chiyoda-ku, Tokyo 102
Tel:(03)3234-5601
Fax:(03)3265-2409

Kansai Association of Corporate Executives (Kansai Keizai Doyukai)
6-2-27 Nakanoshima,
Kita-ku, Osaka 530
Tel:(06)441-1031
Fax:(06)441-1030

Kansai Economic Federation
Nakanoshima Center Bldg.,
6-2-27 Nakanoshima,
Kita-ku, Osaka 530
Tel:(06)441-0101
Fax:(06)443-5347

Industrial Organizations

Aerospace

Society of Japanese Aerospace Companies
Hibiya Park Bldg.,
1-8-1 Yurakuhco,
Chiyoda-ku, Tokyo 100
Tel:(03)3211-5678
Fax:(03)3211-5018

Agriculture, Forestry and Fisheries

Central Association of Livestock Industry
Zenkoku Choson Kaikan,
1-11-35 Nagatacho,
Chiyoda-ku, Tokyo 100
Tel:(03)3581-6676
Fax:(03)5511-8205

Central Union of Agricultural Cooperatives (Zenchu)
JA Bldg.,
1-8-3 Otemachi,
Chiyoda-ku, Tokyo 100
Tel:(03)3245-7500
Fax:(03)5255-7356

Federation of Japan Tuna Fisheries Cooperative Associations
2-3-22 Kudan-kita,
Chiyoda-ku, Tokyo 102
Tel:(03)3264-6161
Fax:(03)3264-7235

Japan Fisheries Association
Sankaido Bldg.,
1-9-13 Akasaka,
Minato-ku, Tokyo 107
Tel:(03)3585-6683
Fax:(03)3582-2337

Japan Salmon Fisheries Cooperative Association
Sankaido Bldg.,
1-9-13 Akasaka,
Minato-ku, Tokyo 107
Tel:(03)3582-1736
Fax:(03)3505-1736

Japan Whaling Association
2-8-3 Higashi Nihonbashi,
Chuo-ku, Tokyo 103
Tel:(03)3851-2584
Fax:(03)3851-1312

National Federation of Agricultural Cooperative Associations (Zenno)
1-8-3 Otemachi,
Chiyoda-ku, Tokyo 100
Tel:(03)3245-7111
Fax:(03)3245-7442

National Federation of Dairy Cooperative Associations
Chikusan Kaikan,
4-9-2 Ginza,
Chuo-ku, Tokyo 104
Tel:(03)3542-6131
Fax:(03)3544-0393

National Federation of Fisheries Cooperative Associations
1-1-12 Uchi-Kanda,
Chiyoda-ku, Tokyo 101
Tel:(03)3294-9611
Fax:(03)3294-9609

National Federation of Livestock Agricultural Cooperative Associations
Baji Chikusan Kaikan,
1-2 Kanda Surugadai,
Chiyoda-ku, Tokyo
Tel:(03)3292-3031
Fax:(03)3295-1016

Automobiles

Japan Auto-Body Industries Association
Kishimoto Bldg.,
2-2-1 Marunouchi,
Marunouchi,
Chiyoda-ku, Tokyo 100
Tel:(03)3213-2031
Fax:(03)3213-2034

Japan Auto Parts Industries Association
1-16-15 Takanawa,
Minato-ku, Tokyo 108
Tel:(03)3445-4211
Fax:(03)3447-5372

Japan Automobile Dealers Association
5-7-17 Minami Aoyama,
Minato-ku, Tokyo 107
Tel:(03)3400-8404
Fax:(03)3400-8413

Japan Automobile Manufacturers Association
Otemachi Bldg.,
1-6-1 Otemachi,
Chiyoda-ku, Tokyo 100
Tel:(03)3216-5771
Fax:(03)3287-2072

Japan Electric Vehicle Association
2-5-5 Toranomon,
Minato-ku, Tokyo 105
Tel:(03)3503-3651
Fax:(03)3503-8493

Japan Industrial Vehicles Association
Tobu Bldg.,
1-5-26 Moto-Akasaka,
Minato-ku, Tokyo 107
Tel:(03)3403-5556
Fax:(03)3403-5057

Japan Small Vehicle Association
3-20-4 Nishi Shinbashi,
Minato-ku, Tokyo 105
Tel:(03)3436-2381
Fax:(03)3436-2385

Banking and Finance

Federation of Bankers Associations of Japan
1-3-1 Marunouchi,
Chiyoda-ku, Tokyo 100
Tel:(03)3216-3761
Fax:(03)3201-5608

Japan Federation of Consumer Credit Companies
No. 2 Muneyasu Bldg.,
1-23 Kanda Nishikicho,
Chiyoda-ku, Tokyo 101
Tel:(03)5259-2901
Fax:(03)5259-2909

National Association of Prefectural Credit Federations of Agricultural Cooperatives
JA Bldg., 1-8-3 Otemachi,
Chiyoda-ku, Tokyo 100
Tel:(03)3270-2808
Fax:(03)3270-4546

National Association of Labour Banks
2-5-15 Kanda Surugadai,
Chiyoda-ku, Tokyo 101
Tel:(03)3295-6721
Fax:(03)3295-6752

National Association of Shinkin Banks
3-8-1 Kyobashi,
Chuo-ku, Tokyo 104
Tel:(03)3563-4821
Fax:(03)3561-1576

National Central Society of Credit Cooperatives
1-9-1 Kyobashi,
Chuo-ku, Tokyo 104
Tel:(03)3567-2451
Fax:(03)3567-9225

National Federation of Credit Cooperatives
1-9-1 Kyobashi,
Chuo-ku, Tokyo 104
Tel:(03)3562-5111
Fax:(03)3567-3496

National Federation of Credit Guarantee Corporations
3-1-3 Kyobashi,
Chuo-ku, Tokyo 104
Tel:(03)3271-7201
Fax:(03)3272-7364

Regional Banks Association of Japan
3-1-2 Uchi-Kanda,
Chiyoda-ku, Tokyo 101
Tel:(03)3252-5171
Fax:(03)3254-8664

Second Association of Regional Banks
5 Sanbancho,
Chiyoda-ku, Tokyo 102
Tel:(03)3262-2181
Fax:(03)3262-2339

Trust Companies Association of Japan
Nihon Bldg.,
2-6-2 Otemachi,
Chiyoda-ku, Tokyo 100
Tel:(03)3241-7135
Fax:(03)3241-7200

Zenshinren Bank (Central Cooperative Bank for Shinkin Banks)
3-8-1 Kyobashi,
Chuo-ku, Tokyo 104
Tel:(03)3563-4111
Fax:(03)3564-4766

Chemicals

Federation of Pharmaceutical Manufacturers' Associations of Japan
Tokyo Yakugyo Kaikan,
2-1-5 Nihonbashi Honcho,
Chuo-ku, Tokyo 103
Tel:(03)3270-0581
Fax:(03)3241-2090

Japan A.B.S. Resin Industry Association
Sogo Nagatacho Bldg.,
1-11-28 Nagatacho,
Chiyoda-ku, Tokyo 100
Tel:(03)3581-2468
Fax:(03)3581-2055

Japan Ammonium Chloride Fertilizer Association
Morichu Bldg.,
1-8-11 Nihonbashi Bakurocho,
Chuo-ku, Tokyo 103
Tel:(03)3249-3939
Fax:(03)3249-3940

Japan Chemical Industry Association
Tokyo Club Bldg.,
3-2-6 Kasumigaseki,
Chiyoda-ku, Tokyo 100
Tel:(03)3580-0751
Fax:(03)3580-0764

Japan Cosmetic Industry Association
Hatsumei Bldg.,
2-9-14 Toranomon,
Minato-ku, Tokyo 105
Tel:(03)3502-0576
Fax:(03)3502-0829

Japan Paint Manufacturers Association
Tobu Bldg.,
1-5-26 Moto Akasaka,
Minato-ku, Tokyo 107
Tel:(03)3478-3451
Fax:(03)3405-5565

Japan Petrochemical Industry Association
Iino Bldg.,
2-1-1 Uchisaiwaicho,
Chiyoda-ku, Tokyo 100
Tel:(03)3501-2151
Fax:(03)3501-3895

Japan Phosphatic & Compound Fertilizers Manufacturers Association
Rinsan Kurabu Bldg.,
3-1-6 Nihonbashi Muromachi,
Chuo-ku, Tokyo 103
Tel:(03)3241-0101
Fax:(03)3241-0919

Japan Plastics Industry Federation
Tokyo Club Bldg.,
3-2-6 Kasumigaseki,
Chiyoda-ku, Tokyo 100
Tel:(03)3580-0771
Fax:(03)3580-0775

Japan PVC Association
Iino Bldg.,
2-1-1 Uchisaiwaicho,
Chiyoda-ku, Tokyo 100
Tel:(03)3506-5481
Fax:(03)3506-5487

Japan Soap & Detergent Association
Yushi Kogyo Kaikan,
3-13-11 Nihonbashi,
Chuo-ku, Tokyo 103
Tel:(03)3271-4301
Fax:(03)3281-1870

Japan Soda Industry Association
Horiuchi Bldg.,
2-6-1 Kajicho,
Chiyoda-ku, Tokyo 101
Tel:(03)3254-2471
Fax:(03)3254-2470

Japan Thermosetting Plastics Industry Association
3-2-6 Kasumigaseki,
Chiyoda-ku, Tokyo 100
Tel:(03)3580-0881
Fax:(03)3580-0832

Japan Urea & Ammonium Sulphate Industry Association
Aroma Bldg.,
3-5-2 Nihonbashi Kayabacho,
Chuo-ku, Tokyo 103
Tel:(03)3662-6371
Fax:(03)3662-1717

Japan Vinyl Goods Manufacturers' Association
Tobu Bldg.,
1-5-26 Moto Akasaka,
Minato-ku, Tokyo 107
Tel:(03)3408-7201
Fax:(03)4301-9351

Photo-sensitized Materials Manufacturers Association
JCII Bldg.,
25 Ichibancho,
Chiyoda-ku, Tokyo 102
Tel:(03)5276-3561
Fax:(03)5276-3563

Commodities

All Japan Grain Exchange Association
1-12-5 Nihonbashi Kakigaracho,
Chuo-ku, Tokyo 103
Tel:(03)3668-9311
Fax:(03)3661-4564

Commodity Futures Association of Japan

Kakigaracho F Bldg.,
1-28-5 Nihonbashi Kakigaracho,
Chuo-ku, Tokyo 103
Tel:(03)3664-4731
Fax:(03)3667-8256

Japan Federation of Commodity Exchanges

1-1-10 Nihonbashi Ningyocho,
Chuo-ku, Tokyo 103
Tel:(03)3667-4381
Fax:(03)3667-4139

Construction

Japan Civil Engineering Contractors' Association

Tokyo Kensetsu Kaikan,
2-5-1 Hacchobori,
Chuo-ku, Tokyo 104
Tel:(03)3552-3201
Fax:(03)3552-3206

Japan Dam Association

Ginza GT Bldg.,
2-14-2 Ginza,
Chuo-ku, Tokyo 104
Tel:(03)3545-8361
Fax:(03)3545-5055

Japan Road Association

Shoyu Kaikan,
3-3-1 Kasumigaseki,
Chiyoda-ku, Tokyo 100
Tel:(03)3581-2211
Fax:(03)3581-2231

Japan Road Contractors Association

3-3-1 Marunouchi,
Chiyoda-ku, Tokyo 100
Tel:(03)3211-8876
Fax:(03)3201-4540

Electric Machinery

Communications Industry Association of Japan

Sankei Bldg. Annex,
1-7-2 Otemachi,
Chiyoda-ku, Tokyo 100
Tel:(03)3231-3156
Fax:(03)3246-0495

Electronic Industries Association of Japan

3-2-2 Marunouchi,
Chiyoda-ku, Tokyo 100
Tel:(03)3211-2765
Fax:(03)3287-1712

Japan Battery & Appliance Industries Association

No.9 Mori Bldg.,
1-2-2 Atago,
Minato-ku, Tokyo 105

Japan Business Machine Makers Association

Daiichi Mori Bldg.,
1-12-1 Nishi Shinbashi,
Minato-ku, Tokyo 105
Tel:(03)3503-9821
Fax:(03)3591-3646

Japan Electrical Manufacturers' Association

2-4-15 Nagatacho,
Chiyoda-ku, Tokyo 100
Tel:(03)3581-4841
Fax:(03)3593-3198

Japan Electronic Industry Development Association

Kikai Shinko Kaikan,
3-5-8 Shibakoen,
Minato-ku, Tokyo 105
Tel:(03)3433-1922
Fax:(03)3433-6350

Semiconductor Equipment Association of Japan

Fujika Bldg.,
3-2-2 Yotsuya.
Shinjuku-ku, Tokyo 160
Tel:(03)3353-7651
Fax:(03)3353-7970

Energy

Federation of Electric Power Companies

Keidanren Kaikan,
1-9-4 Otemachi,
Chiyoda-ku, Tokyo 100
Tel:(03)3279-2180
Fax:(03)3241-1513

Japan Electric Association

Shinbashi SY Bldg.,
1-14-2 Nishi Shinbashi,
Minato-ku, Tokyo 105
Tel:(03)3216-0551
Fax:(03)3214-6005

Japan Gas Association

1-15-12 Toranomon,
Minato-ku, Tokyo 105
Tel:(03)3502-0111
Fax:(03)3502-0013

Japan LP-Gas Association

1-1-21 Nishi Shinbashi,
Minato-ku, Tokyo 105
Tel:(03)3503-5741
Fax:(03)3580-7776

Japan Natural Gas Association

No.5 Mori Bldg.,
1-17-1 Toranomon,
Minato-ku, Tokyo 105
Tel:(03)3501-1396
Fax:(03)3501-1398

Petroleum Association of Japan

Keidanren Kaikan,
1-9-4 Otemachi,
Chiyoda-ku, Tokyo 100
Tel:(03)3279-3811
FAx:(03)3242-5688

Foodstuffs

All Japan Liquor Merchants Association

2-1-26 Naka Meguro,
Meguro-ku, Tokyo 153
Tel:(03)3714-0171
Fax:(03)3710-8230

Brewers Association of Japan

2-8-18 Kyobashi,
Chuo-ku, Tokyo 104
Tel:(03)3561-8386
Fax:(03)3561-8380

Japan Baking Industry Association

15-6 Nihonbashi Kabutocho,
Chuo-ku, Tokyo 103
Tel:(03)3667-1976
Fax:(03)3667-2049

Japan Canners Association

Marunouchi Bldg.,
2-4-1 Marunouchi,
Chiyoda-ku, Tokyo 100
Tel:(03)3213-4751
Fax:(03)3211-1430

Japan Frozen Food Association

No.2 Katsuraya Bldg.,
10-6 Nihonbashi Kofunecho,
Chuo-ku, Tokyo 103
Tel:(03)3667-6671
Fax:(03)3669-2117

Japan Fruit Juice Association

Nihonbashi Fuji Bldg.,
2-5-13 Nihonbashi,
Chuo-ku, Tokyo 103
Tel:(03)3275-1031
Fax:(03)3275-1067

Japan Soft Drinks Association

3-23-1 Hongo,
Bunkyo-ku, Tokyo 113
Tel:(03)3814-0666
Fax:(03)3813-9739

National Rice Association
Shokuryo Kaikan,
3-3-6 Kojimachi,
Chiyoda-ku, Tokyo 102
Tel:(03)3222-9581
Fax:(03)3264-1771

General Machinery

Japan Farm Machinery Manufacturers' Association
3-5-8 Shiba Koen,
Minato-ku, Tokyo 105
Tel:(03)3433-0415
Fax:(03)3433-1528

Japan Industrial Robot Association
3-5-8 Shiba Koen,
Minato-ku, Tokyo 105
Tel:(03)3434-2919
Fax:(03)3578-1404

Japan Machine Tool Builders' Association
3-5-8 Shiba Koen,
Minato-ku, Tokyo 105
Tel:(03)3434-3961
Fax:(03)3434-3763

Japan Machinery Federation
3-5-8 Shiba Koen,
Minato-ku, Tokyo 105
Tel:(03)3434-5381
Fax:(03)3434-2666

Japan Society for the Promotion of Machine Industry
3-5-8 Shiba Koen,
Minato-ku, Tokyo 105
Tel:(03)3434-8324
Fax:(03)3434-8003

Japan Society of Industrial Machinery Manufacturers
3-5-8 Shiba Koen,
Minato-ku, Tokyo 105
Tel:(03)3434-6821
Fax:(03)3434-4767

Japan Vending Machine Manufacturers' Association
Shinbashi Tanaka Bldg.,
2-37-6 Nishi Shinbashi,
Minato-ku, Tokyo 105
Tel:(03)3431-7443
Fax:(03)3431-1967

Glass and Ceramics

Ceramic Society of Japan
2-22-17 Hyakunincho,
Shinjuku-ku, Tokyo 169
Tel:(03)3362-5231
Fax:(03)3362-5714

Flat Glass Association of Japan
Shin Tokyo Bldg.,
3-3-1 Marunouchi,
Chiyoda-ku, Tokyo 100
Tel:(03)3212-8631
Fax:(03)3216-3726

Glass Fiber Association of Japan
Kawate Bldg.,
1-5-8 Nishi Shinbashi,
Minato-ku, Tokyo 105
Tel:(03)3591-5406
Fax:(03)3591-5408

Japan Cement Association
Hattori Bldg.,
1-10-3 Kyobashi,
Chuo-ku, Tokyo 104
Tel:(03)3561-8632
Fax:(03)3567-8570

Japan Fine Ceramics Association
Nishikan Toranomon Bldg.,
1-22-13 Toranomon,
Minato-ku, Tokyo 105
Tel:(03)3508-8461
Fax:(03)3508-4485

Insurance

Japan Trade and Investment Insurance Organization
Akasaka Twin Tower Main Bldg.,
2-17-22 Akasaka,
Minato-ku, Tokyo 107
Tel:(03)3224-1201
Fax:(03)3224-0527

Life Insurance Association of Japan
Shinkokusai Bldg.,
3-4-1 Marunouchi,
Cyiyoda-ku, Tokyo 100
Tel:(03)3286-2624
Fax:(03)3201-6713

Marine and Fire Insurance Association of Japan
2-9 Kanda Awajicho,
Chiyoda-ku, Tokyo 101
Tel:(03)3255-1211
Fax:(03)3255-1270

Management

Japan Management Association
3-1-22 Shiba Koen,
Minato-ku, Tokyo 105
Tel:(03)3434-6211
Fax:(03)3434-1087

Japan Management Institute
Sumitomo Seimei Bldg.,
3-1-30 Minami Aoyama,
Minato-ku, Tokyo 107
Tel:(03)3478-7581
Fax:(03)3478-7587

Japan Productivity Center
3-1-1 Shibuya,
Shibuya-ku, Tokyo 150
Tel:(03)3409-1111
Fax:(03)3409-1986

Metal and Metal Products

Japan Alminium Federation
Nihonbashi Asahi Seimei Kaikan,
2-1-3 Nihonbashi,
Chuo-ku, Tokyo 103
Tel:(03)3274-4551
Fax:(03)3274-3179

Japan Iron & Steel Federation
Keidanren Kaikan
1-9-4 Otemachi,
Chiyoda-ku, Tokyo 100
Tel:(03)3279-3611
Fax:(03)3245-0144

Japan Light Metal Association
Nihonbashi Asahi Seimei Kaikan,
2-1-3 Nihonbashi,
Chuo-ku, Tokyo 103
Tel:(03)3273-3041
Fax:(03)3213-2918

Kozai Club
Tekko Kaikan,
3-2-10 Nihonbashi Kayabacho,
Chuo-ku, Tokyo 103
Tel:(03)3669-4811
Fax:(03)3664-1457

Mining

Japan Coal Association
1-8-1 Yurakucho,
Chiyoda-ku, Tokyo 100
Tel:(03)3271-3481
Fax:(03)3214-0585

Japan Mining Industry Association
Shin Hibiya Bldg.,
1-3-6 Uchisaiwaicho,
Chiyoda-ku, Tokyo 100
Tel:(03)3502-7451
Fax:(03)3591-9841

News Media

Japan Newspaper Publishers and Editors Association
Nippon Press Center Bldg.,
2-2-1 Uchisaiwaicho,
Chiyoda-ku, Tokyo 100
Tel:(03)3591-4401
Fax:(03)3591-6149

National Association of Commercial Broadcasters in Japan
Bungei Shunju Bldg.,
3-23 Kioicho,
Chiyoda-ku, Tokyo 102
Tel:(03)3265-7481
Fax:(03)3261-2860

Paper and Pulp

Japan Paper Association
Kami Pulp Kaikan,
3-9-11 Ginza,
Chuo-ku, Tokyo 104
Tel:(03)3248-4801
Fax:(03)3248-4826

Precision Machinery

Japan Camera Industry Association
JCII Bldg.,
25 Ichibancho,
Chiyoda-ku, Tokyo 102
Tel:(03)5276-3891
Fax:(03)5276-3893

Japan Clock & Watch Association
Kudan TS Bldg.,
1-9-16Kudan-kita,
Chiyoda-ku, Tokyo 102
Tel:(03)5276-3411
Fax:(03)5276-3414

Japan Optical Industry Association
Kikai Shinko Bldg.,
3-5-8 Shiba Koen,
Minato-ku, Tokyo 105
Tel:(03)3431-7073

Retail

Japan Chain Stores Association
Toranomon 40 Mori Bldg.,
5-13-1 Toranomon,
Minato-ku, Tokyo 105
Tel:(03)3433-1290
Fax:(03)3433-1297

Japan Consumers' Co-operative Union
Seikyo Kaikan,
4-1-13 Sendagaya,
Shibuya-ku, Tokyo 151
Tel:(03)3497-9111
Fax:(03)3402-8246

Japan Department Stores Association
2-1-10 Nihonbashi,
Chuo-ku, Tokyo 103
Tel:(03)3272-1666
Fax:(03)3281-0381

Kanto Department Stores Association
2-1-10 Nihonbashi,
Chuo-ku, Tokyo 103
Tel:(03)3278-8781
Fax:(03)3278-8783

Kinki Department Stores Association
1-15-27 Higashi-Shinsaibashi,
Chuo-ku, Osaka 542
Tel:(06)261-4207

Rubber Goods

Japan Automobile Tire Manufacturers Association
1-1-12 Toranomon,
Minato-ku, Tokyo 105
Tel:(03)3503-0191
Fax:(03)3503-0199

Japan Rubber Manufactures Association
1-5-26 Moto-Akasaka,
Minato-ku, Tokyo 107
Tel:(03)3408-7101
Fax:(03)3408-7106

Securities

Japan Securities Dealers Association
1-5-8 Nihonbashi Kayabacho,
Chuo-ku, Tokyo 103
Tel:(03)3667-8451
Fax:(03)3666-8009

Shipbuilding

Shipbuilders' Association of Japan
Senpaku Shinko Bldg.,
1-15-16 Toranomon,
Minato-ku, Tokyo 105
Tel:(03)3502-2010
Fax:(03)3502-2816

Textiles

Japan Apparel Federation
6-12-22 Jingumae,
Shibuya-ku, Tokyo 150
Tel:(03)3486-1605
Fax:(03)3486-1645

Japan Chemical Fibers Association
3-1-11 Nihonbashi,
Chuo-ku, Tokyo 103
Tel:(03)3241-2311
Fax:(03)3246-0823

Japan Spinners' Association
Mengyo Kaikan Bldg.,
2-5-8 Bingomachi,
Chuo-ku, Osaka 541
Tel:(06)231-8431
Fax:(06)229-1590

Japan Wool Spinners' Association
1-15-4 Ueno,
Taito-ku, Tokyo 110
Tel:(03)3837-7916
Fax:(03)3837-7918

Trade

Japan Foreign Trade Council
2-4-1 Hamamatsucho,
Minato-ku, Tokyo 105
Tel:(03)3435-5952
Fax:(03)3435-5969

Transportation

All Japan Freight Forwarder Association
Yamashiro Bldg.,
1-1 Kanda Ogawacho,
Chiyoda-ku, Tokyo 101
Tel:(03)3291-4511
Fax:(03)3291-4510

Japan Automobile Carriers Association
Okamoto Bldg.,
1-11-15 Shinjuku,
Shinjuku-ku, Tokyo 160
Tel:(03)3356-3977
Fax:(03)3356-3427

Japan Harbor Transportation Association
Kouun Kaikan,
6-11-10 Shinbashi,
Minato-ku, Tokyo 105
Tel:(03)3432-1050
Fax:(03)3432-5900

Japan Non-Government Railways Association
1-6-4 Marunouchi,
Chiyoda-ku, Tokyo 100
Tel:(03)3211-1401
Fax:(03)3213-0446

Japan Port & Harbor Association
1-2-8 Toranomon,
Minato-ku, Tokyo 105
Tel:(03)3503-6968
Fax:(03)3503-6975

Japan Shipping Club
2-6-4 Hirakawacho,
Chiyoda-ku, Tokyo 102
Tel:(03)3264-1825
Fax:(03)3221-0228

Japan Tanker Owners' Association
1-7-20 Hirakawacho,
Chiyoda-ku, Tokyo 102
Tel:(03)3265-7576
Fax:(03)3265-7577

Japan Trucking Association
3-2 Yotsuya,
Shinjuku-ku, Tokyo 160
Tel:(03)3357-6271
Fax:(03)3357-8265

Japanese Shipowners' Association
2-6-4 Hirakawacho,
Chiyoda-ku, Tokyo 102
Tel:(03)3264-7171
Fax:(03)3262-4760

National Railway Express Carriers Association
3-12-9 Soto Kanda,
Chiyoda-ku, Tokyo 101
Tel:(03)5256-2380

Warehousing

Japan Warehousing Association
1-13-3 Eitai,
Koto-ku, Tokyo 135
Tel:(03)3643-1221
Fax:(03)3643-1252

Economic Research Institutes

Japan Center for Economic Research
2-6-1 Nihonbashi Kayabacho,
Chuo-ku, Tokyo 103
Tel:(03)3639-2801
Fax:(03)3639-2839

Japan Economic Research Institute
2-7-1 Hirakawacho,
Chiyoda-ku, Tokyo 102
Tel:(03)3230-1261
Fax:(03)3230-4791

Japan Research Institute
3-12 Kioicho,
Chiyoda-ku, Tokyo 102
Tel:(03)3288-4600
Fax:(03)3288-4688

Mitsubishi Economic Research Institute
3-3-1 Marunouchi,
Chiyoda-ku, Tokyo 100
Tel:(03)3214-4416
Fax:(03)3214-4415

Nippon Research Center
2-8-5 Hatcchobori,
Chuo-ku, Tokyo 104
Tel:(03)3552-2411
Fax:(03)3553-0024

Nomura Research Institute
Dai-ni Edobashi Bldg.,
1-10-1 Nihonbashi,
Chuo-ku, Tokyo 103
Tel:(03)5255-1800
Fax:(03)5255-9303

Research Institute on the National Economy
2-24-15 Minami Aoyama,
Minato-ku, Tokyo 107
Tel:(03)3403-5271
Fax:(03)3403-5272

Foreign Chambers of Commerce in Japan

American Chamber of Commerce in Japan
3-25-2 Toranomon,
Minato-ku, Tokyo 105
Tel:(03)3433-5381

Australian and New Zealand Chamber of Commerce in Japan
P.O. Box 1096
Tokyo 100-910
Tel:(03)3212-8787

Belgian-Luxembourg Chamber of Commerce in Japan
Ichibancho Central Bldg.,
22-1 Ichibancho,
Chiyoda-ku, Tokyo 102
Tel:(03)3237-9281

British Chamber of Commerce in Japan
Kenkyusha Bldg.,
1-2 Kagurazaka,
Shinjuku-ku, Tokyo 162
Tel:(03)3269-1901

Canadian Chamber of Commerce in Japan
7-4-7 Akasaka,
Minato-ku, Tokyo 107
Tel:(03)3224-7824

Danish Chamber of Commerce Western Japan
Kobe CIT Bldg.,
5-1-14 Hamabe Dori,
Chuo-ku, Kobe 651
Tel:(078)232-1333

French Chamber of Commerce and Industry in Japan
Hanzomon MK Bldg.,
1-8-1 Kojimachi,
Chiyoda-ku, Tokyo 102
Tel:(03)3288-9621

German Chamber of Commerce and Industry in Japan
Akasaka Tokyu Bldg.,
2-14-3 Nagatacho,
Chiyoda-ku, Tokyo 100
Tel:(03)3581-9881

Indian Chamber of Commerce-Japan
Satonam Bldg.,
1-5-8 Minami Honmachi,
Chuo-ku, Osaka 541
Tel: (06)261-1741

Italian Chamber of Commerce in Japan
Sankaido Bldg.,
1-9-13 Akasaka,
Minato-ku, Tokyo 107
Tel:(03)3583-7984

Netherlands Chamber of Commerce in Japan
C.P.O. Box 1296
Tokyo 100-91
Tel:(03)5210-0300

Philippine Chamber of Commerce & Industry in Japan
Sangyo Boeki Center Bldg.,
2 Yamashitacho,
Naka-ku, Yokohama 231
Tel:(045)663-8575

Swiss Chamber of Commerce and Industry in Japan
CS Tower,
1-11-30 Akasaka,
Minato-ku, Tokyo 107
Tel:(03)3587-1122

Trade Unions

Japanese Trade Union Confederation (JTUC-RENGO)
3-2-11 Kanda-Surugadai, Chiyoda-ku
Tokyo 101
Tel:(03)5295-0550
Affiliated union federation: 80
Total membership: 7,957,518

Major RENGO-Affiliated Union Federations

All Japan Prefectural and Municipal Workers' Union (Jichiro)
1 Rokubancho, Chiyoda-ku, Tokyo 102
Tel:(03)3263-0263
Membership: 1,012,173

Confederation of Japan Automobile Workers' Unions (Jidosha Soren)
U-life Center, 1-4-26 Kaigan, Minatoku, Tokyo 105
Tel:(03)3434-7641
Membership: 795,073

Japanese Federation of Electrical Electronic and Information Union (Denki Rengo)
1-10-3 Mita, Minato-ku, Tokyo 108
Tel:(03)3455-6911
Membership: 774,765

Japanese Federation of Textile, Garment, Chemical, Mercantile, Food and Allied Industries Workers' Unions (Zensen Domei)
4-8-16 Kudan-Minami, Chiyoda-ku, Tokyo 101
Tel:(03)3288-3549
Membership: 584,375

National Federation of Life Insurance Worker's Unions (Seiho Roren)
3-9-15 Yushima, Bunkyo-ku, Tokyo 103
Tel:(03)3837-2031
Membership: 413,882

Japan Teachers Union (Nikkyoso)
2-6-2 Hitotsubashi, Chiyoda-ku, Tokyo 101
Tel:(03)3265-2171
Membership: 393,989

Japanese Federation of Metal Industry Workers' Unions (Zenkin Rengo)
2-20-12 Shiba, Munato-ku, Minato-ku, Tokyo 105
Tel:(03)3451-2141
Membership: 322,611

Japan Federation of Telecommunications, Electronic Information and Allied Workers (Jyoho Roren)
3-6 Kanda Surudagai, Chiyoda-ku, Tokyo 101
Tel:(03)3219-2231
Membership: 279,960

Confederation of Electric Power Related Industry Workers' Union of Japan (Denryoku Soren)
2-7-15 Mita, Minato-ku, Tokyo 108
Tel:(03)3454-0231
Membership: 244,391

National Federation of Iron and Steel Workers' Unions (Tekko Roren)
1-23-4 Shinkawa, Chuo-ku, Tokyo 104
Tel:(03)3555-0401
Membership: 206,077

National Metal and Machinery Workers' Unions of Japan (Kinzoku Kikai)
6-2 Sakuragaoka, Shibuya-ku, Tokyo 150
Tel:(03)3463-4231
Membership: 205,000

General Federation of Private Railway Workers' Unions (Shitetsu Soren)
4-3-5 Takanawa, Minato-ku, Tokyo 108
Tel:(03)3473-0166
Membership: 189,335

Japan Postal Workers' Union (Zentei)
1-2-7 Koraku, Bunkyo-ku, Tokyo 112
Tel:(03)3812-4260
Membership: 161,388

All Japan Federation of Transport Workers' Unions (Unyu Roren)
3-3-3 Kasumigaseki, Chiyoda-ku, Tokyo 100
Tel:(03)3503-2171
Membership: 133,898

Japan Confederation of Shipbuilding and Engineering Workers' Unions (Zosenjuki Roren)
2-20-12 Shiba, Minato-ku, Tokyo 105
Tel:(03)3451-6783
Membership: 133,898

Japan Federation of Commercial Workers Unions (Shogyo Roren)
2-23-1 Yoyogi, Shibuya-ku, Tokyo 151
Tel:(03)3370-4121
Membership: 126,475

Japanese Federation of Chemical and General Workers' Unions (Zenka Rengo)
2-20-12 Shiba, Minato-ku, Tokyo 105
Tel:(03)3453-3801
Membership: 122,828

National Federation of General Workers' Unions (Ippan Domei)
2-20-12 Shiba, Minato-ku, Tokyo 105
Tel:(03)3453-5969
Membership: 111,154

Japan Federation of Transport Workers Unions (Kotsu Roren)
2-20-12 Shiba, Minato-ku, Tokyo 105
Tel:(03)3451-7243
Membership: 103,400

Japanese Federation of Synthetic Chemistry Workers Unions (Goka Roren)
5-26-30 Shiba, Minato-ku, Tokyo 108
Tel:(03)3452-5591
Membership: 98,478

Japan Confederation of Railway Workers' Unions (JR Soren)
3-2-13 Nishi-Gotanda, Shinagawa-ku, Tokyo 141
Tel:(03)3491-7191
Membership: 76,475

National Council of General Amalgamated Workers Unions (Zenkoku Ippan)
3-5-6 Misaki-cho, Chiyoda-ku, Tokyo 101
Tel:(03)3230-4071
Membership: 65,096

All Japan Seamen's Union (Kaiin Kumiai)
7-15-26 Roppongi, Minato-ku, Tokyo 106
Tel:(03)5410-8328
Membership: 55,000

Japanese Federation of Pulp and Paper Workers' Unions (Kamipa Rengo)
2-12-4 Kita-Aoyama, Minato-ku, Tokyo 107
Tel:(03)3402-7656
Membership: 54,063

Japan Federation of Leisure and Service Industries Workers' Unions (Leisure Service Rengo)
3-5-6 Misaki-cho, Chiyoda-ku, Tokyo 101
Tel:(03)3230-1724
Membership: 48,900

Securities Markets

Sapporo Stock Exchange
5-14-1 Minami Ichijo Nishi
Chuo-ku, Sapporo 060
Tel:(011)241-6171

Niigata Securities Exchange
1245 Hachibancho, Kami-
Okawamaedori, Niigata 951
Tel:(0252)22-4181

Tokyo Stock Exchange
2-1 Nihonbashi-Kabutocho,
Chuo-ku, Tokyo 103
Tel:(03)3666-0141

Nagoya Stock Exchange
3-3-17 Sakae, Naka-ku,
Nagoya 460
Tel:(052)262-3171

Kyoto Securities Exchange
66 Tachiuri Nishimachi, Shijodori,
Higashitoin Higashi-iru,
Shimogyo-ku, Kyoto 600
Tel:(075)221-1171

Osaka Securities Exchange
1-8-16 Kitahama, Chuo-ku,
Osaka 541
Tel:(06)226-0058

Hiroshima Stock Exchange
14-18 Kanayamacho, Naka-ku,
Hiroshima 730
Tel:(082)541-1121

Fukuoka Securities Exchange
2-14-2 Tenjin, Chuo-ku,
Fukuoka 810
Tel:(092)741-8231

Commodity Exchanges

Hokkaido Grain Exchange
5-3 Ohdori Nishi, Chuo-ku,
Sapporo 060
Tel:(011)221-9131

Maebashi Dried Cocoon Exchange
1-49-1 Furuichimachi,
Maebashi, Gunma 371
Tel:(0272)52-1401

Tokyo Grain Exchange
1-12-5 Nihonbashi-kakigaracho
Chuo-ku, Tokyo 103
Tel:(03)3668-9311

Tokyo Commodity Exchange
1-10-8 Nihonbashi-Horidomecho
Chuo-ku, Tokyo 103
Tel:(03)3661-9191

Yokohama Raw Silk Exchange
Silk Center, 1 Yamashitacho,
Naka-ku, Yokohama 231
Tel:(045)641-1341

Nagoya Grain & Sugar Exchange
2-3-2 Meieki Minami,
Nakamura-ku, Nagoya 450
Tel:(052)571-8161

Nagoya Textile Exchange
3-2-15 Nishiki, Naka-ku,
Nagoya 460
Tel:(052)951-2171

Toyohashi Dried Cocoon Exchange
2-52 Ekimaeohdori, Toyohashi,
Aichi 440
Tel:(0532)52-6231

Kansai Agricultural Commodities Exchange
1-10-14 Awaza, Nishi-ku,
Osaka 550
Tel:(06)531-7931

Osaka Textile Exchange
2-5-28 Kyutarocho,
Chuo-ku, Osaka 541
Tel:(06)253-0031

Kobe Raw Silk Exchange
Kobe Silk Center Bldg.,
126 Higashimachi, Chuo-ku, Kobe 650
Tel:(078)331-7141

Kobe Rubber Exchange
49 Harimacho, Chuo-ku, Kobe 650
Tel:(078)331-4211

Kanmon Commodity Exchange
1-5 Nabecho, Shimonoseki,
Yamaguchi 750
Tel:(0832)31-1313

ORGANIZATION STRUCTURE OF TOKYO STOCK EXCHANGE

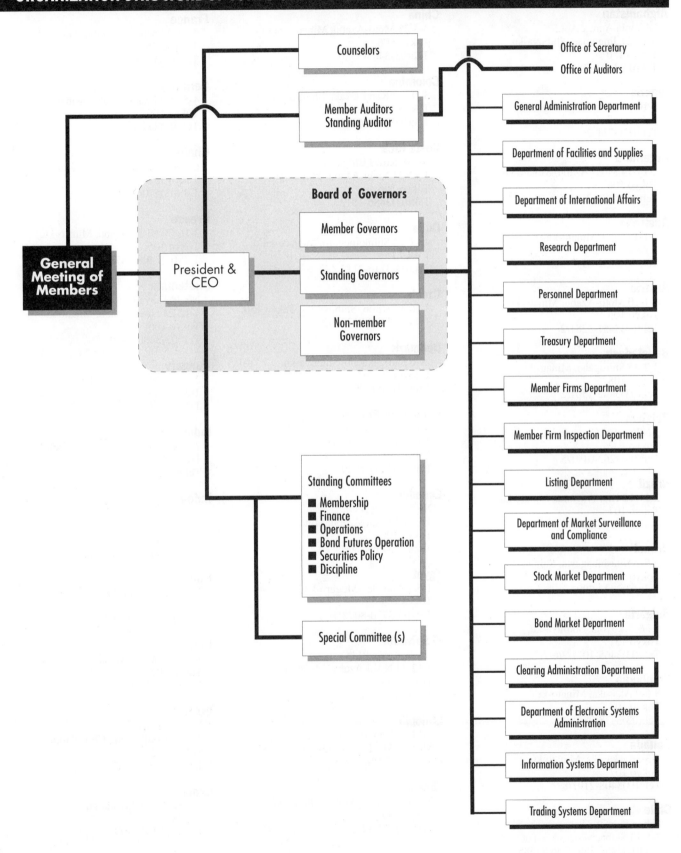

General Meeting of Members

President & CEO

Counselors

Member Auditors
Standing Auditor

Board of Governors

Member Governors

Standing Governors

Non-member Governors

Standing Committees

■ Membership
■ Finance
■ Operations
■ Bond Futures Operation
■ Securities Policy
■ Discipline

Special Committee (s)

Office of Secretary
Office of Auditors

General Administration Department

Department of Facilities and Supplies

Department of International Affairs

Research Department

Personnel Department

Treasury Department

Member Firms Department

Member Firm Inspection Department

Listing Department

Department of Market Surveillance and Compliance

Stock Market Department

Bond Market Department

Clearing Administration Department

Department of Electronic Systems Administration

Information Systems Department

Trading Systems Department

Foreign Embassies in Japan

Afghanistan
Olympia Annex Apt.,
6-13-21 Jingumae, Shibuya-ku,
Tokyo 150
Tel:(03)3407-7900

Algeria
2-10-67 Mita, Meguro-ku,
Tokyo 153
Tel:(03)3711-2661

Argentina
2-14-14 Moto-Azabu, Minato-ku,
Tokyo 106
Tel:(03)5420-7101/5

Australia
2-1-14 Mita, Minato-ku,
Tokyo 108
Tel:(03)5232-4111

Austria
1-1-20 Moto-Azabu, Minato-ku,
Tokyo 106
Tel:(03)3451-8281/2

Bangladesh
2-7-45 Shirogane, Minato-ku,
Tokyo 108
Tel:(03)3442-1501/2

Belgium
5 Nibancho, Chiyoda-ku,
Tokyo 102
Tel:(03)3262-0191/5

Brazil
2-11-12 Kita-Aoyama, Minato-ku,
Tokyo 107
Tel:(03)3404-5211/8

Brunei
6-5-2 Kitashinagawa, Shinagawa-ku
Tokyo 141
Tel:(03)3447-7997

Bulgaria
5-36-3 Yoyogi, Shibuya-ku,
Tokyo 151
Tel:(03)3465-1021/2/6/7

Cambodia
8-6-9 Akasaka, Minato-ku,
Tokyo 107
Tel:(03)3478-0861

Canada
7-3-38 Akasaka, Minato-ku,
Tokyo 107
Tel:(03)3408-2101/8

Chile
Nihon Seimei Akabanebashi Bldg.,
3-1-14 Shiba, Minato-ku, Tokyo 105
Tel:(03)3452-7561/7562/7585

China
3-4-33 Moto-Azabu, Minato-ku,
Tokyo 106
Tel:(03)3403-3380

Colombia
3-10-53 Kami-Osaki, Shinagawa-ku,
Tokyo 141
Tel:(03)3440-6451

Costa Rica
No.38 Kowa Bldg.,
4-12-24 Nishi-Azabu, Minato-ku,
Tokyo 106
Tel:(03)3486-1812

Cuba
4-11-12 Shimomeguro, Meguro-ku,
Tokyo 153
Tel:(03)3716-3112

Czech
2-16-14 Hiroo, Shibuya-ku, Tokyo 150
Tel:(03)3400-8122/3/5

Denmark
29-6 Sarugakucho, Shibuya-ku,
Tokyo 150
Tel:(03)3496-3001

Dominican Republic
No.38 Kowa Bldg.,
4-12-24 Nishi-Azabu, Minato-ku,
Tokyo 106
Tel:(03)3499-6020

Ecuador
No.38 Kowa Bldg.,
4-12-24 Nishi-Azabu, Minato-ku,
Tokyo 106
Tel:(03)3499-2800

Egypt
1-5-4 Aobadai, Meguro-ku,
Tokyo 153
Tel:(03)3770-8022/4

El Salvador
No.38 Kowa Bldg.,
4-12-24 Nishi-Azabu, Minato-ku,
Tokyo 106
Tel:(03)3499-4461

Ethiopia
1-14-15 Midorigaoka,
Meguro-ku, Tokyo 152
Tel:(03)3718-1003/5

Finland
3-5-39 Minami-Azabu, Minato-ku,
Tokyo 106
Tel:(03)3442-2231

France
4-11-44 Minami-Azabu, Minato-ku,
Tokyo 106
Tel:(03)5420-8800

Germany
4-5-10 Minami-Azabu, Minato-ku,
Tokyo 106
Tel:(03)3473-0151/7

Ghana
6-2-4 Fukazawa, Setagaya-ku,
Tokyo 158
Tel:(03)5706-3201

Greece
3-16-30 Nishi-Azabu, Minato-ku,
Tokyo 106
Tel:(03)3403-0871/2

Guatemala
No.38 Kowa Bldg.,
4-12-24 Nishi-Azabu, Minato-ku,
Tokyo 106
Tel:(03)3400-1830

Hungary
2-17-14 Mita, Minato-ku,
Tokyo 108
Tel:(03)3798-8801/4

India
2-2-11 Kudan-Minami, Chiyoda-ku,
Tokyo 102
Tel:(03)3262-2391/7

Indonesia
5-2-9 Higashi-Gotanda,
Shinagawa-ku,
Tokyo 141
Tel:(03)3441-4201

Iran
3-10-32 Minami-Azabu, Minato-ku,
Tokyo 106
Tel:(03)3446-8011/5

Iraq
8-4-7 Akasaka, Minato-ku,
Tokyo 107
Tel:(03)3423-1727/28/29/30

Ireland
Ireland House
2-10-7 Koujimachi, Chiyoda-ku,
Tokyo 102
Tel:(03)3263-0695

Israel
3 Nibancho, Chiyoda-ku.
Tokyo 102
Tel:(03)3264-0911

Italy
2-5-4 Mita, Minato-ku,
Tokyo 108
Tel:(03)3453-5291/6

Jordan
Chiyoda House,
2-17-8 Nagatacho, Chiyoda-ku,
Tokyo 100
Tel:(03)3580-5856

Kenya
3-24-3 Yakumo, Meguro-ku,
Tokyo 152
Tel:(03)3723-4006/7

Korea
1-2-5 Minami-Azabu, Minato-ku,
Tokyo 106
Tel:(03)3452-7611/9

Kuwait
4-13-12 Mita, Minato-ku,
Tokyo 108
Tel:(03)3455-0361

Laos
3-3-22 Nishi-Azabu, Minato-ku,
Tokyo 106
Tel:(03)5411-2291/2

Lebanon
Chiyoda House,
2-17-8 Nagatacho, Chiyoda-ku,
Tokyo 100
Tel:(03)3580-1227

Libya
10-14 Daikanyamacho, Shibuya-ku,
Tokyo 150
Tel:(03)3477-0701/4

Luxembourg
Nibancho TS Bldg.,
2-1 Nibancho, Chiyoda-ku,
Tokyo 102
Tel:(03)3265-9621/2/3

Malaysia
20-16 Nanpeidaicho, Shibuya-ku,
Tokyo 150
Tel:(03)3476-3840

Mexico
2-15-1 Nagatacho, Chiyoda-ku,
Tokyo 100
Tel:(03)3581-1131/5

Mongolia
21-4 Kamiyamacho, Shibuya-ku,
Tokyo 150
Tel:(03)3469-2088, 2091/2

Morocco
Silva Kingdom Bldg.,
3-16-3 Sendagaya, Shibuya-ku,
Tokyo 151Tel:(03)3478-3271/4

Myanmar
4-8-26 Kita-Shinagawa,
Shinagawa-ku,
Tokyo 140
Tel:(03)3441-9291/5

Nepal
7-14-9 Todoroki, Setagaya-ku,
Tokyo 158
Tel:(03)3705-5558/9

Netherlands
3-6-3 Shibakoen, Minato-ku,
Tokyo 105
Tel:(03)5401-0411

New Zealand
20-40 Kamiyamacho, Shibuya-ku,
Tokyo 150
Tel:(03)3467-2271/5

Nigeria
5-11-17 Shimomeguro, Meguro-ku,
Tokyo 153
Tel:(03)5721-5391/3

Norway
5-12-2 Minami-Azabu, Minato-ku,
Tokyo 106
Tel:(03)3440-2611

Oman
2-28-11 Sendagaya, Shibuya-ku,
Tokyo 151
Tel:(03)3402-0877/0749

Pakistan
2-14-9 Moto-Azabu, Minato-ku,
Tokyo 106
Tel:(03)3454-4861/4

Panama
No.38 Kowa Bldg.,
4-12-24 Nishi-Azabu, Minato-ku
Tokyo 106
Tel:(03)3499-3741

Peru
4-4-27 Higashi, Shibuya-ku,
Tokyo 150
Tel:(03)3406-4240/4243/4249

Philippines
11-24 Nanpeidaicho,
Shibuya-ku, Tokyo 150
Tel:(03)3496-2731

Poland
2-13-5 Mita, Meguro-ku,
Tokyo 153
Tel:(03)3711-5224/6

Portugal
Olympia Annex Apt.,
6-13-21 Jingumae, Shibuya-ku,
Tokyo 150Tel:(03)3400-7907/8

Qatar
6-16-22 Shirogane, Minato-ku,
Tokyo 108
Tel:(03)3446-7561

Romania
3-16-19 Nishi-Azabu, Minato-ku,
Tokyo 106
Tel:(03)3479-0311

Russian Federation
2-1-1 Azabudai, Minato-ku,
Tokyo 106
Tel:(03)3583-4224,5982

Saudi Arabia
1-53 Azabu-Nagasakacho, Minato-ku,
Tokyo 106
Tel:(03)3589-5241

Singapore
5-12-3 Roppongi, Minato-ku,
Tokyo 106
Tel:(03)3586-9111/2

Slovakia
2-16-14 Hiroo, Shibuya-ku,
Tokyo 150
Tel:(03)3400-8122/3/5

Slovenia
7-5-15 Akasaka, Minato-ku,
Tokyo 107
Tel:(03)5570-6275

South Africa
Zenkyoren Bldg.,
2-7-9 Hirakawacho, Chiyoda-ku,
Tokyo 102
Tel:(03)3265-3366/9

Spain
1-3-29 Roppongi, Minato-ku,
Tokyo 106
Tel:(03)3583-8531/3

Sri Lanka
1-14-1 Akasaka, Minato-ku,
Tokyo 107
Tel:(03)3585-7431/2

Sudan
Kindai-Shinsetsu Bldg.,
1-13-4 Aobadai, Meguro-ku,
Tokyo 153
Tel:(03)3476-0811/2

Sweden
1-10-3-100 Roppongi, Minato-ku,
Tokyo 106
Tel:(03)5562-5050

Switzerland
5-9-12 Minami-Azabu, Minato-ku,
Tokyo 106
Tel:(03)3473-0121

Syria
Homat-Jade,
6-19-45 Akasaka, Minato-ku,
Tokyo 107
Tel:(03)3586-8977

Tanzania
4-21-9 Kamiyoga, Setagaya-ku,
Tokyo 158
Tel:(03)3425-4531

Thailand
3-14-6 Kami-Osaki, Shinagawa-ku,
Tokyo 141
Tel:(03)3441-7352

Tunisia
1-18-8 Wakaba, Shinjuku-ku,
Tokyo 160
Tel:(03)3353-4111/3

Turkey
2-33-6 Jingumae, Shibuya-ku,
Tokyo 150
Tel:(03)3470-5131/5

United Arab Emirates
9-10 Nanpeidaicho, Shibuya-ku,
Tokyo 150
Tel:(03)5489-0804

United Kingdom of Great Britain and Northern Ireland
1 Ichibancho, Chiyoda-ku,
Tokyo 102
Tel:(03)3265-5511

United States of America
1-10-5 Akasaka, Minato-ku,
Tokyo 107
Tel:(03)3224-5000

Uruguay
No.38 Kowa Bldg.,
4-12-24 Nishi-Azabu, Minato-ku,
Tokyo 106
Tel:(03)3486-1888/1750

Venezuela
No.38 Kowa Bldg.,
4-12-24 Nishi-Azabu, Minato-ku,
Tokyo 106
Tel:(03)3409-1501/4

Vietnam
50-11 Motoyoyogicho, Shibuya-ku,
Tokyo 151
Tel:(03)3466-3311/3313

Yemen
No.38 Kowa Bldg.,
4-12-24 Nishi-Azabu, Minato-ku,
Tokyo 106
Tel:(03)3499-7151/2

Yugoslavia
4-7-24 Kita-Shinagawa,
Shinagawa-ku,
Tokyo 140
Tel:(03)3447-3571/2

Zaire
Harajyuku Green Heights.,
3-53-17 Sendagaya, Shibuya-ku,
Tokyo 151
Tel:(03)3423-3981/2

Zambia
1-10-2 Ebara, Shinagawa-ku,
Tokyo 142
Tel:(03)3491-0121

Japanese Embassies Abroad

Algeria
1,Chemin Macklay (Al Bakri),
Ben-Aknoun, Alger
(B.P.80,El-Biar)
Tel:(213-2)912004

Argentina
Bouchard 547 Piso-17,
Buenos Aires
Tel:(54-1)318-8200

Australia
112 Empire Circuit, Yarralumla,
Canberra A.C.T. 2600
Tel:(61-6)273-3244

Austria
1040 Wien, Argentinierstrasse
21, Osterreich
Tel:(43-1)501710

Bangladesh
Plot No.5&7,
Dutabash Road, Baridhara,
Dhaka
Tel:(880-2)870087

Belgium
Avenue des Arts 58, 1040 Bruxelles
Tel:(32-2)513-2340

Bolivia
Calle Rosendo Gutierrez
No.497 esq. Sanchez Lima, La Paz
(P.O. Box 2725)
Tel:(591-2)373151

Brazil
Avenida das Nacoes,
Lote 39, 70425, Brasilia
(Caixa Postal 07-0891)
Tel:(55-61)242-6866

Bulgaria
UI. Lyulyakova Gradina 14, Sofia
Tel:(359-2)72-39-84

Canada
255 Sussex Drive, Ottawa,
Ontario K1N 9E6
Tel:(1-613)241-8541

Chile
Av.Providencia 2653,
19 Piso, Casilla 124,
Correo 35, Santiago
Tel:(56-2)2321807

China
7 Ri Tan Road, Jian Guo Men Wai, Beijing
Tel:(86-1)532-2361

Colombia
Carrera 9a. A No.99-02,(Piso 6)
Edificio Latinoamericana de Seguros,
Santa Fe De Bogota
Tel:(57-1)618-2800

Costa Rica
Barrio Rohrmoser,
Sabana Oeste de la Primera Entrada,
500 Mts. Oeste y 100 Mts. Norte
San Jose (Apartado No.501 y No.10145)
Tel:(506)232-1255

Cuba
Calle N No.62 Esq.15,
Vedado, Ciudad de La Habana
(Apartado No.752)
Tel:(53-7)33-3355

Czech
Maltezske namesti 6,
Praha 1-Mala Strana
Tel:(42-2)24510753

Denmark
Pilestraede 61, 1112,
Copenhagen K
Tel:(45)33-11-33-44

Dominican Republic
Torre BHD 8 Piso, Avenida Winston
Churchill, Esquina Luis F.
Thomen Santo Domingo
(P.O.Box 1236)
Tel:(1-809)566-8023

Ecuador
Calle Juan Leon Mera
No.130 y Avenida Patria,
Edificio de la Corporacion
Financiera Nacional, 7-Piso, Quito
(P.O.Box 1721-01518)
Tel:(593-2)561-899

Egypt
3rd Floor Cairo Center Bldg.,
2, Abdel Kader Hamza Street,
Garden City, Cairo (P.O. Box 281)
Tel:(20-2)3553962

El Salvador
Calle Loma Linda #258,
Colonia San Benito,
San Salvador (Apartado #115)
Tel:(503)224-4740

Ethiopia
House No.653, Kebele 7,
Woreda 18, Addis Ababa
(P.O.Box 5650)
Tel:(251-1)51-10-88

Finland
Etelaranta 8, 00130, Helsinki
Tel:(358-0)633011

France
7, Avenue Hoche, 75008 Paris
Tel:(33-1)4888-6200

Germany
Godesberger Allee 102-104,
53175 Bonn
Tel:(49-228)81910

Ghana
No.8 Josif Broz Tito Ave.,
Off Jawaharlal Nehru Ave., Accra
Tel:(233-21)775615

Greece
2-4, Messoghion Avenue,
Athens Tower Bldg., 21st Floor, Athens
Tel:(30-1)775-8101

Guatemala
Ruta 6, 8-19, Zona 4,
Ciudad de Guatemala 01901
(Apartado Postal No.531)
Tel:(502-2)31-9668

Honduras
Colonia San Carlos,
Calzada Rep. Paraguay,
Tegucigalpa, D.C.
(Apartado Postal 3232)
Tel:(504)36-5511

Hungary
1125 Zalai ut 7,
Budapest, XII (P.O.Box 78)
Tel:(36-1)275-1275

India
50-G, Chanakyapuri, New Delhi
Tel:(91-11)6876564

Indonesia
Jalan M.H. Thamrin 24,Jakarta
Tel:(62-21)324308

Iran
Bucharest Avenue,
Corner of the 5th Street, Tehran
Tel:(98-21)8717923

Iraq
Hay Babil 929/17/70, Baghdad
(P.O. Box 2369, ALWIYAH)
Tel:(964-1)7195156

Ireland
Nutley Bldg., Merrion Center,
Nutley Lane, Dublin 4
Tel:(353-1)269-40-33

Israel
Asia House, 4, Weizman Street,
64 239 Tel-Aviv
Tel:(972-3)6957292

Italy
Via Quintino Sella, 60
00187 Roma
Tel:(39-6)487991

Jamaica
32 Trafalger Road, 3f Atrium
Bldg., Kingston 10
Tel:(1-809)9293338

Jordan
Between 4th and 5th Circles,
A1-Aqsa Street, Jabal Amman,
Amman (P.O. Box 2835)
Tel:(962-6)672486

Kenya
15F ICEA Bldg., Kenyatta Ave.,
Nairobi
(P.O. Box 60202, Nairobi)
Tel:(254-2)332955

Korea
18-11, Choonghak-dong
Chongro-ku, Seoul
Tel:(82-2)733-5626

Kuwait
Area No.9 Plot No.496,
Jabriya, Kuwait (P.O. Box 2304 Safat)
Tel:(965)5312870

Laos
Road Sisangvone,
Vientiane
Tel:(856-21)41-4400

Lebanon
Officers' Club Street,
Quarter of the Presidential Place,
Lot No.2963-BAABDA, Beirut
(P.O.Box 3360)
Tel:(961-1)464255

Libya
Organization of African
Unity Road, Dhat Al-Imad,
Tower No.4, Halls No.13&14,
Tripoli
(P.O.Box 3265)
Tel:(218-21)607462

Luxembourg
17 Rue Beaumont,
L-1219 Luxembourg
Tel:(352)464151

Malaysia
No.11 Pesiaran Stonor,
Off Jalan Tun Razak, 50450,
Kuala Lumpur
Tel:(60-3)242-7044

Mexico
Paseo de la Reforma No.395,
Col. Cuauhtemoc, 06500 Mexico,
D.F. (Apartado 5-101)
Tel:(52-5)211-0028

Mongolia
Ulaanbaatar 13,
Zaluuchuudyn Gudamj 12, Ulaanbaatar
(P.O. Box 1011)
Tel:(976-1)324408

Morocco
70, Ave., des Nations Unies,
Agdal, Rabat
Tel:(212-7)67-41-63

Myanmar
No.100, Natmauk Road, Yangon
(P.O. Box 841)
Tel:(95-1)39644

Nepal
Durbar Marg, Kathmandu
(P.O.Box 264)
Tel:(977-1)226061

Netherlands
Tobias Asserlaan 2,
2517 KC, The Hague
Tel:(31-70)3469544

New Zealand
7th Floor, Norwich Insurance House,
3-11 Hunter Street, Wellington 1,
(P.O. Box 6340)
Tel:(64-4)473-1540

Nicaragua
Plaza Espana 1 cuadra abajo y
1 cuadra al lago,
Bolonia, Managua
(Apartado Postal 1789)
Tel:(505-2)668668

Nigeria
Plot 24-25 Apese Street, Victoria
Island, Lagos, (P.O. Box 2111)
Tel:(234-1)2614929

Norway
Parkveien 33-B, 0244, Oslo 2
Tel:(47-22)55-10-11

Pakistan
Plot No.53-70, Ramna 5/4
Diplomatic Enclave 1, Islamabad
Tel:(92-51)219721

Panama
Calle 50 y 60E,
Obarrio, Apartado No.1411,
Panama 1
Tel:(507)263-6155

Peru
Avenida San Felipe 356,
Jesus Maria, Lima
(Apartado No.3708)
Tel:(51-14)63-0000

Philippines
375 Senator Gil J.Puyat Avenue,
Makati, Metro Manila
Tel:(63-2)818-9050

Poland
Ul. Grazyny 11, 02-548, Warszawa
Tel:(48-22)49-87-81

Portugal
Av. da Liberdade,
245-6, 1250 Lisboa
Tel:(351-1)3110560

Romania
Strada Polona No.4,
Sector 1, Bucharest
Tel:(40-1)210-07-90

Russian Federation
Kalashny Pereulok 12, Moscow
Tel:(7-095)291-85-00

Saudi Arabia
A-11 Diplomatic Quarter,
Riyadh (P.O. Box 4095)
Tel:(966-1)488-1100

Singapore
16 Nassim Road, Singapore 1025
Tel:(65)2358855

South Africa
2nd Fl., Sanlam Bldg., Hatfield
353 Festival St., Hatfield, Pretoria 0083
Tel:(27-12)342-2100

Spain
Calle de Joaquin Costa, 29,
28002-Madrid
Tel:(34-1)562-5546

Sri Lanka
No.20, Gregory's Road, Colombo 7
(P.O.Box 822 Colombo)
Tel:(94-1)693831

Sudan
House No.24, Block,
10 A, E., Street No.3,
New Extension, Khartoum
Tel:(249-11)451600

Sweden
Gardesgatan 10, 115 27, Stockholm
Tel:(46-8)663-0440

Switzerland
43 Engestrasse, 3012 Berne
Tel:(41-31)302-08-11

Tanzania
Plot No.1018, Upanga,
Dar es Salaam (P.O. Box 2577)
Tel:(255-51)46356

Thailand
1674 New Petchburi Road,
Bangkok 10310
Tel:(66-2)252-6151

Trinidad and Tobago
5 Hayes Street, St. Clair,
Port of Spain (P.O.Box 1039)
Tel:(1-809)628-5991

Tunisia
10 rue Mahmoud El Matri,
1002 Tunis-Belvedere
(B.P.95, 1002 Tunis-Belvedere)
Tel:(216-1)791-251

Turkey
Resit Galip Caddesi 81,
Gaziosmanpasa, Ankara
(P.O. Box P.K. 31-Kavaklidere)
Tel:(90-312)446-0500

United Arab Emirates
Abu Dhabi (P.O.Box 2430)
Tel:(971-2)435696

United Kingdom of Great Britain and Northern Ireland
101-104, Piccadilly, London
W1V 9FN
Tel:(44-171)465-6500

United States of America, The
2520 Massachusetts Avenue,
N.W., Washington D.C.,
20008-2869
Tel:(1-202)939-6700

Uruguay
Bulevar Artigas 953,
Montevideo
(Casilla de Correo 1273)
Tel:(598-2)48-7645

Venezuela
Quinta "Sakura", Avenida San Juan
Bosco, Entre 8a.y 9a.
Transversal, Altamira, Caracas
Tel:(58-2)261-8333

Vietnam
61 Truong Chinh Road,
Phuong Mai Quarter,
Dong Da District, Hanoi
Tel:(84-4)69-2600

Yemen
South Safiyah, off 35 Meter Rd.,
Street No.38,
House No.2, Sana'a,
(P.O. Box 817)
Tel:(967-1)207356

Yugoslavia
Genex Apartments,
Vladimira Popovica 6,
11070 Novi Beograd
Tel:(381-11)222-1434

Zambia
No.5218, Haile Selassie Ave.,
Lusaka (P.O. Box 34190)
Tel:(260-1)251555

Goverment Financial Institutions

Agriculture, Forestry and Fisheries Finance Corp.
1-9-3 Otemachi, Chiyoda-ku, Tokyo 100
Tel:(03)3270-2261

Environmental Sanitation Business Finance Corp.
1-9-13 Akasaka, Minato-ku, Tokyo 107
Tel:(03)3582-5411

Export-Import Bank of Japan
1-4-1 Otemachi, Chiyoda-ku, Tokyo 100
Tel:(03)3287-9101

Hokkaido-Tohoku Development Finance Corp.
1-9-3 Otemachi, Chiyoda-ku, Tokyo 100
Tel:(03)3270-1656

Housing Loan Corp.
1-4-10 Koraku, Bunkyo-ku, Tokyo 112
Tel:(03)3812-1111

Japan Development Bank
1-9-1 Otemachi, Chiyoda-ku, Tokyo 100
Tel:(03)3270-3211

Japan Finance Corp. for Municipal Enterprises
Hotel New Otani Annex Bldg., 4-1 Kioi-cho, Chiyoda-ku, Tokyo 102
Tel:(03)5210-5900

National Finance Corp.
1-9-3 Otemachi, Chiyoda-ku, Tokyo 100
Tel:(03)3270-1361

Okinawa Development Finance Corp.
1-7-1 Kumoji, Naha, Okinawa 900
Tel:(098)867-6611

Small Business Credit Insurance Corp.
1-8-2 Otemachi, Chiyoda-ku, Tokyo 100
Tel:(03)3270-2361

Small Business Finance Corp.
1-9-3 Otemachi, Chiyoda-ku, Tokyo 100
Tel:(03)3270-1261

Government-Affiliated Corporations, Institutes and Companies

Central Japan Railway Co.
2-14-19 Meieki Minami,
Nakamura-ku, Nagoya
Aichi Prefecture 450
Tel:(052)564-2338

East Japan Railway Co.
1-6-5 Marunouchi,
Chiyoda-ku, Tokyo 100
Tel:(03)3212-3782

Electric Power Development Co.
6-15-1 Ginza, Chuo-ku,
Tokyo 104
Tel:(03)3546-2211

Electrotechnical Laboratory
1-1-4 Umezono, Tsukuba City,
Ibaraki Prefecture 305
Tel:(0298)54-5021

Employment Promotion Corp.
2-1 Kojimachi,
Chiyoda-ku, Tokyo 102
Tel:(03)3222-8001

Facilitation Fund for Industrial Structural Adjustment
Kaigin Bldg., 1-9-1 Otemachi,
Chiyoda-ku, Tokyo 100
Tel:(03)3241-6283

Foreign Press Center
6th Flr. Nippon Press Center Bldg.,
2-1 Uchisaiwaicho, Chiyoda-ku,
Tokyo 100
Tel:(03)3501-3401

Forest Development Corp.
Fukuda Bldg., 3-29 Kioicho,
Chiyoda-ku, Tokyo 102
Tel:(03)3222-1211

Geological Survey of Japan
1-1-3 Higashi, Tsukuba City,
Ibaraki Prefecture 305
Tel:(0298)54-3521

Government Industrial Research Institute, Osaka
1-8-31 Midorigaoka,
Ikeda City, Osaka 563
Tel:(0727)51-8351

Hokkaido Railway Co.
4 Kita Gojo Nishi, Chuo-ku,
Sapporo, Hokkaido 060
Tel:(011)222-6122

Honshu-Shikoku Bridge Authority
45 Mori Bldg., 5-1-5 Toranomon,
Minato-ku, Tokyo 105
Tel:(03)3434-7281

Housing and Urban Development Corp.
1-14-6 Kudankita, Chiyoda-ku,
Tokyo 102
Tel:(03)3263-8111

Institute of Developing Economies
42 Ichigaya-Honmuracho, Shinjuku-ku,
Tokyo 162
Tel:(03)3353-4231

Institute of Physical and Chemical Research
2-1 Hirosawa, Wako City,
Saitama Prefecture 351-01
Tel:(048)462-1111

Institute of Population Problems
1-2-2 Kasumigaseki,
Chiyoda-ku, Tokyo 100
Tel:(03)3503-1711

Japan Atomic Energy Research Institute
Fukoku Seimei Bldg.,
2-2-2 Uchisaiwaicho,
Chiyoda-ku, Tokyo 100
Tel:(03)3592-2111

Japan Environment Corp.
1-4-1 Kasumigaseki, Chiyoda-ku,
Tokyo 100
Tel:(03)3501-3251

Japan External Trade Organization (JETRO)
2-2-5 Toranomon, Minato-ku,
Tokyo 105
Tel:(03)5251-1014

Japan Foundation
Ark Mori Bldg., 1-12-32 Akasaka,
Minato-ku, Tokyo 107
Tel:(03)5562-3511

Japan Freight Railway Co.
1-6-5 Marunouchi,
Chiyoda-ku, Tokyo 100
Tel:(03)3240-9607

Japan Highway Public Corp.
3-3-2 Kasumigaseki, Chiyoda-ku,
Tokyo 100
Tel:(03)3506-0111

Japan Information Center of Science and Technology
5-2 Yonbancho, Chiyoda-ku,
Tokyo 102
Tel:(03)5214-8401

Japan Institute for Social and Economic Affairs
1-6-1 Otemachi, Chiyoda-ku,
Tokyo 100
Tel:(03)3201-1411

Japan International Cooperation Agency (JICA)
2-1-1 Nishi-Shinjuku, Shinjuku-ku, Tokyo 163
Tel:(03)3346-5311

Japan International Research Center for Agricultural Sciences
1-2 Owashi, Tsukuba City, Ibaraki Prefecture 305
Tel:(0298)38-6313

Japan Key Technology Center
1-12-32 Akasaka, Minato-ku, Tokyo 107
Tel:(03)3505-6811

Japan Marine Fishery Resource Research Center
3-27 Kioicho, Chiyoda-ku, Tokyo 102
Tel:(03)3265-8301

Japan Marine Science and Technology Center
2-15 Natsushimacho, Yokosuka City, Kanagawa Prefecture 237
Tel:(0468)66-3811

Japan National Oil Corp.
Fukoku Seimei Bldg., 2-2-2 Uchisaiwaicho, Chiyoda-ku, Tokyo 100
Tel:(03)3597-7522

Japan National Tourist Organization
2-10-1 Yurakucho, Chiyoda-ku, Tokyo 100
Tel:(03)3216-1901

Japan Railway Construction Public Corp.
Sanno Grand Bldg., 2-14-2 Nagatacho, Chiyoda-ku, Tokyo 100
Tel:(03)3506-1813

Japan Regional Development Corp.
3-8-1 Kasumigaseki, Chiyoda-ku, Tokyo 100
Tel:(03)3501-5211

Japan Society for the Promotion of Science
Yamato Bldg., 5-3-1 Kojimachi, Chiyoda-ku, Tokyo 102
Tel:(03)3263-1721

Japan Tobacco Inc.
4-12-62 Higashi Shinagawa, Shinagawa-ku, Tokyo 140
Tel:(03)3474-3111

JNR Settlement Corp.
1-6-5 Marunouchi, Chiyoda-ku, Tokyo 100
Tel:(03)3215-3270

Kansai International Airport Co.
1 Senshu Kuko-Kita, Izumisano, Osaka Prefecture 549
Tel:(0724)55-2103

Kyushu Railway Co.
1-1 Hakataeki Chuogai, Hakata-ku, Fukuoka City, Fukuoka Prefecture 812
Tel:(092)474-2501

Livestock Industry Promotion Corp.
2-2-1 Azabudai, Minato-ku, Tokyo 106
Tel:(03)3582-3381

Maritime Credit Corp.
Iino Bldg., 2-1-1 Uchisaiwaicho, Chiyoda-ku, Tokyo 100
Tel:(03)3501-2146

Mechanical Engineering Laboratory
1-2 Namiki, Tsukuba City, Ibaraki Prefecture 305
Tel:(0298)58-7000

Metal Mining Agency of Japan
Tokiwa Bldg., 1-24-14 Toranomon, Minato-ku, Tokyo 105
Tel:(03)3503-2801

Metropolitan Expressway Public Corp.
1-4-1 Kasumigaseki, Chiyoda-ku, Tokyo 100
Tel:(03)3502-7311

National Aerospace Laboratory
7-44-1 Jindaiji-Higashimachi, Chofu City, Tokyo 182
Tel:(0422)47-5911

National Agricultural Insurance Fund
19 Ichibancho, Chiyoda-ku, Tokyo 102
Tel:(03)3239-3101

National Agriculture Research Center
3-1-1 Kannondai, Tsukuba City, Ibaraki Prefecture 305
Tel:(0298)38-8481

National Consumer Information Center
3-13-22 Takanawa, Minato-ku, Tokyo 108
Tel:(03)3443-6211

National Food Research Institute
2-1-2 Kannondai, Tsukuba City, Ibaraki Prefecture 305
Tel:(0298)38-7971

National Institute for Advanced Interdisciplinary Research
1-1-4 Higashi, Tsukuba City, Ibaraki Prefecture 305,
Tel:(0298)54-2500

National Institute for Research Advancement
34th Flr. Garden Place Tower, 4-20-3 Ebisu, Shibuya-ku, Tokyo 150
Tel:(03)5448-1700

National Institute for Research in Inorganic Materials
1-1 Mamiki, Tsukuba City, Ibaraki Prefecture 305
Tel:(0298)51-3351

National Institute for Resources and Environment
16-3 Onogawa, Tsukuba City, Ibaraki Prefecture 305
Tel:(0298)58-8100
National Institute of Agrobiological Resources
2-1-2 Kannondai, Tsukuba City, Ibaraki Prefecture 305
Tel:(0298)38-7406

National Institute of Agro-Environmental Sciences
3-1-1 Kannondai, Tsukuba City, Ibaraki Prefecture 305
Tel:(0298)38-8148

National Institute of Bioscience and Human-Technology
1-1 Higashi, Tsukuba City, Ibaraki Prefecture 305
Tel:(0298)54-6000

National Institute of Materials and Chemical Research
1-1 Higashi, Tsukuba City, Ibaraki Prefecture 305
Tel:(0298)54-6228

National Institute of Radiological Sciences
4-9-1 Anagawa, Inage-ku, Chiba City, Chiba 263
Tel:(043)251-2111

National Institute of Science and Technology Policy
1-11-39 Nagatacho, Chiyoda-ku, Tokyo 100
Tel:(03)3581-2391

National Research Institute of Agricultural Economies
2-2-1 Nishigahara, Kita-ku,
Tokyo 114
Tel:(03)3910-3946

National Research Institute of Agricultural Engineering
2-1-2 Kannondai, Tsukuba City,
Ibaraki Prefecture 305
Tel:(0298)38-7513

National Research Laboratory of Metrology
1-1-4 Umezono, Tsukuba City,
Ibaraki Prefecture 305
Tel:(0298)54-4148

National Space Development Agency of Japan (NASDA)
2-4-1 Hamamatsucho, Minato-ku,
Tokyo 105
Tel:(03)5470-4111

New Energy and Industrial Development Organization (NEDO)
Sunshine 60,
3-1-1 Higashi Ikebukuro,
Toshima-ku, Tokyo 170
Tel:(03)3987-9312

New Tokyo International Airport Authority
2-4 Nihonbashi-Honcho,
Chuo-ku, Tokyo 103
Tel:(03)3639-6200

Overseas Economic Cooperation Fund
1-4-1 Otemachi, Chiyoda-ku,
Tokyo 100
Tel:(03)3215-1311

Pension Welfare Service Public Corp.
1-4-1 Kasumigaseki, Chiyoda-ku,
Tokyo 100
Tel:(03)3502-2481

Power Reactor and Nuclear Fuel Development Corp.
1-9-13 Akasaka, Minato-ku,
Tokyo 107
Tel:(03)3587-3311

Research Development Corp. of Japan
4-1-8 Honcho, Kawaguchi City,
Saitama 332
Tel:(048)226-5601

Shikoku Railway Co.
1-10 Hamanocho,
Takamatsu City,
Kagawa Prefecture 760
Tel:(0878)51-1880

Small Business National Corp.
37 Mori Bldg.,
3-5-1 Toranomon, Minato-ku,
Tokyo 105
Tel:(03)3433-8811

Social Development Research Institute
Annex Bldg., 2-19-8 Akasaka,
Minato-ku, Tokyo 107
Tel:(03)3589-1381

Social Welfare and Medical Service Corp.
4-3-13 Toranomon, Minato-ku,
Tokyo 105
Tel:(03)3438-0211

Training Institute of International Trade and Industry
5-4-36 Fujimicho,
Higashimurayama, Tokyo 189
Tel:(0423)93-2521

Water Resources Development Public Corp.
5-3-3 Akasaka, Minato-ku,
Tokyo 107
Tel:(03)3584-1251

West Japan Railway Co.
2-4-24 Shibata, Kita-ku,
Osaka, Osaka 530
Tel:(06)375-8935

Statistics

GROSS DOMESTIC PRODUCT

Nominal (Seasonally adjusted annual rates for quarterly figures)

Items	Gross domestic product	Change from preceding year or quarter	Final private spending	Final government spending	Gross domestic fixed capital formation	Gross fixed capital formation	Private housing investment	Private plant & equipment investment	Govt.'s fixed capital formation	Increase in public inventory	Exports of goods & services (NET) (S.A)	Exports of goods & services (S.A)	Imports of goods & services (S.A)
1993(CY)	465,972.4	0.6%	270,919.4	44,666.4	139,475.8	138,814.8	23,764.8	74,561.5	40,488.4	661.0	10,910.8	44,243.8	33,333.1
1994	469,148.7	0.7	277,676.8	46,108.0	135,338.7	134,063.9	25,874.4	66,236.5	41,953.0	1,274.8	10,025.2	44,449.2	34,424.0
1995													
1993(FY)	466,763.8	0.6	272,976.7	44,987.1	138,085.3	137,265.4	24,214.2	71,924.7	41,126.5	819.9	10,714.8	43,643.5	32,928.7
1994	468,233.7	0.3	277,565.7	46,600.9	134,796.7	133,350.4	26,204.8	65,502.8	41,642.8	1,446.3	9,270.4	44,453.3	35,182.9
1995													
1994–Jan.–Mar.	469,540.9	1.0	277,709.6	45,618.2	135,186.4	134,313.0	24,401.6	68,291.9	41,619.5	873.4	11,026.7	44,374.5	33,347.8
Apr.–June	470,364.4	0.2	277,594.5	46,335.0	136,502.6	134,338.6	26,261.5	65,867.7	42,209.4	2,164.0	9,932.3	44,103.5	34,171.2
July–Sept.	471,250.5	0.2	277,954.7	47,023.9	136,543.8	134,916.9	27,020.3	65,653.6	42,243.0	1,626.9	9,728.1	44,033.0	34,304.9
Oct.–Dec.	465,799.3	-1.2	277,710.1	45,710.4	132,959.9	132,517.8	25,589.4	65,132.8	41,795.6	442.1	9,418.9	45,274.3	35,855.4
1995–Jan.–Mar.	466,220.0	0.1	277,201.7	47,776.2	133,259.0	131,688.5	25,877.0	65,419.6	40,391.9	1,570.5	7,983.1	44,360.9	36,377.8
Apr.–June	467,360.3	0.2	278,398.5	47,291.3	133,998.7	131,680.1	24,380.6	65,941.1	41,358.4	2,318.6	7,671.8	43,001.7	35,329.9
July–Sept.													
Oct.–Dec.													

Real (In constant 1985 prices; Seasonally adjusted annual rates for quarterly figures)

Items	Gross domestic product	Change from preceding year or quarter	Final private spending	Final government spending	Gross domestic fixed capital formation	Gross fixed capital formation	Private housing investment	Private plant & equipment investment	Govt.'s fixed capital formation	Increase in public inventory	Exports of goods & services (NET) (S.A)	Exports of goods & services (S.A)	Imports of goods & services (S.A)
1993(CY)	419,765.1	-0.2	243,483.6	36,200.8	136,488.6	135,541.3	19,972.6	79,143.2	36,425.5	947.3	3,592.0	62,022.0	58,430.0
1994	421,922.5	0.5	248,781.6	37,227.9	134,094.1	132,238.8	21,909.8	72,094.2	38,234.8	1,855.4	1,818.9	65,173.1	63,354.3
1995													
1993(FY)	419,490.4	-0.2	244,859.6	36,454.1	135,382.2	134,250.9	20,376.8	76,721.8	37,152.4	1,131.3	2,794.5	62,055.7	59,261.2
1994	421,902.3	0.6	248,953.8	37,591.1	134,104.8	132,090.0	22,197.6	71,856.9	38,035.6	2,014.8	1,252.6	66,200.6	64,948.0
1995													
1994–Jan.–Mar.	420,613.6	0.8	248,352.7	36,956.3	133,003.5	131,584.4	20,654.7	73,138.8	37,790.9	1,419.1	2,301.1	63,012.9	60,711.8
Apr.–June	421,314.3	0.2	247,619.8	36,963.1	134,275.6	132,198.2	22,285.7	71,585.9	38,326.6	2,077.4	2,455.8	65,134.0	62,678.2
July–Sept.	424,934.1	0.9	250,418.7	37,501.9	135,135.2	133,254.0	22,872.9	71,777.8	38,603.3	1,881.2	1,878.3	65,459.1	63,580.8
Oct.–Dec.	420,720.5	-1.0	248,825.4	37,524.1	133,734.8	131,689.3	21,634.0	71,815.9	38,239.4	2,045.5	636.2	67,041.7	66,405.5
1995–Jan.–Mar.	420,657.0	-0.0	249,070.8	38,355.3	133,175.8	131,147.2	21,950.1	72,198.2	36,999.6	2,028.6	55.1	67,099.0	67,043.9
Apr.–June	423,871.6	0.8	251,112.3	37,861.5	134,984.8	132,601.2	20,743.9	73,997.2	37,860.1	2,383.6	-87.0	69,792.4	69,879.4
July–Sept.													
Oct.–Dec.													

Note: Figures are in billions of yen except for percent.
Source: Economic Planning Agency

BANKING ACCOUNTS

Items	Bank notes issued (end of month or year)	Yr-to-yr change	Deposits (end of month or year)	Loans & discounts (end of month or year)	Securities (end of month or year)	Official discount rate	Average contracted interest rates on loans & discounts of all banks (end of month or year)	Call rates unsecured, overnight Tokyo; central rates; monthly average	*M1 outstanding (end of month or year)	Yr-to-yr change	**M2 + CD outstanding (end of month or year)	Yr-to-yr change	Long-term prime rate
1993	41,625.9	6.7%	446,001.8	479,907.5	120,802.0	2.361%	4.414%	3.0594%	126,027.8	3.0%	508,978.7	1.1%	4.9%
1994	42,880.3	3.0	453,226.9	480,133.0	121,402.0	1.750	4.047	2.1957	132,833.2	5.4	519,421.2	2.1	4.4
1995													
1995–Jan.	37,536.1	4.2	445,483.2	474,481.2	122,067.5	1.750	4.046	2.2500	137,999.6	5.5	530,035.4	3.2	4.9
Feb.	37,720.5	2.6	446,138.8	474,724.0	123,441.1	1.750	4.032	2.2172	133,434.5	4.9	527,382.7	3.7	4.9
Mar.	38,126.6	4.6	458,929.7	477,661.8	122,335.9	1.750	3.997	2.1889	138,917.6	4.5	532,199.0	3.6	4.6
Apr.	39,051.6	3.1	455,669.9	474,182.4	124,493.6	1.000	3.902	1.5250	142,362.8	5.6	536,568.7	3.2	3.9
May	36,611.7	4.1	453,697.7	468,898.4	125,907.8	1.000	3.740	1.3100	142,072.7	5.9	534,661.4	3.3	3.6
June	39,392.8	4.3	455,271.7	470,428.9	124,611.6	1.000	3.575	1.2800	140,407.9	7.0	534,688.9	3.3	3.3
July	38,778.4	3.9				1.000	3.454	0.9500	144,654.3	7.2	538,207.4	2.9	2.8
Aug.	38,565.6	5.4				1.000			144,011.2	9.0	536,705.1	2.8	2.7
Sept.						0.500							
Oct.													
Nov.													
Dec.													

Notes: Figures are in billions of yen except for percent.
*M1: Cash and demand deposits
**M2: M1 and time deposits
Source: Bank of Japan

PRICES

Items	Wholesale prices (national)								Export price index		Import price index		Corporate service price index	Consumer price index (Tokyo)		a) Consumer price index (national) General	
	Overall index					Domestic price index											
	All commodities		Primary materials	Inter-mediate goods	Final goods	All commodities		Consumer goods									
		Yr-to-yr change					Yr-to-yr change			Yr-to-yr change		Yr-to-yr change			Yr-to-yr change		Yr-to-yr change
Units & base	1990=100	%	1990=100			1990=100	%	1990=100	1990=100	%	1990=100	%	1990=100	1990=100	%	1990=100	%
1993	95.0	−2.9	83.5	95.4	99.3	98.6	−1.5	99.8	83.9	−8.0	77.3	−10.3	105.0	106.6	1.2	106.4	1.3
1994	93.1	−2.0	80.2	93.3	97.9	96.9	−1.7	98.5	81.6	−2.7	73.0	−5.6	104.0	107.3	0.7	107.1	0.7
1995																	
1995–Jan.	93.0	−1.1	81.6	93.9	96.9	96.4	−1.0	97.5	81.2	−5.1	76.7	3.5	102.9	107.3	0.5	107.2	0.6
Feb.	92.9	−0.6	81.8	94.0	96.8	96.5	−0.9	97.4	80.8	−2.4	76.4	5.5	103.1	106.9	0.0	106.8	0.2
Mar.	92.3	−1.1	80.3	93.8	96.6	96.5	−0.7	97.2	77.8	−5.7	73.7	2.1	103.3	106.9	−0.4	106.7	−0.4
Apr.	91.6	−1.5	77.7	93.5	96.3	96.4	−0.6	96.9	74.9	−8.4	70.0	−1.7	103.1	107.1	−0.2	107.1	−0.2
May	91.4	−1.8	77.5	93.2	96.1	96.2	−0.7	96.8	75.2	−8.3	69.5	−3.9	103.0	107.4	−0.1	107.4	0.0
June	91.3	−1.8	77.4	93.0	96.0	96.1	−0.8	96.7	75.2	−8.0	69.0	−5.2	102.9	107.2	0.0	107.3	0.3
July	91.5	−1.4	77.1	93.1	96.0	96.1	−0.8	96.6	76.9	−3.8	69.3	−3.5	103.0	106.6	−0.1	106.6	0.1
Aug.	92.1	−1.0	78.3	93.2	96.0	96.0	−0.9	96.7	80.6	0.1	71.5	−2.2		106.7	−0.5		
Sept.																	
Oct.																	
Nov.																	
Dec.																	

Sources: Bank of Japan: a) Management & Coordination Agency

LABOR & WAGES

Items	a) Population		Employed	Unemployed	Unemployment rate	b) All-industry employment index of regular workers	b) All-industry wage index			b) Job-offers-to-applicants ratio (S.A.)	c) Labor productivity index		Wages earned (all industries)	Total hours worked
	Aged 15 or over	Labor force					Nominal	Real	Yr-to-yr change		Manufac-turing	Yr-to-yr change		
Units & base	in 1,000 persons				%	1990=100	1990=100		%	fold	1990=100	%	in yen	1990=100
1993	103,700	66,150	64,500	1,660	2.5	106.7	106.0	99.8	−0.5	0.76	95.6	−1.4	393,224	93.0
1994	104,440	66,450	64,530	1,920	2.9	106.7	108.2	101.4	1.6	0.64	98.4	2.9	401,128	92.6
1995														
1995–Jan.	104,870	65,190	63,240	1,960	3.0	106.0	89.6	84.0	2.4	0.66	101.0	9.5	331,997	84.6
Feb.	104,840	65,140	63,150	1,990	3.1	105.5	82.8	78.0	3.0	0.66	100.8	8.2	306,760	92.3
Mar.	104,950	66,000	63,810	2,190	3.3	105.0	90.6	85.3	3.4	0.66	111.6	7.0	335,646	93.5
Apr.	104,880	66,900	64,750	2,140	3.2	106.7	85.4	80.1	2.8	0.65	100.8	8.3	316,338	96.0
May	105,060	67,340	65,260	2,080	3.1	106.7	84.3	78.9	2.3	0.63	103.4	6.5	312,145	88.4
June	105,130	67,600	65,590	2,020	3.0	106.7	165.9	155.5	0.1	0.61	99.8	3.2	614,462	97.3
July	105,040	67,440	65,420	2,020	3.0	106.6	139.9	132.1	4.1	0.61			518,202	95.7
Aug.														
Sept.														
Oct.														
Nov.														
Dec.														

Sources: Economic Planning Agency; a) Management & Coordination Agency; b) Ministry of Labor; c) Japan Productivity Center

INDUSTRIAL ACTIVITY

Items	Production index*				Producer shipment index				Producer inventory index of finished goods*			Index of producer inventory ratio to shipment*			Operating rate index*
	All industries	Mining-mfg.	Yearly or monthly change	Mfg.	All industries	Mining-mfg.	Yearly or monthly change	Mfg.	Mining-mfg.	Yearly or monthly change	Mfg.	Mining-mfg.	Yearly or monthly change	Mfg.	Mfg.
Units & base	1990=100		%	1990=100	1990=100		%	1990=100		%	1990=100		%	1990=100	
1993	92.0	91.2	−4.5	91.2	93.4	92.7	−3.7	92.7	107.0	−3.5	107.0	119.8	2.1	119.8	84.3
1994	93.1	92.0	0.9	92.0	94.8	93.9	1.3	93.9	102.1	−4.6	102.1	114.3	−4.6	114.3	84.2
1995															
1995–Jan.	94.7	93.8	−1.3	93.7	96.0	94.8	−2.3	94.8	103.8	1.1	103.9	115.1	5.6	115.1	85.8
Feb.	96.8	95.7	2.0	95.8	98.0	97.1	2.4	97.1	104.5	0.7	104.5	110.6	−3.9	110.6	87.9
Mar.	97.9	97.0	1.4	97.0	97.9	97.0	−0.1	97.0	106.1	1.5	106.1	112.5	1.7	112.5	89.3
Apr.	97.0	96.1	−0.9	96.1	99.2	98.3	1.3	98.3	106.9	0.8	106.9	114.0	1.3	114.1	88.7
May	96.5	95.6	−0.5	95.6	98.1	97.3	−1.0	97.3	107.0	0.1	107.0	115.8	1.6	115.8	86.8
June	95.7	94.9	−0.7	94.9	97.1	96.4	−0.9	96.4	106.9	−0.1	106.9	115.5	−0.3	115.5	86.2
July	93.5	92.3	−2.7	92.3	94.3	93.2	−3.3	93.2	107.4	0.5	107.4	120.9	4.7	120.9	83.0
Aug.															
Sept.															
Oct.															
Nov.															
Dec.															

*Figures are seasonally adjusted.

BALANCE OF PAYMENTS

Items	Trade balance	Exports	Imports	Invisible balance	Transfer balance	Current balance	Long-term capital balance	Short-term capital balance	Overall balance (errors & omissions adjusted)	Chg. of foreign exchange reserves	Financial accounts & others	Foreign exchange reserves (end of year or month)
1993	141,514	351,292	209,778	-3,949	-6,117	131,448	-78,336	-14,426	38,426	26,904	11,522	95,589
1994	145,944	384,176	238,232	-9,296	-7,508	129,140	-82,037	-8,897	20,428	27,256	-6,828	122,845
1995												
1995-Jan.	5,382	26,581	21,199	-1,512	-481	3,389	-3,174	12,841	16,344	1,020	15,324	123,865
Feb.	13,165	34,238	21,073	-236	-785	12,144	-5,391	11,165	15,356	2,076	13,280	125,941
Mar.	16,470	41,553	25,083	-187	-1,708	14,575	8,717	6,516	42,595	15,582	27,013	141,523
Apr.	12,472	38,562	26,090	-661	-466	11,345	-7,019	-5,048	3,803	12,147	-8,344	153,670
May	10,007	34,347	24,340	-496	-572	8,939	-18,960	2,191	-10,067	604	-10,671	154,274
June	13,998	38,627	24,629	-2,618	-445	10,935	-17,661	9,928	3,995	2,760	1,235	157,034
July	12,123	36,635	24,512	-1,989	-916	9,218	-12,613	6,601	-4,497	1,358	-5,855	158,392
Aug.												166,393
Sept.												
Oct.												
Nov.												
Dec.												

Note: Figures are in millions of dollars
Source: Bank of Japan

OTHER BUSINESS INDICATORS

Items	e) Orders for machinery: Private (excl. ships and electric power; sea. adj.)	e) Yearly or monthly change	f) Department store sales: Domestic national	f) Yr-to-yr change	g) Construction orders: Private (big 50 contractors)	g) Yearly or monthly change	New car registration	g) Housing starts (new construction)	d) Bankruptcies	d) Yr-to-yr change	d) Debts	h) Stock price index (*1): Nikkei Stock Average (225 issues) (TSE 1st section; closing average)	h) Commodity price index (*1): Nikkei index of 17 items
	in bil. yen	%	in bil. yen	%	in bil. yen	%	in number of units	in 1,000 homes		%	in bil. yen	in yen	1970 = 100
1993	10,577.2	-12.5	11,263.6	-6.2	12,107.5	-24.1	4,199,451	1,485.7	14,564	3.5	6,847.7	19,086.95	90.524
1994	10,923.3	2.7	11,024.9	-2.6	11,419.5	-5.7	4,210,168	1,570.3	14,061	-3.5	5,629.4	19,918.49	94.502
1995													
1995-Jan.	930.7	-3.1	841.9	-5.2	611.0	-23.5	241,926	100.2	1,076	-2.5	303.9	18,948.41	96.132
Feb.	915.3	-1.7	704.5	-3.2	774.8	-11.2	384,769	114.4	1,170	10.9	554.3	18,065.03	91.778
Mar.	910.1	-0.6	920.8	-2.6	1,874.8	7.0	647,798	113.2	1,338	4.1	1,455.9	16,447.56	90.045
Apr.	1,045.4	14.9	849.2	-2.5	808.5	13.2	321,728	124.1	1,353	10.0	873.9	16,322.09	87.587
May	960.9	-8.1	841.7	-2.0	785.4	18.0	293,379	115.6	1,194	0.2	403.6	16,265.89	86.177
June	1,043.6	8.6	841.4	-1.4	896.0	7.4	397,398	124.7	1,162	0.2	356.2	15,039.44	85.502
July	978.4	-6.3	1,142.0	-2.1	823.1	-7.4	426,914	129.1	1,104	-1.4	483.2	16,188.70	84.338
Aug.							253,196		1,408	30.0	820.0	17,410.72	88.260
Sept.													
Oct.													
Nov.													
Dec.													

Sources: d) Tokyo Shoko Research: e) Economic Planning Agency: f) Ministry of International Trade & Industry: g) Ministry of Construction: h) Nihon Keizai Shimbun

FOREIGN AND OVERSEAS INVESTMENTS

Items	Direct foreign investment in Japan (notification basis)	Non-residents' investment in Japanese stocks (settlement basis)			Non-residents' investment in Japanese long-term securities (settlement basis)				Residents' investment in overseas stocks (settlement basis)			Residents' investment in overseas long-term securities (settlement basis)			Bonds issued abroad by Japanese corporations (notification basis)	Bonds issued in Japan by non-residents (notification basis)
		Buying	Selling	Balance	Buying	Selling	Balance	Gensaki balance*	Buying	Selling	Balance	Buying	Selling	Balance		
1993	1,895	187,629	140,906	46,724	186,377	176,067	10,310	1,190	64,751	48,499	16,252	1,249,548	1,228,219	21,329	49,667	9,936
1994	3,159	179,114	163,386	15,729	148,741	141,204	7,537	449	52,543	43,491	9,052	947,474	871,612	75,862	16,947	12,051
1995																
1995-Jan.	127	13,140	14,073	-933	11,514	7,884	3,630	-149	2,374	3,542	-1,168	71,145	68,039	3,106	972	565
Feb.	443	16,222	15,632	591	12,898	11,384	1,514	247	3,385	3,954	-570	85,494	83,523	1,971	2,103	2,020
Mar.	387	15,300	11,658	3,642	25,822	17,942	7,880	484	5,233	7,511	-2,278	94,128	94,674	-546	2,077	151
Apr.	308	11,722	9,854	1,867	12,629	10,515	2,113	-504	2,631	2,074	557	69,360	64,778	4,582	1,042	828
May	63	11,928	10,685	1,243	9,727	11,710	-1,983	-244	3,989	3,032	957	106,423	93,068	13,355	906	1,111
June	68	12,453	9,773	2,680	17,529	18,763	-1,235	-63	4,492	4,297	194	132,539	112,340	20,199	840	1,515
July	68	20,024	12,765	7,258	14,962	14,607	354		3,926	3,962	-36	107,291	92,102	15,189	1,479	1,112
Aug.																
Sept.																
Oct.																
Nov.																
Dec.																

Notes: Figures are in millions of dollars
*Trading with repurchase agreement.
Source: Ministry of Finance

FOREIGN TRADE (1)

(1) Exports
— By country —

Item	k) Customs-cleared exports	Asia	Republic of Korea	Taiwan	China	Indonesia	Thailand	Singapore	Hong Kong	Iran	Europe	EU	U.K.	France	Germany	Italy	Russia
1993	360,911	147,620	19,115	22,081	17,273	6,022	12,261	16,601	22,686	1,452	67,405	56,412	12,047	5,454	18,021	3,211	1,501
1994	395,600	167,836	24,359	23,792	18,682	7,672	14,702	19,605	25,740	911	67,642	57,480	12,734	5,260	17,788	3,357	1,167
1995																	
1995—Jan.	27,191	10,835	1,809	1,533	935	516	1,077	1,327	1,486	57	4,793	4,422	901	356	1,219	253	51
Feb.	35,238	15,331	2,392	2,316	1,485	766	1,469	1,662	2,289	19	5,973	5,523	1,045	463	1,619	355	75
Mar.	42,592	18,799	3,056	2,750	2,007	881	1,776	2,062	2,625	80	7,618	6,969	1,376	608	2,007	439	88
Apr.	40,060	18,053	2,904	2,649	1,800	917	1,689	1,983	2,530	58	6,788	6,272	1,248	553	1,829	350	69
May	35,538	16,285	2,623	2,485	1,718	755	1,474	1,787	2,402	51	6,126	5,602	1,178	483	1,596	321	130
June	40,155	18,327	2,927	2,639	1,939	931	1,837	2,083	2,577	86	6,758	6,084	1,373	493	1,728	329	209
July	38,070	17,738	2,727	2,651	1,909	882	1,739	2,101	2,443	21	6,326	5,754	1,199	459	1,706	278	105
Aug.	35,225		2,591	2,445	1,775	832	1,692	1,923	2,262	61		5,454	1,117	482	1,603	316	87
Sept.																	
Oct.																	
Nov.																	
Dec.																	

Note: Figures are in millions of dollars

(2) Imports

Items	North America	U.S.A.	South America	Brazil	Africa	Oceania	Australia	k) Customs-cleared imports	Asia	Republic of Korea	Taiwan	China	Indonesia	Thailand	Iran	Saudi Arabia
1993	122,930	105,405	5,690	1,624	7,482	9,784	7,694	240,670	109,652	11,678	9,678	20,565	12,478	6,502	2,419	8,887
1994	136,219	117,560	5,993	1,881	6,989	10,920	8,718	274,742	125,052	13,509	10,754	27,566	12,917	8,184	2,758	8,385
1995																
1995—Jan.	9,983	8,234	452	207	460	667	548	24,384	11,441	1,254	927	2,331	1,122	694	204	888
Feb.	11,847	10,135	615	276	612	859	679	23,944	10,982	1,094	857	2,238	1,107	720	251	853
Mar.	13,841	11,770	718	331	606	1,011	783	28,721	13,173	1,386	1,216	2,813	1,143	886	335	1,053
Apr.	12,966	11,114	642	266	679	932	731	29,170	13,149	1,475	1,169	3,156	1,074	847	275	856
May	11,109	9,636	634	260	557	827	649	28,549	12,913	1,502	1,302	2,827	1,287	840	263	811
June	12,521	10,834	602	211	950	996	737	28,502	12,797	1,473	1,234	2,730	1,221	922	133	805
July	11,951	10,366	579	188	576	900	724	28,636	12,916	1,480	1,289	2,991	1,209	912	265	704
Aug.		9,275		197			614	29,258		1,515	1,276	3,312	1,190	910	202	755
Sept.																
Oct.																
Nov.																
Dec.																

Note: Figures are in millions of dollars

Items	Europe	EU	U.K.	France	Germany	Italy	Switzerland	Sweden	Russia	North America	U.S.A.	South America	Brazil	Africa	Oceania	Australia
1993	40,193	30,149	4,951	5,122	9,786	3,828	2,828	1,543	2,769	65,489	55,236	6,325	2,848	3,897	15,111	12,218
1994	47,196	35,479	5,914	5,683	11,133	4,937	3,067	1,826	3,490	74,031	62,659	7,248	3,261	4,156	17,054	13,627
1995																
1995—Jan.	4,332	3,517	513	399	1,074	421	250	208	365	6,054	5,046	696	255	384	1,476	1,153
Feb.	43,11	3,522	500	511	1036	472	296	162	336	6,308	5,282	665	293	336	1,342	1,015
Mar.	5,195	4,183	677	482	1,270	537	434	200	405	7,734	6,671	691	257	417	1,510	1,165
Apr.	5,078	4,011	582	601	1,121	480	350	191	493	7,723	6,598	1,124	426	458	1,638	1,281
May	5,276	4,298	663	689	1,170	457	349	233	435	7,570	6,326	855	382	381	1,553	1,210
June	5,084	4,112	682	592	1,109	504	336	200	468	7,884	6,589	752	305	399	1,585	1,255
July	5,194	4,269	572	542	1,178	632	358	238	410	7,776	6,497	753	346	428	1,569	1,250
Aug.		4,423	650	565	1,138	729			364		6,333	0	339			1,346
Sept.																
Oct.																
Nov.																
Dec.																

Note: Figures are in millions of dollars
Source: k) Ministry of Finance

FOREIGN TRADE (2)
— By commodity —

(1) Exports

Items	k) Customs-cleared exports	Foodstuffs	Textiles	Chemicals	Fertilizers	Non-metallic mineral manufactures	Metals	Steel	Metal products	Nonferrous metals	Machinery & equipment	Textile machines
1993	360,911	2,007	8,239	20,199	111	4,047	22,939	14,524	5,711	2,703	274,388	3,505
1994	395,600	2,038	8,385	23,669	106	4,698	24,237	14,842	6,270	3,124	300,837	3,270
1995												
1995–Jan.	27,191	137	371	1,822	68	333	1,613	983	401	229	20,722	191
Feb.	35,238	152	711	2,445	110	418	2,115	1,278	528	309	26,624	265
Mar.	42,592	186	808	2,908	164	508	2,612	1,604	634	374	32,424	360
Apr.	40,060	179	764	2,784	92	498	2,335	1,392	592	352	30,287	296
May	35,538	172	786	2,573	98	472	2,332	1,343	650	338	26,350	259
June	40,155	177	915	2,682		500	2,588	1,553	648	388	29,979	294
July	38,070	171	816	2,507		465	2,527	1,495	650	382	28,400	270
Aug.	35,225	183	728	2,387		470	2,657	1,677	590	390		
Sept.												
Oct.												
Nov.												
Dec.												

Note: Figures are in millions of dollars

(2) Imports

Items	Telecom. equipment	ICs	Scientific & optical equipment	Copiers	TV sets	VCRs	Automobiles	Ships	Others	i) Customs-cleared imports	Foodstuffs	Wheat	Maize (for feed)	Sugar	Textile materials	Wool	Raw cotton
1993	8,119	13,103	14,260	2,841	2,245	4,133	58,390	9,951	29,093	240,670	39,413	1,138	1,498	456	1,523	486	683
1994	8,578	18,274	15,895	3,031	2,445	4,136	56,914	10,946	31,736	274,742	46,652	1,348	1,568	498	1,869	676	658
1995																	
1995–Jan.	500	1,532	1,106	217	170	215	3,895	1,057	2,193	24,384	3,354	107	114	24	174	77	60
Feb.	629	1,741	1,463	268	224	309	4,927	885	2,773	23,944	3,387	122	105	41	157	60	62
Mar.	904	2,113	1,844	333	261	314	5,529	975	3,146	28,721	4,246	102	134	41	199	56	86
Apr.	669	2,086	1,628	280	197	274	5,491	1,113	3,212	29,170	4,610	93	114	77	182	71	66
May	589	2,003	1,573	271	160	272	4,253	737	2,854	28,549	4,607	114	132	35	160	52	70
June	664	2,282	1,685	270	164	319	4,683	1,242	3,314	28,502	4,647	117	118	60	168	53	81
July	612	2,359	1,824	300	169	286	4,230	718	3,184	28,636	4,753	125	105	47	141	38	72
Aug.	579	2,358	1,421	264	184	262	3,588	561	3,119	29,258	4,406	119	129			45	50
Sept.																	
Oct.																	
Nov.																	
Dec.																	

Note: Figures are in millions of dollars

Items	Metal ores & scrap	Iron ore	Non-ferrous metal ores	Raw materials (others)	Soybean	Natural rubber	Wood	Mineral fuels	Coal	Petroleum, crude & partly refined	Petroleum products	Chemicals	Machinery & equipment	Office machines	Others
1993	6,956	3,029	2,975	27,213	1,374	541	10,160	48,840	5,913	27,991	5,141	17,964	46,634	6,834	26,848
1994	7,452	2,898	3,440	28,569	1,395	644	9,743	47,785	5,699	27,634	4,973	20,216	59,591	9,034	31,899
1995															
1995–Jan.	810	257	413	2,658	111	78	827	4,532	525	2,560	472	2,012	5,661	893	2,543
Feb.	727	242	359	2,563	121	76	789	4,439	443	2,575	456	1,903	5,456	972	2,615
Mar.	749	245	354	2,827	110	116	917	5,052	517	3,030	488	2,079	7,052	1,425	3,404
Apr.	802	273	402	2,825	119	83	899	4,576	512	2,729	418	2,165	6,561	1,054	3,543
May	840	260	451	3,043	105	103	989	4,303	531	2,411	456	2,245	6,998	1,128	3,305
June	792	258	399	3,014	137	107	975	4,383	549	2,385	553	2,134	7,111	1,355	3,248
July	805	276	415	2,872	121	106	932	4,146	550	2,202	433	2,166	7,338	1,338	3,171
Aug.		286	467		107		895	4,389	645	2,309	499	2,032	7,195	1,365	3,430
Sept.															
Oct.															
Nov.															
Dec.															

Note: Figures are in millions of dollars
Source: i) Ministry of Finance

OUTPUT OF PRINCIPAL PRODUCTS

Items	Electric power	Coal	Crude oil	Pig iron	Ferro-alloys	Crude steel	Semi-finished steel	Ordinary hot rolled steel	Special hot rolled steel	Electrolytic gold	Electrolytic Silver	Electrolytic copper	Lead	Zinc
	in mil. kWh	in 1,000 tons	in kiloliters	in 1,000 tons						in kilograms		in tons		
1993..................	751,236	7,217	910,589	73,738	952	99,623	94,313	79,077	14,767	108,769	2,159,517	1,188,776	258,128	695,687
1994..................	802,692	6,932	869,591	73,776	877	98,295	93,138	76,631	15,014	102,778	2,020,223	1,119,168	234,253	665,502
1995..................														
1995–Jan..........	69,448	440	74,849	6,398	84	8,583	8,146	6,661	1,286	8,299	172,893	95,553	19,772	56,559
Feb.............	65,826	529	70,911	5,718	67	8,131	7,699	6,374	1,278	8,348	167,116	89,925	19,507	54,247
Mar............	69,541	633	75,966	6,335	81	8,831	8,354	6,955	1,464	9,904	178,687	97,235	20,672	56,014
Apr.............	61,542	401	73,079	6,211	84	8,702	8,253	6,789	1,399	9,636	169,949	96,890	19,831	53,449
May............	60,937	434	73,700	6,405	93	9,036	8,572	6,973	1,454	9,319	173,650	100,657	20,679	59,800
June...........	63,248	528	73,579	6,264	79	8,699	8,238	6,841	1,390	8,761	174,834	98,260	19,705	58,527
July...........	76,563	559	70,823	6,486	75	8,679	8,269	6,703	1,402	10,106	164,030	101,075	15,514	44,088
Aug.............	83,078													
Sept...........														
Oct.............														
Nov.............														
Dec.............														

Source: Ministry of International Trade & Industry

Items	Aluminum	Optical fiber products (electric wire cable)	Copper electric wire & cable	Internal combustion engines for industry	Tractors	Shovel-type excavators	Chemical machinery	Injection molding machines	Printing machinery	Wood-working machinery	Pumps	Power tillers (incl. walking tractors)	Metal cutting machinery
	in tons	in kilometers	in tons	in 1,000 PS (*1)	in number of units			in tons		in number of units	in tons	in number of units	in tons
1993..................	18,263	2,824,049	1,014,817	59,427	155,497	101,645	188,235	94,661	61,407	73,293	125,993	225,564	213,730
1994..................	16,956	3,063,490	1,006,142	61,508	167,686	112,712	165,761	96,533	57,330	66,772	128,947	212,539	215,621
1995..................													
1995–Jan...........	1,602	152,468	76,896	4,924	13,063	8,428	15,600	7,359	3,342	4,661	8,979	16,855	17,918
Feb.............	1,446	186,566	88,467	5,937	16,309	9,801	8,989	9,363	4,571	5,590	11,105	17,446	20,971
Mar............	1,533	338,502	94,541	6,462	18,350	11,100	41,195	12,221	11,499	5,385	14,526	21,991	30,080
Apr.............	1,470	270,451	86,439	6,209	15,397	10,149	33,541	8,959	4,472	5,423	10,588	19,835	22,971
May............	1,579	256,784	76,474	4,989	12,606	8,992	14,744	7,561	4,676	4,434	8,762	16,663	20,190
June...........	1,538	333,529	85,582	6,118	13,705	9,942	15,609	10,756	4,997	5,113	9,403	16,801	23,420
July...........		331,054	82,370	5,467	12,290	8,967	21,619	8,833	4,860	5,618	9,745	16,363	23,234
Aug.............													
Sept...........													
Oct.............													
Nov.............													
Dec.............													

Note: (*1) PS stands for Pferderstaerke, meaning horsepower

Items	Desktop electronic calculators (handy type) (*2)	Type-writers (*3)	Electro-static copying machines (indirect-method)	Cash registers	Indus-trial robots	Vending machines (beverages)	Air conditioners	Electric tools	Bearings (finished goods)	General engine generators	Standard trans-formers	Automatic washing machines	Electric refrigerators
	in 1,000 units	in number of units			in mil. yen	in number of units		in 1,000 units		in kVA	in number of units	in 1,000 units	
1993..................	26,369	802,054	2,047,789	1,251,910	192,328	366,003	15,532,908	10,950	2,588,343	4,481,665	513,392	5,163	4,350
1994..................	11,674	436,173	1,952,159	904,515	207,305	344,494	17,421,902	11,302	2,661,975	4,188,478	451,944	5,042	4,952
1995..................													
1995–Jan...........	390	21,819	144,829	59,309	14,291	21,829	1,414,540	819	220,370	391,123	40,299	356	322
Feb.............	371	22,921	160,372	67,922	18,235	31,723	1,679,588	933	234,768	460,359	41,951	443	417
Mar............	436	16,087	173,297	67,200	25,138	36,680	2,031,747	980	259,511	450,513	41,369	517	464
Apr.............	272	16,751	155,990	58,113	22,855	37,055	1,887,960	1,006	244,342	424,564	42,852	451	453
May............	333	19,652	143,673	50,389	21,731	31,040	1,617,494	872	231,456	400,198	41,579	359	393
June...........	315	14,645	156,409	52,812	24,859	30,896	1,903,579	987	261,761	436,947	46,263	431	492
July...........	145	26,151	155,891	49,228	23,635	26,701	1,855,214	939	253,671	456,334	43,896	403	437
Aug.............													
Sept...........													
Oct.............													
Nov.............													
Dec.............													

(*2) excluding functional calculation; (3*) with keys for Japanese letters.

Items	Vacuum cleaners	Microwave ovens	Facsimiles	Radio-cassette tape recorder	Color TV sets (excl. kits)	VCRs	Stereo sets	Transistors	Semi-conductor integrated circuits (ICs)	Computers (processors)	Passenger cars	Buses	Trucks	Motorcycles
Unit	in 1,000 units									in mil. yen	in 1,000 units			
1993	6,331	3,459	5,109	3,065	10,717	15,839	2,795	23,545,065	17,051,534	1,002,109	8,494	48.1	2,675	3,023
1994	6,355	3,167	5,288	2,346	9,445	15,390	2,616	25,834,396	19,724,618	939,101	7,801	49.1	2,689	2,725
1995														
1995–Jan.	517	221	402	149	585	976	175	2,154,027	1,593,785	45,708	571	3.4	186	201
Feb.	588	275	436	106	693	1,171	174	2,230,505	1,719,972	55,957	712	4.0	227	241
Mar.	653	330	488	137	846	1,265	191	2,500,876	1,809,078	71,802	811	5.0	265	297
Apr.	568	284	445	120	722	1,090	140	2,570,810	1,827,037	56,975	648	4.1	216	260
May	478	249	405	143	568	950	170	2,638,968	1,788,648	32,924	555	2.7	193	227
June	504	292	462	162	602	1105	195	2,841,550	1,968,953	46,410	662	4.3	233	261
July	503	245	477	172	590	1,032	179	2,757,066	1,998,710	49,344	642	3.8	223	233
Aug.														
Sept.														
Oct.														
Nov.														
Dec.														

Items	Bicycles	Video cameras	35mm still cameras (includ. half-frame cameras)	Watches	Cement	Sheet glass	Ammonium sulphate	Urea	Calcium carbide	Caustic soda	Sulfuric acid	Synthetic dyes	Caprolactam	Polyvinyl chloride resin
Unit	in 1,000 units	in number of units	in 1,000 units		in 1,000 tons	in 1,000 blocks	in 1,000 tons					in tons		
1993	6,858	7,698,906	12,428	390,596	88,046	33,059	1,681	725	245	3,777	6,937	67,395	510,056	1,979,848
1994	6,701	7,996,942	11,842	393,187	91,624	31,830	1,709	694	246	3,785	6,594	71,161	519,352	2,110,745
1995														
1995–Jan.	491	501,436	799	29,582	6,398	2,978	162	78	25	348	594	5,508	49,937	193,492
Feb.	567	603,461	865	32,175	7,254	2,927	140	71	20	318	525	6,050	44,433	188,118
Mar.	742	805,192	1,050	38,854	8,015	2,911	150	56	23	338	581	6,567	45,090	188,442
Apr.	740	694,860	851	34,499	7,100	2,778	139	64	28	333	557	6,453	39,543	195,725
May	541	746,253	890	31,248	7,041	2,791	153	65	30	318	598	5,439	47,861	183,503
June	473	856,268	892	35,078	7,609	2,690	140	61	28	303	588	6,222	46,393	176,575
July	497	749,581	954	35,013	7,218	2,580	155	45	19	334	527	6,178	47,482	174,232
Aug.														
Sept.														
Oct.														
Nov.														
Dec.														

Items	Poly-ethylene	Polypropylene	Synthetic rubber	Photographic films	Synthetic detergent for household	Paint	Oil distillation	Gasoline	Naphtha	Kerosene	Gas oil	Fuel oil C	Paper pulp
Unit	in tons			in 1,000 sq.m.	in tons		in 1,000 kiloliters						in tons
1993	2,761,533	2,031,122	1,309,792	269,952	1,053,820	1,955,713	232,227	47,991	17,358	26,960	41,260	48,239	10,440,347
1994	2,944,112	2,224,755	1,350,822	284,680	1,095,170	2,006,854	242,940	49,857	17,460	27,198	43,943	52,479	10,438,230
1995													
1995–Jan.	296,269	220,327	135,208	18,779	52,886	144,033	22,886	4,214	1,792	3,246	3,507	4,580	864,589
Feb.	253,373	203,476	122,051	25,656	79,383	161,461	21,376	3,816	1,894	3,096	3,411	4,558	876,477
Mar.	272,466	205,231	116,414	24,091	89,511	183,730	23,395	4,269	1,917	3,083	3,990	4,509	944,164
Apr.	270,481	197,190	131,623	25,609	87,388	167,192	21,465	4,152	1,652	2,209	4,173	4,208	901,473
May	275,180	214,816	141,354	22,711	78,195	153,615	17,683	4,051	1,195	1,616	3,554	3,458	930,867
June	256,044	210,604	112,790	26,793	97,992	168,743	15,374	3,689	919	1,135	3,445	3,352	947,811
July	241,234	182,091	136,277	22,827	90,470	162,385	19,084	4,156	1,168	1,609	3,867	3,972	903,223
Aug.													
Sept.													
Oct.													
Nov.													
Dec.													

Items	Container boards	Synthetic fiber (filament)	Synthetic fiber (staple)	Cotton yarn	Woollen yarn	Cotton fabrics	Woollen fabrics	Silk fabrics	Synthetic fabrics	Automobile tires & tubes	Mechanical rubber products	Leather	Plastic products
Units	in tons					in 1,000 sq.m.				in tons			
1993................	8,394,285	693,581	748,344	284,140	84,060	1,205,412	286,811	71,364	2,265,105	915,624	200,688	170,104	5,264,048
1994................	8,748,168	688,856	786,592	234,767	89,543	1,180,444	285,546	65,444	2,142,775	923,975	207,932	150,712	5,478,245
1995................													
1995~Jan...........	696,192	60,677	66,077	16,146	6,593	84,819	19,876	4,616	170,374	74,883	16,580	10,054	452,506
Feb...........	715,126	57,813	62,599	17,796	7,062	92,788	19,398	5,099	173,146	81,191	17,876	9,790	476,921
Mar...........	801,703	63,185	68,472	19,100	7,279	96,111	19,865	4,924	179,474	91,152	19,938	11,024	518,592
Apr...........	764,899	60,661	66,370	18,638	6,705	93,204	20,323	5,215	176,911	88,974	18,431	10,621	503,378
May...........	747,374	62,766	67,871	17,608	6,241	85,890	21,650	4,853	168,727	81,362	16,480	10,628	466,413
June...........	787,783	60,908	65,218	19,500	6,423	91,398	22,870	5,067	175,407	89,235	18,065	10,495	495,866
July...........	743,095	61,358	67,368	19,195	6,017	87,841	22,262	5,064	174,129	90,851	17,592	10,881	497,933
Aug...........													
Sept...........													
Oct...........													
Nov...........													
Dec...........													

GENERAL ACCOUNT BUDGET FOR FY1995

(Initial budget; in millions of yen)

	FY1995 (A)	FY1994 (B)	A—B	Change (%)
Revenues				
Taxes and stamps	53,731,000	53,665,000	66,000	0.1
NTT stock sale proceeds	172,541	172,541	0	0.0
Other revenues	4,485,579	5,601,128	−1,115,549	−19.9
Bonds	12,598,000	13,643,000	−1,045,000	−7.7
Total	**70,987,120**	**73,081,669**	**−2,094,549**	**−2.9**
Expenditures				
Social security				
Public assistance	1,053,180	1,052,382	798	0.1
Social welfare	3,472,812	3,187,472	285,340	9.0
Social insurance	8,469,994	8,288,559	181,435	2.2
Public health service	634,802	660,426	−25,624	−3.9
Measures for unemployed	293,624	292,788	836	0.3
Subtotal	13,924,412	13,481,627	442,785	3.3
Education and science promotion				
National government's share of compulsory education expenses	2,766,137	2,750,952	15,185	0.6
Transfer to the national schools' special account	1,557,599	1,520,352	37,247	2.4
Promotion of science and technology	684,357	636,421	47,936	7.5
Public shcool facilities	270,435	272,531	−2,096	−0.8
School education assistance	699,311	681,650	17,661	2.6
Scholarship on loan basis to students	98,622	95,890	2,732	2.8
Subtotal	6,076,461	5,957,796	118,665	2.0
Debt servicing	13,221,300	14,360,242	−1,138,942	−7.9
Pensions for public officials				
For civil servants	89,617	93,727	−4,110	−4.4
For veterans and war-bereaved families of soldiers	1,510,201	1,540,178	−29,977	−1.9
Administrative expenses for pension payments	5,622	5,700	−78	−1.4
Aid to war-bereaved families and families of the un-repatriated	121,112	122,414	−1,302	−1.1
Subtotal	1,726,552	1,762,019	−35,467	−2.0
Tax grants for local governments	13,215,395	12,757,752	457,643	3.6
Defense	4,723,610	4,683,548	40,062	0.86
Public works				
Erosion and flood control	1,573,173	1,980,826	−407,653	−20.6
Road improvement	2,586,547	3,105,893	−519,346	−16.7
Improvement of harbors ,fishing ports and airports	705,101	860,736	−155,635	−18.1
Promotion of housing and urban regions	1,157,832	1,266,806	−108,974	−8.6
Improvement of sewerage systems	1,612,158	1,973,282	−361,124	−18.3
Improvement of conditions for agricultural production	1,196,639	1,490,367	−293,728	−19.7
Forest roads water for industrial use, etc.	325,097	385,875	−60,778	−15.8
Adjustment expenses	14,997	14,108	889	6.3
(Subtotal)	9,171,544	11,077,893	−1,906,349	−17.2
Disaster reconstruction	68,215	68,215	0	0.0
Subtotal	9,239,759	11,146,108	−1,906,349	−17.1
Economic cooperation	1,035,114	999,160	35,954	3.6
Promotion of smaller businesses	185,691	187,651	−1,960	−1.0
Energy measures	681,862	675,928	5,934	0.9
Food control	272,318	274,318	−2,000	−0.7
Public works financed by NTT proceeds	1,281,226	172,541	1,108,685	642.6
Others	5,053,420	4,728,211	325,209	6.9
Reserves	350,000	350,000	0	0.0
Compensations		1,544,768		
Total	**70,987,120**	**73,081,669**	**−2,094,549**	**−2.9**

TREASURY INVESTMENT AND LOANS PROGRAMS FOR FY1991-1995

(In billions of yen)

	FY95	FY94	FY93	FY92	FY91
Fund resources					
Industrial Investment Special Account	65.6	55.7	57.7	58.1	65.7
Trust Fund Bureau Fund	36,692.50	36,370.50	37,659.50	33,489.10	29,134.90
Postal-office Life Insurance	8,182.00	8,682.00	7,053.40	6,055.00	6,305.00
Government-guaranteed bond and borrowing	3,250.00	2,750.00	2,000.00	1,800.00	1,900.00
Total	**48,190.10**	**47,858.20**	**46,770.60**	**41,402.20**	**37,405.60**
By category disbursement					
Housing	14,192.70	13,073.00	10,798.90	9,799.30	9,474.50
Improvement of living environment	6,611.50	6,387.80	6,069.60	5,157.90	4,293.30
Welfare	1,611.30	1,406.70	1,397.10	1,109.70	1,026.10
Education	817.20	755.20	649.90	582.90	582.40
Small businesses	5,873.80	5,873.80	5,341.60	4,830.10	4,494.50
Agriculture forestry and fisheries	1,050.30	1,050.30	914.50	907.90	908.20
(Subtotal)	30,576.50	28,546.80	25,171.60	22,387.80	20,779.00
Disaster reconstruction	510.40	495.10	531.80	374.00	330.60
Roads	3,125.40	3,473.50	3,626.90	3,375.30	2,983.20
Transportation and communications	1,851.10	2,209.70	2,889.80	2,230.40	1,468.10
Local development	1,050.80	1,089.00	981.50	824.60	709.00
(Subtotal)	6,537.70	7,267.30	8,030.00	6,804.30	5,490.90
Industry and technology	1,232.40	1,312.50	1,289.00	965.60	937.70
Trade and economic cooperation	1,893.50	2,021.30	2,105.00	2,104.50	1,898.00
Total	**40,240.10**	**39,147.90**	**36,595.60**	**32,262.20**	**29,105.60**
By Institution					
Special accounts	5,853.70	5,635.30	5,595.30	4,728.60	4,140.30
Government financial corporations	22,240.20	17,903.40	16,132.90	15,153.10	13,215.50
Other government corporations	12,471.10	16,141.10	13,911.40	12,165.60	10,407.80
Local public entities	7,250.00	5,700.00	4,895.00	4,365.00	4,170.00
Special companies	375.10	390.80	267.60	393.30	287.00
Total	**48,190.10**	**45,770.60**	**40,802.20**	**36,805.60**	**32,220.60**

FINANCIAL INSTITUTIONS IN JAPAN
(as of end of March 1995)

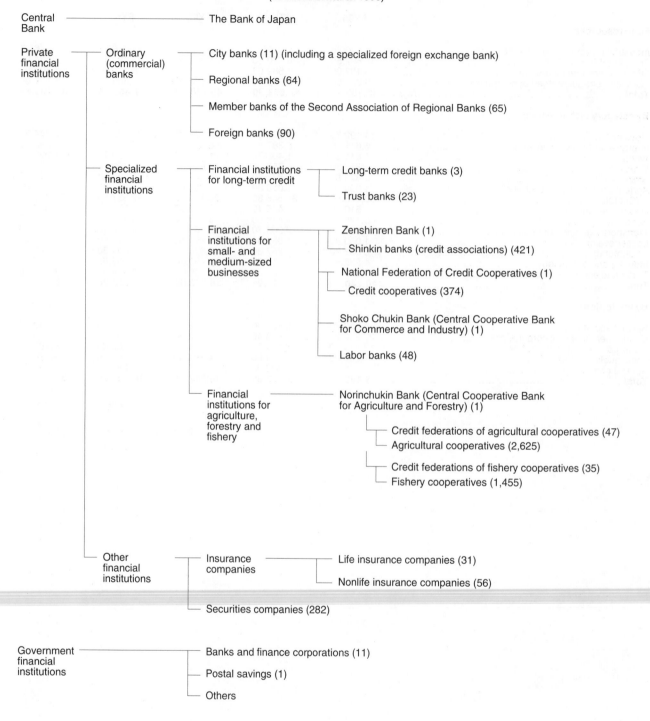

Central Bank ——————————— The Bank of Japan

Private financial institutions

- Ordinary (commercial) banks
  - City banks (11) (including a specialized foreign exchange bank)
  - Regional banks (64)
  - Member banks of the Second Association of Regional Banks (65)
  - Foreign banks (90)

- Specialized financial institutions
  - Financial institutions for long-term credit
    - Long-term credit banks (3)
    - Trust banks (23)
  - Financial institutions for small- and medium-sized businesses
    - Zenshinren Bank (1)
    - Shinkin banks (credit associations) (421)
    - National Federation of Credit Cooperatives (1)
    - Credit cooperatives (374)
    - Shoko Chukin Bank (Central Cooperative Bank for Commerce and Industry) (1)
    - Labor banks (48)
  - Financial institutions for agriculture, forestry and fishery
    - Norinchukin Bank (Central Cooperative Bank for Agriculture and Forestry) (1)
      - Credit federations of agricultural cooperatives (47)
      - Agricultural cooperatives (2,625)
      - Credit federations of fishery cooperatives (35)
      - Fishery cooperatives (1,455)

- Other financial institutions
  - Insurance companies
    - Life insurance companies (31)
    - Nonlife insurance companies (56)
  - Securities companies (282)

Government financial institutions
- Banks and finance corporations (11)
- Postal savings (1)
- Others

OUTSTANDING BALANCE OF FUND VOLUME BY TYPE OF BANK

(As of end of March 95; in billions of yen; as of Sept. 94 in parentheses)

	Total fund volume	Percent change from a year earlier	Loans & discounts	Percent change from a year earlier	Loan-deposit ratio
Long-term credit banks					
1 Industrial Bank of Japan	30,333.7 (30,761.0)	−7.6	23,209.1 (23,183.2)	−0.4	76.4 (75.2)
2 Long-Term Credit Bank of Japan	25,061.5 (24,881.1)	17.7	18,889.7 (18,989.1)	−1.3	75.3 (76.3)
3 Nippon Credit Bank	14,163.5 (14,391.5)	−2.0	10,338.0 (10,590.8)	−3.8	72.9 (73.5)
Trust banks					
1 Mitsubishi Trust & Banking	30,475.4 (31,334.7)	0.0	13,571.1 (13,998.8)	−5.3	44.5 (44.6)
2 Sumitomo Trust & Banking	29,251.7 (28,874.8)	2.9	13,287.7 (13,334.5)	−2.6	45.4 (46.1)
3 Mitsui Trust & Banking	27,179.6 (28,233.5)	−1.5	11,422.2 (11,571.8)	−5.6	42.0 (40.9)
4 Yasuda Trust & Banking	22,709.3 (22,586.6)	2.9	9,569.1 (9,737.2)	−4.3	42.1 (43.1)
5 Toyo Trust & Banking	19,419.4 (19,335.4)	4.4	8,309.6 (8,459.8)	−1.7	42.7 (43.7)
6 Chuo Trust & Banking	12,081.7 (11,671.0)	5.9	4,642.4 (4,645.4)	−1.8	38.4 (39.8)
7 Nippon Trust & Banking	3,593.7 (3,647.4)	−1.4	1,551.9 (1,736.0)	−14.1	43.1 (47.5)
City banks					
1 Sanwa Bank	39,696.3 (37,248.2)	8.7	33,251.5 (33,273.9)	−0.3	83.7 (89.3)
2 Dai-Ichi Kangyo Bank	38,909.1 (38,389.7)	0.1	33,757.8 (33,697.0)	−0.4	86.7 (87.7)
3 Sumitomo Bank	37,604.7 (37,774.6)	−2.9	33,819.0 (33,981.8)	−1.0	89.9 (89.9)
4 Sakura Bank	37,233.8 (38,719.4)	−5.1	35,795.8 (35,806.5)	−1.2	96.1 (92.4)
5 Mitsubishi Bank	37,011.8 (37,075.2)	0.6	30,825.7 (30,798.4)	−1.1	83.2 (83.0)
6 Fuji Bank	36,799.6 (38,082.4)	−4.5	30,967.5 (31,055.6)	−2.0	84.1 (81.5)
7 Tokai Bank	22,070.5 (21,877.9)	−3.5	19,690.0 (19,631.5)	−1.4	88.9 (89.7)
8 Asahi Bank	21,794.0 (21,476.1)	1.5	20,289.5 (20,339.7)	−1.3	93.0 (94.7)
9 Bank of Tokyo	15,691.3 (15,571.8)	0.9	10,718.1 (10,950.6)	−4.2	68.3 (70.3)
10 Daiwa Bank	13,201.8 (13,473.4)	1.9	10,633.0 (10,409.6)	−0.2	80.5 (77.2)
11 Hokkaido Takushoku Bank	8,768.9 (8,844.4)	−3.7	7,305.0 (7,249.5)	−1.5	83.3 (81.9)
Regional banks					
1 Bank of Yokohama	9,573.7 (8,945.4)	7.0	8,931.4 (8,995.0)	−0.7	93.2 (100.5)
2 Chiba Bank	7,046.9 (6,875.8)	2.5	5,867.7 (5,796.1)	1.2	83.2 (84.2)
3 Shizuoka Bank	6,712.9 (6,610.8)	1.5	4,593.2 (4,607.6)	−0.3	68.4 (69.6)
4 Hokuriku Bank	6,644.9 (6,333.8)	4.9	5,438.2 (5,420.5)	0.3	81.8 (85.5)
5 Joyo Bank	6,609.7 (6,323.0)	4.5	4,957.7 (4,895.0)	1.3	75.0 (77.4)
6 Ashikaga Bank	5,753.2 (5,791.5)	−0.7	4,823.5 (4,860.1)	−0.8	83.8 (83.9)
7 Hiroshima Bank	5,730.9 (5,698.5)	−0.6	4,268.5 (4,288.2)	−0.5	74.4 (75.2)
8 Bank of Fukuoka	5,553.1 (5,348.2)	3.8	4,319.9 (4,119.1)	4.9	77.7 (77.0)
9 Hachijuni Bank	4,869.3 (4,781.7)	1.8	3,607.0 (3,531.4)	2.1	74.0 (73.8)
10 Gunma Bank	4,713.0 (4,590.8)	2.7	3,721.3 (3,663.6)	1.6	78.9 (79.8)
11 Chugoku Bank	4,211.0 (4,168.7)	1.0	2,879.1 (2,732.0)	5.4	68.3 (65.5)
12 Yamaguchi Bank	4,102.5 (3,984.6)	3.0	2,750.4 (2,664.5)	3.2	67.0 (66.8)
13 77 Bank	3,984.8 (3,783.6)	5.3	2,670.4 (2,609.6)	2.3	67.0 (68.9)
14 Nishi-Nippon Bank	3,725.4 (3,633.0)	2.5	3,106.4 (3,016.4)	3.0	83.3 (83.0)
15 Bank of Kyoto	3,419.1 (3,298.9)	3.6	2,466.1 (2,439.7)	1.1	72.1 (73.9)
16 Juroku Bank	3,292.9 (3,169.7)	3.9	2,506.1 (2,428.3)	3.2	76.1 (76.6)
17 Nanto Bank	3,249.7 (3,211.6)	1.2	2,520.2 (2,494.1)	1.0	77.5 (77.6)
18 Iyo Bank	3,216.5 (3,158.3)	1.8	2,421.9 (2,361.1)	2.6	75.2 (74.7)
19 Daishi Bank	3,143.0 (3,066.5)	2.5	2,314.2 (2,272.3)	1.8	73.6 (74.1)
20 Shiga Bank	3,108.4 (3,055.8)	1.7	2,214.1 (2,214.0)	0.0	71.2 (72.3)
21 Hyakujushi Bank	3,104.9 (2,923.6)	6.2	2,458.0 (2,393.2)	2.7	79.1 (81.8)
22 Hokkaido Bank	2,985.3 (2,990.2)	−0.2	2,569.2 (2,553.4)	0.6	86.0 (85.3)
23 San-in Godo Bank	2,835.0 (2,717.1)	4.3	2,096.6 (2,004.7)	4.6	73.9 (73.7)
24 Suruga Bank	2,814.9 (2,656.9)	5.9	2,017.0 (1,924.8)	4.8	71.6 (72.4)
25 Kiyo Bank	2,795.1 (2,742.0)	1.9	2,076.9 (2,044.8)	1.6	74.3 (74.5)
26 Hyakugo Bank	2,737.7 (2,651.2)	3.3	1,840.6 (1,767.8)	4.1	67.2 (66.6)
27 Hyogo Bank	2,655.9 (2,670.4)	−0.5	2,770.2 (2,778.9)	−0.3	104.3 (104.0)
28 Tokyo Sowa Bank	2,619.0 (2,557.2)	2.4	2,185.9 (2,135.8)	2.3	83.4 (83.5)
29 Higo Bank	2,582.1 (2,541.8)	1.6	1,724.0 (1,644.8)	4.8	66.7 (64.7)
· 30 Ogaki Kyoritsu Bank	2,488.2 (2,449.7)	1.6	1,841.9 (1,824.3)	1.0	74.0 (74.4)
31 Fukuoka City Bank	2,487.6 (2,412.1)	3.1	2,203.8 (2,155.9)	2.2	88.5 (89.3)
32 Hokkoku Bank	2,412.8 (2,335.0)	3.3	1,966.2 (1,931.1)	1.8	81.4 (82.7)
33 Bank of Nagoya	2,346.3 (2,289.0)	2.5	1,856.6 (1,826.0)	1.7	79.1 (79.7)
34 Toho Bank	2,258.5 (2,180.1)	3.6	1,627.9 (1,583.3)	2.8	72.0 (72.6)
35 Bank of Kinki	2,236.6 (2,210.8)	1.2	1,968.2 (1,967.7)	0.0	88.0 (89.0)
36 Tokyo Tomin Bank	2,222.3 (2,180.8)	1.9	1,899.6 (1,881.0)	1.0	85.4 (86.2)
37 Keiyo Bank	2,196.6 (2,149.7)	2.2	1,939.6 (1,909.9)	1.6	88.3 (88.8)
38 Musashino Bank	2,119.8 (2,032.3)	4.3	1,665.1 (1,629.8)	2.2	78.5 (80.1)
39 Kagoshima Bank	2,106.2 (2,074.2)	1.5	1,462.9 (1,413.4)	3.5	69.4 (68.1)
40 Shikoku Bank	2,043.2 (1,984.8)	2.9	1,500.4 (1,428.7)	5.0	73.4 (71.9)

RANKING OF BANKS
Fund Volume
(March 1995)

#	Bank	In millions of yen	Percent change from March 1994	#	Bank	In millions of yen	Percent change from March 1994
1	Sanwa Bank	39,696,347	8.7	61	Shizuoka Pref. C.F.A.C.	2,481,576	1.1
2	Norinchukin Bank	39,438,185	−0.8	62	Hokkoku Bank	2,412,855	3.1
3	Dai-Ichi Kangyo Bank	38,909,192	0.2	63	Bank of Nagoya	2,346,339	4.5
4	Sumitomo Bank	37,604,751	−2.9	64	Toho Bank	2,258,428	7.5
5	Sakura Bank	37,233,867	−5.2	65	Bank of Kinki	2,236,656	3.6
6	Mitsubishi Bank	37,011,806	0.7	66	Tokyo Tomin Bank	2,222,365	1.9
7	Fuji Bank	36,799,617	−4.6	67	Keiyo Bank	2,196,631	3.0
8	Mitsubishi Trust & Banking	30,475,484	0.0	68	Kanagawa Pref. C.F.A.C.	2,189,933	2.5
9	Industrial Bank of Japan	30,333,824	−4.7	69	Musashino Bank	2,119,883	2.5
10	Sumitomo Trust & Banking	29,251,701	2.9	70	Kagoshima Bank	2,106,291	2.5
11	Mitsui Trust & Banking	27,179,608	−1.5	71	Saitama Pref. C.F.A.C.	2,056,239	2.7
12	Long-Term Credit Bank of Japan	25,061,658	4.0	72	Shikoku Bank	2,043,272	5.8
13	Daiwa Bank	24,317,591	4.5	73	Okazaki Shinkin Bank	2,012,311	9.4
14	Yasuda Trust & Banking	22,709,386	2.9	74	Kyoto Shinkin Bank	1,954,015	5.8
15	Tokai Bank	22,070,505	−3.6	75	Akita Bank	1,952,246	7.3
16	Asahi Bank	21,794,003	1.6	76	Kofuku Bank	1,932,722	2.2
17	Toyo Trust & Banking	19,419,469	4.4	77	Nagano Pref. C.F.A.C.	1,918,631	1.5
18	Bank of Tokyo	15,691,321	1.0	78	Kyoto Chuo Shinkin Bank	1,912,545	5.5
19	Shoko Chukin Bank	14,992,234	0.3	79	Osaka Pref. C.F.A.C.	1,910,562	0.1
20	Nippon Credit Bank	14,163,555	−0.1	80	Aichi Bank	1,880,732	1.8
21	Zenshinren Bank	13,254,518	13.4	81	Yamanashi Chuo Bank	1,863,312	4.3
22	Chuo Trust & Banking	12,081,768	6.0	82	Chiba Kogyo Bank	1,860,508	1.4
23	Bank of Yokohama	9,573,773	4.3	83	Oita Bank	1,857,924	2.7
24	Hokkaido Takushoku Bank	8,768,935	−3.8	84	Fukui Bank	1,832,647	2.1
25	Chiba Bank	7,046,903	3.4	85	Bank of Osaka	1,829,113	0.5
26	Shizuoka Bank	6,712,906	1.5	86	Hiroshima-Sogo Bank	1,829,073	2.3
27	Hokuriku Bank	6,644,932	1.8	87	Awa Bank	1,799,598	4.6
28	Joyo Bank	6,609,745	2.6	88	Bank of Iwate	1,767,360	1.4
29	Ashikaga Bank	5,753,225	−2.2	89	Amagasaki Shinkin Bank	1,745,089	6.0
30	Hiroshima Bank	5,730,981	−1.3	90	Gifu Shinkin Bank	1,721,970	4.4
31	Bank of Fukuoka	5,553,113	−3.3	91	Gifu Pref. C.F.A.C.	1,713,575	1.5
32	Hachijuni Bank	4,869,345	1.5	92	Fukutoku Bank	1,708,424	0.7
33	Gunma Bank	4,713,054	0.4	93	Aomori Bank	1,684,060	5.1
34	Chugoku Bank	4,211,038	2.1	94	Hokkaido C.F.A.C.	1,675,986	2.0
35	Yamaguchi Bank	4,102,562	1.7	95	Hokuetsu Bank	1,673,252	−0.4
36	77 Bank	3,984,876	5.2	96	Eighteenth Bank	1,667,145	0.5
37	Nishi-Nippon Bank	3,725,414	1.2	97	Yachiyo Bank	1,664,803	−0.2
38	Nippon Trust Bank	3,593,736	−1.5	98	Towa Bank	1,598,179	2.2
39	Bank of Kyoto	3,419,140	3.5	99	North Pacific Bank	1,519,671	5.0
40	Shinkumi Federation Bank	3,379,641	4.4	100	Senshu Bank	1,496,958	2.8
41	Juroku Bank	3,292,945	1.8	101	Bank of Saga	1,492,691	3.1
42	Nanto Bank	3,249,710	3.2	102	Higashi-Nippon Bank	1,486,274	4.0
43	Iyo Bank	3,216,571	2.8	103	Chukyo Bank	1,474,914	1.8
44	Daishi Bank	3,143,001	2.9	104	Hiroshima Pref. C.F.A.C.	1,467,245	0.0
45	Shiga Bank	3,108,497	2.4	105	Shinwa Bank	1,465,270	1.3
46	Hyakujushi Bank	3,104,940	3.6	106	Michinoku Bank	1,457,512	3.7
47	Hyogo Pref. C.F.A.C.	3,050,628	3.0	107	Tochigi Bank	1,418,397	4.4
48	Hokkaido Bank	2,985,391	0.2	108	Daisan Bank	1,418,175	0.8
49	Aichi Pref. C.F.A.C.	2,900,253	1.3	109	Bank of The Ryukyus	1,415,825	1.3
50	San-in Godo Bank	2,835,059	3.1	110	Miyazaki Bank	1,409,534	5.4
51	Jonan Shinkin Bank	2,832,919	10.2	111	Bank of Ikeda	1,390,001	2.8
52	Suruga Bank	2,814,960	6.9	112	Niigata Pref. C.F.A.C.	1,372,738	1.6
53	Kiyo Bank	2,795,170	2.0	113	Mie Pref. C.F.A.C.	1,364,092	0.1
54	Hyakugo Bank	2,737,728	2.3	114	Chiba Pref. C.F.A.C.	1,352,185	1.1
55	Hyogo Bank	2,655,938	2.9	115	Okayama Pref. C.F.A.C.	1,326,032	−1.2
56	Tokyo Sowa Bank	2,619,048	3.1	116	Fukuoka Pref. C.F.A.C.	1,317,108	0.1
57	Higo Bank	2,582,136	4.4	117	Yamagata Bank	1,310,124	3.1
58	Rokinren Bank	2,573,881	8.6	118	Ehime Bank	1,296,472	1.8
59	Ogaki Kyoritsu Bank	2,488,267	2.1	119	Saitama Shinkin Bank	1,262,180	5.1
60	Fukuoka City Bank	2,487,682	5.1	120	Kumamoto Family Bank	1,253,864	5.1

RANKING OF SECURITIES COMPANIES
Pretax Profits
(For fiscal year ended March '95)

		In millions of yen	Percent change from a year earlier			In millions of yen	Percent change from a year earlier
1	Cosmo Securities	8,494	—	23	Warburg Investment Trust Management	112	—
2	Nikko Securities Investment Trust Management	7,029	−23.5	24	Toyo Investment Trust Management	98	308.3
3	Nomura Securities	6,797	−86.6	25	Cosmo Investment Trust Management	96	−27.3
4	Nomura Securities Investment Trust Management	6,296	−38.2	26	Universal Investment Trust Management	63	−33.7
5	Daiwa Securities Investment Trust Management	4,557	−42.6	27	Taiheiyo Investment Trust Management	62	−69.2
6	Japan Securities Finance	4,179	−41.6	28	Marufuku Securities	35	−93.6
7	Yamaichi Investment Trust Management	2,671	−55.4	29	Hikari Securities	18	−93.7
8	Japan Bond Trading	2,516	−35.4	30	Chubu Securities Financing	15	−88.9
9	Nichiei Securities	2,263	—	31	Miyako Securities	12	−89.2
10	Kokusai Investment Trust Management	2,071	−39.5	32	Dojima Securities	7	−95.4
				33	Fukuyama Securities	0	−100.0
11	Osaka Securities Finance	843	−12.6	34	Naka Securities	−21	−105.5
12	Asahi Investment Trust Management	789	−21.7	35	Tsuyama Securities	−44	—
13	Taiyo Investment Trust and Management	521	−42.0	36	Okachi Securities	−50	−112.3
14	Shin-Wako Securities Investment Trust and Management	461	−31.1	37	Invesco Investment Trust Management	−56	−609.1
15	Jardine Fleming Investment Trust Management	449	—	38	Nisshin Securities	−94	−270.9
16	Kosei Securities	322	−33.9	39	Daitoku Securities	−108	—
17	Utsumiya Securities	246	−72.9	40	SBIM Investment Trust Management	−112	—
18	Japan Investment Trust Management	243	−21.4	41	IBJ Investment Trust Management	−112	—
19	Norinchukin Investment Trust Management	169	−99.5	42	Kotobuki Securities	−113	—
20	Dai-ichi Investment Trust Management	164	13.9	43	Daiman Securities	−122	−630.4
				44	Joko Securities	−123	−592.0
21	Sanyo Investment Trust Management	143	−68.4	45	Toho Securities	−123	—
22	Matsui Securities	112	−63.2	46	Kaneman Securities	−131	−196.3
				47	Shinwa Securities	−136	−151.5
				48	Central Investment Trust Management	−139	—
				49	Omori Securities	−141	—
				50	Rokuwa Securities	−161	—

OUTSTANDING BALANCE OF PERSONAL SAVINGS BY TYPE OF INSTITUTION
(In billions of yen; percentage distribution in parentheses)

	Mar. 1995	(%)	Mar. 1994	(%)	Mar. 1993	(%)	Mar. 1992	(%)
Total	923,879.7	(100.0)	884,512.1	(100.0)	842,197.7	(100.0)	800,917.9	(100.0)
Deposits	586,594.7	(63.5)	554,969.0	(62.7)	528,070.4	(62.7)	505,011.4	(63.1)
(1) Banks	227,101.4	(25.6)	215,853.9	(24.4)	208,361.9	(24.7)	205,589.5	(25.7)
(2) Shinkin banks	67,931.7	(7.4)	64,337.7	(7.3)	61,963.4	(7.4)	59,646.2	(7.4)
(3) Credit cooperatives	17,705.9	(1.9)	17,263.4	(2.0)	16,436.0	(2.0)	15,685.0	(2.0)
(4) Agricultural & fishery cooperative	67,637.5	(7.3)	65,608.2	(7.4)	63,350.4	(7.5)	61,098.4	(7.6)
(5) Postal offices	197,339.1	(21.4)	183,534.8	(20.7)	170,090.6	(20.2)	155,600.7	(19.4)
(6) Labor banks	8,879.1	(1.0)	8,371.0	(0.9)	7,868.1	(0.9)	7,391.6	(0.9)
Trust	49,507.0	(5.4)	49,670.5	(5.6)	48,087.2	(5.7)	44,480.3	(5.6)
Insurance	219,599.8	(23.8)	206,222.9	(23.3)	188,318.3	(22.4)	171,877.8	(21.5)
Securities	68,178.2	(7.4)	73,649.7	(8.3)	77,721.8	(9.2)	79,723.3	(10.0)
(1) Public and corporate bonds	40,203.9	(4.4)	39,379.0	(4.5)	40,906.1	(4.9)	45,759.9	(5.7)
(2) Investment trusts	27,974.3	(3.0)	34,270.7	(3.9)	36,815.7	(4.4)	33,963.4	(4.2)

Figures for postal offices are settled on a counter basis.
Trust consists of money trust and loan trust.
Insurance consists of private life insurance, postal life insurance and agricultural mutual aid.
Securities consists of public and corporate bonds and investment trust held by individual investors.

Notes: Source: Bank of Japan

NUMBER OF BRANCHES OF MAJOR FINANCIAL INSTITUTIONS

Branches	Dec. 1994	Dec. 1993	Dec. 1992	Dec. 1991	Dec. 1990	Dec. 1989	Dec. 1988
Banks	16,740	16,767	16,762	16,560	16,191	15,878	11,016
1) Long-term credit banks	75	75	77	77	74	70	67
2) City banks	3,516	3,534	3,579	3,553	3,474	3,400	3,303
3) Regional banks	7,986	7,978	7,864	7,729	7,546	7,414	7,270
4) Trust banks	391	393	400	395	389	379	376
5) Second regional banks	4,772	4,787	4,842	4,806	4,708	4,615	4,497
Shinkin banks	8,515	8,439	8,354	8,208	8,122	7,909	7,730
Shoko Chukin Bank	104	101	104	100	97	96	96
Credit cooperatives	2,997	3,005	3,004	2,989	2,974	2,943	2,921
Labor banks	668	664	660	657	652	645	642
Norinchukin Bank	39	39	39	38	38	38	38
Agricultural cooperatives	—	—	—	16,164	16,218	16,321	16,314
Securities companies	2,784	2,838	2,988	3,212	3,117	2,933	2,747
Post offices	24,503	—	—	24,190	24,107	23,408	23,236
Head Office							
Banks	150	150	151	153	154	155	87
1) Long-term credit banks	3	3	3	3	3	3	3
2) City banks	11	11	11	11	12	13	13
3) Regional banks	64	64	64	64	64	64	64
4) Trust banks	7	7	7	7	7	7	7
5) Second regional banks	65	65	66	68	68	68	68
Shinkin banks	422	429	435	443	451	454	455
Credit cooperatives	376	383	393	398	407	414	419
Labor banks	47	47	47	47	47	47	47
Agricultural cooperatives	—	—	—	3,446	3,322	3,493	3,712
Securities companies	208	213	209	210	210	210	210

Notes: Excluding overseas branches.

OUTSTANDING BAD LOANS

(As of end of March 1995; in millions of yen)

1	Sakura Bank	1,410,787
2	Dai-Ichi Kangyo Bank	1,192,986
3	Fuji Bank	1,162,134
4	Sumitomo Bank	945,861
5	Long-Term Credit Bank of Japan	784,354
6	Sanwa Bank	734,546
7	Tokai Bank	724,011
8	Nippon Credit Bank	611,736
9	Mitsui Trust & Banking	577,424
10	Mitsubishi Bank	526,460
11	Industrial Bank of Japan	519,784
12	Sumitomo Trust & Banking	497,001
13	Hokkaido Takushoku Bank	479,305
14	Asahi Bank	448,053
15	Mitsubishi Trust & Banking	441,853
16	Yasuda Trust & Banking	418,269
17	Daiwa Bank	298,619
18	Toyo Trust & Banking	283,362
19	Bank of Tokyo	206,871
20	Chuo Trust & Banking	173,826
21	Nippon Trust Bank	109,048
22	Ashikaga Bank	79,750
23	Hyogo Bank	60,959
24	Hokuriku Bank	51,952
25	Bank of Yokohama	45,736
26	Kofuku Bank	36,032
27	Nanto Bank	34,797
28	Tokyo Sowa Bank	33,732
29	Fukutoku Bank	30,060
30	Taiheiyo Bank	27,506

RATIO OF BAD LOANS TO TOTAL OUTSTANDING LOANS

(%)

1	Nippon Trust Bank	7.0
2	Hokkaido Takushoku Bank	6.6
3	Nippon Credit Bank	5.9
4	Mitsui Trust & Banking	5.1
5	Yasuda Trust & Banking	4.4
6	Long-Term Credit Bank of Japan	4.2
7	Sakura Bank	3.9
8	Taiheiyo Bank	3.9
9	Fuji Bank	3.8
10	Kokumin Bank	3.8
11	Tokai Bank	3.7
12	Chuo Trust & Banking	3.7
13	Sumitomo Trust & Banking	3.7
14	Dai-Ichi Kangyo Bank	3.5
15	Toyo Trust & Banking	3.4
16	Mitsubishi Trust & Banking	3.3
17	Sumitomo Bank	2.8
18	Wakayama Bank	2.7
19	Daiwa Bank	2.5
20	Industrial Bank of Japan	2.2
21	Asahi Bank	2.2
22	Sanwa Bank	2.2
23	Hyogo Bank	2.2
24	Fukutoku Bank	2.1
25	Kanagawa Bank	2.0
26	Kofuku Bank	2.0
27	Shimane Bank	2.0
28	Bank of Tokyo	1.9
29	Tokuyo City Bank	1.9
30	Kyoto Kyoei Bank	1.8

FOREIGN BANKS' BRANCHES IN JAPAN
(As of March 1995; in millions of yen)

	Fund volume	Deposits	Securities	Loans
U.S.A.				
American Express Bank	2,513	2	—	—
Bank of America	—	—	—	—
Bank of California	34,377	80	—	18,330
Bank of Hawaii	41,453	2,506	0	37,570
Bank of New York	61,389	5,672	1	19,544
Bankers Trust	120,839	12,405	2,923	28,851
Chase Manhattan Bank	503,640	49,412	7,663	29,445
Chemical Bank	259,497	19,378	15,066	58,370
Citibank	1,539,486	484,725	130,393	263,179
CoreStates Bank	10,790	—	1	—
First National Bank of Boston	15,348	271	0	7,978
First National Bank of Chicago	101,363	40,008	0	4,965
Morgan Guaranty Trust Co. of New York	294,952	11,647	51,083	115,163
NBD Bank	41,886	2,670	3,840	20,091
Republic National Bank of New York	32,244	2,358	2,354	4,690
State Street Bank and Trust	56,094	33,122	—	—
Germany				
Bayerische Landesbank	289,728	20,012	78,521	84,817
Bayerische Vereinsbank	273,332	43,131	2,630	206,119
BHF Bank	84,524	1,781	3,370	56,911
Commerzbank	457,113	59,106	15,424	321,557
Deutsche Bank	1,053,435	92,013	282,288	437,485
Dresdner Bank	—	—	—	—
Lehman Brothers Bankhaus	24,243	14,111	7,446	170
Merrill Lynch Bank	10,155	862	—	—
Morgan Stanley Bank	13,535	5,874	—	—
Salomon Brothers AG	136,523	112,535	84,725	10,223
Westdeutsche Landesbank	774,974	304,173	33,501	338,302
South Korea				
Cho Hung Bank	139,814	11,041	9,549	68,309
Commercial Bank of Korea	151,693	18,350	26,706	57,072
Hanil Bank	221,823	21,560	24,890	105,163
Industrial Bank of Korea	32,374	3,503	5,613	9,586
Kookmin Bank	38,405	2,717	8,172	11,866
Korea Development Bank	—	22,606	29,717	60,726
Korea Exchange Bank	238,809	69,124	4,394	150,356
Korea First Bank	186,104	27,140	10,329	112,945
SEOULBANK	134,081	16,462	14,462	52,514
Shinhan Bank	163,345	46,294	19,142	84,443
France				
Banque Indosuez	353,485	29,210	53,088	147,012
Banque Nationale de Paris	1,280,087	369,196	212,478	473,729
Banque Paribas	372,539	22,418	133,640	37,677
Credit Commercial de France	157,903	6,945	77,798	35,746
Credit Lyonnais	1,077,219	213,124	38,412	360,170
Societe Generale	1,517,616	460,105	53,959	580,088
Union de Banques Arabes et Francaises	123,240	35,717	6,103	41,626
U.K.				
Barclays Bank	408,238	15,335	30,189	231,060
Goldman Sachs	23,101	1,775	—	—
Lloyds Bank	114,990	7,503	21,077	30,323
Midland Bank	—	73,809	261,468	8,244
National Westminster Bank	512,790	156,371	58,778	151,882
Standard Chartered Bank	70,465	3,720	757	9,870
Canada				
Bank of Montreal	60,161	13	6,141	9
Bank of Nova Scotia	52,764	12,832	5	11,886
Canadian Imperial Bank of Commerce	49,588	341	883	19,201
Royal Bank of Canada	66,139	1,078	0	22,917
Toronto-Dominion Bank	106,497	22,901	47,858	5,497
Australia				
Australia and New Zealand Banking Group	134,882	18,886	1,851	11,847
Commonwealth Bank of Australia	94,993	306	23,047	7,945
National Australia Bank	66,608	51,888	1,681	10,767
Westpac Banking	298,146	21,772	16,316	81,353
Singapore				
Development Bank of Singapore	108,929	411	374	88,193
Oversea-Chinese Banking	53,293	137	1	35,680
Overseas Union Bank	35,221	161	—	30,695
United Overseas Bank	10,775	206	0	5,430

	Fund volume	Deposits	Securities	Loans
Italy				
Banca Commerciale Italiana	336,274	111,123	67,103	80,914
Credito Italiano	169,828	91,258	13,627	55,713
Istituto Bancario San Paolo di Torino	547,839	32,961	52,972	59,091
Spain				
Banco Bilbao Vizcaya	138,319	377	45,266	51,581
Banco Central Hispanoamericano	76,594	7,305	2,690	21,156
Banco Santander	73,166	2,792	561	49,624
Switzerland				
Credit Suisse	314,464	41,132	4,472	108,999
Swiss Bank	478,790	34,467	965	136,020
Union Bank of Switzerland	1,045,777	11,903	46,880	235,251
Taiwan				
International Commercial Bank of China	68,277	6,379	13,885	14,743
Chang Hwa Commercial Bank	6,980	1,433	0	1,219
First Commercial Bank	1,833	188	0	618
Brazil				
Banco do Brasil	134,227	112,559	892	18,254
Banco do Estado de Sao Paulo	98,306	29,023	286	40,071
India				
Bank of India	83,550	53,059	1,968	15,253
State Bank of India	80,548	1,316	1,442	33,738
Indonesia				
Bank Bumi Daya	58,398	18,498	0	17,818
Bank Negara Indonesia	124,032	32,829	1,004	45,096
Netherlands				
ABN AMRO Bank N.V.	1,194,959	9,659	51,618	623,728
International Nederlanden Bank N.V.	314,794	2,540	10,914	143,180
China				
Bank of China	904,256	77,979	371,116	42,667
Hong Kong				
Hongkong and Shanghai Banking	224,926	12,734	4,104	135,421
Malaysia				
Bank Bumiputra Malaysia	25,490	7,117	151	21,149
Pakistan				
National Bank of Pakistan	7,092	4,627	1	79
Sweden				
Skandinaviska Enskilda Banken	21,686	153	0	20,180
Thailand				
Bangkok Bank	68,630	2,961	1,638	9,300

NIKKEI SURVEY

Market share survey

Seven industries saw market leadership change places in 1994, and two of those changes came as the result of mergers, reveals the annual Market Share Survey of 100 Key Goods and Services by The Nihon Keizai Shimbun.

Twenty-six companies and groups in 21 sectors made it into the top five for the first time, compared with 17 firms in 16 sectors a year earlier. In the imported car market, Honda Motor Co. drove Mercedes-Benz AG out of first place thanks to sales growth triggered in part by price cuts on its Accord Wagon.

Mega-mergers turned Chichibu Onoda Cement Corp. into the top cement maker and earned Mitsubishi Chemical Corp. the leading market share for low-density polyethylene.

New faces shook up the home video game market, with Sony Computer Entertainment Inc. clinching third place out of the blue, thanks to solid sales of the Sony PlayStation.

Market leader Nintendo Co. lost ground, while Sega Enterprises Ltd. and Matsushita Electric Industrial Co. both increased their market shares. This points out a change of generations.

In the market for color photo film, Agfa-Gevaert Japan Ltd. boosted its presence by marketing low-cost, store-brand film.

100 KEY GOODS & SERVICES

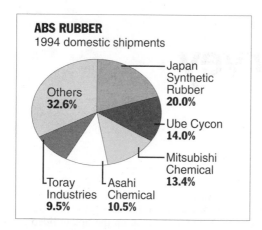

ABS RUBBER
1994 domestic shipments

- Japan Synthetic Rubber **20.0%**
- Ube Cycon **14.0%**
- Mitsubishi Chemical **13.4%**
- Asahi Chemical **10.5%**
- Toray Industries **9.5%**
- Others **32.6%**

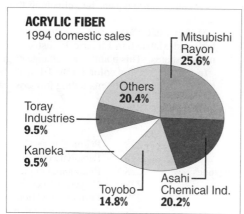

ACRYLIC FIBER
1994 domestic sales

- Mitsubishi Rayon **25.6%**
- Asahi Chemical Ind. **20.2%**
- Toyobo **14.8%**
- Kaneka **9.5%**
- Toray Industries **9.5%**
- Others **20.4%**

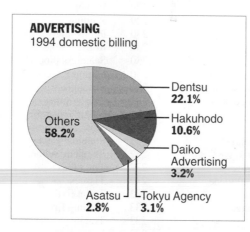

ADVERTISING
1994 domestic billing

- Dentsu **22.1%**
- Hakuhodo **10.6%**
- Daiko Advertising **3.2%**
- Tokyu Agency **3.1%**
- Asatsu **2.8%**
- Others **58.2%**

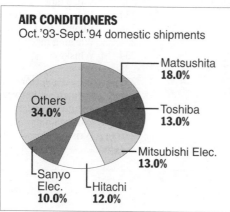

AIR CONDITIONERS
Oct.'93-Sept.'94 domestic shipments

- Matsushita **18.0%**
- Toshiba **13.0%**
- Mitsubishi Elec. **13.0%**
- Hitachi **12.0%**
- Sanyo Elec. **10.0%**
- Others **34.0%**

ABS RUBBER

Shipments of ABS rubber totaled 596,466 tons in 1994, up 5.3% over the previous year, according to a Nikkei survey. Domestic shipments were up 1% to 440,700 tons, while exports jumped 18% to 155,700 tons due to strong demand from Japanese manufacturers in Southeast Asia.

As styrene monomer was in short supply worldwide, there was strong demand for ABS resin for use in car bodies and consumer electronics casings.

Market leader Japan Synthetic Rubber Co. lost 1.0 point to 20.0%, and Ube Cycon Ltd. slid by the same margin to 14.0%. Mitsubishi Chemical Corp. stood third with 13.4%, up 0.4 point, followed by Asahi Chemical Industry Co. which gained 0.5 point to 10.5%.

ACRYLIC FIBER

Total shipments of acrylic fiber by domestic producers grew 7.1% in 1994 to 397,600 tons, recovering to levels in 1986-1988, according to a Nikkei survey. The growth was mainly attributed to exports, which accounted for 70% of the total.

Mitsubishi Rayon Co. remained the top supplier with a 25.6% share, down 0.2 of a point from 1993. Asahi Chemical Industry Co. kept second spot with 20.2%, down 0.4, followed by Toyobo Co. at 14.8%, down 0.8. The three firms' share declines reflected aggressive output increases by other producers.

In 1994, insect damage reduced cotton crops, which pushed up replacement demand for acrylic fiber in Asia, mainly in cotton-producing China and Pakistan.

ADVERTISING

Advertising billings grew 0.8% from a year earlier to 5,168.2 billion yen in 1994 to mark the first increase in three years. Newspaper ad billings rose 1.1%, the first gain in four years; TV ad billings rose for the first time in three years, by a healthy 3.4%. The gains are attributed to 1994's extremely hot summer and a cut in income taxes.

Dentsu Inc. slightly increased its market dominance to 22.1%, up 0.2 of a percentage point. Hakuhodo Inc. followed at 10.6%, up 0.3 of a point. Daiko Advertising Inc. recaptured third place for the first time since 1988 with a 3.2% share.

Of the top four only Tokyu Agency Inc. saw lower billings, and shed 0.2 of a point to drop to fourth at 3.1%.

AIR CONDITIONERS

Shipments of air conditioners in the year through September 1994 totaled 6,724,000, up 33.2% from the previous year and the second-largest figure on record, according to a Nikkei survey. The steep increase was attributed to last year's unusually hot summer.

The top five makers expanded combined share by 1.5 percentage points to 66.0%. They were able to meet soaring demand in the July-September period while smaller firms could not. Matsushita Electric Industrial Co. retained first place with 18.0% of the market, up 1.0 point. Toshiba Corp. jumped from third to share second place with Mitsubishi Electric Corp. at 13.0%. Toshiba's share was unchanged, while Mitsubishi lost 0.5 point.

ALUMINUM SASHES

Domestic sales of aluminum sashes and doors expanded 5.6% to 751.9 billion yen thanks to brisk housing starts in fiscal 1994. Tostem Corp. maintained the largest market share by shifting its focus to this particular segment ahead of rivals. It commanded a share of 34.3%, up 0.5 point.

YKK Architectural Products Inc. had the second-biggest share of 30.4%, unchanged. The company stepped up sales efforts in the Tokyo metropolitan area and also established products catering to differing regional climates.

Shin Nikkei Co. retained its third-place ranking even though its market share contracted 0.1 point to 10.9% on slow sales of high-grade products.

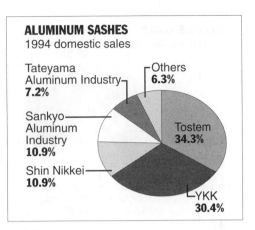

ALUMINUM SASHES
1994 domestic sales

- Tateyama Aluminum Industry **7.2%**
- Sankyo Aluminum Industry **10.9%**
- Shin Nikkei **10.9%**
- Others **6.3%**
- Tostem **34.3%**
- YKK **30.4%**

BEARINGS

Sales of bearings including exports totaled 556.8 billion yen in 1994, up 2.0% from 1993 for the first rise in four years. Total domestic sales including imports dipped 0.6% to 419.6 billion yen, according to a Nikkei survey.

Market leader NSK Ltd. raised its share by 0.4 of a point to 34.4% on strong sales of small bearings for hard disk drives and air conditioners. NTN Corp. gained 0.3 of a point to 26.2% thanks to strong demand for bearings used in automobile. Third-ranked Koyo Seiko Co. also gained 0.4 to 25.5% on growing demand from truck makers.

Domestic demand has shown growth since the second half of 1994, but bearing makers are anxious about automakers' moves to expand purchases from abroad.

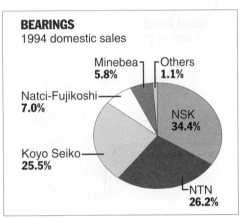

BEARINGS
1994 domestic sales

- Minebea **5.8%**
- Natci-Fujikoshi **7.0%**
- Koyo Seiko **25.5%**
- Others **1.1%**
- NSK **34.4%**
- NTN **26.2%**

BEER

Breweries routed 597.93 million cases of beer (one case holds 20 633ml bottles) to thirsty consumers in 1994, up 7.8%, according to a Nikkei survey. The strong demand for beer was directly related to last year's scorching summer, say industry analysts.

Kirin Brewery Co. saw its share fall for the third straight year to 47.0%, down 1.6 points, but still well ahead of its rivals. Asahi Breweries Ltd. boosted share by 1.0 point to 24.9%, while third-ranked Sapporo Breweries Ltd. held a 17.4% share, down 0.9 of a point.

Suntory Ltd., unable to capitalize on the heat wave, saw its shared slide 1.1 points to 5.6%. Imported beers posted a powerful performance, climbing 2.6 points to 4.2%.

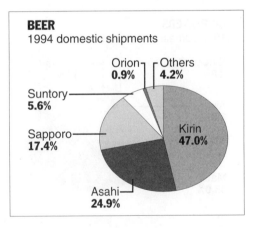

BEER
1994 domestic shipments

- Orion **0.9%**
- Suntory **5.6%**
- Sapporo **17.4%**
- Others **4.2%**
- Kirin **47.0%**
- Asahi **24.9%**

CAMCORDERS

Sharp Corp. captured more of the camcorder market in 1994, raising its share by 9.8 percentage points to 25% and moving up from third to second. The firm saw continued strong demand for its 8mm liquid crystal ViewCam series, released in autumn 1992.

Top maker Sony Corp. held 40.4% of the market, down 0.8 point. Matsushita Electric Industrial Co. slid from second to third place as stagnant sales pushed down its share by 9.5 points to 15.5%. Victor Co. of Japan Ltd. expanded its share by 4.0 points to 11.0%. Domestic camcorder shipments rose 8.7% to 1.27 million units, rising for the second straight year. The lasting popularity of Sharp's ViewCam prompted other firms to release LCD models.

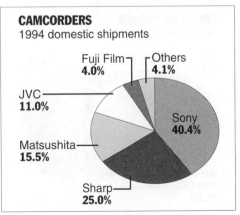

CAMCORDERS
1994 domestic shipments

- Fuji Film **4.0%**
- JVC **11.0%**
- Matsushita **15.5%**
- Sharp **25.0%**
- Others **4.1%**
- Sony **40.4%**

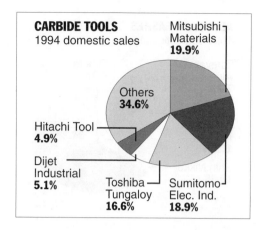

CARBIDE TOOLS
1994 domestic sales

Mitsubishi Materials **19.9%**
Others **34.6%**
Hitachi Tool **4.9%**
Dijet Industrial **5.1%**
Toshiba Tungaloy **16.6%**
Sumitomo Elec. Ind. **18.9%**

CARBIDE TOOLS

Domestic shipments of carbide tools in 1994 declined 2.2% year on year to 163 billion yen, falling for the third straight year, according to an industry survey. Mitsubishi Materials Corp., the market leader, saw its share rise 1.0 point to 19.9% on strong sales of wear-resistant carbide tips.

Sumitomo Electric Industries Ltd. came in second with 18.9%, down 0.3 point. In third place, Toshiba Tungaloy Co. took 16.6%, down 0.2.

Domestic tool makers are likely to face stiff competition from their overseas rivals, which are keen to take advantage of the yen's appreciation in early 1995 to broaden their market share. Imports now hold just under 10% of the Japanese market.

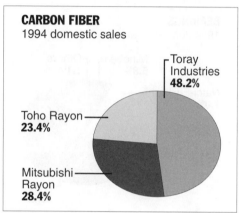

CARBON FIBER
1994 domestic sales

Toray Industries **48.2%**
Toho Rayon **23.4%**
Mitsubishi Rayon **28.4%**

CARBON FIBER

Domestic sales of polyacrylonitrile (PAN) carbon fibers dropped 2.2% from a year earlier to 40,454 million yen in fiscal 1994. Toray Industries Inc. again grabbed the largest market share, up 2.3 percentage points to 48.2%. Mitsubishi Rayon Co. stayed in second place with 28.4%, up 0.6 point. Toho Rayon came in third at 23.4%, up 2.0 points. Asahi Kasei Carbon Fiber Co. withdrew from the market last year.

The total PAN carbon fiber output capacity of the three Japanese makers stands at 7,650 tons, accounting for more than 60% of worldwide production capacity of 12,000 tons. The three firms will boost output capacity in 1995 in anticipation of growth in worldwide demand.

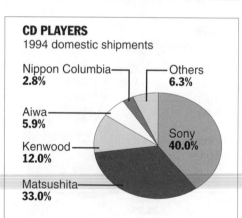

CD PLAYERS
1994 domestic shipments

Nippon Columbia **2.8%**
Others **6.3%**
Aiwa **5.9%**
Kenwood **12.0%**
Sony **40.0%**
Matsushita **33.0%**

CD PLAYERS

Shipments of compact disc players soared 17.6% year on year to 1,974,000 units in 1994, according to an industry survey. The consumer electronics manufacturers that offer portable models, which accounted for 86% of total shipments last year, occupied the top four places.

Sony Corp. remained market leader with 40.0%, down 2.0 percentage points. Matsushita Electric Industrial Co. came in second with 33.0%, also down 2.0 points, followed by Kenwood Corp. with an unchanged 12.0% share.

Aiwa Co. raised its share by 2.0 points to 5.9% on strong sales of low-priced models produced at its overseas plants.

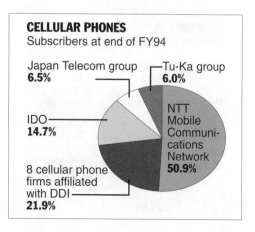

CELLULAR PHONES
Subscribers at end of FY94

Japan Telecom group **6.5%**
Tu-Ka group **6.0%**
IDO **14.7%**
NTT Mobile Communications Network **50.9%**
8 cellular phone firms affiliated with DDI **21.9%**

CELLULAR PHONES

The number of cellular phone subscribers rose 103.3% to 4,331,400 in fiscal 1994, according to a Nikkei survey. The record-high increase was triggered by sharp declines in terminal prices and subscription fees.

The share of market leader NTT Mobile Communications Network group slipped 11.2 percentage points to 50.9%. In second position, the eight DDI Corp.-affiliated cellular telephone firms lost 0.2 point to 21.9%, and third-ranked Nippon Idou Tsushin Corp. dropped 1.1 points to 14.7%.

The remaining chunk of the market was shared by new entrants. Japan Telecom Co.-affiliated firms grabbed 6.5% and Nissan Motor Co.-affiliated Tu-Ka Cellular companies took 6.0%.

CEMENT

Domestic cement sales rose 1.5% to 80.2 million tons in 1994 thanks to active housing construction and public works projects. Due to corporate mergers in October, Chichibu Onoda Cement Corp. leapt into first place with a 23.7% share and Sumitomo Osaka Cement Co. placed second with an 18.1% share. The newly created firms displaced Nihon Cement Co., which fell from first to third place, and Mitsubishi Materials Corp. which was bumped to fourth place.

Despite this, Nihon Cement used its extensive sales channels and reduced costs to increase its share 0.3 of a percentage point. The top five firms raised their combined share by 0.7 of a percentage point to 81.6%, which ate into the business of smaller producers.

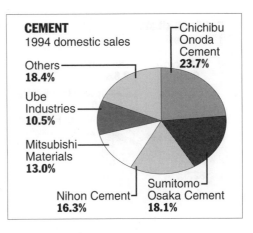

CEMENT
1994 domestic sales

- Chichibu Onoda Cement **23.7%**
- Sumitomo Osaka Cement **18.1%**
- Nihon Cement **16.3%**
- Mitsubishi Materials **13.0%**
- Ube Industries **10.5%**
- Others **18.4%**

COLOR FILM

Domestic shipments of 35mm color film grew 2.7% to 17.36 million sq. meters in 1994. Fourth-ranked Agfa-Gevaert Japan Ltd. saw its market share grow 4.1 percentage points to 5.0%, the largest increase among the top four film makers. The surge is attributed to the firm's arrangement with Daiei Inc. to supply private brand film.

Fuji Photo Film Co. continued to dominate the market with a 69.4% share, though it shed 4.4 points. The decline is almost a mirror image of Agfa-Gevaert's gain. The cheaper private brand film was the primary cause of the shift.

Konica Corp. held on to second place with 17.0%, down 0.5 of a point. The share of third-ranked Kodak Japan Ltd. rose 1.1 points to 8.6%.

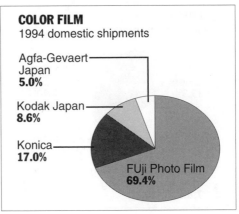

COLOR FILM
1994 domestic shipments

- Agfa-Gevaert Japan **5.0%**
- Kodak Japan **8.6%**
- Konica **17.0%**
- FUji Photo Film **69.4%**

COLOR TVS

Domestic shipments of color television sets totaled 10.3 million units in 1994, according to a Nikkei survey. In particular, shipments of TVs with a height-to-width ratio of 9 to 16, so called wide TVs, soared to 1.4 million from 300,000 in 1993.

Matsushita Electric Industrial Co. retained its top share position in the color TV market, but saw its market share drop 0.5 of a point to 16.3% when it fell behind the competition in the wide-screen TV market.

Sharp Corp. ranked second with a 12.2% share, down 0.2 of a point. Toshiba Corp. which expanded its share by 0.3 of a point to 11.9% on strong sales of its TV that can show two programs simultaneously, placed third.

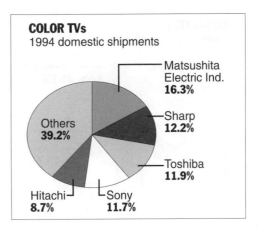

COLOR TVs
1994 domestic shipments

- Matsushita Electric Ind. **16.3%**
- Sharp **12.2%**
- Toshiba **11.9%**
- Sony **11.7%**
- Hitachi **8.7%**
- Others **39.2%**

COMPACT DISCS

The value of music compact discs produced in Japan in 1994 came to 492,241 million yen, up 2.5% from a year earlier, according to an industry survey. Although a total of 18 singles and 14 albums sold over 1 million copies, growth in the market as a whole slowed. Price cuts in imported compact discs in the wake of the yen's appreciation helped sustain what growth there was in the market, analysts say.

Sony Music Entertainment (Japan) Inc. remained the market leader with a 17.7% share, up 0.2 percentage point. Toshiba EMI Ltd. held onto second with 12.3%, dropping 2.4 points after many popular artists left the label in 1993.

Polydor KK moved up to third place from fourth with 9.3%, up 1.3 points.

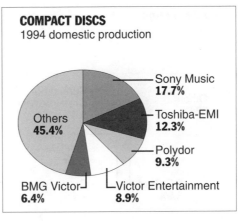

COMPACT DISCS
1994 domestic production

- Sony Music **17.7%**
- Toshiba-EMI **12.3%**
- Polydor **9.3%**
- Victor Entertainment **8.9%**
- BMG Victor **6.4%**
- Others **45.4%**

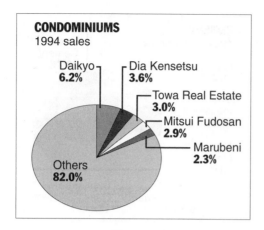

CONDOMINIUMS
1994 sales

Daikyo 6.2%
Dia Kensetsu 3.6%
Towa Real Estate 3.0%
Mitsui Fudosan 2.9%
Marubeni 2.3%
Others 82.0%

CONDOMINIUMS

Condominium sales soared 80.0% year on year to 188,343 units in 1994, an all-time high, thanks to price cuts and low interest rates. While the number of condominiums put on sale grew drastically in every region, prices continued to plunge.

Daikyo Inc. retained the top spot for the 17th straight year, though its market share shrank by 2.0 percentage points to 6.2%. Dia Kensetsu Co. jumped two slots to second place with a 3.6% share, up 1.0 point, followed by Towa Real Estate Development Co. with 3.0%, down 0.5 point.

Mitsui Fudosan Co. dropped to fourth from second position with 2.9%, down 1.6 points. The firm's stable-supply policy prevented it from rapidly expanding its condominium supply.

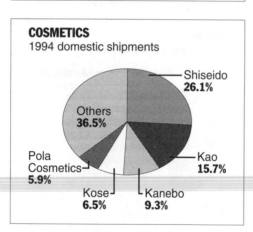

COPPER
1994 domestic production

Nippon Mining 19.2%
Mitsubishi Materials 17.7%
Sumitomo Metal Mining 11.2%
Mitsui Mining & Smelting 10.8%
Dowa Mining 7.8%
Others 33.3%

COPPER

Rankings in sales of copper in 1994 remained unchanged from 1993. All producers cut output last year, however, because tight global supplies of copper ore prevented them from buying on favorable terms. Slight changes in specific market shares seem to have depended on the extent to which individual firms cut production.

Top producer Nippon Mining & Metals Co. raised its share by 0.6 of a percentage point to 19.2%, while second-ranked Mitsubishi Materials Corp. lost 0.6 of a point to 17.7%. Sumitomo Metal Mining Co. held third at 11.2%, down 0.1 point, followed by Mitsui Mining & Smelting Co. at 10.8%, up 0.2. Domestic sales of copper last year totaled 1,358,939 metric tons, down 2.6% from 1993.

COSMETICS
1994 domestic shipments

Shiseido 26.1%
Kao 15.7%
Kanebo 9.3%
Kose 6.5%
Pola Cosmetics 5.9%
Others 36.5%

COSMETICS

The combined market share of five major cosmetics makers fell by 3.7 percentage points to 63.5% in 1994. This indicates a steady growth in market share for small and midsize firms, which typically offer products such as less-abrasive or wholly natural cosmetics, selling by mail order and personal networking. The overall market saw no major hit product emerge.

Shiseido Co. remained the market leader in 1994, though it dropped 1 percentage point of share to 26.1%. Second-ranked Kao Corp. raised its share by 0.2 of a point to 15.7%, while Kanebo Ltd., ranked third, saw its share fall by 1.7 points to 9.3%.

Price cutting is likely to effect changes in the market share rankings of cosmetics makers.

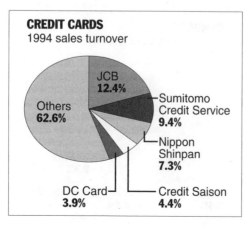

CREDIT CARDS
1994 sales turnover

JCB 12.4%
Sumitomo Credit Service 9.4%
Nippon Shinpan 7.3%
Credit Saison 4.4%
DC Card 3.9%
Others 62.6%

CREDIT CARDS

Credit card usage rose 4.5% to 13.47 trillion yen in 1994 after staying flat in 1993, according to a Nihon Keizai Shimbun survey. The gain appears to stem from more young people saying charge it and rising discount store sales in contrast to the continuing decline in business at department stores and supermarkets. The top three Japanese firms held their ground in market share rankings. JCB ranked first with a 12.4% share and Sumitomo Credit Service Co. placed second with 9.5%, followed by Nippon Shinpan Co.'s 7.3%. They kept their edge with extensive networks of businesses accepting their cards and thorough customer service. They should maintain their market leadership for some time, industry watchers say.

CRUDE STEEL

Fiscal 1994 crude steel output by Japan's steelmakers grew 4.4% to 101.38 million tons, topping 100 million for the first time in three years. Exports dropped 3.6% to 23.62 million tons due to the strong yen. Shipments to construction firms, automobile and home electric appliance manufacturers increased.

Nippon Steel Corp. produced 26.57 million tons, up 5.7% year on year and its market share rose 0.3 percentage point to 26.2%. NKK Corp. was second with an 11.1% market share, down 0.1 point, followed by Sumitomo Metal Industries Ltd. with 10.4%, up 0.1 point. Kobe Steel Ltd., ranked fifth, cut output by 360,000 tons because its facilities were damaged by the Great Hanshin Earthquake of Jan. 17.

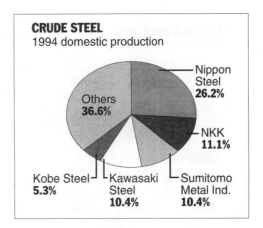

CRUDE STEEL
1994 domestic production

- Nippon Steel 26.2%
- NKK 11.1%
- Sumitomo Metal Ind. 10.4%
- Kawasaki Steel 10.4%
- Kobe Steel 5.3%
- Others 36.6%

DOOR-TO-DOOR DELIVERY

The number of parcels delivered door-to-door in fiscal 1994 rose 6.6% year on year to 1,318.3 million. The rise was due to brisk demand from corporate clients, including mail-order firms. Yamato Transport Co. held onto the lead with a 44.6% market share, up 0.3 of a point from the previous year. Its expansion of services helped increase orders from corporate clients. Second-ranked Nippon Express Co. saw its share fall for the third straight year, shrinking 1.0 point to 25.2%. The all-round transport firm lost out to Yamato in winning corporate orders. Footwork Express Co. retained third place with a 9.1% share, up 0.3 point, on the strength of its sales expansion campaign.

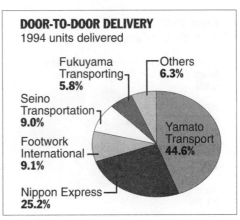

DOOR-TO-DOOR DELIVERY
1994 units delivered

- Fukuyama Transporting 5.8%
- Others 6.3%
- Seino Transportation 9.0%
- Footwork International 9.1%
- Nippon Express 25.2%
- Yamato Transport 44.6%

EDIBLE OILS

Sales of edible vegetable oils (excluding palm oil) totaled 1,774,000 tons in 1994, growing 1.3% despite weak demand during the unusually hot summer. Thanks to strong sales of canola oil for consumer use, Nisshin Oil Mills Ltd. retained the largest market share at 21.4%, down 0.2 of a percentage point from 1993.

Honen Corp. held the second-largest share at 13.7%, also down 0.2 of a point, on the strength of its marketing power for commercial-use products. Ajinomoto Co. kept third place with 13.2% of the market, down 0.1 point, supported by favorable consumer demand. Imports grew 27% from 1993, to 99,000 tons, thanks to the strong yen; that slightly cut into the shares of the five market leaders.

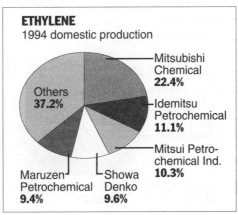

EDIBLE OILS
1994 domestic sales

- Nisshin Oil Mills 21.4%
- Honen 13.7%
- Ajinomoto 13.2%
- Showa Sangyo 10.0%
- Yoshihara Oil Mill 9.5%
- Others 32.2%

ETHYLENE

Domestic production of ethylene totaled 6,124,000 tons in 1994, up 6.1% over the previous year for the first gain in three years, according to a Nikkei survey. The unexpectedly large jump in output was due to a mild recovery in the domestic economy, a steep increase in exports to Southeast Asia and the unusually hot summer, analysts say.

Mitsubishi Chemical Corp., created through the October merger of Mitsubishi Petrochemical Co. and Mitsubishi Kasei Corp., accounted for 22.4% of total output, up 1.1 points over their combined share in 1993.

Idemitsu Petrochemical Co. ranked second with an 11.1% share, down 1.1 points. Third-place Mitsui Petrochemical Industries Ltd. increased its share by 0.8 point to 10.3%.

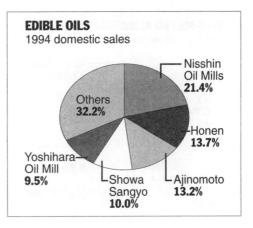

ETHYLENE
1994 domestic production

- Mitsubishi Chemical 22.4%
- Idemitsu Petrochemical 11.1%
- Mitsui Petrochemical Ind. 10.3%
- Showa Denko 9.6%
- Maruzen Petrochemical 9.4%
- Others 37.2%

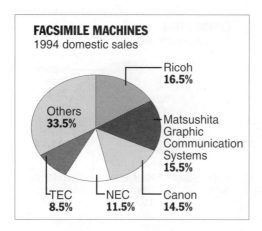

FACSIMILE MACHINES
1994 domestic sales

- Ricoh **16.5%**
- Matsushita Graphic Communication Systems **15.5%**
- Canon **14.5%**
- NEC **11.5%**
- TEC **8.5%**
- Others **33.5%**

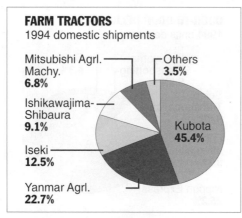

FARM TRACTORS
1994 domestic shipments

- Mitsubishi Agrl. Machy. **6.8%**
- Others **3.5%**
- Ishikawajima-Shibaura **9.1%**
- Kubota **45.4%**
- Iseki **12.5%**
- Yanmar Agrl. **22.7%**

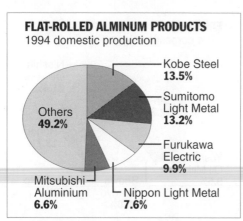

FLAT-ROLLED ALMINUM PRODUCTS
1994 domestic production

- Kobe Steel **13.5%**
- Sumitomo Light Metal **13.2%**
- Furukawa Electric **9.9%**
- Nippon Light Metal **7.6%**
- Mitsubishi Aluminium **6.6%**
- Others **49.2%**

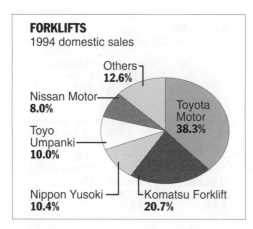

FORKLIFTS
1994 domestic sales

- Others **12.6%**
- Nissan Motor **8.0%**
- Toyo Umpanki **10.0%**
- Nippon Yusoki **10.4%**
- Komatsu Forklift **20.7%**
- Toyota Motor **38.3%**

FACSIMILE MACHINES

Domestic sales of facsimile machines in 1994 jumped by 16.7% year on year to 210 billion yen. Sales of business-use products leveled off due to slow replacement demand during the prolonged recession. In contrast, growing sales of personal-use models with cordless phone or answering machine functions boosted the overall market.

Ricoh Co. stayed on top as sales of two new laser plain paper models increased, although its share was unchanged at 16.5%. Matsushita Graphic Communication Systems Inc. stood second after shedding 0.5 percentage point to 15.5%.

Third-ranked Canon Inc. also saw its share fall 0.5 point, to 14.5%, despite brisk sales of its new plain paper and multifunction models.

FARM TRACTORS

The domestic market for farm tractors in 1994 saw no change in rankings among the five leading producers, which held a combined share of over 95%. Market leader Kubota Corp. raised its share by 0.3 of a point to 45.4% on sales of new models. Second-ranked Yanmar Agricultural Equipment Co. held 22.7%, up 0.1, followed by Iseki & Co. with 12.5%, down 1.0.

Domestic shipments of tractors totaled 161,788 in 1994, up 12.1%, according to a Nikkei survey. Japanese preference for domestic rice and a bumper crop last year prompted farmers to replace equipment. Imports of lower priced large tractors have shown rapid growth, though these are mainly used in Hokkaido. Tractor demand remains strong.

FLAT-ROLLED ALUMINUM PRODUCTS

Domestic output of sheet and extruded aluminum amounted to an all-time high of 2,355,110 tons in 1994, up 9.2%, reflecting sharp growth in beverage can and air conditioner fin demand due to the hot summer.

Kobe Steel Ltd. regained the top spot. It boosted output by 20.6% to raise its share 1.3 points to 13.5%, largely because of expanded output of materials for cans at its domestic joint venture with Aluminum Co. of America (Alcoa).

Sumitomo Light Metal Industries Ltd., slid to second place, though it upped its share 0.4 of a point to 13.2%. Furukawa Electric Co. remained third at 9.9%, down 0.3 of a point, followed by Nippon Light Metal Co. at 7.6%, down 0.9 of a point.

FORKLIFTS

Domestic forklift sales inched up 0.1% in 1994 to 69,370 vehicles, ending a fall that saw sales drop from a peak of 103,862 units in 1991 to 69,299 in 1993, according to a Nikkei survey. Toyota Motor Corp. added 1.3 points for a market share of 38.3%, leader for the 29th straight year.

Analysts say Toyota overwhelms the competition through its dealership network. The company argues that it also competes on a price basis, thanks to strict cost cutting.

Second-ranked Komatsu Forklift Co. lost 0.7 of a percentage point to 20.7%. It produces more value-added forklifts, seeking profit rather than market share, the firm says.

Nippon Yusoki Co., third, fell 0.3 point to 10.4%, while Toyo Umpanki Co., fourth, lost 0.7 point to 10.0%.

4-MEGABIT DRAMS

The domestic market for 4-megabit dynamic random-access memory chips grew 60% in 1994 from the previous year to 360 billion yen, thanks to strong demand from makers of personal computers, printers and other equipment. Imports accounted for 20% of the total, up 5 points.

Hitachi Ltd. retained its leading position with a 19.5% share, down 2.0 points, followed by NEC Corp. which saw its share fall 1.0 point to 13.0%. Toshiba Corp. came in third with 12.5%, down 5.0.

Samsung Electronics Co. of South Korea ranked fourth with a 6.0 point share gain to 12.0%, its first appearance in the top five. It was the only leading maker to score a share increase.

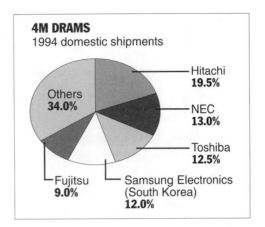

4M DRAMS
1994 domestic shipments

- Hitachi **19.5%**
- NEC **13.0%**
- Toshiba **12.5%**
- Samsung Electronics (South Korea) **12.0%**
- Fujitsu **9.0%**
- Others **34.0%**

FROZEN FOOD

Sales of frozen food in 1994 rose to 774.2 billion yen, up 4.2% from the previous year, according to a Nikkei survey.

Nichirei Corp. retained top spot with a 20.0% share, up 0.4 point. The increase was mainly attributed to brisk sales of its new home-use frozen croquettes, which can be quickly warmed up in a microwave oven. Katokichi Co. saw its share rise 0.6 point to 12.0% and strengthened its grip on second place, thanks to the popularity of its low-cost frozen noodle and rice products.

Ajinomoto Co. held down third spot with 11.1%, up 0.1 point and only 0.7 point ahead of Nippon Suisan Kaisha Ltd., primarily a seafood producer whose market share remained flat last year.

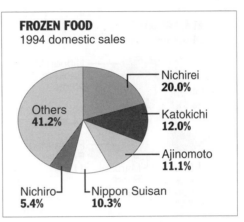

FROZEN FOOD
1994 domestic sales

- Nichirei **20.0%**
- Katokichi **12.0%**
- Ajinomoto **11.1%**
- Nippon Suisan **10.3%**
- Nichiro **5.4%**
- Others **41.2%**

GASOLINE

Domestic sales of gasoline totaled 50,577,000 kiloliters in fiscal 1994, up 4.1% over the previous year, as the unusually hot summer increased the use of car air-conditioners. But earnings at oil firms fell due to price-cutting ahead of the liberalization of gasoline imports.

Market share rankings were unchanged. In first place, Nippon Oil Co. grabbed 16.4% of the market, down 0.3 point. Idemitsu Kosan Co. was second with 14.3% and third-ranked Showa Shell Sekiyu K.K. took 12.5% for the second year, both unchanged from the preceding year. Cosmo Oil Co. was fourth with 12.0%, down 0.1 point. While the larger oil firms failed to increase sales as they struggled to maintain prices, some smaller ones saw market shares expand.

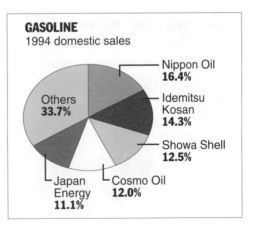

GASOLINE
1994 domestic sales

- Nippon Oil **16.4%**
- Idemitsu Kosan **14.3%**
- Showa Shell **12.5%**
- Cosmo Oil **12.0%**
- Japan Energy **11.1%**
- Others **33.7%**

GOLF CLUBS

Shipments of golf clubs in fiscal 1994 totaled 10,720,000 units, down 7.8% from fiscal 1993 and the fourth straight year of decline, according to a Nikkei survey. The market showed two tendencies: one toward high-function, high-value-added clubs and the other to low-tech, low-priced products.

Market leader Mizuno Corp., boosting shipments of low-priced clubs and increased its share 2.8 percentage points to 31.2%. Second-ranked Maruman Golf Co., rebuilding after two straight years of red ink, limited shipments, which cut its share by 2.3 points to 20.5%.

Bridgestone Sports Co. held onto third place at 13.0%, up 0.1 point, while Sumitomo Rubber Industries Ltd. gained 1.0 point to take fourth with an 11.3% share.

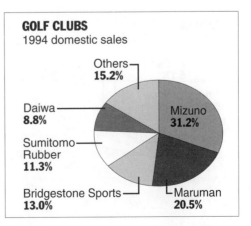

GOLF CLUBS
1994 domestic sales

- Others **15.2%**
- Daiwa **8.8%**
- Sumitomo Rubber **11.3%**
- Bridgestone Sports **13.0%**
- Mizuno **31.2%**
- Maruman **20.5%**

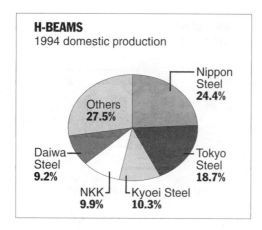

H-BEAMS
1994 domestic production

- Nippon Steel **24.4%**
- Others **27.5%**
- Tokyo Steel **18.7%**
- Kyoei Steel **10.3%**
- NKK **9.9%**
- Daiwa Steel **9.2%**

H-BEAMS

Nippon Steel Corp. raised its market share in H-beams, a key construction material, by 4.2 percentage points to 24.4% in fiscal 1994, dethroning Tokyo Steel Mfg. Co. to take over segment leadership, according to a Nikkei survey. Blast-furnace steelmakers increased their share of the on the back of intensified streamlining efforts and lower materials costs with the strong yen. Overall domestic production of H-beams stood at 5.869 million tons last year, marking a gain of 9.7% year on year.

Electric furnace maker Tokyo Steel lost 4.4 percentage points to 18.7, while Kyoei Steel & Structural Ltd., a subsidiary of Sumitomo Metal Industries Ltd., placed third with a 10.3% share, a gain of 4.5 points.

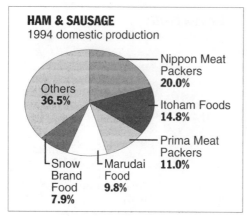

HAM & SAUSAGE
1994 domestic production

- Nippon Meat Packers **20.0%**
- Others **36.5%**
- Itoham Foods **14.8%**
- Prima Meat Packers **11.0%**
- Marudai Food **9.8%**
- Snow Brand Food **7.9%**

HAM & SAUSAGE

Domestic production of ham and sausage in 1994 rose a mere 0.4% year on year to 548,090 tons, after slipping slightly the previous year. In value terms, however, production dropped from a year earlier due to tough price competition, particularly from supermarkets' private brands. The rankings of the five major producers remained unchanged.

Nippon Meat Packers Inc. stayed on top with a market share of 20%, up 0.5 of a percentage point. The company has the largest number of delivery trucks and salespersons in the industry. Itoham Foods Inc. retained second place with a 14.8% share, unchanged from a year ago.

Third-ranked Prima Meat Packers Ltd. saw its share fall by 1 point to 11%.

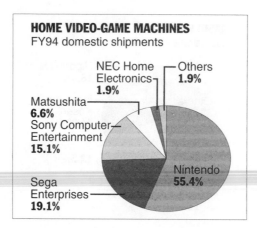

HOME VIDEO-GAME MACHINES
FY94 domestic shipments

- NEC Home Electronics **1.9%**
- Others **1.9%**
- Matsushita **6.6%**
- Sony Computer Entertainment **15.1%**
- Nintendo **55.4%**
- Sega Enterprises **19.1%**

HOME VIDEO-GAME MACHINES

Domestic shipments of home video-game machines in 1994 are estimated at 5.29 million, up 7.9% from the previous year, according to a Nikkei survey. The rise is attributed to brisk demand for 32-bit machines with enhanced graphics capabilities.

Although Nintendo Co. suffered a sharp 20-point drop in its share to 55.4%, it still commanded an overwhelming 55.4% of the market. Sega Enterprises Ltd. held second place with 19.1%, up 7.6 points. Sony Computer Entertainment Inc., which debuted on the market with its 32-bit PlayStation machine, ranked third at 15.1%.

Matsushita Electric Industrial Co. moved up one rank to fourth, raising its share 4.5 percentage points to 6.6%.

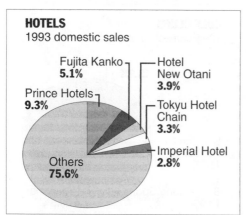

HOTELS
1993 domestic sales

- Fujita Kanko **5.1%**
- Hotel New Otani **3.9%**
- Prince Hotels **9.3%**
- Tokyu Hotel Chain **3.3%**
- Imperial Hotel **2.8%**
- Others **75.6%**

HOTELS

Hotel revenues toppled, for the second straight year, 4.5% to 1,647.6 billion yen last fiscal year. Though the average occupancy rate, which has been on the decline for several years, is bottoming out, the average room price continues to ebb. Sales of all the top five hoteliers saw sales fall over the past year.

Top-ranked Prince Hotels Inc. saw its market share rise 0.4 of a percentage point to 9.3% thanks to sound business at its Shinagawa Prince Hotel New Tower, which features low prices. Fujita Kanko Inc. remained second with 5.1%, up 0.2 of a point, on the strength of diversified operations. Third-ranked Hotel New Otani shed 0.1 share point to 3.9%.

HYDRAULIC EXCAVATORS

Domestic shipments of hydraulic excavators totaled 44,369 units in 1994, up 11.7% from 1993 and the first increase in four years, according to a Nikkei survey which this year switched from production as the key index. An increase in public works projects in a government economic stimulus package helped boost demand for construction machinery.

Komatsu Ltd. kept the top spot at 30.3%, down 0.4 of a point from 1993, followed by Hitachi Construction Machinery Co., which rode sales of new models to gain 1.4 points to 25.0%. Shin Caterpillar Mitsubishi Ltd. stayed in third at 18.0%, gaining 1.1 points with its new Rega series.

Kobe Steel Ltd. held on to fourth at 13.0%, down 0.1 point.

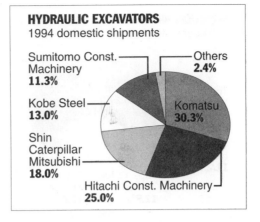

HYDRAULIC EXCAVATORS
1994 domestic shipments

- Sumitomo Const. Machinery **11.3%**
- Kobe Steel **13.0%**
- Shin Caterpillar Mitsubishi **18.0%**
- Hitachi Const. Machinery **25.0%**
- Komatsu **30.3%**
- Others **2.4%**

ICE CREAM

Domestic sales of ice cream, including imports, in 1994 were estimated to be 420 billion yen, up 12.4%. While the blistering summer contributed to overall sales, the inability of producers to meet the sizzling demand was reflected in changes in market share.

Ezaki Glico Co., which remained the top Japanese purveyor, saw its share down by 0.5 of a point to 11.3%. Morinaga Milk Industry Co. was in a virtual tie losing 0.3 of a point, unable to produce enough to meet demand.

Meanwhile, Meiji Milk Products Co. enjoyed a 19% rise in sales thanks to its new products, gaining 0.2 of a point to 11.2%. Snow Brand Milk Products Co. wasn't frozen out either thanks to revived demand for premium ice cream.

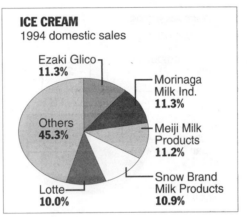

ICE CREAM
1994 domestic sales

- Ezaki Glico **11.3%**
- Others **45.3%**
- Lotte **10.0%**
- Morinaga Milk Ind. **11.3%**
- Meiji Milk Products **11.2%**
- Snow Brand Milk Products **10.9%**

IMPORTED CARS

Sales of imported cars rose 41.6% in 1994 to 276,161 units. Sales of U.S. cars swelled on lower prices made possible by the yen's climb. Honda of America Mfg. witnessed a sharp sales rise to capture a leading 17.1% share of Japan's imported car market, up 3.3 percentage points.

Chrysler Corp. and Ford Motor Co. both saw sales in Japan more than double from 1993.

Meanwhile, overall sales of German cars fell to make up only 43.8% of the market, almost half the 80% share of 1985. The Volkswagen-Audi group had the second biggest share of 12.5%, down 0.3 point, even though it led foreign automakers in sales with 34,621 units, up 39.2%. Mercedes-Benz AG was third with a 12.1% share, down 2.2 points.

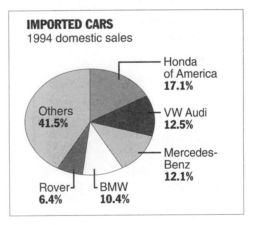

IMPORTED CARS
1994 domestic sales

- Others **41.5%**
- Rover **6.4%**
- BMW **10.4%**
- Honda of America **17.1%**
- VW Audi **12.5%**
- Mercedes-Benz **12.1%**

INDUSTRIAL ROBOTS

Production of industrial robots recovered to some 400 billion yen in 1994 for the first time in two years, up 1.5% from 1993, thanks to brisk exports to the U.S. and Southeast Asia, says the Japan Robot Association. Production of robots used to make telecommunications equipment and automobiles particularly increased.

Industry leader Matsushita Electric Industrial Co. manufactured 24.0% of the sector's output, up 3.8 percentage points. Strong demand from makers of telecommunications gear boosted its output 19.0% from 1993. Second-ranking Fuji Machine Mfg. Co. also increased share, by 1.8 points to 14.0%. Fanuc Ltd., third at 12.5%, up 0.6 of a point, enjoyed brisk exports to U.S. automakers.

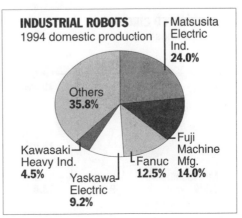

INDUSTRIAL ROBOTS
1994 domestic production

- Others **35.8%**
- Kawasaki Heavy Ind. **4.5%**
- Yaskawa Electric **9.2%**
- Fanuc **12.5%**
- Fuji Machine Mfg. **14.0%**
- Matsusita Electric Ind. **24.0%**

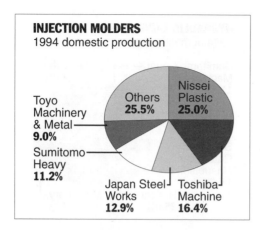

INJECTION MOLDERS
1994 domestic production

Nissei Plastic 25.0%
Others 25.5%
Toyo Machinery & Metal 9.0%
Sumitomo Heavy 11.2%
Japan Steel Works 12.9%
Toshiba Machine 16.4%

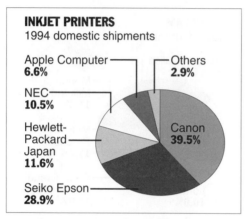

INKJET PRINTERS
1994 domestic shipments

Apple Computer 6.6%
Others 2.9%
NEC 10.5%
Hewlett-Packard Japan 11.6%
Canon 39.5%
Seiko Epson 28.9%

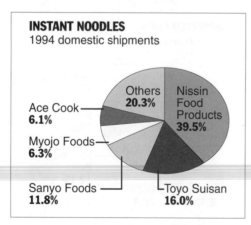

INSTANT NOODLES
1994 domestic shipments

Others 20.3%
Nissin Food Products 39.5%
Ace Cook 6.1%
Myojo Foods 6.3%
Sanyo Foods 11.8%
Toyo Suisan 16.0%

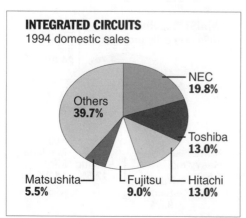

INTEGRATED CIRCUITS
1994 domestic sales

NEC 19.8%
Others 39.7%
Toshiba 13.0%
Matsushita 5.5%
Fujitsu 9.0%
Hitachi 13.0%

INJECTION MOLDERS

Output of plastic injection molding machines in 1994 dipped 0.2% from the year earlier to 11,183 units. While slow corporate capital investment dampened domestic sales, exports were strong because more and more manufacturers transferred operations overseas.

Top firms, in terms of market share, managed to increase sales in the year by introducing cheaper models.

Market leader Nissei Plastic Industrial Co. widened its share by 1.0 percentage point to 25%. Second-ranked Toshiba Machine Co. increased its share by 1.9 points to 16.4%, while Japan Steel Works Ltd. saw its share rise 0.9 point to 12.9% for the third largest market share.

INKJET PRINTERS

Domestic shipments of inkjet printers in 1994 totaled 760,000 units, a sharp 94.9% jump from 1993. The rise was spurred mainly by demand for color inkjet printers, particularly among users of the Windows operating environment for personal computers.

Canon Inc. maintained top position, with a 39.5% share of the market, despite losing 9.2 percentage points. Seiko Epson Corp. recorded a 3.3-point increase to 28.9%, followed by Hewlett-Packard Japan Ltd., which lost 14.0 points to finish third with 11.6%. Canon released its 120,000-yen color inkjet printer last year, prompting fierce price competition. NEC Corp. also released a color printer in 1994, and seized a 10.5% share its first year in the market.

INSTANT NOODLES

Domestic shipments of instant noodles in fiscal 1994 stood at 5.037 billion packages, up barely 0.3% from the previous year, reported the Japan Convenience Foods Industry Association. While a fiercely hot summer depressed noodles in bags by nearly 6% year on year, semi-fresh noodles soared more than 30% from the previous year.

Nissin Food Products Co. remained the market leader with a commanding 39.5% share, up 2.0 percentage points, thanks to brisk sales of its semi-fresh noodle series.

Toyo Suisan Kaisha Ltd. held onto second with a 16% share, unchanged from a year ago, while Sanyo Foods Co. retained the third place with 11.8%, down 3.0 points. Fourth-ranked Myojo Foods Co. shed 2.0 share points to 6.3%.

INTEGRATED CIRCUITS

The Japanese market for integrated circuits (ICs) grew 16.7% in 1994 to 2.45 trillion yen. Imports accounted for 25% of the market, up 3 percentage points.

NEC Corp. maintained the top spot, with micro controllers, ASICs and analog ICs all contributing to the effort. Despite in-house demand for the chips, used in its 98-series PCs, NEC's market share fell 1.5 percentage points to 19.8%, eroded by imports.

Hitachi Ltd. tied Toshiba Corp. for second, each holding 13% of the market. Focusing on 16M DRAMs, Toshiba apparently became the top supplier of memory chips. Fujitsu was fourth. Intel Corp. and Samsung Co. enjoyed strong sales among foreign semiconductor manufacturers.

INTERNATIONAL PHONE SERVICES

Japan's international telephone service market totaled 286.4 billion yen in fiscal 1994, up 5.1%, according to a Nikkei survey. Industry analysts suggest the pace of growth may be slowing if one compares this number to 1993's double-digit gain.

Kokusai Denshin Denwa Co. (KDD) saw its share drop 1.9 points to 68.6%, but the bleeding seems to have eased in view of a 3.7 point fall in fiscal 1993. International Digital Communications Inc. (IDC) gained 1.1 points to 16.3%, and International Telecom Japan Inc. (ITJ) expanded its share by 0.8 of a point to 15.1%.

Those figures reflect a tacit understanding that KDD should maintain a 70% share, according to industry sources.

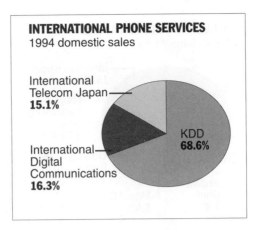

INTERNATIONAL PHONE SERVICES
1994 domestic sales

International Telecom Japan **15.1%**
International Digital Communications **16.3%**
KDD **68.6%**

JAPANESE WORD PROCESSORS

Sales of Japanese-language word processors fell 5% in 1994 from a year earlier to 2.11 million units, marking a year-on-year decline for the third straight year, according to a Nikkei survey. The decline was sharper than in 1993 due to phenomenal sales growth in low-priced personal computers.

Sharp Corp. stayed on top with a 21.0% share, up 1 percentage point, thanks to brisk sales of its home-use models. NEC Corp. came in second with 15.4%, up 0.9 point. Fujitsu Ltd. jumped to third place with 14.3%, up 0.8 point, after enhancing its lineup of home-use models.

The combined share of the top five makers grew 3.4 percentage points as lower-ranking firms suffered sluggish sales in a dwindling market.

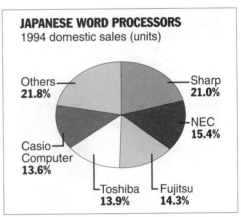

JAPANESE WORD PROCESSORS
1994 domestic sales (units)

Others **21.8%**
Sharp **21.0%**
NEC **15.4%**
Casio Computer **13.6%**
Toshiba **13.9%**
Fujitsu **14.3%**

LAUNDRY DETERGENT

Domestic shipments of laundry detergent edged up 1.3% to 720,886 tons in 1994. Kao Corp. remained the largest producer, but its market share slipped 2.0 percentage points to 35.0%. Lion Corp. roared to a solid hold on second with its share unchanged at 27.0%. Procter & Gamble Corp. lost 1.0 percentage point to 17.0%.

Complicating the market is the entry of private brands. Supermarket giant Daiei Inc., got a 1.5% foot in the door thanks to strong sales of its house brand laundry soap. Major manufacturers have no choice but to combat the rising tide of private labels by improving their concentrated detergents. They have been adding value, for example, by giving more cleaning power to ever smaller amounts of laundry soap.

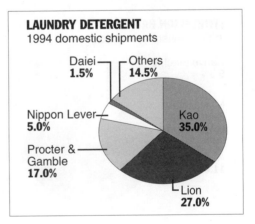

LAUNDRY DETERGENT
1994 domestic shipments

Daiei **1.5%**
Others **14.5%**
Nippon Lever **5.0%**
Procter & Gamble **17.0%**
Kao **35.0%**
Lion **27.0%**

LEASING

The total value of leasing contracts signed in fiscal 1994 grew 3.1% from the previous year to ¥6.16 trillion, the first year-on-year increase since fiscal 1991, said the Japan Leasing Association. The surge is attributed to the growing need to replace information-related equipment, which accounts for 40% of the leasing market. Orix Corp. remained the top leasing company with 6.0% of the market, up 0.3 percentage point. The firm's continued success is attributed to its powerful sales network. Second-ranked Japan Leasing Corp. saw its market share increase 0.5 point to 4.7%. SB Leasing Co. held third place with a 4.5% share, up 0.5 point, followed by Century Leasing System Inc. with 3.4%, up 0.2 point, and Hitachi Leasing Ltd. unchanged at 3.3%.

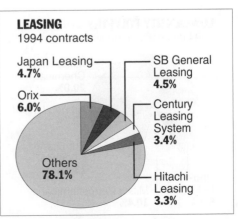

LEASING
1994 contracts

Japan Leasing **4.7%**
SB General Leasing **4.5%**
Orix **6.0%**
Century Leasing System **3.4%**
Others **78.1%**
Hitachi Leasing **3.3%**

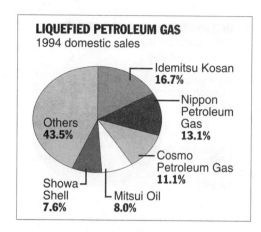

LIQUEFIED PETROLEUM GAS
1994 domestic sales

- Idemitsu Kosan **16.7%**
- Nippon Petroleum Gas **13.1%**
- Cosmo Petroleum Gas **11.1%**
- Mitsui Oil **8.0%**
- Showa Shell **7.6%**
- Others **43.5%**

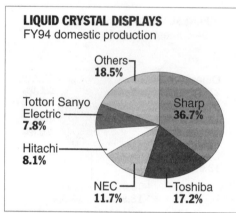

LIQUID CRYSTAL DISPLAYS
FY94 domestic production

- Others **18.5%**
- Tottori Sanyo Electric **7.8%**
- Hitachi **8.1%**
- NEC **11.7%**
- Toshiba **17.2%**
- Sharp **36.7%**

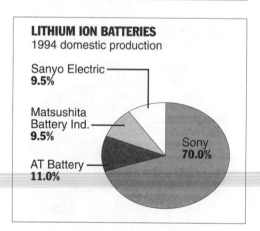

LITHIUM ION BATTERIES
1994 domestic production

- Sanyo Electric **9.5%**
- Matsushita Battery Ind. **9.5%**
- AT Battery **11.0%**
- Sony **70.0%**

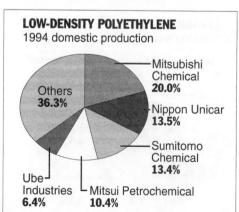

LOW-DENSITY POLYETHYLENE
1994 domestic production

- Mitsubishi Chemical **20.0%**
- Nippon Unicar **13.5%**
- Sumitomo Chemical **13.4%**
- Mitsui Petrochemical **10.4%**
- Ube Industries **6.4%**
- Others **36.3%**

LIQUEFIED PETROLEUM GAS

Domestic sales of liquefied petroleum gas (LPG) fell 1.6% from a year earlier to 19.56 million tons in fiscal 1994 due to the sweltering summer heat of last year and a rise in import prices. The summer heat wave cut into demand for household LPG, while the import price hike forced industrial users to shift to other fuels. Idemitsu Kosan Co. remained market leader with 16.7%, up 0.2 of a percentage point due to an increase in sales to Idemitsu Petrochemical Co. Nippon Petroleum Gas Co. stayed at second with a 13.1% share, up 0.1, on brisk sales of LPG as a fuel for automobiles, including taxis. Third-ranked Cosmo Petroleum Gas Co. lost 0.4 of a point for an 11.1% share, primarily because liquefied natural gas replaced LPG as a power generation fuel.

LIQUID CRYSTAL DISPLAYS

Domestic output of liquid crystal displays rose 33.3% to 640 billion yen in fiscal 1994 on strong worldwide sales of notebook computers and growing demand for car navigation monitors, according to a Nikkei survey. Thin-film transistor (TFT) panels are estimated to have topped 50% of the market.

Sharp Corp. held on to the top spot with a 36.7% share, down 2.4 points from fiscal 1993. Second-ranked Toshiba Corp. raised its share 5.7 points to 17.2%, and NEC Corp. stood at third with a 2.9 point gain to 11.7%.

Hitachi Ltd. rose to fourth place with 8.1%, up 2.1 points, followed by Tottori Sanyo Electric Co. with 7.8%, up 3.9 points.

LITHIUM ION BATTERIES

Domestic output of lithium ion batteries jumped by 200% to 12 million units in 1994, and demand is expected to continue outstripping supply, industry sources say. Sony Corp., which held a monopoly in 1993, saw its share drop 30 percentage points in 1994 as a number of rivals entered the market.

In 1995, output of the batteries, for use in such devices as notebook computers and cellular phones, is expected to grow another 200% to 36 million units.

However, the eight firms now competing are likely to have difficulty raising output capacity to keep up with demand because of the high degree of technical sophistication required in the manufacturing process, say the sources.

LOW-DENSITY POLYETHYLENE

Domestic output of low-density polyethylene totaled 1.83 million tons in 1994, up 5.4% year on year. The rise was due to a 10% rise in exports, which made up just over 10% of shipments.

Mitsubishi Chemical Corp., born of the October 1994 merger of Mitsubishi Petrochemical Co. and Mitsubishi Kasei Corp., took the lead with a 20.0% share, or 0.3 of a percentage point more than the combined 1993 shares of the two firms.

Nippon Unicar Co. dropped to second at 13.5%, down 0.4. Sumitomo Chemical Corp. saw its share jump 2.3 points to 13.4% on being commissioned to produce linear low-density polyethylene for Ube Industries Ltd., which closed its own plant in October 1993.

MACHINING CENTERS

The value of machining centers produced in Japan in 1994 totaled 129,222 million yen, down 9.1% from 1993, according to a Nikkei survey. Makino Milling Machine Co. jumped from fifth place to third, increasing its market share by 3.6 percentage points to 12.0%. Yamazaki Mazak Corp. remained the market leader with 19.5%, up 3.0 points. Mori Seiki Co. followed with 15.5%, up 2.3 points.

The top three manufacturers accounted for 47.0% of the market, up 8.9 points from a year ago.

Even as the strong yen shaves points off the international competitiveness of Japanese manufacturers, the U.S. market for machining centers has turned down sharply and demand is not expected to pick up anytime soon.

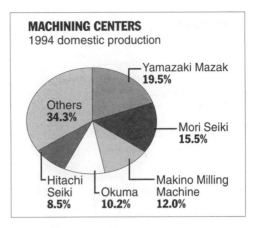

MACHINING CENTERS
1994 domestic production

- Yamazaki Mazak **19.5%**
- Mori Seiki **15.5%**
- Makino Milling Machine **12.0%**
- Okuma **10.2%**
- Hitachi Seiki **8.5%**
- Others **34.3%**

MAINFRAME COMPUTERS

Growth in the market for mainframe computers decelerated in 1994 for the second year in a row due to ongoing downsizing at corporations. Newly installed mainframes amounted to 12.02 trillion yen in value, up 1.8% from the year before. The increase fell short of the 2.0% expansion seen in 1993.

According to a Nikkei survey, Fujitsu Ltd. remained Japan's top maker of mainframes with a 25.5% market share, up 0.3 point. It expanded the share by introducing higher cost-performance models. Second ranked IBM Japan Ltd. also increased its share by 0.1 point to 23.7% through the introduction of lower-priced models. Third-ranked Hitachi Ltd. saw its share shrink by 0.1 point to 17.7%.

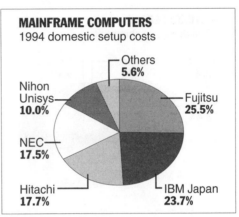

MAINFRAME COMPUTERS
1994 domestic setup costs

- Others **5.6%**
- Fujitsu **25.5%**
- Nihon Unisys **10.0%**
- NEC **17.5%**
- Hitachi **17.7%**
- IBM Japan **23.7%**

MEN'S OUTERWEAR

Domestic sales of men's outerwear fell 4.2% to 1,491.7 billion yen in 1994, according to a Nikkei survey. The decline is attributed to decreased sales of expensive suits, due to growing popularity for less costly fashions and a consumer preference for more casual designs.

Onward Kashiyama Co. retained the top spot, with its share unchanged at 5.7%. The firm enjoyed brisk demand for suits and casual wear targeted at men in their 20s and 30s. D'urban Inc. ranked second at 2.9%, down 0.2 of a point.

Sanyo Shokai Ltd. saw its market share drop 0.6 of a percentage point to 2.4%, falling to fourth place from third. Changing place, Renown Inc. ranked third at 2.7%, down 0.2 point.

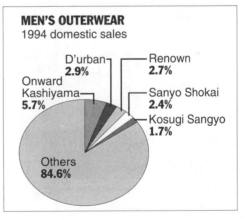

MEN'S OUTERWEAR
1994 domestic sales

- D'urban **2.9%**
- Renown **2.7%**
- Onward Kashiyama **5.7%**
- Sanyo Shokai **2.4%**
- Kosugi Sangyo **1.7%**
- Others **84.6%**

MINI-COMPONENT STEREOS

Domestic shipments of mini-component stereo systems rose 12.7% to 1.94 million units in 1994. Aiwa Co. led its rivals with a 26.4% market share. The firm enhanced its price competitiveness by shifting more production abroad. Kenwood Corp. moved up from third to second place with 16.5%, displacing Sony Corp., whose share fell to 14%.

Aiwa has remained the market leader for the past three years because of the popularity of its model able to display still images on the TV and another model with a 3-disc compact disc player. The company also sharply cut prices because overseas production now accounts for 80% of total output. Other firms were forced to challenge Aiwa by cutting prices.

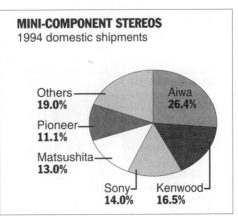

MINI-COMPONENT STEREOS
1994 domestic shipments

- Others **19.0%**
- Aiwa **26.4%**
- Pioneer **11.1%**
- Matsushita **13.0%**
- Sony **14.0%**
- Kenwood **16.5%**

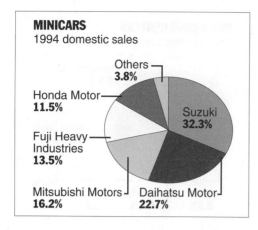

MINICARS
1994 domestic sales

Others **3.8%**
Honda Motor **11.5%**
Fuji Heavy Industries **13.5%**
Mitsubishi Motors **16.2%**
Daihatsu Motor **22.7%**
Suzuki **32.3%**

MINICARS

Domestic sales of minicars (engine displacement of 660cc or less) grew 2.2% to 1,616,316 vehicles in 1994. Although market shares remained unchanged, the popularity of sports utility vehicles and low-priced light trucks resulted in some changes in the overall picture.

Market leader Suzuki Motor Corp. expanded its share by 2.5 points to 32.3%, thanks to the lasting popularity of its Wagon R model. No. 2 Daihatsu Motor Co. saw its share shrink by 0.7 point due to sluggish sales of its mainline Mira.

Third-ranked Mitsubishi Motors Corp.'s share contracted 0.2 point to 16.2%. Strong sales of its sports utility vehicles were eclipsed by its weakened competitiveness in the lower-priced light-truck market.

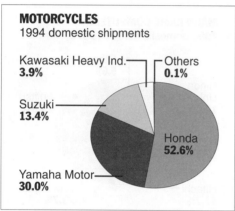

MOTORCYCLES
1994 domestic shipments

Kawasaki Heavy Ind. **3.9%**
Others **0.1%**
Suzuki **13.4%**
Honda **52.6%**
Yamaha Motor **30.0%**

MOTORCYCLES

Domestic motorcycle shipments declined 4.8% in 1994 to 1,194,000 vehicles, falling for a sixth straight year. The drop came on continued sluggish demand for scooters, especially 50cc models which make up 70% of the total market.

The rankings of the four major manufacturers remained unchanged, with their market shares well spread out. Honda Motor Co. lost 0.5 of a percentage point to take 52.6%; it saw a 22% falloff in shipments of motorcycles with engines displacing more than 400cc.

Yamaha Motor Co. boosted its second-place share to 30.0%, building on growth seen in 1993. Suzuki Motor Corp. enjoyed strong sales of new versions of its main models to gain 0.5 point to 13.4%.

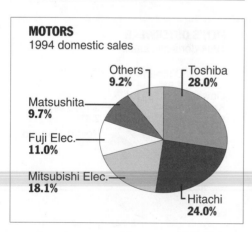

MOTORS
1994 domestic sales

Others **9.2%**
Toshiba **28.0%**
Matsushita **9.7%**
Fuji Elec. **11.0%**
Mitsubishi Elec. **18.1%**
Hitachi **24.0%**

MOTORS

Domestic sales of general-purpose motors grew 1.4% from a year earlier to 1.37 million units in 1994, marking the first year-on-year increase in four years. The surge is attributed to reviving demand for motors installed in manufacturing equipment and to brisk sales of motors for air conditioners in the wake of the sweltering summer heat last year.

There was no change in the ranking of the top five manufacturers. Their combined share stood at 90.8%, up 0.6 percentage point.

Toshiba Corp. held onto the top spot, although its share remained unchanged at 28.0%. Second-ranked Hitachi Ltd. gained 0.4 point to 24.0%. Mitsubishi Electric Corp. came in third with 18.1%, down 0.4 point.

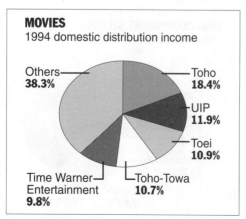

MOVIES
1994 domestic distribution income

Others **38.3%**
Toho **18.4%**
UIP **11.9%**
Toei **10.9%**
Toho-Towa **10.7%**
Time Warner Entertainment **9.8%**

MOVIES

Film distribution revenues in 1994 fell 10.7% to 64.15 billion yen, according to the Motion Picture Producers Association of Japan. The drop was attributed to the lack of mega-hit movies. The lone box office smash this year was "Heisei Tanuki Gassen Ponpoko," an animated movie released by Toho Co.

Toho raised its market share by 3.4 percentage points to 18.4 regaining top position. United International Pictures Far East Inc. dropped to second with 11.9%, down 8.1 points.

Toei Co. raised its share by 2.0 points to 10.9% and jumped to third place.

Japanese films' share of total revenues rose slightly to 40% in 1994 from 35%.

NC LATHES

Domestic output of numerically controlled lathes rose 7.5% to 134.69 billion yen in 1994, marking the first year-on-year gain in four years. The release of low-priced models early in the year served to boost demand as users moved away from high-end products.

Output rankings changed little, with Mori Seiki Co. gaining 0.9 share point to retain control of the largest share of the market at 22.3%. Coming a close second was Yamazaki Mazak Corp. which also posted a 0.9 point gain to take 21.9%, followed by Okuma Corp. with 15.4%.

Orders for NC lathes last year jumped 19.7% year on year to 170.67 billion yen, accounting for 50.7% of the growth in the entire machine-tool sector.

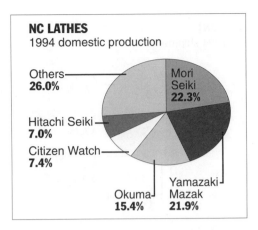

NC LATHES
1994 domestic production

Mori Seiki 22.3%
Others 26.0%
Hitachi Seiki 7.0%
Citizen Watch 7.4%
Okuma 15.4%
Yamazaki Mazak 21.9%

NYLON FIBER

Total output of nylon fiber in 1994 shrank 3.8% from a year ago to 245,700 tons, marking a decline for the fourth straight year. The fall is ascribed to continuing sluggish demand from such industrial users as auto and carpet makers.

Toray Industries Inc. remained the market leader with a 32.8% share, up 0.5 percentage point. Thanks to its diligent cost-cutting efforts, the firm was the only company to post profits in nylon fiber making operations.

Asahi Chemical Industry Co. moved up from third to second with 14.9%, down 0.6 point. Unitika Ltd. fell to third from second by losing 2.7 points to 14.6%. Both firms plan to restructure their nylon fiber divisions to score profits, even at the cost of a production cut.

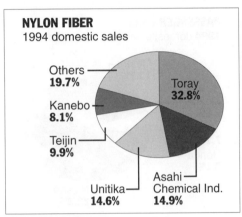

NYLON FIBER
1994 domestic sales

Toray 32.8%
Others 19.7%
Kanebo 8.1%
Teijin 9.9%
Unitika 14.6%
Asahi Chemical Ind. 14.9%

OPTICAL FIBER

Optical fiber shipments totaled 2.91 million kilometers in fiscal 1994, up 5.8%. But the growth rate was 7.1 percentage points smaller than in fiscal 1993, as development of the telecommunications infrastructure lags.

Sumitomo Electric Industries Ltd., Fujikura Ltd. and Furukawa Electric Co. retained the three largest shares, combining to take more than 80% of the market.

Among the five top makers, only Sumitomo Electric lost share. It remained the leader, however, with 31.7%, the industry's largest production facilities and strongest marketing power. NTT was seen buying more fiber from Siecor International Corp., as the U.S. manufacturer used the strong yen to hone its price competitiveness.

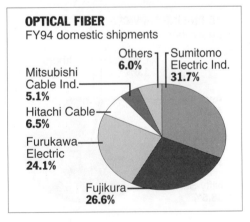

OPTICAL FIBER
FY94 domestic shipments

Others 6.0%
Sumitomo Electric Ind. 31.7%
Mitsubishi Cable Ind. 5.1%
Hitachi Cable 6.5%
Furukawa Electric 24.1%
Fujikura 26.6%

OVERSEAS TRAVEL

Bookings of overseas travel packages in 1994 increased by 5.7% to 3,532.3 billion yen, rising for the first time in two years. But lower unit prices per customer because of growing price consciousness among consumers weighed heavily on bookings and deteriorated earnings of travel agencies.

Top-ranking Japan Travel Bureau Inc. gained 0.1 of a percentage point of market share, to 13.7%, by cutting prices sharply on its two main lines of package tours. Kinki Nippon Tourist Co. held onto second place with an increase of 0.1 point to 7.9%, thanks to its success in mail-order sales.

Nippon Travel Agency Co., third ranked, lost share due to sluggish corporate demand.

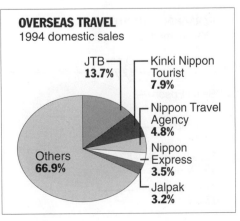

OVERSEAS TRAVEL
1994 domestic sales

JTB 13.7%
Kinki Nippon Tourist 7.9%
Nippon Travel Agency 4.8%
Nippon Express 3.5%
Jalpak 3.2%
Others 66.9%

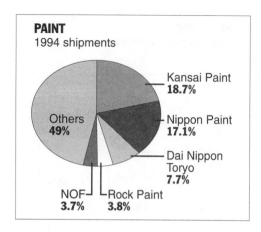

PAINT
1994 shipments

- Kansai Paint **18.7%**
- Nippon Paint **17.1%**
- Dai Nippon Toryo **7.7%**
- Rock Paint **3.8%**
- NOF **3.7%**
- Others **49%**

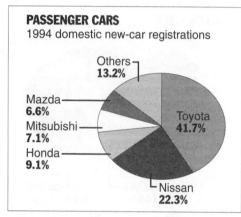

PASSENGER CARS
1994 domestic new-car registrations

- Others **13.2%**
- Mazda **6.6%**
- Mitsubishi **7.1%**
- Honda **9.1%**
- Toyota **41.7%**
- Nissan **22.3%**

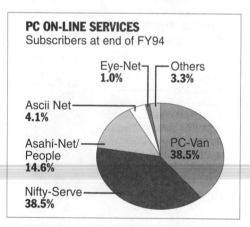

PC ON-LINE SERVICES
Subscribers at end of FY94

- Eye-Net **1.0%**
- Others **3.3%**
- Ascii Net **4.1%**
- Asahi-Net/People **14.6%**
- Nifty-Serve **38.5%**
- PC-Van **38.5%**

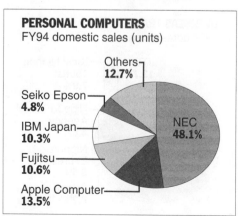

PERSONAL COMPUTERS
FY94 domestic sales (units)

- Others **12.7%**
- Seiko Epson **4.8%**
- IBM Japan **10.3%**
- Fujitsu **10.6%**
- Apple Computer **13.5%**
- NEC **48.1%**

PAINT

Domestic paint sales in fiscal 1994 totaled 744,952 million yen, up 1.7% from a year earlier. Imports soared 27.2% in value to 11,815 million yen and 44.0% in volume to 28,705 tons. Since paint makers are expanding production overseas, imports are likely to grow further.

Kansai Paint Co. retained the largest share of the market, despite losing 0.7 percentage point to 18.7%. The company set up four automobile-paint joint ventures in China to cope with intensifying competition to discount prices.

Second-ranked Nippon Paint Co. also suffered a loss of market share, dropping 1.1 points to 17.1%. Dai Nippon Toryo Co. came in third with 7.7%, up 0.3 point, due to brisk sales of powdered paint used in the printing of metal products.

PASSENGER CARS

Registrations of new passenger cars, excluding minicars, in 1994 fell for the fourth straight year to 3,400,145 units, down 0.8% year on year. The fall was attributed to a scarcity of new models to stimulate potential purchasers. Registrations of imported cars, meanwhile, jumped 40% to 276,161 units.

Among the top five automakers, only fourth-ranked Mitsubishi Motors Corp. saw its share rise, reaching 7.1%, up 0.4 point, thanks to surging sales of sports-utility models.

Industry leader Toyota Motor Corp. shed 1.3 share points to finish at 41.7%. Next came Nissan Motor Co., which saw its share drop 1.7 points to 22.3%. Third-place Honda Motor Co. held a 9.1% share, down 1.6 points.

PC ON-LINE SERVICES

On-line services expanded at an unprecedented pace during fiscal 1994 to a total 2.5 million subscribers, up 46.1%. The strong growth was linked to lower prices for computers and cheaper and faster modems.

Nifty Serve tied PC-VAN for top spot with 38.5% of the market each in terms of the number of subscribers. Nifty increased its share by 1.4 percentage points, while PC-Van gave up 1.3 points. The Asahi Net/People joint service grabbed 14.6%, up from 10.5% for Asahi Net in fiscal 1993. People started service in April 1994. Ascii Net shed 1.3 points to 4.1%.

PERSONAL COMPUTERS

Shipments of personal computers in fiscal 1994 jumped 47.2% to 3.62 million systems. Particularly noticeable were strong sales of IBM-compatible DOS/V models, believed to now make up some one-third of the entire DOS/V PC market.

NEC Corp. saw shipments grow more than 30%, but could not keep pace with the market expansion and lost 4.6 percentage points of market share, down to 48.1%, according to a Nikkei survey.

Apple Japan Inc. held onto second place at 13.5%, up 1.3 points, followed by Fujitsu Ltd. with 10.6%, down 0.7 of a point. IBM Japan Ltd. increased its share by 2.2 points to 10.3%, thanks to brisk sales of sub-notebook PCs and models integrating system and display into a single unit.

PLAIN PAPER COPIERS

Domestic shipments of plain paper copiers totaled 633,000 units in 1994, up 2.1% from a year earlier, according to a Nikkei survey. The strong showing after a weak 1993 was attributed to brisk corporate investment in information equipment and growing demand for digital models to replace analog.

There were no major changes in the shares of the three leading copier makers. Their combined share stood at 82.9%, up 0.3 of a point from the previous year. Ricoh Co. remained on top with 32.2% of the market, up 0.7 point, thanks to brisk sales of its digital copiers and color copiers. Canon Inc. ranked second with 27.5%, down 0.3 point, followed by Fuji Xerox Co. with 23.2%, down 0.1 point.

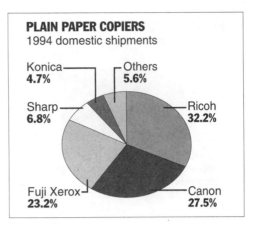

PLAIN PAPER COPIERS
1994 domestic shipments

POLYESTER FIBER

Domestic polyester fiber shipments in 1994 grew 4.6% from a year earlier to 511,000 tons. Though total output of the eight domestic polyester fiber makers rose only 0.4% year on year, a gain in polyester fiber imports contributed to the increase in shipments.

There was no change in the rankings of the top five manufacturers. Teijin Ltd. remained market leader with a 22.1% share, down 0.9 of a percentage point, followed by Toray Industries Inc. with 21.9%, down 0.4.

Third-ranked Toyobo Co. raised its share by 0.1 to 9.4% by boosting output. The company was the only maker among the top five that saw an increase in market share.

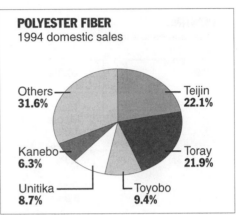

POLYESTER FIBER
1994 domestic sales

PREFABRICATED HOUSES

Housing starts for prefabricated homes dropped 2.2% year on year to 290,551 in fiscal 1994. The decline is attributed to an ebbing of the boom that hit apartment construction after taxes on agricultural land were raised to the same level as residential land.

Sekisui House Ltd. remained the market leader at 24.9% though it lost 1.4 percentage points on declining condominium sales. Daiwa House Industry Co. jumped one slot to second after increase 0.3 of a point to 15.0%. Sekisui Chemical Co. remained in fourth place, also with a gain of 0.3 point to 10.5%. Misawa Homes Co. dropped to third at 13.1%, down 1.9 points; its sales of single-family houses could not make up for falling condo sales.

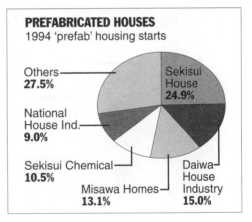

PREFABRICATED HOUSES
1994 'prefab' housing starts

PRERECORDED VIDEOTAPES

Sales of prerecorded videotapes grew 1.1% to 154.82 billion yen in 1994. Although demand from rental shops was unchanged, sales in the retail market rose for the first time in three years on the popularity of Walt Disney animation movies.

Market leader Pony Canyon Inc.'s share slipped 1.2 points to 23.8%. But it saw brisk sales of "REX", a Japanese dinosaur movie for children. Second-ranked Victor Entertainment Inc. widened its share by 2.1 points to 20.6% on sound demand for "Jurassic Park" from rental shops.

Both Toei Video Co., third with 8.4%, and Time Warner Entertainment Japan Inc., fourth with 8.1%, saw their shares shrink because neither had videotapes of hit movies.

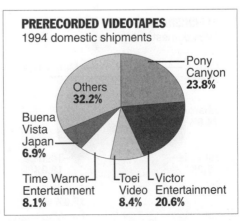

PRERECORDED VIDEOTAPES
1994 domestic shipments

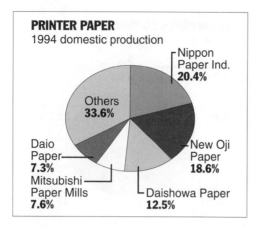

PRINTER PAPER
1994 domestic production

- Nippon Paper Ind. **20.4%**
- Others **33.6%**
- Daio Paper **7.3%**
- Mitsubishi Paper Mills **7.6%**
- Daishowa Paper **12.5%**
- New Oji Paper **18.6%**

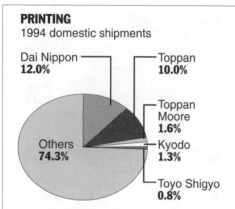

PRINTING
1994 domestic shipments

- Dai Nippon **12.0%**
- Toppan **10.0%**
- Toppan Moore **1.6%**
- Kyodo **1.3%**
- Others **74.3%**
- Toyo Shigyo **0.8%**

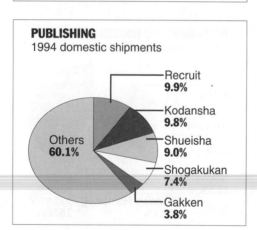

PUBLISHING
1994 domestic shipments

- Recruit **9.9%**
- Kodansha **9.8%**
- Shueisha **9.0%**
- Shogakukan **7.4%**
- Others **60.1%**
- Gakken **3.8%**

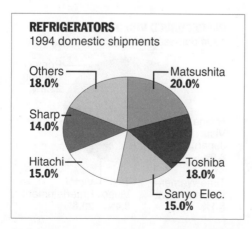

REFRIGERATORS
1994 domestic shipments

- Others **18.0%**
- Matsushita **20.0%**
- Sharp **14.0%**
- Hitachi **15.0%**
- Toshiba **18.0%**
- Sanyo Elec. **15.0%**

PRINTER PAPER

Domestic shipments of paper for computers, copiers and other printed matter in 1994 grew 4.1% to 9,720,351 tons, mainly because of a recovery in demand in the latter half of the year. Both shipments and production in 1994 surpassed those of 1991, the largest in the recent past.

With no new installments of paper machines in the industry for the past five years, there was no major change in rankings or share figures.

Nippon Paper remained the market leader with a 20.4% share, up 0.1 of a percentage point. New Oji Paper Co. held on to second place, though its share dropped 0.9 of a point to 18.6%. Daishowa Paper Mfg. Co. ranked third with 12.5%, down 0.5 of a point.

PRINTING

The value of domestic printing shipments totaled 8,702 billion yen in fiscal 1994, posting the first yearly gain in three years, according to a Nikkei survey. The gain reflects strong sales of paperbacks, comic books and mail-order catalogues as well as the rising popularity of such new media as magazines with CD-ROMs attached.

Share rankings of top firms remained unchanged. Dai Nippon Printing Co. held the biggest share of 12.0%, up 0.2 point, as its new businesses, such as shadow masks for computer displays, start to get on track. Toppan Printing Co. followed, with share unchanged at 10.0%.

Trailing the big two were Toppan Moore Co. with a 1.6% share, also unchanged, and Kyodo Printing Co. with 1.3%.

PUBLISHING

The value of books and periodicals published in 1994 totaled 2,006.8 billion yen, up 2.0% from a year earlier. Retail sales of books and periodicals grew 2.1% to 2,542.6 billion yen, marking the smallest year-on-year increase since 1981 due to sluggish sales of periodicals.

Recruit Co. was top publisher again with 9.9% of the market, down 0.1 percentage point as advertising in its recruitment magazines fell.

Second-ranked Kodansha Ltd. boosted its share 0.1 point to 9.8%, with the firm's largest sales ever both in books and magazines in the business year ended November 1994.

Shueisha Inc. came in third with 9.0%, down 0.2 point, followed by Shogakukan Inc. with 7.4%, also down 0.2 point.

REFRIGERATORS

Domestic shipments of refrigerators through September 1994 jumped by 10.2% to 4,546,000, ending a four-year long slump. Buoyed by growing replacement demand due to the 1994 heat wave, shipments saw double-digit growth from a year earlier during the late summer. Sales of all sizes and models were brisk.

Matsushita Electric Industrial Co. stayed on top with a 20% share, unchanged from 1993. Second-ranked Toshiba Corp. increased its share by 2 points to 18% through sales of models with freezers located near the middle of the cabinet. Sanyo Electric Co. and Hitachi Ltd. tied at 15% with Sanyo unchanged and Hitachi's share down a point. Sharp Corp. gained one point for a close fifth at 14% of the market.

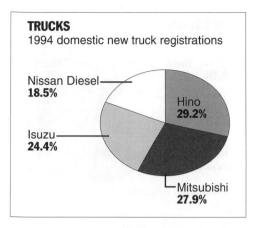

TRUCKS
1994 domestic new truck registrations

Nissan Diesel **18.5%**
Hino **29.2%**
Isuzu **24.4%**
Mitsubishi **27.9%**

TRUCKS

Domestic sales of trucks totaled 135,450 units in 1994, up 16.5%. Market share rankings of the four leading manufacturers remained unchanged, as they have for over 10 years. Top-ranked Hino Motors Ltd. controlled a 29.2% share, down 0.3 percentage point. Mitsubishi Motors Corp. held 27.9%, up 0.4 point, Isuzu Motors Ltd. had 24.4%, up 0.1 point, and Nissan Diesel Motor Co. 18.5%, down 0.2 point.

For large trucks, Hino and Mitsubishi expanded their market shares because they were able to meet a surge in demand resulting from tightened loading rules.

For midsize trucks, Mitsubishi regained the No.1 position from Hino as clients shunned Hino's high-priced new model equipped with a clean-air engine.

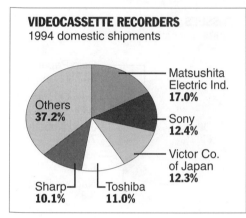

VIDEOCASSETTE RECORDERS
1994 domestic shipments

Matsushita Electric Ind. **17.0%**
Others **37.2%**
Sony **12.4%**
Victor Co. of Japan **12.3%**
Sharp **10.1%**
Toshiba **11.0%**

VIDEOCASSETTE RECORDERS

Domestic shipments of videocassette recorders totaled 5.5 million units in 1994, up 7.8% over the previous year for the first gain in six years. Demand was stimulated by the rapid increase in low-cost "reverse" imports by major electronics makers.

Matsushita Electric Industrial Co. retained the top spot with a 17.0% share, but dropped 3.2 points on weak sales of its high-priced S-VHS VCR, which was undercut by rivals' lower-priced models.

Sony Corp. was second with a 12.4% share, up 0.1 point. It was followed by Victor Co. of Japan (JVC) with 12.3%, unchanged. In 1994, Japanese manufacturers' offshore production of VCRs topped domestic output for the first time.

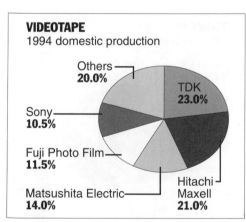

VIDEOTAPE
1994 domestic production

Others **20.0%**
TDK **23.0%**
Sony **10.5%**
Fuji Photo Film **11.5%**
Matsushita Electric **14.0%**
Hitachi Maxell **21.0%**

VIDEOTAPE

Domestic videotape production in 1994 fell 8% from a year earlier to 549 million rolls (in terms of 120-minute tape units), marking a year-on-year drop for the fourth straight year. The decline was attributed to a shift of production overseas by Japanese manufacturers.

There was no change in the ranking of the top five manufacturers. TDK Corp. retained the top spot for the seventh consecutive year with a 23.0% share, up 0.5 of a percentage point. It boosted productivity by integrating manufacturing from two domestic facilities at a plant in Oita Prefecture.

Hitachi Maxell Ltd. came in second with 21.0%, up 0.5 point, followed by Matsushita Electric Industrial Co. with 14.0%, up 1.0 point.

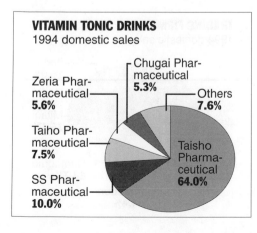

VITAMIN TONIC DRINKS
1994 domestic sales

Chugai Pharmaceutical **5.3%**
Zeria Pharmaceutical **5.6%**
Others **7.6%**
Taiho Pharmaceutical **7.5%**
Taisho Pharmaceutical **64.0%**
SS Pharmaceutical **10.0%**

VITAMIN TONIC DRINKS

Shipments of 100-milliliter bottled vitamin drinks in fiscal 1994 were worth an estimated 76 billion yen, up 3.4% from fiscal 1993, according to a Nikkei survey. Demand rose for the first time in three years, reflecting last summer's record hot summer.

Rankings remained unchanged. Taisho Pharmaceutical Co., the producer of Lipovitan-D, held an overwhelming share of 64.0%, down 0.1 of a point. SS Pharmaceutical Co. remained second at 10.0%, down 0.4, followed by Taiho Pharmaceutical Co. at 7.5%, up 1.1. Taiho's growth is attributed to cuts in retail prices of its Tiovita since January. With the exception of Taisho, rankings in fiscal 1995 may change after price cuts kick in and new products are introduced.

SEAMLESS PIPE

Domestic production of seamless steel pipe and tubing fell 9.2% in fiscal 1994 to 2.209 million tons due to weak overseas demand and reduced competitiveness of Japanese products on the global market, caused by the yen's strength.

Of the top four manufacturers, only first-ranked Sumitomo Metal Industries Ltd. saw its market share expand, growing 4.8 points to 40%. NKK Corp. moved into second from third, even though its share shrank by 2.2 points to 20.6%. Nippon Steel Corp. fell to third from second with 20.5%, down 3.1 points, and Kawasaki Steel Corp. kept fourth with 12.5%, down 0.7 point.

While Sumitomo raised output by some 3%, the other three firms all saw double-digit decreases in output.

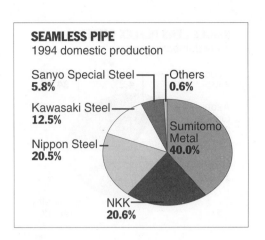

SEAMLESS PIPE
1994 domestic production

Sanyo Special Steel **5.8%**
Others **0.6%**
Kawasaki Steel **12.5%**
Sumitomo Metal **40.0%**
Nippon Steel **20.5%**
NKK **20.6%**

SHAMPOO, CONDITIONER

The value of shipments of shampoos, conditioners, body and facial soaps totaled 308.8 billion yen in 1994, up 6.8% from the previous year, statistics compiled by the Ministry of International Trade and Industry show. There was a surge in the popularity of high value-added products designed for specific purposes, such as revitalizing damaged hair.

Shiseido Co. stayed on top with a 15.2% share of shipments, up 1.1 points. Sales of its mainline Super Mild shampoo grew about 9%, while the firm's mineral-enhanced shampoo also sold well.

Kao Corp. came in second with 13.4%, down 0.5 point. The company lost many users of its Biore U body shampoo to rival products.

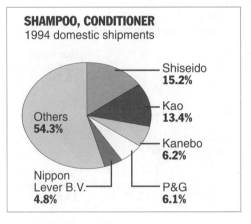

SHAMPOO, CONDITIONER
1994 domestic shipments

Shiseido **15.2%**
Kao **13.4%**
Others **54.3%**
Kanebo **6.2%**
Nippon Lever B.V. **4.8%**
P&G **6.1%**

SHEET GLASS

Domestic sales of sheet glass in 1994 fell 3.8% from a year earlier to 257.9 billion yen. The rate of decline was half the previous year's. Domestic output was also down 3.7%, marking the fourth straight year of decrease.

Combined sales of the local units of two U.S. sheet glass makers -- PPG Industries Inc. and Guardian Industries Corp. -- stood at about 4 billion yen, accounting for some 30% of total imports. Imports took 3.9% of the market last year, down 0.5 point from 1993.

Asahi Glass Co. continued to dominate with a 46.3% share, down 0.2 percentage point from 1993. Nippon Sheet Glass Co. came in second with 32.0%, also off 0.2 point, while Central Glass Co. gained 0.9 point to 17.8%.

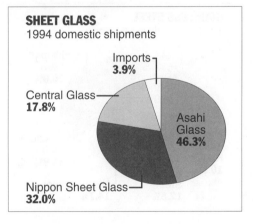

SHEET GLASS
1994 domestic shipments

Imports **3.9%**
Central Glass **17.8%**
Asahi Glass **46.3%**
Nippon Sheet Glass **32.0%**

SHIPBUILDING

The gross tonnage of ships built in Japan in 1994 fell 5.3% to 8.60 million tons, the first decline since 1988, but still well ahead of archrival South Korea, according to a Nikkei survey. The tonnage completed in Korean shipyards came to 4.08 million last year.

Mitsubishi Heavy Industries Ltd. shed 0.3 percentage point but remained No. 1 with 12.6%. Ishikawajima-Harima Heavy Industries Co. came in second with a 7.9% share, down a sharp 2.3 points. Imabari Shipbuilding Co. gained 1.5 points and jumped to third from fifth with a 7.1% share, followed by NKK Corp. with 6.6%, down 0.5. Kawasaki Heavy Industries Ltd. boosted its share 1.8 points and returned to the ranks of the top five with 6.3%.

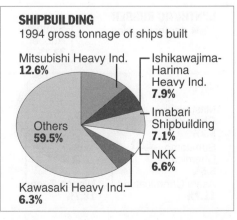

SHIPBUILDING
1994 gross tonnage of ships built

Mitsubishi Heavy Ind. **12.6%**
Ishikawajima-Harima Heavy Ind. **7.9%**
Imabari Shipbuilding **7.1%**
Others **59.5%**
NKK **6.6%**
Kawasaki Heavy Ind. **6.3%**

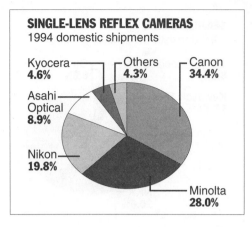

SINGLE-LENS REFLEX CAMERAS
1994 domestic shipments

- Kyocera 4.6%
- Others 4.3%
- Canon 34.4%
- Asahi Optical 8.9%
- Nikon 19.8%
- Minolta 28.0%

SINGLE-LENS REFLEX CAMERAS

Domestic shipments of single-lens reflex cameras totaled 718,534 units in 1994, up 21%, for the first year-on-year rise in four years, according to a Nikkei survey. Growth was spurred by the release of new products and demand from photography enthusiasts. Demand for compact cameras was weak.

Canon Inc. stayed on top, with a market share of 34.4%, up 1.0 point on imports of low-priced models made in Taiwan. Minolta Co. was second with 28.0%, pushed up 0.9 point by its new user-friendly models. In third place, Nikon Corp. grabbed 19.8%, down 0.3 The success of the G1 system camera released by Kyocera Corp. last September propelled the firm to fifth position with 4.6%, up 2.0.

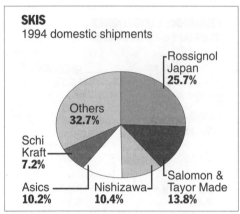

SKIS
1994 domestic shipments

- Rossignol Japan 25.7%
- Others 32.7%
- Schi Kraft 7.2%
- Asics 10.2%
- Nishizawa 10.4%
- Salomon & Tayor Made 13.8%

SKIS

Shipments of skis for the 1994-1995 winter fell 4.7% from the previous season to 1.01 million pairs, posting a third straight drop, according to a Nikkei survey. The retail market experienced a severe price war caused by chronic inventory stockpiles.

Rossignol Japan Corp. stayed on top with 25.7% of the market, up 0.2 of a percentage point, followed by Salomon & Taylor Made Co. with 13.8%, up 2.5 points. Both companies used aggressive marketing tactics. Nishizawa International Inc. remained third with 10.4%, unchanged, followed by Asics Corp. with 10.2%, up 0.3. Schi Kraft Inc. rose to fifth, replacing Yamaha Corp.

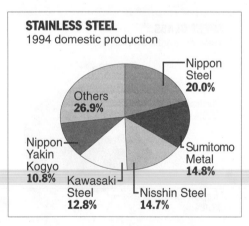

STAINLESS STEEL
1994 domestic production

- Nippon Steel 20.0%
- Others 26.9%
- Nippon Yakin Kogyo 10.8%
- Kawasaki Steel 12.8%
- Nisshin Steel 14.7%
- Sumitomo Metal 14.8%

STAINLESS STEEL

Hot-rolled stainless steel output rose 8.1% to 2.86 million tons in 1994 in Japan thanks to stronger sales of autos and home electronics and brisk demand from Asia. The market started to rise in May 1994 and producers, who had been forced by anemic demand to cut prices, have been operating at full capacity since last summer.

The top six producers' domestic sales rankings showed no change from 1993, according to a Nikkei survey. Nippon Steel Corp. ranked first with 20.0% and Sumitomo Metal Industries Ltd. came in second with 14.8%, followed by Nisshin Steel Corp.'s 14.7%. Only Nippon Steel and Nisshin Steel saw a rise in market share.

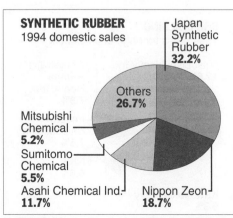

SYNTHETIC RUBBER
1994 domestic sales

- Japan Synthetic Rubber 32.2%
- Others 26.7%
- Mitsubishi Chemical 5.2%
- Sumitomo Chemical 5.5%
- Asahi Chemical Ind. 11.7%
- Nippon Zeon 18.7%

SYNTHETIC RUBBER

Domestic sales of synthetic rubber totaled 1,058,000 tons in 1994, up 2.6% over the previous year for the first increase in two years, according to a Nikkei survey. The rise was attributed to the brisk exports. Still, domestic makers saw their market share shrink due to an increase in imports by tire makers looking to reduce costs.

Japan Synthetic Rubber Co. remained on top with a 32.2% share, down 0.6 point, followed by Nippon Zeon Co., which captured 18.7%, down 0.4 point.

Asahi Chemical Industry Co. came in third with an 11.7% share, down 0.2 point. Fourth-ranked Sumitomo Chemical Co. posted a 0.2-point decline to 5.5% and Mitsubishi Chemical Corp. also dropped 0.2 point to 5.2%.

TIRE TUBES

Domestic production of tires totaled 931,529 tons in 1994, up slightly for the first time in four years, according to a Nikkei survey. The gain was due to a 7% rise in production for export which more than offset a 3% drop in output for domestic sales.

Bridgestone Corp. remained Japan's biggest tire maker with a dominant share of 48.3%, up 1.6 points, as it increased exports to its U.S. subsidiary during a marathon strike.

Yokohama Rubber Co. kept second place with an 18.5% share, down 1.0 point. Sumitomo Rubber Industries Ltd. and other manufacturers also saw their shares decline due to increased overseas production caused by the yen's appreciation.

TISSUES

Domestic shipments of tissues and toilet paper in 1994 rose 1.3% to 1,547,958 tons, according to a Nikkei survey. Shipments of toilet paper increased 3.9%, and paper towels rose 3.4%, while tissue shipments fell by 0.9%. Sanitary paper shipments were slightly higher last year, up 1.9% over 1993.

The two leading producers, Daio Paper Corp. and New Oji Paper Co., both increased their market shares thanks to stable sales of their mainstay brands of household paper products.

Daio retained the top spot with a 12.7% share, up 0.6 of a point from 1993. New Oji gained 0.7 of a point to 9.4%. Third-ranked Jujo Kimberly KK lost 0.1 of a percentage point to 7.8%, due primarily to fierce price competition.

TOILET FIXTURES

Domestic shipments of toilet fixtures including bowls, washstands and watertanks in 1994 rose sharply to 11.63 million units, up 13.9% from 1993, according to a Nikkei survey. The rise was attributed to an increase in housing starts to 1.57 million units and brisk demand for house refurbishment.

Toto Ltd. enjoyed overwhelming predominance, although its share remained unchanged from a year earlier at 62.6% due to a slowdown in construction of office buildings. In second place, Inax Corp. saw its share rise by 0.3 point to 23.5%, through active sales to prefabricated housing makers.

Janis Ltd. retained third place with a 4.7% share, down 1.4 points.

TRADING FIRMS

Aggregate sales at Japan's top nine trading firms dipped 3.3% to 99.77 trillion yen in fiscal 1994, falling for the fourth straight year. All the traders saw lower revenues due to the yen's 8% advance to the dollar, compared with a year ago, as well as a decrease in gold dealings, which had previously padded revenues.

Itochu Corp. retained the top market share of 16% by posting sales of 15.94 trillion yen, down from over 16 trillion yen in fiscal 1993. Mitsui & Co. remained second.

Marubeni Corp. moved down from third to fourth. Its market share contracted 0.3 point to 14.4% due mainly to a plunge in foods sales. Sumitomo advanced a notch to the third slot to 14.7%, up 0.1 point.

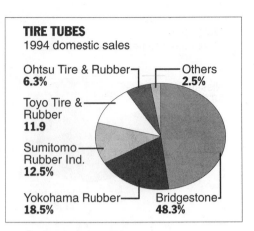

TIRE TUBES
1994 domestic sales

- Ohtsu Tire & Rubber 6.3%
- Others 2.5%
- Toyo Tire & Rubber 11.9
- Sumitomo Rubber Ind. 12.5%
- Yokohama Rubber 18.5%
- Bridgestone 48.3%

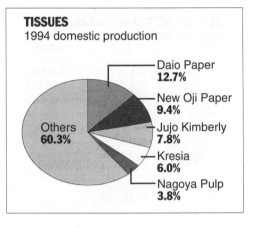

TISSUES
1994 domestic production

- Daio Paper 12.7%
- New Oji Paper 9.4%
- Jujo Kimberly 7.8%
- Kresia 6.0%
- Nagoya Pulp 3.8%
- Others 60.3%

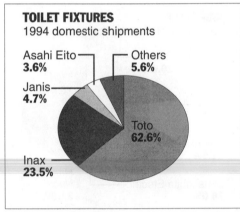

TOILET FIXTURES
1994 domestic shipments

- Asahi Eito 3.6%
- Others 5.6%
- Janis 4.7%
- Toto 62.6%
- Inax 23.5%

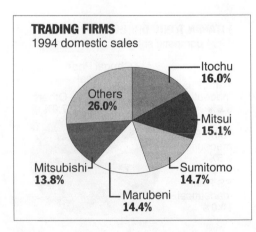

TRADING FIRMS
1994 domestic sales

- Itochu 16.0%
- Mitsui 15.1%
- Sumitomo 14.7%
- Marubeni 14.4%
- Mitsubishi 13.8%
- Others 26.0%

WASHING MACHINES

Domestic shipments of washing machines grew 1.5% from a year earlier to 4,685,000 units in 1994, marking the first year-on-year increase in three years. Although there was no change in the ranking of the top five manufacturers, their combined share stood at 91% of the market, up 2.0 percentage points from a year ago.

Shipments of the most popular type, fully automatic models with a stainless steel tub, accounted for about 50% of all automatic models in 1994, up 15 points from the previous year.

Matsushita Electric Industrial Co. stayed on top with a 23.0% share, up 0.5 of a point. Hitachi Ltd. was second with an unchanged 20.0% share, followed by Toshiba Corp. also unchanged at 19.0%.

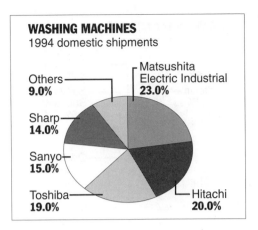

WASHING MACHINES
1994 domestic shipments

- Matsushita Electric Industrial **23.0%**
- Others **9.0%**
- Sharp **14.0%**
- Sanyo **15.0%**
- Toshiba **19.0%**
- Hitachi **20.0%**

WHISKEY

Whiskey shipments were sluggish in 1994, falling 7.8% to 171,290 kiloliters. Imports declined 2.4% to 42,208kl, while domestic brands lost 9.3% to 129,082kl. Demand for gift goods was slack and business-related consumption was low.

Suntory Ltd. continued to dominate with 59.5% of the market, down 1.4 percentage points. Its canned whiskey-and-water product didn't sell as well last year, however, as in its 1993 debut.

Nikka Whisky Distilling Co., ranked second, also saw its share dip, by 0.3 of a point to 11.7%. The popularity of new inexpensive brands was offset by poor demand for its mainstay labels. Kirin Seagram Co. gained 0.2 of a point to 3.3%, even though its shipments slipped 3.8% last year.

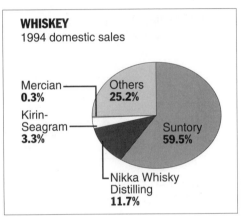

WHISKEY
1994 domestic sales

- Mercian **0.3%**
- Others **25.2%**
- Kirin-Seagram **3.3%**
- Suntory **59.5%**
- Nikka Whisky Distilling **11.7%**

WINE

Taxable shipments of domestically produced wine totaled 61,219kl in 1994, falling below shipments of imported wine for the first time. Overall shipments in Japan, both domestic and foreign wine, hit a record 138,300kl, lifted by strong demand for low-priced imports.

Mercian Corp. retained its hold on the market for domestic wine by shipping 15,000kl for a 24.5% share, up 1.8 percentage points. Second-ranked Suntory Ltd.'s share contracted 3.2 points to 17.6% because its shipments of imports grew while that of domestic wine fell.

Sapporo Breweries Ltd. raised its share 0.4 point for 9.1% of the market for domestically produced wine. It raised shipments 13.7% from 1993 to 5,560kl.

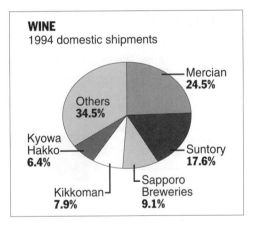

WINE
1994 domestic shipments

- Mercian **24.5%**
- Others **34.5%**
- Kyowa Hakko **6.4%**
- Suntory **17.6%**
- Kikkoman **7.9%**
- Sapporo Breweries **9.1%**

WIRE CONNECTORS

Shipments of connectors reached a total value of 418.5 billion yen in fiscal 1994, up 8.1% from fiscal 1993, according to a Nikkei survey. Shipments for audiovisual equipment declined as more production was shifted overseas, but demand from makers of personal computers and communications equipment rose.

AMP Japan Ltd. remained on top with a 16.6% share, unchanged from fiscal 1993. Japan Solderless Terminal Mfg. Co. followed at 12.3%, also unchanged, and Hirose Electric Co. at 12.2%, up 0.8 of a point. User demands for lower prices are increasing, say industry sources, making cost-cutting an urgent task. Some connector makers are expanding overseas production to remain price competitive.

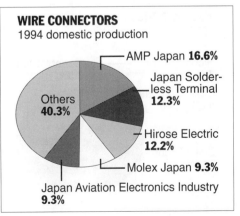

WIRE CONNECTORS
1994 domestic production

- AMP Japan **16.6%**
- Japan Solderless Terminal **12.3%**
- Hirose Electric **12.2%**
- Molex Japan **9.3%**
- Japan Aviation Electronics Industry **9.3%**
- Others **40.3%**

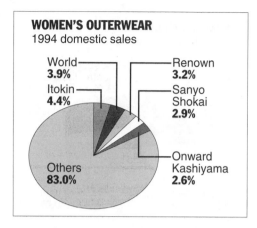

WOMEN'S OUTERWEAR
1994 domestic sales

World 3.9%
Itokin 4.4%
Renown 3.2%
Sanyo Shokai 2.9%
Onward Kashiyama 2.6%
Others 83.0%

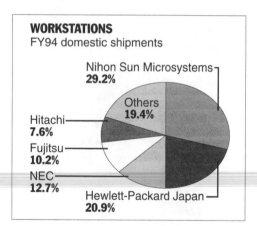

WOMEN'S UNDERWEAR
1994 domestic sales

Wacoal 23.0%
Others 46.7%
Cecile 12.0%
Charle 7.3%
Trimph 5.4%
Gunze 5.6%

WORKSTATIONS
FY94 domestic shipments

Nihon Sun Microsystems 29.2%
Others 19.4%
Hitachi 7.6%
Fujitsu 10.2%
NEC 12.7%
Hewlett-Packard Japan 20.9%

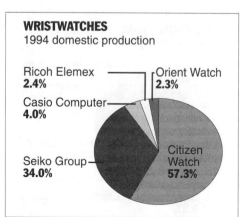

WRISTWATCHES
1994 domestic production

Ricoh Elemex 2.4%
Orient Watch 2.3%
Casio Computer 4.0%
Seiko Group 34.0%
Citizen Watch 57.3%

WOMEN'S OUTERWEAR

Sales of women's outerwear in 1994 fell 1.1% from the previous year to 2,800.8 billion yen, according to a Nikkei survey. The drop was smaller than the 2.8% in 1993, however, due to replacement demand and the effect of a tax cut.

Fifth-ranked Onward Kashiyama Co. was the only maker that saw its share rise. The firm gained 0.1 of a point to 2.6%, thanks to brisk demand for its Kumikyoku and 23 Ku casual design brands for working women in their 20s and 30s. Fourth-ranked Sanyo Shokai Ltd. also enjoyed a rise in sales of its brand for working women but its share was unchanged at 2.9% Itokin Co. retained the top spot, though its share dropped 0.1 of a percentage point to 4.4%. World Co. held on to second place with a 3.9% share, down 0.4 of a point.

WOMEN'S UNDERWEAR

Domestic sales of women's underwear in 1994 slipped 0.7% year on year to 436.5 billion yen, pulled down by sluggish demand for higher-priced lingerie. Sales of foundation garments such as bras and girdles played a crucial role in determining market share. Among the top five manufacturers, only Cecile Co. saw its market share decline.

Wacoal Corp. stayed on top with 23%, up 0.8 percentage point, thanks to robust sales of support bras and girdles. Second-ranked Cecile saw its share fall 0.5 point to 12% as the appeal of the firm's low-priced products apparently faded.

Charle Co. ranked third with a 7.3% share, up 0.1 point, thanks to brisk sales of its comfortable foundation garments.

WORKSTATIONS

Domestic sales of workstations grew 12.5% year on year to 157,580 units in fiscal 1994, for the second year of double-digit growth, as companies continued to downsize their computer systems. Nihon Sun Microsystems KK remained the market leader with a 29.2% share, despite losing 0.6 percentage point. Hewlett-Packard Japan Ltd. (formerly Yokogawa-Hewlett-Packard), expanded its share a hefty 5.4 points to 20.9%. The rise was attributed to expanded OEM sales, which accounted for 29% of its total sales last year. NEC Corp. maintained its third-place ranking with an unchanged 12.7% share, thanks largely to a fourth-quarter order for 2,300 units to a convenience store chain in the Daiei group.

WRISTWATCHES

Domestic output of wristwatches, both finished products and movements, dropped 4.5% in 1994 to 303.7 million units. The decrease was attributed to growth in demand for imported products, which could be priced lower due to the strong yen.

Production market share rankings of the top three firms remained unchanged, but third-ranked Casio Computer Co. saw its share fall by 3.4 percentage points to 4% because the company increased assembly abroad.

Citizen Watch Co. retained the top spot with a 57.3% share, up 1.9 points, and the second-ranked Seiko Corp. group gained 5.2 points to 34%. Both firms expanded domestic output of movements to account for about 90% of their overall domestic production.

WASHING MACHINES

Domestic shipments of washing machines grew 1.5% from a year earlier to 4,685,000 units in 1994, marking the first year-on-year increase in three years. Although there was no change in the ranking of the top five manufacturers, their combined share stood at 91% of the market, up 2.0 percentage points from a year ago.

Shipments of the most popular type, fully automatic models with a stainless steel tub, accounted for about 50% of all automatic models in 1994, up 15 points from the previous year.

Matsushita Electric Industrial Co. stayed on top with a 23.0% share, up 0.5 of a point. Hitachi Ltd. was second with an unchanged 20.0% share, followed by Toshiba Corp. also unchanged at 19.0%.

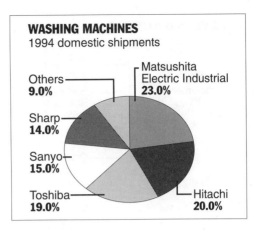

WASHING MACHINES
1994 domestic shipments

- Others 9.0%
- Sharp 14.0%
- Sanyo 15.0%
- Toshiba 19.0%
- Matsushita Electric Industrial 23.0%
- Hitachi 20.0%

WHISKEY

Whiskey shipments were sluggish in 1994, falling 7.8% to 171,290 kiloliters. Imports declined 2.4% to 42,208kl, while domestic brands lost 9.3% to 129,082kl. Demand for gift goods was slack and business-related consumption was low.

Suntory Ltd. continued to dominate with 59.5% of the market, down 1.4 percentage points. Its canned whiskey-and-water product didn't sell as well last year, however, as in its 1993 debut.

Nikka Whisky Distilling Co., ranked second, also saw its share dip, by 0.3 of a point to 11.7%. The popularity of new inexpensive brands was offset by poor demand for its mainstay labels. Kirin Seagram Co. gained 0.2 of a point to 3.3%, even though its shipments slipped 3.8% last year.

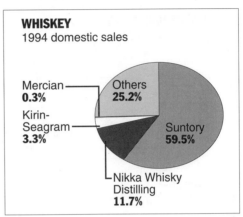

WHISKEY
1994 domestic sales

- Mercian 0.3%
- Kirin-Seagram 3.3%
- Others 25.2%
- Suntory 59.5%
- Nikka Whisky Distilling 11.7%

WINE

Taxable shipments of domestically produced wine totaled 61,219kl in 1994, falling below shipments of imported wine for the first time. Overall shipments in Japan, both domestic and foreign wine, hit a record 138,300kl, lifted by strong demand for low-priced imports.

Mercian Corp. retained its hold on the market for domestic wine by shipping 15,000kl for a 24.5% share, up 1.8 percentage points. Second-ranked Suntory Ltd.'s share contracted 3.2 points to 17.6% because its shipments of imports grew while that of domestic wine fell.

Sapporo Breweries Ltd. raised its share 0.4 point for 9.1% of the market for domestically produced wine. It raised shipments 13.7% from 1993 to 5,560kl.

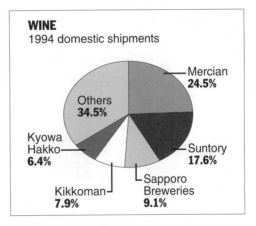

WINE
1994 domestic shipments

- Others 34.5%
- Kyowa Hakko 6.4%
- Kikkoman 7.9%
- Mercian 24.5%
- Suntory 17.6%
- Sapporo Breweries 9.1%

WIRE CONNECTORS

Shipments of connectors reached a total value of 418.5 billion yen in fiscal 1994, up 8.1% from fiscal 1993, according to a Nikkei survey. Shipments for audiovisual equipment declined as more production was shifted overseas, but demand from makers of personal computers and communications equipment rose.

AMP Japan Ltd. remained on top with a 16.6% share, unchanged from fiscal 1993. Japan Solderless Terminal Mfg. Co. followed at 12.3%, also unchanged, and Hirose Electric Co. at 12.2%, up 0.8 of a point. User demands for lower prices are increasing, say industry sources, making cost-cutting an urgent task. Some connector makers are expanding overseas production to remain price competitive.

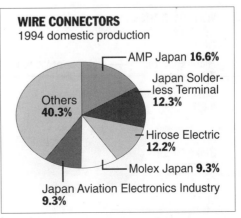

WIRE CONNECTORS
1994 domestic production

- AMP Japan 16.6%
- Japan Solderless Terminal 12.3%
- Hirose Electric 12.2%
- Molex Japan 9.3%
- Japan Aviation Electronics Industry 9.3%
- Others 40.3%

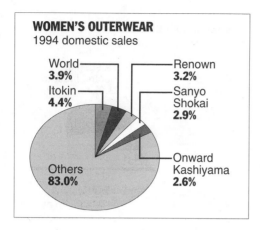

WOMEN'S OUTERWEAR
1994 domestic sales

WOMEN'S OUTERWEAR

Sales of women's outerwear in 1994 fell 1.1% from the previous year to 2,800.8 billion yen, according to a Nikkei survey. The drop was smaller than the 2.8% in 1993, however, due to replacement demand and the effect of a tax cut.

Fifth-ranked Onward Kashiyama Co. was the only maker that saw its share rise. The firm gained 0.1 of a point to 2.6%, thanks to brisk demand for its Kumikyoku and 23 Ku casual design brands for working women in their 20s and 30s. Fourth-ranked Sanyo Shokai Ltd. also enjoyed a rise in sales of its brand for working women but its share was unchanged at 2.9% Itokin Co. retained the top spot, though its share dropped 0.1 of a percentage point to 4.4%. World Co. held on to second place with a 3.9% share, down 0.4 of a point.

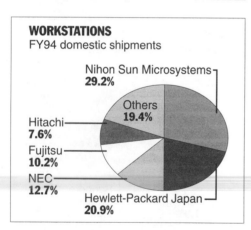

WOMEN'S UNDERWEAR
1994 domestic sales

WOMEN'S UNDERWEAR

Domestic sales of women's underwear in 1994 slipped 0.7% year on year to 436.5 billion yen, pulled down by sluggish demand for higher-priced lingerie. Sales of foundation garments such as bras and girdles played a crucial role in determining market share. Among the top five manufacturers, only Cecile Co. saw its market share decline.

Wacoal Corp. stayed on top with 23%, up 0.8 percentage point, thanks to robust sales of support bras and girdles. Second-ranked Cecile saw its share fall 0.5 point to 12% as the appeal of the firm's low-priced products apparently faded.

Charle Co. ranked third with a 7.3% share, up 0.1 point, thanks to brisk sales of its comfortable foundation garments.

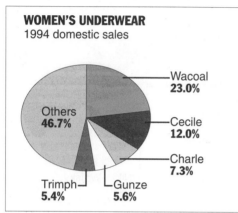

WORKSTATIONS
FY94 domestic shipments

WORKSTATIONS

Domestic sales of workstations grew 12.5% year on year to 157,580 units in fiscal 1994, for the second year of double-digit growth, as companies continued to downsize their computer systems. Nihon Sun Microsystems KK remained the market leader with a 29.2% share, despite losing 0.6 percentage point. Hewlett-Packard Japan Ltd. (formerly Yokogawa-Hewlett-Packard), expanded its share a hefty 5.4 points to 20.9%. The rise was attributed to expanded OEM sales, which accounted for 29% of its total sales last year. NEC Corp. maintained its third-place ranking with an unchanged 12.7% share, thanks largely to a fourth-quarter order for 2,300 units to a convenience store chain in the Daiei group.

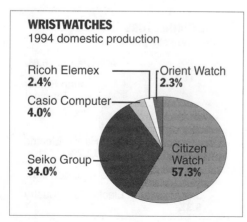

WRISTWATCHES
1994 domestic production

WRISTWATCHES

Domestic output of wristwatches, both finished products and movements, dropped 4.5% in 1994 to 303.7 million units. The decrease was attributed to growth in demand for imported products, which could be priced lower due to the strong yen.

Production market share rankings of the top three firms remained unchanged, but third-ranked Casio Computer Co. saw its share fall by 3.4 percentage points to 4% because the company increased assembly abroad.

Citizen Watch Co. retained the top spot with a 57.3% share, up 1.9 points, and the second-ranked Seiko Corp. group gained 5.2 points to 34%. Both firms expanded domestic output of movements to account for about 90% of their overall domestic production.

SEAMLESS PIPE

Domestic production of seamless steel pipe and tubing fell 9.2% in fiscal 1994 to 2.209 million tons due to weak overseas demand and reduced competitiveness of Japanese products on the global market, caused by the yen's strength.

Of the top four manufacturers, only first-ranked Sumitomo Metal Industries Ltd. saw its market share expand, growing 4.8 points to 40%. NKK Corp. moved into second from third, even though its share shrank by 2.2 points to 20.6%. Nippon Steel Corp. fell to third from second with 20.5%, down 3.1 points, and Kawasaki Steel Corp. kept fourth with 12.5%, down 0.7 point.

While Sumitomo raised output by some 3%, the other three firms all saw double-digit decreases in output.

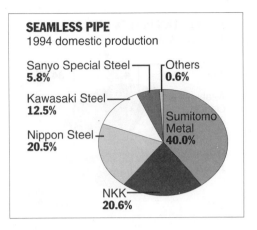

SEAMLESS PIPE
1994 domestic production

- Sanyo Special Steel **5.8%**
- Others **0.6%**
- Kawasaki Steel **12.5%**
- Sumitomo Metal **40.0%**
- Nippon Steel **20.5%**
- NKK **20.6%**

SHAMPOO, CONDITIONER

The value of shipments of shampoos, conditioners, body and facial soaps totaled 308.8 billion yen in 1994, up 6.8% from the previous year, statistics compiled by the Ministry of International Trade and Industry show. There was a surge in the popularity of high value-added products designed for specific purposes, such as revitalizing damaged hair.

Shiseido Co. stayed on top with a 15.2% share of shipments, up 1.1 points. Sales of its mainline Super Mild shampoo grew about 9%, while the firm's mineral-enhanced shampoo also sold well.

Kao Corp. came in second with 13.4%, down 0.5 point. The company lost many users of its Biore U body shampoo to rival products.

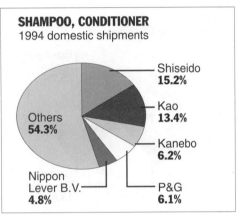

SHAMPOO, CONDITIONER
1994 domestic shipments

- Shiseido **15.2%**
- Kao **13.4%**
- Kanebo **6.2%**
- P&G **6.1%**
- Nippon Lever B.V. **4.8%**
- Others **54.3%**

SHEET GLASS

Domestic sales of sheet glass in 1994 fell 3.8% from a year earlier to 257.9 billion yen. The rate of decline was half the previous year's. Domestic output was also down 3.7%, marking the fourth straight year of decrease.

Combined sales of the local units of two U.S. sheet glass makers -- PPG Industries Inc. and Guardian Industries Corp. -- stood at about 4 billion yen, accounting for some 30% of total imports. Imports took 3.9% of the market last year, down 0.5 point from 1993.

Asahi Glass Co. continued to dominate with a 46.3% share, down 0.2 percentage point from 1993. Nippon Sheet Glass Co. came in second with 32.0%, also off 0.2 point, while Central Glass Co. gained 0.9 point to 17.8%.

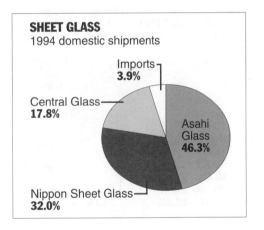

SHEET GLASS
1994 domestic shipments

- Imports **3.9%**
- Central Glass **17.8%**
- Asahi Glass **46.3%**
- Nippon Sheet Glass **32.0%**

SHIPBUILDING

The gross tonnage of ships built in Japan in 1994 fell 5.3% to 8.60 million tons, the first decline since 1988, but still well ahead of archrival South Korea, according to a Nikkei survey. The tonnage completed in Korean shipyards came to 4.08 million last year.

Mitsubishi Heavy Industries Ltd. shed 0.3 percentage point but remained No. 1 with 12.6%. Ishikawajima-Harima Heavy Industries Co. came in second with a 7.9% share, down a sharp 2.3 points. Imabari Shipbuilding Co. gained 1.5 points and jumped to third from fifth with a 7.1% share, followed by NKK Corp. with 6.6%, down 0.5. Kawasaki Heavy Industries Ltd. boosted its share 1.8 points and returned to the ranks of the top five with 6.3%.

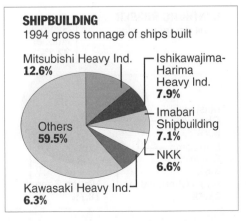

SHIPBUILDING
1994 gross tonnage of ships built

- Mitsubishi Heavy Ind. **12.6%**
- Ishikawajima-Harima Heavy Ind. **7.9%**
- Imabari Shipbuilding **7.1%**
- NKK **6.6%**
- Kawasaki Heavy Ind. **6.3%**
- Others **59.5%**

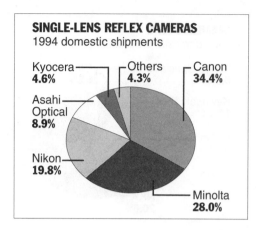

SINGLE-LENS REFLEX CAMERAS
1994 domestic shipments

Kyocera 4.6%
Others 4.3%
Canon 34.4%
Asahi Optical 8.9%
Nikon 19.8%
Minolta 28.0%

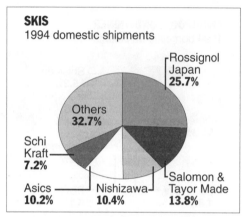

SKIS
1994 domestic shipments

Rossignol Japan 25.7%
Others 32.7%
Schi Kraft 7.2%
Asics 10.2%
Nishizawa 10.4%
Salomon & Tayor Made 13.8%

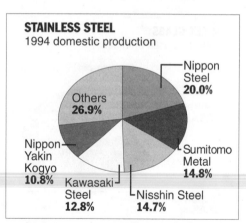

STAINLESS STEEL
1994 domestic production

Nippon Steel 20.0%
Others 26.9%
Nippon Yakin Kogyo 10.8%
Kawasaki Steel 12.8%
Nisshin Steel 14.7%
Sumitomo Metal 14.8%

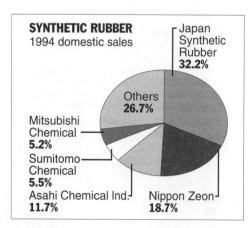

SYNTHETIC RUBBER
1994 domestic sales

Japan Synthetic Rubber 32.2%
Others 26.7%
Mitsubishi Chemical 5.2%
Sumitomo Chemical 5.5%
Asahi Chemical Ind. 11.7%
Nippon Zeon 18.7%

SINGLE-LENS REFLEX CAMERAS

Domestic shipments of single-lens reflex cameras totaled 718,534 units in 1994, up 21%, for the first year-on-year rise in four years, according to a Nikkei survey. Growth was spurred by the release of new products and demand from photography enthusiasts. Demand for compact cameras was weak.

Canon Inc. stayed on top, with a market share of 34.4%, up 1.0 point on imports of low-priced models made in Taiwan. Minolta Co. was second with 28.0%, pushed up 0.9 point by its new user-friendly models. In third place, Nikon Corp. grabbed 19.8%, down 0.3 The success of the G1 system camera released by Kyocera Corp. last September propelled the firm to fifth position with 4.6%, up 2.0.

SKIS

Shipments of skis for the 1994-1995 winter fell 4.7% from the previous season to 1.01 million pairs, posting a third straight drop, according to a Nikkei survey. The retail market experienced a severe price war caused by chronic inventory stockpiles.

Rossignol Japan Corp. stayed on top with 25.7% of the market, up 0.2 of a percentage point, followed by Salomon & Taylor Made Co. with 13.8%, up 2.5 points. Both companies used aggressive marketing tactics. Nishizawa International Inc. remained third with 10.4%, unchanged, followed by Asics Corp. with 10.2%, up 0.3. Schi Kraft Inc. rose to fifth, replacing Yamaha Corp.

STAINLESS STEEL

Hot-rolled stainless steel output rose 8.1% to 2.86 million tons in 1994 in Japan thanks to stronger sales of autos and home electronics and brisk demand from Asia. The market started to rise in May 1994 and producers, who had been forced by anemic demand to cut prices, have been operating at full capacity since last summer.

The top six producers' domestic sales rankings showed no change from 1993, according to a Nikkei survey. Nippon Steel Corp. ranked first with 20.0% and Sumitomo Metal Industries Ltd. came in second with 14.8%, followed by Nisshin Steel Corp.'s 14.7%. Only Nippon Steel and Nisshin Steel saw a rise in market share.

SYNTHETIC RUBBER

Domestic sales of synthetic rubber totaled 1,058,000 tons in 1994, up 2.6% over the previous year for the first increase in two years, according to a Nikkei survey. The rise was attributed to the brisk exports. Still, domestic makers saw their market share shrink due to an increase in imports by tire makers looking to reduce costs.

Japan Synthetic Rubber Co. remained on top with a 32.2% share, down 0.6 point, followed by Nippon Zeon Co., which captured 18.7%, down 0.4 point.

Asahi Chemical Industry Co. came in third with an 11.7% share, down 0.2 point. Fourth-ranked Sumitomo Chemical Co. posted a 0.2-point decline to 5.5% and Mitsubishi Chemical Corp. also dropped 0.2 point to 5.2%.

TIRE TUBES

Domestic production of tires totaled 931,529 tons in 1994, up slightly for the first time in four years, according to a Nikkei survey. The gain was due to a 7% rise in production for export which more than offset a 3% drop in output for domestic sales.

Bridgestone Corp. remained Japan's biggest tire maker with a dominant share of 48.3%, up 1.6 points, as it increased exports to its U.S. subsidiary during a marathon strike.

Yokohama Rubber Co. kept second place with an 18.5% share, down 1.0 point. Sumitomo Rubber Industries Ltd. and other manufacturers also saw their shares decline due to increased overseas production caused by the yen's appreciation.

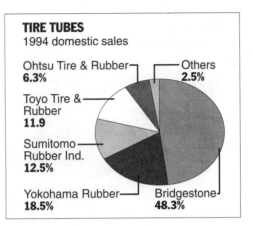

TIRE TUBES
1994 domestic sales

Ohtsu Tire & Rubber **6.3%**
Toyo Tire & Rubber **11.9**
Sumitomo Rubber Ind. **12.5%**
Yokohama Rubber **18.5%**
Others **2.5%**
Bridgestone **48.3%**

TISSUES

Domestic shipments of tissues and toilet paper in 1994 rose 1.3% to 1,547,958 tons, according to a Nikkei survey. Shipments of toilet paper increased 3.9%, and paper towels rose 3.4%, while tissue shipments fell by 0.9%. Sanitary paper shipments were slightly higher last year, up 1.9% over 1993.

The two leading producers, Daio Paper Corp. and New Oji Paper Co., both increased their market shares thanks to stable sales of their mainstay brands of household paper products.

Daio retained the top spot with a 12.7% share, up 0.6 of a point from 1993. New Oji gained 0.7 of a point to 9.4%. Third-ranked Jujo Kimberly KK lost 0.1 of a percentage point to 7.8%, due primarily to fierce price competition.

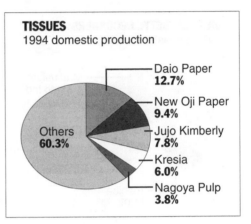

TISSUES
1994 domestic production

Daio Paper **12.7%**
New Oji Paper **9.4%**
Jujo Kimberly **7.8%**
Kresia **6.0%**
Nagoya Pulp **3.8%**
Others **60.3%**

TOILET FIXTURES

Domestic shipments of toilet fixtures including bowls, washstands and watertanks in 1994 rose sharply to 11.63 million units, up 13.9% from 1993, according to a Nikkei survey. The rise was attributed to an increase in housing starts to 1.57 million units and brisk demand for house refurbishment.

Toto Ltd. enjoyed overwhelming predominance, although its share remained unchanged from a year earlier at 62.6% due to a slowdown in construction of office buildings. In second place, Inax Corp. saw its share rise by 0.3 point to 23.5%, through active sales to prefabricated housing makers.

Janis Ltd. retained third place with a 4.7% share, down 1.4 points.

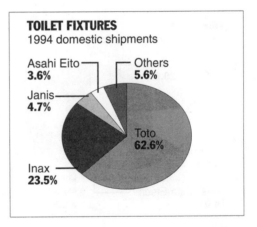

TOILET FIXTURES
1994 domestic shipments

Asahi Eito **3.6%**
Janis **4.7%**
Inax **23.5%**
Others **5.6%**
Toto **62.6%**

TRADING FIRMS

Aggregate sales at Japan's top nine trading firms dipped 3.3% to 99.77 trillion yen in fiscal 1994, falling for the fourth straight year. All the traders saw lower revenues due to the yen's 8% advance to the dollar, compared with a year ago, as well as a decrease in gold dealings, which had previously padded revenues.

Itochu Corp. retained the top market share of 16% by posting sales of 15.94 trillion yen, down from over 16 trillion yen in fiscal 1993. Mitsui & Co. remained second.

Marubeni Corp. moved down from third to fourth. Its market share contracted 0.3 point to 14.4% due mainly to a plunge in foods sales. Sumitomo advanced a notch to the third slot to 14.7%, up 0.1 point.

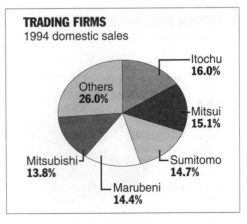

TRADING FIRMS
1994 domestic sales

Itochu **16.0%**
Mitsui **15.1%**
Sumitomo **14.7%**
Marubeni **14.4%**
Mitsubishi **13.8%**
Others **26.0%**

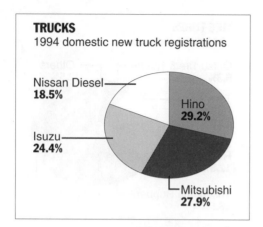

TRUCKS
1994 domestic new truck registrations

Nissan Diesel
18.5%

Isuzu
24.4%

Hino
29.2%

Mitsubishi
27.9%

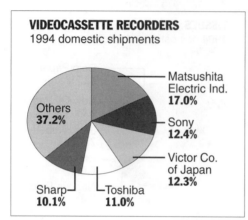

VIDEOCASSETTE RECORDERS
1994 domestic shipments

Others
37.2%

Matsushita
Electric Ind.
17.0%

Sony
12.4%

Victor Co.
of Japan
12.3%

Sharp
10.1%

Toshiba
11.0%

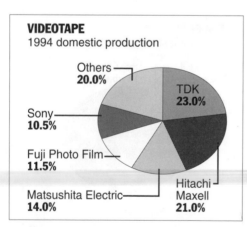

VIDEOTAPE
1994 domestic production

Others
20.0%

TDK
23.0%

Sony
10.5%

Fuji Photo Film
11.5%

Matsushita Electric
14.0%

Hitachi
Maxell
21.0%

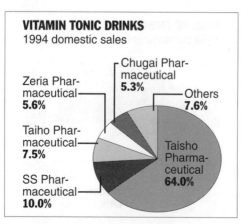

VITAMIN TONIC DRINKS
1994 domestic sales

Chugai Pharmaceutical
5.3%

Zeria Pharmaceutical
5.6%

Others
7.6%

Taiho Pharmaceutical
7.5%

Taisho
Pharmaceutical
64.0%

SS Pharmaceutical
10.0%

TRUCKS

Domestic sales of trucks totaled 135,450 units in 1994, up 16.5%. Market share rankings of the four leading manufacturers remained unchanged, as they have for over 10 years. Top-ranked Hino Motors Ltd. controlled a 29.2% share, down 0.3 percentage point. Mitsubishi Motors Corp. held 27.9%, up 0.4 point, Isuzu Motors Ltd. had 24.4%, up 0.1 point, and Nissan Diesel Motor Co. 18.5%, down 0.2 point.

For large trucks, Hino and Mitsubishi expanded their market shares because they were able to meet a surge in demand resulting from tightened loading rules.

For midsize trucks, Mitsubishi regained the No.1 position from Hino as clients shunned Hino's high-priced new model equipped with a clean-air engine.

VIDEOCASSETTE RECORDERS

Domestic shipments of videocassette recorders totaled 5.5 million units in 1994, up 7.8% over the previous year for the first gain in six years. Demand was stimulated by the rapid increase in low-cost "reverse" imports by major electronics makers.

Matsushita Electric Industrial Co. retained the top spot with a 17.0% share, but dropped 3.2 points on weak sales of its high-priced S-VHS VCR, which was undercut by rivals' lower-priced models.

Sony Corp. was second with a 12.4% share, up 0.1 point. It was followed by Victor Co. of Japan (JVC) with 12.3%, unchanged. In 1994, Japanese manufacturers' offshore production of VCRs topped domestic output for the first time.

VIDEOTAPE

Domestic videotape production in 1994 fell 8% from a year earlier to 549 million rolls (in terms of 120-minute tape units), marking a year-on-year drop for the fourth straight year. The decline was attributed to a shift of production overseas by Japanese manufacturers.

There was no change in the ranking of the top five manufacturers. TDK Corp. retained the top spot for the seventh consecutive year with a 23.0% share, up 0.5 of a percentage point. It boosted productivity by integrating manufacturing from two domestic facilities at a plant in Oita Prefecture.

Hitachi Maxell Ltd. came in second with 21.0%, up 0.5 point, followed by Matsushita Electric Industrial Co. with 14.0%, up 1.0 point.

VITAMIN TONIC DRINKS

Shipments of 100-milliliter bottled vitamin drinks in fiscal 1994 were worth an estimated 76 billion yen, up 3.4% from fiscal 1993, according to a Nikkei survey. Demand rose for the first time in three years, reflecting last summer's record hot summer.

Rankings remained unchanged. Taisho Pharmaceutical Co., the producer of Lipovitan-D, held an overwhelming share of 64.0%, down 0.1 of a point. SS Pharmaceutical Co. remained second at 10.0%, down 0.4, followed by Taiho Pharmaceutical Co. at 7.5%, up 1.1. Taiho's growth is attributed to cuts in retail prices of its Tiovita since January. With the exception of Taisho, rankings in fiscal 1995 may change after price cuts kick in and new products are introduced.

Company Directory

— Firms listed on first sections of Tokyo, Osaka and Nagoya stock exchanges —

A

Achilles Corp.	03-3341-5111
Advantest Corp.	03-3342-7500
Aica Kogyo Co.	052-202-6911
Aichi Bank	052-251-3211
Aichi Corp.	052-263-5191
Aichi Electric Co.	0568-31-1111
Aichi Machine Industry Co.	052-681-1111
Aichi Steel Works Ltd.	052-604-1111
Aichi Tokei Denki Co.	052-661-5151
Aida Engineering Ltd.	0427-72-5231
Aisin Seiki Co.	0566-24-8231
Aiwa Co.	03-3827-3111
Ajinomoto Co.	03-5250-8111
Akai Electric Co.	03-3745-9880
Akebono Brake Industry Co.	03-3668-5171
Akita Bank	0188-63-1212
All Nippon Airways Co.	03-3592-3065
Alpine Electronics Inc.	03-3494-1101
Alps Electric Co.	03-3726-1211
Amada Co.	0463-96-1111
Amada Metrecs Co.	0463-91-8001
Amada Sonoike Co.	0463-96-3550
Amada Wasino Co.	0568-77-8221
Amano Corp.	045-401-1441
Ando Corp.	03-3457-0111
Anritsu Corp.	03-3446-1111
Aoki Corp.	06-458-5851
Aoki International Co.	045-941-1888
Aomori Bank	0177-77-1111
Aoyama Trading Co.	0849-20-0050
Aplus Co.	06-245-7771
Arabian Oil Co.	03-3214-4319
Arai-Gumi Ltd.	0798-26-3111
Araya Industrial Co.	06-253-0221
Asahi Bank	03-3287-2111
Asahi Breweries Ltd.	03-5608-5112
Asahi Chemical Industry Co.	03-3507-2730
Asahi Denka Kogyo KK	03-5255-9002
Asahi Diamond Industrial Co.	03-3222-6311
Asahi Glass Co.	03-3218-5741
Asahi Kogyosha Co.	03-3432-5711
Asahi Optical Co.	03-3960-5151
Asahi Organic Chemicals Industry Co.	0982-35-0880
Asahi Tec Corp.	0537-36-3111
Asakawagumi Co.	0734-23-7161
Asanuma Corp.	06-768-5222
Asatsu Inc.	03-3547-2013
Ashikaga Bank	0286-22-0111
Ashimori Industry Co.	06-533-9250
Asics Corp.	078-303-3333
Ask Corp.	045-503-7711
AT & T Global Information Solutions Japan Ltd.	03-3582-6111
Atsugi Nylon Industrial Co.	0462-31-1111

Autobacs Seven Co.	06-873-2767
Awa Bank	0886-23-3131

B

Bandai Co.	03-3847-5005
Bando Chemical Industries Ltd.	078-232-2923
Bank of Fukuoka	092-723-2131
Bank of Ikeda	0727-51-3521
Bank of Iwate	0196-23-1111
Bank of Kansai	06-213-0213
Bank of Kinki	06-945-2121
Bank of Kyoto	075-361-2211
Bank of Nagoya	052-951-5911
Bank of Okinawa	098-867-2141
Bank of Osaka	06-538-1021
Bank of Saga	0952-24-5111
Bank of The Ryukyus	098-866-1212
Bank of Tokyo	03-3245-1111
Bank of Yokohama	045-225-1111
Banyu Pharmaceutical Co.	03-5203-8111
Best Denki Co.	092-781-7161
Biwako Bank	0775-24-9311
Bridgestone Corp.	03-3567-0111
Brother Industries Ltd.	052-824-2511
Bunka Shutter Co.	03-3968-6600

C

Cabin Co.	03-3779-6811
Calpis Food Industry Co.	03-3463-2111
Calsonic Corp.	03-5385-0111
Canon Inc.	03-3758-2111
Canon Sales Co.	043-211-9071
Casio Computer Co.	03-3347-4811
Central Finance Co.	052-203-1111
Central Glass Co.	03-3259-7111
Chain Store Okuwa Co.	0734-25-2481
Chiba Bank	043-245-1111
Chiba Kogyo Bank	043-243-2111
Chichibu Onoda Cement Corp.	03-5512-5222
Chino Corp.	03-3956-2111
Chisan-Tokan Co.	03-3400-7101
Chiyoda Corp.	03-3456-1211
Chiyoda Fire and Marine Insurance Co.	03-3281-3311
Chori Co.	06-228-5000
Chubu Electric Power Co.	052-951-8211
Chubu-Nippon Broadcasting Co.	052-241-8111
Chubu Steel Plate Co.	052-661-3811
Chudenko Corp.	082-291-7411
Chuetsu Pulp & Paper Co.	03-3544-1524
Chugai Pharmaceutical Co.	03-3281-6611
Chugai Ro Co.	06-441-8931
Chugoku Bank	086-223-3111
Chugoku Electric Power Co.	082-241-0211
Chugokukogyo Co.	082-221-8111
Chugoku Marine Paints Ltd.	082-248-3191
Chukyo Bank	052-262-6111

Chukyo Coca-Cola Bottling Co.	052-723-3131
Chuo Paperboard Co.	0573-66-1511
Chuo Spring Co.	052-623-1111
Chuo Trust & Banking Co.	03-3567-1451
Citizen Watch Co.	03-3342-1231
CKD Corp.	0568-77-1111
Clarion Co.	03-3400-1121
Cleanup Corp.	03-3894-4771
CMK Corp.	03-5323-0231
Co-op Chemical Co.	03-3230-0011
Copal Co.	03-3965-1111
Cosmo Oil Co.	03-3798-3211
Cosmo Securities Co.	06-203-2331
Credit Saison Co.	03-3988-2111
CSK Corp.	03-3344-1811

D

Daibiru Corp.	06-441-1932
Daicel Chemical Industries Ltd.	0722-27-3111
Dai-Dan Co.	06-441-8231
Daido Concrete Co.	03-5600-3311
Daidoh Ltd.	03-3257-5050
Daido Hoxan Inc.	06-252-1757
Daido Kogyo Co.	07617-2-1234
Daido Steel Co.	052-201-5111
Daido Steel Sheet Corp.	06-487-1717
Daiei Inc.	078-302-5001
Daiei OMC Inc.	03-3495-8511
Daifuku Co.	06-472-1261
Daihatsu Motor Co.	0727-51-8811
Daihen Corp.	06-301-1212
Daiho Corp.	03-3553-4311
Daiichi Cement Co.	044-322-5361
Daiichi Chuo Kisen Kaisha	03-3278-6800
Daiichi Corp.	082-247-5111
Dai-Ichi Hotel Ltd.	03-3501-4411
Daiichi Jitsugyo Co.	03-5214-8500
Dai-Ichi Kangyo Bank	03-3596-1111
Dai-Ichi Katei Denki Co.	03-3352-7241
Dai-ichi Kogyo Seiyaku Co.	075-343-1181
Daiichi Pharmaceutical Co.	03-3272-0611
Dai-ichi Securities Co.	03-3244-2600
Daiken Corp.	06-228-3321
Daikin Industries Ltd.	06-373-4312
Daikyo Inc.	03-3475-1111
Daimaru Inc.	06-281-9003
Daimei Telecom Engineering Corp.	03-5434-1121
Dainichiseika Colour & Chemicals Mfg. Co.	03-3662-7111
Dai Nippon Construction	0582-76-1111
Dainippon Ink and Chemicals Inc.	03-3272-4511
Dainippon Pharmaceutical Co.	06-203-5321
Dai Nippon Printing Co.	03-3266-2111
Dainippon Screen Mfg. Co.	075-414-7111
Dai Nippon Toryo Co.	06-466-6661
Daio Paper Corp.	03-3271-1961

Daisan Bank	0598-23-1111
Daishi Bank	025-222-4111
Daishinku Corp.	0794-26-3211
Daishowa Paper Mfg. Co.	0545-30-3000
Daiso Co.	06-443-5501
Daisue Construction Co.	06-456-3737
Daito Kogyo Co.	03-3685-2111
Dai-Tokyo Fire and Marine Insurance Co.	03-3272-8811
Daito Trust Construction Co.	03-3473-9111
Daito Woolen Spinning & Weaving Co.	03-3665-7816
Daiwa Bank	06-271-1221
Daiwabo Co.	06-281-2325
Daiwa Danchi Co.	06-532-6251
Daiwa House Industry Co.	06-538-5111
Daiwa Kosho Lease Co.	06-942-8012
Daiwa Securities Co.	03-3243-2111
Daiwa Seiko Inc.	0424-75-2111
Dantani Corp.	093-561-6331
Danto Corp.	06-448-6251
Denki Kagaku Kogyo KK	03-3507-5055
Denki Kogyo Co.	03-3216-1671
Denny's Japan Co.	03-3459-3548
Descente Ltd.	06-774-0365
Diamond Lease Co.	03-3274-0731
Dijet Industrial Co.	06-791-6781
Dowa Fire and Marine Insurance Co.	06-363-1121
Dowa Mining Co.	03-3201-1062
D'urban Inc.	03-5496-8120
Dynic Corp.	03-5210-9266

E

Eagle Industry Co.	03-3438-2291
East Japan Railway Co.	03-3212-3772
Ebara Corp.	03-3743-6111
Eime Bank	0899-33-1111
Eighteenth Bank	0958-24-1818
Eisai Co.	03-3817-3700
Enshu Ltd.	053-447-2111
Ezaki Glico Co.	06-477-8351

F

FamilyMart Co.	03-3989-6600
Fanuc Ltd.	0555-84-5555
FDK Corp.	03-3434-1271
First Baking Co.	03-3738-0131
France Bed Co.	03-3463-1011
Fudo Construction Co.	03-3831-9111
Fuji Bank	03-3216-2211
Fuji Car Mfg. Co.	06-213-2711
Fuji Denki Reiki Co.	03-3832-1251
Fuji Electric Co.	03-3211-7111
Fuji Fire and Marine Insurance Co.	06-271-2741
Fuji Heavy Industries Ltd.	03-3347-2111
Fujii & Co.	06-271-2311
Fujiko Co.	03-3449-1111
Fuji Kosan Co.	03-3580-3571
Fujikura Ltd.	03-5606-1111
Fuji Kyuko Co.	0555-22-7112
Fuji Machine Mfg. Co.	0566-81-2111
Fuji Oil Co.	06-213-8151
Fuji Photo Film Co.	03-3406-2111
Fujirebio Inc.	03-3348-0691
Fujisawa Pharmaceutical Co.	06-202-1141
Fuji Spinning Co.	03-3665-7777
Fujita Corp.	03-3402-1911
Fujita Kanko Inc.	03-3433-5153
Fujitec Co.	0726-22-8151
Fujitsu General Ltd.	044-861-7627

Fujitsu Ltd.	03-3216-3211
Fujiya Co.	03-3572-4150
Fukuda Corp.	025-266-9111
Fukui Bank	0776-24-2030
Fukuoka City Bank	092-441-2222
Fukusuke Corp.	06-577-3600
Fukutoku Bank	06-252-1101
Fukuyama Transporting Co.	0849-24-2000
Furukawa Battery Co.	045-331-1221
Furukawa Co.	03-3212-6561
Furukawa Electric Co.	03-3286-3001
Furuno Electric Co.	0798-65-2111
Fuso Pharmaceutical Industries Ltd.	06-969-1131
Futaba Corp.	0475-24-1111
Futaba Industrial Co.	0564-31-2211

G

Ga-jo-en Kanko KK	03-3495-9501
Gakken Co.	03-3726-8111
Gastec Service Inc.	0532-32-5161
General Sekiyu KK	03-3595-8300
Gifu Bank	058-275-1111
Godo Shusei Co.	03-3575-2711
Godo Steel Ltd.	06-346-1031
Graphtec Corp.	045-825-6200
Green Cross Corp.	06-227-4625
Gun Ei Chemical Industry Co.	0273-53-1818
Gunma Bank	0272-52-1111
Gunze Ltd.	06-348-1313
Gunze Sangyo Inc.	03-5211-1800

H

Hachijuni Bank	0262-27-1182
Hakone Tozan Railway Co.	0465-24-2111
Hakuyosha Co.	03-3460-1111
Hankyu Corp.	06-373-5088
Hankyu Department Stores Inc.	06-361-1381
Hankyu Realty Co.	06-313-3341
Hanshin Bank	078-331-8141
Hanshin Department Store Ltd.	06-345-1201
Hanshin Electric Railway Co.	06-457-2121
Hanwa Bank	0734-23-8181
Hanwa Co.	03-3544-2171
Harima Ceramic Co.	0794-43-1401
Harima Chemicals Inc.	06-201-2461
Haseko Corp.	03-3456-5451
Hayashikane Sangyo Co.	0832-66-0210
Hazama Corp.	03-3405-1111
Heiwado Co.	0749-23-3111
Heiwa Real Estate Co.	03-3666-0181
Higashi-Nippon Bank	03-3273-6221
Higo Bank	096-325-2111
Hino Motors Ltd.	0425-86-5011
Hirose Electric Co.	03-3491-5300
Hiroshima Bank	082-247-5151
Hiroshima-Sogo Bank	082-241-3131
Hisaka Works Ltd.	06-201-3531
Hisamitsu Pharmaceutical Co.	0942-83-2101
Hitachi Cable Ltd.	03-3216-1616
Hitachi Chemical Co.	03-3346-3111
Hitachi Construction Machinery Co.	03-3245-6305
Hitachi Credit Corp.	03-3503-2111
Hitachi Electronics Ltd.	03-5821-5311
Hitachi Koki Co.	03-3270-6130
Hitachi Ltd.	03-3258-1111
Hitachi Maxell Ltd.	0726-23-8101
Hitachi Metals Ltd.	03-3284-4511
Hitachi Plant Engineering & Construction Co.	03-3292-8111

Hitachi Seiki Co.	0471-84-1111
Hitachi Software Engineering Co.	045-681-2111
Hitachi Transport System Ltd.	03-5634-0333
Hitachi Zosen Corp.	06-466-7500
Hochiki Corp.	03-3444-4111
Hodogaya Chemical Co.	044-549-6600
Hohsui Corp.	03-3297-8200
Hokkai Can Co.	03-3213-5111
Hokkaido Bank	011-261-7111
Hokkaido Electric Power Co.	011-251-1111
Hokkaido Gas Co.	011-231-9511
Hokkaido Takushoku Bank	011-271-2111
Hokko Chemical Industry Co.	03-3279-5151
Hokkoku Bank	0762-63-1111
Hoko Fishing Co.	03-3542-5411
Hokuetsu Bank	0258-35-3111
Hokuetsu Paper Mills Ltd.	03-3245-4500
Hokuriku Bank	0764-23-7111
Hokuriku Electrical Construction Co.	0764-31-6551
Hokuriku Electric Industry Co.	0764-67-1111
Hokuriku Electric Power Co.	0764-41-2511
Hokuriku Seiyaku Co.	0779-88-5111
Honda Motor Co.	03-3423-1111
Honen Corp.	03-3211-6511
Honshu Paper Co.	03-5467-1001
Horiba Ltd.	075-313-8121
Hosiden Corp.	0729-93-1010
Hosokawa Micron Corp.	06-233-3966
Hotel New Hankyu Co.	06-372-5101
House Foods Corp.	06-788-1231
Howa Machinery Ltd.	052-408-1111
Hoya Corp.	03-3952-1151
Hyakugo Bank	0592-27-2151
Hyakujushi Bank	0878-31-0114
Hyogo Bank	078-231-6150

I

Ibiden Co.	0584-81-3111
Ichida & Co.	03-3663-1411
Ichikawa Co.	03-3816-1111
Ichiken Co.	078-252-2114
Ichikoh Industries Ltd.	03-3443-7281
Idec Izumi Corp.	06-398-2500
Ihara Chemical Industry Co.	03-3822-5223
Iino Kaiun Kaisha Ltd.	03-3506-3066
Ikegai Corp.	03-5470-1431
Ikegami Tsushinki Co.	03-5700-1111
Inabata & Co.	06-267-6051
Inageya Co.	0425-37-5111
INAX Corp.	0569-35-2700
Industrial Bank of Japan	03-3214-1111
Ines Corp.	03-3505-6131
Intec Inc.	0764-44-1111
International Reagents Corp.	078-231-4151
Inui Steamship Co.	078-331-3366
Iseki & Co.	03-5604-7602
Isetan Co.	03-3352-1111
Ishihara Sangyo Kaisha Ltd.	06-444-1451
Ishii Iron Works Co.	03-3562-3210
Ishikawajima-Harima Heavy Industries Co.	03-3244-5111
Ishikawa Seisakusho Ltd.	0762-22-2111
Ishizuka Glass Co.	052-871-3311
Isolite Insulating Products Co.	06-345-7231
Isuzu Motors Ltd.	03-5471-1111
Itochu Corp.	06-241-2121
Itochu Fuel Corp.	03-3584-8521

Itoham Foods Inc.	0798-66-1231
Itoki Crebio Corp.	06-935-2200
Ito-Yokado Co.	03-3459-2111
Iwasaki Electric Co.	03-3452-5351
Iwata Air Compressor Mfg. Co.	03-3711-7232
Iwatani International Corp.	06-267-3131
Iwatsu Electric Co.	03-5370-5111
Iyo Bank	0899-41-1141
Izumi Co.	082-264-3211
Izumiya Co.	06-657-3355
Izutsuya Co.	093-522-3111

J

Jaccs Co.	03-5448-1311
Janome Sewing Machine Co.	03-3277-2071
Japan Aircraft Mfg. Co.	045-773-5100
Japan Airlines Co.	03-3284-2511
Japan Airport Terminal Co.	03-3201-7111
Japan Aviation Electronics Industry Ltd.	03-3780-2711
Japan Bridge Corp.	06-571-5511
Japan Carlit Co.	03-5821-2020
Japan Digital Laboratory Co.	03-3348-6751
Japan Energy Corp.	03-5573-6000
Japan Metals & Chemicals Co.	03-3667-1341
Japan Oil Transportation Co.	03-3213-5511
Japan Paper Industry Co.	03-3251-3101
Japan Pulp & Paper Co.	03-3270-1311
Japan Radio Co.	03-3584-8711
Japan Securities Finance Co.	03-3666-0571
Japan Steel Works Ltd.	03-3501-6111
Japan Storage Battery Co.	075-312-1211
Japan Synthetic Rubber Co.	03-5565-6519
Japan Tobacco Inc.	03-3582-3111
Japan Transcity Corp.	0593-53-5211
Japan Vilene Co.	03-3258-3333
Japan Wool Textile Co.	06-205-6600
JDC Corp.	03-3403-3311
JEOL Ltd.	0425-43-1111
JGC Corp.	03-3279-5441
JMS Co.	082-243-5844
Joban Kosan Co.	03-3663-3411
Joshin Denki Co.	06-631-1221
Joyo Bank	0292-31-2151
Jujiya Co.	03-3864-2511
Juken Sangyo Co.	0829-32-3333
Juki Corp.	03-3480-1111
Juroku Bank	0582-65-2111
Jusco Co.	043-212-6000

K

Kagawa Bank	0878-61-3121
Kagome Co.	052-951-3571
Kagoshima Bank	0992-25-3111
Kajima Corp.	03-3404-3311
Kaken Pharmaceutical Co.	0473-90-6111
Kamei Corp.	022-264-6111
Kamigumi Co.	078-271-5110
Kanaden Corp.	03-3433-1211
Kanagawa Chuo Kotsu Co.	0463-22-8800
Kandenko Co.	03-5476-2111
Kanebo Ltd.	06-922-8151
Kaneka Corp.	06-226-5050
Kanematsu Corp.	03-5440-8111
Kanematsu Electronics Ltd.	03-5703-2111
Kanematsu-NNK Corp.	03-3521-8421
Kankaku Securities Co.	03-5640-5111
Kansai Electric Power Co.	06-441-8821
Kansai Kisen Kaisha	06-574-9131

Kansai Paint Co.	06-203-5531
Kansei Corp.	048-652-5051
Kanto Auto Works Ltd.	0468-61-5111
Kanto Bank	0298-21-8111
Kanto Denka Kogyo Co.	03-3216-4561
Kanto Natural Gas Development Co.	03-3241-5511
Kanto Special Steel Works Ltd.	0466-33-7111
Kao Corp.	03-3660-7111
Kasho Co.	03-3276-7726
Kasumi Co.	0298-31-0031
Katakura Industries Co.	03-3281-3161
Katokichi Co.	0875-56-1100
Kato Works Co.	03-3458-1111
Katsumura Construction Co.	03-3876-0111
Kawada Industries Inc.	03-3915-4321
Kawai Musical Instruments Mfg. Co.	053-457-1213
Kawasaki Heavy Industries Ltd.	078-371-9530
Kawasaki Kisen Kaisha Ltd.	03-3595-5082
Kawasaki Steel Corp.	03-3597-3111
Kawashima Textile Manufacturers Ltd.	075-414-9700
Kawasho Corp.	03-3578-5111
Kayaba Industry Co.	03-3435-3511
KDD	03-3347-7111
Keihan Electric Railway Co.	06-944-2521
Keihanshin Real Estate Co.	06-202-7331
Keihin Co.	03-3456-7801
Keihin Electric Express Railway Co.	03-3280-9120
Keihin Seiki Mfg. Co.	03-3341-8588
Keio Teito Electric Railway Co.	0423-37-3112
Keisei Electric Railway Co.	03-3621-2242
Keiyo Bank	043-222-2121
Keiyo Co.	043-255-1111
Kenwood Corp.	03-5457-7111
Keyence Corp.	06-379-1111
Kikkoman Corp.	0471-23-5111
Kimmon Mfg. Co.	03-3960-2151
Kimura Chemical Plants Co.	06-488-2501
Kimuratan Corp.	078-241-4351
Kinden Corp.	06-375-6000
Kinki Nippon Railway Co.	06-775-3444
Kinki Nippon Tourist Co.	03-3255-7116
Kinki Sharyo Co.	06-746-5222
Kinseki Ltd.	044-952-8101
Kinsho-Mataichi Corp.	03-3297-7111
Kinugawa Rubber Industrial Co.	043-259-3111
Kioritz Corp.	0428-32-6111
Kirin Brewery Co.	03-5540-3411
Kishu Paper Co.	06-345-6471
Kissei Pharmaceutical Co.	0263-25-9081
Kitagawa Iron Works Co.	0847-45-4560
Kita-Nippon Bank	0196-53-1111
Kitano Construction Corp.	0262-33-5111
Kitz Corp.	043-299-0111
Kiyo Bank	0734-23-9111
KOA Corp.	0265-78-2121
Koa Fire and Marine Insurance Co.	03-3593-3111
Koa Oil Co.	03-3241-8611
Koatsu Gas Kogyo Co.	06-311-1361
Kobayashi Metals Ltd.	06-535-3690
Kobe Electric Railway Co.	078-582-5800
Kobe Kiito Co.	078-251-4901
Kobe Steel Ltd.	078-261-5111
Kogi Corp.	078-576-5081
Koito Manufacturing Co.	03-3443-7111
Kokune Corp.	03-3222-8600
Kokusai Electric Co.	03-3368-6111

Kokusai Kogyo Co.	03-3262-6221
Kokusai Securities Co.	03-3297-2111
Kokuyo Co.	06-976-1221
Komai Tekko Inc.	03-3833-5101
Komatsu Construction Co.	03-3434-5131
Komatsu Forklift Co.	03-3224-6522
Komatsu Ltd.	03-5561-2616
Komatsu Seiren Co.	0761-55-1111
Komatsu Zenoah Co.	0425-61-2148
Komori Corp.	03-5608-7811
Konami Co.	03-3432-5678
Konica Corp.	03-3349-5251
Kosei Securities Co.	06-943-6770
Kotobukiya Co.	096-366-3111
Kowa Spinning Co.	052-963-3417
Koyo Seiko Co.	06-271-8451
Krosaki Corp.	093-622-7224
Kubota Corp.	06-648-2111
Kumagai Gumi Co.	03-3260-2111
Kumiai Chemical Industry Co.	03-3822-5036
Kurabo Industries Ltd.	06-266-5111
Kuraray Co.	06-348-2111
Kureha Chemical Industry Co.	03-3249-4666
Kurimoto Ltd.	06-538-7731
Kurita Water Industries Ltd.	03-3347-3111
Kyocera Corp.	075-592-3851
Kyodo Printing Co.	03-3817-2111
Kyodo Shiryo Co.	045-461-5711
Kyoei Tanker Co.	03-5280-1331
Kyokuyo Co.	03-3211-0134
Kyosan Electric Manufacturing Co.	045-501-1261
Kyotaru Co.	03-3665-6111
Kyoto Kintetsu Department Store Co.	075-361-1111
Kyowa Exeo Corp.	03-5570-8001
Kyowa Hakko Kogyo Co.	03-3282-0007
Kyowa Leather Cloth Co.	053-425-2121
Kyudenko Corp.	092-523-1231
Kyushu Bank	0956-24-7111
Kyushu Electric Power Co.	092-761-3031
Kyushu Matsushita Electric Co.	092-431-2111

L

Lecien Corp.	075-241-6000
Life Co.	03-3233-9111
Life Corp.	06-815-2600
Lintec Corp.	03-5248-7711
Lion Corp.	03-3621-6211
L Kakuei Corp.	03-3350-4340
Long-Term Credit Bank of Japan	03-5511-5111

M

Mabuchi Motor Co.	0473-84-1111
Maeda Corp.	03-3265-5551
Maeda Road Construction Co.	03-3447-0781
Magara Construction Co.	0762-31-1266
Makino Milling Machine Co.	03-3717-1151
Makita Corp.	0566-97-1711
Marubeni Corp.	03-3282-2111
Marudai Food Co.	0726-61-2518
Maruei Department Store Co.	052-264-1211
Maruetsu Inc.	03-3590-1110
Maruha Corp.	03-3216-0232
Maruichi Steel Tube Ltd.	06-531-0101
Marui Co.	03-3384-0101
Maruman Securities Co.	052-264-1111
Marusan Securities Co.	03-3272-5211
Maruwn Corp.	03-3433-0111
Maruyama Mfg. Co.	03-3252-2271

Company	Phone
Maruzen Co.	03-3272-7211
Maruzen Showa Unyu Co.	045-671-5713
Matsui Construction Co.	03-3553-1151
Matsumura-Gumi Corp.	06-353-1131
Matsuo Bridge Co.	06-552-1551
Matsushita Communication Industrial Co.	045-531-1231
Matsushita Electric Industrial Co.	06-908-1121
Matsushita Electric Works Ltd.	06-908-1131
Matsushita-Kotobuki Electronics Industries Ltd.	0878-51-7228
Matsushita Refrigeration Co.	06-784-7000
Matsushita Seiko Co.	06-939-1161
Matsuya Co.	03-3567-1211
Matsuyadenki Co.	06-643-5461
Matsuzakaya Co.	052-251-1111
Max Co.	03-3669-0311
Mazda Motor Corp.	082-282-1111
Meidensha Corp.	03-5641-7000
Meiji Milk Products Co.	03-3281-6118
Meiji Seika Kaisha Ltd.	03-3272-6511
Meiji Shipping Co.	03-3792-0811
Meisei Industrial Co.	06-447-0271
Meitetsu Department Store Co.	052-585-1111
Meito Sangyo Co.	052-521-7111
Meiwa Trading Co.	03-3240-9534
Mercian Corp.	03-3231-3922
Michinoku Bank	0177-74-1111
Mie Bank	0593-53-3111
Mie Kotsu Co.	0592-29-5511
Mikuni Coca-Cola Bottling Co.	048-774-1111
Minebea Co.	03-5434-8611
Minolta Co.	06-271-2251
Misawa Homes Co.	03-3345-1111
Misawa Resort Co.	03-3344-8811
Mitsuba Electric Mfg. Co.	0277-52-0111
Mitsubishi Bank	03-3240-1111
Mitsubishi Cable Industries Ltd.	03-3216-1551
Mitsubishi Chemical Corp.	03-3283-6274
Mitsubishi Corp.	03-3210-2121
Mitsubishi Electric Corp.	03-3218-2111
Mitsubishi Estate Co.	03-3287-5100
Mitsubishi Gas Chemical Co.	03-3283-5000
Mitsubishi Heavy Industries Ltd.	03-3212-3111
Mitsubishi Kakoki Kaisha Ltd.	03-3454-4811
Mitsubishi Materials Corp.	03-5252-5201
Mitsubishi Motors Corp.	03-3456-1111
Mitsubishi Oil Co.	03-3472-7500
Mitsubishi Paper Mills Ltd.	03-3213-3751
Mitsubishi Pencil Co.	03-3458-6221
Mitsubishi Plastics Inc.	03-3283-4006
Mitsubishi Rayon Co.	03-3245-8675
Mitsubishi Shindoh Co.	03-3561-9281
Mitsubishi Steel Mfg. Co.	03-3536-3111
Mitsubishi Trust and Banking Corp.	03-3212-1211
Mitsubishi Warehouse & Transportation Co.	03-3278-6611
Mitsuboshi Belting Ltd.	078-360-5931
Mitsui & Co.	03-3285-1111
Mitsui Construction Co.	03-5821-7001
Mitsui Engineering & Shipbuilding Co.	03-3544-3147
Mitsui Fudosan Co.	03-3246-3065
Mitsui High-tec Inc.	093-614-1111
Mitsui Home Co.	03-3346-4411
Mitsui Marine and Fire Insurance Co.	03-3259-3111
Mitsui Matsushima Co.	092-771-2171
Mitsui Mining Co.	03-3241-1334
Mitsui Mining and Smelting Co.	03-3246-8000
Mitsui O.S.K.Lines Ltd.	03-3587-7111
Mitsui Petrochemical Industries Ltd.	03-3580-2012
Mitsui Real Estate Sales Co.	03-5381-4070
Mitsui-Soko Co.	03-3667-5331
Mitsui Sugar Co.	03-3663-3111
Mitsui Toatsu Chemicals Inc.	03-3592-4111
Mitsui Trust and Banking Co.	03-3270-9511
Mitsukoshi Ltd.	03-3241-3311
Mitsumi Electric Co.	03-3489-5333
Mitsuuroko Co.	03-3279-6311
Miura Co.	0899-79-1111
Miyaji Iron Works Co.	03-3639-2111
Miyakoshi Corp.	03-5493-8111
Miyazaki Bank	0985-27-3131
Miyoshi Oil & Fat Co.	03-3603-1111
Miyuki Keori Co.	052-509-1600
Mizuno Corp.	06-614-8000
Mochida Pharmaceutical Co.	03-3358-7211
Morimoto Corp.	06-779-1451
Morinaga & Co.	03-3456-0112
Morinaga Milk Industry Co.	03-3798-0111
Mori Seiki Co.	07435-3-1121
Morita Fire Pump Mfg. Co.	06-756-0100
Morozoff Ltd.	078-822-5000
Mory Industries Inc.	0721-54-1121
Mr. Max Corp.	092-623-1111
Murata Mfg. Co.	075-951-9111
Musashino Bank	048-641-6111
Mutoh Industries Ltd.	03-5486-1111
Mutow Co.	053-464-1123

N

Company	Phone
Nabco Ltd.	078-251-8080
Nachi-Fujikoshi Corp.	03-3435-5111
Nagasakiya Co.	03-3661-3810
Nagase & Co.	06-535-2114
Nagatanien Co.	03-3432-2511
Nagoya Railroad Co.	052-571-2111
Naigai Co.	03-3293-1511
Nakabayashi Co.	06-943-5555
Nakamuraya Co.	03-3352-6161
Nakano Corp.	03-3265-4661
Nakayama Steel Works Ltd.	06-555-3028
Namco Ltd.	03-3756-2311
Namura Shipbuilding Co.	06-543-3561
Nankai Electric Railway Co.	06-644-7121
Nanto Bank	0742-22-1131
National House Industrial Co.	06-834-5111
National Securities Co.	03-3666-0321
Navix Line Ltd.	03-3282-7550
NEC Corp.	03-3454-1111
NEC System Integration & Construction Ltd.	03-5463-1111
Neturen Co.	03-3443-5441
New Japan Chemical Co.	06-202-0624
New Japan Securities Co.	03-3219-1111
New Oji Paper Co.	03-3563-1111
NGK Insulators Ltd.	052-872-7230
NGK Spark Plug Co.	052-872-5915
NHK Spring Co.	045-786-7511
Nichias Corp.	03-3433-7251
Nichia Steel Works Ltd.	06-416-1021
Nichiban Co.	03-5978-5601
Nichiboshin Ltd.	03-3271-4602
Nichicon Corp.	075-231-8461
Nichido Fire and Marine Insurance Co.	03-3571-5141
Nichiei Co.	045-521-6161
Nichiei Construction Co.	03-3734-6211
Nichii Co.	06-203-5075
Nichimen Corp.	06-223-5111
Nichimo Co.	03-3245-4718
Nichimo Corp.	06-672-2201
Nichirei Corp.	03-3248-2101
Nichireki Co.	03-3265-1511
Nichiro Corp.	03-3240-6211
Nifco Inc.	045-825-7900
Nihon Cement Co.	03-3201-1731
Nihon Kentetsu Co.	0474-35-5111
Nihon Kohden Corp.	03-5996-8000
Nihon Matai Co.	03-3843-2111
Nihon Nohyaku Co.	03-3274-3374
Nihon Nosan Kogyo KK	045-224-3700
Nihon Parkerizing Co.	03-3278-4333
Nihon Spindle Mfg. Co.	06-499-5551
Nihon Tokushu Toryo Co.	03-3913-6131
Nihon Unisys Ltd.	03-5546-4111
Niigata Chuo Bank	025-229-1111
Niigata Engineering Co.	03-5710-7700
Nikken Chemicals Co.	03-3544-8701
Nikkiso Co.	03-3443-3711
Nikko Co.	078-947-3131
Nikko Securities Co.	03-3283-2211
Nikon Corp.	03-3214-5311
Nintendo Co.	075-541-6111
Nippon Beet Sugar Mfg. Co.	03-3273-4383
Nippon Carbide Industries Co.	03-3240-8600
Nippon Carbon Co.	03-3552-6111
Nippon Chemical Industrial Co.	03-3636-8111
Nippon Chemi-Con Corp.	0428-22-1251
Nippon Chemiphar Co.	03-3863-1211
Nippon Chutetsukan KK	03-3252-4661
Nippon Columbia Co.	03-3584-8111
Nippon Comsys Corp.	03-3448-7031
Nippon Concrete Industries Co.	03-3573-0363
Nippon Conlux Co.	03-3502-1811
Nippon Conveyor Co.	0720-72-2205
Nippon Credit Bank	03-3263-1111
Nippon Denko Co.	03-3546-9319
Nippon Densetsu Kogyo Co.	03-3822-8811
Nippondenso Co.	0566-25-5511
Nippon Denwa Shisetsu Co.	052-263-5011
Nippon Dry-Chemical Co.	03-5460-6011
Nippon Electric Glass Co.	0775-37-1700
Nippon Electric Industry Co.	0298-89-3111
Nippon Express Co.	03-3253-1111
Nippon Felt Co.	03-3213-5611
Nippon Fine Chemical Co.	06-231-4781
Nippon Fire and Marine Insurance Co.	03-3272-8111
Nippon Flour Mills Co.	03-3350-2311
Nippon Formula Feed Mfg. Co.	045-316-7200
Nippon Gas Co.	03-3553-1281
Nippon Hodo Co.	03-3563-6751
Nippon Housing Loan Co.	03-3504-1031
Nippon Hume Pipe Co.	03-3433-4111
Nippon Kakoh Seishi Co.	03-3584-2671
Nippon Kasei Chemical Co.	03-3506-6211
Nippon Kayaku Co.	03-3237-5111
Nippon Kinzoku Co.	03-3212-8111
Nippon Koei Co.	03-3238-8030
Nippon Koshuha Steel Co.	03-3231-6761
Nippon Lace Co.	075-255-1201
Nippon Light Metal Co.	03-3456-9211
Nippon Meat Packers Inc.	06-282-3031
Nippon Metal Industry Co.	03-3345-5555
Nippon Oil Co.	03-3502-1111

Nippon Paint Co.	06-458-1111
Nippon Paper Industries Co.	03-3218-8000
Nippon Pipe Manufacturing Co.	0473-22-3322
Nippon Piston Ring Co.	03-3234-4171
Nippon Road Co.	03-3571-4891
Nippon Sanso Corp.	03-3581-8200
Nippon Sharyo Ltd.	052-882-3316
Nippon Sheet Glass Co.	03-5443-9522
Nippon Shinpan Co.	03-3811-3111
Nippon Shinyaku Co.	075-321-1111
Nippon Shokubai Co.	06-223-9111
Nippon Signal Co.	03-3287-4500
Nippon Soda Co.	03-3245-6054
Nippon Steel Chemical Co.	03-3248-5053
Nippon Steel Corp.	03-3242-4111
Nippon Suisan Kaisha Ltd.	03-3244-7000
Nippon Synthetic Chemical Industry Co.	06-314-3110
Nippon Telegraph and Telephone Corp.	03-5359-5111
Nippon Television Network Corp.	03-5275-1111
Nippon Thompson Co.	03-3448-5811
Nippon Trust Bank	03-3245-8111
Nippon Valqua Industries Ltd.	03-3212-8571
Nippon Yakin Kogyo Co.	03-3272-1511
Nippon Yusen KK	03-3284-5151
Nippon Yusoki Co.	075-951-7171
Nippon Zeon Co.	03-3216-1772
Nishimatsu Construction Co.	03-3502-0211
Nishi-Nippon Bank	092-476-2525
Nishi-Nippon Railroad Co.	092-734-1217
Nissan Chemical Industries Ltd.	03-3296-8111
Nissan Construction Co.	03-3402-8161
Nissan Diesel Motor Co.	048-781-2301
Nissan Fire & Marine Insurance Co.	03-3404-4111
Nissan Motor Co.	03-3543-5523
Nissan Shatai Co.	0463-21-8001
Nissei Build Kogyo Co.	0762-68-1111
Nissei Sangyo Co.	03-3504-7111
Nisseki House Industry Co.	03-5424-1811
Nissha Printing Co.	075-811-8111
Nisshinbo Industries Inc.	03-5695-8833
Nisshin Fire and Marine Insurance Co.	03-3231-8000
Nisshin Flour Milling Co.	03-3660-3111
Nisshin Oil Mills Ltd.	03-3206-5025
Nisshin Steel Co.	03-3216-5511
Nissho Corp.	06-372-2331
Nissho Iwai Corp.	06-209-2111
Nissin Corp.	03-3238-6663
Nissin Electric Co.	075-212-7222
Nissin Food Products Co.	06-305-7711
Nitsuko Corp.	044-811-1111
Nittetsu Mining Co.	03-3284-0516
Nitto Boseki Co.	03-3865-6689
Nitto Chemical Industry Co.	03-3271-0251
Nitto Denko Corp.	0726-22-2981
Nitto Flour Milling Co.	03-3553-8781
Nitto Seiko Co.	0773-42-3111
Nitto Seimo Co.	03-3572-5376
Nittoc Construction Co.	03-3542-9126
NKK Corp.	03-3212-7111
NOF Corp.	03-5424-6600
Nohmi Bosai Ltd.	03-3265-0211
NOK Corp.	03-3432-4211
Nomura Securities Co.	03-3211-1811
Noritake Co.	052-561-7110
Noritz Corp.	078-391-3361
North Pacific Bank	011-261-1311

Nozaki & Co.	03-5641-4320
NSK Ltd.	03-3779-7111
NTN Corp.	06-443-5001

O

Obayashi Corp.	03-3292-1111
Obayashi Road Corp.	03-3796-6500
Odakyu Construction Co.	03-3376-3101
Odakyu Electric Railway Co.	03-3349-2054
Odakyu Real Estate Co.	03-3370-1110
Ogaki Kyoritsu Bank	0584-74-2111
Ohki Corp.	03-3255-4111
Ohkura Electric Co.	03-3398-5111
Oita Bank	0975-34-1111
Okabe Co.	03-3624-5111
Okamoto Industries Inc.	03-3817-4111
Okamura Corp.	045-319-3401
Okasan Securities Co.	03-3272-2211
Oki Electric Cable Co.	044-754-4351
Oki Electric Industry Co.	03-3501-3111
OKK Corp.	06-376-6611
Okuma Corp.	0587-95-7822
Okuma & Howa Machinery Ltd.	0587-55-1172
Okumura Corp.	06-621-1101
Okura & Co.	03-3566-6000
Okura Industrial Co.	0877-56-1111
Olympus Optical Co.	03-3340-2121
O-M Ltd.	06-350-1200
Omron Corp.	075-344-7000
Ono Pharmaceutical Co.	06-222-5551
Ono Sokki Co.	045-935-3888
Onward Kashiyama Co.	03-3272-2317
Optec Dai-Ichi Denko Co.	03-3212-6928
Organo Corp.	03-5689-5100
Orient Corp.	03-3989-6111
Origin Electric Co.	03-3983-7111
Orix Corp.	03-3435-6641
Osaka Gas Co.	06-202-2221
Osaka Sanso Kogyo Ltd.	06-396-3181
Osaka Securities Finance Co.	06-233-4510
Osaka Uoichiba Co.	06-469-2001
Osaki Electric Co.	03-3443-7171
OSG Corp.	05338-2-1111
Oyo Corp.	03-3234-0811

P

Pacific Industrial Co.	0584-91-1111
Pacific Metals Co.	03-3201-6681
Parco Co.	03-3477-5731
Pasco Corp.	03-5722-7600
Penta-Ocean Construction Co.	03-3816-7111
Pilot Corp.	03-5487-8111
Pioneer Electronic Corp.	03-3494-1111
Pokka Corp.	052-932-1471
Press Kogyo Co.	044-266-2581
Prima Meat Packers Ltd.	03-3593-6710

Q

Q.P. Corp.	03-3486-3331

R

Raito Kogyo Co.	03-3265-2551
Rasa Industries Ltd.	03-3278-3801
Rengo Co.	06-202-2371
Renown Inc.	03-3403-2211
Renown Look Inc.	03-3794-9100
Rheon Automatic Machinery Co.	0286-65-1111
Rhythm Watch Co.	03-3833-7311
Ricoh Co.	03-3479-3111

Riken Corp.	03-3230-3911
Riken Vinyl Industry Co.	03-3663-7991
Rinnai Corp.	052-361-8211
Rohm Co.	075-311-2121
Rohto Pharmaceutical Co.	06-758-1231
Royal Co.	092-471-2414
Ryobi Ltd.	03-3257-1500
Ryoden Trading Co.	03-5396-6112
Ryosan Co.	03-3862-2591
Ryoyo Electro Corp.	03-3543-7711

S

Saeki Kensetsu Kogyo Co.	06-203-0161
Sagami Co.	03-5461-7111
Sagami Railway Co.	045-319-2111
Saibu Gas Co.	092-633-2211
Sakai Chemical Industry Co.	0722-23-4111
Sakai Heavy Industries Ltd.	03-3434-3401
Sakai Ovex Co.	0776-36-5800
Sakata Inx Corp.	06-447-5812
Sakata Seed Corp.	045-945-8800
Sakura Bank	03-3230-3111
Sakurada Co.	043-274-8511
San-Ai Oil Co.	03-5479-3113
Sanden Corp.	0270-24-1211
Sangetsu Co.	052-564-3311
San-in Godo Bank	0852-26-7111
Sankei Building Co.	03-3231-7171
Sanken Electric Co.	048-472-1111
Sanki Engineering Co.	03-3502-6111
Sanko Metal Industrial Co.	03-3567-3551
Sankyo Aluminium Industry Co.	0766-20-2214
Sankyo Co.	03-5255-7111
Sankyo Seiki Mfg. Co.	03-3502-3711
Sankyo Seiko Co.	06-268-5000
Sankyu Inc.	03-5484-3939
Sanoyas Hishino Meisho Corp.	06-202-1221
Sanrio Co.	03-3779-8111
Sansui Electric Co.	0248-75-4171
Santen Pharmaceutical Co.	06-321-7000
Sanwa Bank	06-206-8111
Sanwa Shutter Corp.	03-3346-3019
Sanyo Chemical Industries Ltd.	075-541-4311
Sanyo Electric Co.	06-991-1181
Sanyo Electric Railway Co.	078-612-2032
Sanyo Industries Ltd.	03-3685-3451
Sanyo Securities Co.	03-3666-1233
Sanyo Shokai Ltd.	03-3357-4111
Sanyo Special Steel Co.	0792-35-6111
Sapporo Breweries Ltd.	03-5423-2111
Sasaki Glass Co.	03-3663-1211
Sasebo Heavy Industries Co.	03-3211-2989
Sata Construction Co.	0272-51-1551
Sato Co.	06-309-6301
Sato Kogyo Co.	03-3661-1231
Sato Shoji Corp.	03-3553-7005
Sawafuji Electric Co.	03-5999-3355
Secaicho Corp.	06-374-0071
Secom Co.	03-3348-7511
Sega Enterprises Ltd.	03-5736-7111
Seibu Railway Co.	0429-26-2035
Seika Corp.	03-5221-7102
Seikitokyu Kogyo Co.	03-3434-3251
Seiko Corp.	03-3563-2111
Seino Transportation Co.	0584-81-1111
Seiren Co.	0776-35-2111
Seiyo Food Systems Inc.	03-3984-0662

Seiyu Ltd.	03-3989-4590	Snow Brand Milk Products Co.	03-3226-2111
Sekisui Chemical Co.	06-365-4122	Soda Nikka Co.	03-3245-1802
Sekisui House Ltd.	06-440-3111	Sogo Co.	06-281-3111
Sekisui Jushi Corp.	06-365-3204	Sokkia Co.	03-3465-5211
Sekisui Plastics Co.	06-365-3014	Sony Corp.	03-5448-2111
Senko Co.	06-372-1611	Sotetsu Rosen Co.	045-319-7064
Senshu Bank	0724-23-2131	SS Pharmaceutical Co.	03-3668-4511
Senshukai Co.	06-881-3100	Stanley Electric Co.	03-3710-2727
Settsu Corp.	06-488-2530	Star Micronics Co.	054-263-1111
Seven-Eleven Japan Co.	03-3459-3711	S.T. Chemical Co	03-3364-2551
Seventy-Seven(77) Bank	022-267-1111	Subaru Enterprise Co.	03-3213-2861
Sharp Corp.	06-621-1221	Suminoe Textile Co.	06-251-6801
Shibaura Engineering Works Co.	03-3586-2119	Sumisho Computer Systems Corp.	03-5624-1600
Shibusawa Warehouse Co.	03-3660-4040	Sumisho Lease Co.	06-346-6000
Shibuya Kogyo Co.	0762-62-1201	Sumitomo Bakelite Co.	03-5462-4111
Shiga Bank	0775-24-2141	Sumitomo Bank	06-227-2111
Shikibo Ltd.	06-268-5493	Sumitomo Chemical Co.	06-220-3891
Shikoku Bank	0888-23-2111	Sumitomo Coal Mining Co.	03-5404-0401
Shikoku Chemicals Corp.	0877-22-4111	Sumitomo Construction Co.	03-3353-5111
Shikoku Electric Power Co.	0878-21-5061	Sumitomo Corp.	06-220-6000
Shimachu Co.	048-623-7711	Sumitomo Electric Industries Ltd.	06-220-4141
Shimadzu Corp.	075-823-1111	Sumitomo Forestry Co.	03-3349-7521
Shimamura Co.	048-652-2111	Sumitomo Heavy Industries Ltd.	03-5488-8000
Shimano Inc.	0722-23-3330	Sumitomo Light Metal Industries Ltd.	03-3436-9700
Shima Seiki Mfg. Ltd.	0734-71-0511	Sumitomo Marine and Fire Insurance Co.	03-3297-1111
Shimizu Bank	0543-53-5151	Sumitomo Metal Industries Ltd.	06-220-5111
Shimizu Corp.	03-5441-1111	Sumitomo Metal Mining Co.	03-3436-7704
Shimura Kako Co.	03-3216-6431	Sumitomo Osaka Cement Co.	03-3296-9600
Shinagawa Fuel Co.	03-5470-7100	Sumitomo Precision Products Co.	06-482-8811
Shinagawa Refractories Co.	03-3273-4511	Sumitomo Realty & Development Co.	03-3346-1011
Shindengen Electric Mfg. Co.	03-3279-4431	Sumitomo Rubber Industries Ltd.	
Shin-Etsu Chemical Co.	03-3246-5011	078-265-3000	
Shin-Etsu Polymer Co.	03-3279-1712	Sumitomo Seika Chemicals Co.	06-220-8508
Shin-Kobe Electric Machinery Co.	03-3344-2811	Sumitomo Sitix Corp.	06-411-4300
Shinko Electric Co.	03-3274-1112	Sumitomo Special Metals Co.	06-220-8822
Shinko Shoji Co.	03-5721-2111	Sumitomo Trust and Banking Co.	06-220-2121
ShinMaywa Industries Ltd.	0798-47-0331	Sumitomo Warehouse Co.	06-581-1181
Shin Nippon Air Technologies Co.	03-3279-5671	Sunstar Inc.	0726-82-5541
Shinsho Corp.	06-206-7001	Suntelephone Co.	03-3665-1500
Shintom Co.	045-563-3111	Sun Wave Corp.	03-5371-4311
Shinto Paint Co.	06-426-3355	Suruga Bank	0599-62-0080
Shinwa Bank	0956-24-5111	Suzuki Motor Corp.	053-440-2061
Shinwa Kaiun Kaisha Ltd.	03-5627-7550	Suzutan Co.	052-263-1191
Shinyei Kaisha	078-392-6911		
Shionogi & Co.	06-202-2161	**T**	
Shiroki Corp.	045-473-4691	Tabai Espec Corp.	06-358-4741
Shiseido Co.	03-3572-5111	Tada Corp.	03-3683-3111
Shizuoka Bank	054-261-3131	Tadano Ltd.	0878-39-5555
Sho-Bond Corp.	03-3292-8101	Taihei Dengyo Kaisha Ltd.	03-5213-7211
Shochiku Co.	03-3542-5555	Taihei Kogyo Co.	03-5543-6000
Shoko Co.	03-3459-5111	Taiheiyo Bank	03-3230-8811
Shokusan Jutaku Sogo Co.	03-3370-1214	Taiheiyo Kaiun Co.	03-5445-5800
Showa Aluminum Corp.	03-3239-5311	Taiheiyo Kouhatsu Inc.	03-3591-1271
Showa Corp.	0485-54-1151	Taiheiyo Securities Co.	03-5695-3111
Showa Denko KK	03-5470-3111	Taikisha Ltd.	03-3344-1851
Showa Electric Wire & Cable Co.	03-3597-7011	Taisei Corp.	03-3348-1111
Showa Highpolymer Co.	03-3293-8844	Taisei Fire and Marine Insurance Co.	03-3234-3111
Showa Line Ltd.	03-3581-8535	Taisei Prefab Construction Co.	03-3493-4941
Showa Sangyo Co.	03-3257-2011	Taisei Rotec Corp.	03-3567-9431
Showa Shell Sekiyu KK	03-3580-0123	Taisho Pharmaceutical Co.	03-3985-1111
Silver Seiko Ltd.	03-3356-6111	Taito Co.	03-3663-3851
Sintokogio Ltd.	052-582-9211	Taiyo Toyo Sanso Co.	06-449-7000
Skylark Co.	03-3349-7070	Taiyo Yuden Co.	03-3832-0101
S x L Corp.	06-315-1131	Takada Kiko Co.	06-649-5100
SMC Corp.	03-3502-8271	Takaoka Electric Mfg. Co.	03-3211-1671
SMK Corp.	03-3785-1111	Taka-Q Co.	03-5248-4100
		Takarabune Corp.	0774-46-6002

Takara Co.	03-3603-2131
Takara Shuzo Co.	075-241-5110
Takara Standard Co.	06-962-1531
Takasago International Corp.	03-3442-1211
Takasago Thermal Engineering Co.	03-3255-8212
Takasaki Paper Mfg. Co.	03-3257-0931
Takashima & Co.	03-3567-0211
Takashimaya Co.	06-631-1101
Takeda Chemical Industries Ltd.	06-204-2111
Takiron Co.	06-267-2800
Takuma Co.	06-346-5161
Tamura Corp.	03-3978-2111
Tamura Electric Works Ltd.	03-3493-5113
Tanabe Seiyaku Co.	06-205-5555
Tasaki Shinju Co.	078-302-3321
Tateho Chemical Industries Co.	07914-2-5041
Tatsuta Electric Wire and Cable Co.	06-721-3331
Tayca Corp.	06-243-5811
TDK Corp.	03-3278-5111
Teac Corp.	0422-52-5009
Tec Corp.	03-3292-6223
Teijin Ltd.	06-268-2132
Teijin Seiki Co.	06-448-6001
Teikoku Hormone Mfg. Co.	03-3583-8361
Teikoku Oil Co.	03-3466-1237
Teikoku Sen-i Co.	03-3281-3023
Teikoku Tsushin Kogyo Co.	044-422-3171
Teisan KK	03-3502-0551
Tekken Corp.	03-3262-3411
Tenma Corp.	03-3598-5511
Terumo Corp.	03-3374-8111
Tesac Co.	06-227-1821
Tetra Co.	03-3342-0151
Titan Kogyo KK	0836-31-4156
Toa Corp.	03-3262-5102
Toa Doro Kogyo Co.	03-3405-1811
Toagosei Co.	03-3597-7215
Toa Steel Co.	03-3221-7121
Toa Wool Spinning & Weaving Co.	06-203-3001
Tobishima Corp.	03-3263-3151
Tobu Railway Co.	03-3621-5055
Tobu Store Co.	03-3989-8211
TOC Co.	03-3494-2111
Tochigi Bank	0286-33-1241
Tochigi Fuji Industrial Co. Ltd.	0282-27-1111
Toda Corp.	03-3562-6111
Toda Kogyo Corp.	082-231-2181
Todentu Corp.	03-3434-5111
Toei Co.	03-3535-4641
Toenec Corp.	052-221-1111
Toho Bank	0245-23-3131
Toho Co.	03-3591-1221
Toho Gas Co.	052-871-3511
Toho Rayon Co.	03-3278-7615
Toho Real Estate Co.	03-3504-3333
Toho Zinc Co.	03-3272-5611
Tohoku Electric Power Co.	022-225-2111
Tohpe Corp.	0722-43-6411
Tohto Suisan Co.	03-3541-5666
Tokai Bank Ltd.	052-211-1111
Tokai Carbon Co.	03-3746-5100
Tokai Corp.	054-254-8181
Tokai Kanko Co.	03-5488-1010
Tokai Kogyo Co.	03-5200-5141
Tokai Pulp Co.	0547-36-5151
Tokai Rika Co.	0587-95-5211

Tokai Senko KK	052-581-7911	Totetsu Kogyo Co.	03-3268-4211	Wakita & Co.	06-251-1901
Tokico Ltd.	044-244-3126	Totoku Electric Co.	03-5273-2121	Wako Securities Co.	03-3667-8111
Tokimec Inc.	03-3732-2111	Toto Ltd.	093-951-2111	**Y**	
Tokin Corp.	022-308-0014	Towa Bank	0272-34-1111	Yahagi Construction Co.	052-935-2351
Tokio Marine and Fire Insurance Co.	03-3212-6211	Towa Real Estate Development Co.	03-3272-6331	Yahagi Iron Co.	052-611-1511
Toko Electric Corp.	03-3214-5281	Toyama Chemical Co.	03-3348-6611	Yakult Honsha Co.	03-3574-8960
Toko Inc.	03-3727-1161	Toyo Aluminium KK	06-271-3151	Yamagata Bank	0236-23-1221
Tokushima Bank	0886-23-3111	Toyobo Co.	06-348-3111	Yamaguchi Bank	0832-23-3411
Tokushu Paper Mfg. Co.	0559-88-1111	Toyo Chemical Co.	0467-45-1111	Yamaha Corp.	053-460-2071
Tokuyama Corp.	03-3449-8710	Toyo Communication Equipment Co.	03-5462-9700	Yamaha Motor Co.	0538-32-1115
Tokuyo City Bank	022-222-0171	Toyo Construction Co.	03-3296-4611	Yamaichi Securities Co.	03-3276-3181
Tokyo Broadcasting System Inc.	03-3746-1111	Toyo Corp.	03-3279-0771	Yamamura Glass Co.	0798-32-2300
Tokyo Denki Komusho Co.	03-3434-0151	Toyoda Automatic Loom Works Ltd.	0566-22-2511	Yamanashi Chuo Bank	0552-33-2111
Tokyo Dome Corp.	03-3811-2111	Toyoda Boshoku Corp.	0566-23-6611	Yamanouchi Pharmaceutical Co.	03-3244-3000
Tokyo Electric Power Co.	03-3501-8111	Toyoda Gosei Co.	052-400-1055	Yamatake-Honeywell Co.	03-3486-2031
Tokyo Electron Ltd.	03-5561-7000	Toyoda Machine Works Ltd.	0566-25-5111	Yamatane Corp.	03-3820-1111
Tokyo Gas Co.	03-3433-2111	Toyo Denki Seizo K.K.	03-3271-5041	Yamatane Securities Co.	03-3669-3211
Tokyo Kikai Seisakusho Ltd.	03-3451-8141	Toyo Engineering Corp.	03-3592-7411	Yamato International Inc.	06-262-1661
Tokyo Nissan Auto Sales Co.	03-3405-2236	Toyo Exterior Co.	03-3354-3211	Yamato Kogyo Co.	0792-73-1061
Tokyo Ohka Kogyo Co.	044-722-7181	Toyo Information Systems Co.	06-385-0888	Yamato Transport Co.	03-3541-3411
Tokyo Rakutenchi Co.	03-3631-3121	Toyo Ink Mfg. Co.	03-3272-5731	Yamazaki Baking Co.	03-3864-3111
Tokyo Rope Mfg. Co.	03-3211-2851	Toyo Kanetsu KK	03-5690-7777	Yamazen Corp.	06-534-3021
Tokyo Securities Co.	03-3214-3211	Toyo Kohan Co.	03-3502-6611	Yaohan Japan Corp.	0559-23-3234
Tokyo Seimitsu Co.	0422-48-1011	Toyo Radiator Co.	03-3373-1101	Yaskawa Electric Corp.	093-645-8800
Tokyo Sowa Bank	03-3586-3111	Toyo Securities Co.	03-3274-0211	Yasuda Fire and Marine Insurance Co.	03-3349-3111
Tokyo Steel Mfg. Co.	03-3501-7721	Toyo Seikan Kaisha Ltd.	03-3508-2113	Yasuda Trust and Banking Co.	03-3278-8111
Tokyo Style Co.	03-3262-8111	Toyo Shutter Co.	06-943-6571	Yodogawa Steel Works Ltd.	06-245-1113
Tokyo Tanabe Co.	03-3241-5151	Toyo Sugar Refining Co.	03-3668-7871	Yokogawa Bridge Corp.	03-3453-4111
Tokyo Tatemono Co.	03-3274-0111	Toyo Suisan Kaisha Ltd.	03-3458-5111	Yokogawa Electric Corp.	0422-52-5555
Tokyo Tekko Co.	03-5276-9011	Toyota Auto Body Co.	0566-36-2121	Yokohama Matsuzakaya Ltd.	045-261-2121
Tokyo Theatres Co.	03-3561-8531	Toyota Motor Corp.	0565-28-2121	Yokohama Reito Co.	045-461-6611
Tokyo Tomin Bank	03-3582-8251	Toyota Tsusho Corp.	052-584-5000	Yokohama Rubber Co.	03-3432-7111
Tokyotokeiba Co.	03-3271-9105	Toyo Tire & Rubber Co.	06-441-8801	Yomeishu Seizo Co.	03-3462-8111
Tokyu Car Corp.	045-701-5155	Toyo Trust and Banking Co.	03-3287-2211	Yomiuri Land Co.	044-966-1111
Tokyu Construction Co.	03-5466-5111	Toyo Umpanki Co.	06-441-9151	Yondenko Corp.	0878-36-1111
Tokyu Corp.	03-3477-6079	Toyo Warehouse Co.	052-581-0251	York-Benimaru Co.	0249-24-3111
Tokyu Department Store Co.	03-3477-3111	Toyo Wharf & Warehouse Co.	03-3503-5351	Yoshihara Oil Mill Ltd.	06-441-8851
Tokyu Hotel Chain Co.	03-3264-0111	Tsubakimoto Chain Co.	06-911-1221	Yoshimoto Kogyo Co.	06-643-1122
Tokyu Land Corp.	03-5458-0633	Tsubakimoto Machinery & Engineering Co.	06-489-2891	Yoshitomi Pharmaceutical Industries Ltd.	06-201-1600
Tokyu Store Chain Co.	03-3711-0109	Tsubakimoto Precision Products Co.	06-489-2891	Yuasa Corp.	0726-61-9811
Tokyu Tourist Corp.	03-5704-3750	Tsudakoma Corp.	0762-42-1111	Yuasa Trading Co.	03-3665-6511
Toli Corp.	06-492-1331	Tsugami Corp.	03-5470-7890	Yuken Kogyo Co.	0466-23-2111
Tomato Bank	086-221-1010	Tsukamoto Co.	03-3279-1310	Yurtec Corp.	022-296-2111
Tomen Corp.	03-3588-7111	Tsukishima Kikai Co.	03-5560-6511	**Z**	
Tomoe Corp.	03-3571-8681	Tsumura & Co.	03-3221-0001	Zenchiku Co.	03-3471-5521
Tomoegawa Paper Co.	03-3272-4111	Tsurumi Mfg. Co.	06-911-2351	Zenitaka Corp.	06-531-6431
Tomoku Co.	03-3213-6811	Tsutsunaka Plastic Industry Co.	06-229-5000	Zexel Corp.	03-3400-1551
Tonami Transportation Co.	0766-21-1073	TYK Corp.	03-3201-0821	Zuken Inc.	045-942-1511
Tonen Corp.	03-3286-5115	**U**			
Topcon Corp.	03-3966-3141	Ube Industries Ltd.	03-5460-3311		
Toppan Printing Co.	03-3835-5111	Uchida Yoko Co.	03-5634-6043		
Topre Corp.	03-3271-0711	Ueki Corp.	0257-23-2200		
Topy Industries Ltd.	03-3265-0111	Uni Charm Corp.	03-3447-5111		
Toray Industries Inc.	03-3245-5111	Uniden Corp.	03-5543-2800		
Torishima Pump Mfg. Co.	0726-95-0551	Unisia Jecs Corp.	0462-25-8025		
Toshiba Ceramics Co.	03-5381-5815	Unitika Ltd.	06-281-5695		
Toshiba Corp.	03-3457-4511	Uny Co.	0587-24-8111		
Toshiba Engineering & Construction Co.	03-5404-6005	Ushio Inc.	03-3242-1811		
Toshiba Machine Co.	03-3567-0520	Utoc Corp.	045-201-6931		
Toshiba Tungaloy Co.	044-548-9500	**V**			
Toshoku Ltd.	03-3245-2211	Victor Company of Japan Ltd.	045-450-1583		
Tosho Printing Co.	03-3473-7300	**W**			
Tosoh Corp.	03-3585-3311	Wacoal Corp.	075-682-5111		
Tostem Corp.	03-3638-8115	Wakachiku Construction Co.	03-3492-0271		
Tostem Viva Corp.	048-773-3815	Wakamoto Pharmaceutical Co.	03-3279-0371		
Totenko Co.	03-3828-6272				

Japan map

POPULATION: about 125.1 million (1995)

LAND AREA: 377,765 sq. km., roughly the size of the American state of California. Japan has four main islands, Hokkaido, Honshu, Shikoku and Kyushu, plus about 3,000 small islands.

PREFECTURES: 47, including Hokkaido.

TIME ZONE: It's noon in Tokyo when it's 10 p.m. in New York City a day before, 7 p.m. in San Francisco a day before and 3 a.m. in London.

GEOLOGY: The islands are largely mountainous, and include more than 160 volcanoes, 54 of which are active. About 1,500 earthquakes occur each year, but most go unnoticed.

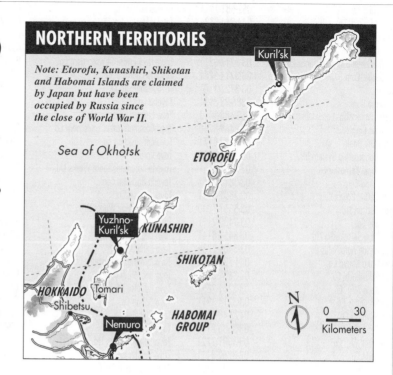

NORTHERN TERRITORIES

Note: Etorofu, Kunashiri, Shikotan and Habomai Islands are claimed by Japan but have been occupied by Russia since the close of World War II.

Kuril'sk

Sea of Okhotsk

ETOROFU

Yuzhno-Kuril'sk

KUNASHIRI

SHIKOTAN

HOKKAIDO

Tomari

Shibetsu

Nemuro

HABOMAI GROUP

N

0   30
Kilometers

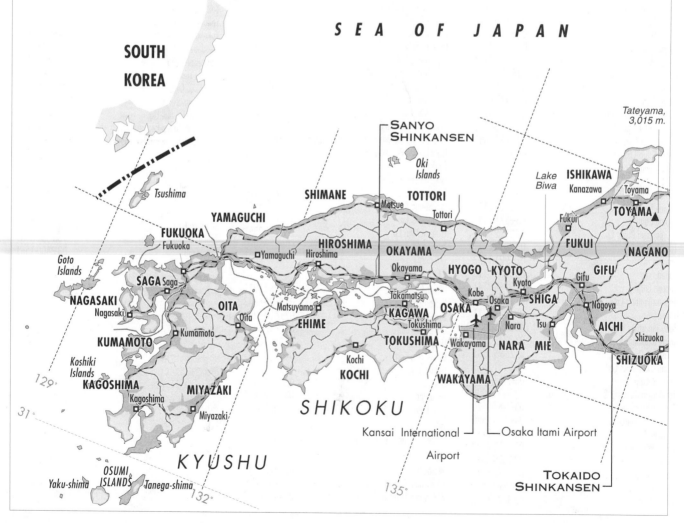

SEA OF JAPAN

SOUTH KOREA

Tsushima

Goto Islands

FUKUOKA
Fukuoka

YAMAGUCHI

Yamaguchi

SHIMANE

Matsue

Oki Islands

SANYO SHINKANSEN

TOTTORI

Tottori

Lake Biwa

ISHIKAWA
Kanazawa

Toyama

TOYAMA

Tateyama, 3,015 m.

HIROSHIMA
Hiroshima

OKAYAMA

Okayama

HYOGO

KYOTO
Kyoto

Fukui

FUKUI

NAGANO

GIFU
Gifu

SAGA Saga

NAGASAKI
Nagasaki

OITA
Oita

Matsuyama

EHIME

Takamatsu

KAGAWA
Tokushima

Kobe
Osaka

OSAKA

Nara

SHIGA

Nagoya

Tsu

AICHI

Shizuoka

KUMAMOTO
Kumamoto

Koshiki Islands

KAGOSHIMA
Kagoshima

MIYAZAKI
Miyazaki

TOKUSHIMA

Kochi

KOCHI

SHIKOKU

Wakayama

NARA

MIE

SHIZUOKA

WAKAYAMA

Kansai International Airport

Osaka Itami Airport

129°

31°

KYUSHU

OSUMI ISLANDS

Yaku-shima

Tanega-shima

132°

135°

TOKAIDO SHINKANSEN

200 kilometers

125 miles

✈ Major international airports
Japan Railways lines
Shinkansen lines
Prefectural boundaries

144°

Rebun
Wakkanai
Rishiri

HOKKAIDO

Rumoi
HOKKAIDO
Abashiri
Asahikawa
Kitami
Iwamizawa
Sapporo

(See inset map)
KUNASHIRI

Obihiro

Okushiri

Kushiro

43°
Nemuro

Hakodate

Sapporo
(Chitose)
Airport

AOMORI
Aomori

138°
40°

AKITA
Akita
Morioka
IWATE

JOETSU
SHINKANSEN

Sado

TOHOKU SHINKANSEN

YAMAGATA
Niigata
Yamagata
Sendai
NIIGATA
MIYAGI
Nagaoka
Fukushima
FUKUSHIMA

HONSHU

129°

Nagano
TOCHIGI
NAGANO
GUNMA
Maebashi
Utsunomiya
Mito
37°

Kofu
SAITAMA
Omiya
IBARAKI
YAMANASHI
Urawa
TOKYO
Chiba
Yokohama
KANAGAWA
CHIBA

NORTH

*Amami
Islands*
*Amami
O-shima*

Tokuno

EAST
CHINA
SEA

Yoron

KAGOSHIMA

OKINAWA

126°

Naha

Okinawa

Tokyo International
Airport At Narita

Naha
Airport

PACIFIC
OCEAN

*Mt. Fuji,
3,776 m.*
O-shima
Miyake
IZU
ISLANDS
Mikura

123°

Senkaku Islands

Miyako

Hachijo

Yonaguni
Ishigaki
Iriomote

123°

126°

129°

Index

Multimedia	98
Multimedia age	94
Multimedia PCs	146
Multiple-system operator	90,91
Murayama cabinet	14
Murayama, Tomiichi	14
Musicland Group Inc.	144
Myanmar	18
NAFTA	22
Nakauchi, Isao	122
NASDA	60
NASDAQ	66
National brand	158
National Land Agency	54
National Space Development Agency	60,105
National supermarket chains	148
Near-zero growth	34
NEC Corp.	86
Nerve-gas attack	26
Net equity sales by life insurers	64
New electoral system	14
New Fiber Vision Plan	118
New products & services	146
New strategic alliance	23
New Zealand	41
Nickel	129
NIEs	18
Nifty-Serve	94
Nikkei 225 futures	65
Nikkei 300 futures	65
Nikkei 300 stock index fund	65
Nikkei Commodity Index	73
Nikkei OTC Average	67
Nikkei OTC index	66
Nikkei Stock Average	44,64
Nikkei World Commodity Index	72
Nippon Television Network Corp.	98
Nokia Corp.	92
Nominal GDP	30
Nomura Securities Co.	144
Non-affiliated voters	15
Nonbank	82
Nonbank financial institution	82
Nonferrous metal	128
Nonferrous metal recycling	129
Nonlife insurance subsidiary	80
Nonlife insurers	80
Nonperforming loans	12,28,76
North American Free Trade Agreement	22
NTT breakup	90
NTT procurement	23
Nuclear Non-Proliferation Treaty	33
Nuclear power	46
Nuclear power program	60
Numerical targets	22
Numerically controlled lathe	106
Nynex Corp.	92
ODA	52
Official development assistance	52
Official discount rate	16,31,34,44,64,70,132
Offshore R&D	17
Oil distributors	122
Oil refiners	122
Olivetti & C.SpA	144
Open competitive bidding	134
Open-pricing system	116
Orderly reversal	44,70
Ordinary rolled steel	127
Orix Corp.	39
OTC entry criteria	67
OTC market	67
OTC registration	66
OTC trust fund	66
OTC-registered issue	66
Outdoor sports	138
Over-the-counter market	66
Overnight call rate	44,68
Overprescription	112
Overseas investment	38
Overseas investment insurance	39
Overseas package tours	154
Overseas touring	138
Overseas travelers	139
Overseas trip	138
PAC system	49
Packard Bell Electronics Inc.	86,145
Pajero Mini	146
Paperboard	120
Parent bank responsibility	83
PC-Van	94
PDA	92
Pension assets in Japan	59
Pension funds	59
Pentium	89
Performance bond system	134,135
Permanent membership of the U.N. Security Council	13
Perry, William	32
Personal computer	86,146
Personal digital assistants	92
Personal handy-phone system	23,90,91,92,146
Petrochemical industry	110
Petroleum	122
Pharmaceuticals	112
Pharmaceuticals & health-care products	150
Pharmacy market	112
PHS	90,92
PHS handset sales	92
PHS operator	92
Piezoelectric ceramic	130
Pig iron	126
Pizza delivery franchises	156
PlayStation	96,151
Plaza Accord	13,118
Plutonium	47
Political Action Committee	49
Political donation	49
Polyethylene	110,111
Polypropylene	110,111
Polystyrene	111
Polyvinyl chloride resin	110
Population	58
Postal savings deposits	28
Power Reactor and Nuclear Fuel Development Corp.	60
Pre-offering auction	66
Prepaid cards	156
Price busting	72
Price-cutting strategy	158
Price-discounting war	158
Printing paper	120
Private brand	158
Private housing construction	134
Private power generators	125
Private-brand beer	117
Problem loans	54
Product Liability Law	112,113
Provisional Measures Law	122
Public spending	34
Public-works spending	35,42
Pulp and paper	120
Pump-priming measure	35
R&D bases overseas	38
R&D spending	60
R&D-related budget	60
RAM memory	88
Ratio of finished goods imports	37
Real estate	132
Real Estate Economic Research Institute	132
Real estate market	54
Real estate price	54
Real GDP	30
Recycle 55 Project	121
Recycling Promotion Law	63
Regional supermarkets	148
Religious Corporation Law	27
Research and development	60
Residential land prices	30
Resources	46
Restaurants	156
Return on assets	76
Rice imports	56
Rice market	56,143
Rice Price Council	56
Rice retailing	143
Risk management	25
Rokkasho	47
Rolled steel product	126
Saber	136
Sakamoto, Tsutsumi	26,27